DATE DUE

MAR 0 8 2010	
JAN 24 2010	
GAYLORD	PRINTED IN U.S.A.

Labor
in the American
Economy

St. Martin's Press

New York

Labor
in the American
Economy

Everett Johnson Burtt
Boston University

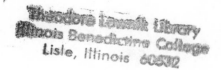

Library of Congress Catalog Card Number: 78-73037
Copyright © 1979 by St. Martin's Press, Inc.
All rights reserved.
Manufactured in the United States of America.
32109
fedcba
For information, write St. Martin's Press, Inc.,
175 Fifth Avenue, New York, N.Y. 10010.

cover design: Mark Berghash

ISBN: 0-312-46248-4

Acknowledgment

Edward F. Denison: From *Accounting for United States Economic Growth,
1929–1969* (The Brookings Institution, 1974), p. 138. Copyright 1974 by
The Brookings Institution.

To my wife,
Cynthia Webb Burtt

Preface

This book offers a comprehensive introduction to the concepts and theories of labor economics and to those issues that pertain to the position of the worker in the American economy. It examines labor markets and how they function, unions and their policies, collective bargaining in the private and public sectors, and those government programs, both macro and micro, that affect labor markets and their institutions.

The field of labor economics is necessarily a broad one, because labor economists must consider not only the economic forces of the market but also the specific institutions and the socio-political environment within which those market forces operate. There are those who would restrict labor market analysis to a subfield of a micro theory based upon the prescriptions of an abstract competitive model. But such attempted restriction fails for two reasons. One is that labor markets are too complex, participants' motivations too diverse, and the limitations of the competitive hypothesis too pervasive to lead to satisfactory analyses. The other is that unless labor economics deals with realities and with significant social issues it loses its relevance and *raison d'être*.

Historically, the vitality of the field of labor economics in the United States has stemmed primarily from the willingness of labor economists to advance new hypotheses for the analysis of issues that mainstream economics has so often ignored or treated as anomalies. It was the period of labor unrest during the transformation of the American economy in the latter part of the last century and early years of this one that led to the first studies of labor markets, wages, unions and the labor movement, and the labor policies of the expanding oligopolistic sectors of American industry. During the Great Depression, World War II, and the immediate postwar years, problems of achieving and maintaining full employment stimulated the development of labor force statistics and monthly measures of unemployment, studies of labor mobility, and research concerning the nature and implications of the industrial relations system which had spread throughout basic American industries.

With the civil rights movement and turmoil in big city ghettoes during the 1960s, labor economists focused their research on discriminatory labor market practices, measures of poverty, and the reasons for the successes and failures of governmental manpower programs. The dual market theory and concepts of labor market segmentation were among the important new hypotheses that helped explain wage and income disparities which failed to conform to orthodox theories of human capital investment.

The decade of the 1970s stimulated new research interests. The expansion of unionism and collective bargaining among government employees at the federal, state, and local levels has led to investigations of the multilateral character of labor relations in the public sector and its implications. Environmental problems, particularly those of the workplace, are just beginning to be explored. As negative externalities they raise controversial issues of government policy because remedial action can be taken only politically.

Probably the most fundamental issue of the recent years has been the inflationary pressures within the American economy and the slowdown in the rate of increase of workers' real earnings. Studies of the wage and price controls imposed in the early 1970s have revealed some of the implications of that type of governmental intervention, both for controlling price rises and for industrial relations.

In dealing with these and other issues and concepts in the present text, I have followed to some extent the organizational plan of my earlier book, *Labor Markets, Unions, and Government Policies* (New York, St. Martin's, 1963), and I have also incorporated some of its historical material. I have benefited greatly from discussions of labor market concepts, policies, and the vast array of materials in the field of labor with my colleagues at Boston University, particularly Peter B. Doeringer, Blanche Fitzpatrick, Robert E. B. Lucas, Paul Osterman, and William Spring of the Department of Economics and S. M. Miller of the Department of Sociology. I am especially indebted to Wendell D. Macdonald and his staff at the Boston regional office of the U.S. Bureau of Labor Statistics for their willingness to provide and appraise statistical information so essential for labor studies. I also appreciate very much the suggestions of Professor Bruno Stein of New York University, who read the manuscript in its entirety, for clarification, elaboration, and correction of a number of points. Finally, I wish to thank Carole Ringler, who typed the manuscript.

For any errors of fact or misinterpretations, I alone am responsible.

E.J.B.

January 1979

Contents

10

Union Objectives in Collective Bargaining: Wages and Wage Supplements   218

11

Union Objectives in Collective Bargaining: Hours of Work, Security, Seniority, and Work Rules   241

xiv Contents

16

Unemployment: Its Costs, Characteristics, and Causes   388

17

Full-Employment Policies   411

Labor
in the American
Economy

1

Introduction

Labor markets have a direct and intimate effect upon the lives of most adult Americans. The United States has become a nation of employees who are dependent upon the income from wages and salaries earned at jobs. This situation is quite unlike that of a hundred years ago, when independent farmers, small businessmen, and individual craftsmen dominated the American economic structure. How labor markets work and how well they perform their functions are not only matters of importance to those who participate in them; they are also vital to the performance of the entire economy.

THE SUBJECT MATTER OF LABOR ECONOMICS

Labor economics is that branch of general economics that deals systematically with the economic forces operating within labor markets. It uses the tools of economic analysis and research to study the characteristics of labor supply, labor demand, the price of labor (wages), and employment.

Labor economics is necessarily concerned with the institutions through which the forces of supply, demand, wages, and employment are expressed. There are four major types of institutions: households, firms, unions, and governments.

Households (both single persons and multiperson families) are, from an economic point of view, sources of labor. As consumers these decision-making units, living within a universe of interrelated prices and markets, purchase food, clothes, entertainment, and other goods and services in product markets. As producers they rent out property, invest capital, and organize business enterprises for profit or sell labor services for income in factor markets. In 1975 about 72 million households in the United States supplied an average of 92.6 million persons to the civilian labor force per week. In that relatively depressed year, 84.8 million had jobs during the average week, while 7.8 million were unemployed. Of those with jobs, some 7 million were proprietors of firms and farms, managers, or officials, while 77 million individuals were employees working under the direction of others at wages and salaries which

1

usually constituted the main source of the income of their households. As the unemployed are well aware, labor markets do not automatically provide jobs and income for those who want them.

Firms are economic organizations that use factors of production (inputs) in the production of goods and services. Legally, an individually owned firm is considered a household; a partnership is several households. A corporation is a legal entity divorced from households, although its owners—the shareholders—are households that supply the capital. In 1973 there were about 13.5 million business firms in nonagricultural industries in the United States— 10.5 million proprietorships, a million partnerships, and about 2 million corporations. The latter, especially the larger corporations, are the dominant force in the American industrial system. In 1976, according to *Fortune* magazine, the top 500 industrial corporations alone had assets of nearly $750 billion, received a net income of $50 billion, and employed nearly 15 million workers. Ten corporations alone employed over 3 million workers. Managers of large modern corporations are often able to exercise economic decision-making power independently of its owners, the stockholders, and even to influence the world of markets within which they operate. Governments may exert restraints where market forces are inadequate, although it is not altogether certain whether government controls, on balance, abet or limit corporate power.

In any case, the firm, whether a household or corporation, depends for its survival upon the returns from sales in product markets in relation to the prices it must pay for factors of production in the factor markets. Of special significance to firms are the costs of labor, which amount on the average to about two-thirds of total costs. Firms are therefore strongly motivated to control costs by resisting demands for wage increases and by seeking out labor in markets where wages are lower.

Unions comprise a third group of institutions concerned with decisions in labor markets. With some 23 million members in over 200 national unions and public and professional employee associations in 1974, these nonprofit organizations have been recognized by law as representatives of workers in the sale of labor services. Although the union is not a selling agency as such, it acts as an intermediary to regularize and better the conditions under which workers' services are sold. Although responsible to their members, who authorize their policies and actions, union leaders, like corporation officials, may enjoy a range of independence in policy formation and bargaining. Nonetheless, unions operate within constraints imposed by the marketplace. On the one hand they face firms with varying abilities to resist wage demands; on the other hand they must contend with possible displacement from lower-wage, nonunionized workers.

Governments—local, state, and national—are directly and indirectly involved in labor markets. Like private firms, governments are buyers of labor services and often bargain with public employee unions over the terms and conditions of employment. Governments exercise regulatory powers that affect the procedures of bargaining and the content of wage and employment relationships in the private sector through laws, such as the Civil Rights Act of 1964, and through administrative agencies, such as the National Labor Relations Board. Governments have an impact on workers' welfare through monetary, tax, and expenditure policies. The effect can be felt immediately when the Social Security payroll tax is increased; it is indirect when the government restricts the monetary supply and raises interest rates, which in turn cuts back demands for new home financing and adversely affects jobs for construction workers. In times of emergency—often but not always associated with wars—governments may even override privately negotiated labor contracts and set wages unilaterally with a system of wage controls. Finally, governments provide for transfer payments to households directly for reasons other than for work performed. Using designated tax revenues, governments pay benefits to individuals under a variety of unemployment, old age, and other social insurance programs, and through antipoverty measures designed to help those who cannot find income to meet basic needs through labor markets.

Although labor economics stresses the market relationships of supplies and demands, and of wages and employment, it also includes other aspects of work and of employee-employer relationships. Workers, firms, unions, and governments are not motivated solely by considerations of wage rates.

To the individual worker, a job is more than a source of income, because his or her efforts and person must be directly involved at a place and under conditions assigned by the employer. He or she comes under the direction of others and is subject to the administrative decisions and working rules that enforce the industrial discipline characteristic of modern industry. A worker becomes immersed in the complex net of interpersonal relationships with fellow employees that characterizes industrial society. The worker's adjustments to these conditions, controls, and relationships become an integral part of his or her participation in a labor market as a seller of labor services for a price. Such adjustments are not occasional events, for the typical male worker remains in the labor market for some 40 to 45 years, while a woman can expect to work for perhaps 20 to 25 years. It is true that work environments do not dominate a person's life span today as much as they did 50 years ago, that young people enter the labor force later in life, that older workers have more years of retirement because they live longer, and that hours of work per week are fewer. Yet it is still true that work environments and their hazards, the nature of the work performed, and controls over work performance profoundly shape the lives and attitudes of workers. The stresses of work environments may provoke dissension and unrest as surely as disputes over the size of a wage increase.

Similarly, firms are concerned with more than wage rates, which are only one dimension of the labor costs of production. To maximize profits, a firm attempts to raise labor productivity and worker efficiency through control over work assignments, work speeds, and even the time allowed for coffee breaks. General working rules and plant regulations become a part of labor agreements between unions and managements, and attempts by management to change them in the name of greater efficiency may trigger strikes as easily as a refusal to grant a wage increase.

Employers may also have other goals besides profit maximization. Some may prefer a relaxed, casual atmosphere for employees, while others insist on a strict accounting of time and effort. Among the objectives not included in the balance sheet may be the gain of employee good will or a reputation for being a "good" employer. Investigators differ in their evaluation of the non-economic motives of the business firm, and some critics claim that broader goals are either the result of a protected, monopolistic position in an industry (which full-fledged competition would not allow) or simply more sophisticated devices to raise labor productivity.

The diversity of objectives in unions' participation in labor markets stems from their political nature and from the complexity of the environment in which they act. As political organizations, unions have both leaders and members, and the relationships between them, among leaders, and among unions and managements sometimes create the impression that final decisions on wages and the terms of employment are matters of personality and not of economics at all. Unions as well as managements must operate within the basic limitations of the economic situation, however, and, as we shall see, the range within which discretion and negotiation can affect the value of the labor transaction may be fairly small. Nonetheless, the nature of the institutional structure of unions, the internal pressures from the members upon their leaders, and the leaders' pressure on members influence behavior in the labor market and the final terms and conditions of work.

Through governments the public attempts to supplement, modify, or otherwise control market forces for a variety of purposes. Certain desirable goods and services either would not be produced adequately by the market system or would not be provided at all. For example, the system of public education and of public subsidies for private schools and colleges rests upon the proposition that an educated populace economically benefits society as a whole, and that without subsidy the level of that education would be far lower because the system would be wholly dependent upon those who could afford to pay the cost.

Governments establish standards to which employment conditions must conform. For example, in the interests of health, governments outlaw child labor, require elimination of certain types of hazardous work, and ban use of dangerous materials. Similarly, environmental controls for cleaner air and water, like zoning laws to keep industry out of residential areas, set standards concerning the "quality of life" which the market system cannot provide.

OBJECTIVES AND METHODS OF LABOR ECONOMICS

Understanding how markets allocate labor and other inputs in the production of goods and services is one of the primary objectives of the labor economist. In view of the diversity of interests and motivations among the individuals and institutions that participate in labor markets, the questions are: How satisfactorily does the market system, supplemented by the political process, adjust demands and supplies to meet the conflicting desires of consumers and producers? How adequately does it take into account the costs, both social and individual, of producing various goods and services? Utilizing most effectively an economy's resources is a problem basic to all economies.

A second objective is to examine the stability or instability of the system as a whole. Is the economy subject to booms and recessions? Can it grow at a rate that provides adequate jobs for an increasing population at rising income levels?

Finally, the labor economist looks at the distributional problem, the question of how income in the form of the produced goods and services is distributed to workers and households within the economy. The distributional problem includes the analysis of wage differentials by occupation, sex, or race. It also includes the macro aspect of distribution between wages and salaries for those who work and the nonlabor returns of interest, profits, and rents.

The labor economist investigates facts, theories, and policies that relate to these objectives. All scientific research includes the gathering of accurate, objective information, but it is important to appraise the different methods used in gathering facts and recognize their limitations. The discovery of facts is not as simple as it may appear to be. Just as an automobile accident will be described differently by the different participants and bystanders, so economic facts have different meanings for different people depending upon the point of view. Apart from ideological differences, emotionally induced blind spots, or unsuppressed subjectivity, scientific observation and measurement are still dependent upon the tools, instruments, and procedures that the individual analyst chooses to utilize. Each method of collecting facts has certain advantages and limitations.

The *historical method* includes the search in primary source materials for records of actions concerned with the problem to be investigated and, if the data permit, some generalization concerning the facts. Often a situation may be illuminated by other events that occurred at or about the same time. Historical research is especially useful in analyzing institutions and policy decisions. For example, an economist might want to find out why the presidential decision on August 15, 1971, to invoke wage and price controls in the United States was made despite previously stated commitments to the maintenance of free markets. Care must be taken in historical research to avoid the error known as *post hoc, propter hoc*—the fallacy of imputing causality to a sequence of events. Because of the interdependence of many variables in a real situation, there is always the possibility that under other conditions a particular series of events might have other outcomes.

The *case-study method* has been used in a variety of situations. A case study is an intensive and thorough investigation of one or more situations, including not only their historical background but also firsthand observation and interviews. For example, case studies of the work experience of selected types of workers over a period of time have been used to examine factors influencing geographical and occupational mobility. One difficulty with case studies is that motivations of participants may not be fully understood even by the interviewees themselves, and that responses may conceal rather than reveal true attitudes and motivations. Moreover, generalizations from case studies are necessarily restricted: the analyst must always face the possibility that a different set of cases might produce a different set of results.

The *statistical method*, a variant of the historical method, is limited to the analysis of numerical quantities. Defined broadly, statistics includes the collection, analysis, and presentation of numerical data. The problems of collecting basic and comprehensive economic statistics are generally so immense that governments are the primary collection agencies, since they have the financial resources to obtain and process data as well as the power to secure certain types of desired information. But even governmental resources are limited. If Congress or a state legislature is concerned with economy, the collection of certain types of labor statistics may be pruned from the budget, or statistical samples may be so limited in size that their significance and reliability are impaired. Collection costs of statistics also play an important part in determining the size and significance of smaller, privately conducted studies of the labor market. The techniques of securing statistical data, the phrasing of questions, and the skill of the interviewer must also be considered in evaluation of final information. Even what may appear the simplest problem of counting can be enormously complicated.

Analysis must occur simultaneously with the gathering of statistics and other information. Determining which facts to collect depends upon the importance assigned to them by a theoretical formulation of relevant variables. The task of theory is to identify the key relationships from the many influences that are found in economic and social situations. Although a deductive theory, if logically correct, may be considered true by definition, it is useful only if it leads to understanding situations that others find perplexing and significant, or if it can predict the consequences of specified actions. In the field of labor economics, there are a number of competing theories; they differ because of the nature of the problems with which they are concerned, and there are contradictory opinions as to their usefulness. The *theory of competitive equilibrium in the long run*, for example, assumes that with mobility of factors of production, occupational wage differentials (other things equal) will be consistent with the costs of the education and training acquired by the individual worker—with his or her human capital investment, in short. The *dual labor market theory*, on the other hand, attempts to explain why in some markets workers, despite their training, are confined to low-paying jobs with little or no payoff for education and skills.

Theories are a fertile source of hypotheses about labor markets, but the actual testing of hypotheses through research is not simple; in fact, in few if any scientific fields of study is basic knowledge obtained easily and without controversy. In labor economics, as in most social sciences, experimentation is generally precluded because of the difficulty in controlling the variables that might affect the result. Certain experiments have occasionally been tried; a recent one attempted to see whether work incentives would be impaired if poor families received cash subsidies.[1] Despite the best controls, the experimenter must interpret results carefully, if for no other reason than that the individuals who know they are under observation may behave differently than they otherwise would.

Without experimentation, hypothesis-testing must rely upon a reasoned analysis based on whatever information throws light on the relationship to be investigated. For certain types of problems where statistical information is available, econometric techniques are useful. They enable one to estimate the relative influence of different independent variables and identify relationships that might otherwise lie buried in masses of data. Multicorrelation analyses, for example, have given quantitative estimates of the effects that an increase in job opportunities has had in inducing individuals to enter or reenter the labor force, thus supporting the hypothesis that unemployment rates as now defined probably understate the amount of unemployment. Nonetheless, statistical data, like other historical information, must be used with care. Econometric techniques cannot improve the quality of the raw data, nor can they guarantee that the underlying relationships that they attempt to lay bare will necessarily persist under new and different conditions.

In testing hypotheses, investigators often come to different and sometimes contradictory conclusions. In view of the complexities of the real world of economics, the various interests of investigators, and the vast range of empirical

[1] This was the Work Incentive Experiment conducted among a sample of New Jersey households from 1968 to 1972. For interpretation of results, see Harold W. Watts and Albert Rees, eds., *The New Jersey Income-Maintenance Experiment*, vol. 2: *Labor-Supply Responses*, Institute for Research on Poverty (New York: Academic Press, 1977). Similar experiments have since been initiated in other areas, both urban and rural.

data, the lack of unanimity should not be surprising, nor even undesirable. Although there is much that investigators do agree upon, new labor issues call for new points of view when old solutions fail. If economic analysis did not adjust to emerging problems, it would quickly become irrelevant.

In contrast to facts and theories are recommendations for specific labor policies, usually expressed in terms of what the government should or should not do. A policy reflects a value judgment, or a standard of right or wrong, that is not verifiable in the above sense of hypothesis-testing. Recommendations for changes in labor legislation express certain value judgments. Although theories can point to consequences of particular policies, the relevance and importance of policies and their consequences are determined through a political, not a scientific, process, which may lead to legislative enactment, executive enforcement (or nonenforcement), and judicial interpretations. In this sense, the development of law becomes in effect the record of the changes in the dominant social values of a nation.

In the following chapters we consider the major areas of labor economics: labor force, supply, demand, and labor markets, the development of union organizations and union policy, collective bargaining and its regulation, wages and unemployment, and governmental policy for full employment and economic security. In each area we are concerned not only with basic materials, but also with the hypotheses that labor economists have developed to attempt to explain observed behavior in labor markets and with the policy recommendations proposed by various writers.

DISCUSSION QUESTIONS

1. The United States is becoming more and more a nation in which workers are employees working under the direction of others. Do you believe this is a gain or a loss for the individual? for the nation? Explain.
2. If you could choose between two jobs, each with similar responsibilities and pay, but one with a large firm and the other with a small one, which would you prefer? What are your reasons?
3. In labor controversies, it is sometimes said that "the facts of the matter," if correctly known, are all that is necessary to resolve the dispute. Do you agree? Explain.
4. Give examples of the distinction between economic and noneconomic objectives of management, unions, and governments. How important do you believe noneconomic objectives are in an analysis of a labor dispute? Can you illustrate, drawing upon some current labor dispute?

SELECTED READINGS

The scientific study of labor economics, like many fields, requires a foundation in both theory and empirical observations. While nearly everyone agrees in general with this proposition, labor economists disagree about the application of theory and the interpretation of empirical information. For a discussion, see Simon Rottenberg, "On Choice in Labor Markets," in the *Industrial and Labor Relations Review*, 9 (January 1956), 183–199. Robert J. Lampman criticized this position in "On Choice in Labor Markets: Comment," in the same journal, 9 (July 1956), 629–636. See also Rottenberg's reply in the same issue, pp. 636–641. All three statements have been republished in John F. Burton, Jr., et al., eds., *Readings in Labor Market Analysis* (New York: Holt, Rinehart and Winston, 1971), pp. 37–65.

PART ONE

The Economics of the Labor Market

2

The Labor Force

MEASURING THE LABOR FORCE

Definition of "Labor"

Like many words in ordinary speech that are taken over by social scientists for specific concepts, the term "labor" has many meanings. To the economist, labor means the service rendered by individuals in the production of goods and services; labor—like capital, land, and the organizing and risk-taking activities of the entrepreneur—is a factor of production.

This meaning is often modified, however, to include only those labor services rendered in a market for a price. This limitation is justified on the grounds that our economy is primarily a market economy and that society is not concerned with labor services to produce goods or services for personal or family consumption, such as parents' meal preparation or home repairs, or chores performed by children. Although we will normally follow the procedure of excluding this type of labor from consideration, we will see that it cannot be wholly neglected in analyzing certain types of situations, such as those relating to the amount of labor supplied.

A second limitation considers only the labor of those who work for others, and not the labor of the self-employed. The employee typically receives a wage or salary in payment for services performed in accordance with a contract with the employer or with the buyer of the services. The self-employed person receives a profit (or loss) after paying contractual obligations and other expenses.[1] Although both the employee and the self-employed perform ser-

---

[1] In the commercial fisheries, fishermen who work for the owner of the boat may not receive a wage or salary but a share of the profits of the voyage according to the terms of the "lay." In this instance, the fishermen share in the risk by "venturing" their labor, in a manner formally similar to the owner who "ventures" his capital. They are "employed" by the boat owner, but they receive "profits."

Naturally, the fishermen consider their returns as wages, but the courts do not always do so. For example, attempts by fishermen to control the price of fish, as workers in other industries try to control their "wages," have in some states been held to violate antitrust laws.

vices, labor economics generally deals with persons employed by others, not because the self-employed have no problems, but because theirs are dwarfed in public discussion by the sheer magnitude of the problems of employees.

A third qualification sometimes made in the definition of labor is to distinguish those employed persons who have the power to hire (and fire) from those who do not. This is useful because in a corporation everyone from president of the firm to the janitor is an employee. The owners are the shareholders who, in theory at least, exercise control through an elected board of directors. The board hires a president, who in turn hires vice presidents and staff, who in turn hire others, and so forth. In this situation, only those at the lower end of the chain would be considered workers to be dealt with in labor economics.[2]

Another qualification, less commonly advanced by economists but perhaps more generally accepted by the public, concerns income level. In an economy in which half the income units receive less than $12,000 per year, the public may wonder whether the "problems" of $70,000-a-year airline pilots should be included in a discussion of "labor." The implication is usually that labor economics is concerned with the *poor* wage earner, not the wealthy one. Nonetheless, the practical difficulty is how to determine the income level at which the distinction should be made, and that difficulty is compounded by the decision as to where the line should be tomorrow, and the day after, when incomes have changed.

Gainful Workers and the Labor Force[3]

Although the measurement of the amount of labor in the United States, a function of the U.S. Bureau of the Census, began with the decennial census

[2] But again it is not always so simple. In some industries, the lower echelons of management, the foremen, have argued that they have "labor problems" and have formed unions to assist them in their contract. The basic federal labor law, the Labor Management Relations Act of 1947 (the Taft-Hartley Act), draws a line between those with and those without the power to hire by withholding legal protection for unions of foremen.

[3] For a general presentation of the methods of data collection, see Bureau of Labor Statistics, U.S. Department of Labor, *How the Government Measures Unemployment*, Report 418 (1973), and Bureau of Labor Statistics and Bureau of the Census, *Concepts of Methods Used in Labor Force Statistics Derived from the Current Population Survey*, Report 463 (1976). Complete statistics of the labor force are published in the monthly periodical, *Employment and Earnings*, Bureau of Labor Statistics (Washington, D.C.: U.S. Government Printing Office).

A National Commission on Employment and Unemployment Statistics has been established under the Emergency Jobs Programs Extension Act of 1976 to reappraise the present system. An earlier examination of the labor force statistics was made in 1962 by the President's Committee to Appraise Employment and Unemployment Statistics. Its report was *Measuring Employment and Unemployment* (Washington, D.C.: U.S. Government Printing Office, 1962); this was called the Gordon Report after its chairman, Professor Robert A. Gordon.

of 1820, it was not until 1890 that standardized concepts for the collection of comparable statistics were successfully employed. From 1890 to 1930 the decennial census defined labor for statistical purposes as the gainful worker, a person who usually earned money, or a money equivalent, or assisted in the production of marketable goods. Although the concept of the gainful worker did yield information on the size of the experienced labor force, its disadvantages gradually became obvious. The techniques of data collection were relatively crude, according to present standards; there was considerable variation in interpretation of questions, such as the question about the usual (as distinguished from the occasional) occupation; unemployment was not measured except by supplementary questions on unemployment asked in certain census years; the tabulation did not provide a logical basis for counting the occasional, the inexperienced, and the would-be worker, nor did it provide a continuous statistical series. The use of a time period of reference to determine whether a person was unemployed came only in the census of 1930.

The concept of the labor force, developed by economists of the Works Progress Administration and introduced by the Bureau of the Census in the decennial census of 1940, measures the number of persons currently attached to the labor market. The "labor force" is the sum of the employed and unemployed during a particular week in a month. On the basis of a sample of households, a monthly estimate of employed and unemployed is prepared and published by the Bureau of Labor Statistics of the U.S. Department of Labor. (The Bureau of the Census conducts the interviews of the households in its Current Population Survey.)

Current attachment to the labor market is measured only for persons 16 years old and over who are not inmates of hospitals, prisons, and detention and nursing homes. The cutoff age of 16—previously the minimum age had been 10 through the census of 1930, and 14 from 1940 to 1967—reflects the decreasing importance of child labor but does not, of course, imply that there are no workers below that age.[4] The number of those in the armed forces is added to the civilian labor force to give the total labor force.

Attachment to the labor market is indicated by a person's activity during a specified period of time. Each household interviewed is asked to report the labor market activity of each member of the household during the calendar week containing the twelfth day of the month. The types of activities are three: employed, unemployed, and out of the labor force. The first two categories constitute the labor force.

Employed persons include two categories. The first is defined as those who worked during the calendar week in their own business or profession, on their own farm, or in a business operated by a member of the family. A person is

---

[4] In 1975, the average number of 14- and 15-year-olds employed was estimated to be 1.66 million.

considered employed if he or she works one hour or more a week, except for unpaid workers on a family farm or business, where 15 hours is the minimum. The second category is defined as those who had a job or business but did not work during the reference week because of illness, bad weather, a strike, or similar reasons. These are the nonworking employed. Persons who have a new job to which they will report within 30 days or who are laid off but waiting to be recalled are not considered employed.

The unemployed are those who did no work at all during the survey week, who are currently available for work (except for temporary sickness), and who are looking for work. The last criterion requires that, to be counted as unemployed, a person must have actively looked for work during the previous four weeks; the search may include registering at an employment office, writing letters, or simply checking with friends or relatives. The only exception to this requirement is in the case, noted above, of the worker who will start a job within 30 days or who is laid off and awaiting recall.

The group considered "out of the labor force" consists of the remainder of the noninstitutional population 16 years of age and over: namely, those who are neither employed, unemployed, nor members of the armed forces. In this group are homemakers, students, those unable to work because of long-term disabilities, the retired, the voluntarily idle, and unpaid workers in a family enterprise working less than 15 hours per week. The voluntarily idle are those who are financially independent, those who work only at other times during the year, and those who are called "discouraged workers." The latter group consists of those who want full- or part-time work but who have not looked for work during the previous four weeks because they do not believe that suitable jobs are available in the community.[5]

Problems of Measurement

Household Reporting Information concerning the labor force is obtained by household interviews. In the decennial censuses all households are interviewed, while in the regular monthly survey interviews are obtained from about 47,000 households in 461 sample areas throughout the United States.

How satisfactory are data obtained from households rather than from employers? Statistics on employment derived from household interviews never agree exactly with the employment data reported by firms, such as those recorded in the current nonagricultural employment series of the Bureau of Labor Statistics or farm employment estimates of the Department of Agriculture. In household interviews the respondent, usually the housewife, must

[5] In 1975, "discouraged workers" totaled nearly 1 million persons; if they had been included in the unemployment totals, the unemployment estimate of 7.8 million workers would have been increased by 11.5 percent, and the nation's unemployment rate for the year would have been 9.3 percent instead of 8.5.

rely on memory to describe the labor activity during the previous week of each member of the household 16 years of age and over. When a firm reports the number it employed, it can refer to its records. Another difference is that households report persons, while establishments report jobs held. If one person holds two or more jobs, he or she is counted once in household reports but twice or more by the employers. Furthermore, household statistics report the labor force by residence, while establishment statistics do so by place of work; for any particular city, county, or state, interarea commuting may cause the two types of statistical reports to differ.

The estimate of those unemployed, as derived from household interviews, is larger than the number of persons who receive weekly unemployment compensation benefits. Such benefits are paid only to those who qualify for them by working in industries covered by the respective state laws—in 1974, about two-thirds of the labor force—who meet specific eligibility tests and who have not already received the maximum number of weeks of benefits to which they were entitled. Another divergence between labor force unemployment estimates and the number reported as receiving benefits results from the fact that the latter total includes those who are working part time and drawing "partial" unemployment benefits. In the relatively prosperous month of December 1973, about 1.7 million workers were reported as the "insured unemployed," or 2.8 percent of those in covered employments; the labor force unemployment estimate for that month was 4.1 million, or a seasonally adjusted rate of 4.9 percent.

Because monthly labor force estimates are derived from a sample, they may not exactly equal the totals that would be obtained from interviews of the entire population. The reliability of the estimates varies with the size of the sample; in the case of unemployment, in recent years the chances were about 19 out of 20 that the unemployment estimate would not differ by more than 180,000 persons from the figure derived from the sample, an error not significant enough to distort the unemployment picture.

On the other hand, data from the sample must be related to the total population in order to achieve historical comparability. Following each decennial census adjustments are made to bring year-to-year estimates of total population into line with the comprehensive counts of population.[6] Moreover, it must be recognized that even the decennial data have limitations. Various procedures have been used to check the completeness of census enumeration, but all leave little doubt that there have been significant undercounts. The number of unenumerated persons in the 1970 census has been estimated at 5.3 million, or about 2.6 percent of the population. The incidence of those

[6] From the 1970 census, information was introduced into the estimating procedure that raised the civilian noninstitutional population by 800,000 and the labor force and employment total by a little more than 300,000. See *Employment and Earnings*, 20 (January 1974), 178.

missed is greater for males than for females, and for nonwhites than for whites.[7]

Period of Reference   The time period for which labor activity is reported has a direct effect on the size of the labor force. In both the decennial census and the monthly reports, the period of reference is one week. If it were one day, the resulting statistics would be considerably different from those now collected. There would probably be fewer persons reported at work and more unemployment would be recorded, because persons working less than a week might be interviewed on an off day and would be classified as either unemployed (if they were looking for more work) or not in the labor force. On the other hand, if the time period were greater than a week—for example, a year—the statistical results would show a larger number of workers and less unemployment. Seasonal workers would be included as employed, since they would have been employed at some time during the longer period. In fact, any worker who had participated in any way in the labor market during any portion of the year would be considered a member of the labor force; to be considered unemployed, he or she would have had to be fully unemployed for the entire length of time spent in the labor force.

A change in the period of reference, therefore, changes the statistics collected. What time period is best? The answer depends upon the purposes the statistics are intended to serve. In the United States, a one-week period is particularly suitable to our demands for *current* information on employment and unemployment. Other time periods are useful, however, and the Bureau of the Census has instituted its work experience report based on the calendar year. The term "work experience" distinguishes the statistics from "labor force." In 1975, for example, the United States work experience study indicated that 104.4 million persons worked at some time during the year. In contrast, civilian employment determined by the current activity reports for a specific week in each month averaged 84.8 million during the year. The work experience survey showed that 21.1 million workers were unemployed at some time during the year, or nearly three times the 7.8 million reported as unemployed for the average month; 3.2 million persons who looked for work during the calendar year did not find work at all.

These two surveys of the monthly labor force and of annual work experience yield valuable information about mobility in the labor force—that is, the

---

[7] U.S. Bureau of the Census, *Developmental Estimates of the Coverage of the Population of States in the 1970 Census: Demographic Analysis,* Current Population Reports, Special Studies, Series P-23, No. 65, Table I-B. See also Deborah P. Klein, "Determining the Labor Force Status of Men Missed in the Census," *Monthly Labor Review,* 93 (March 1970), 26–32. After the 1970 census, various groups challenged the Bureau of the Census counts, especially of blacks in large cities and of Chicanos, on the grounds that undercounts cost cities and minorities a loss of federal funds when such disbursements were made on the basis of population size.

movement of persons in and out of it. Certain groups display a marked tendency to go in and out of the labor force during the year, while others remain in it throughout the year. The ratio of those in the labor force at some time during the year to the average monthly size of the labor force (times 100) gives a measure called *labor force turnover*. The labor force turnover of women is higher than that of men, with ratios in 1975 of 121.0 and 107.2 respectively. Over a fifth more women were in the labor force at some time during the year compared to the average number for the twelve months; the movement in and out for males was less. Youthful workers, both male and female, and older workers of both sexes have the higher turnover rates.[8]

The Unemployed One problem encountered in measuring unemployment has to do with criteria for classifying the partially employed worker. According to Bureau of the Census procedures, a worker who works at least one hour or more a week is classified as employed and not unemployed, even though he or she may have been actively looking for more work. This classification has been questioned on the grounds that if persons consider themselves unemployed and are looking for work, they should be so counted. On the average in 1975, there were some 10.6 million part-time workers in nonagricultural industries, about 12 percent of those at work. Most of these did not want full-time work, but 3.5 million of them did. Either their search for a full-time job had not been successful, or their workweek had been cut below 35 hours (defined as full time) by adverse economic conditions.[9]

A second difficulty in measuring unemployment is the blurred line between unemployment and the out-of-the-labor-force category. In addition to the "discouraged workers" noted above, persons marginally attached to the labor force may leave the labor force when their jobs come to an end. Seasonal workers, young people after summer employment, and women who hold temporary jobs may not become unemployed as such but rather move directly from the employment to the out-of-the-labor-force category. This group, sometimes known as the secondary work force, may in fact be "unemployed" although classified at any given time as at school or as housewives. The household interview technique cannot identify the extent to which these workers would participate more fully in the labor force under other conditions. As will be pointed out in the following chapter, however, the statistical record provides evidence that there is a substantial amount of "hidden unemployment"—that is, people who would participate in the labor force above the number counted officially if economic conditions in the market, even in normal years, were improved.

[8] U.S. Department of Labor, Bureau of Labor Statistics, *Work Experience of the Population in 1975*, Special Labor Force Report 192 (Washington, D.C.: U.S. Government Printing Office, 1976).

[9] Data are from *Employment and Training Report of the President*, 1976 (Washington, D.C.: U.S. Government Printing Office), pp. 181–183.

Table 2-1
Employment Status of the Noninstitutional Population 16 Years and Over, Annual Averages, 1947–1977
(Numbers in thousands)

Year	Total Noninstitutional Population	Total Labor Force, Including Armed Forces		Civilian Labor Force						Not in Labor Force
					Employed			Unemployed		
		Number	Percent of Noninstitutional Population	Total	Total	Agriculture	Nonagricultural Industries	Number	Percent of Labor Force	
1947	103,418	60,941	58.9	59,350	57,039	7,891	49,148	2,311	3.9	42,477
1948	104,527	62,080	59.4	60,621	58,344	7,629	50,711	2,276	3.8	42,447
1949	105,611	62,903	59.6	61,286	57,649	7,656	49,990	3,637	5.9	42,708
1950	106,645	63,858	59.9	62,208	58,920	7,160	51,752	3,288	5.3	42,787
1951	107,721	65,117	60.4	62,017	59,962	6,726	53,230	2,055	3.3	42,604
1952	108,823	65,730	60.4	62,138	60,254	6,501	53,748	1,883	3.0	43,093
1953	110,601	66,560	60.2	63,015	61,181	6,261	54,915	1,834	2.9	44,041
1954	111,671	66,993	60.0	63,643	60,110	6,206	53,898	3,532	5.5	44,678
1955	112,732	68,072	60.4	65,023	62,171	6,449	55,718	2,852	4.4	44,660
1956	113,811	69,409	61.0	66,552	63,802	6,283	57,506	2,750	4.1	44,402
1957	115,065	69,729	60.6	66,929	64,071	5,947	58,123	2,859	4.3	45,336

Year										
1958	116,363	70,275	60.4	67,639	63,036	5,586	57,450	4,602	6.8	46,088
1959	117,881	70,921	60.2	68,369	64,630	5,565	59,065	3,740	5.5	46,960
1960	119,759	72,142	60.2	69,628	65,778	5,458	60,318	3,852	5.5	47,617
1961	121,343	73,031	60.2	70,459	65,746	5,200	60,546	4,714	6.7	48,312
1962	122,981	73,442	59.7	70,614	66,702	4,944	61,759	3,911	5.5	49,539
1963	125,154	74,571	59.6	71,833	67,762	4,687	63,076	4,070	5.7	50,583
1964	127,224	75,830	59.6	73,091	69,305	4,523	64,782	3,786	5.2	51,394
1965	129,236	77,178	59.7	74,455	71,088	4,361	66,726	3,366	4.5	52,058
1966	131,180	78,893	60.1	75,770	72,895	3,979	68,915	2,875	3.8	52,288
1967	133,319	80,793	60.6	77,347	74,372	3,844	70,527	2,975	3.8	52,527
1968	135,562	82,272	60.7	78,737	75,920	3,817	72,103	2,817	3.6	53,291
1969	137,841	84,239	61.1	80,733	77,902	3,606	74,296	2,831	3.5	53,602
1970	140,182	85,903	61.3	82,715	78,627	3,462	75,165	4,088	4.9	54,280
1971	142,596	86,929	61.0	84,113	79,120	3,387	75,732	4,993	5.9	55,666
1972	145,775	88,991	61.0	86,542	81,702	3,472	78,230	4,840	5.6	56,785
1973	148,263	91,040	61.4	88,714	84,409	3,452	80,957	4,304	4.9	57,222
1974	150,827	93,240	61.8	91,011	85,936	3,492	82,443	5,076	5.6	57,587
1975	153,449	94,793	61.8	92,613	84,783	3,380	81,403	7,830	8.5	58,655
1976	156,048	96,917	62.1	94,773	87,485	3,297	84,188	7,288	7.7	59,130
1977	158,559	99,534	62.8	97,401	90,546	3,244	87,302	6,855	7.0	59,025

Sources: Employment and Training Report of the President, 1977 (Washington, D.C.: U.S. Government Printing Office), p. 135, and Employment and Earnings, 25 (January 1978), 136.

COMPOSITION OF THE LABOR FORCE

In the remainder of this chapter, we shall be concerned with the composition of the American labor force in terms of demographic characteristics and the extent of part-time versus full-time employment. We shall also turn our attention to changing trends in the distribution of occupational employments and the importance of the increasing metropolitan concentration of the labor force.

Age-Sex Composition

In 1977, the total labor force of the United States of 99.5 million workers constituted 62.8 percent of the total noninstitutional population of 158.6 million persons 16 years old and over (see Table 2–1). Of the civilian labor force of 97.4 million, 90.5 million were employed and 6.9 million (7.0%) were unemployed.

In the period from 1947 to 1977, the total labor force had increased by some 39 million workers, or nearly two-thirds (63.3%).[10] The increase reflects a substantial growth in population and, to a lesser extent, a slight rise in the overall percentage of the population 16 years of age and over who participate in the labor force (from 58.9% in 1947 to 62.8% in 1977).

Two significant changes have occurred in the composition of the labor force by age and sex groups since World War II. First, the average age of the labor force has declined, as the "baby boom" generation of the postwar period entered the labor force in the 1960s and early 1970s. The percentage of the total labor force under 25 years of age rose from one out of five (19.6%) in 1947 to one out of four (25%) in 1977. Secondly, women members of the labor force have increased both absolutely and relatively. The actual numbers more than doubled during the period, from about 17 to 40 million workers, and the female proportion of the total labor force rose from 27.3 percent in 1947 to 40.3 percent in 1977. The percentage of women 16 years of age and over who were in the labor force rose from 31.8 to 48.5, while the percentage of men declined from 86.8 to 78.3. Another way of describing the change is by saying that of the 38.6-million worker increase in the labor force in the last 30 years, three out of every five additional workers were women.

The participation rates, or the percent of the noninstitutional population

[10] Published data on labor force and employment for 1947 and 1977 are not precisely comparable because of certain changes made in estimating procedures, and also because of the inclusion of the new states of Alaska and Hawaii beginning in 1960. The two new states added about 500,000 to the population and about 300,000 to the labor force, four-fifths of which was in nonagricultural industries. See *Employment and Earnings*, 20 (January 1974), 177–178.

in the labor force, give a more detailed picture of these work patterns (see Figure 2–1). In 1977, for males, half (50.6%) of youth (16 and 17 years of age) were in the labor force, and the rates rise rapidly to over 95 percent for the age group 25–44, the peak in the age-specific participation rates. In the age group 45–54 the rate falls slightly to 91.2, declines to 74.0 for those in the 55–64 group, and then drops sharply to 20.1 for those 65 years old and over. The participation rates for females are not so high as the male rates. From

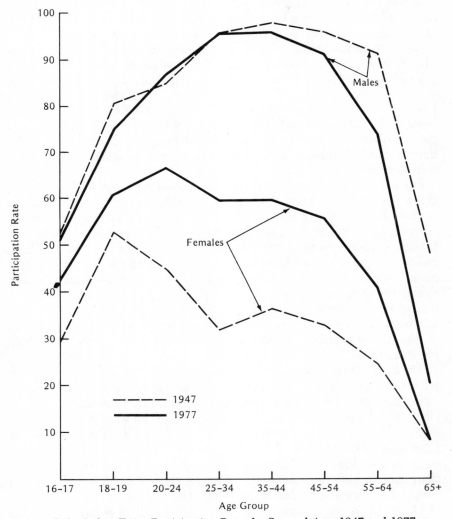

FIGURE 2–1 Labor Force Participation Rates by Sex and Age, 1947 and 1977

Source: Employment and Training Report of the President, 1978 (Washington, D.C.: U.S. Government Printing Office).

42.2 percent for young women 16 and 17 years of age, the participation rate rises to a high of 66.7 for those in the 20–24 group, then falls steadily, dropping to 8.1 for those 65 years of age and over. The drop in rates after the age of 25, although far less than in earlier years, reflects the outflow from the labor market as women marry and raise families.

Since World War II, participation rates for males have declined for every age group except the 20–24 group, although the rate for this group is lower than that reached during the decade of the 1950s. For the teenagers and for the 20–24 age group since the 1950s, the declining rates are explained by the increasing emphasis on education at the college and post-secondary levels. However, a counter-trend in participation rates has occurred in the 1970s. The most substantial declines in male participation rates have been in the older age groups. For the male 55–64 age group, the rate dropped from 89.6 in 1947 to 74.0 in 1977, while for the category of 65 and over, the rate in 1947 was 47.8, more than twice the 1977 rate. This decline has occurred because of the increased benefits and extension of Social Security coverage and the virtual revolution in private pension schemes that enabled, and sometimes compelled, workers to retire with an income, however modest, rather than to continue working after 65.

For women, the long-run rise in participation rates has affected all age groups, except for the group 65 and over, for which the rate has remained the same as 30 years ago. The expansion of job opportunities for women, especially in the rapidly growing clerical, white-collar, and professional fields has brought women into the labor force in far greater numbers than had been predicted. Especially significant has been the increased participation of older married women who seek jobs after their children begin to attend school. The availability of many new houshould appliances, prepared foods, and commercial services has lightened housework and freed married women for outside work. The long-run decline in birth rates and the general disappearance of the three-generation family have also tended to reduce household responsibilities.

The long-run trends in labor participation rates by specific age-sex groups are expected to continue into the near future, but because of the changing size and composition of the United States population, the projected 1990 civilian labor force will be different in certain ways from what it is now. In the first place, according to the Bureau of Labor Statistics,[11] the flow into the labor force of persons born during the postwar "baby boom" will have been completed by 1980, and labor force growth rates will begin to decline. The sharp drop in birth rates that occurred during the 1960s will be reflected in a lower labor force growth during the 1980s. The 1990 labor force is projected at 113.8 million, compared to the total of 101.7 million projected for 1980

[11] Howard N. Fullerton, Jr., and Paul D. Flaim, *New Labor Force Projections to 1990,* Special Labor Force Report 197, U.S. Bureau of Labor Statistics (December 1976).

and the actual annual average of 82.7 million in 1970. While the labor force was increasing by 2 million workers a year during the period from 1970 to 1975, the net annual additions will be under 1 million by the last half of the 1980s; the annual rate of change will have fallen from 2.26 in 1970 to 0.94 by 1990.

Second is the matter of age composition. The youth labor force (age 16 to 24), which is already growing at a slower rate than it did in the early 1970s, is expected to fall in absolute numbers by over 3 million workers between 1980 and 1990. The prime age labor force—those 25 to 54 years of age—will grow more rapidly than other age groups, again reflecting the aging of persons born during the post–World War II baby boom. The older labor force (those over 55 years), on the other hand, is expected to decline in absolute numbers by the last half of the 1980s. Toward the end of this century and into the next, this trend will be reversed as the "baby boom" population cohorts begin to affect these age groups; the implications of this trend with respect to the Social Security system will be considered in chapter 18.

Finally, projections for 1990 show a continued increase in the proportion of women in the labor force. Of the total 31.1 million people that will be added to the civilian labor force between 1970 and 1990, it is estimated that 17.1 million, or more than half of them, will be women. Men will still predominate, constituting an estimated 57.3 percent of the labor force in 1990, but their participation rates are likely to fall while those of women continue their long-run rise. Although many more women will soon be reaching the age of childbearing, their participation rates are not likely to fall as much as formerly for two reasons. One is that birth rates are lower; the other is that mothers of young children are now increasingly likely to remain at work.

Race

Negroes and other nonwhites (the Bureau of the Census does not report separate data for blacks, who compromise approximately 90 percent of the nonwhites) totaled over 11 million members of the labor force in 1976, or 11.7 percent of the civilian labor force. This was a slightly higher percentage than immediately after World War II.[12] Participation rates for nonwhite males are lower than for white males in all age groups, but especially so among teenagers; earlier, nonwhite male participation rates averaged slightly above the white male rates, except in the middle age groups. In the case of females, on the other hand, nonwhite participation rates have continued to

[12] Because controls over collection of data were not established by the Bureau of the Census until 1954, absolute numbers by color are not available for earlier years. The number of nonwhites in the civilian labor force in 1954 was 6,824,000, or 10.7 percent of the aggregate. See *Manpower Report of the President* (Washington, D.C.: U.S. Government Printing Office, 1974), Table A–3. Participation rates by color are, however, available back to 1948.

be higher than those of whites although differences have been decreasing. In terms of the average civilian labor force participation rate, the nonwhite female rate rose from 45.6 to 51.0 between 1948 and 1977, while the white female rate increased from 31.3 to 48.2. By age groups, the black female pattern of participation is lower than that of white females below the age of 25 but higher in older age groups.

The labor force participation rates for black women have been far higher than for white women primarily because black families have had to rely on incomes from more than one working person to meet family needs. For males, the substantial drop in participation rates in the postwar period to some extent reflects the shift of the 1940s and 1950s of workers out of agricultural areas, where male participation rates are generally higher, to urban areas, where job opportunities have been fewer. Lower levels of education and job discrimination have also been important deterrents to fuller participation in the labor force, especially by young blacks in urban areas. The reported high unemployment rates of black youth in central cities, shocking in themselves, probably underestimate the true situation because of the discouraging effect on labor force participation.

Full-Time and Part-Time Participants

Primary workers are those with a continuing attachment to the labor force. They are the "hard core" of the labor force. *Secondary workers* (who are not the same as "second workers" in a household) are those with a temporary attachment to the labor force. Measurement of these two groups is expressed in terms of part-time work per week and part-year work. By both measures, the size of the secondary labor force is substantial, although it does not seem to have been increasing significantly in recent years.

On the average, one-fourth of the labor force works less than 35 hours per week, a convenient line separating the part-time from full-time weekly work: in 1977, the number was 21.2 million out of a total of 85.1 million employed persons. Of the part-time workers, a third usually worked full-time, and the remaining two-thirds (or about 14.1 million workers) usually worked part-time.[13]

The "usually part-time" workers are primarily women (some of whom have household responsibilities), youths (still in the process of making the transition from school to the world of work), and older persons (who may be seeking partial income supplements to their retirement pensions). In nonagricultural industries in 1977, women had a voluntary part-time employment average of 23.4 percent in contrast to the male average of 7.4. The percentage of employed male youths 16 and 17 years of age on voluntary

---

[13] These and the following data are taken from *Employment and Earnings*, U.S. Bureau of Labor Statistics, 25 (January 1978), 162–164, Tables 32–35.

part-time work was 65.9. The percentage at first declined as the age increased: for males 25 to 44 years of age it was only 1.9 percent. But at higher age levels it rose again: for those 65 years and older, 43.6 percent of the employed were working at less than full-time jobs.

Studies of work experience, which deal with the extent to which persons enter the labor market over the course of a year, provide a measure of the extent of part-year versus full-year participation in the labor market. In 1975, of the 101.2 million persons who worked at some time during the year, only 55 million, or 54.7 percent, worked 50 to 52 weeks at full-time jobs of 35 or more hours a week; some 7 million worked throughout the year at part-time jobs.[14] In short, over one-third of those with work experience worked at less than full-year jobs. The reasons for working less than a full year included seasonal work, returning to school, and, among women, pregnancy, marriage, and the assumption of full-time household responsibilities. What is particularly significant about the extent of this part-year work experience of 38 million persons is that the number is over twice as high as the 17.7 million who reported unemployment during the year. In short, the movement of workers into and out of the employment category is far greater than would seem possible according to labor force statistics of unemployment. Workers can lose their jobs or quit work and not become reported as unemployed at all: they move directly to the out-of-the-labor-force category.

TRENDS IN EMPLOYMENT

The labor force of a country tends to adjust itself to the changing structure and distribution of employment by industries and occupations. As a nation develops industrially, there are four trends in the types of employment. One is a decline in agricultural employment and an expansion in manufacturing and then in service industries. The second trend is a decline of the self-employed and an increase of those dependent upon the market for wages and salaries. Third is the development of more and more specialized types of jobs so that the labor force becomes more heterogeneous in terms of occupations. And fourth is the growing concentration of population in urban and metropolitan areas.

The Shift from Agriculture

The massive shift of labor out of agriculture and into other industries constitutes one of the most fundamental economic changes experienced by the United States in the twentieth century. Until 1880, more than half of those

[14] U.S. Bureau of Labor Statistics, *Work Experience of the Population in 1975*, Special Labor Force Report 192, p. 4, Table 1.

gainfully employed were in agriculture. The absolute number began to decline just before World War I. Both relative and absolute declines continued steadily after World War II, when some 7.6 million, or 13.1 percent of all employed persons, were in agriculture. By 1973, the number had contracted sharply to less than 3.5 million, or 4.1 percent of total employment. There is currently some evidence that at last the absolute level is stabilizing.

Farm employment fell by nearly 55 percent in the last quarter of a century; at the same time, however, farmers raised enough food not only for a population that increased by over 50 million but also for export. This was possible because of a tremendous gain in labor productivity as the result of technological changes, improved crops and livestock, and greater capital investment per worker. The emergence and dominance of large-scale production caused a contraction of employment among small, self-employed farmers and unpaid family workers. Mechanization in the cotton-raising areas of the deep South, for example, put many blacks and tenant farmers out of work.

The most important of the nonagricultural industries in the United States is manufacturing, the heart of any industrialized country; in 1977, it employed 19.6 million persons, or about a fourth (23.9%) of those in nonagricultural employment.[15] (See Figure 2–2.) Some 15.5 million were employed in manufacturing in 1947, and the total rose to peaks of about 20 million in 1969, 1973, and 1974; but manufacturing's *share* of nonfarm jobs in this period fell from over a third to about one-fourth.

The great expansion—from 44 to over 82 million jobs—in nonagricultural industries in the period from 1947 to 1977 came in three major industry groups: government, with a net growth of 9.7 million workers; services, with a gain of 10.2 million; and trade, with a gain of 9.3 million. In 1977, these three groups, in absolute numbers, accounted for 15.2, 15.3, and 18.3 million workers. This total of nearly 49 million amounted to nearly three out of every five nonagricultural jobs in the United States. The increases in other industry groups were less significant: finance, insurance, and real estate more than doubled the number of workers to about 4.5 million, or 5.5 percent of the total; construction employment, which rose from about 2 to 3.8 million workers, has had a relative position of about 5 percent of total employment since World War II; transportation and public utility employment, remaining above 4 million, has fallen relatively, to 5.6 percent of total employment; and mining, which experienced the greatest absolute decline, fell from about 1 million to 831,000 workers, a level somewhat above its lowest point earlier in this decade.

The dominance of service-type, over goods-producing, industries has some-

---

[15] These data are drawn not from labor force reports but from the establishment-reporting statistics of the Bureau of Labor Statistics of the U.S. Department of Labor. These are included in the *Employment and Training Report of the President, 1977* (Washington, D.C.: U.S. Government Printing Office), and *Employment and Earnings* 25 (March 1978).

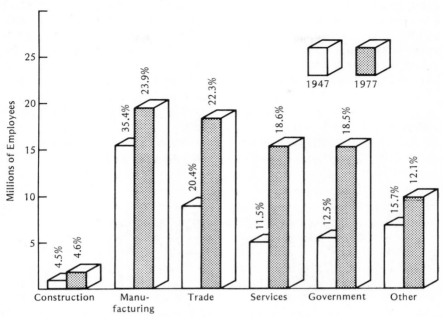

FIGURE 2–2   Change in Nonagricultural Employment by Industry and Its Distribution, 1947–1977

Sources: *Employment and Training Report of the President,* 1977 (Washington, D.C.: U.S. Government Printing Office), Table C–1, and *Employment and Earnings,* 25 (March 1978), 61.

times been hailed as the mark of the post-industrial society, where, because the production of goods is automated, individuals can turn increasingly to the purchase of services of all kinds.[16] Productivity gains in the goods-producing industries (including agriculture) made possible employment shifts into service industries. More recently, however, world shortages of food, energy, and raw materials, at a time when world population growth is accelerating, have led some observers to question whether these trends can continue. Moreover, the rapid employment expansion in government (primarily at the state and local levels) reflected to some degree an education boom, which is now lessening.

Wage and Salary Workers

Labor force data are not adequate indicators of the supply of labor, as defined earlier in this chapter, because they include self-employed, unpaid fam-

[16] A leading exponent of this view is Daniel Bell. See his *The Coming of Post-Industrial Society, A Venture in Social Forecasting* (New York: Basic Books, 1973).

ily workers as well as managers and supervisory personnel. The number of wage and salary workers has been increasing more rapidly than the aggregates of the civilian labor force. The reason for this rise is that the total of self-employed persons, both in agriculture and in nonagricultural industries, has declined in absolute numbers. In agriculture, where the contraction has been the greatest, the number fell from nearly 4.7 million in 1948 to 1.6 million in 1977, for a loss of 66.0 percent. In nonagricultural industries the decline from 6.1 to 5.7 million was minimal, 6.9 percent. Unpaid family workers, estimated for 1948 at 1.3 million and 400,000 in agriculture and nonagricultural industries respectively, stood at 350,000 and 500,000 in 1977. Working for a wage or salary is becoming more and more the predominate way of life, as seen in Table 2–2.

Table 2–2
Relative Increase of Wage and Salary Workers, 1948–1977

	Percentage Increase
Noninstitutional population (16 years and over)	51.7
Civilian labor force (employed and unemployed)	60.7
Total employed	67.2
Wage and salary workers	79.1

In 1977, wage and salary workers constituted 90.7 percent of all employed persons; in 1948, the percentage was 78.6.

Occupational Composition

One of the primary characteristics of industrial development is the increasing differentiation and specialization of occupations that require greater training and education on the part of the labor force. It is a long and costly process to transform the labor force from one that satisfies the relatively simple occupational requirements of an agricultural society to one with the vast array of skills demanded by the complex needs of an advanced, technologically sophisticated economy. For this reason, increasing human capital investment—the development of abilities and skills through training and education—has been an integral, necessary part of modern industrial systems.

Although it does not give a wholly adequate picture of the proliferation of skills that has occurred with industrialization, the occupational breakdown of employed workers shown in Table 2–3 illustrates the types of changes that have occurred. Long-run trends in major occupational groupings parallel industrial changes. Farm workers declined; manual and service workers gained slightly in proportion to the total; white-collar workers not only quadrupled in number from 1900 to 1950, but their proportion of the total doubled from

Table 2–3
Percentage Distribution by Major Occupation Group for the Economically
Active Civilian Population of the United States, 1900–1950

Major Occupation Group, Both Sexes	1900	1910	1920	1930	1940	1950
White-collar workers	17.6	21.3	24.9	29.4	31.1	36.6
Professional, technical and kindred workers	4.3	4.7	5.4	6.8	7.5	8.6
Managers, officals, and proprietors, except farm	5.8	6.6	6.6	7.4	7.3	8.7
Clerical and kindred workers	3.0	5.3	8.0	8.9	9.6	12.3
Sales workers	4.5	4.7	4.9	6.3	6.7	7.0
Manual and service workers	44.9	47.7	48.1	49.4	51.5	51.6
Manual workers	35.8	38.2	40.2	39.6	39.8	41.1
Craftsmen, foremen, and kindred workers	10.5	11.6	13.0	12.8	12.0	14.1
Operatives and kindred workers	12.8	14.6	15.6	15.8	18.4	20.4
Laborers, except farm and mine	12.5	12.0	11.6	11.0	9.4	6.6
Service workers	9.0	9.6	7.8	9.8	11.7	10.5
Private household workers	5.4	5.0	3.3	4.1	4.7	2.6
Service workers, except private household	3.6	4.6	4.5	5.7	7.1	7.9
Farm workers	37.5	30.9	27.0	21.2	17.4	11.8
Farmers and farm managers	19.9	16.5	15.3	12.4	10.4	7.4
Farm laborers and foremen	17.7	14.4	11.7	8.8	7.0	4.4
	100.0	100.0	100.0	100.0	100.0	100.0

Source: U.S. Bureau of the Census.

17.6 percent in 1900 to 36.6 percent in 1950. Within the white-collar groups, the numbers of clerical and kindred workers grew most rapidly, followed by the numbers of professional and sales workers. Among manual and service workers, expansion occurred primarily among semiskilled workers in factories, service workers (except domestic servants), and craftsmen and foremen, while sharp relative declines are found among laborers and domestic servants (especially after 1940).

Some of these long-run employment trends by occupations have been accelerated since World War II. For the ten years from 1960 to 1970, the annual average increase in employment amounted to nearly 1.3 million per year. Of these, about 950,000, or nearly three-fourths, entered white-collar occupations. The average annual growth of white-collar workers consisted of 395,000 into clerical occupations and 367,000 into professional and technical ones. About as many, 375,000, entered annually into blue-collar occupations, and 169,000 entered service jobs. Farm employment showed an average annual decline of 205,000 persons.

White-collar workers became the largest sector of total civilian employment in the 1950s. By 1976, white-collar workers reached half of all employed workers (see Table 2–4). Within the white-collar occupations, the fastest growing group was that of professional and technical workers; this was in contrast with the period before World War II, when the number of clerical workers had expanded most rapidly.

Among blue-collar workers, the significant change has been the decline in the relative numbers of nonfarm laborers—that is, of unskilled workers. Not only was the rate of growth during the period from 1958 to 1976 one of the lowest of all major nonfarm categories, but the total of these workers amounted to less than 5 percent of the employed labor force. At the turn of the century, one of every eight nonfarm workers was unskilled.

Increasing occupational differentiation and the growth of the white-collar work force does not mean that the relative size of the American working class is in decline. Although the definition of "class" is open to various interpretation in terms of status, attitude, income, and other criteria, jobs of a manual nature are still a majority. Not only are blue-collar workers, who have generally been considered the core of the working class, still a significant group within the economy, but those in service occupations (as distinguished from service industries)—guards, waiters, hospital attendants, and the like—are also manual workers. In addition, many people in white-collar occupations actually perform manual work (at relatively low pay): typists, key-punch operators, and those employed in routine technical jobs. Even excluding these white-collar workers, the manual workers in the blue-collar occupations, service occupations, and agricultural labor composed half of all employed workers in 1976, and over half (55.1%) of all those in nonmanagerial occupations.

Metropolitan Concentration

The long-run movement of workers from rural to urban areas was a response both to industrialization and to the expansion of service industries so characteristic of modern large metropolitan areas. By 1970, seven out of ten Americans lived in 243 metropolitan areas, or Standard Metropolitan Statistical Areas (SMSAs), each with a population of 50,000 or more in its central city or cities. Although there is some evidence that the urban flow, so high during the post–World War II period, began to ebb during the 1970s, the American civilian labor force is now heavily concentrated geographically in the larger metropolitan areas. In 1973, the 30 largest metropolitan areas had over 33.4 million workers, or 37.7 percent of the nation's total.[17]

[17] See U.S. Department of Labor Report 431, *Geographical Profile of Employment and Unemployment, 1973.*

Table 2-4
Percentage Distribution of Employed Persons 16 Years and Over, by Occupation Group, Annual Averages, 1958–1977[a]

Year	Total Employed	White-Collar Workers Total	Professional and Technical	Managers and Administrators ex. Farm	Sales Workers	Clerical Workers	Blue-Collar Workers Total	Craft and Kindred Workers	Operatives Total	Operatives Except Transport	Operatives Transport Equipment	Nonfarm Laborers	Service Workers Total	Private Household Workers	Other Service Workers	Farmworkers Total	Farmers and Farm Managers	Farm Laborers and Supervisors
1958	100.0	42.6	11.0	10.8	6.3	14.5	37.0	13.4	18.1	(b)	(b)	5.5	11.9	3.1	8.8	8.5	4.9	3.4
1959	100.0	42.7	11.0	10.7	6.5	14.4	37.1	13.2	18.3	(b)	(b)	5.6	11.9	3.0	8.9	8.3	4.7	3.6
1960	100.0	43.4	11.4	10.7	6.4	14.8	36.6	13.0	18.2	(b)	(b)	5.4	12.2	3.0	9.2	7.9	4.2	3.3
1961	100.0	43.9	11.7	10.8	6.4	15.0	36.0	13.1	17.8	(b)	(b)	5.1	12.6	3.1	9.5	7.5	4.1	3.9
1962	100.0	44.4	12.0	11.1	6.2	15.1	36.1	13.0	18.0	(b)	(b)	5.1	12.6	3.0	9.5	6.9	3.9	3.4
1963	100.0	44.2	12.2	10.8	6.1	15.1	36.6	13.2	18.4	(b)	(b)	5.0	12.8	3.0	9.8	6.4	3.5	2.3
1964	100.0	44.5	12.3	10.7	6.1	15.3	36.6	13.0	18.6	(b)	(b)	5.0	12.8	2.9	9.9	6.1	3.3	2.6
1965	100.0	44.8	12.5	10.3	6.3	15.7	36.9	13.0	18.8	(b)	(b)	5.2	12.6	2.8	9.8	5.7	3.1	2.1
1966	100.0	45.4	12.8	10.2	6.2	16.2	37.0	13.2	19.0	(b)	(b)	4.8	12.6	2.6	10.0	5.0	2.9	2.0
1967	100.0	46.0	13.3	10.1	6.1	16.6	36.7	13.2	18.7	(b)	(b)	4.8	12.5	2.4	10.2	4.8	2.6	2.4
1968	100.0	46.8	13.6	10.2	6.1	16.9	36.3	13.2	18.4	(b)	(b)	4.7	12.4	2.3	10.1	4.6	2.5	2.3
1969	100.0	47.3	13.8	10.2	6.0	17.2	36.2	13.1	18.4	(b)	(b)	4.7	12.2	2.1	10.1	4.2	2.4	1.5
1970	100.0	48.3	14.2	10.5	6.2	17.4	35.3	12.9	17.7	(b)	(b)	4.7	12.4	2.0	10.4	4.0	2.2	1.7
1971	100.0	48.3	14.0	11.0	6.4	17.0	34.4	12.9	16.4	(b)	(b)	5.1	13.5	1.9	11.6	3.8	2.1	1.7
1972	100.0	47.8	14.0	9.8	6.6	17.4	35.0	13.2	16.6	12.7	3.9	5.2	13.4	1.8	11.7	3.8	2.1	1.7
1973	100.0	47.8	14.0	10.2	6.4	17.2	35.4	13.4	16.9	13.0	3.9	5.1	13.2	1.6	11.6	3.6	2.0	1.6
1974	100.0	48.6	14.4	10.4	6.3	17.5	34.6	13.4	16.2	12.4	3.8	5.1	13.2	1.4	11.8	3.5	1.9	1.6
1975	100.0	49.8	15.0	10.5	6.4	17.8	33.0	12.9	15.2	11.4	3.8	4.9	13.7	1.4	12.4	3.5	1.9	1.6
1976	100.0	50.0	15.2	10.6	6.3	17.8	33.1	12.9	15.3	11.5	3.7	4.9	13.7	1.3	12.4	3.2	1.7	1.5
1977	100.0	49.9	15.1	10.7	6.3	17.8	33.4	13.1	15.2	11.4	3.8	5.0	13.7	1.3	12.4	3.0	1.6	1.4

[a] Data are limited to 1958 forward because occupational information for only 1 month of each quarter was collected prior to 1958 and the adjustment for the exclusion of 14- and 15-year-olds was not possible for earlier years.
[b] Not available.

Note: Beginning 1971, occupational data are not strictly comparable with statistics for earlier years as a result of changes in the occupational classification system for the 1970 Census of Population that were introduced into the Current Population Survey (CPS) in January 1971. Moreover, data from 1972 forward are not completely comparable with 1971 because of the addition of a question to the CPS in December 1971 relating to major activities and duties. For further explanation, see the Note on Historic Comparability of Labor Force Statistics at the beginning of the Statistical Appendix.

Sources: Employment and Training Report of the President, 1977 (Washington, D.C.: U.S. Government Printing Office), p. 162, and Employment and Earnings, 25 (January 1978), 152.

Within the metropolitan areas, the growth of population has occurred primarily in the suburbs, while many of the central cities have actually lost population. In terms of population growth between 1960 and 1970, the central cities of all SMSAs managed to grow by 6.4 percent while their suburbs grew by 26.8 percent; for the nonmetropolitan areas of the United States, the rate of growth was 6.8 percent. Although census data refers to location of residence, jobs have also moved from the central cities into suburbs, probably at about the same rate as population in the older SMSAs of the North and East and perhaps more rapidly in the South and West.[18]

Because of the contraction in agricultural employment, especially in the South since World War II, many blacks migrated to urban areas in the South and to cities in the North and West as well. Although the first signs of the South-to-North migration appeared after World War I, the larger and more recent movement has transformed the geographical distribution of blacks. At the turn of the century 83 percent of black Americans lived in nonurban areas and 90 percent in the South; in 1970 the South had a bare majority of the 22 million blacks in the United States, and three-fourths of them lived in urban areas. Those who migrated to the North and West became almost completely urbanized. Within the metropolitan areas, they found their new homes primarily in the central cities. In fact, nearly half (47.5%) of the black civilian labor force of the entire United States resided in the 30 largest SMSAs in 1973. And over three-fourths of these workers lived in the central cities.

SUMMARY

Statistics on the labor force of the United States are published monthly. The data refer to those persons 16 years of age and over, outside of institutions, who are employed and unemployed as determined from interviews with a sample of households conducted monthly by the Bureau of the Census. The period of reference is the week containing the twelfth day of the month. The decennial census aims at a complete count and uses the same labor force definitions.

The unemployment rate, calculated as a percentage of the labor force (both employed and unemployed), includes those who did not work during the reference week but who had looked for work during the previous month. "Discouraged workers," or those who did not work and who did not look for jobs because they believed none were available, are considered out of the labor force. Workers who worked part-time during the week but wished to work more hours are counted as employed, not as unemployed.

Another useful set of data is the annual work experience study, which indi-

---

[18] For a summary of evidence see James Heilbrun, *Urban Economics and Public Policy* (New York: St. Martin's Press, 1974), pp. 40ff. Some of the changes in metropolitan area growth are the result of changes in city and area boundaries.

cates the number of people who worked or looked for work during a calendar year. The number is substantially higher than the average monthly labor force: in 1975, 104.4 million persons worked or looked for work during the year, but the average monthly labor force was 84.8 million.

The labor force has not only been growing substantially but its composition has also been changing. Since the early post–World War II period, the average age has fallen and the percentage of women has risen sharply to over 40 percent in 1977. In terms of labor force participation rates—the percentage of a particular age/sex population group in the labor force—male rates have generally declined, most noticeably for males age 55 and up. For women the participation rates have been increasing; the rate for all women went from 31.8 in 1947 to 48.5 in 1977.

Part-time employment of the American labor force is significant: about one-fourth work less than 35 hours per week. If full-year employment is defined as 50 to 52 weeks of work per year, then about a third of the persons reported by work experience studies are employed at part-year jobs.

In the composition of the labor force there has been a long-run downward trend in agricultural employment, a declining relative trend in manufacturing, and an expansion in three industry groups—government (particularly at the state and local levels), services, and trade. About three out of every five jobs added since the end of the World War II have been in these three fields.

With a decline in those who are self-employed, both on farms and in nonagricultural industries, a higher percentage of the employed labor force are wage and salary workers. The white-collar sector contains the fastest growing occupations, especially those in the professional and technical categories. Blue-collar workers have been declining proportionately, even though their numbers have increased absolutely. The greatest declines over the long run have been among laborers, both farm and nonfarm. The category of service workers (other than private household) has shown the greatest expansion in recent years. Manual labor is still the most prevalent type of employment among American workers.

The increasing concentration of employment in metropolitan areas reflects the long-term decline in agricultural employment. Because of the dramatic technological revolution in southern agriculture since World War II, the impact was greatest upon black workers, nearly half of whom reside in the largest metropolitan areas.

DISCUSSION QUESTIONS

1. The text points out that labor statistics depend on the definitions and methods used in the collection of data. If definitions (say, of unemployment) vary, the numbers will change. Does this fact limit the usefulness of labor statistics? Is the problem unique to labor economics?
2. What are the trends in the labor force participation rates of youths, women, older

persons, and males of prime working age? What factors explain these trends? Do you expect such trends to continue?
3. What are the arguments for classifying "discouraged workers" as out of the labor force, rather than as unemployed? Do you agree?
4. There has been a historical rise in the following types of employment: (a) part-time and part-year, (b) white-collar, (c) metropolitan. For each, explain the reasons for the trends.
5. Do you believe the concept of class—whether working class or middle class—is relevant in analyzing the labor force?

SELECTED READINGS

For the theoretical basis of the present system of labor force statistics, see the Gordon Report, noted above: President's Committee to Appraise Employment and Unemployment Statistics, *Measuring Employment and Unemployment* (Washington, D.C.: U.S. Government Printing Office, 1962). Current statistics of the labor force are found in the U.S. Bureau of Labor Statistics monthly publication, *Employment and Earnings*; annual data are found in the *Employment and Training Report of the President*. The latter also has articles interpreting labor force developments.

A major review of labor force concepts is currently being undertaken by the National Commission on Employment and Unemployment Statistics, established by law in 1976. Under the chairmanship of Sar A. Levitan, the commission will evaluate present methodology and procedures in the collection of data on employment and unemployment and recommend methods of improvement. Although many issues are to be considered by the commission, one concerns the appropriateness and interpretation of the presently calculated unemployment rate. For an examination of some of the viewpoints on this issue, see Julius Shiskin, "Employment and Unemployment: The Doughnut or the Hole," *Monthly Labor Review*, 99 (February 1976), 3–10.

Standard works on the labor force include Peter Blau and Otis D. Duncan, *The American Occupational Structure* (New York: John Wiley & Sons, 1967); Gertrude Bancroft, *The American Labor Force* (New York: John Wiley & Sons, 1958); William G. Bowen and T. Aldrich Finegan, *The Economics of Labor Force Participation* (Princeton, N.J.: Princeton University Press, 1969); and Clarence D. Long, *The Labor Force under Changing Income and Employment* (Princeton, N.J.: National Bureau of Economic Research, 1958).

On the changing occupational and industrial structure of the modern American economy, see Daniel Bell, *The Coming of Post-Industrial Society, A Venture in Social Forecasting* (New York: Basic Books, 1973); Niles M. Hansen, *Rural Poverty and the Urban Crisis: A Strategy for Regional Development* (Bloomington, Ind.: Indiana University Press, 1970); Richard Parker, *The Myth of the Middle Class* (New York: Liveright, 1972); and Bertram Silverman and Murray Yanovitch, eds., *The Worker in "Post-Industrial Capitalism": Liberal and Radical Responses* (New York: Free Press, 1974).

For different aspects of the American economy, see Robert T. Averitt, *The Dual Economy* (New York: Norton, 1968); Victor R. Fuchs, *The Service Economy* (New York: National Bureau of Economic Research, 1968); and Eli Ginsberg, Dale L. Hiestand, and Beatrice G. Reubens, *The Pluralistic Economy* (New York: McGraw-Hill, 1965).

3

The Economics
of Labor Supply

The composition of employment by occupations, industries, and areas represents the outcome of actions taken by workers and employers in countless labor markets. In these markets, the forces of demand and supply establish the price and quantity sold of particular labor services; in a market economy the price of labor governs its allocation among alternative uses. In attempting to maximize profits, employers adjust their employment of labor when wages go up or down relative to the costs of other factor inputs and to the prices of their products. Workers also respond to market changes: they may try to seek out higher-paying jobs, they may decide to do more or less work, or they may invest their time in training or education in the hope of improving their job prospects at some future date.

The nature of the responses by workers and employers to changes in wages and employment can be complex. In this chapter we shall examine some of the factors that influence workers' reactions; in the next several chapters we shall look at the labor market adjustments made by employers and the interactions that occur in the market itself.

To explain changes in the supply of labor, it is important to recognize that some influences lie beyond the scope of the usual economic analysis. Individuals have attitudes toward work that reflect their own tastes as developed within the social and intellectual environment in which they have been reared. From the economic point of view, however, given some set of ethical values, individuals relate the amount and type of work they perform to the income they expect to receive. This chapter presents the theory of these relationships and some of the relevant evidence in terms of hours of work and labor force participation rates. In addition the chapter considers the nature and significance of human capital investments in the form of education and training that individuals undertake in order to improve their future income.

INCOME AND WORK

The concept of a relationship between the wage paid and the amount of work performed is an old one, but there have been differences of opinion as to the exact nature of that relationship. Even before Adam Smith wrote his *Wealth of Nations* in 1776, mercantilists in Great Britain had considered the effect wages might have upon the supply of labor. They more or less unanimously accepted the view of the "backward-bending" supply curve—that is, if wages rose, workers would work less than before, for they would spend time in ale-houses and in general be less efficient. For the glory of England, as well as to compete with the Dutch, these writers felt that a low-wage policy was most efficient because it would force the "sturdy beggars" to go to work. Adam Smith, on the other hand, subscribed to the "forward-sloping" supply curve—that is, if wages rose, workers would have the incentive to work more, and therefore more goods would be produced at a higher wage than at a lower one.

A new line of attack from a deductive point of view was made by the British economist Sir Stanley Jevons, who said in 1871 that the worker compared the marginal gain from income with the marginal disutility of work. Although Jevons did not state that all work necessarily was accompanied by "pain," he suggested that after the first hours of work, when there might be some positive pleasure, eventually—and perhaps quickly—the marginal disutility of further work would increase. At the same time the workers' marginal gain in utility from the goods and services obtained by extra work would steadily fall. Equilibrium—or the amount of work the individual would be just willing to perform—could be found at the point where the marginal utility of the additional goods obtained and the marginal disutility of working for those goods were equal. An increase in the wage rate would enable the worker to secure more goods for each hour of work, and the worker would tend to work less than before. Jevons's supply curve of labor was thus in the short run negatively inclined, since at higher wages less work would be performed.

A slightly different approach has been emphasized in this century by the American economist Frank H. Knight, who focused on the crucial choice between leisure and work. Disutility may be a relevant factor, but the important alternatives are leisure and work, expressed in terms of the goods and services purchased by work. A worker cannot work for an unlimited period to obtain goods and services and at the same time enjoy an unlimited amount of leisure; a choice must be made. This is not an all-or-nothing choice, however, but rather a decision about how much more income in terms of goods and services a person would be willing to work for in comparison with how much more leisure he or she would be willing to give up for it. Knight assumed that if the rate of pay were raised, people would certainly divide their time so as to earn more money, but they would also work fewer hours.[1]

An analysis of work and income using the indifference-curve technique arrives at a less specific conclusion. The impact of a wage increase upon the amount of work to be offered for sale is separated into two parts: the "income effect," meaning that the worker will offer less labor because of a desire for more leisure, much as in Knight's theory; and the "substitution effect," meaning that leisure hours will be replaced with work, since higher wages will make work more attractive than before. It cannot be determined which effect will offset the other, nor can either effect be isolated in any particular case. For example, if a worker decides to work, not 40 hours a week, but only 35 when his wage rises from $4.00 to $5.00 per hour, he gains five hours of leisure and $15.00 of income in the form of goods per week as his weekly wages rise from $160 to $175. The income effect can be said to have outweighed the substitution effect, but the specific influence of each effect on his decision cannot be established. Of course, if the worker decides to work the same number of hours as before, or even more, at the higher wage, the substitution effect plainly overbalances the income effect.

These relationships are demonstrated in Figure 3–1, where II is an individual's indifference curve, representing the worker's choice between income, on the vertical axis, and division of time between leisure and work, on the horizontal axis.[2] Leisure is measured from the origin to the right, while work is

[1] Frank H. Knight, *Risk, Uncertainty and Profit* (Boston: Houghton Mifflin, 1921), p. 117, and see footnote 1, pp. 117–118.

Knight's conclusion has been criticized on the grounds that no *a priori* "law" can be deduced as to the effect of a wage change on the amount of work performed. Lionel Robbins showed that the effect depended upon what he called the "elasticity of demand for material income in terms of effort." He felt that the fact that when wages rise the *effort price* of commodities falls, overlooked by Knight, prohibited a deductive solution to the question of whether the worker would work more or less. If the effort price of income increased (that is, if the real wage fell), the worker would "demand" fewer goods and services and, in more realistic terminology, would be willing to work for a smaller total income, whereas if the effort price fell (if the real wage rose), he would demand an increase in income, the exact amount depending on his individual preferences. According to Robbins, only inductive studies could reveal the actual shape of the demand curve for income; it could not be deduced by armchair reasoning. Lionel Robbins, "On the Elasticity of Demand for Income in Terms of Effort," reprinted in American Economic Association, *Readings in the Theory of Income Distribution* (Philadelphia: Blakiston, 1949), pp. 237–244.

[2] An indifference curve represents those various combinations of income and leisure that yield the worker the same satisfaction. Any point to the right of, or above, an indifference curve means that the new combination of income and leisure is viewed by the worker as an improvement in welfare; at a combination below or to the left, the worker's situation is perceived as worse.

The slope of the curve represents the additional income a worker believes would be necessary to compensate for the loss of additional leisure time. As hours of work increase (and hence as leisure time is reduced), the assumption is that the worker would have to receive more and more income in order not to feel worse off than before. That is, the slope increases as hours of work are greater.

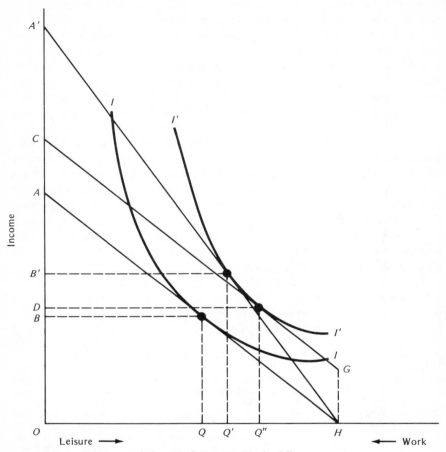

FIGURE 3-1 Income and the Work-Leisure Trade-Off

measured to the left from point H, the maximum number of hours that can be devoted to both. The wage line, HA, indicates the amount of income received by the individual as the hours devoted to work increase; its slope is the wage rate (that is, income/hours of work). The equilibrium position of the individual in Figure 3-1 is determined by the tangency of the wage line with the highest possible indifference curve. In this case, the individual will work HQ hours, have OQ hours of leisure, and receive an income measured by OB. If the wage were increased so that the new wage line were raised to HA', the indifference curve would be higher, I'I'; the individual would work fewer hours, HQ', and yet receive more income, OB'.

The income effect of the wage increase can be illustrated by indicating how much work an individual would be willing to perform if he or she were willing to work at the old wage and yet remain at the higher preference level. This can be shown by a wage line parallel to the former wage and tangent to the higher indifference curve. The line GC indicates that the individual would have reduced the amount of work to HQ'' and would receive OD income. In terms of hours of work, the income effect is the number of reduced hours of work, QQ''; the amount of income needed to produce this effect is measured by the nonwage income the individual would have to receive, namely HG, in order to reach the higher indifference curve if he or she worked at the old wage rate.

The substitution effect, on the other hand, represents the tendency of the individual to work more if the wage is higher—that is, the opportunity cost of not working is greater. The individual will substitute work for leisure to the amount measured by the distance $Q''Q'$. Because (in this case) the distance is less than the income effect, the higher wage rate leads on balance to a diminished work effort from the initial position of HQ hours.

Douglas's Study

There have been attempts to investigate statistically the relationships existing between income and the amount of work. In a major pioneering study of the short-run labor supply curve in the United States, Paul H. Douglas used a variety of statistical devices.[3] First, he compared participation rates of age and sex groups in selected cities in the United States from statistical materials of the census of 1920 with real annual earnings of adult males for 1919; by adjusting the data for each city to a standardized sex-and-age distribution to eliminate variations resulting from different population compositions, he found that the regression line that best fitted the data for separate cities yielded a coefficient of elasticity of from −0.13 to −0.16 for the urban labor force. That is, for a 1 percent income increase, the labor force declined by a seventh to a sixth of 1 percent. Douglas's results substantiated the position that the supply curve did bend backward, although slightly. The negative inclination of the supply curve, however, was the result almost exclusively of the effect on participation of "children, youths, old people and women over 25 years." By specific groups, the negative elasticity was greatest for the juvenile groups of 14 and 15 years and particularly high for women over 65. Douglas found the effect of differences in real earnings on the labor participation of adult men "very slight."

Douglas also approached the short-run supply curve in terms of the relationship between hours of work and real income. Here again he found a slight negative correlation: the higher the wage, the fewer hours worked. He estimated the elasticity of labor in terms of hours to lie between −0.1 and −0.2: that is, an increase in wages of 1 percent would cause a decrease of 0.1 to 0.2 percent in the hours normally worked.

[3] Paul H. Douglas, *The Theory of Wages* (New York: Macmillan, 1934), ch. 11.

By combining both approaches, Douglas estimated the elasticity of the short-run supply curve of the amount of labor (number of persons times the number of hours worked) to be in the range of −0.24 to −0.33. He concluded that Knight had been correct: workers tended to divide an increase in hourly wages into two parts, with about "two-thirds to three-quarters of the gain" being used for a higher material standard of living, and the remainder for increased leisure.[4]

Hours of Work

As to hours of work, subsequent studies have generally confirmed Douglas's findings on the relative importance of the income effect. On the average the number of hours of work per worker tends to decrease as wages increase. The shorter work week in American industry illustrates the general trend. The average work week decreased from about 53 hours in the latter part of the nineteenth century to about 40 hours by the end of the 1960s; this was a drop of 13 hours, or about one-fourth. The decline, however, was a product of a number of factors, not all of which were related to increasing incomes. The shift of workers out of agriculture, where hours are longer, was one factor. Others were the greater importance of service industries, where significant numbers of part-time workers are employed, and legislation such as the Fair Labor Standards Act, which was designed to reduce hours in order to share the work. Nonetheless, studies attempting to isolate the wage and working hour variables from other influences support the dominance of the income over the substitution effect. These studies have been both cross-sectional (comparing various groups of workers in one time period) and longitudinal (comparing the same group of workers over time). T. A. Finegan, in a cross-sectional analysis, showed that for male workers the relationship was indeed negative with respect to wages, although other variables, such as marriage, increasing age, and more schooling were associated with an increase in the number of hours worked.[5]

The technical requirements of industry may limit an individual's decision with respect to the number of hours worked. Efficiency in production can require uniform sets of rules governing hours of operation, machine speeds, intensity of work, and other dimensions of work performance to which the preferences of individuals must be adjusted for the economic survival of the

[4] Ibid., p. 314.

[5] T.A. Finegan, "Hours of Work in the United States: A Cross-Sectional Analysis," *Journal of Political Economy* (October 1962), 452–470. Finegan's analysis of data for 1950 showed that "a work week shorter by one hour was associated [with] (1) higher hourly earnings of about $.12, (2) a lower marriage ratio of about six percentage points, (3) less schooling of about one year, (4) about fifteen fewer years of age, (5) a higher Negro-employment ratio of about eighteen percentage points, and (6) a higher female-employment ratio of about forty-three percentage points."

firm. Yet certain options exist that can alter what might appear to be otherwise inflexible arrangements. A worker may quit one firm where the work situation is undesirable and take a job elsewhere. If the worker wants less work, he or she can be absent from the job, providing this does not jeopardize employment. If the worker wants more work, he or she may be able to obtain overtime work within the firm, or take a second job.[6] Moreover, the work year, rather than the work week, may be shortened with paid holidays and longer vacations. In manufacturing in 1968, for example, only 18 percent of the workers had no paid vacation. For the private nonfarm economy as a whole, the total number of weeks that workers spent on vacations increased by almost 50 percent between 1960 and 1969, with the average length per full-time worker rising from 1.8 to 2.2 weeks per year. The number of paid holidays for plant workers increased from 6.8 to 7.5 days in the period between 1960 and 1968.

To employers the cost of various types of leave—holidays, vacations, and civic and personal leave—has been rising. Employer expenditures in 1972 amounted to the equivalent of $0.28 an hour for production workers in manufacturing, or 6.2 percent of the worker's total compensation of $4.51; for office workers in manufacturing, the amount was $0.49, or 7 percent of the average total compensation of $7.03. (Total compensation includes wages and fringe benefits such as pensions and Social Security expenditures.) Leave expenditures have been rising more rapidly than pay for working time. From 1968 to 1972, the expenditures of manufacturing employers for leave time rose 40.0 and 36.1 percent for production workers and office employees respectively, while pay for working time increased by 26.2 percent for production workers and 29.6 percent for office employees.[7]

Labor Force Participation

The analysis of substitution and income effects of wage changes furnishes insights into the trends of labor force participation rates by major demographic groups, as discussed in chapter 2. The long-run decline of participa-

---

[6] In May 1975 "moonlighters" (those who hold two or more jobs) constituted about 4 million workers, or about 4.7 percent of all workers. The percentage tends to rise during booms and decline during recessions; for example, in 1973, a boom year, the percentage rose to 5.1. See Kopp Michelotti, "Multiple Job Holders in May 1975," *Monthly Labor Review*, 98 (November 1975), 56ff.

In an earlier study, it was evident that moonlighting is directly related to need. The rate of moonlighting was 4 percent for single men, 6 percent for married men with no children under 18, 11 percent for those with five children or more. See Geoffrey H. Moore and Janice Neipert Hedges, "Trends in Labor and Leisure," *Monthly Labor Review*, 94 (February 1971), 7.

[7] Calculated from series on Employer Expenditures for Employee Compensation, U.S. Department of Labor, Bureau of Labor Statistics, *Handbook of Labor Statistics, 1975— Reference Edition* (Washington, D.C.: U.S. Government Printing Office), Table 118.

tion rates of older men reflects the availability of nonwage income in the form of pensions and Social Security payments that make retirement possible. However, the substitution effects are clearly in evidence when the lifetime view of a worker's career is taken into consideration. The labor force participation rates of men in their prime working years, say from 25 to 55, are relatively insensitive to changes in wages. It is reasonable to infer that the substitution effect is dominant: the individual will work most during those years of greatest energy when earning power is highest, and withdraw from the labor force in later years, when earning abilities are curtailed.

One must also be careful in explaining the long-run decline in the labor force participation of young people. To the extent that this decline reflects a lengthier education, it is more rightly viewed as a form of increased human capital investment than as an increase in leisure. As an investment, the time spent in schools and colleges becomes a way of acquiring a greater amount of future goods. The rewards from such investment can be considered a higher wage. To the extent that education is made attractive by the expectation of higher future wages, the substitution effect is dominant: leisure time—that is, time not spent in working and studying—is reduced.

In the case of women workers, the historically rising participation rate at first seems to contradict the earlier findings of Douglas as well as the theory of choice between income and work. In Douglas's cross-sectional analysis, the participation rate of women declined as the wages of males increased, a conclusion that seemed both practically and theoretically appropriate, particularly for married women. As husbands earned more money, there was less economic pressure for wives to enter the labor market, in terms of the indifference curve analysis, because to the wife the husband's wage was like nonwork income. A 1958 study by Clarence D. Long in fact added to the puzzle with confirmation of the short-run, backward-bending supply curve of women.[8] In the long run, however, on the basis of Long's estimates, the rise in real disposable personal income per equivalent adult employed male nearly tripled from about $1,000 in 1890 to $2,700 in 1950 (in 1929 dollars), and the female participation rate, which should have fallen from around 199 per 1,000 females in 1890 to about 124 per 1,000 in 1950, instead rose to 284! In brief, there was a marked difference between the short-run and long-run view of the labor supply of women workers.

During the 1960s a number of econometric studies used a new approach to the issue of rising participation rates for married women.[9] They examined the

[8] Clarence D. Long, *The Labor Force Under Changing Income and Employment*, National Bureau of Economic Research (Princeton, N.J.: Princeton University Press, 1958).

[9] Jacob Mincer, "Labor Force Participation of Married Women," in National Bureau of Economic Research, *Aspects of Labor Economics* (Princeton, N.J.: Princeton University Press, 1962), pp. 63–97; Glen C. Cain, *Married Women in the Labor Force* (Chicago: University of Chicago Press, 1966); William G. Bowen and T. Aldrich Finegan, *The Economics of Labor Force Participation* (Princeton, N.J.: Princeton University Press, 1969).

relative strengths of the substitution and income effects of wage changes and nonwage income upon labor market participation of individuals and members of households. The studies also included the effects of labor market variables, such as unemployment, and of demographic factors, such as age, race, and number of children.

For married women, both Jacob Mincer and Glen C. Cain included in their analyses the comparison of work in the market, work at home, and income derived from the work of the husband. When the wage for outside work increased sufficiently in comparison with the value received from work at home, it was argued that the substitution effect would lead the housewife to enter the market. Although rising income received by the household, from both husband and wife, was found to have the anticipated income effect of reducing the wife's participation, on balance their econometric studies showed the greater strength of the substitution relative to the income effect over time.

In their study, William G. Bowen and T. Aldrich Finegan agreed that historically the substitution effect had overwhelmed the income effect, but they also pointed to a variety of other influences on the participation rates of married women. Demographic factors, such as the number of children, rural residence, and age, tended to lower participation rates. On the other hand, higher levels of educational attainment strongly motivated entry into the market, along with greater job opportunities for women—what the authors called the greater "femininity" of employment—even though higher family income, other things being equal, partially offset this trend. Unlike Mincer, however, they still found a large unexplained residual. For the period from 1948 to 1965, when the participation rate of married women 14 to 55 years of age rose by 14.6 points (adjusted for demographic changes), they could attribute less than half of the rise (46.6%) to wage and income variables.[10] One explanation of this discrepancy is that families have rising income aspirations: women have been entering the market in order to attain ever-higher standards of living. In other words, they enter the market in order to purchase those home appliances, prepared foods, and other services that make their market participation possible![11]

The Bowen and Finegan study investigated the participation rates of five population groups: prime-age males, 25–54 years of age; married women, 14–54 years of age; single females, 25–54 years old; older persons, 55 and over; and younger persons, 14–24 years of age. With regression analyses, the authors examined demographic and economic variables using both time series and cross-sectional analyses. The time series were drawn from decennial censuses and from the Current Population Surveys over a period from 1947 to 1967. The cross-sectional analyses, based on the One-in-a-Thousand Sample drawn from the 1960 Censuses of Population and Housing, provided information for over 180,000 individuals.

[10] Bowen and Finegan, *Economics of Labor Force Participation*, p. 226.

[11] One of the results of this "merry-go-round" syndrome is the increasing number of children being reared in homes of women who work. In March 1974, 27 million children,

With greater labor market participation of women, their average number of hours of work for pay has also risen, but it is not known whether the total number of hours both in the market and in the home on housework and child care has increased or decreased. The introduction of labor-saving devices at home, as well as the trend towards smaller families, has undoubtedly lightened the home burden. Yet it is also true that goods purchased for consumption often require more time for their enjoyment. And certain types of services formerly furnished by sellers must now be performed by the buyer, such as "self-service" supermarket buying.[12] Moreover, more time outside the labor market may have to be spent by consumers, both male and female, to maintain, repair, and service the goods purchased. There seems to be no method of determining quantitatively the net balance of these costs and benefits.

The participation of both men and women may also be approached in terms of work during one's life span. Between 1900 and 1970, the worklife expectancy of a woman on the average more than tripled, from 6.3 years to 22.9 years, an absolute increase of 16.6 years (see Table 3-1). Because of the increase in the number of years she can be expected to live, however, she has more time "left over" than before—51.9 years in 1970 compared to 44.4 years in 1900, a gain of 7.5 years. Men, who spend more time in the labor

Table 3-1
Life and Worklife Expectancy (in years) at Birth, by Sex, 1900 and 1970

	1900[a]	1970	Increase 1900–1970
Men			
Life expectancy	48.2	67.1	18.9
Worklife expectancy	32.1	40.1	8.0
Difference	16.1	27.0	10.9
Women			
Life expectancy	50.7	74.8	24.1
Worklife expectancy	6.3	22.9	16.6
Difference	44.4	51.9	7.5

[a] Data in 1900 are for white persons in death registration states.

Source: Howard N. Fullerton, Jr., and James J. Byrne, "Length of Working Life for Men and Women, 1970," *Monthly Labor Review*, 99 (February 1976), 32.

or about 42 percent of the total of 65,755,000 children under the age of 18, had mothers in the labor force. Earlier, in 1970, the number was 25.5 million, or 38.8 percent of all children, who had mothers either working or looking for work. See U.S. Bureau of Labor Statistics, *Children of Working Mothers*, Special Labor Force Report, September 1974.

[12] See Steffan Linder, *The Harried Leisure Class* (New York: Columbia University Press, 1970); Gary Becker, "A Theory of the Allocation of Time," *Economic Journal*, 75 (September 1965), 493–517.

force, have also experienced both a gain in worklife and in nonworking years. As the life expectancy for men increased (less so than for women), work expectancy rose from 32.1 to 40.1 years, for a net gain of 8 years; men's time out of the labor force also rose from 16.1 to 27.0 years, for a net gain of 10.9 years.

Part of the increase in nonworking years over the 70-year period has been spent attending school, a form of investment incurred by individuals that has undoubtedly helped them achieve longer work spans. It seems clear, however, that increased labor input in the American economy has come about because individuals now perform more work during their lifetimes than before. Combining the work years of an average man and woman reveals that they furnished in 1970 a total of 63 years of work in comparison with 38.4 years in 1900, a gain of 64.1 percent. Their combined years of not working on the average increased from 60.5 years to 78.9, a gain of 30.4 percent.

The Effect of Business Conditions

The size of the labor force changes in response to changes in general business conditions. During the depression of the 1930s, W. S. Woytinsky advanced the "additional worker" hypothesis, which stated that if the principal breadwinner of a family lost his or her job, not only the breadwinner but others in the household would begin to look for work.[13] In other words, if one worker were to lose a job, unemployment would increase by two or more. The implication of this hypothesis was that during a depression estimates of unemployment *overstated* the actual number of new jobs required in order to restore high levels of employment. When a man was rehired, for example, unemployment would drop by more than one as his wife returned to her kitchen and the children to school.

A contrary analysis, known as the "discouraged worker" hypothesis, gained support during and after World War II. It stated that rising unemployment discouraged those who lose their jobs from continuing the search for work, as well as those who might otherwise be likely to enter or reenter the labor market.[14] Hence during periods of recession the estimates of unemployment *understate* the actual number of new jobs required to restore high levels of

---

[13] W. S. Woytinsky, "Additional Workers and the Volume of Unemployment in the Depression," Committee on Social Security (Washington, D.C.: Social Science Research Council, 1904), mimeographed. In 1953 Woytinsky modified his position by proposing that the labor force increases "both in severe depression and in a boom." The modification is found in his *Employment and Wages in the United States* (New York: Twentieth Century Fund, 1953), pp. 322–323.

[14] The discouraged worker hypothesis is different from the term "discouraged worker" used in chapter 2. The latter—a labor force statistical concept—refers to those individuals, out of the labor force, who identify themselves as discouraged because of lack of job opportunities. The hypothesis attempts to explain how individuals react to changes in job opportunities—irrespective of what they may say.

employment. That is, as the number of jobs increases, not only will the unemployed return to work but there will also be others, heretofore hidden in
the out-of-the-labor-force categories, who will enter the labor force to take
jobs. These individuals, in other words, will substitute work in the market for
nonmarket activities and/or leisure.

Evidence for the discouraged worker hypothesis was furnished by the experience during World War II, with its immense demands for military and civilian manpower. From 1940, a year of considerable unemployment, the total
labor force of the United States (including the armed forces) rose from some
58 million to a peak of an estimated 68 million persons in 1944. Since it was
estimated that the normal expansion between 1940 and 1945 would have
been around 3 million, some 7 to 8 million persons who would not normally
have entered the labor force did so during the war. Approximately half of
these were women, who were drawn into the labor force by economic
pressure when their husbands were drafted into the armed forces, by patriotism, or by the availability of employment opportunities. The other half
consisted of younger individuals who either entered the armed forces or left
school or college to take jobs in war industries.

The great expansion of the labor force during World War II, plus the sizable unemployment of around 8 million persons that existed in 1940, provided an enormous reservoir of usable manpower that enabled civilian
employment to increase by about 7 million while the armed forces added 12
million men. The relative expansion of the labor force was about the same in
Canada but much less in Great Britain and in Germany, where in 1940 the
rate of labor force participation was already far higher than that in the United
States. With demobilization and the ending of war employment, the American labor force contracted rapidly. Though a good part of the additional war
workers returned to their former activities outside the labor force, not all of
them did so. The postwar labor force participation rate of women was higher
than its former level, but it is difficult to determine whether this reflected a
long-run upward trend or whether the rate was higher because of the social
and economic changes wrought by the war.[15]

The Korean hostilities offered another opportunity to test nationally the
effect of wartime demands on labor force participation, and again, there was
an increase in participation rates, especially for women 35 to 64 years of age.
The overall change in rates was slight, however, and the exact increase in the
labor force that resulted from partial mobilization of the economy cannot be

[15] The problem in separating these influences stems from various interpretations of the
1940 census. If that census is considered to have measured satisfactorily labor force participation rates, there was a net gain in additional workers by the end of World War II. If, on
the other hand, the 1940 census underestimated such rates, one could argue that female
labor force participation rates in the postwar period continued their long-run secular rise,
and that the effects of World War II were nil. See Long, *Labor Force Under Changing
Income*, p. 16.

definitely determined because of the uncertainties as to the "normal" trends in the post–World War II economy.[16]

Subsequent investigations of the labor force under conditions of changing aggregate demands substantiate the dominance of the substitution effect: namely, that greater availability of jobs (and therefore income) encourages, and diminished job opportunities discourage, labor force participation.[17] While it is possible that in some families the additional worker concept is applicable, the opposite relationship is more important quantitatively. Bowen and Finegan's econometric analysis of participation rates found the discouraged worker hypothesis pertinent to all population groups—not only among women and younger and older persons, where the relationship was especially strong, but also among males in the prime working age group (from 25 to 54 years).[18]

By how much is unemployment understated when the economy is operating at less than full employment? Although answers depend upon the method of estimating, one approach relies on reports from the Current Population Survey of those persons now classified as outside the labor force who state that they wish to work but believe that no work is available for them (the "discouraged workers"). If to this group are added those part-time workers who explicitly say they wish to work more, the total of both categories generally moves cyclically with the number of reported unemployed. During the recession in the fall of 1974, for example, the number of reported discouraged workers increased from 676,000 to 845,000 between the second and fourth quarters, a rise of 25 percent. The number of workers on part-time schedules for "economic reasons" alone increased by 820,000 workers from August to December.[19]

The census also reports on a broader category of those outside the labor force who state that they wish to work but are not now looking for work. It is not necessarily discouragement that holds them back: they may have household responsibilities or be sick, disabled, in school, or retired. It is likely that some of these persons would enter the labor market if jobs were available. This group, which totaled nearly 4 million in 1974, not including the discouraged workers as such, has been called the "labor reserve."[20]

---

[16] See Philip M. Hauser, "Mobility in Labor Force Participation," in B. E. Wight Bakke et al., *Labor Mobility and Economic Opportunity* (New York: John Wiley, 1954), pp. 28–31.

[17] For a review of the literature, see Herbert S. Parnes, "Labor Force and Labor Markets," in Woodrow L. Ginsburg et al., *A Review of Industrial Relations Research* (Madison, Wis.: Industrial Relations Research Association, 1970), vol. I, pp. 15–21.

[18] Bowen and Finegan, *Economics of Labor Force Participation*, p. 77.

[19] See *Manpower Report of the President*, including reports by the U.S. Department of Labor and the U.S. Department of Health, Education, and Welfare (Washington, D.C.: U.S. Government Printing Office, 1975), pp. 27–28.

[20] Christopher G. Gellner, "Enlarging the Concept of Labor Reserve," *Monthly Labor Review*, 98 (April 1975), 20–28.

A different approach estimates hidden unemployment. This is calculated by subtracting actual participation rates of demographic groups within the population from the participation rates existing in periods of full employment. Because estimating procedures may have different assumptions and refer to different periods of time, estimated hidden unemployment can vary widely. Alfred Tella arrived at an estimate of 762,000 hidden unemployed workers for 1964, using a target full-employment level of 4.2 percent. Thomas Dernburg and Kenneth Strand estimated hidden unemployment in 1962 at 2.3 million on the basis of a 4.0 full-employment rate. Bowen and Finegan, who concentrated on the period of the 1963–1967 boom, estimated that the improvement in economic conditions had induced a net increase of 1.6 million persons—about 1 million women and 600,000 men—to enter or to remain in the labor force.[21]

From the point of view of the theory of labor supply, the existence of hidden unemployment raises the question whether the supply curve of labor, at least as suggested by the evidence of labor force participation, is not actually forward-rising rather than backward-bending as Douglas and others assumed. When the aggregate demand for labor increases, some of those outside the labor force will now enter the labor market and substitute the income from jobs for lower-valued nonmarket activities.

HUMAN CAPITAL INVESTMENT

Labor supplies are differentiated in terms of skills, abilities, and experience, and any analysis of a nation's labor resources must consider what the economist calls human capital. Human capital, in its broadest sense, is investment in the development of an individual's economic productivity. Given a person's initial abilities, human capital investment includes the education, both formal and informal, and the experience and training that enhance income from work. In its broadest usage, the term also includes investments in health (if it enhances earning power), acquisition of labor market information, mobility, and job search. The key to the concept of human capital is this: investment to acquire greater future income exacts a cost in the loss of returns that resources could have produced through other uses. Hence the sacrifice of present returns for expected future income characterizes an investment proc-

[21] For a review of other models that have yielded still different results, see Joseph L. Gastwirth, "Estimating the Number of 'Hidden Unemployed,' " Monthly Labor Review, 96 (March 1973), 17–26. Alfred Tella's model is presented in "Labor Force, Sensitivity to Employment by Age, Sex," Industrial Relations, 4 (February 1965), 69–83. For the model of Thomas Dernburg and Kenneth Strand, see "Hidden Unemployment 1953–62: A Quantitative Analysis by Age and Sex," American Economic Review, 56 (March 1966), 71–95; the Bowen and Finegan analysis is found in Economics of Labor Force Participation, part III.

ess in humans just as it does for those investing in machines, inventories, or other nonhuman capital goods.

The human capital concept has its roots in classical economics. Adam Smith called the "acquired and useful abilities" of individuals part of the fixed capital of a nation, and early writers held that the wages of skilled workers must be high enough in the long run to cover the costs of the training required. The modern approach to human capital began in the 1960s. One of the first exponents was Theodore W. Schultz, who showed how the increase in the "stock" of educational capital in the United States could help explain the nation's economic growth rate.[22] Previous explanations relying on increases in the quantity of labor and in inputs of nonhuman capital had consistently underestimated actual growth rates. Schultz argued that it was improvement in the quality of the labor force through human capital investment that could account for the difference. Gary S. Becker[23] and others developed the human capital concept as an explanation of labor market behavior.

The modern approach has sometimes been identified as neoclassical because of two assumptions: (1) that human capital investment decisions represent the rational choices of individuals concerned with utility maximization; and (2) that workers receive returns to cover their investments, as one would expect in a competitive market. Hence differences in wages can be explained, albeit in a more sophisticated manner than Smith's, by the differences in the amount of human capital invested in individuals. But the human capital approach to the supply of labor is not intrinsically dependent on these assumptions. Human capital can be the product of community decisions with respect to public education, rather than reflecting individual choice. Moreover, wages may not reflect investment outlays, as human capital research in the case of racial and sex discrimination has shown. Here we shall review the theory of investment choices and its implications, and examine some of the empirical findings that relate to it. The question of the relationship between human capital and the process of wage determination is reserved for the following chapter.

Theory

The modern theory of human capital investment begins with the choices an individual can make in allocating the time spent on current income as opposed to investments that will yield a higher return in the future. It is also likely that a person will have to choose among several types of investment

---

[22] Theodore W. Schultz, "Investment in Human Capital," *American Economic Review*, 51 (March 1961), 1ff., and "Reflections on Investment in Man," in Supplement, *Investment in Human Beings, Journal of Political Economy*, 70, part 2 (October 1962), 1–8.

[23] Gary S. Becker, *Human Capital* (New York: Columbia University Press, 1964).

possibilities. For a particular investment proposal, the individual would estimate not only the direct costs but also the earnings forgone—namely, what could have been earned if time had not been devoted to investment in a new learning process. The gains have to be estimated in the form of a time profile of extra earnings for future years. A person would not compare the aggregate earnings with aggregate costs, however, because future earnings anticipated over the life of the asset must be discounted to the present. Discounting is necessary in order to account for the fact that an individual tends to value a dollar today more highly than a dollar tomorrow, even if the general level of prices is expected to remain unchanged. The difference, expressed as a rate of interest, is known as the individual's rate of time preference; the community's rate of time preference can be said to be represented by the going rate of interest in the market. The higher the rate of time preference, the lower will be the present value of a future dollar.

EQUATIONS OF HUMAN CAPITAL

The calculation of human capital investment is expressed in the following equation, in which PV is the present value anticipated of future annual earnings, E, for years 1, 2, 3 . . . n, and the rate of interest is r.

$$(1) \qquad PV = \frac{E_1}{1 + r} + \frac{E_2}{(1 + r)^2} + \frac{E_3}{(1 + r)^3} \cdots \frac{E_n}{(1 + r)^n}$$

This equation can also be written as

$$PV = \sum_1^n \frac{E_t}{(1 + r)^t}$$

where t is time.

The present value of all costs of investment C, incurred over years 1, 2, 3, . . . m, is

$$(2) \qquad C = \frac{C_1}{1 + r} + \frac{C_2}{(1 + r)^2} + \frac{C_3}{(1 + r)^3} \cdots \frac{C_m}{(1 + r)^m}$$

$$C = \sum_1^m \frac{C_t}{(1 + r)^t}$$

The net present value of human capital (NPV) is then

$$(3) \qquad NPV = \sum_1^n \frac{E_t}{(1 + r)^t} - \sum_1^m \frac{C_t}{(1 + r)^t}$$

For the internal rate of return on human investment, the following equation would be solved for r.

$$(4) \qquad \sum_1^m \frac{C_t}{(1 + r)^t} = \sum_1^n \frac{E_t}{(1 + r)^t}$$

There are two formulations of the investment process (see equations on p. 52). One is to find the *net present value* of a specific investment proposal. This requires the use of some interest rate, such as the current market rate, to obtain the present values of the anticipated benefits and of the costs of the investment. The difference between the two is the net present value. The second is to calculate what is called the *internal rate of return* on the investment. This is the interest rate that would equate the present values of both benefits and costs: it is essentially the rate of return on the costs of the investment. Under the first procedure, an individual would presumably select from various investment possibilities the one that would yield the greatest net present value. Using the second approach, a person would be able to compare the internal rates of return of various projects and select the one with the highest rate. In this case an individual would compare the rate of return with market interest rates. The implication is that if people had their own funds to finance an investment, they would not use them to pursue their own education if investment opportunities in nonhuman capital would give them a greater future return. On the other hand, if these nonhuman alternatives offered a lower return, they would invest in themselves and would even be willing to borrow money to do so.

Because human capital investments, like other investments, involve future returns, decisions to invest necessarily are based on estimates, not certainties. Both risks and uncertainties must be taken into consideration. Risks are those future events whose probabilities are known; uncertainties, in this case, are variations in the future income stream whose probabilities cannot be calculated. Although no mathematical formulas can be a substitute for informed judgment, an individual considering a human capital investment decision can view the probability of risk as a coefficient applied to estimated earnings in future years. Uncertainty is a premium added to the interest rate: the effect of greater uncertainty is to reduce even more the present value of future returns.

Human capital theorists emphasize the implications of capital market constraints on the "production" of human capital. Although a particular investment opportunity may be worthwhile, funds are required to meet the costs if the investment is to be made. In the case of public education, it is the taxpayers who, as the result of a political decision-making process, pay the social costs of providing resources. While such political decisions may not be finely calculated in terms of estimates of net capital values, deliberations in the political process are nonetheless concerned with estimates of investment costs, including the price that must be paid to borrow funds if necessary, the future social gains, the rate of discount, and the risks and uncertainties.

To an individual considering a particular investment, such as going to college, the availability of funds can be crucial, even though many of the social costs of the investment are subsidized by state or private endowments. He or she must usually rely on individual savings or those of the family. As schooling is prolonged in the modern economy, educational costs rise, not only because tuition and other costs go up but also because foregone earnings are higher the older the student. Private lenders are usually reluctant to invest in individuals' education because of the lack of a negotiable collateral for the loan. Moreover, the lender is legally prohibited in a "free" labor market from requiring the performance of work by the individual to pay off a loan. In addition, future earnings from a given human capital investment are never certain; they depend on factors, such as other assets and investments of the borrower, which the lender cannot control.[24]

For these reasons, people with savings and ready access to funds can finance human capital investment more easily than those who lack resources. An unequal initial distribution of wealth and income therefore gives rise to greater inequality as the result of differential rates of human capital investment. Not only do privately funded educational investments promote greater inequality; public education programs may have a similar effect. Educational funds derived from local property taxes are less per student in poorer communities than in wealthier ones. Studies have shown that even state funds distributed at both the public school and college levels often accentuate inequalities in educational opportunity.[25]

Formal Education

Empirical research on human capital investment was at first largely centered on the returns to formal education. The procedure was to compare average earnings of workers with different amounts of schooling. In general, the findings indicated that the returns to education were substantial. According to an estimate by Gary S. Becker, the returns received by white males who had graduated from college averaged about 9 percent, a rate about as high as that received from investments in physical capital. For nonwhite male college graduates, Becker found the rate to be two points less.[26] W. Lee Hansen, using 1949 data, found that for males at age 14 who had completed the eighth grade, the additional lifetime income rose sharply with further education, although the internal rate of return, which was 15.3 percent for those with four years of high school, declined to 12.9 percent for those with four years of college.[27] Calculations by others using later data indicate rates of re-

[24] Lester Thurow, *Investment in Human Capital* (Belmont, Calif.: Wadsworth, 1970), pp. 77ff.
[25] See W. Lee Hansen and Burton A. Weisbrod, *Benefits, Costs and Finance of Higher Education* (Chicago: Markham, 1969).
[26] Gary S. Becker, "Underinvestment in College Education?" *American Economic Review*, 50 (May 1960), 346–354.
[27] W. Lee Hansen, "Rates of Return to Investment in Schooling in the United States," in M. Blaug, *Economics of Education: Selected Readings* (Baltimore: Penguin Books, 1968); see Table 6, p. 152.

turn that fall mainly within the 5 to 15 percent range. These studies substantiate the conclusion that rates of return tend to be lower as individuals increase their human capital investments. Graduate school education, for example, leads to the lowest rates of return.[28]

Although the statistical evidence indicating the importance of educational investments in enhancing income can hardly be controverted, certain problems do arise with respect to calculating and interpreting rates of return. The estimation procedures for rates of return from education rely primarily on cross-sectional profiles of earnings by age groups during a particular year; it is assumed that these earnings will be attained by a given educational group as it advances in age through its own lifetime. But past statistical relationships should not be interpreted as invariable indices of future returns. The calculated rates reflect differing qualities of educational inputs in the past, as well as varying supply and demand conditions governing earnings; future returns will differ. Moreover, as human investments are made in specific skills and careers, individuals may find their training obsolete and suffer a capital loss.[29] Reinvestment in other skills is possible but not always feasible because rates of return tend to fall as people grow older. As already pointed out, on the one hand the costs of such reinvestments mount as individuals age, while on the other hand benefits are less because the worker has fewer remaining years in which to work.

Interpretations of the relationships between schooling and economic returns vary widely. Statistical correlations offer no proof of causality. The fact that earnings can differ substantially for those with similar amounts of education, even when controlling for other obvious influences (such as sex, race, or region), indicates that a given amount of formal instruction does not guarantee a specific return. Lester Thurow has pointed to some statistics for 1966: among males 25 and over, high school graduates had a median income of nearly $3,000 less per year than college graduates; yet 18 percent of them earned more than the median income of college graduates. Conversely, over a fourth of the latter earned less than the median income of those with only a high school diploma.[30]

On the supply side, earnings differentials have been attributed to differences in the ability of individuals, in social backgrounds, and in the quality of

[28] See rates of return estimated by Giora Hanoch, "An Economic Analysis of Earnings and Schooling," *The Journal of Human Resources*, 2 (Summer 1967), 322. Mark Blaug reviews some of the literature in "The Empirical Status of Human Capital Theory: A Slightly Jaundiced Survey," *The Journal of Economic Literature*, 14 (September 1976), 840.

[29] The recessions of 1971–1972 and 1974–1975 affected certain professional occupations severely. For example, the demand for school teachers reached a 20-year low in 1971; nearly 300,000 new teachers were available for only 19,100 new positions excluding replacement needs. See Michael F. Crowley, "Professional Manpower: The Job Turnaround," *Monthly Labor Review*, 95 (October 1972), 12.

[30] Thurow, *Investment in Human Capital*, pp. 22–23.

schools and colleges. Because individuals with greater ability tend to acquire more education and have a higher motivation, bigger returns may be the result of their ability, not of the education as such. Students of a higher socio-economic status also tend to make greater educational investments: their earnings would reflect the advantages of home environments—including more informal education, better knowledge of labor markets, and better health—rather than the effects of schooling per se.[31] Finally it should be noted that education has nonmonetary rewards. It may be sought for itself—for consumption and not for investment purposes.

On the demand side, the remuneration of human investment is affected by a variety of influences. Because of discriminatory hiring and wage policies, the returns on education are lower for women than men and lower for blacks than whites. As already noted, wages can vary from occupation to occupation and from place to place, and if the costs of transfering from one market to another are too high in relation to the gains, the differentials will continue. Furthermore, nonmonetary returns from an occupation may weigh heavily in workers' job choices. Job security, good working conditions, or the amenities of a particular job location may offset the desire to maximize one's monetary income.

Training and Work Experience

Even more important than the relationship between formal education and monetary returns is the investment made in workers on the job in the form of training by the employer and of work experience. Firms play an important role in training and developing the capabilities of their own employees for specific jobs within the firm. Such human investments range from formal in-plant training programs through general supervision and guidance of trainees by management or fellow-employees to the less specific and even unplanned orientation and adjustments that a worker makes in a new job environment. In firms where workers have opportunities for advancement up ladders of promotion—the so-called internal, or structured, markets, to be discussed in chapter 5—employers can select, evaluate, and invest in the workers they believe offer promise for better positions. The process of evaluation and training, however informal, can continue during the worklife of individuals as they continue to move up promotional ladders.

Distinctions have been made by human capital theorists, particularly Becker and Mincer, between general and specific training. The former term refers to those forms of in-plant investment that add to workers' productivity whether they remain with the firm or transfer elsewhere; specific training

---

[31] For a review of recent findings, see Finis Welch, "Human Capital Theory: Education, Discrimination, and Life Cycles," *American Economic Review*, 65 (May 1975), 63–73.

refers to investments that enhance a worker's productivity only within a specific firm. According to this analysis, employers will not bear the costs of general training because workers who quit gain an advantage for which the employer is not compensated. Employers will underwrite specific training because they believe that they will recoup their investments later in the form of increased worker productivity that cannot be transfered elsewhere.

In practice, however, differentiation between the two types of in-plant investment is often difficult, and there are grounds for assuming that both types are involved as the worker enters and remains with a firm. Hence the costs of such investments tend to be shared by the worker and employer; the worker takes lower wages in exchange for increased earnings later, and the employer incurs certain costs that are paid back later through the worker's increased productivity.

One important factor affecting the extent of an employer's investment is the current state of the labor market. In boom times, when labor is in short supply, firms are inclined to absorb more training costs not only in order to recruit new workers but also to retain those already employed. Employers may also find it necessary to lower hiring standards because workers with the skills normally demanded are not available. In this situation, the employer in effect is willing to substitute on-the-job training for the general training (human investment) that the worker would normally present in order to qualify for employment. When the unemployment rate is higher, the employer can raise hiring standards and hence reduce training costs by shifting them to the worker.

Specific and general training are related in yet another way. Hiring decisions by firms involve estimations of future productivity that cannot fully be known until the worker has been on the job. Thus the employer tends to rely on whatever evidence can be found in the applicant's educational qualifications, work experience, personality traits, or even family background to indicate not only productivity but also the ability to absorb and benefit from specific training. This gives rise to what has been called credentialism, or statistical discrimination—namely, the use of certain attributes as proxies for productivity estimations. For example, an employer may require a high school diploma for a given job rather than a specific test for competency. From the firm's point of view, such a procedure may be the most efficient way of recruitment and selection of new personnel. Yet it can attenuate the relationship between human capital investment and productivity. Hiring standards may be applied arbitrarily without reference to an individual's specific capabilities. They may not be relevant to actual job requirements or for estimating a worker's trainability. And the procedure provides an opportunity for inadvertent as well as deliberate discrimination. Women who return to the labor market after rearing a family, for example, may arbitrarily be considered as less trainable for certain positions solely on the grounds that they have not had continuous work experience.

SUMMARY

According to the theory of labor supply, an individual's choice concerning the amount of work he or she is willing to perform depends on a valuation of the leisure time forgone. If the wage rate for work should change, the theory holds that the amount of work an individual would be willing to offer is affected in two opposite ways. One, the "income effect," leads a worker to seek more leisure (that is, to work less) if the wage is higher. The other, the "substitution effect," leads a worker to work more if the wage goes up.

The relative strengths of these two effects cannot be determined *a priori*, and empirical studies indicate various responses among different groups. In one of the first studies, Douglas argued that the income effect dominated both with respect to labor force participation (other than among males) and in terms of hours of work. The long-run decline in average hours of work and the reduction in the work year through paid vacations and paid holiday time tends to support the dominance of the income effect.

In terms of labor force participation, the analysis is more complex. The decline in participation of older persons is sometimes viewed as the result of the income effect provided by pensions. But viewed within the context of the individual's worklife, the older person is more likely substituting leisure at a time when wages are low, having participated more fully during the early and middle years, when the remuneration was greater. For youth, lower participation reflects—in part at least—not an income effect but a desire for higher wages later through educational investments in the present.

In the case of married women workers, the substitution effect appears to have been stronger by far than the income effect. Other factors, particularly reductions in the amount of housework and the increased availability of jobs for women in the market, have accentuated this tendency.

The availability of jobs, as measured by general business conditions, also affects labor force participation of both men and women. The evidence strongly supports the "discouraged worker" hypothesis; essentially this is akin to the dominance of the substitution effect. Although the number of discouraged workers during periods of recession has been variously estimated by different writers, the existence of such hidden unemployment tends to controvert the belief that the supply curve of labor is backward-bending.

The concept of labor supply takes into consideration the skills and quality of labor resources. Known as human capital investment, outlays for education and training, as well as forgone earnings during the learning process, are investment costs, while the resulting higher earnings expected in the future are the benefits. As an investment decision, human capital outlay can be analyzed in terms of either net present value or the internal rate of return on the investment. Unless supported by public funds (and perhaps even then), the process of human capital investment is likely to accentuate income inequalities because of the unequal access by individuals to capital funds for investment purposes. Although empirical studies substantiate the positive returns on human capital investment, it is clear that such other factors as ability, social background, and discrimination significantly affect the rate of return.

Training on the job is another form of capital investment. It may be either general training that is transferable to other firms, or specific to the job. One approach argues that employers will bear only the costs of specific training, but on practical grounds the distinction between the two types is difficult to make. In determining whether to make human capital investments in their work force, employers may sometime resort to arbitrary hiring criteria as guidelines for determining trainability.

DISCUSSION QUESTIONS

1. Review your understanding of the meaning of income and substitution effects as applied to the labor supply function of an individual. In economic terms, how would you distinguish a person who shuns work from one who is a "workaholic"? How important do you believe leisure is as an objective for society as a whole?
2. In terms of the economic theory of labor supply, can you explain the long-run decline in hours of work for the labor force as a whole? the recent relative stability in hours of work per week in manufacturing?
3. What do you believe would be the likely effect (if any) upon women's labor force participation rates if (a) the rate of marriages declined, (b) the birth rate rose, or (c) women's wages rose in relation to men's?
4. What is meant by human capital? How is it measured? How is it similar to and different from physical capital?
5. Similar amounts of human capital investment often yield wide differences in rates of return among individuals; how do you explain such variations?
6. What is meant by the financial constraints of the market with respect to human capital investments? Contrast free public higher education with public loans to college students in terms of their advisability in overcoming those limitations.

SELECTED READINGS

In addition to the Bowen and Finegan and Long studies already cited, other references on the economics of labor supply include Gary Becker, "A Theory of the Allocation of Time," *Economic Journal* (September 1965), 493–517; Glen G. Cain, *Married Women in the Labor Force* (Chicago: University of Chicago Press, 1966); and Jacob Mincer, "Labor-Force Participation and Unemployment: A Review of Recent Evidence," in Robert A. Gordon and Margaret S. Gordon, eds., *Prosperity and Unemployment* (New York: John Wiley & Sons, 1966), pp. 73–112.

For basic human capital theory, see articles in *Investment in Human Beings,* Supplement, *Journal of Political Economy*, 70 (October 1962); and Gary S. Becker, *Human Capital* (New York: Columbia University Press, 1964). As the literature is vast, the student will find helpful Jacob Mincer's "Distribution of Labor Income: A Survey with Special Reference to the Human Capital Approach," in *Journal of Economic Literature*, 8 (March 1970), 1–26.

Critiques of human capital theory are plentiful. A few are: Ivar Berg, *Education and Jobs: The Great Training Robbery* (Boston: Beacon Press, 1971); Samuel S. Bowles and Herbert Gintis, "The Problem with Human Capital Theory, A Marxist Approach," *American Economic Review*, 65 (May 1975), 74–82; Richard B. Freeman, *The Overeducated American* (New York: Harcourt Brace Jovanovich, 1976); and Bennett Harrison, *Education, Training, and the Urban Ghetto* (Baltimore: Johns Hopkins Press, 1972). A review that evaluates the impact of such criticisms is Mark Blaug, "The Empirical Status of Human Capital Theory: A Slightly Jaundiced Survey," *Journal of Economic Literature*, 14 (September 1976), 827–855.

4

The Economics
of Labor Demand

While wages are income to workers, they are costs of production to employers. In general, employers will incur such costs if they believe that worker productivity justifies the outlay. Broadly interpreted, this principle can be applied to the private profit and the private nonprofit sectors as well as to the public sector of the economy. In the private profit sector, an employer measures productivity in terms of the revenue to the firm resulting from the worker's output. Such measurement may be relatively simple—for example, if a worker is engaged on piecework—or highly complex and arbitrary—as when a clerk is considered part of a firm's overhead. In the private nonprofit sector, productivities are estimated not only in terms of monetary returns from sale of services but also, as in the case of nonprofit hospitals or educational institutions, in terms of their value to the community as measured by the ability to raise funds from endowments or charitable grants. In the public sector, the administrative decisions that determine whether productivities justify costs occur within a political process through which the public balances benefits against costs in terms of taxes.

This chapter examines the theory of labor demand in the private profit sector, primarily on the grounds that demand theory for other sectors has not as yet been well developed. The obvious justification is that despite the growth of the modern mixed economy, in which government has come to take an increasing part, the private sector is the heart of modern capitalist economies. In dealing with the theory of the firm and industry, the chapter falls within the field of microeconomics.

We shall consider first the neoclassical theory of marginal productivity under competition; secondly, the effect of monopolistic conditions in the product market on the demand for labor; and thirdly, an analysis of the market demand for labor, including conditions under competition, monopsony, and economic discrimination.

THE DEMAND FOR LABOR
UNDER COMPETITIVE CONDITIONS

The analysis of the demand for labor relates to the theory of distribution, or how the output resulting from a production process involving the interaction of several factors of production is divided up among those factors. The modern theory of distribution, known as neoclassical theory, rests upon the assumption that in a market economy, where firms attempt to maximize profits, the remuneration of units of a factor will be governed by the marginal product of that factor. Firms are considered to be intermediaries between factors used to produce goods and the ultimate consumer. According to this theory, firms, guided by the lure of profits, are able to identify the marginal contribution of any factor to total output, and will pay no more for each unit of the factor than the value placed on that marginal output in the product market. Thus the theory integrates distribution with production and relates the consumers' valuations of goods and services to the determination of wages as the value of the workers' marginal output.

The Short Run

Basic to this analysis is the concept of the production function of a firm—namely, the technical relationships that describe the possible combinations of inputs of various factors and the resulting outputs. This analysis assumes that the firms operate within a given technological framework, that the units of each factor are homogeneous, and that the proportions among the various factors are variable. Under these conditions the theory states that for any firm in the short run, where units of one factor are added to a fixed quantity of other factors, the resulting additions to output will diminish after some point. For our purposes, we will treat the capital equipment of the firm as fixed and the amount of labor as the variable factor.

The technical production function, derived from the earlier classical law of diminishing returns,[1] is described in Figure 4–1. In a firm in which all factors but labor are held constant, the additional output, called the marginal physical product (MPP) of labor, at first rises to W_1 and then declines ultimately to zero as more units of labor are added. The total product (TP), which is the sum of the marginal outputs, rises as long as the marginal product is greater

---

[1] The British classical writers of the early nineteenth century applied the theory of variable proportions only to agriculture. Land was considered fixed in quantity. As population increased (and hence the amount of labor applied to food production), the law of diminishing returns held that food supplies would not rise proportionately, with the result that the amount of subsistence per worker would diminish. According to Robert Malthus, who first expounded this principle in stark, bold strokes in 1798, unless population growth were restrained, the world was headed for famine, disease, and war.

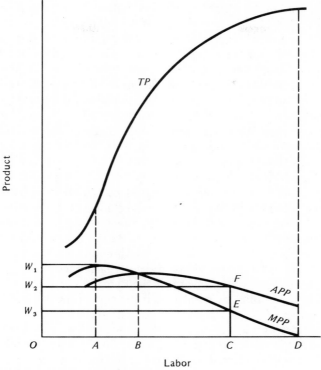

FIGURE 4–1   Productivity Curves of a Firm

than zero, and its rate of increase declines after point A. It reaches a maximum at D where the marginal product, which is the rate of increase in the total product curve, becomes zero. The average physical product curve (APP) is the total product divided by the number of units of labor employed. It rises when the marginal output curve lies above it and falls when the marginal outputs are below it.

The marginal physical product curve can be readily converted into the demand curve for labor. With the output of the firm sold in a competitive market at a price that is not affected by the amount of product the firm offers for sale, the marginal product, multiplied by the price, gives the marginal revenue product of labor (MRP). This is the amount the firm would be willing to pay for labor. If the marginal product of the tenth worker is 20 units per day and if the firm can sell any and all of its product for $1 per unit, the marginal revenue product of 10 workers is $20; the firm would be unwilling to pay the worker any larger amount if it wished to maximize its profits. On the grounds that the tenth worker is exactly equal in ability and skill to the other 9 workers, the firm would pay each of the 10 workers $20. If the firm hired an eleventh worker, it might find that the marginal output had dropped to 18 units, and hence the *MRP* to $18 (assuming that the selling price of the output was unchanged). The firm would not employ the eleventh worker unless the wage, and the wage for the other 10 workers, was no higher than $18. The demand curve of labor can be read as follows: if the wage is $20, the firm will employ 10 workers; if the wage is $18, the firm will employ 11 workers. The curve is downward-sloping because of the principle of diminishing marginal physical productivity—the *MPP* curve of Figure 4–1.

In real terms, what is the relationship of the marginal and average product curves? In terms of the total product of the firm, workers receive the equivalent of the wage times the number of workers. If *OC* workers are employed at the wage W_3, which equals the marginal product *CE*, the total wage bill is the rectangle OW_3EC; the amount received by the owners of fixed factors would be the rectangle W_3W_2FE; the two rectangles together represent the total product. The share going to the fixed factors increases steadily as the firm employs more workers at lower wages. At the extreme limits the total product goes to labor when *OB* are employed; none goes to them when employment is *OD*. In absolute terms, the aggregate wage payment going to workers depends upon the elasticity of the demand curve for labor: as the wage is lowered, the total payment rises if the curve is elastic and falls if the curve is inelastic.

For an industry in the short run, the demand curve for labor is not the sum of the demand curves of the individual firms. This follows because the price of the product will be affected as all firms in the industry expand or contract their output. At a lower wage, for example, firms would hire more workers and produce more goods; the price of the product would fall instead of remaining constant, as in the case of the individual firm. In short, the derived demand curve for labor for the industry as a whole is less elastic than the curve for a single firm. As elasticity refers to the percentage change in employment resulting from a small percentage change in wages, the increase in employment from a given fall in wage levels would be relatively less if it affected all firms in an industry than if it affected only one.

The Long Run

While in the short run other factors of production are held constant, the long-run analysis of a firm's demand for labor must take into consideration the possibility of the adjustments in plant, equipment, and other inputs of the productive process. The reason is that the return to "other factors" obtained in the short run must be sufficient to cover their costs or they will eventually be employed elsewhere. In the terminology of Alfred Marshall, one of the early developers of neoclassical theory, the return to the fixed factors in the short run may be considered a quasi-rent. (In Figure 4–1, the quasi-rent in real terms is designated by the rectangle W_3W_2FE.) If that rent is greater than the costs of those facilities, the firm will find it expedient to increase its investment in them; if less than costs, the facilities will be withdrawn.

The effect of such changes is to shift the short-run productivity curve of labor, and hence labor demand. (See Figure 4–2A.) If a firm expands its fixed equipment, for example, the labor demand curve would be shifted to the right, from D to D', because workers employed with more capital per worker are more productive. In this case, where the competitive wage rate, W, remains the same in the market, the number of workers employed will increase from E to E'.

A wage change can initiate new combinations of resources. If the wage should rise from W_1 to W_2 (Figure 4–2B), the firm would reduce employment as a short-run adjustment from E_1 to E_2, but would find that the return to its other factors had been reduced. If the firm then decided to withdraw some of its equipment for investment elsewhere, the result would be to shift the short-run labor demand curve to the left from D to D' as the decline in the amount of fixed equipment per worker caused labor productivities to fall. Employment would now decline further, from E_2 to E_3. With higher wages, the long-run demand curve for labor, LD, will therefore be more elastic than the short-run curve: that is, the percentage reduction in employment that results from a given percentage increase in wages will be higher.

Long-run adjustments include not only those made within firms but also those affecting the number of firms. When the returns to fixed factors—capital in the broad sense—are high, new firms will enter an industry; when low, firms will leave. If wages differ in various regions, there will be a tendency for firms to transfer their operations to a low-wage region in order to improve their returns on capital.

In the long run, firms may introduce new technology (analytically defined as an innovation) or a new production function. Historically, when changes are made in the amount of capital invested in old firms, technological improvements are often embodied in a new plant and equipment, so it is difficult to separate the effects of capital as such from technical modernization. Nonetheless, technical change raises labor productivities, although whether it leads to an expansion or contraction of employment at a given wage rate depends upon the type of innovation and general market conditions. A labor-saving innovation is one that reduces labor's share of the total product, while a capital-saving innovation is one that raises it. In a static analysis where other variables are held constant, the effect of labor-saving innovations would be to increase the elasticity of the demand curve for labor. Some writers have held that as wages have risen, labor-saving innovations have in fact been induced to offset a reduction in the share that would otherwise have been received by capital. In a static world labor-saving devices will reduce employment. But in

A. Short run

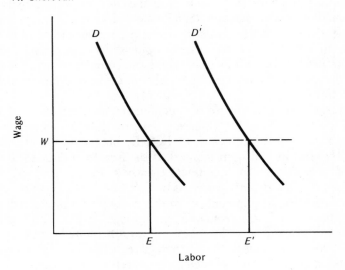

B. Long run

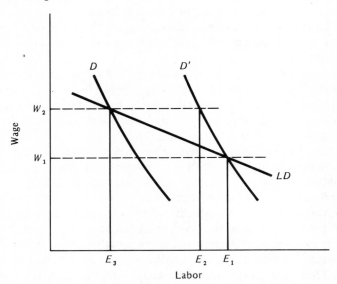

FIGURE 4–2 Short- and Long-Run Labor Demand Curves

a dynamic world this need not necessarily happen: if the innovation lowers costs, a particular firm may expand its employment through increased sales at lower prices.

THE DEMAND FOR LABOR
UNDER MONOPOLISTIC CONDITIONS

When firms have monopolistic power over the prices at which they sell their products, the competitive model of the demand for labor must be modified. The consumer no longer is the ultimate source of valuations of the worker's marginal product; the firm itself can influence valuations by restricting the level of output. Monopolistic power is derived from size with respect to a particular market. Whereas under perfect conditions there are many firms, none of which is large enough to have its output affect the product price perceptibly—as in the case of a small wheat farmer—in a monopolistic situation a firm is large enough, relative to the market, to make its presence felt. And because such a firm can sell less in order to raise the price of its product and improve its profits, its demand curve for labor in the short run will be affected adversely from the point of view of labor. In technical terms, the labor demand curve will be shifted to the left and become less elastic.

The Short Run

Under equilibrium conditions in the short run, economists classify noncompetitive product markets into three types, each of which has somewhat different implications for the demand for labor: (1) those in which there are a number of firms producing similar but differentiated products; (2) those characterized by only a few sellers (oligopoly); and (3) those in which there are only monopolists.

In the first case (known as monopolistic competition), a firm can raise its price without losing all of its customers because some will prefer the unique qualities of its product even at a higher price; other customers, however, may shift to similar products made by other firms. The firm's product demand curve will be unlike that of a firm in a perfectly competitive market; it will tilt downward to the right instead by being horizontal. Such a monopolistic firm has the power to influence the price of its product by changing its output. (See Figure 4–3.)

This situation directly affects the derived demand for labor. Although the production function of the firm is unchanged, the price of the output will decrease as more is produced. The result is that although the schedule of the marginal physical product of labor (MPP) has not been changed, the marginal revenue product (MRP) will be less than under perfect competition. The derived demand curve for labor will have a steeper slope than would

A. Product Demand

Perfect Competition

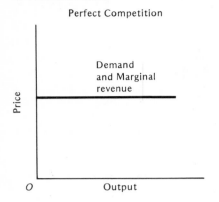

Monopolistic Competition

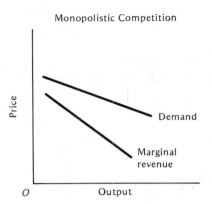

B. Derived Demand for Labor

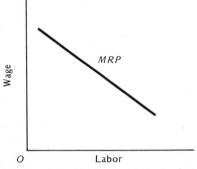

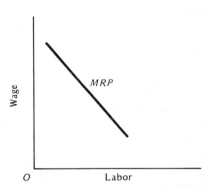

FIGURE 4–3 Product and Derived Demand Curves Under Perfect and Monopolistic Competition

otherwise be the case. The firm's most profitable position is found in the same way as under competitive conditions—namely, by equating MRP with the wage rate—but the MRP will be less than the MPP times the price at which that quantity of output is sold. The capturing of a part of the product market by the firm through product differentiation, advertising, or similar means then changes the pattern of resource allocation. In this case, it puts a burden on workers; if at every level of output the marginal revenue product of labor is lower, the firm will employ fewer workers.

Under conditions of oligopoly, where only a relatively few firms are selling in the product market, the demand curve for labor becomes discontinuous. Each of the few firms will hesitate to lower product prices, fearing that the other firms will follow, so that no one firm will gain a differential advantage;

similarly, each will fear to raise prices because other firms might not raise theirs. In this cat-and-mouse situation, each oligopolist tends to keep the product price and production at the current level within a wide range of different wage rates. In short, a change in the wage rate within that range will have no "employment effect." Under oligopoly, the demand curve in the product market is usually described as kinked (see Figure 4–4). To the firm under these circumstances total revenue declines (or is expected to decline) no matter whether the product price is raised or lowered. The derived *MRP* would have a shape as indicated in Figure 4–5, so that for any change in the wage rate between *L* and *W* the firm would continue to hire *OL* workers.

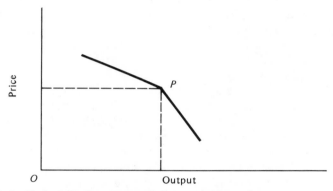

FIGURE 4–4   Kinked Product Demand Curve of Oligopolist

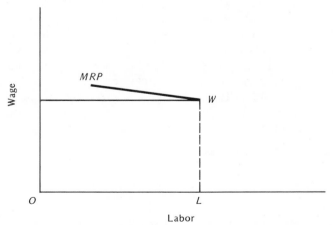

FIGURE 4–5   Discontinuity in Labor Demand Curve of Oligopolist

Finally, in the case of a single seller (monopolist) in the product market, the demand curve for the product is the industry demand curve. As it is less than perfectly elastic, it gives rise to a marginal revenue curve for labor that lies below the curve respresenting the marginal physical product of labor times the price of the output. The monopolist gains by paying workers less than their full marginal product. To the extent that oligopolists act together on a common price policy, either explicitly or by recognizing a price leader that others will follow, the monopolistic case is applicable.

The Long Run

The long-run demand for labor must be viewed differently in monopolistic industries than in competitive industries. The large oligopolistic corporation, which occupies such a dominant role in the American economy, engages in pricing practices and investment policies that can take into consideration economic influences likely to occur over a long period far more readily than can a smaller competitive firm. Indeed, the large firm must do so. With its need to protect and develop its substantial investments in fixed plant and equipment, its most important management skill is successful long-run planning. In fact, concern for the long run takes precedence over the short run; as some observers have pointed out, the concept of short-run profit maximization in its neoclassical version loses relevance, and may even be misleading.[2] Long-run objectives can deter the firm from making short-term adjustments to market conditions that are temporary, or considered temporary.

Although economists disagree as to their prevalence, the existence of administered pricing practices and the establishment by firms in such industries as steel, autos, and oil of target goals for rates of profits support the view that the monopolistic sector tends to be less responsive in the short run to market forces. Administered prices are likely to be set by firms to achieve certain long-run goals.[3] One approach is to set prices so that with the expected level of revenue a firm would be able to cover its costs plus a designated, or target, rate of profits. The latter would be planned to provide not only a desired rate of return on invested capital but also profits for reinvestment in the enterprise. Under these circumstances, the administered price would be increased if wages or other costs were increased, or if the firm wanted to make greater investments in its plant and equipment through retained earnings. The price

[2] For example, see Robert T. Averitt, *The Dual Economy: The Dynamics of American Industry Structure* (New York: W. W. Norton, 1968), esp. ch. 6; John Kenneth Galbraith, *The New Industrial State* (Boston: Houghton Mifflin, 1967), chs. 2–4.

[3] On target profit objectives, see A. D. H. Kaplan, Joel Dirlam, and Robert Lanzillotti, "Pricing in Big Business" (Washington, D.C.: Brookings Institution, 1958); Donaldson Brown, "Pricing Policy in Relation to Financial Control," *Management and Administration* (February-April 1974).

might also be increased if demand for products declined on the grounds that a decline in output would be likely to raise unit costs.

A further factor important in oligopolistic pricing is the implicit or explicit agreement among firms to follow suit. As noted above, an oligopolist acting independently is likely to suffer economic losses through retaliatory actions by others in the industry. By acting together, however, all can gain. In such a situation, one firm may become accepted as a price leader, on the grounds that it will take actions designed to achieve the "best" results for the group. Other guidelines may be developed in terms of respect for one another's historical share of the market. Finally, if the existing firms are to protect their oligopoly successfully, they must bar new entrants. In some industries where the capital requirements of a new firm are large, size alone can deter entry; research and development funds spent on new processes and products, with patent protection, can often be barriers, too. Vertical integration—backward to control material supplies or forward to control consumer outlets—is a strategy frequently used to preserve a firm's position over the years.

In terms of the demand for labor, what are the economic effects of these price and investment policies of the oligopolistic enterprises that constitute, in Averitt's terminology, the "center" firms of the American economy? They are threefold. The first is that the demand curve for labor at any particular time tends to be less elastic: wage increases can be passed on to the consumer more easily than in competitive markets. Secondly, because administered prices are less flexible with respect to changes in the general level of business conditions, employment fluctuates over the business cycle more widely than in competitive industries. Thirdly, the elasticity of the long-run demand for labor is probably enhanced. This follows for several reasons. Oligopolistic firms are better able organizationally to introduce new technologies with a labor-saving bias; they also have larger, internally generated funds to finance such innovations. And through greater command of information, they can relocate plant and facilities more easily and readily to take advantage of areas, at home or overseas, where wages are lower.

THE MARKET DEMAND FOR LABOR

In a labor market the demand for labor is the sum of the demand schedules of the individual firms. It is appropriate for this analysis to concentrate on a market for a particular type of labor at a particular time, and convenient to assume that the market is localized spatially—that is, one in which workers commute regularly to established centers of demand. Such a market is described in Figure 4-6. The aggregate demand curve will slope downward to the right, while the supply curve rises to the right, indicating that as wages

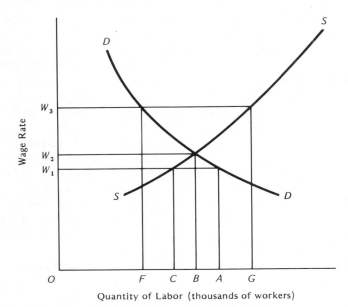

FIGURE 4-6   Supply and Demand Curves in a Labor Market

increase more units of labor will be offered. Under these circumstances, a shortage or a surplus of labor could exist if the wage were too low or too high. On our graph, W_1 indicates a wage that is too low because the quantity demanded, OA, is greater than the quantity supplied, OC. The labor shortage would be resolved if the wage were to rise to the equilibrium wage, W_2, defined as that wage at which the quantity demanded, OB, is exactly equal to the quantity supplied.

On the other hand, W_3, a wage higher than equilibrium, creates a labor surplus—namely, unemployment to the amount of FG. A wage decrease to W_2 will eliminate unemployment, since the quantity demanded will then be equal to the quantity supplied. When the wage falls, one part of FG—represented by FB—becomes employed, since employers will hire more workers at the lower wage. The other part, BG, consists of those workers who no longer look for work in this market because the lower wage is not attractive to them. They either become voluntarily unemployed or seek jobs in other markets.

Competitive Conditions

If this is a perfectly competitive market, (1) each worker seeks the highest wage he or she can get and will leave one employer for another if the wage offered by the latter is higher; (2) each employer seeks the worker who will be willing to work at the lowest wage and will hire him or her to replace any other; and (3) there are enough employers so that no one of them, acting independently, can perceptibly influence the wage rate, and, *pari passu*, workers act independently, and not through organizations such as unions, so that no one of them can influence the wage rate. The first of these characteristics refers to "perfect mobility," the second to "profit maximization," and the third to a perfectly competitive "market structure."

If these admittedly abstract conditions were actually to exist, there would be only one wage existing in a market for a particular labor service, such as typing. If any firm employed workers at less than the equilibrium rate, other employers would immediately bid for them and thus either cause the firm to lose its employees or force it to raise the wage to the equilibrium level if it wished to keep them. On the other hand, if one firm paid a higher wage than others in the market, workers from other firms, would bid for employment there, with the result that the firm could either replace its labor force with workers who would work for less or else force its own employees to accept a lower wage if they wanted to keep their jobs.

To each firm, the supply of labor in such a market would be perfectly elastic at the equilibrium rate. In terms of labor market *power*, the perfectly elastic supply curve means that the firm has no bargaining power. The wage rate that must be paid is "fixed" by the market, and the firm cannot influence it.[4]

Graphically, the curve of the labor supply to a firm in a perfect market would be represented by a straight line, parallel to the base (see Figure 4–7). Such a supply curve is, of course, consistent with a rising supply curve for the market as a whole. (Note the difference in the units of labor as measured on the horizontal axis of Figures 4–6 and 4–7.)

Next let us assume that there are two perfectly competitive markets for the

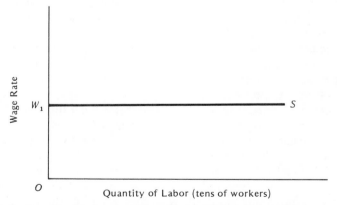

FIGURE 4–7   Supply of Labor to a Firm Under Perfect Competition

[4] Nor does the nonunionized worker have any bargaining power, since the rate is "fixed" by the market for workers as well.

same type of labor, but that the wages differ. What would happen? If the buyers and sellers were governed by their economic self-interest, the theory of competitive market behavior would predicate that workers, or at least some of them, would transfer to the higher wage market, and that some firms would move their operations to the lower wage market. Shifts in the market demand and supply schedules would bring about wage equality in the two markets. But this would be the world of perfect intermarket and intramarket mobility. It is more realistic to recognize three limiting factors.

One is incomplete information. Workers and employers are never fully informed about different levels of wages. If knowledge of market conditions were entirely lacking, there would be no mobility at all. But knowledge is never either perfectly complete or nonexistent, and most actions are taken on the basis of incomplete information. With respect to the supply side, if some knowledge of the market leads a few workers to leave an employer and take higher paying jobs elsewhere, it can be argued that there would be a tendency towards wage equalization; the process of readjustment would be speeded up as more information became available and more workers sought to take advantage of the wage difference. On the demand side of the market, the problem is more complex. While wages are likely to be the sole source of income for workers, the cost of labor for employers is only one of various input costs; a firm must consider not only other input costs, but also the transportation costs of its products to market. A wage differential between one area and another may not be a sufficient cause for relocating. Nonetheless, the better its knowledge, the more profitable a firm's investment decisions are likely to be.

If acquisition of knowledge is costly, however—and better information usually is—wage differentials between markets may still persist because at some point a worker or firm will limit the time and money spent in searching for better opportunities. As a form of capital investment, market information is subject to the limitations that affect other forms of investment. For example, people are more likely to search when they have capital funds available. Workers with high incomes are likely to have a greater knowledge of market conditions than those with less money; larger firms are better able to search out market possibilities than are small ones.

A second limiting condition is the uncertainty of future events. To the worker, a higher-paying job with an uncertain future may be less attractive than a present stable position where the wage is lower. In terms of the human capital investment theory discussed in chapter 3, uncertainties raise the rate at which future returns are discounted. Uncertainties about future job levels, promotional opportunities, and job security cause workers to adjust in the market more slowly and cautiously than they would in the world of perfect mobility.

Uncertainties affect the behavior of employers, too. All policy formulation necessarily requires ex ante evaluations of future events. To be prudent, a firm may avoid wage cutting, even though unemployment exists in the market, if it feels that business will soon improve; it may hold back in order not to lose key personnel or incur bad feeling among its workers. When labor is short, a firm may resort to greater recruitment efforts on a temporary basis rather than raise wages on the grounds that, once increased, wages tend to remain high even if the labor supply eventually expands, while the extra costs of recruitment can be quickly eliminated.

A third limitation is transfer costs. In an occupational change, the worker incurs monetary costs in terms of both acquiring necessary skills or experience and income forgone during the training period. In geographical shifts, the transfer costs include the outlays for moving oneself and one's family as well as losses during the transfer. The latter may be capital losses, such as those resulting from the sale of nonmovable assets (like a house) and the income forgone during the move itself. There may also be the psychic costs of breaking with established social relationships and adjusting to new ones.

Transfer costs are essentially human capital costs, as previously indicated, and will be compared with the discounted, anticipated gains from the job shift. The theory helps to explain the persistence of lower wages in distressed communities abandoned by industries. Youths with lower transfer costs leave, but older workers, with more assets and ties to the community and fewer productive years remaining, are reluctant to bear the heavier transfer cost burdens.

Monopsony

The perfect market assumes that there are so many buyers that no single one is able perceptibly to influence the wage by buying more or less labor, but there are various types of situations where this condition is not met. It may be that only one firm exists in the market. One firm that is relatively large with respect to smaller employers of similar types of labor may act as a wage leader for the group. Groups of firms may agree among themselves either to pay certain wages, or to refuse to hire workers from each other (that is, they may have antipirating agreements). Several large firms may compete with each other in the same market. Or firms may have differing nonwage characteristics.

Each of these situations affects the labor market and the curve of labor supply. Where there is only one buyer of a particular type of labor in a market (the *monopsonist* case), that firm will "see" the supply curve as the upward-sloping curve of the market as a whole and not as the straight, horizontal line of a firm in a perfectly competitive market. When one large firm dominates a market in which there are other smaller firms and where joint wage agreements exist, the monopsonist principle would also apply.

When a few large firms dominate the labor market (the *oligopsonist* case), the labor supply is analogous to the demand curve for products of one of several sellers. Each firm's view of the supply curve is dependent upon the actions taken by the others. If one firm raises wages to attract more labor, the others follow by increasing their wages, so that the original firm will not gain as much labor as it otherwise would. If a firm lowers its wages and the others decide not to follow, the firm tends to lose workers to the other firms. Therefore, if each of the oligopsonists so analyzes the labor market, the supply curve will appear with a "kink" or a sharp corner at the current wage level, and there will be little incentive for any one firm to change its wage level. On the other hand, if the firms agree to some common labor-market policy, their power to control wages will be the same as that of the monopsonists described above.

Finally, the situation is different where many firms existing in an area hire similar types of labor but have differing nonwage policies and conditions of work. These might include the physical conditions of the plant and such benefits as holiday pay, pensions, or sickness allowances. They could also include differences in location that affect commuting costs. If firms are *employment differentiated*, workers may place certain values on these nonwage differences and be willing to accept different wages in order to equalize the total advantage. A situation in which workers are not indifferent to their choice of employer is clearly analogous to that in product markets where elements of both monopoly and competition are present. It is also related to the occupational preferences discussed earlier. For the labor market, "monopsonistic competition" has two implications: (1) since the wage differs among firms, each firm with differentiated employment policies becomes a separate market; and (2) the supply curve of labor to each firm is sloped upward.

If one of these employers can exert a bargaining influence over the wage rate in the market by hiring more or fewer workers, fewer workers will be hired and the wage rate will be lower than that in a competitive market. This can be shown by comparing the firm's average and marginal expenditures for labor under conditions of a perfectly elastic labor supply (the perfect market) and of less than perfectly elastic labor supply.

In Table 4–1, Firm A has a perfectly elastic supply curve of labor. It can hire more workers at the same wage of $3.00 per hour. If it increases its labor force from 100 to 200 workers, its total labor expenditures rise by an additional $300, from $300 to $600. Since the firm obtains an additional 100 workers with an additional $300, its marginal expenditure per worker is $3.00. As long as the supply curve is perfectly elastic, the marginal expenditure per worker will be the same as the wage (or the average expenditure).

In the case of Firm B, which has a rising supply curve of labor, an increase in the labor force from 1,000 to 1,100 workers will force the average wage up from $3.00 to $3.10 per hour. Since this increase will be applied to the entire labor force, the total cost of the 1,100 workers will be $3,410, or $410 more

Table 4-1
Hypothetical Average and Marginal Labor Expenditures Under Different
Market Conditions

	Flat Labor Supply Curve Firm A				Rising Labor Supply Curve Firm B		
Wage	Number of Workers	Total Expenditures	Marginal Expenditure per Worker	Wage	Number of Workers	Total Expenditures	Marginal Expenditure per Worker
$3.00	100	$300	—	$3.00	1,000	$3,000	—
3.00	200	600	$3.00	3.10	1,100	3,410	$4.10
3.00	300	900	3.00	3.20	1,200	3,840	4.30
3.00	400	1,200	3.00	3.30	1,300	4,290	4.50

than the firm paid before. Thus the marginal expenditure for each of the 100
workers is $4.10 per hour. It is the marginal expenditure of $4.10 and not the
average expenditure of $3.10 that the firm must consider in hiring the addi-
tional 100 workers. In such circumstances, Firm B would expand employment only if it anticipated a return of $4.10 per hour or more from employing
the additional workers.

Such a steeply rising marginal expenditure curve puts a damper on expansion (see Figure 4–8) and prevents the wage of the worker ($3.10) from equal-
ing the marginal product of the worker ($4.10). Consequently, fewer workers
are hired and the wage is lower than under competition.

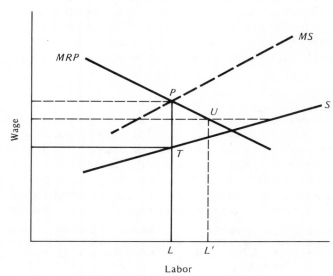

Labor

FIGURE 4-8   Wage Determination with Rising Supply Curve

In Figure 4–8, which shows this situation, the rising supply curve S produces a marginal expenditure curve MS above it. A firm will hire labor up to the point L, where MS is equal to MRP, but the wage paid will be LT, or less than the MRP, which is equal to the distance LP. It should be noted that this monopsonistic situation leads to a lower wage rate and a smaller number of employed workers than under perfect competition. If perfect competition were the case in the labor market, a flat supply curve located above the LT wage rate would give a higher wage *and* more employment, so long as it did go as high as LP. For example, a flat supply curve at the higher wage rate $L'U$ would increase employment by LL'.

Two factors offset this implication of the rising curve of labor supply. One is that the hiring of additional labor at a higher wage may not cause the wages of those already employed to be increased. The example assumes that all workers are of the same skill or occupational level, but if the initial plant labor force of 1,000 were employed at various occupations, each of which paid a different wage, an increase in the wage at one level (say, unskilled labor) from $3.00 to $3.10 an hour might not have so direct an effect upon the wages paid for other jobs within the firm; to the extent that the wage increase could be confined to one component of the firm's internal wage structure, the gap between the marginal and average expenditures could be reduced.[5]

The second offsetting factor is the existence of unemployment within a given labor market. Unemployment is a normal characteristic of most labor markets, and its effect is to make the supply curve of labor flat rather than rising, unless the unemployment consists of workers with different abilities than those demanded. The very existence of such unemployment implies the failure of the market to adjust wages to prevailing supply and demand conditions. If unemployment is eliminated by increasing demands for labor, the firm will face a rising curve of marginal expenditure.

Discrimination

Economic discrimination as applied to groups of workers on the basis of race, sex, age, or other differences means that wages differ among groups even though productivities are the same—that is, even when ability and human capital investments are equal. There are other forms of discrimination. One of the most important is the discriminatory social environment that affects the supply side of the labor market. In this case the pervasiveness of beliefs concerning inferiority becomes institutionalized so that individuals who fall

[5] Whether one part of the wage structure of the firm can be isolated from other parts is another matter. In accordance with competitive theory, which assumes that occupational wage differentials can be explained in terms of costs of training and preferences, such wage differentials should in the long run persist, or at least reassert themselves, if temporarily compressed. At the present point, we need only note the possibility that all wages might not be increased.

within a particular group are not educated or trained for certain types of economic activity. Such discrimination creates a vicious circle. Inferior education perpetuates an inferior economic position because the individual does not acquire the necessary human capital for economic advancement, and the failure to be hired for better-paying jobs serves as a justification for providing that inferior education.

Unlike such discrimination, economic discrimination has long been considered by neoclassical analysts to be self-correcting in the long run under competitive conditions. The argument is that for workers of equal productivity employers will ultimately pay equal wages, irrespective of race, sex, or other attributes that do not impair productivity. In the short run, however, some employers may discriminate against a group of workers either by refusing to hire them or by paying them a lower wage. The lowered wage would eventually motivate other employers to hire those discriminated against when they discover these equally productive workers at bargain prices. The bargain hunters would undersell the discriminators, make greater profits, expand, and in the long run drive wages upward: the original discriminatory firms either would not be able to survive or would be forced to modify their hiring practices.

But racial and sex discrimination in wages has continued to exist in market economies over long periods of time, contrary to this analysis, and explanations based upon the competitive hypothesis have not been considered satisfactory. One explanation, already referred to, is statistical discrimination—the use by employers of easily identifiable characteristics of the individual as proxies for measures of productivity without adequate investigations of the individual's true worth. Even though trained as an engineer, a woman may be considered unqualified because she is a woman. But the practice of statistical discrimination leaves unanswered the question of why discrimination does not fade away.[6] To explain that, the theory would have to assume that employers are misinformed in setting their hiring proxies, that they remain misinformed, and that they are unable to discover the fallacy of their misconceptions.

Another and somewhat older theory refers to an employer's "tastes" for discrimination.[7] By this is meant that an employer has a particular desire to discriminate in favor of or against a particular group. This view implies that an employer would be willing to pay a higher wage to the favored group because the gain in utility from employing them would offset profit losses. The model, however, does not explain successfully why such employers would

[6] Kenneth J. Arrow, "The Theory of Discrimination," in Orley Ashenfelter and Albert Rees, *Discrimination in Labor Markets* (Princeton, N.J.: Princeton University Press, 1973), esp. pp. 23ff.

[7] Gary S. Becker, *The Economics of Discrimination* (Chicago: University of Chicago Press, 1957).

make this sacrifice, and why they would not be pushed out of business eventually by other employers who had less "taste" for discrimination and as a result lower costs of production.

A more satisfactory explanation is that employers, no less than other members of a community, are affected by its social value structure. They are indeed most often the leaders in the social establishment, and their demands for labor are conditioned by beliefs concerning inferiority. When such beliefs are pervasive in the social structure, they can become self-justifying in the economic domain as well. An example is what has been called the "crowding effect."[8] If firms discriminate in hiring for a particular job, those discriminated against are forced into less attractive occupations with lower pay. Such occupations become identified as jobs suitable for women, or blacks, because in the social scale of values they are less desirable. In the economic scale of values, these workers are paid their marginal products, which are lower because of the nature of the job and the oversupply of labor. As a result of the initial economic discrimination, the competitive system does not lead to corrective, equalizing wage changes but to the perpetuation of misallocation and a strengthening of the original beliefs of inferiority.

SUMMARY

The demand for labor by an individual firm depends on its technical production function and on the extent of competition in the product market in which it sells its output. The production function, which relates output to various combinations of factor inputs, determines the physical productivity of the factors. In the short run where the firm can be analyzed as having two factors—capital, which is fixed in amount, and labor, which is variable—the theory states that after some point the marginal physical product of labor will decline. If the product market is competitive, so that the firm cannot influence the selling price, the marginal physical product of a labor valued at its selling price becomes the downward-sloping marginal revenue product curve, which is the demand curve for labor. In the long run, the curve is affected by the fact that firms can vary the size of their plant and equipment and introduce labor-saving technology when wages rise. The labor demand curve is therefore more elastic in the long run than in the short run.

Product markets that are not perfectly competitive affect the demand curve for labor. When the product market is not perfectly competitive, a firm sells a larger output only at lower prices. This reduces the firm's total revenue so that the marginal revenue product is less than physical output times price. Under market conditions of monopolistic competition, oligopoly, and monopoly (in comparison with competition in product markets), fewer workers are employed at wages that are less than their marginal output times price. In

[8] Barbara R. Bergman, "The Effect on White Incomes of Discrimination in Employment," *Journal of Political Economy*, 79 (March/April 1971), 294–313.

the oligopolistic case the wage is not uniquely determined but is subject to bargaining. However, the fact that large oligopolies tend to include the accumulation of investment funds in their pricing (and wage) decision-making means that they are more able to offset wage increases directly by introducing labor-saving innovations and relocating plants.

The competitive demand for labor in a market tends to establish a single wage rate for a particular skill, although this is subject to the limitations of knowledge about wage differences and uncertainties characteristic of the real world. Among different local markets these imperfections are even more likely; in addition, the transfer costs of worker relocation increase the possibility that wages wlll not be equalized for specific skills.

Workers will not receive wages equal to their marginal revenue products when labor markets are monopsonistic or where employers practice economic discrimination. In the first case, an employer or group of employers acting together are so large relative to the local market that they can influence the wage by hiring more or fewer workers; they will adjust their employment in accordance with marginal labor expenditures rather than labor's supply price. In the case of economic discrimination, employers will pay some particular group of workers, as distinguished by race, sex, or other noneconomic characteristic, less than their marginal revenue products. The lower wage will persist as long as the beliefs behind the discrimination continue to be held. Workers discriminated against enter other occupations where lower wages and social status often serve to perpetuate discriminatory beliefs.

DISCUSSION QUESTIONS

1. Explain why the demand curve for labor is considered to be a "derived" demand curve. Why is the demand curve—for a firm, for an industry—downward-sloping?
2. Would you expect the demand curve for labor to be more elastic in the short run or in the long run? Why?
3. Where firms sell their products in markets that are not perfectly competitive, workers receive less than the value of their marginal product (as defined by marginal physical product times price), even when labor markets are perfectly competitive. Why is this so?
4. Under conditions of oligopoly, it can be argued that the wage/employment relationships of the labor demand curve are "indeterminate"—that is, the number of workers the firm will hire is not affected by changes in wages, at least within a range. What is the key principle upon which this argument is based?
5. In the perfectly competitive model of the labor market, it is assumed that wages will be the same for workers of equal efficiency. Show how uncertainty, lack of knowledge, and worker transfer costs modify this conclusion.
6. Other things being equal, how will the wage and employment levels differ between a firm that hires competitively in a labor market and one that has monopsonistic power?

7. Explain the economic terms: statistical discrimination, the "taste" for discrimination, the crowding effect. Show how each can be related to the persistence of wage differentials by sex or race even under conditions where abilities and human capital investments are equal.

SELECTED READINGS

For the theory of labor demand, see Allan M. Cartter, *Theory of Wages and Employment* (Homewood, Ill.: Irwin, 1959); Belton M. Fleisher, *Labor Economics, Theory and Evidence* (Englewood Cliffs, N.J.: Prentice-Hall, 1970), esp. chs. 6–10. Still worth study is John R. Hicks's classic work, *The Theory of Wages* (New York: Macmillan, 1932). A critical view of marginal productivity theory as applied to labor markets is presented by Lester C. Thurow, *Generating Inequality: Mechanisms of Distribution in the U.S. Economy* (New York: Basic Books, 1975).

On the theory of discrimination see articles in Orley Ashenfelter and Albert Rees, eds., *Discrimination in Labor Markets* (Princeton, N.J.: Princeton University Press, 1973); Gary S. Becker, *The Economics of Discrimination* (Chicago: University of Chicago Press, 1957); Lester C. Thurow, *Poverty and Discrimination* (Washington, D.C.: Brookings Institution, 1969).

5

Internal Labor Markets, Segmentation, and Labor Mobility

The existence of labor market imperfections, such as lack of knowledge, uncertainties, and transfer costs, and the limitations of competitive demand arising from monopsony and economic discrimination clearly contribute to labor market segmentation, or the lack of mobility among different markets as determined by skill and location. But there are other approaches to segmentation.

This chapter examines internal labor markets, or those administrative units of firms (and government agencies) in which the allocation and pricing of labor are determined in accordance with organizational policies and rules. While these structured markets cannot be considered as enclaves free from the price and wage changes in the outside world, they nonetheless segment labor markets by creating inflexibilities (in both the short and long runs) in wage and employment adjustments to market forces. Similarly structured by administrative rules are union-controlled markets, such as those for construction, maritime, and other craftworkers. Both types of markets are known as primary markets.

By contrast, secondary markets are those employments in firms, generally small in size, in which there are few opportunities for advancement, low wages, little or no unionism, and high turnover. This chapter also examines these markets, which are often segmented by geographical area, race, sex, and industry. Finally we shall concern ourselves with some of the studies of labor mobility and labor turnover as they pertain to labor market segmentation.

Labor in the American Economy First, however, it should be pointed out that economists for many years have noted that labor markets do not function in accord with the usual analysis of demand and supply forces. The modern dual labor market theory, with its analysis of primary and secondary markets, has developed out of this historical background, as have other present-day theories of segmentation.

THE IMPORTANCE OF IMPERFECTIONS

Adam Smith was one of the first writers to show that, in making labor market choices, workers were not motivated solely by the wages paid but also by nonmarket considerations.[1] Jobs that were in pleasant surroundings would attract more workers than jobs that were disagreeable; hence the wages paid for the former would be lower than those for the latter. Because higher wages would tend to compensate for disagreeable tasks, competition would, it was said, lead to "equalizing wage differences."

But Smith himself seemed to abandon the concept of equalizing wages under competition when, in a famous passage, he decried the effects of the division of labor upon those whose efforts were confined to a "few very simple operations." Having no occasion to exert his understanding, said Smith, such a worker "generally becomes as stupid and ignorant as it is possible for a human creature to become. . . . His dexterity at his own particular trade seems, in this manner, to be acquired at the expense of his intellectual, social, and martial virtues . . . unless government takes some pains to prevent it."[2]

In the nineteenth century, British economist John Stuart Mill expressed strong reservations about the tendency toward equalization of net advantages. If greater pain or disutility were indeed to merit higher wages, then, said Mill, the competitive system actually worked in reverse. The largest output went to

> those who have never worked at all, the next largest to those whose work is almost nominal, and so in descending scale, the remuneration dwindling as the work grows harder and more disagreeable, until the most fatiguing and exhausting bodily labour cannot count with certainty on being able to earn even the necessaries of life.[3]

In 1869 a follower of Mill, John E. Cairnes, wrote of "non-competing groups," or workers who competed with each other for jobs within their own group but not for other types of occupations. Lack of knowledge, training, and funds to acquire such training effectively prohibited mobility among groups. Cairnes delineated four such groups: the unskilled laborers; artisans and certain skilled trades; higher skilled workers, including superintendents and other business groups; and, finally, the professional classes, such as lawyers and doctors.[4]

---

[1] Adam Smith, *The Wealth of Nations* (New York: Modern Library, 1937), pp. 100ff.
[2] Ibid., pp. 734–735.
[3] John Stuart Mill, *Principles of Political Economy with Some of Their Applications to Social Philosophy,* in *Collected Works of John Stuart Mill* (Toronto: University of Toronto Press, 1965), vol. II, p. 207.
[4] John E. Cairnes, *Some Principles of Political Economy Newly Expounded* (London: Macmillan, 1874), pp. 69ff.

By the end of the nineteenth century, Alfred Marshall, who reformulated the classical theories into what became known as neoclassical economies, believed that adjustments in the labor market to changes in demand and supply were so slow in coming that a market disequilibrium was a more or less permanent state of affairs in a dynamic world. Marshall recognized that the proper adjustment of the supply of labor to demand might require shifts of workers from one occupation to another and shifts of workers and their families from one area to another. A period of time for adjustment would have to exist, for example, so that children of workers in declining occupations could learn and become experienced in the expanding ones. He implied that even one generation might not be enough time for certain types of adjustment to be made.[5]

In the 1930s, John R. Hicks, a British economic theorist, also indicated the importance of imperfections of the labor market in retarding adjustments. His realistic picture of a market where demand is increasing indicated the stickiness of wages, and he concluded that the "transmission of an increase must be a slow process." He said that "this slowness is largely responsible for those local differences in wages which present a picture of such bewildering complexity in many trades."[6]

Despite these limitations, the hallmark of what today is called the neoclassical position in labor market analysis is that imperfections may be important in the short run but not in the long run. Given enough time for competitive forces to work themselves out, and in the absence of specific monopolistic restraints, it is argued that whatever wage differentials do persist can be adequately explained by the differential human capital costs of transfers and by workers' occupational preferences.

But the competitive hypothesis of labor markets has been challenged from other viewpoints. The central criticism has been that the imperfections of the marketplace are more important than orthodox economists are willing to admit. It was the critics, backed by social reformers, who in the nineteenth century in the United States pressed for investigations of poverty and poor working conditions and secured the establishment of the first government agencies to collect statistics concerning the labor market.[7] The field of labor economics was developed early in this century by those like John R. Com-

[5] Marshall pointed out that the ability of poor parents to invest in the education of their children is limited, and this limitation carries over to the next and following generations. Alfred Marshall, *Principles of Economics*, 8th ed. (London: Macmillan, 1922), p. 562.

[6] John R. Hicks, *The Theory of Wages* (New York: Macmillan, 1932), p. 74.

[7] The Massachusetts Bureau of Statistics of Labor, established in 1869, was the first state agency; the federal Bureau of Labor Statistics came in 1885. Although the political support was reformist, the agencies discovered that objective, factual reporting was the best insurance for political survival. See James Leiby, *Carroll Wright and Labor Reform: The Origin of Labor Statistics* (Cambridge, Mass.: Harvard University Press, 1960), ch. III.

mons, who found competition in labor markets detrimental to worker welfare and therefore supported unionization and protective social legislation.

Beginning with the 1930s, research became concerned more directly with the economics of the labor market as such. As this study flourished after World War II, investigators consistently turned up evidence that the theory of the long-run tendency toward equalization of net advantages was not supportable. In 1950 Clark Kerr wrote that "abundant evidence now testifies that it would, in the absence of collusion, be almost more correct to say that wages tend to be unequal rather than the other way around," even in terms of net advantage.[8] In a 1957 review of empirical studies, Charles A. Myers concluded that "the over-all impression of local labor markets which emerges . . . is one of considerable haphazard and apparently purposeless movement, many imperfections, and a weak link between mobility and the equalizations of net advantages in different jobs."[9] In a 1970 survey of more recent literature, Herbert S. Parnes wrote that those who observe labor makets directly see them as "less orderly, rational, and efficient than those who study aggregate data on job changing with the simple framework of economic theory."[10]

With the War on Poverty and the urban crises of the 1960s, research on labor markets turned to investigations of the experience of the disadvantaged, the unemployed, and underemployed in the big city ghettoes, and the causes of the successes and failures of federal manpower programs. Out of these studies came the concepts of dual markets and segmentation, and further criticism of the traditional neoclassical analysis of labor market behavior.[11]

INTERNAL LABOR MARKETS

The flaw of traditional theory was the failure to recognize that many employed workers are effectively removed, or insulated, from the market influences of supply and demand by virtue of the "structure of job rights or privileges" that they acquire within the employing firm. Kerr called this type of relationship the "institutional" labor market;[12] Lloyd Fisher, the "struc-

---

[8] Clark Kerr, "Labor Markets: Their Character and Consequences," *Papers and Proceedings of the American Economic Association*, 11 (May 1950), 280.

[9] Charles A. Myers, "Labor Market Theory and Empirical Research," in John T. Dunlop, ed., *The Theory of Wage Determination* (London: Macmillan, 1957), p. 321.

[10] Herbert S. Parnes, "Labor Force Participation and Labor Mobility," in Woodrow L. Ginsburg et al., eds., *A Review of Industrial Relations Research* (Madison, Wis.: Industrial Relations Research Association, 1970), vol. 1, p. 64.

[11] Glen C. Cain reviews this history briefly in "The Challenge of Segmented Labor Market Theories to Orthodox Theory: A Survey," *Journal of Economic Literature*, 14 (December 1976), 1215–1257. See also David M. Gordon, *Theories of Poverty and Underemployment*, Orthodox, Radical, and Dual Labor Market Perspectives (Lexington, Mass.: D.C. Heath, 1972).

[12] Kerr, "Labor Markets," 280–283.

tured" labor market;[13] John T. Dunlop, the "internal" labor market.[14] Peter B. Doeringer and Michael J. Piore used the concept of primary markets (including internal and craft labor markets) in conjunction with secondary, or unstructured, labor markets to develop the dual labor market theory.[15] The terms "structured" and "unstructured" are essentially interchangeable with "primary" and "secondary" labor markets.

The essential characteristic of the internal market is that the allocation and pricing of labor are made administratively in accordance with internal rules that have a rigidity that can "interrupt or transform" external market forces.[16] The administrative unit may be a firm—most likely a large one—a governmental agency, a nonprofit institution, or even workers in a particular geographical area who are within the jurisdictional direction of a craft union, or a group of craft unions. The development of structured markets, however, can precede the formation of unions. Although historical origins have not as yet been thoroughly explored, the structured market seems to have evolved from the internal, administrative needs of firms to organize large numbers of workers efficiently and to have a stable work force.[17] In unionized firms the union contract provides a written, detailed set of rules and regulations that govern the conditions of hiring, promotion, transfer, and layoffs of workers. In governmental employment, civil service regulations spell out the terms of the allocation of labor and what is considered to be its appropriate remuneration. For 1965, Orme W. Phelps estimated that some 45 percent of the American civilian wage and salary workers were employed in "fully structured" labor markets and an additional 19 percent in partially structured ones. Only a little more than one-third (36%) worked in unstructured ones.[18]

The structured market is characterized by hierarchies of jobs that are connected by promotional ladders and matched by appropriate wage differentials. Hiring of new workers takes place mainly at the bottom of the ladder. It

[13] Lloyd H. Fisher, "The Harvest Labor Market," reprinted in G. P. Shultz and J. R. Coleman, eds., *Labor Problems: Cases and Readings*, 2nd ed. (New York: McGraw-Hill, 1959), pp. 382ff. Fisher's original study appeared in 1953.

[14] John T. Dunlop, "Job Vacancy Measures and Economic Analysis," in National Bureau of Economic Research, *The Measurement and Interpretation of Job Vacancies* (New York: Columbia University Press, 1966), pp. 32ff.

[15] Peter B. Doeringer and Michael J. Piore, *Internal Labor Markets and Manpower Analysis* (Lexington, Mass.: D. C. Heath, 1971). An earlier statement of the theory was Piore's "On-the-Job Training in a Dual Labor Market," in Arnold R. Weber et al., eds., *Public-Private Manpower Policies* (Madison, Wis.: Industrial Relations Research Association, 1969).

[16] Doeringer and Piore, *Internal Labor Markets*, p. 5.

[17] A significant attempt to analyze the early development of structured markets in American industry is the paper of David M. Gordon, Richard C. Edwards, and Michael Reich, *Labor Market Segmentation in American Capitalism*, presented at the Conference on Labor Market Segmentation, Harvard University, March 16–17, 1973, an unpublished report submitted to the Manpower Administration of the U.S. Department of Labor.

[18] Orme W. Phelps, *Introduction to Labor Economics*, 4th ed. (New York: McGraw-Hill, 1967), Table 3–2, p. 49.

is here that the firm makes contact with the external labor market, usually at the level of unskilled or semiskilled labor. Depending upon the nature of its occupations, the firm may have other "ports of entry,"[19] where workers are recruited directly from the outside market rather than from within. Maintenance machinists, truck drivers, and electronic engineers often fall into this category.

The advantages to a firm of a structured work force are many. First, by establishing promotion ladders and by defining pensions, fringe benefits, and other job rights, a firm can acquire a relatively stable labor force of workers who consider themselves attached to it. During temporary layoffs, these workers may be reluctant to search for other jobs because of the hope that when rehired they will pick up former job rights. Such attachment to the firm by workers is a clear gain to employers, who save on costs of recruitment and training.

Secondly, a firm can invest in the types of on-the-job training for its labor force that are best suited to its needs. Even where the actual costs to the firm are minimal, the experience derived from a worker's exposure to a job can enable her or him to perform better as a "member of the production team." If the training is specific to the operations of the firm, there is an added gain. The worker's dependence upon the firm is also increased; workers are less likely to quit if they believe that they would not be compensated for their experience by any other firm.

Thirdly, the internal wage structure can be more readily rationalized and administered if it is isolated, at least to some extent, from external market forces. When going rates of pay for certain occupations in external markets diverge from traditional patterns, firms often believe that an uncontrolled introduction of such changes in their own occupational wage structure could lead to "morale problems"—dissension and demoralization within the work force. On the other hand, if the internal market wage pattern is so out of line with market rates at ports of entry that the firm experiences recruitment difficulties, it may be able to hold down costly adjustments in the wages of employees in other occupations. That is, it may be able to prevent marginal labor expenditures from rising above the actual cost of hiring new workers, as discussed in chapter 4.

The advantages of the structured market to the worker parallel those to the firm. The worker who enters such a market can look forward, after a trial period, to a stable work-relationship with advancements in position, pay, and additional benefits. A stable job reduces the costs and uncertainties of job search just as it reduces costs to the employer of excessive turnover. Although there might be a better job around the corner, the employed worker, unless

---

[19] The term was used by Clark Kerr in "The Balkanization of Labor Markets, in E. Wight Bakke et al., *Labor Mobility and Economic Opportunity* (Cambridge, Mass.: Technology Press of M.I.T., 1954), pp. 101–103.

strongly motivated to do otherwise, may be content to save the costs of attempting to investigate the greener grass on the other side of the fence, and just stay put. Finally, a structured market offers some protection against the vagaries and what often appear to be the injustices of external market forces. "The rules which govern an internal market are thought to effectuate standards of equity that a competitive market cannot or does not respect."[20]

The concept of the internal or structured market provides an explanation for the limitations of the competitive hypothesis as often applied to labor markets. First, it helps to demonstrate why rates of pay remain inflexible in situations of excess demand or excess supply where wage changes would appear to be called for. The labor market becomes "job competitive," not "wage competitive."[21] Employers are concerned with filling "slots" rather than making wage adjustments; workers are motivated by job opportunities rather than trying to underbid other workers by offering their services at lower wages.

The concept also serves to explain not only the limited mobility of many American workers and their willingness to seek goals of job stability within a firm, but also workers' concern about loss of bargaining power. In the case of a firm with only one port of entry for new workers at the bottom rung, competition determines the wage only at the lowest level. According to human capital theory, wages at the higher rungs would be negotiated at the time of the initial employment decision insofar as general and specific on-the-job investments are considered. But, as pointed out earlier, those distinctions are difficult if not impossible to make in practice and hence become subject to bargaining not only when a worker enters a firm but also during the course of employment. At higher levels the employer has monopsonistic power because the worker's disadvantage is the difference between current wage and the lowest wage at the entry level of another firm, not the wage of the equivalent position. With unionization and collective bargaining, workers believe that they participate in the determination of the wage structure and thus offset their inferior bargaining position.

But there are limitations to administrative decisions even within a structured market. First, wages for occupations in which workers are recruited from the market impose points around which the internal wage structure tends to be organized. Secondly, wages in the market-isolated occupations must fall within the range of worker expectations for remuneration. Such expectations may not be precise, and ranges may be highly elastic; yet there are limits, however broad, beyond which a firm will discover increasing dissatisfaction, turnover, or difficulties in recruitment. Thirdly, where unions and collective bargaining exist, wage decisions within the firm are more likely to

[20] Doeringer and Piore, *Internal Labor Markets*, p. 29.
[21] Lester C. Thurow uses this terminology in *Generating Inequality: Mechanisms of Distribution in the U.S. Economy* (New York: Basic Books, 1975), ch. 4.

be highly sensitive to conditions in other firms. Similarly, if a firm that does not recognize a union is fearful of a union organizing campaign, it is also likely to be sensitive to the "going" level of wages. Finally, economic expansion tends to break down the market isolation of jobs in the firm. In any market where new firms are entering or old firms are expanding, staffing cannot be done by promoting or training unskilled workers. The firm must enter the market to hire workers with a variety of skills. With new job opportunities available; it is now possible for employed workers to compare their own positions with the new opportunities—in short, to indulge in a calculation of net advantages.

SECONDARY, UNSTRUCTURED MARKETS

In unstructured markets workers acquire few or no rights in their jobs, and promotional ladders are short or nonexistent. In these markets, capital equipment costs per worker are usually low, and few skills are required. With no need for on-the-job investments, employers have no interest in maintaining a stable labor force as long as they can recruit at will in the market. Examples of unstructured markets include migratory farm work (for which the term was first developed), casual and part-time jobs in smaller firms where employees are paid little for often unpleasant jobs and where advancement possibilities are rare, and those departmental operations of larger firms with dead-end jobs carefully segregated from promotional ladders in the rest of the firm.

Investigations during the 1960s of the poverty and manpower problems of big city ghettoes revealed the pervasiveness of these unstructured markets and gave rise to the newer theories of the dual labor market and of segmentation.[22] These theories point out that the two markets present not only two types of employments from the demand side but also a parallel differentiation of labor supplies. The use of the terms "primary" and "secondary" markets to identify structured and unstructured markets respectively is consciously designed to convey the connotation.[23] In labor supply terminology, primary workers are those who have a stable, long-term attachment to the labor force, while secondary workers are those whose participation is weak, intermittent, or occasional. Secondary workers include teenagers, disadvantaged blacks, some women, various minority groups, and people with low skills, propensity for

[22] See, for example, Bennett Harrison, *Education, Training, and the Urban Ghetto* (Baltimore: Johns Hopkins University Press, 1972), esp. ch. 5.

While most of these writers tended to emphasize the supply side of the secondary market, others focused on the firms. See Averitt, *The Dual Economy*, and Barry Bluestone, "The Tripartite Economy: Low-Wage Industries and the Working Poor," *Poverty and Human Resources* (July-August 1970).

[23] Doeringer and Piore, who use these terms, state that the association "is not altogether misleading." *Internal Labor Markets*, p. 166.

absenteeism, and high turnover rates; they are found in the unstructured markets because only secondary market employers are willing to hire them. Primary workers, on the other hand, with the qualities of stability that primary employers prefer, tend to gravitate towards those markets.

The central question which dual labor market analysis confronted was why workers in low-paying jobs, especially those in unstructured urban labor markets, did not seek employment at the ports of entry to structured markets, where they would be able to work up promotional ladders to better jobs. One group of analysts has explained the problem in terms of the human capital costs of transfer, illustrated by the hiring queue for primary markets.[24] An employer in a structured market views those seeking jobs as if they formed a queue; individuals are ranked in accordance with the employer's best estimate of their potential productivity. A firm would hire only from the front of the queue—that is, the applicants with the best qualifications in terms of ability and human investments. Such new recruits would have higher probabilities of success in advancing up the ladder. Through appropriate education, training, and cultivation of desired work habits, workers would be able to move toward the front of the queue. Workers who did not make the requisite capital investments in themselves stood at the end of the queues and usually had to accept low-wage, secondary employments. The implications of this approach were twofold. One was that through extension of education and manpower training programs workers could be advanced out of poverty conditions by progressing up the queues towards the better—that is, structured—jobs. The other was that general economic conditions of boom facilitated the movement of such workers into structured markets. In times of labor scarcity, queues were shortened as employers became willing to hire less qualified workers.

Another group of writers, however, has been less sanguine about the transfer of workers from secondary to primary employments. They have tended to emphasize the institutional rigidities that lead to market segmentation.[25] First, structured labor markets necessarily result in the segmentation of primary workers; moreover, in hiring at ports of entry, firms have more difficulty in evaluating estimated productivities of applicants than the queue theory suggests. Secondly, the characteristics of the labor force in unstructured markets that appear to defer advancement to primary jobs reflect the nature of secondary jobs and actually serve to prevent the outflow of the cheap labor on which secondary sector firms depend. Thirdly, several institutionalized policies reinforce the segmentation of urban markets. Racial discrimination prac-

---

[24] Lester C. Thurow develops this concept in *Poverty and Discrimination* (Washington, D.C.: Brookings Institution, 1969).

[25] This group includes the dual labor market theorists. See Gordon, *Theories of Poverty*, ch. 4.

ticed by structured firms at their ports of entry prevents many blacks, even with equivalent training, from competing with whites for new positions. In large metropolitan areas where the black proportion of central city populations has been growing, racial discrimination in suburban housing has effectively prevented blacks from relocating near suburban employments, and commuting systems are ill-designed to carry ghetto workers from city cores to suburban jobs.

LABOR MOBILITY

One of the key dimensions of labor markets is labor mobility. To economists who view labor markets as a vital institution in the efficient operation of the economy as a whole, mobility has a high priority in social policy. It enables the economy to allocate labor resources efficiently in response to changing consumer demands for goods and services. Yet, as evidence of the structured labor market indicates, neither employers nor workers may be impressed by arguments favoring mobility. Employers want to avoid the costs of rapid turnover; workers are reluctant to leave jobs, given the uncertainties of job search and alternative positions. Nor does the high mobility in the unstructured labor markets mean that these markets are operating with greater economic efficiency.

Job Mobility

Various definitions of labor mobility are used in empirical studies. One, called job mobility, refers to the frequency with which workers change employers during a particular period of time. Such job changes can be classified as voluntary or involuntary, and as simple or complex. Voluntary changes are those initiated by the worker, while involuntary ones are those that result from layoffs, firing, or compulsory retirement. A simple job change occurs when a worker takes a position doing the same work with another employer in the same industry. Complex job changes involve occupational or industrial shifts or both. (Job mobility may further be analyzed in terms of geographical mobility—defined as a change in the worker's residence—which is discussed later in this chapter.)

A broader definition of labor mobility includes not only job changes but other changes in the worker's position in the labor market, such as the shift from employment to unemployment and vice versa, as well as movements in and out of the labor force. (These have already been dealt with in the discussion of labor force mobility in chapter 2.)

One important disadvantage of these definitions of mobility is that they exclude intrafirm job changes, the changes in workers' positions within the internal market of a firm. Such changes, which may be more important to a worker's career than interfirm mobility, are most likely to be occupational changes as the worker moves up, or down, the occupational ladder; in a large firm with different plants, they may even include industrial and geographical shifts. A few mobility studies have sought to measure the extent of both interfirm and intrafirm occupational changes.[26]

Extent and Characteristics   A historical perspective on the extent of job mobility in the United States is provided by the comprehensive surveys based on the household sample used in the Current Population Survey for the years 1955 and 1961. They indicated that about one out of ten workers changed employers one or more times a year (10.1% in 1961, and 11.1% in 1955).[27] In absolute numbers for 1961, this meant that 8.1 million out of 80.3 million workers 14 years of age and over, who had worked at some time during the year, changed their jobs. The job mobility rate was higher for males (11.0 %) than for females (8.6%). Because some workers changed jobs several times during the year, there were a total of 10.9 million job shifts, with 37 percent of the male and 25 percent of the female job changers changing jobs more than once.

The job mobility studies pointed up the strong inverse relationship of job mobility and age. In 1961, nearly a fourth (24.1%) of the males aged 18 to 24 who worked were job changers. In contrast, the percentage of job changers was 12.5 percent for males in the age group 25–44, and only 5.5 percent for males 45 and over. For women, a similar pattern of job changing was found, although the rates were lower than for males in each age group.

By broad occupational groupings, job changing was more frequent for

[26] The more comprehensive and systematic job and occupational mobility studies are based on information derived from interviews of households in the Current Population Survey. Other useful sources of data are the decennial censuses and the Work History Sample of the Social Security Administration. The former, however, yields information only every ten years on net changes by occupations and industries; the latter is somewhat limited in its coverage (about 90 percent of the labor force), has no occupational or educational information, and does not distinguish between voluntary and involuntary job changes. For an attempt to deduce the extent of voluntary job mobility from the sample, see Lowell E. Gallaway, *Interindustry Labor Mobility in the United States, 1957 to 1960*, U.S. Department of Health, Education, and Welfare, Research Report No. 18 (Washington, D.C.: U.S. Government Printing Office, 1967).

In specialized mobility studies, the National Longitudinal Surveys of labor market behavior offer many opportunities for analytical work. These surveys are ongoing work histories of cohorts of workers selected to be representative of demographic groups in terms of age, sex, and color. For an overall view, see Herbert S. Parnes, "The National Longitudinal Surveys: New Vistas for Labor Market Research," Papers and Proceedings, *American Economic Review*, 64 (May 1974), 244–249.

A general review of mobility studies is found in Herbert S. Parnes, "Labor Force Participation and Labor Mobility," in Woodrow L. Ginsburg et al., *A Review of Industrial Relations Research* (Madison, Wis.: Industrial Relations Research Association, 1970), vol. I, pp. 33–66.

[27] See Gertrude Bancroft and Stuart Garfinkle, "Job Mobility of Workers in 1961," *Monthly Labor Review*, 86 (August 1963), 897–906.

those whose jobs required less training and education. The rate of job changing was 8.5 percent for male professional and technical workers and less than 5 percent for nonfarm managers, officials, and proprietors. But for craftsmen and operatives, the largest male occupational group, about 13 percent changed employers. Occupational rates were also related to the nature of the industry, with higher rates in construction and lower ones in manufacturing, public utilities, and transportation. About one-third of the job shifts were simple, involving no shift in either major occupational classification or major industry group.

One of the significant findings in the 1961 survey was that many job changers had suffered involuntary job losses of regular or temporary employment, or had left the labor market; only a third of those changing jobs had done so voluntarily to improve their status. Consistent with the relatively low voluntary job mobility was the finding that many workers did not improve their economic position through job mobility. One study compared the earnings of male full-time workers on their first and second jobs; of those who earned between $40 and $150 a week on their first job, a third (33.3%) improved their earnings, half (48.5%) stayed at the same level, and the rest (18.2%) suffered loss.[28]

Occupational Mobility Studies   The relatively limited extent of mobility revealed in earlier studies was confirmed by investigations of occupational mobility for the years 1965 and 1972. These studies, also based on the household sample for the Current Population Survey, used the 440 3-digit occupational categories of the U.S. Bureau of the Census to determine occupational changes. The percentage of workers who were in a different occupation in mid-January 1964 as compared to mid-January 1963 was 8.9; nearly the same figure—8.7 percent—was reported for the year 1972.[29] Both of these reports included occupational changes within a firm. In 1972, 9.7 percent of the men and 7.0 percent of the women who changed occupations stayed with the

[28]Ibid., p. 900.
[29] Samuel Saben, "Occupational Mobility of Employed Workers," *Monthly Labor Review*, 90 (June 1967), 31–38, and James J. Bryne, "Occupational Mobility of Workers," *Monthly Labor Review*, 98 (February 1975), 53–59.

It should be noted that a different system of classifying occupations would yield different results: a less-detailed breakdown of occupations, for example, would reduce the reported number of occupational shifts.

Moreover, the shift data do not indicate the degree of relatedness between the occupations. Some of the changes may be advancement up career ladders; others may involve changes within a group of occupations, known as "clusters," which have common skill requirements. For analysis of occupations and their classifications, see Peter Blau and Otis Dudley Duncan, *The American Occupational Structure* (New York: John Wiley, 1967); Robert A. Dauffenbach, *The Structure of Occupational Mobility in the U.S. Economy* (Urbana: University of Illinois, Center for Advanced Computation, 1973); and James G. Scoville, *The Job Content of the U.S. Economy 1940–1970* (New York: McGraw-Hill, 1969).

same firm; seven years earlier these proportions had been higher: 19.1 percent of the men and 12.6 percent of the women. These data indicate that occupational mobility of workers within firms plays a significant role in the reallocation of labor supplies, and to that extent diminishes the allocative influences of the external market.[30]

Both occupational studies substantiated the effects of age on worker mobility. For example, of the total number of individuals who were working in both January 1972 and January 1973, less than 40 percent were under 35 years of age. But of those who changed occupations between the two dates, over 70 percent were under the age of 35. Even the fact that male single workers tend to be more mobile than married males seemed to be primarily a function of age.

Mobility rates by broad occupational groups followed expected patterns. Among men for the year 1972, the rate was 15.5 for nonfarm laborers but only 5.4 for professional and technical workers. Women's mobility rates followed a similar occupational pattern.

Most changes occurred within broad occupational categories or ones that were closely related. Blue-collar job changers tended to stay in blue-collar occupations; similarly, when white-collar workers made changes, they found new white-collar jobs. For example, over half (57.7%) of the women entering new clerical positions came from other clerical positions.

A more precise measure of the extent of major occupational shifts is the "mobility ratio." This ratio compares actual experience with what would have occurred solely on the basis of chance. In the case just cited, it could be argued that the large percentage of women entering new clerical positions from old ones would be explained in part by the fact that so many women are already in such occupations. The mobility ratio takes such factors into account. As Table 5–1 shows, the tendency of job changers to remain in their previous occupational category is greater than would occur if mobility were purely random. (A ratio of 1.0 indicates the mobility rate expected through chance.) For example, the mobility ratio of male blue-collar workers moving into white-collar jobs is 0.6, or less than would be expected on the basis of chance, while the ratio of 1.2 for blue-collar males moving into other blue-collar jobs is greater than would otherwise be expected. Women in blue-collar jobs display an even stronger tendency to remain within that occupational classification. The ratios also indicate that the barriers to occupational changes into white-collar jobs seem to be consistently higher than those between service and blue-collar occupations.

[30] A more recent study by Dixie Sommers and Alan Eck, *Occupational Mobility in the American Labor Force*, reprint with corrections from the *Monthly Labor Review* (January 1977), provides data for 1965–1970 that in general supports the above magnitude of occupational changes. But unfortunately it does not identify the extent of intrafirm mobility.

Table 5-1
Mobility Ratios, 1972-1973

January 1973 Occupation	January 1972 Occupation					
	Men			Women		
	White-Collar	Blue-Collar	Service	White-Collar	Blue-Collar	Service
White-collar	1.7	0.6	0.8	1.3	(a)	0.8
Blue-collar	0.6	1.2	1.1	0.5	3.0	1.0
Service	0.8	1.1	(a)	0.7	(a)	1.8

ᵃ Insufficient data.

Explanatory Note: Values greater than 1.0 indicate that more changes occurred between the two occupational groups being compared than could be accounted for on the basis of chance.

Source: James J. Byrne, "Occupational Mobility of Workers," *Monthly Labor Review*, 98 (February 1975), 57.

Geographical Mobility

Although the United States has long been characterized as a country where geographical mobility is relatively high, most job changes are made without residential changes. Census data indicate that the United States does have a highly mobile population. In the period from 1970 to 1973, for example, nearly a third (31.8%) of the population 3 years old and over had changed their place of residence. Of the total 1970 population of 186.1 million 5 years of age and over, 98.6 million, or only 53.0 percent, resided in the same house as in 1965. Because many movers were repeaters, annual mobility rates are higher proportionally than rates covering a longer span of years.[31]

These data cannot be directly related to job mobility for several reasons. First, they include the total population and not simply the labor force. The incidence of geographical mobility by age groups distorts superficial comparisons. The rate of residential change is highest for youth, particularly at the ages of 22 and 23, when individuals are leaving school, shopping for jobs, or making changes associated with marriage and what the census calls "new household formation." Geographical mobility rates decline rapidly after the age of 25. High mobility rates for young families create high geographical mobility rates for very young children. These rates also decline sharply as children reach school age; they hit a low point in the middle teenage bracket before rising again. In terms of lifetime geographical mobility rates, it is estimated that on the average a fourth of all migration moves will occur before an

[31] See U.S. Bureau of the Census, *Statistical Abstract of the United States, 1974*, 95th Annual Edition (Washington, D.C.: U.S. Government Printing Office, 1974), tables 45 and 46.

individual reaches 18 years of age and another fourth before a person's 27th birthday.[32]

Secondly, although economic motivations are significant in geographical mobility, they by no means explain it all. In a 1963 study it was found that one-half (49.5%) of the geographical migrants over a year period indicated work-related motives for their moves: taking a job, looking for a job, or a job transfer. The others reported changes because of health, a desire for a better residence, need to be closer to the workplace, or other reasons.[33] The 1974 *Manpower Report of the President* estimated that exclusively economic decisions explained "perhaps 60 percent" of all moves.[34]

Thirdly, the greater number of residential moves are for short distances, usually defined as within a county. Such moves may involve no job changes. The process of suburbanization that has characterized metropolitan areas in the United States includes relocations from central city to suburb of both households and firms. The interaction between the two leads to significantly more intrametropolitan geographical mobility than job mobility. When a firm makes such a relocation, workers tend to remain with their jobs and may move their residence to shorten commuting time.[35]

Job Tenure

It is apparent that most workers are not mobile. With an annual mobility rate of around 10 percent, nine out of ten workers are immobile. This is a significantly high proportion, though it declines if longer periods of time are considered. The role of the structured market in immobility is emphasized by job tenure studies, which give a cross-sectional analysis of workers in terms of the number of years they have worked continuously for a single employer.[36] In January 1973, about a quarter of the 81 million workers of the United States had held their jobs for 10 years or more; one out of six (16.6%) for 15 years or more. At the other end of the job tenure range, one-fourth (25.1%) had been employed by their present employer for less than a year. The average (median) number of years of tenure was 3.8—4.6 for men and 2.8 for women.

[32] *Manpower Report of the President*, 1974, chart on p. 83.
[33] Samuel Saben, "Geographic Mobility and Employment Status, March 1962–March 1963," *Monthly Labor Review*, 87 (August 1964), 876–877.
[34] *Manpower Report of the President*, 1974, p. 83.
[35] For a study of housing changes by workers in response to relocations of firms from the city core to the suburbs (the Route 128 area of the Boston metropolitan area), see Everett J. Burtt, Jr., *Plant Relocation and the Core City Worker, Commuting and Housing Decisions of Relocated Workers: The Boston Experience* (Washington, D.C.: U.S. Government Printing Office, 1967), esp. ch. V.
[36] Vacations, illnesses, and layoffs of less than 30 days are not considered interruptions in tenure. See Howard Hayghe, "Job Tenure of Workers, January, 1973," *Monthly Labor Review*, 97 (December 1974), 53–57.

Again, as one would expect, the length of service on the job increased with the age of the worker. Young persons not only have not had the opportunity to work at the same job for a lengthy period of time; they also make more job changes. Over half the workers under 25 years of age had been on the same job for less than a year, but among those 55 to 64 years of age, only 8 percent had been employed for that short time. Although, as we have seen, women have lower mobility rates than men, the fact that women workers interrupt their work careers for home responsibilities explains why their job tenure was less than that of males at all age levels. Although the studies have not specifically distinguished between structured and unstructured industries, among male wage earners the highest averages of number of years on the current job were found in industries characterized by large internal markets—6.7 years in public administration, 6.4 in mining, 6.3 in transportation and public utilities, and 5.6 in manufacturing.

There is some evidence that duration of service on the job was somewhat less in 1973 than a decade earlier, but it is not conclusive. Overall job tenure data cannot be used in such comparisons because the incidence of youthful workers and of women in the labor force has changed, and interruptions in job tenure occur for reasons that have little to do with trends in the structured markets. World War II, the Korean War, and the Vietnam War interrupted job service for many. Recessions in general and declines in specific industries also reduce the average number of years on the job. Finally, the recent growth of service industries has increased the number of firms in the secondary labor markets, where job tenure is typically low.

LABOR TURNOVER

Whereas mobility studies are based upon information largely obtained from workers, labor turnover reflects the vantage point of the employer. To the firm, labor turnover consists of workers hired and workers separated from its employment over a specified period of time. Turnover statistics are collected regularly by the U.S. Department of Labor on a monthly basis from a sample of establishments in manufacturing industries. The published statistics pertain to all employees, permanent or temporary, full- or part-time, and in production or management. Although the usefulness of turnover data is limited by its restricted coverage and its lack of specificity with respect to worker characteristics, special studies of turnover have helped to provide more detail in the analysis of labor mobility.

Definition and Measurement

Labor turnover as defined by the Department of Labor is the gross movement of wage and salary workers into and out of employment of individual firms. It includes "accessions" and "separations." Accessions are further divided into new hires and other accessions; the later category includes workers recalled from layoff and workers transferred from other plants of the same firm. Separations are terminations of employment classified in three groups: (1) quits, or voluntary separations initiated by the employee except for retirement, entry into the armed forces, or transfer to another plant of the same firm; (2) layoffs, or terminations because of lack of business and with no prejudice to the worker; and (3) other separations, which include discharge, retirement, death, entrance into the armed forces, or transfer to another plant of the same company. Of the three types of separations, quits and layoffs are the most important, accounting for about 80 percent of the total.

The most common method of measuring labor turnover, and that used by the U.S. Bureau of Labor Statistics, is to estimate the ratios of accessions and separations to a firm's total labor force. Thus the monthly accession rate is the total number of accessions during the month divided by total employment during the middle week of the month, and the separation rate is calculated in a similar way. Although these ratios are useful in analyzing labor mobility, it should be remembered that they are *rates*, not absolute numbers, and that accession and separation rates are not independent of each other, since accessions and separations can each affect the firm's mid-monthly employment, which serves as the basis of comparison for each rate. For example, if a firm with 1,000 workers loses 50 a month and hires another 50 workers a month to replace them, both the accession and separation rates are .05, or 5.0 percent. But if the firm were to lose 50 additional workers through voluntary quits, so that employment is reduced to 950, the accession rate would be increased to 5.3 percent, even though the firm hired only 50 employees as usual. In a similar fashion, a rise in the absolute number of accessions during the month will *reduce* the rate of separations even if the number of separations remains unchanged from previous months.

Although turnover is a two-sided affair, involving both accessions and separations, most attention centers on separations, especially quits. Voluntary separations serve as an indicator of a firm's lack of success in holding workers. If the firm is seeking to maintain or increase its employment, quits impose a cost burden for recruiting and training replacements. On the other hand, if the firm is seeking to reduce employment, quits may prove to be an alternative to discharges or layoffs, although the workers who quit may be those the firm would like to keep.

Fluctuations and Trends in Quit Rates

Because labor turnover rates have been regularly reported over a long period of time, they can give some indication of the cyclical fluctuations and long-run trends in labor mobility in the industries covered (mainly in the primary sector).

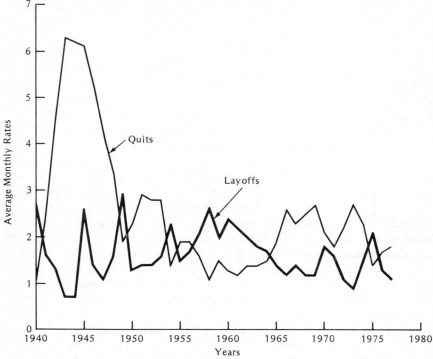

FIGURE 5–1 Average Monthly Quit and Layoff Rates of Manufacturing Workers in the United States, 1940–1977

Source: U.S. Department of Labor.

During business fluctuations, turnover rates show what is called the "scissors effect" between quit and layoff rates. (See Figure 5–1 for this effect for the period 1940 to 1977.) During the upswing of prosperity, the layoff rate declines but the quit rate rises; during the down-swing of recession, the reverse occurs. As the layoff rates of industry are readily explained by the changing level of business activity, the inverse behavior of the quit rate indicates the reaction of workers to changes in market opportunities: they are less willing to quit in the hopes of finding better jobs when layoffs are prevalent and hiring rates are low than when firms are expanding. These relationships are shown by the contrast between the high rate of quits during the prosperous 1920s, when an average of about 75 percent of all separations were quits, and the depression 1930s, when the average was 25 percent; in some years of deep depression, there were few voluntary separations. During the 1940s, as the extensive demands for labor during the war drained labor supplies, quit rates rose again. Quit rates fell as layoff rates increased during the recession years of 1949, 1954, 1957–1958, and 1960–1961, while quit rates were higher during the more prosperous years 1950–1953, 1955–1956, and 1959.

Table 5-2

Annual Average of Monthly Labor Turnover Rates[a] in Manufacturing in the United States

Year	Accessions	Total Separations	Quits	Layoffs
1940	5.4	4.0	1.1	2.6
1941	6.5	4.7	2.4	1.6
1942	9.3	7.8	4.6	1.3
1943	9.1	8.6	6.3	0.7
1944	7.4	8.1	6.2	0.7
1945	7.7	9.6	6.1	2.6
1946	8.1	7.2	5.2	1.4
1947	6.2	5.7	4.1	1.1
1948	5.4	5.4	3.4	1.6
1949	4.3	5.0	1.9	2.9
1950	5.3	4.1	2.3	1.3
1951	5.3	5.3	2.9	1.4
1952	5.4	4.9	2.8	1.4
1953	4.8	5.1	2.8	1.6
1954	3.6	4.1	1.4	2.3
1955	4.5	3.9	1.9	1.5
1956	4.2	4.2	1.9	1.7
1957	3.6	4.2	1.6	2.1
1958	3.6	4.1	1.1	2.6
1959	4.2	4.1	1.5	2.0
1960	3.8	4.3	1.3	2.4
1961	4.1	4.0	1.2	2.2
1962	4.1	4.1	1.4	2.0
1963	3.9	3.9	1.4	1.8
1964	4.0	3.9	1.5	1.7
1965	4.3	4.1	1.9	1.4
1966	5.0	4.6	2.6	1.2
1967	4.4	4.6	2.3	1.4
1968	4.6	4.6	2.5	1.2
1969	4.7	4.9	2.7	1.2
1970	4.0	4.8	2.1	1.8
1971	3.9	4.2	1.8	1.6
1972	4.4	4.2	2.2	1.1
1973	4.8	4.6	2.7	0.9
1974	4.2	4.8	2.3	1.5
1975	3.7	4.2	1.4	2.1
1976	3.9	3.8	1.7	1.3
1977	4.0	3.8	1.8	1.1

[a] Calculated as the number per 100 workers. Beginning with 1943, rates refer to all employees; previously, to production workers only. Beginning with January 1959, transfers between establishments of the same firm are included in total accessions and total separations.

Sources: U.S. Department of Labor, Bureau of Labor Statistics, *Handbook of Labor Statistics 1975—Reference Edition*, Bulletin 1865 (Washington, D.C.: U.S. Government Printing Office, 1975), p. 130; and *Employment and Earnings*, 25 (March 1978), table D–1.

During the employment expansion of the Vietnam War period, the quit rate rose steadily to a peak of 2.7 in 1969. Although this was somewhat below the levels reached during the Korean and World War II periods, it was the highest in 16 years. With the 1970–1971 recession, the quit rate fell sharply, turned up with the recovery of 1972–1973, and then dropped to one of the lowest points since the early 1960s with the recession of 1974–1975. (In the first six months of 1975 it averaged only 1.1.) The layoff rate, as expected, behaved in the opposite manner. (See Table 5–2.)

Since World War II the long-run trend in quit rates has been downward. When the trend was first noted during the 1950s, some writers interpreted it as the growing attachment of workers to their jobs and the increasing role of collective bargaining, rather than quits, as a channel through which workers could express their dissatisfaction with their jobs.[37] In opposition to this hypothesis, Arthur M. Ross argued that the decline in quit rates following World War II was similar to that which occurred during the 1920s after World War I. He questioned the view that unionism, pension plans, and seniority reduced voluntary terminations; such factors affected older workers, whose quit rates were lower in any case. Writing in 1958, Ross believed that quit rates would soon begin to move upward as more and more women and young people entered the labor market, and that fears of a growing "industrial feudalism" were unfounded.[38]

Ross's study, however, did not resolve the issue of whether the trend in quit rates and voluntary mobility in manufacturing has been downward as the result of the growth of structured labor markets. Parker and Burton in a later study applied econometric techniques in an investigation of quit rates in the period from 1930 to 1966.[39] They approached the problem by seeking to explain manufacturing quit rates in terms of incentives for workers to quit, opportunities of workers to change jobs, and other factors such as the extent of unionism. To measure incentives they took a measure of interindustry differentials and a measure of the wage differential between manufacturing and the rest of the economy. For the opportunity variables they included unemployment rates and the rate of accessions. In general their conclusions disputed Ross: "We have . . . found an apparent decline in voluntary mobility in the U.S. manufacturing sector over the past several decades."[40] However, they were not able to explain the drop, which occurred from the period before and during World War II to the postwar era.

[37] Ewan Clague, "Long Term Trends in Quit Rates, *Employment and Earnings* (December 1956), ii–iv, and Joseph Shister, "Labor Mobility: Some Institutional Aspects," Industrial Relations Research Association, *Annual Proceedings*, 1950, pp. 42–59.

[38] Arthur M. Ross, "Do We Have a New Industrial Feudalism?" *American Economic Review*, 48 (December 1958), 903ff.

[39] John E. Parker and John F. Burton, "Voluntary Mobility in the U.S. Manufacturing Sector," Industrial Relations Research Association, *Annual Proceedings*, 1968, pp. 61–70.

[40] Ibid., p. 70.

Mobility and Structured Markets

Whether mobility studies lend support to the competitive hypothesis as an explanatory and predictive theory of labor market behavior has long been a source of controversy among economists. Those who support the competitive model point to long-run tendencies of the labor force to move towards better-paying jobs. Critics tend to emphasize the evidence of immobility and of other institutional factors that impede the movement of workers in response to wage differentials, especially in the short run. Others have taken the middle position that there are both competitive and noncompetitive elements in labor markets.

It is true that in the long run the American economy has had a highly mobile labor force. Whether one goes back in time to consider the westward sweep of population that developed the nation's vast resources, or concentrates on the more limited period since World War II—with its marked industrial, occupational, and geographical shifts in employment—the American labor force has exhibited an impressive ability to adjust to change.

Yet it must also be pointed out that part of the flexibility of the American labor force has come about not through reallocation of the nation's existing work force but rather by drawing on new sources of labor supplies. In the period before World War I, immigration was a major factor in providing labor for the expansion of the nation's industries. In more recent years the growth of clerical occupations brought more and more women into the labor market. Flexibility in the labor supply was also furthered by youths leaving educational institutions and moving into expanding employment fields. The revolution in electronics and computer-based industries, for example, required many new skills; these were provided by an educational system that was able to redesign its instructional programs to train labor supplies to meet the new demands.

Moreover, much of the flexibility of the American labor force has been involuntary. Although interest in mobility had usually been focused on quit rates (voluntary separations), workers who are laid off with little prospect of an early return to their former jobs are forced to seek alternative employment whether or not they want to. As these alternatives are often less desirable than the jobs previously held, mobility under such circumstances can result in a setback in the workers' economic position. General business recessions, as well as employment declines in specific industries—such as those that have occurred in coal mining, northern textiles, and southern agriculture—also cause unwanted mobility. Even in prosperous periods the economy is never free of plant shutdowns, layoffs, and technological displacements: during the relatively prosperous 1960s, for example, layoffs accounted for nearly 40 percent of all separations of workers from manufacturing firms.

Involuntary mobility, even when accompanied by wage losses, is not of course inconsistent with the competitive model of labor markets. The model assumes that both economic incentives and economic pressure are necessary in order to bring about desirable reallocations of labor in accordance with the changing requirements of a dynamic economy. The model, however, excludes from consideration the costs of adjustment imposed on workers through involuntary mobility, and in this sense it is incomplete. To the extent that involuntary mobility has contributed to the flexibility of the American labor force, the gains that reputedly arise from labor reallocations turn out to be ambiguous.

In the short run the competitive model is even less satisfactory. Many workers are relatively immobile, reluctant to make shifts to other employers and other geographical locations even when wage differentials are apparently attractive. This situation arises especially in the case of large firms with structured internal labor markets, which offer incentives to workers to remain with the firm and penalize those who leave through loss of accumulated benefits. Control over a firm's labor force is enhanced by this type of labor market segmentation, unless challenged through unionization of the firm's employees. In the public sector, federal, state, and local governments have had structured employment relationships with their employees for many years as developed through civil service regulations and more recently through collective bargaining arrangements.

In the secondary, unstructured market sector, where the competitive model appears to be more appropriate, there are grounds for believing that mobility is too high and that labor resources are inefficiently used and often wasted.

Because their objective is to participate in the determination of those conditions within firms that enhance workers' employment stability, unions tend to strengthen the forces making for labor immobility. This is the case within large internal markets; it is also pertinent in the markets of the maritime, construction, entertainment, and even agricultural industries, where unions have sought to structure employment relationships.

In summary, labor market segmentation reflects a reality that limits the applicability of competitive models of labor allocation. Although it would be hazardous to predict future trends, it seems clear that the nonmarket allocative mechanisms of the large internal markets and of unions are not going to diminish in importance.

SUMMARY

Modern dual labor market theory expresses the segmentation of employment in the modern economy in terms of primary and secondary markets. The first includes internal markets of firms and of certain unions, where jobs were structured by specific work rules, where wages are higher, and where workers have an attachment to the firm or occupation. In secondary (i.e., unstructured) employments on the other hand, jobs tend to be less stable, promotion opportunities fewer, wages lower, and jobs less attractive. Even these markets are often segmented by geographical area—such as inner city versus suburbs—by sex, and by racial discrimination. Segmentation of labor in market economies is not a new phenomenon: it was recognized by classical economists. But it has been a major subject of study, in one form or another, by labor economists since World War II.

One of the significant effects of segmentation is to reduce mobility of workers in the structured markets and perhaps to accentuate the mobility in the unstructured ones. Various measures of mobility, although not wholly satisfactory, point to the importance of the stability of employment in the primary sector. In general, they show that mobility declines with age, is less for women than men, is greater for jobs requiring less education, and is often involuntary because of layoffs. Shifts from one major occupational grouping to another are less frequent than one would expect on a probability basis. Studies of geographical mobility and of job tenure generally substantiate these findings.

Information on labor turnover throws light on mobility from the viewpoint of the employer. Firms seek to reduce unwanted voluntary separations, or quits, because they impose on the firms additional costs of hiring replacements. The quit rate in American manufacturing has shown some tendency to decline since World War II, although whether the trend is due to greater worker attachment to firms is still the subject of controversy. Quit rates do vary cyclically, in the opposite direction from layoff rates, indicating that the extent of workers' voluntary separations from jobs is in part a function of the general level of business conditions.

In appraising the role of labor mobility in the American economy, one should recognize that the flexibility of labor supplies is not dependent solely on the willingness of workers to leave one job for another. In part the reallocation of labor resources among industries and sections has been made possible by drawing on new labor sources—immigrants, women, and youths entering the labor force for the first time. In addition, labor reallocation need not be necessarily voluntary; it can result from layoff and discharge.

DISCUSSION QUESTIONS

1. What is meant by an internal labor market? What are its advantages from the point of view of the worker? the employer? society in general? What are its disadvantages?
2. In what ways is a "secondary" labor market distinguished from a "primary" one? Would you argue that work in a secondary market is a necessary first step before attempting to obtain a position in a primary one? Why or why not?
3. Who is likely to benefit from on-the-job training—the worker, the employer, or both? Who do you believe should bear the cost of such training? Why?
4. In the structured, internal labor market, wages tend to be less sensitive to supply-

and-demand forces than they are in external labor markets. Why is this the case?
5. Indicate how the extent of labor mobility is likely to be affected by such demographic factors as age, sex, marital status, and race. How would it be affected by economic factors such as general business conditions, the level of skill, or the size of the firm?
6. From general observation do you believe that workers in certain industries have a greater attachment to employment in that industry than those employed in other types of industries? If so, can you offer an explanation?
7. Explain why the quit rate is considered a good indicator of general business conditions.

SELECTED READINGS

For early expositions of the concept of the structured labor market, see John T. Dunlop, ed., *The Theory of Wage Determination* (London: Macmillan, 1957); Lloyd H. Fisher, *The Harvest Labor Market in California* (Cambridge, Mass.: Harvard University Press, 1953); Clark Kerr, "The Balkanization of Labor Markets," in E. Wight Bakke et al., *Labor Mobility and Economic Opportunity* (Cambridge, Mass.: Technology Press of MIT, 1954); Melvin W. Reder, "The Theory of Occupational Wage Differentials," *American Economic Review*, 45 (December 1955), 833–852; and Lloyd G. Reynolds, *The Structure of Labor Markets* (New York: Harper & Row, 1951).

Of the growing literature on the modern theory of the dual and segmented labor market, see Peter B. Doeringer and Michael J. Piore, *Internal Labor Markets and Manpower Analysis* (Lexington, Mass.: D. C. Heath, 1971); David M. Gordon, *Theories of Poverty and Underemployment: Orthodox, Radical, and Dual Labor Market Perspectives* (Lexington, Mass.: D. C. Heath, 1972); and Richard C. Edwards, Michael Reich, and David M. Gordon, eds., *Labor Market Segmentation* (Lexington, Mass.: D. C. Heath, 1975). A review of this literature is found in Glen C. Cain, "The Challenge of Segmented Labor Market Theories to Orthodox Theory: A Survey," *Journal of Economic Literature*, 14 (December 1976), 1215–1257.

On labor mobility, see two studies by Lowell E. Gallaway, *Interindustry Labor Mobility in the United States, 1957 to 1960*, Social Security Administration Office of Research & Statistics, Report No. 18 (Washington, D. C.: U.S. Government Printing Office, 1967), and *Geographic Labor Mobility in the United States, 1957–1960*, Social Security Administration Office of Research & Statistics, Report No. 28 (Washington, D.C.: U.S. Government Printing Office, 1969); J. B. Lansing and E. Mueller, eds., *The Geographic Mobility of Labor* (Ann Arbor: Institute for Social Research, University of Michigan, 1967); Gladys L. Palmer et al., *The Reluctant Job Changer* (Philadelphia: University of Pennsylvania Press, 1962); and Albert Rees and George P. Shultz, *Workers and Wages in an Urban Labor Market* (Chicago: University of Chicago Press, 1970). For reviews of mobility studies, see Harbert S. Parnes, "Labor Force Participation and Labor Mobility," in W. Ginsburg et al., *A Review of Industrial Relations Research* (Madison, Wis.: Industrial Relations Research Association, 1970), and Michael J. Greenwood, "Research on Internal Migration in the United States: A Survey," *Journal of Economic Literature*, 13 (June 1975), 397–433.

PART TWO

The Development of Unions and Union Policy

6

The Nature
and Growth of Unions

The development of industrial society in the Western world has been accompanied by the rise and expansion of organizations of wage earners attempting to improve their economic position as workers within the economy. Unions[1] have now been recognized as an integral part of the natural history of industrialization, and writers and social scientists have tried to discover the reasons for their development and to appraise their nature and their role within the industrial system. While this process of investigation and evaluation is a never-ending one, several significant theories of unions and of the labor movement have been devised. In this chapter, we shall first review the more important theories and then turn to an analysis of the growth of American unions.

THEORIES OF THE LABOR MOVEMENT

Marx and Lenin

In one sense, the analysis of capitalism developed by Karl Marx in the nineteenth century is a theory of the labor movement in terms of its origin, growth, characteristics, and future. Marx held that the early development of capitalism by the process of accumulating capital through the reinvestment of profits created both an expanding industrial system and a class of industrial workers who were separated from the land and from property. He claimed moreover that the owners of capital obtained their profits only by the exploitation of labor, so that economic conflict between worker and employer was

[1] A union, to use the definition of Sidney and Beatrice Webb, is "a continuous association of wage earners for the purposes of maintaining or improving the conditions of their working lives." A labor movement consists of all the varied activities of wage earners to improve their position in society, including political and cooperative actions as well as attempts to seek higher wages.

inevitable. When the accumulation of capital in the hands of a few at one extreme and the accumulation of misery for the many at the opposite pole reached a certain point, Marx believed, the workers would take into their own hands the reorganization of the system for their benefit and would displace the "exploitative" capitalist system with a socialist economy.

Marx felt that unions sprang from the need of workers to protect themselves from the pressure of employers to reduce wages and increase output. Workers would inevitably join labor organizations in an "ever-expanding union," but as the struggle between unions and employers grew into a struggle between classes, the conflict would become political as well as economic. "This organization of the proletarians into a class, and consequently into a political party, is continually being upset again by the competition between the workers themselves. But it ever rises up again, stronger, firmer, mightier."[2]

In 1864 Marx emphasized class solidarity among workers of different countries in his inaugural address before the International Workingmen's Association, usually known as the First International. Although he stressed the economic and political objectives of unions, it was not until 1869 that he advanced a socialist program for the association. This was developed to counteract the anarchist position of Bakunin.

But Marx came to recognize, especially in his later writings, that trade unions did not automatically shift their objectives from purely day-to-day practical problems to the broader political and revolutionary goals of socialism that he wanted to promote. He felt that if the worker's organizations remained only "trade-union minded," they would never be able to break out of the basic limitations of the capitalist system. Accordingly, he believed unions had to be "educated" to socialist thinking and subordinated to socialist political objectives.

These views were supported by such followers of Marx as Karl Kautsky and Nikolai Lenin. The latter, who shaped and led the Communist party to power in Russia in 1917, was explicit in defining the supremacy of the revolutionary party over the trade unions. In his analysis, unions were based only on a feeling of defense against the employer, while a socialist revolutionary party developed its objectives and feelings independently of unions. Of course unions were an important instrument in the struggle for political power, but they were only one of many instruments. Similarly, strikes and other union activities were not desirable in themselves, but only as they served to awaken workers to the inevitability of the class struggle and to the recognition that revolutionary socialism was the only ultimate solution to the workers' problems.

Marx and Lenin thus developed on the one hand an analysis of unionism

---

[2] Karl Marx and Friedrich Engels, "Manifesto of the Communist Party," in Karl Marx, *Capital, The Communist Manifesto and Other Writings*, Max Eastman, ed. (New York: Modern Library, 1932), p. 331.

and on the other a program for socialist action. Trade unions were considered opportunistic and quite incapable of seeing the grand design of the whole battlefield while they engaged in little skirmishes with employers. To Lenin, who planned and attempted to carry out the master strategy of communism, it was essential that members of the Communist party, subordinated to overall direction, be the leaders of the unions, so that the latter, when once controlled, would become subordinates of the Communist party and agencies of the state.

The Webbs

Sidney and Beatrice Webb were lifelong students of labor movements, and especially of British unions, from the last decades of the nineteenth century into the first part of the twentieth. Unlike the Marxists, who considered unions as an instrument for the conquest of political power, the Webbs stressed the role of unions as a means of extending representative democracy in the industrial system, whether it was organized under a form of capitalism or socialism. "Collective bargaining," a term used first by Beatrice Potter (before she married Sidney Webb),[3] symbolized industrial democracy, because employers and unions participated as equals in the determination of the terms and conditions of employment.

In their studies of unions, the Webbs claimed that two principles characterized union behavior: the "device of the common rule" and the "device of the restrictions of numbers."[4] By standardizing employment conditions for all workers in a trade, the common rule eliminated individual bargaining, so detrimental to wages and working conditions, and equalized the bargaining power between employer and workers. Restriction of numbers was practiced by unions to enhance the bargaining power of the union, and the strict apprenticeship rules and similar policies that reduced the labor supply made it possible for union members to secure a higher level of wages. The Webbs thought that such monopolistic devices would work most successfully only in skilled occupations and would become less important as unions tended to be organized in terms of particular industries.

In the formulation of their policies, the Webbs classified the different principles that unions used under different conditions. The "doctrine of vested interests" served to resist technological changes that might wipe out the need for certain skills or might otherwise weaken union controls of jobs, and the "doctrine of supply and demand" allowed unions to jockey for tactical advantage in the market to gain greater concessions from employers. The "doctrine of the living wage" was yet another principle by which unions

[3] Beatrice Potter, *The Cooperative Movement in Great Britain* (London: Sloan Sonnenschein, 1891), p. 217.
[4] Sidney and Beatrice Webb, *Industrial Democracy* (London: Longmans, 1911), p. 560.

stressed the humanitarian idea of meeting the needs especially of persons in less favored bargaining positions.

Finally, the Webbs endorsed political action, social reform, and a moderate democratic socialism. They supported factory legislation and participated in the formation of the Fabian Society, an organization that promoted socialist policies in gradual, democratic terms.[5]

Commons

John R. Commons, professor at the University of Wisconsin for many years, was the acknowledged pioneer in research on the history of the labor movement in the United States. His work gave a strong impetus to other scholarly investigations in the new field of unionism. While Commons was essentially oriented toward basic historical research, his theory of the origin of unions in the United States and his analysis of the special factors that conditioned their growth and their role in creating freedoms for workers were significant contributions.

Commons presented his explanation of the origin of unions primarily in terms of American experience of the nineteenth century. Since unionism developed first among skilled workers outside the factory system, he believed that unions had originated as defensive mechanisms against low-wage competition in a widening market. Although the separation of the worker from property was a necessary condition to the formation of unions, the basic cause was the fact that competition in the product market forced the employer to lower costs in order to survive. Since labor costs were a large proportion of total costs, and since employers had the power to control them, they reduced wages, but at just this point journeymen joined together to resist such actions. Later, as new transportation facilities—turnpikes, canals, and railroads—lowered transfer costs and widened the area of competition, wholesalers and merchant capitalists began to play one firm off against another, and employers were therefore forced to attempt to reduce wages even further.

Commons's analysis was not a monistic theory; rather, it stressed the distinctive characteristics of the American labor movement, such as the effects of a high rate of immigration, the failure to develop a labor party because of the complex federal-state governmental relationships, the importance of cheap land, and the role of the business cycle.[6] As a historian, Commons found the unique and the singular more interesting for study than he did a broad theory of union growth.

Commons's studies of labor were also concerned with workers' freedoms

[5] The group took its name from Quintus Fabius (275–203 B.C.), a Roman general who defeated Hannibal by cautious, nonviolent tactics.

[6] John R. Commons, *Labor and Administration* (New York: Macmillan, 1913). See also John R. Commons et al., *History of Labour in the United States* (New York: Macmillan, 1936), vol. I, pp. 3–21.

and rights. The working rules that defined the rights of workers were established by collective bargaining and thus rested on the unions' protective power, but such rights offered workers greater freedom than did control of their activities by the unilateral decisions of employers or the hazards of the market. Commons held that all employer-worker transactions attempt both to settle economic questions and to determine the specific rights and duties of each party. But such rights and duties must be consistent with existing law: while unions can expand the area of workers' freedoms without state intervention, governments can affect freedoms by redefining rights and duties. Commons's early interest in legal definitions of property rights and in court interpretations that changed the position of the worker in American society led him in later years to a broader theory of institutional economics, in which he sought to extend his analysis to all types of economic relationships.[7]

Hoxie

Writing during World War I, Robert F. Hoxie denied that any one factor or related group of factors could explain either the origin or the development of unions in the United States.[8] He felt that unions were essentially opportunistic, operating in response to specific situations with programs adapted to immediate problems and using the leadership at hand. He was able to classify unions in terms of their purpose, however, though he offered no theory about why workers would form one type of union rather than another or why one would become dominant and others disappeared. Hoxie's four basic functional types of unions were "business," "uplift," "revolutionary," and "predatory."[9]

The business union, which he held to be the most common form in the United States, accepted the capitalistic system, and its members were craft- or industry-conscious rather than class-conscious. Its major objective was the improvement of the position of the union member by collective bargaining over the terms and conditions of employment; it used work rules and restrictive practices to promote economic advantages for its members and political pressure to secure favorable legislation whenever possible. Samuel Gompers, the president of the American Federation of Labor for many years,[10] was the leading advocate of business unionism.

[7] His two major works in the wider field were *Legal Foundations of Capitalism* (New York: Macmillan, 1924) and *Institutional Economics, Its Place in Political Economy* (New York: Macmillan, 1934).

[8] Robert F. Hoxie, *Trade Unionism in the United States* (New York: Appleton, 1928), pp. 34ff. His work first appeared in 1919.

[9] Hoxie also classified unions by structure: the craft union, the crafts or trade union (that is, federations, either local or national), the industrial union, and the labor union. The latter included all workers, irrespective of occupations or industry. Ibid., pp. 38ff.

[10] See the following chapter.

Uplift unionism was idealistic, seeking the economic and social advancement of all workers through educational, legislative, and cooperative actions. The Knights of Labor of the 1880s was the leading American example of this type of union.

Revolutionary unionism, on the other hand, aimed at overturning the economic system and instituting control by the workers. Its two subvarieties were socialist and anarcho-syndicalist, both of which accepted the theory of irreconcilable conflict between capitalists and workers in terms of strong class consciousness. The socialists were willing to bargain collectively and to live up to their agreements, however, even if such action entailed a temporary acceptance of the existing system, while the anarcho-syndicalists held collective bargaining in contempt and favored direct action in the form of strikes, sabotage, and agitation. The Industrial Workers of the World was the best American example of an anarcho-syndicalist union.

Predatory unionism was directed toward the selfish objective of personal gain for its leaders. Its two subvarieties were "holdup" unionism, which involved collusion of the union leaders with employers to enrich themselves at the expense of the consumers or workers by legal or illegal means, and "guerrilla" unionism, which used its power to extort funds from the employer.

Tannenbaum

In the 1920s, Frank Tannenbaum explained that trade unionism originated as a defensive reaction to the introduction of the machine and the factory system.[11] Unlike Commons, who emphasized the role of the wholesaler and merchant-capitalist, Tannenbaum stressed the impact of the machine as a disruptive force in the economic structure of society that preceded the factory system. Workers no longer participated in small workshops, identifying with and feeling the security of belonging to a larger society. Instead, they faced the insecurities and hazards of technological change and economic pressures. The union served as an expression of their desire for a stable work environment and for some means of defending their interests. Tannenbaum believed that unions were essentially conservative in their functions and actions because they attempted to slow the rate of economic change. At the same time he accepted the view that expansion of unions throughout the economy could transform the nature of the competitive system and lead to its eventual modification and replacement by some form of industrial democracy.

Thirty years later, in his second book, Tannenbaum emphasized the conservative nature of unionism, calling it "the counter-revolution," and "a

---

[11] Frank Tannenbaum, *The Labor Movement, Its Conservative Functions and Social Consequences* (New York: Putnam, 1921).

complete repudiation of Marxism."[12] He still considered the Industrial Revolution the destroyer of the older community, but he argued that the unions' attempt to bring forth a new sense of "community" was not consistent with the concept of free markets. Trade unions, he felt, reduce competition and tend to change the basis of society from contract to status. Tannenbaum believed that pensions, seniority, and other union-won rights tended to tie workers to their jobs and to impede the free movement of labor, especially through the "substitution of a life contract for a temporary contract."[13] Eventually, he felt, unions would be concerned with the financial status of their industry and, as they grew financially, they would begin to acquire proprietary rights in that industry. Thus he regarded them as the "real alternative to the authoritarian state," for he predicted that by a merging of corporate and union interests, the rights and duties of all will be recognized and protected through a "common ownership" and "common identity."[14]

Perlman

A Theory of the Labor Movement, written by Selig Perlman, has probably been the most influential interpretation of the American labor movement, even though it was written in 1928, before the New Deal and the rise of the CIO. A colleague of Commons at the University of Wisconsin, Perlman presented a general theory of the labor movement that he claimed was applicable to all areas and times. His work analyzed the development of the labor movements in Russia, Germany, Great Britain, and the United States and was concerned with the underlying forces that shaped and gave each movement its specific character.

Essentially Perlman stated that three basic factors were relevant to the nature of the labor movement of any country: first, the ability of the capitalist group to maintain and exercise its power to rule; secondly, the "role of the so-called 'intellectual,' the 'intelligentsia,' "[15] who were likely to be anticapitalist in viewpoint; and thirdly, and most important, trade unionism, which had its own characteristic objectives and policies of job control. The particular combination of these three factors in any country could explain the nature of that country's labor movement. In Russia, for example, the Marxist intelligentsia proved to be the dominating factor over a weak capitalist class and a weak trade-union movement. In the United States, on the other hand, the employer class was strong, while the unions were definitely on the defensive but strong enough to prevent domination by anticapitalist intellectuals. Al-

---

[12] Frank Tannenbaum, *The Philosophy of Labor* (New York: Knopf, 1951), p. 3.
[13] Ibid., p. 182.
[14] Ibid., pp. 198–199.
[15] Selig Perlman, *A Theory of the Labor Movement,* reprint (New York: Augustus M. Kelley, 1949), p. 5.

though Perlman explained why one group would be strong or weak in a given situation only on the basis of each country's particular historical development, he indicated that the three forces were mutually interdependent; for example, a powerful capitalist class forced workers to eschew revolutionary goals and to turn to "job-control" trade unionism.

"Job-control" was the dominant motif of the American labor movement. According to Perlman, the trade union mentality assumed that jobs and work opportunities were scarce in relation to the supply of labor. In contrast to the businessman's psychological orientation toward abundance, or "consciousness of unlimited opportunity," the groups of manual workers insisted that scarcity was the rule. Workers believed that they should "own" the "totality of economic opportunity" and should ration out such opportunities to members of the group in accordance with policies determined in common.[16] Unions laid down work rules, seniority regulations, rules on apprenticeship, and similar policies in order to parcel out job opportunities among members. Jurisdictional jealousies and make-work policies also resulted from the same philosophy. Although such actions can be identified with what Hoxie called "business unionism," Perlman insisted that the unions were not lacking in philosophy or ideology. On the contrary, a strong union built a loyalty among its members as it helped the individual worker, and as it aspired "to develop in the individual a willingness to subordinate his own interests to the superior interests of the collectivity."[17]

The Inter-University Study

In 1960, four labor economists associated with a research group called the Inter-University Study of Labor Problems in Industrial Development, sponsored by the Ford Foundation, attempted to assess the role of unions within the context of the industrialization process not only in the United States but also in industrializing countries.[18] These economists were Clark Kerr of the University of California at Berkeley, John T. Dunlop of Harvard University, Frederick H. Harbison of Princeton University, and Charles A. Myers of the Massachusetts Institute of Technology. Believing that the approaches of Hoxie, Commons, Perlman, and others were overly limited in their emphasis on American unions, they found that a more generalized statement could be made in terms of the effect of industrialization upon workers, no matter what the particular political nature of the economic system might be. They claimed that:

[The] really universal phenomenon affecting workers [is] the inevitable structuring of the managers and the managed in the course of industrialization. Everywhere

[16] Ibid., p. 6.
[17] Ibid., p. 273.
[18] Clark Kerr, John T. Dunlop, Frederick H. Harbison, and Charles A. Myers, *Industrialism and Industrial Man: the Problems of Labor and Management in Economic Growth* (Cambridge, Mass.: Harvard University Press, 1960).

there develops a complex web of rules binding the workers into the industrial process, to his job, to his community, to patterns of behavior.[19]

They identified five types of elites that provided leadership in the process of industrialization. Characterized as "ideal types" to which particular historical situations would not necessarily conform, these were the dynastic elite (drawn from some preexisting aristocracy or caste with a paternalist attitude toward labor), the middle class (a capitalist-led elite that operated within the system of the open market), revolutionary intellectuals (socialists who directed a centralized state), colonial administrators (who promoted industrial development primarily for the benefit of their home country), and nationalist leaders.

The authors argued that in the early development of industrialization, workers resisted the impact of the new forces that made old skills obsolete, disrupted ways of life, and required unfamiliar work disciplines, but that worker protest peaked early in the historical process and tended to decline. The form of worker organization and the methods by which the emerging labor force adapted to the industrial relations systems of modern industry were conditioned by the particular type of elite-led society.

In general, the four economists concluded that class collaboration tended to replace class warfare, that in all types of industrializing societies there is professionalization of management which includes the rule-making function, but that in all systems that function is shared "in varying ways and degrees with workers and the state."[20]

UNION GROWTH IN THE UNITED STATES

Membership[21]

The long-run trend of union membership in the United States has been upward, reaching its highest point of 20 million in 1974 (see Table 6–1A). Al-

[19] Ibid., pp. 7–8.

[20] Ibid., p. 263.

[21] Considering union membership as a measure of union strength is not wholly satisfactory. Neither the political power of the union movement nor its economic effectiveness is a function solely of numbers, whether viewed absolutely or in relation to other national aggregates. The varieties of union objectives, the quality of leadership, the attitudes of members—none of these is reflected in a single membership total.

Even the data on total membership must be interpreted cautiously. Inaccuracies arise because unions differ in their interpretation of membership. Although the data are presumed to reflect dues-paying members, some unions may count only those whose dues are up-to-date, while others may include those whose dues are in arrears as a result of unemployment. The number of retirees in the memberships reported by unions also varies considerably. See the special study of retirees in the Bureau of Labor Statistics, U.S. Department of Labor, *Directory of National Unions and Employee Associations, 1971,* Bulletin 1750 (Washington, D.C.: U.S. Government Printing Office, 1972), appendix C, p. 104.

Table 6-1
Union and Association Membership in the United States, 1960–1976[a]

Year	Total Membership (thousands)	Total Labor Force Number (thousands)	Total Labor Force Percent Members	Employees in Nonagricultural Establishments Number (thousands)	Employees in Nonagricultural Establishments Percent Members
A. Unions					
1960	17,049	72,142	22.6	54,234	31.4
1961	16,303	73,031	22.3	54,042	30.2
1962	16,586	73,442	22.6	55,596	29.8
1963	16,524	74,571	22.2	56,702	29.1
1964	16,841	75,830	22.0	58,331	28.9
1965	17,299	77,178	22.4	60,815	28.4
1966	17,940	78,893	22.7	63,955	28.1
1967	18,367	80,793	22.7	65,857	27.9
1968	18,916	82,272	23.0	67,951	27.8
1969	19,036	84,240	22.6	70,442	27.0
1970	19,381	85,903	22.6	70,920	27.3
1971	19,211	86,929	22.1	71,222	27.0
1972	19,435	88,991	21.8	73,714	26.4
1973	19,818	91,040	21.8	76,896	25.8
1974	20,199	93,240	21.7	78,413	25.8
1975	19,473	94,793	20.5	77,051	25.3
1976	19,432	96,917	20.1	79,443	24.5
B. Unions and Associations					
1968	20,721	84,272	25.2	67,915	30.5
1969	20,776	84,240	24.7	70,284	29.6
1970	21,248	85,903	24.7	70,920	30.0
1971	21,327	86,929	24.5	71,222	29.9
1972	21,657	88,991	24.3	73,714	29.4
1973	22,239	91,040	24.4	76,896	28.9
1974	22,809	93,240	24.5	78,413	29.1
1975	22,298	94,793	23.5	77,051	28.9
1976	22,463	96,917	23.2	79,443	28.3

[a] Membership includes total reported membership excluding Canada. Also included are members of directly affiliated local unions. Members of single-firm unions are excluded.

Sources: U.S. Department of Labor, Bureau of Labor Statistics, *Directory of National Unions and Employee Associations, 1975,* Bulletin 1937 (Washington, D.C.: U.S. Government Printing Office, 1977), p. 63, and *Labor Union and Employee Association Membership,* 1976.

though this was the highest level in history, union membership has not been rising as rapidly as the total labor force in the past several decades. The percentage of the labor force in unions has edged downward from a peak of slightly over 25 percent in 1953 to a little above 20 percent in the mid-1970s. In terms solely of nonagricultural employment, which is more relevant to unions' organizing activities, the percentage is higher, but the ratio has fallen more rapidly as the agricultural sector has diminished in size; the percentage declined from a high of nearly 36 percent in 1945 to 24.5 percent in 1976.

Because of the growth of organizations of professional and public sector employees that engage in collective bargaining and similar types of union activities, their membership should also be included in any measure of unionization. In 1974 there were 37 such associations. Association members totaled 3 million in 1976; over 90 percent of them were employed in the public sector. One of the fastest-growing forms of union, these associations became actively involved in collective bargaining during the surge of public sector organization in the 1960s. From 1960 to 1976 their membership rose by 1,740,000, while the regular national unions reported a membership increase of only 516,000. Unions and associations in 1976 had a total membership in the United States of almost 22,500,000 or 28.3 percent of the nonagricultural employment of the United States. (See Table 6–1B.)

The growth of unions has not been steady but rather has been concentrated in a few periods. Prior to the 1930s, these periods of advance were generally followed by retreats, usually but not always coinciding with fluctuations in the general level of business activity. Beginning with the mid-1930s, union membership increased dramatically until the end of World War II, and there have been no significant drops since then despite the several postwar recessions after World War II, and the Korean and Vietnam wars. From 1945 to 1956, union membership rose by about 5 million, or 38.1 percent; after a period of stability and minor slippage, it resumed its rise after 1963, with only minor retreats in the recession years of 1971 and 1975–1976. By contrast, union membership after World War I fell sharply from a peak of about 5 million workers in 1920 to 3.1 million in the boom year of 1929, a drop of nearly a third (31.8%).[22] Nine major periods of growth in union membership can be identified.[23]

---

[22] These earlier estimates include foreign memberships of American unions and are derived from a different series than the U.S. Department of Labor data presented in Table 6–1. The earlier series is drawn from Leo Wolman, *The Ebb and Flow in Trade Unionism* (New York: National Bureau of Economic Research, 1936); Irving Bernstein, "The Growth of American Unions," *American Economic Review*, 44 (June 1954), 303–304; and Bernstein's "Growth of American Unions, 1945–1960," *Labor History*, 2 (Spring 1961), 135.

[23] Much of this review of American labor history (including some of the terms describing major periods) is based on John R. Commons et al., *History of Labor*, vols I and II, and on Selig Perlman and Philip Taft, *The History of Labor in the United States, 1896–1932* (New York: Macmillan, 1935).

Early Formation of Local Unions, 1792–1815 This period was marked by the first unions, which were local in scope and limited to a few trades in a few cities. Their total membership is unknown. Business conditions were generally prosperous, and unions disappeared with the depression following the Napoleonic Wars.

"Awakening" of the Labor Movement, 1821–1836 The local unions revived and spread into new trades and cities, especially during the periods of prosperity of 1821–1827 and 1833–1836. During the depressed years of the late 1820s, workers formed the first political parties. Peak union membership was estimated at 300,000 workers in 1836. Following the panic of 1837, unions disappeared, and a variety of social reform schemes were advanced.

Nationalization of the Labor Movement, 1850–1873 A broader advance in the number of unions and in membership began with the prosperity of the early 1850s, was checked by the depression of 1857, and continued during the Civil War and in the postwar period. Although membership in 1872 is estimated at only about 300,000 the period is noteworthy for the establishment of a number of national trade unions that have continued to the present. The long depression from 1873 to 1879 sharply cut back membership but did not wipe out the union movement.

The "Great Upheaval," 1879–1886 A revival of union growth came with the business upswing in 1879, but the greatest rise came during a recession in 1885–1886, when the Knights of Labor expanded from a membership of 104,000 to 702,924. The added growth of other unions, especially those affiliated with the American Federation of Labor (AFL), brought the total number of organized laborers to about 1 million in 1886. After that date membership declined, particularly in the Knights of Labor, and setbacks continued during the depressed 1890s.

"Mass Advancement," 1897–1904 Union membership rose rapidly from about 450,000 in 1897 to approximately 2 million in 1904, a quadrupling during this period of general business revival. The growth occurred in membership in unions affiliated with the American Federation of Labor, the rise from 260,000 to 1,672,000 members representing an increase from about 60 to 80 percent of total union membership. After 1904 the labor movement was more or less stable until 1910, when there was renewed expansion, although at a slower rate. By the beginning of World War I in 1914, total union membership in the United States was about 2.7 million.

World War I Expansion, 1915–1920 With the high level of economic activity during World War I, which began especially after 1915 and lasted until the sharp business recession of 1920, union membership doubled, rising to 5,048,000 in 1920. The gains occurred primarily among existing unions in a small number of industries. With the postwar depression membership quickly declined, the losses being markedly higher among the new members, and by 1923 it stood at about 3.6 million. Throughout the rest of the 1920s and even into the early years of the depression of the 1930s, membership remained at that level. By 1933 membership had sunk to 2,973,000, or only slightly above that in 1914.

The New Deal, 1934–1939 In a second "great upheaval" in American labor, union membership more than doubled as the total rose from about 3 million to 7,735,000 in 1939, a gain of nearly 5 million, equaling the total membership of the previous peak year of 1920. The expansion at this time was characterized by the unionization of mass-production industries by the new organizations affiliated with the Committee for Industrial Organization (CIO). At the same time unions affiliated with the AFL grew rapidly. This period was one of business expansion until 1937, although even in that year unemployment did not fall below 7,700,000 workers, or 14.3 percent of the labor force.

World War II Expansion, 1940–1945 Under the pressure of intense demands for labor by war industries, union membership rose sharply again from about 8 million in 1940 to nearly 13.5 million in 1945. After the war, as already indicated, union membership continued to rise but at a slower rate; it became stabilized after 1956 at about 18 million (17 million if foreign members of American unions are excluded).

Surge in Public Sector Unionism, 1962–1974 Unionization of employees in federal, state, and local governments increased dramatically during this period. At the federal level, Executive Order 10988, which encouraged collective bargaining among federal workers, was issued by President John F. Kennedy in January 1962; in the years that followed many states passed legislation favorable to collective bargaining. Union membership in the public sector rose from 1 million in 1960 to nearly 3 million in 1974. The inclusion of members in the important professional organizations, such as the National Educational Association—which turned to collective bargaining during the 1960s—raised the 1974 total to 5.3 million. Outside of government employment, unions gained about 2 million members, or 11.0 percent, during the period from 1960 to 1974,[24] but this rate of expansion was less than the rates of growth of the total labor force and of nonagricultural employment (29.2 and 44.4 percent respectively).

Changes in National Unions

Union growth can also be examined in terms of changes in the various structural units of the American labor movement. Considered here are only the national unions (or international unions when they have locals outside the United States), because these constitute the major elements in the union organizational hierarchies.

Each national union has a particular jurisdiction, or area within which it

---

[24] These data include membership outside the United States but exclude members of locals directly affiliated with the AFL–CIO. For basic statistics, see U.S. Department of Labor, *Directory of National Unions and Employee Associations, 1975*, p. 71.

organizes; it has its own constitution and officers; it can grant or deny charters to locals; and it is relatively autonomous in determining its policy even when it is affiliated with a national federation. The formation or disappearance of national unions cannot be taken as a sole measure of union activity, but an increase in their number has in the past been an indicator of expansion into new trades, industries, or geographical areas. In an analysis by Lloyd Ulman of the formation and disappearance of national (and international) unions for the period from 1850 to 1947, the statistics point to the importance of the decades of the 1860s, the 1880s, and the 1890s (especially the end of the decade), the first decade of the twentieth century, and the 1930s as active periods in the formation of national unions. Although there have been continual changes in national unions through mergers, secessions, the emergence of new unions, and the expiration of old ones, it was in those five decades that most of the 198 national unions existing in 1947 were formed.[25]

After World War II, and especially after 1954, the number of national unions generally decreased, reaching 173 in 1974. This trend represents the merger and consolidation of various national unions. With the rise in total union membership, the average size of unions has increased, but there has been no significant trend toward greater concentration of total union membership in a few unions. In 1972, the top 10 unions in terms of the number of members had 45.5 percent of all union members; in 1954, the largest 10 unions had 43.4 percent of the total.

What has occurred since 1960, however, has been the development of collective bargaining by employee associations in the public sector. Although a number of unions had previously represented government employees, the number of associations that turned to union action serves as a good indicator of growth. The first separate listing of such associations in the directories compiled by the Department of Labor was made in 1969, when 14 were reported for 1968. The number had increased to 23 by 1970 and to 37 in 1974.

FACTORS IN UNION GROWTH

The expansion or contraction of union membership or the growth or decline of national unions or of any other structural element of the labor movement, like changes in other economic and social institutions, is the result of complex sets of influences.

Worker Motivations

Workers may have no real choice in deciding whether to join a union. There may be no union in the trade, area, or firm that they can join. On the

---

[25] Lloyd Ulman, *The Rise of the National Union* (Cambridge, Mass.: Harvard University Press, 1955). See especially his statistical summary, p. 4.

factors in growth

ɔmatically join a union because a "union shop"
⸴l employees of a firm must become members as a
employment. In all probability, however, at some
⸴rs workers are likely to have the opportunity to de-
to a union. A number of factors influence their deci-
⸴ not meant to be exhaustive, nor is each factor to be
portant.)

ttitudes Toward Unionization Workers from non-
⸴nvironments (such as small towns or rural areas) are
unions, even when they find themselves in communities
⸴ng. On the other hand, members of working-class house-
⸴s a tradition of unionism are likely to join a union as a

ʃlow Workers To be successful in most jobs, a worker
h fellow employees, and joining (or not joining) a union
win friends among others in the work group. This "band-
⸴ be accompanied by pressures, indirect or direct, upon the
⸴n to the group.

Union Leaders The case presented by the leaders or sup-
union may or may not be persuasive. While it is fallacious to
ɔusing speech makes a labor movement, union leaders are on dis-
ɔresentatives of organized labor, and their behavior can be impor-
⸴nning converts.

ɩudes of Management The relationship between managerial poli-
⸴ and the worker's decision to join a union is also complex. For example, if
management expresses strong critical views of unions, workers may become
convinced of the validity of management's position or they may come to fear
reprisals, such as loss of promotion or discharge, if they join the union. Economic pressures on workers to prevent union membership were most significant in the period before federal government protection of the rights of
workers to join unions began in the 1930s. Even with governmental protection, however, a worker may be reluctant to join because of the possibility of
reprisals and the difficulties of making a case against the employer. On the
other hand, managerial policies may backfire. If a worker reacts negatively to
management's leadership, he or she may feel that if management is opposed
to unions, it would be advantageous to join one whenever the opportunity
develops.

Terms of Employment A job situation unsatisfactory to workers can
motivate them to join unions, especially if there are problems that fall within
the typical province of the unions: wages, working conditions, or denial of expectations with respect to "fairness" in promotion and other presumed job
"rights." In recent years such factors have motivated baseball players and
college professors to join unions just as in the case of agricultural workers.
Dissatisfaction with the intrinsic nature of the job appears to be less impor-

tant in stimulating support for unions, primarily because most American unions have not been active in promoting the redesigning of jobs to make them more interesting.[26]

Equality of Participation in Job Control   Whatever the specific incidents or situations that lead into unionism, there is yet a more pervasive element that may strongly affect their attitudes toward unions—the essentially democratic aspiration to have a voice in the control over their jobs and careers and to participate in the determination of wages and working conditions. Because the worker feels that he alone has no bargaining equality with an employer, a union is the most likely channel for such participation, whether in negotiation of a contract or in the grievance process by which disputes over interpretation of contract clauses are settled.

Influences of Business Cycles

The specific factors reviewed above cannot in themselves explain the growth or changes in union membership over a period of time, for more fundamental forces have clearly been at work. One well-known theory relates short-run changes in membership to the business cycle.[27] Even a brief review of the growth of membership in American unions, especially during the nineteenth century, leads one to suspect that the business cycle has had a strong influence. As business conditions improve, unions tend to gain new members. When recessions or depressions occur, membership falls off, unions may even disappear, and labor unrest drifts toward political activity and legislative demands. The upswing of the business cycle improves the bargaining position of unions. Employers, faced with expanding markets but low inventories, are eager to obtain high levels of output, more workers, and uninterrupted production, and are therefore more likely to accede to union demands and threats of strikes. At the same time workers are likely to be motivated to join together to present their demands because consumer prices are rising while wages remain unchanged; moreover, the workers may have grievances that have accumulated during the previous period of depressed conditions.

During the downswing of the business cycle, the opposite conditions are

[26] The issue of the boredom and meaninglessness of certain types of jobs gained attention in 1973 with the publication of *Work in America*, Report of a Special Task Force to the Secretary of Health, Education, and Welfare (Cambridge, Mass.: M.I.T. Press, n.d.). Among other conclusions, the report claimed that because unions were more concerned with the traditional "extrinsic rewards" of employment than with the intrinsic nature of the job itself, workers were becoming alienated from unions as well as from work itself. For a broader perspective, see George Strauss, "Job Satisfaction, Motivation, and Job Redesign," in George Strauss et al., eds., *Organizational Behavior, Research and Issues*, Industrial Relations Research Association Series (Madison, Wis.: University of Wisconsin Press, 1974), esp. pp. 44–45.

[27] One of the first major works on business cycle influences was Leo Wolman, *The Ebb and Flow in Trade Unionism* (New York: National Bureau of Economic Research, 1936).

likely to exist. Employers are more inclined to resist union demands, since their inventories may be high while demand is falling off; under these circumstances, a strike might not be a disaster, since employers may have planned to reduce output in any case. Workers will attempt to avoid a strike, because it may simply lead to earlier unemployment than would otherwise occur. Their key motivation would be to hold on to their jobs, without endangering them by aggressive union action.

The business-cycle theory is a helpful but not entirely satisfactory explanation of union growth. It seems to explain especially well developments through the nineteenth century, although membership statistics for that period are far less reliable than those for modern times, when there has been more interest in statistics and thus more information for checking and analysis. Nevertheless, the experience from the Civil War on shows that all the major periods of union advance—the Civil War, 1886, 1897–1904, World War I, 1933–1939, and World War II—except the 1880s were periods of business revival. We have seen, however, that some years in the 1930s witnessed revival but not prosperity. The tight labor market associated with a business boom was clearly a reality during the three wartime periods. (The Spanish-American War had little economic effect, although the country was undergoing a broad revival at that time.)

The business-cycle explanation has been challenged by a number of writers, among them Horace B. Davis and Irving Bernstein. Davis, who noted that significant union growth had occurred during severe depressions, such as that in the 1930s, argued that workers' accumulation of grievances were expressed in strikes and other union activity as soon as the economy began to recover. Davis believed that the longer a depression, the greater would be the surge of unionism in the following upturn.[28] In a study of union membership from 1897 to 1953, Bernstein concluded that the relationship between changes in membership and the business cycle, whether in terms of costs of living, wholesale prices, employment, or production, was weak; he emphasized instead longer-run secular forces and specific periods of unrest or economic disturbance. Among secular forces Bernstein included the growing size of the labor force, greater acceptance of trade unionism, increased homogeneity of the labor force, and the spread of collective bargaining devices such as the union shop that required membership in unions. Among short-run influences he included severe depressions, governmental intervention, wars, and also the business cycle. Bernstein reaffirmed his position in a subsequent study of union growth in the United States from 1945 to 1960.[29] An econo-

[28] Horace B. Davis, "The Theory of Union Growth," *Quarterly Journal of Economics*, 55 (August 1941), 611–637, reprinted in Francis S. Doody, *Readings in Labor Economics* (Cambridge, Mass.: Addison-Wesley, 1950).

[29] Irving Bernstein, "The Growth of American Unions," *American Economic Review*, 44 (June 1954), 301–318, and "The Growth of American Unions, 1945–1960," *Labor History* (Spring 1961).

metric approach to the growth of union membership between 1900 and 1960, by Orley Ashenfelter and John H. Pencavel, holds that business cycle influences were most important, especially changes in real wages; but the authors also include an index of the "stock of grievances," which increases with the severity of a depression, as well as political factors—the extent of prounion sentiment in Congress as indicated by Democratic party strength.[30]

Secular and Other Forces

The fact that in the last 100 years union growth has been concentrated primarily in a few sharply defined periods, with either declines or little growth registered in such booms as that of the 1920s and the 1950s, indicates that forces other than the business cycle must be at work. Although some of these factors will be reviewed in subsequent chapters on the history of unionism, three will be discussed here.

Protest Against Industrialization   It has been argued that unions are one manifestation of the protest that has occurred in various countries in response to the changes in the economic and social structure wrought by industrialization.[31] "Industrialization" is usually considered to include not only the introduction of machinery and the factory system, but also the accompanying features of impersonal relationships between managers and managed, highly structured enterprises (either private or public), and large geographical concentrations of capital and population in urban areas. The changes that have occurred during the nineteenth and twentieth centuries in one country after another have truly revolutionized society and have brought forth organized attempts by workers to exert controls over the changes in their work environment and over the factory discipline to which they are subjected.

In the United States, although the period of industrialization is usually thought to have begun in the 1880s, the beginnings of the factory system go back to the end of the eighteenth century. By the time of the Civil War the factory system was firmly established in the manufacture of cotton textiles, woolens, and iron. The largest capital investments at that time were in the railroads. The small labor movement in the United States, however, was not centered in either the factories or the railroads, but flourished among the skilled craftsmen and artisans. The nation before the Civil War was still predominantly agricultural, and by 1860 wage earners in manufacturing industries totaled only 1.3 million out of a population of 31 million. There were nearly three times as many slaves as factory workers. The labor force in tex-

[30] Orley Ashenfelter and John H. Pencavel, "American Trade Union Growth, 1900–1960," *Quarterly Journal of Economics*, 83 (August 1969), 434–448.

[31] Clark Kerr, et al., *Industrialism and Industrial Man* (Cambridge, Mass.: Harvard University Press, 1960), esp. ch. 9. The authors also point out, however, that in the underdeveloped countries today the union movement generally does not protest against industrialization but rather seeks to speed and control the process from the beginning.

tiles, especially before 1840, consisted of women and children drawn from rural families.[32]

Furthermore, there was an abundance of land relative to the population. "The empty continent," with its shortage of labor and relatively high wages on the one hand and an abundance of natural resources and low land prices on the other, siphoned away the discontented and adventurous from the eastern seaboard and tended to undermine the growth of unions as a major instrument for the economic betterment of the wage earner. Cheap land, and free land after the Homestead Act of 1862, lured the worker with prospects of economic independence. The "propertyless proletarian" could acquire property and status if willing to incur the cost of moving West and to accept the uncertainties and hazards of the frontier.

It was after the Civil War, and especially during the 1880s, that the major impact of industrialization on the workers of the United States was first felt. The great "safety valve" of the western lands was closing. The Knights of Labor expressed this discontent with considerable force in 1886, but, for a variety of reasons that we will examine later, it was not able to maintain its leadership of the American labor movement. The unions affiliated with the American Federation of Labor, which were based upon different policies and tactics from those of the Knights, were able to survive in the rather unfriendly soil of industrializing America, but even they were not able to penetrate the heartland of manufacturing industries where new corporate giants had become established. Unrest, turmoil, and violence in labor relations, the growth of the pre–World War I socialist movement, and the development of the syndicalist Industrial Workers of the World—all reflected the impact of the rapid social and economic changes of industrialization. The crisis was finally reached during the 1930s, when the industrial-union surge under the leadership of the CIO broke into the mass-production industries, such as steel, automobiles, rubber, and oil. While some writers have attributed the expansion of unionism during the 1930s to the favorable legislation of the New Deal, it would be more appropriate to view the New Deal itself as a part of the same manifestation of economic and political upheaval accompanying the development of industrialization.

Composition of the Labor Force   In terms of national origin, the diversity that characterized the American labor force until the 1920s undoubtedly

[32] These textile workers did not view factory work as a lifelong career. Recruiters for the mills in Lowell, for example, canvassed the agricultural areas of New Hampshire and Massachusetts for young women to live at boardinghouses of their companies. The women were subjected to the strict disciplines, not only of the cotton mill, but also of the boardinghouse, and they engaged in few strikes and developed no permanent unions.

The first recorded strike of women in factories was in Dover, New Hampshire, in 1828, and there were others in New Jersey and Massachusetts, but in none of these was the strike preceded by the formation of a union. Perlman notes that the "agitation among factory workers was ephemeral." See Selig Perlman, *A History of Trade Unionism in the United States* (New York: Macmillan, 1937), pp. 24–25.

slowed unionization. An estimated 38 million immigrants entered the United States between 1820 and 1914, with the high point of 1 million a year being reached around 1910. At first newly arrived immigrants were likely to be impressed by the opportunities for individual advancement and less inclined to accept a union as the most suitable route to economic benefit. But as the nineteenth century wore on, some immigrants who came from European backgrounds that included trade unions or socialism supported and gave leadership to union activity in the United States. On balance it can be seen that immigration probably added to the difficulties of unions by increasing the heterogeneity of the working class. After 1890 the so-called new immigration came increasingly from southern and eastern European countries, in contrast with the immigration from northern and Western Europe that characterized the earlier period. Except for Jews from Eastern Europe, the new arrivals had little experience with unions. The immigrants flowed into the slum areas of the big cities along the eastern seaboard, into the mill towns, and into the coal fields. Divergent customs, languages, and attitudes created barriers to unionization. After the "barring" of the gates to immigration that began during and after World War I, this diversity diminished. The Americanization of second- and third-generation families and their acceptance of common institutions and common standards tended to facilitate unionization among workers.

In more recent years, immigration has once again emerged as a labor market issue. The 1965 Immigration Act abolished the former ethnocentric quota system and established preferences for skilled workers in shortage occupations. More important, other new workers have come either directly, as in the case of Puerto Ricans (who are not aliens but U.S. citizens) or illegally, as in the case of Mexicans who cross the border to work primarily in agriculture but also in urban areas of the West and Midwest.

Trends by industry and occupation have had a number of effects on the composition of the labor force. The absolute and relative decline in agricultural employment—of farm managers as well as farm workers—has meant that one segment of the labor force traditionally indifferent to unions has become a weaker obstacle to the spread of unionism. On the other hand, such industries as railroads, mining, and certain manufacturing industries, which have been heavily organized but have had low growth rates or even suffered employment declines, offer dim prospects for union gains. In addition, many of the more rapidly expanding fields of employment have in the past been resistant to unionization. The concentration of white-collar workers, women employees, and professional occupations in these industries has led some observers to conclude that the union movement may be reaching a plateau in terms of likely recruits. They argue that white-collar workers tend to identify more with management than with production workers, that women have a more limited commitment to the labor market and hence are less inclined to jeopardize their position by affiliation with unions, and that salaried professional workers do not want controls imposed on individual work standards. As a result of these limitations, some theorists, known as the "saturationists," claim that the long-run upward trend of union growth is near an end.

The saturationist argument was most strongly presented in the 1950s.[33] It has been countered by increasing union organization precisely in those industries that were held to be most immune, such as the white-collar fields, industries with high proportions of women workers, and the service industries. Although the number of white-collar members in unions is sometimes difficult to measure because unions do not maintain separate records by occupational groups, the best estimates indicate a steadily rising proportion of white-collar workers in their total membership. For all national unions from 1966 to 1976, the number of such workers increased by over 1 million, from 2,810,000 to 3,857,000, or from 14.7 to 18.4 percent of total union membership. Much of the white-collar membership is concentrated in relatively few unions: the Retail Clerks, Musicians, Teachers, Communications, Railway Clerks, Postal Workers, State, County and Municipal Workers, and the Steelworkers. Together they accounted for nearly 2.2 million members, or nearly two-thirds of all white-collar union members in 1972. The Retail Clerks, Teachers, and the State, County and Municipal Workers have been among the fastest-growing unions in the nation. If to the count of white-collar unionization is added those in professional and public employee associations—most of whom are in the white-collar occupations—the total number rises to nearly 6 million, or 24.3 percent of all union and association membership in 1976.[34]

With respect to women workers, union membership has also been rising steadily. Women members rose from 3.7 million to 4.2 million between 1966 and 1976, or from 19.3 to 20.0 percent of total union membership. If associations are also included, the total is 6 million women members, or a fourth of the total. The number of unionized women has been increasing more rapidly than men, the result primarily of the expansion of unions into the service industries and government employment where female employment is large. Once the extent of part-time work and the nature of the industry are taken into account, claims that women are more difficult to organize than men do not tend to be substantiated. Women's preference for union representation in

---

[33] A leading exponent of the saturationist point of view is Daniel Bell. See his article, "The Next American Labor Movement," *Fortune*, 47 (April 1953), 120 ff, esp. p. 204. Good summaries of the conflicting arguments between the saturationists and the historical school are presented in Albert A. Blum, "Why Unions Grow," *Labor History*, 9 (Winter 1968), 39–72, and in Woodrow Ginsburg, "Review of Literature on Union Growth, Government and Structure—1955–1969," in Ginsburg et al., *A Review of Industrial Relations Research*, vol. I, esp. pp. 207–227.

[34] See U.S. Department of Labor, *Directory, 1973*, pp. 76–78, and Appendix G; *Directory, 1975* and *Labor Union and Employee Association Membership, 1976*.

National Labor Relations Board white-collar elections has not differed significantly from that of men.[35]

Although women's participation in the labor movement is increasing, their representation on union governing boards is relatively low. In 1974, only 7 percent of board members were female even though women comprised 21.3 percent of the union membership. The boards of bargaining associations had 12 percent female representation with a total membership that was 55 percent female. To promote their interests, women formed the Coalition of Labor Union Women (CLUW) in 1974. With a membership drawing from 85 unions, the organization has set as its goals increased organizing efforts among women workers, reduction in sex discrimination, more participation in union affairs, and improved health and welfare legislation.[36]

The Role of the Government   In a slave economy, workers are regarded simply as one of the instruments of production: if they were to organize to promote their interests by a refusal to work, their rebellious action would be countered by the power of the state to force them to work. Even in an economy characterized by free contract, the conditions that make negotiation legal—that is, enforceable in the courts—and the rules that govern collective bargaining are set by the government. The ultimate sanction is the power to enforce those rules, whether by jailing strike leaders who violate a court injunction or by compelling an employer to rehire and pay back wages to workers discharged for union activity.

Before the 1930s the policies of the American government were not favorable to the development of unions. Those of the early nineteenth century can be described as repressive: from 1806 to 1842, for example, some 18 prosecutions of labor organizations on charges of conspiracy were recorded in state courts, and it was not until the famous *Commonwealth* v. *Hunt* case in Massachusetts in 1842 that the threat of the conspiracy doctrine finally came to an end.

But even after they were technically lawful, unions still faced a handicap: the government would not protect the workers' right to organize by preventing others from interfering with unionization. As a result, a union could be recognized by an employer and bargain collectively only if the latter was willing or forced by economic pressure to do so, but under certain circumstances the employer could use the law to prohibit union activity. Numerous state legislatures from the 1890s until 1908 passed laws to give to workers a protected right to organize, but in the famous *Coppage* v. *Kansas* case in 1908 such action was declared unconstitutional by the Supreme Court, on the grounds that it violated the Fourteenth Amendment. A federal law, the Erd-

[35] Lucretia M. Dewey, "Women in Labor Unions," *Monthly Labor Review*, 94 (February 1971), 44.
[36] See *Directory, 1977*, pp. 54, 66–67.

man Act, passed in 1898, also contained a section that protected the rights of railroad workers to choose a union without interference by employers, but this too was declared unconstitutional in *Adair v. United States* (1905), on the grounds that it violated the due process clause of the Fifth Amendment and thus was an undue interference with the rights of property. As we will see in a later chapter, until the 1930s the labor injunctions based upon the authority of a court in equity to prevent property damage were almost always interpreted so that strikes, picketing, organizing, and related union activity could be considered unlawful actions. The Clayton Act, passed in 1914, included several sections to relieve unions from injunctive proceedings and from antitrust prosecution, but they were weakened by subsequent interpretation in the courts.

During the 1930s the movement to give labor a protected right to organize won victories in Congress and in the courts. Railroad workers had gained the right in 1926, and the labor injunction was curbed in 1932; but under the New Deal, first section 7 (a) of the National Industrial Recovery Act of 1933 and then the National Labor Relations Act of 1935 put the power of the federal government behind unionization and collective bargaining. There is little doubt that these acts gave a strong impetus to union growth: corporations with long records of antiunion activity were forced to accept the verdict of government-sponsored workers' elections to bargain with union representatives.

The Taft-Hartley Act of 1947 and the Landrum-Griffin Act of 1959 represented new shifts in governmental policy toward a stricter control of union activities. Without altering the fundamental government protection of labor's rights to organize, they modified certain privileges and created duties and obligations for both unions and management. The Taft-Hartley Act may have increased the difficulty of new union organization in certain areas, such as the South or small towns, but those areas had always been difficult to organize, and the fact that union membership rose moderately during the 1950s does not in itself support either the position that the Taft-Hartley Act had no effect on the labor movement or the idea that it was a disastrous blow to union organization. The expansion of public sector unions and collective bargaining, beginning in the 1960s, has been directly related to changes in laws concerning public employees. Although some governmental workers, like the postal workers, had a long tradition of collective bargaining, the new upsurge of unionization began at the federal level after issuance of Executive Order 10988 in 1962, later elaborated under Executive Order 11491, issued in 1969. Many states passed legislation supporting unionization during this period. In 1966, six states had collective bargaining statutes for public workers; by 1970 the number had risen to 21.

While this brief review indicates that governmental policy can affect the growth of unions, it leaves unsolved the more basic questions of what determines governmental policy and why such policies change. Government actions are not only a *cause*, but also an *effect*, of other forces. The changes in the governmental approach to unions in the United States from repression to toleration and eventually to encouragement and control have roots in the changing industrial and social environment of the American economy.

SUMMARY

Unions are organizations of wage and salary earners concerned with the protection and advancement of their interests. Their formation and growth have been an integral part of the development of industrial societies of the Western world. Although various writers and students of the labor movement have emphasized different aspects of the nature and role of unions in industrialized economies, the common theme is that workers are not content to allow managers to run industrial organizations without participation in decisions concerning income, job security, and the rules governing employment relations.

Union membership in the United States, growing to over 20 million in 1974, has nonetheless declined as a percentage of nonagricultural employment since the mid-1950s, with about a fourth of workers organized. Associations of professional and public employees engaged in collective bargaining expanded more rapidly and bring the percentage to 28.3 in 1976.

Over the years, union membership has grown in spurts, often related to economic booms and war periods, such as the Civil War and World Wars I and II, but sometimes occurring during depressions, such as that of the 1930s. The number of national unions has stabilized and is showing some decline through consolidations.

Among the factors contributing to union growth are the business cycle, which affects labor's bargaining power, and the accumulation of worker grievances during severe depressions, such as the one in the 1930s. Longer-run influences include protests against industrialization and loss of alternative jobs (such as self-employment in agriculture). The changing composition of labor, with growing numbers of women, white-collar employees, and professional workers, had at one time been considered detrimental to union growth, but evidence indicates that in the late 1960s and early 1970s union membership among these groups expanded. Although unions grew even when government policy was unsympathetic, legislation favorable to union activity provided a significant stimulus to union growth.

DISCUSSION QUESTIONS

1. Do you believe that unions are "natural" developments in the course of industrialization in market-organized, capitalist societies? Give reasons to support your position.

2. What particular interests or desires do you believe motivate workers to form and join unions? What are the reasons given by the various writers discussed in this chapter?
3. What factors do you believe have spurred the recent growth of unions of white-collar and professional employees?
4. The business-cycle theory of union growth has its proponents and critics. What are their respective arguments?
5. What are the arguments of the "saturationists" concerning the prospects of future union growth? Do you agree? What reasons can you give?
6. As women participate more and more in the labor force, do you believe their participation in the labor movement will also increase?

SELECTED READINGS

Both the Perlman theory of unions and the Kerr-Dunlop-Harbison-Myers approach are widely referred to today. For the former, see Selig Perlman, *The Theory of the Labor Movement* (New York: Augustus Kelley, 1949); and Charles A. Gulick and Melvin K. Bers, "Insight and Illusion in Perlman's Theory of the Labor Movement," reprinted in Ray Marshall and Richard Perlman, *An Anthology of Labor Economics* (New York: John Wiley & Sons, 1972), pp. 33–45. On the Inter-University Study of Labor Problems—the KDHM project—see Clark Kerr, John T. Dunlop, Frederick H. Harbison, and Charles A. Myers, *Industrialism and Industrial Man* (Cambridge, Mass.: Harvard University Press, 1960); and Dunlop et al., *Industrialism and Industrial Man Reconsidered: Some Perspectives on a Study over Two Decades of the Problems of Labor and Management in Economic Growth* (Princeton, N.J.: the Inter-University Study of Labor Problems in Economics Development, 1975).

For various perspectives on the role of labor and unions in the United States, the following are suggestive: Harry Braverman, *Labor and Monopoly Capital: The Degradation of Work in the Twentieth Century* (New York: Monthly Review Press, 1976); Derek Bok and John T. Dunlop, *Labor and the American Community* (New York: Simon and Schuster, 1970); and Richard A. Lester, *As Unions Mature: An Analysis of the Evolution of American Unionism* (Princeton, N.J.: Princeton University Press, 1958).

On some of the newer areas of unionization, see E. D. Duryea and Robert S. Fish, *Faculty Unions and Collective Bargaining* (San Francisco: Jossey-Bass, 1973); Daniel S. Hammermesh, ed., *Labor in the Public and Non-Profit Sectors* (Princeton, N.J.: Princeton University Press, 1975); Everett M. Kasslow, "White-Collar Unionism in the United States," in Adolf Sturmthal, ed., *White-Collar Trade Unions, Contemporary Developments in Industrialized Societies* (Urbana: University of Illinois Press, 1967); and Jack Steiber, *Public Employee Unionism* (Washington, D.C.: Brookings Institution, 1973).

7

Development
of Union Organization
in the United States

The present structure of organized labor in the United States is the outgrowth of a long history of struggle against hostile employers and governments and of internal conflicts over policies and ideologies. The first local unions were formed nearly 200 years ago, while the basic structure of the modern labor movement took shape in the 1880s and the organization of the mass production, industrial "heartland" of the American economy began in the 1930s. In this chapter we shall review some of the highlights of the history of unions as they pertain to the development of economics and social forms of policies and organization. We shall also describe the present structure of the AFL-CIO, the dominant federation in the United States since 1955.[1]

UNIONS BEFORE THE KNIGHTS OF LABOR

The First Unions

The first organization of wage earners with a continuous existence was formed by Philadelphia journeymen cordwainers (shoemakers) in 1792. Be-

[1] Basic references for the history of labor are John R. Commons, ed., *A Documentary History of American Industrial Society*, 11 vols. (Glendale, Calif.: Arthur H. Clark Co., 1910–1911); John R. Commons et al., *History of Labor in the United States*, 2 vols. (New York: Macmillan, 1918); Selig Perlman and Philip Taft, *History of Labor in the United States, 1896–1932* (New York: Macmillan, 1936), vol. IV; and Selig Perlman, *A History of Trade Unionism in the United States* (New York: Macmillan, 1937). Other more recent histories of the American labor movement are Philip S. Foner, *History of the Labor Movement in the United States*, vols. 1–4 (New York: International Publishers, 1947, 1955, 1964, and 1965); Joseph G. Rayback, *A History of American Labor* (New York: Macmillan, 1959); Philip Taft, *Organized Labor in American History* (New York: Harper & Row, 1964); and Irving Bernstein, *The Lean Years*, vol. 1, and *The Turbulent Years*, vol. 2 (Boston: Houghton Mifflin, 1960 and 1970).

fore 1819 journeymen's societies were organized in New York, Boston, Pittsburgh, and other cities, not only among cordwainers, but also among printers, carpenters, tailors, and sailors. These societies were local trade unions, each built around a specific skill, with little if any connection between one society and another, even in the same community. Although the first societies were short-lived and left few records, their objectives and policies were amazingly modern. They sought to maintain what they considered proper wages and conditions of work, and they fought off competition from the less-skilled laborers, or "inferior workers," as well as from other skilled journeymen who did not accept their standards. They demanded control of the number of apprentices and minimum wages; they even wanted the "closed shop," to force the employer to discharge those who would not become members of the journeymen's society or accept its wage objectives.

The early trade unions died out because of depressions and employers' charges—which the courts upheld—that associations of workers were illegal conspiracies. But with the business revival of the 1820s, new unions sprang up that were similar in organization to their predecessors but involved more trades in more towns and cities. Women workers and factory laborers organized for the first time between 1820 and 1837. In Philadelphia in 1827 several trade-union societies formed the Mechanics' Union of Trade Associations, the first federation of various local trade unions that today would be called a city central or city council.

In 1828 the Mechanics Union organized the first workingmen's political party. Thus began a form of political agitation that spread first to New York, where a workingmen's party won a seat in the state legislature in 1828, and then to New England. The movement, which eventually found its national leadership in Andrew Jackson and his supporters, was complete with labor newspapers and its left and right wings. Its members wanted to bring into their ranks all workingmen, whether employers or wage earners. They did not oppose property ownership, but rather supported equal opportunity and "equal citizenship." Thus they demanded free public education, the abolition of imprisonment for debt, a mechanics' lien to protect wages in case of employers' bankruptcy, and shorter working hours. Intellectuals also played an important role in the movement's early development. Robert Dale Owen and Frances Wright, leaders of a faction of the New York Workingmen's party, advocated "state guardianship," a system of public education through which children would receive general and industrial instruction in state schools. Factional rivalry and bitter public reaction to their "radical" proposals turned workers away from politics and the leadership of the labor intellectuals and toward more strictly economic action. The movement nonetheless spurred nonlabor groups and regular political parties to take over some of these objectives for themselves.

Other new types of labor organization were formed in the 1830s. One was the national trade union, a federation of local unions in the same trade. These were generally short-lived and ineffective. Another was the National Trades' Union (NTU), a federation of unions representing different trades. Between 1834 and 1837 the NTU claimed to speak for some 300,000 workers against the factory system, long hours of work, employment of women and children, and prison labor. Unlike the trade unions that sought economic improvement by raising members' wages, the National Trades' Union represented a facet of the political reform movement.

Reformism

The panic of 1837 and the ensuing depression brought the early trade-union movement to an end. Shortly thereafter began the "utopian" period in labor history, which lasted until 1850. During that time a number of reform schemes were advocated to benefit workers. In general the reformers dreamed of the independent worker, perhaps working and owning property cooperatively with others, free of control by middlemen and the state. Unlike the intellectuals of developing countries today, most reformers of the 1840s saw only grief in industrialization.

There were three types of reform movements. Each was strongly committed to the idea that only through ownership of property, even if communal, could individualism flourish. One included advocacy of small communistic societies such as those based sometimes on theories of cooperative socialism and sometimes on religious philosophies, in which members shared work and property.

A second type of reform, the producers' cooperative, stemmed more directly from the workers themselves than from intellectuals. But the efforts of workers' owning their shops cooperatively and running them for profit were not successful—neither in the 1840s nor later, when the Knights of Labor also supported the goal of cooperative self-employment. The failure of most of these efforts reflected the workers' lack of capital and business ability, which prevented their withstanding aggressive competition of other firms and unfavorable business conditions.

Most important of the reform programs for the independence of the workingman was the free-land movement. Although a variety of advocates supported the movement, it was George Henry Evans who articulated a specific philosophy of free land for workers. Evans believed that they were entitled to share in the resources of nature and to own the products of their labor. Land should be made available freely to all individuals on an equal basis and should be held inalienably. Evans did not advocate a redistribution of property, but rather the distribution of existing public lands to homesteaders, with specific limitations on the size of grants. Evans argued that the government should bear the cost of transporting workers to the free land, which would be less expensive than paying relief to the unemployed; the scheme would raise wages in the East and lower land prices. The free-land movement, which won support in the North, eventually led to passage of the Homestead Act in 1862.

National Unions

Renewed prosperity in the early 1850s brought a reawakening of unionism among the skilled trades, unaccompanied this time by political goals or ideas of cooperation, but laying a foundation for truly national trade unions on a lasting basis. The National Typographical Society, formed by printers in 1850, was the first national union to last to the present. Other national trade unions of the 1850s were formed among locomotive engineers, hat finishers, molders, and blacksmiths. Although some of these were unable to survive the panic of 1857, the economic prosperity of the Civil War and the subsequent postwar boom led to the formation of additional national unions; during the decade of the 1860s alone their number increased from 6 to 29.

One short-lived attempt was made to form a national organization that would promote the interests of labor generally. This was the National Labor Union, founded in 1866; its first convention was attended by 77 delegates from 13 states, mostly from local unions. Its head was one of the most vigorous leaders of the period, William H. Sylvis, who had successfully organized the International Molders Union. The National Labor Union at first had as its central objective the promotion of such trade-union programs as the eight-hour day and the boycott of goods made by low-paid convict labor. But Sylvis also advocated a broader range of goals: women's rights (Sylvis won support from the women's suffrage movement), workers' cooperation, free land for settlers, and monetary reform. Eventually the National Labor Union split over the question of independent political action and reformist programs. Splinter labor groups later joined with farmers in the Greenback-Labor party, which polled more than a million votes and elected 14 representatives to Congress in 1878.

THE KNIGHTS OF LABOR

From its inauspicious beginning in December 1869, when a group of nine garment cutters met in Philadelphia as a secret society, the Grand and Noble Order of the Knights of Labor grew modestly during the depression of the 1870s and then broke into national prominence with its successful strikes against Jay Gould's railroads in the early 1880s. It went on to reach the highest pinnacle then attained by a union, with over 700,000 members in 1886, but by the end of the century it was a lost cause. Three aspects of the Knights of Labor are important to consider: its philosophy and objectives, its method of organization, and the causes of its spectacular rise and subsequent fall.

Philosophy and Objectives

The program of the leaders of the Knights was a curious combination of reformism and trade unionism, with the former predominating. One of the first principles of the Knights emphasized the solidarity of all workers, which implied a union not only of wage earners, but also of those who had once been wage earners or had worked with their hands. Though Uriah S. Stephens, the founder and Master Workman of the first national assembly, said that "capital has its combinations; labor must have its," he felt, surprisingly, that there were no grounds for antagonism between labor and "necessary" capital. None of the Knights' leaders believed in strikes, and Terence V. Powderly, who was Grand Master Workman during the years of greatest turbulence, expressed approval of arbitration of disputes.

The main problem, as the leaders saw it, was to prevent monopolies from taking from the "industrial masses" the "full share of the wealth" that labor created; but strikes or direct economic action did not seem the most effective method of attaining that goal. Producers' cooperatives would hinder exploitation, and the Knights devoted money and energy to them. But they could neither duplicate the necessary facilities of larger private firms nor protect themselves when competitors chose to employ their superior economic power.

In political philosophy the Knights stressed reform of the land laws to prevent railroads and large corporations from acquiring large tracts, and they advocated child-labor laws, the eight-hour day, equal-pay-for-equal-work laws, and expansion of the monetary supply to ease the problems of debtors. Both Stephens and Powderly had been connected with the Greenback-Labor party; later the Knights supported the free-silver movement.

Organization

In organization, the Knights felt that the separation of workers into trades undermined the unity based upon the common interests of all workers, and it therefore set up a combination of both craft and area organizations. At the lowest level was the local assembly, which was either "pure" (organized, like the original garment cutters, on a single-trade basis), or "mixed" (comprised of workers from different trades and industries). At the next level was the district assembly, usually either a citywide or a regionwide organization, that, like the older local trades' unions, brought together workers of different occupations. In several cases, however, the district assemblies were in fact national trade unions, consisting of locals drawn from the same trade, such as telegraph operators. At the third and highest level was the General Assembly, first held in 1878, consisting of representatives from the district assemblies.

This form of organization, unlike that of the American Federation of Labor that came later, tended to submerge the narrow trade-union interests of the workers in larger problems. The fact that power was channeled through the district assemblies, which were largely area organizations, had definite advantages to the Knights: organizational distinctions between trades and between the skilled and unskilled tended to disappear, and more effective political action could be taken.

Rise and Fall

The growth of the Knights of Labor was a manifestation of continuing labor unrest. Unskilled workers who found no entrance into the national trade unions, even though the latter continued to grow after the upturn of business in 1879, were welcomed into the Knights with open arms. The successful strikes of 1885 against Jay Gould's railroads increased the prestige of the Knights, even though the leaders deplored the strike action. The very fact that the Knights were the first to deal with one of the most powerful capitalists in the country made them a champion of the oppressed.

The great rush into unions in 1886 was one of those relatively rare events in union history, repeated only at the end of World War I and again in the 1930s, when workers did not wait for organizers but joined together on their own initiative and often ran their organizations with little heed to the niceties of proclaimed union policy. In 1886, when the major upheaval brought the Knights raw recruits who had little knowledge of the methods and stated objectives of Powderly, the shorthanded and inexperienced leaders lost administrative control of the movement.

The Knights lost members almost as quickly as they gained them. Their decline was precipitated by violence at Chicago's Haymarket Square in 1886, which, although unrelated to the Knights, created an atmosphere of hostility toward all unions; by the decline of class solidarity among the unskilled; and, above all, by the conflicts with the national trade unions over jurisdictions. By 1888 it was clear that the Knights had lost its hold on the imagination of the American worker.[2]

THE ERA OF THE AMERICAN FEDERATION OF LABOR, 1886 TO 1933

The turning of the tide against the Knights of Labor after 1886 marked the end of the social-reform movements that tended to dominate the nineteenth

---

[2] For a sympathetic treatment of the movement, see Norman J. Ware, *The Labor Movement in the United States, 1860–1895: A Study in Democracy* (New York: Random House, 1964). This study was first published in 1929.

century. In the harsh world of industrial change it was the trade organizations of skilled workers that were able to win the fight for survival, rather than the broadly based farmer-worker coalitions, the industrial unions of the unskilled, or the socialists, however strong their connections. The trade unions that banded together in the American Federation of Labor were able to survive and dominate the American labor movement until the mid-1930s, and it was during this 50-year period that the labor movement acquired its modern form.

The AFL was formed in 1886 as a rallying center for the national trade unions that wished to promote and defend the interests of the trade unions yet leave each union alone to develop its own policies. Control of the AFL resided in the annual convention. Since each of the state federations of labor and the city centrals—the geographical organizations so favored by the Knights—was given only one vote irrespective of the size of its membership, the larger national unions, which were represented by one vote for every 1,-000 members, could control the election of officers. A president, two vice presidents (later there were to be more), a secretary, and a treasurer were elected for one-year terms, and they in turn formed an executive council that carried out the wishes of the convention.

Samuel Gompers, who served as president of the AFL for every year except one until his death in 1924, and who came to symbolize the trade-union position in the public eye, best personified the viewpoint of the national trade unions. A believer in strong national unions, he successfully fought to rebuild his own union, the Cigar Makers International, along the lines of the new British unions. He emphasized increased power of the national officers over the locals to prevent ill-conceived strikes that would tend to weaken the union's prestige and sap financial resources, and advocated higher dues and an extensive benefit system for members. Moreover, Gompers believed that labor organization should rest on a trade, not on an industrial structure. He argued that, since skilled workers had a stable interest in controlling their jobs and maintaining job standards, they would be willing to give more substantial and longer-lasting support to a union made up of fellow workers in their own trade.

Gompers rejected any ideas of abolishing the wage system through cooperation, self-employment, or socialism. Although he had earlier supported socialist ideas, he shifted his views on the grounds that promotion of socialism would bring down on workers the full force of the economic and political power of society, so that more would be lost than could ever be gained. These views hardened as time went on, and AFL leaders fought vigorous battles with socialists as "disrupters" and "wreckers" of the labor movement. In line with his earlier socialist views, however, was Gompers' conviction that wage earners should act in their own interests, of which they themselves were the best judges, and forswear the beguiling enticements of those who would try to abolish the wage system. Separate from intellectuals, farmers, free-silverites and other miscellaneous social reformers, union members should concentrate on immediate economic gains for themselves through collective bargaining—a view labeled "pure and simple" unionism.

One of Gompers's basic tenets was "voluntarism"—the right of a national union freely to determine its own policies without interference from the government, employers, other unions, or even the federation itself. This was labor's equivalent of a laissez-faire doctrine. The federation's leaders could use only their persuasive powers, not force, in presenting to member unions their points of view on such issues as trade versus industrial unionism or on political issues. The federation could serve as the voice for labor in public forums and could support legislative programs desired by its members; it could help national unions in times of strikes (if other nationals would contribute funds), help in organizing workers (if this did not contravene the desires of an existing national union), and resolve jurisdictional disputes. It could not, however, intervene in the affairs of the national unions, which were the key building blocks of the labor movement. Each national union wrote its own constitution and bylaws, elected its own officers, determined its own policies, and defined its own jurisdiction. The national unions operated autonomously, and, as Gompers himself said, the federation was a "rope of sand."

The principal exception to the doctrine of voluntarism was in connection with jurisdictional disputes among nationals—that is, disputes about the types of workers who were eligible for membership within a particular union. Although the extent of its jurisdiction was determined by each union, the federation insisted upon "exclusive jurisdiction," or the right of only one union to organize a given class of workers, since rivalry would otherwise lead to interunion warfare and would be destructive of the unions themselves. Gompers and other federation leaders were bitterly opposed to internecine strikes in the "house of labor," labeling overlapping jurisdictions as "dualism." If a jurisdictional dispute among members did occur, the federation attempted to resolve it by moral persuasion or mediation, and the Executive Council, with the approval of the convention, issued a final decision. A recalcitrant national union that refused to abide by an adverse jurisdictional decision by the federation could be suspended and expelled— though such action would not resolve the dispute, because the expelled union could continue to exist and organize workers outside the federation.

Limited Success of the Trade Unions

After 1886 the trade unions continued to hold and increase their membership, and when membership did not fall during the depression of the 1890s, AFL leaders claimed that the validity of the federation's principles had been proved. Membership expanded rapidly from 1897 to 1904 and again during World War I, but—as noted in the previous chapter—it never included a very high percentage of the number of organizable workers.

The objective of the unions was to gain a jointly negotiated "trade" agreement with employers that would govern the terms and conditions of employment. The idea of a "trade" agreement originated in the "price list" of the early days of the labor movement and in certain agreements found in the 1830s. Although written contracts were the exception before 1890, in the iron industry a written wage scale was introduced in 1866, and trade agreements had been negotiated in the building trades in the 1880s; there was even an example of multiple-employer bargaining negotiated by bricklayers in Chicago in 1887. One of the first national agreements was negotiated in the stove industry between the National Union of Iron Molders and the Stove Founders Defense Association in 1890, an arrangement that has continued down through the years. "Trade agreements" become increasingly important in the late 1890s. At the turn of the century, collective bargaining spread widely through the construction industry and through such other fields as printing, pottery, and machine shops.

The most successful union organization at that time was in the coal fields, where the work was dirty and hard, where the towns were isolated and under the thumb of the operators, where workers had few alternative employment opportunities, and where there had been a long history of unrest, strikes, and attempts at unionization. In 1898 the United Mine Workers of America won a major victory in organizing miners of bituminous ("soft") coal. One reason for this victory was the desire of the many operators scattered throughout a number of states to end a period of ruinous price cutting by stabilizing wages. The 1898 conference established an agreement among bituminous operators in western Pennsylvania, Ohio, Indiana, and Illinois—called the Central Competitive Field (CCF)—in which the union was recognized and the workers obtained the eight-hour day, uniform tonnage rates, and a uniform wage scale for day men. This victory proved to be a boon to the United Mine Workers, and the union shortly became the largest within the AFL. The voices of its leaders—especially that of youthful John Mitchell, who was president from 1898 to 1908, and later that of John L. Lewis, who became president in 1919—carried weight in public as well as in labor circles.

For the miners of anthracite coal, the story was different. Anthracite, or "hard," coal, used primarily by households, was concentrated geographically in five counties in eastern Pennsylvania. The relatively few large and integrated corporations that employed anthracite workers felt no need to stabilize their labor costs and resisted attempts at union organization.

Unions also had less success in bargaining collectively in other industries dominated by a few large firms that were determined not to recognize them. Only the exercise of substantial economic power could force such employers to deal with the union, and unions were no match for large corporations in such contests of strength. For example, the United States Steel Corporation—which, when it was formed in 1901, was the first billion-dollar corporation—was able to close the door to unionism (already more than half shut after the Homestead strike of 1892) not only in its own plants, but in related industries in which its influence was strong, such as the structural iron-erection industry and the carrying trade of the Great Lakes.

The one major exception to the limited success of collective bargaining came during World War I. With the economic pressure of a wartime boom and rising prices, with the support of a friendly administration, and with a wartime spirit of cooperation prevailing among employers, the trade unions were able to penetrate new occupational groups and secure recognition from formerly reluctant firms. Government support could be decisive to labor's cause, and the appointment of labor representatives to government emergency boards, and especially the acceptance by the National War Labor Board of the desirability of the equal rights of workers and employers to organize and bargain collectively, led unions into such new fields as meat packing, shipbuilding, and the occupations of nonoperating railroad workers. But the situation suddenly changed after the armistice in November 1918 had removed the basis for governmental intervention, and after the breakdown of a joint industrial conference called by President Wilson in 1919 to provide a basis for voluntary cooperation between labor and management in peacetime. A major effort to organize steel in 1919 failed, and unions once more had to rely on their own resources to force employers to recognize them.

Socialist Criticism of AFL Policies

The "pure and simple" unionism of the AFL did not go unchallenged by other labor leaders. In the period before World War I the major critics were the socialists, who accepted the idea that strong trade unions could battle employers effectively to achieve immediate economic gains for their members, but broke sharply with AFL leaders on three other issues: industrial unionism, political action, and long-run objectives.

With regard to industrial unions, the socialists believed that all the workers in any industry, the unskilled as well as the skilled, should be enrolled in unions, and that the AFL emphasis on organization in terms of craft or trade split the labor movement and limited the benefits of unionism to only a few. Labor's political activity, they thought, should supplement its economic action, so that the state, which then supported the employers, could be brought under labor's control. The socialists' ultimate ends were abolition of the wage system by means of worker control and ownership of the means of production (that is, the capital equipment of the nation).

There were a number of socialist organizations opposed to the AFL. One center of agitation was the Socialist Labor party, the oldest socialist party in the United States, founded in 1876. Coming under the leadership of Daniel De Leon in 1889, the party sought to capture leadership of the American labor movement and to guide it in accordance with "pure" Marxist principles in two ways: by "boring from within" existing unions to convert (if possible) their membership and leaders to socialism, or by setting up rival socialist organizations to lure workers from their existing affiliations ("dualism"). De Leon set up the Socialist Trade and Labor Alliance in 1895 and issued an appeal to both trade unions and assemblies of the Knights to rally around his banner. The organization attracted only a few unions, however; in 1898 its membership was estimated at between 15,000 and 30,000 workers.

A second center of socialist activity was connected with Eugene V. Debs, who had long been an advocate of industrial unionism. Debs was not a socialist when he first gained national prominence in the 1894 strike of his American Railway Union (ARU) supporting Pullman employees at Chicago. The ARU's refusal to handle Pullman cars unless the company agreed to arbitration led to the issuance of a federal injunction and the use of federal troops on orders from President Grover Cleveland. Debs was jailed on grounds of contempt of court for refusing to obey the injunction, and his conviction was upheld by the Supreme Court. The strike collapsed, and Debs turned to socialism and participated in the formation of the Socialist party in 1901. Debs was the party's candidate for president of the United States in most elections through 1920, and he was by all odds the most influential of the socialist leaders during this era. Unlike De Leon, who was dogmatic, theoretical and doctrinaire, Debs was a midwestern populist converted to a humanitarian version of socialist policies. Although Debs attracted nearly a million votes in each of the elections of 1912 and 1920—campaigning in the latter from the federal penitentiary in Atlanta, to which he had been sentenced for opposition to America's participation in World War I—he had no systematic plan for remaking the labor movement of the United States.

A third center of left-wing opposition to AFL policies was the Industrial Workers of the World (IWW), organized in 1905. Both Debs and De Leon participated in its founding, but its principal strength was in the West, where the "hard-rock" miners in the Rockies who had formed the aggressive Western Federation of Miners (WFM) on an industrial basis comprised the largest share of the membership. Later, after Debs, De Leon, and the WFM had withdrawn, the IWW came to represent primarily the migratory workers of the West—such as harvest hands and lumberjacks—who had no attachment to home, property, or permanent employment, and advocated "direct action" against a world they believed was organized against them. The preamble to the IWW constitution began: "The working class and the employing class have nothing in common. . . . Between these two classes a struggle must go on until the workers of the world organize as a class, take possession of the earth and the machinery of production, and abolish the wage system."[3]

After World War I a new center of agitation was found in the Workers (and later Communist) party, which supported the revolution in Russia and attempted to gain a foothold in the labor movement of the United States. At first the tactics of boring from within were followed, with the Trade Union Educational League as a "front" organization. Then, in 1929, the communists turned to a strategy of dualism, set up a federation called the Trade Union Unity League and organized several national unions on an industrial basis in coal, textiles, and the needle trades. Neither of these programs made substantive inroads in the area organized by noncommunist unions, however, except possibly in the garment and fur industries.

Industrial Structure and Political Action

The issue of industrial unionism that had been seized upon by socialists had certain serious implications for the AFL. It has already been noted that one of the principles of the organization was that the autonomy of each national union was limited only by the requirement that there be no overlapping jurisdictions. In practice, however, no hard-and-fast rule could be used to demarcate jurisdictions as new trades developed out of old ones, and former distinctions in skill became blurred and even disappeared; unions whose jurisdictions had once been clearly defined found themselves in conflict with other unions.[4] Moreover, since the jurisdictions of trade unions were established first, industrial jurisdictions had to overlap with them. An industrial union would seek as its jurisdiction all the workers in all the firms producing the same product, irrespective of their particular jobs. But a trade union that claimed jurisdictional rights over all workers in one occupation, in any firms,

---

[3] There has been a revival of interest in the IWW during the last decade or so. A recent history is Melvyn Dubofsky, *We Shall Be All: A History of the Industrial Workers of the World* (Chicago: Quadrangle Books, 1969). An earlier and still widely respected analysis is Paul F. Brissenden, *The I.W.W.: A Study of American Syndicalism* (New York: Columbia University Press, 1919).

[4] A distinction can be made among different types of "trade unions." In the narrow sense, a *trade union* includes all who follow a particular trade—normally, the journeymen (that is, those who have attained a particular level of skill), apprentices, and helpers. A *craft union*, although often used as identical with a trade union, more precisely includes only journeymen. An *amalgamated trade union* refers to a union of two or more related trades, often the result of a merger of trade or craft unions. Most trade unions have historically changed their jurisdiction as a result of amalgamations: examples are the Bricklayers, Masons and Plasterers, and the Painters, Decorators and Paperhangers. The reverse process of a trade union splitting into unions of subtrades is less common, although the International Typographical Union is a well-known example of a union that originally contained within its jurisdiction pressmen, bookbinders, photoengravers, and others who later formed separate unions.

could forestall AFL approval of the industrial union's jurisdiction by virtue of its prior claim, whether the workers in that industry were actually organized or not.

Furthermore, the mass of semiskilled and unskilled workers in the manufacturing industries were denied the opportunity to form an industrial union that would be consistent with the AFL principle of nonoverlapping jurisdictions established in terms of "trades." The "semi-industrial union," in which all the workers in an industry except those already in recognized trades would be eligible for membership, was one solution to this difficulty. The amalgamation of "subdivided crafts" and the formation of councils of related trades were others.

On the national level a formal Building and Construction Trades Department and a Metal Trade Department were established in 1908, a Railway Employees' Department in 1909, and a Mining Department (which lasted only ten years) in 1912. These departments attempted to bring together the national trade unions in each industry to make arrangements for settling jurisdictional disputes in addition to promoting their common interests.

As much as the AFL leaders may have disliked union participation in political action and the proposals of the socialists, the plain fact had to be faced that the power of government agencies—and especially that of the courts— was affecting union growth and collective bargaining. Gompers felt that labor should not form its own party, as it had in England; without committing themselves politically, unions could carry out a form of bargaining with existing parties to secure legislative support. The slogan was "reward your friends and punish your enemies," and the power of labor was in the voting booth. In 1906 a national meeting of union leaders passed a "Bill of Grievances," which was submitted to all members of Congress; its two items of primary importance were control of the labor injunction and exemption from the antitrust laws. In the 1908 presidential election, the federation found the Democratic party willing to support its demands, and with the election in 1912 of President Woodrow Wilson and a Democratic Congress, labor finally gained the opportunity it had been seeking. It secured passage of such favorable legislation as the Clayton Act of 1914—hailed as labor's Magna Charta because it limited the use of the injunction and antitrust laws in labor cases—the creation of the U.S. Department of Labor in 1913, and the LaFollette Seamen's Act of 1915, which wiped out the worst feature of involuntary servitude in the merchant marine.

Until 1924 the federation refrained from endorsing presidential candidates on the grounds that such endorsement would indicate commitment to an entire platform and to all the candidates of one political party. When neither the Republicans nor the Democrats gave support to labor's goals, it endorsed Robert M. LaFollette and Burton K. Wheeler, the candidates of the Conference for Progressive Political Action, for the presidency and vice presidency;

these men pledged government protection of labor's right to organize and abolition of the injunction in labor disputes. After the election, in which La-Follette polled nearly 5 million votes but carried only his own state of Wisconsin, the coalition of farm and labor groups supporting him broke up, and no further major excursions into politics were made by the federation until the 1930s.

Gompers, until his death in December 1924, and William Green, who succeeded him as president of the AFL, held that the principle of voluntarism was consistent with the political policy of rewarding friends and punishing enemies to attain legislative goals. Gompers and Green sought guarantees of the right of workers to organize and acceptance of collective bargaining, and they favored government action to end unfair competition from convict and child labor. Generally they opposed determination of the terms and conditions of work by the government. Shunning such social legislation as minimum-wage laws for all workers on the grounds that labor should rely on its own efforts to secure its goals, they believed that what the government could give it could take away, but what the union gained through its own strength it could keep.

THE CIO AND THE RISE OF INDUSTRIAL UNIONISM

The depression that began in 1929, one of the worst in the country's history, set the stage for the boom in unionism. At first the AFL's very basis of existence was undermined as industrial production and gross national product fell precipitously to about half of the 1929 level before an upturn came in 1933. Unemployment rose to an estimated 12.8 million workers, or a fourth of the civilian labor force, in the building trades, where much of the federation's membership was located, new construction dropped off by more than 70 percent in the years from 1929 to 1933.

But the depression created the conditions out of which came a new labor "upheaval." Wage cuts, reduction in hours, unemployment, and the fears of an uncertain insecure future meant an "accumulation of grievances." Distrust of business leadership and disillusionment with values of laissez faire in the face of hunger in the midst of plenty accounted in part for the election of Franklin D. Roosevelt as president in 1932 and for his New Deal with its three R's—relief, recovery, and reform. They also led to a major wave of enthusiasm for unionism.

Beginning in 1933, the rush to join unions occurred even in many firms where no organization existed and where no organizer appeared, and existing unions found their membership growing effortlessly. The workers who had organized themselves would ask the American Federation of Labor for a charter. Overwhelmed by requests, the federation could only enroll them in "federal labor unions," local organizations directly under the control of the Executive Council of the federation; these were considered temporary expedients, pending the transfer of new members either to the existing nationals that would claim them or to new nationals formed to represent new jurisdictions. Federal labor unions sprang up in steel, automobiles, and rubber and in many industries where unionism had never been successful.

There were several significant characteristics of the rush into unions in this period of the early New Deal. First, the existing industrial unions—such as the International Ladies Garment Workers (ILGWU), the textile workers, and the miners—increased in far greater proportion than did the craft unions. Secondly, among workers in newly organized industries there was strong interest in the industrial union; workers in rubber plants, for example, did not wish to be identified with specific craft unions that claimed jurisdiction over their jobs. Thirdly, the craft-minded of the AFL showed a noticeable lack of enthusiasm for organizing campaigns in the mass-production industries, either within the limits of their own jurisdictions, or through new industrial national unions.

Formation of the CIO

The conflict within the federation over industrial versus craft unions broke into the open at the San Francisco convention in 1934. The leaders of industrial unions within the federation said that the old forms of union structure would not work in the mass-production industries, and that unless the federation rapidly set up industrial unions, the biggest opportunity in 50 years to organize those industries would be frustrated. Opponents to industrial unionism, on the other hand, charged invasion of existing jurisdictions and violation of the constitutional basis of the federation. Both factions were able to agree on a compromise resolution, The San Francisco Declaration, which stated, first, that union jurisdictions must be protected and, second, that in many industries "a new condition exists requiring organization upon a different basis to be effective."[5]

The San Francisco Declaration proved to be unworkable. Representatives of the craft opposition, centered primarily among the unions in the Metal and the Building Trades departments, commanded a majority in the Executive Council, and they demanded that the new industrial unions exclude from their control jobs that fell within their jurisdictions.

At the Atlantic City convention of the federation in October 1935, the clash over these issues centered on the reports of the resolutions committee. The majority report, presented by John P. Frey of the Metal Trades Department, upheld the historic rights of craft unions, while the minority report interpreted the San Francisco Declaration to mean that all workers in an

[5] Quoted in Philip Taft, *The A.F. of L. from the Death of Gompers to the Merger* (New York: Harper, 1959), p. 80.

industry were to be enrolled in one union. Speaking for the minority view, John L. Lewis charged "breach of faith." The minority report was defeated by the convention by a vote of 18,024 to 10,933. While 60 of the AFL's national and international unions voted solidly against the resolution, 21 supported it, 2 split, and 11 abstained. A majority of the state federations, the city centrals, and the federal labor unions voted in favor of the minority report.

Although the convention ended with John L. Lewis's renominating William Green for president, the split was deep. Three weeks after the convention, a meeting of officers of eight AFL unions[6] set up the Committee for Industrial Organization, to promote the organization of workers in industrial unions in the mass-production industries while still operating as members of the federation. But when Green requested that the committee disband, Lewis resigned as vice president of the AFL, and in January 1936 the United Mine Workers withheld payment of its per capita dues. Shortly afterward, the UMW contributed $500,000 to a newly formed Steel Workers Organizing Committee (SWOC), and its leaders, Philip Murray and John Brophy, offered to head the drive to organize the steel industry. The automobile workers, rubber workers, flat glass workers, and the radio and electrical workers also soon joined the committee. The AFL Executive Council charged the CIO unions with "dualism." In November the delegates to the 1936 convention at Tampa, where the CIO unions were not represented, formally endorsed suspension with a vote of 21, 679 to 2,043.

In 1937 the federation ordered state and city bodies to expel locals of CIO unions, and the committee in retaliation took steps to set up its own state and local organization. After the failure of an attempt to reunite the two groups, the committee organized itself as a permanent labor organization in November 1938, calling itself the Congress of Industrial Organization in order to preserve its initials. There were 34 national and international unions, 8 organizing committees, and a number of state and local councils and local industrial unions.

Structure of the CIO

Structurally, the CIO was remarkably similar to the AFL. The annual convention was the source of authority, and voting strength was concentrated in the national and international unions. The convention elected a president

---

[6] They were John L. Lewis, United Mine Workers; Charles P. Howard, International Typographical Union; Sidney Hillman, Amalgamated Clothing Workers of America; David Dubinsky, International Ladies' Garment Workers' Union; Thomas F. McMahon, United Textile Workers; Harvey C. Fremming, Oil Field, Gas and Refinery Workers of America; Max Zaritsky, United Hatters, Cap and Millinery Workers' International Union; and Thomas H. Brown, International Union of Mine, Mill and Smelter Workers. Lewis was named chairman and Howard secretary. Of the eight leaders, Howard and Zaritsky acted as individuals; their unions neither then nor later joined the CIO.

(Lewis), two vice presidents (Hillman and Murray), and a secretary (James Carey of the United Electrical Workers). An executive board consisting of one representative from each national union was granted powers to act between conventions. Later the constitution was amended to provide for an executive committee composed of the officers.

The similarity of the organizational structures of the two federations was not surprising. CIO leaders had gained their experience within the AFL, and the idea that national unions should be the foundation of the new federation was naturally accepted. But as the unions drew together to carry out their goals of "organizing the unorganized," certain differences emerged. Organizing committees within different industries—steel, textiles, utilities—were created by the national CIO. Each was given staff, funds, and initial overall direction by the CIO national organization, usually in the form of sponsorships by one of the large CIO unions. This practice served to tie together the CIO unions even after the organizing committees became national unions. Furthermore, the basic objective of organizing the mass-production industries, a crusade that united the CIO as a whole, tended for a while to submerge the interests of the nationals and weaken their autonomy. The tendency toward centralization of authority was also furthered by the strong personalities of such leaders as John L. Lewis, the symbol of the crusade, Murray, and Hillman, who were able to exert a decisive influence in the strike strategies of their constituents. Although Lewis was the "five-star general," at least in the early days of the CIO, by 1940, when Lewis supported Wendell Willkie's candidacy for president and resigned when the Republicans lost the election, the CIO was able to survive the loss of the man who had played such an important role in its formation. It later suffered little from the withdrawal of the UMW[7] in 1942.

Policies of the CIO

In terms of union policies, the major differences between the AFL and CIO leaders were, of course, concerned with the form of newly created unions. However, as the new industrial unions achieved a permanent position in industry, the craft-industrial controversy began to recede. The strategies of the AFL were revised when it became apparent that the semiskilled and unskilled workers could be organized after all. The International Association of Machinists, which had played an important role in blocking industrial unionism in the AFL Executive Council, became one of the first to recognize that it was going to have to form industrial locals "in self-defense" against CIO

[7] The mine workers' union remained independent until 1946, when it reaffiliated briefly with the AFL. Lewis's protest of the AFL decision that leaders should sign the noncommunist affidavit required by the Taft-Hartley Act was the grounds for withdrawal from the federation in 1947. Since then, the UMWA has remained independent.

invasions, and this view won support at a special conference of the AFL unions in May 1937. Thereafter the original controversy over *principles* of craft and industrial unionism came to an end.

The CIO leaders, generally younger men who were not imbued with Gompers's philosophy of voluntarism and a distrust of government intervention, were far more sympathetic to social legislation and political action than were the leaders of the older federation. Moreover, since industrial workers were generally less skilled and lower paid than the craft unionists, job, old age, and unemployment insecurities weighed on them more heavily, and governmental programs of relief and social insurance and guarantees of work and wage standards therefore had a direct and beneficial impact on them. There was also little doubt in the minds of CIO unionists that federal action had broken down the barricades against unionism in the major industries. Under these circumstances, political action to influence governmental legislation was inevitable.

Labor's Non-Partisan League was formed in 1936 by national unions from the CIO and by some AFL unions. Though it tried to avoid becoming a third party, the league did more than offer support to its friends in the Gompers tradition: it entered some of its own candidates in primary elections, and in New York state it initiated the American Labor party. When in 1943 the Wartime Labor Disputes Act (Smith-Connally Act) banned political contributions by labor unions, the CIO organized a Political Action Committee (PAC), which was to conduct "a broad and intensive program of education . . . for effective labor action on the political front." Although the AFL was less inclined to engage in broad political action, in 1948 it formed a similar organization, called Labor's League for Political Education (LLPE).

The issue of Communists in labor unions was also treated differently by the AFL and the CIO. The Communist party's dualistic tactics met with little success, and in the mid-1930s it attempted to capture control of membership and leadership of existing unions. At first the Communists concentrated on the AFL unions, but soon they turned to the CIO, which, in its own search for organizers, recruited some with known or suspected Communist affiliations. But many CIO leaders who had a long experience in fighting Communists in their own industries—Lewis, Hillman, and Dubinsky, for example—were careful to keep them out of their unions. Communist infiltration served to arouse not only the opposition of employers and the middle classes to the CIO, but also the enmity of AFL leaders, who considered their own organizations practically impenetrable.

On another important issue, the CIO accused the AFL of harboring racketeers, especially in the craft unions. As in the case of Communism, there was some substance to the charge: as we will see later, the use of union positions to extort money from employers or to reap personal benefits from members' dues is likely to be found in the less democratic unions and in those connected with local markets, such as organizations in building services, long-shoring, and construction.

A final difference in policy related to the racial issue. The constitutions of some AFL unions banned blacks from membership; in terms of the narrower job-control philosophy of craft unionism, such provisions were designed to limit competition for jobs and to maintain "standards." Since CIO unions, on the other hand, aimed at enrolling every worker in a particular plant to secure the greatest possible strength in collective bargaining, racial discrimination in membership was contrary to their objective. Top AFL leadership might complain about racial and racketeering practices, but respect for national union autonomy effectively prevented punitive action.

When the first CIO unions joined together in the winter of 1935–1936, their membership totaled about 1 million. By 1937 the CIO had 3,718,000 members, while the AFL had 2,861,000, and by the time of its first convention in 1938, the CIO was still the largest labor group in the country, representing over 4 million workers. During the recession in business activity that occured from 1937 until America's entry into World War II, however, the CIO made no further significant gains. Then, with the expansion of defense industries, its membership reached 5 million by 1941 and 6 million by 1945. But by 1939 the unions of the AFL had again risen to the top position in terms of membership, and, except in 1941, they remained there, with about 7 million members at the end of World War II.

The great boom in union membership occurred in 1936 and 1937, when the CIO added close to 3 million new workers to its ranks, mostly from the mass-production industries of steel, automobiles, electrical equipment, and coal.

THE AFL–CIO

The Road to Merger

By 1941 there was no doubt that the CIO had established itself firmly in the major basic industries of the United States and was a force to be reckoned with by the AFL as well as by employers. During World War II AFL and CIO leaders sat together as equal representatives of labor with employers on governmental boards. Organized labor worked with management in a variety of ways to stimulate and streamline production of war material. Most important, both unions and employers entrusted the final resolution of disputes to the National War Labor Board, composed of representatives from management, labor, and the public. Although both AFL and CIO unions pledged that there would be no strikes for the duration, John L. Lewis, who was then independent of both organizations, gave no pledge and did not participate in the governmental labor boards.

The public had feared that the end of the war would lead to a reopening of the disputes of the 1930s. These fears were not eased when the labor-management conference called by President Truman in the winter of 1945–1946 broke down and when the strikes that erupted in 1946 made that the worst year in terms of worker days lost. The post–World War II unrest was substantially different from that in the 1930s and from the 1919 strike wave after World War I: the principle of collective bargaining had been accepted by labor and management. President Truman's conference agreed on the principle of collective bargaining and the desirability of strengthening the government's conciliation service, but could find no answer to the problem of placing limits on unions' objectives by defining management's rights. Reflecting the new position that labor had won, the 1946 strikes were concerned with wages. With the prospect that wages and prices would no longer be controlled by governmental agencies after the end of World War II, unions demanded substantial wage increases and the resolution of a backlog of grievances. After lengthy strikes in steel, autos, and other industries, and with the intervention of fact-finding boards appointed by President Truman, wage hikes of about 18.5 cents per hour were accepted by both sides. The postwar militancy of labor then spread to other industries, such as coal and railroads. Although the disputes involved little physical violence, the strikes aroused the public, which showed concern for the strikes' impact upon the reconversion of the economy from war to peacetime production, the operation of public services, and the price level. These attitudes supported the first major revision of the basic labor law—the Labor Management Relations Act of 1947 (the Taft-Hartley Act). Passed over President Truman's veto with its provisions designed to restrict labor's power, this act was denounced by both AFL and CIO leaders as a "slave-labor law"; thus, at the beginning of a new chapter in labor history, the act unwittingly provided an impetus for the merger of the two labor organizations.

Although both labor groups had a new common objective—modification of the Taft-Hartley Act—the steps toward merger were not easy. The background of conflict, interunion warfare, and charge and countercharge was not easily forgotten. Nonetheless, leaders on both sides had uneasy feelings about the split in the "house of labor," for the idea that "labor united" was far stronger than "labor divided" was fundamental union gospel. Several meetings striving for unity between the two camps had, in fact, taken place before 1946, but each attempt had been unable to resolve the conflict between "functional" and "organic" unity. The AFL believed that the CIO unions should individually reunite with the federation, merging organically with others in the same jurisdiction. The CIO leaders, on the other hand, favored functional unity, in which their unions would be accepted en masse, without losing their identity as independent industrial unions.

The common goals of opposing restrictive legislation at the national level and of seeking effective representation of labor in governmental defense agencies during the Korean War were strong motivations for merger. Meanwhile, two divisive issues were resolved. In 1949–1950, the CIO expelled 11 national unions that were considered to be Communist-led, dropped its affiliation with the World Federation of Trade Unions (which the AFL had long opposed as an instrument of Soviet policy), and joined with the federation in helping to form a rival International Conference of Free Trade Unions. And in 1953 the AFL expelled the International Longshoremen's Association on grounds of racketeering, following investigations by the New York State Crime Commission into criminal activities on the New York docks.

Conditions were ripe for new unity talks when in the late fall of 1952 the presidents of the two labor organizations, Philip Murray and William Green, died within two weeks of each other. Although both had originally come up through the ranks of the United Mine Workers, they symbolized to the American public the split in the labor movement. The two men who took their places, George Meany in the AFL and Walter Reuther in the CIO, were committed to unity and wasted no time in initiating new negotiations. By June 1953 the joint unity committee took the first steps to prevent further warfare between the two organizations by accepting a no-raid agreement. Approved unanimously by both the AFL and CIO in their conventions in the fall of 1953, the agreement provided that it should be basic policy that no union affiliated with each federation should attempt to organize employees already in an "established bargaining relationship . . . between their employer and a union in the other federation," and that each federation "should urge" its affiliates to become parties to the agreement; if disputes could not be settled by the respective parties themselves, they were to be referred for arbitration to an individual designated as an impartial umpire.

Even though all the unions did not participate in the no-raid agreement, the road to unity was open. The meetings of the Joint AFL–CIO Unity Committee in October 1954 and February 1955 produced the basic plan for a complete merger. The essence of the proposal was (1) equal recognition of craft and industrial unionism, (2) acceptance of each national union's current jurisdiction, (3) settlement of jurisdictional conflicts at a later date through negotiation, (4) creation of a department of industrial unions, to which all eligible unions could belong, (5) prohibitions against racial discrimination, and (6) power of the central organization to eliminate corruption and communism within its affiliates.

The AFL and the CIO each held their last separate conventions in December 1955—the seventy-fourth and seventeenth, respectively—then voted to merge, and adjourned to meet together to form the new AFL–CIO at the constitutional convention on December 5.

Organization of the AFL–CIO

The new organization was based on the existing structure of both the AFL and the CIO. All affiliated unions of each organization—including the national and international unions, the directly affiliated locals, the state and local federations and councils, and the various departments—were brought intact into the new organization. The national and international unions were the most important of these organizations: their representation at the convention was based on the size of their membership, and this gave them control of the new federation. Each of the other organizations was entitled to one vote.

International and National Unions The autonomy of each of the nationals affiliated with the federation was protected, no matter whether the union's jurisdiction was craft or industrial or overlapped with another union. The constitution stated that "both craft and industrial unions are appropriate, equal, and necessary as methods of trade union organization" (Article VII), and—"each affiliated national and international union is entitled to have its autonomy, integrity, and jurisdiction protected and preserved" (Article III, Sec. 7); affiliates were to respect the established collective bargaining relationship of other unions. Plainly the old doctrine of exclusive jurisdiction, already made obsolete by the representation-election procedure under the National Labor Relations Board, had been abandoned. "Past trespass of jurisdiction" was no ground for claims against national unions. Affiliated unions were to respect the existing positions of unions in the established collective bargaining relationship, even though under the Taft-Hartley Act noncertified unions could try to win over another's members after a 12-month period. The no-raid pact, at first continued under the constitution, was reformulated as Article XXI, Settlement of Internal Disputes, effective January 1, 1962.[8] Although two or more unions could be tolerated within the federation

---

[8] The article provides for the settlement of a jurisdictional dispute among member unions through a procedure of several steps. The first is appointment of a mediator by the president from a panel comprised of those "within the labor movement." If no settlement is forthcoming, the case is referred to an impartial umpire, chosen from a panel of "prominent and respected persons." An appeal can be made from that decision to the Executive Council of the AFL–CIO for a final decision. The sanctions against noncomplying unions range from loss of the right to use the dispute settlement procedure to expulsion.

From 1962 to 1971 a total of 1,171 cases had been filed under the plan, over half of which were settled by mediation. Of the decisions made by impartial umpires, only 17 were rejected by unions found in noncompliance. In those cases sanctions were imposed by the Executive Council. See U.S. Department of Labor, *Directory of National Unions and Employee Associations*, Bulletin 1750 (Washington, D.C.: U.S. Government Printing Office, 1972), p. 66.

even if their jurisdictions overlapped, they were urged to merge. A few mergers have been made but not to the extent originally anticipated.[9]

State and Local Federations All the existing AFL and CIO state and local bodies were initially brought together in the new federation, but the plan to merge the former rivals in every territorial jurisdiction within two years proved to be overly optimistic. At the state level some time extensions had to be granted before the former AFL organization and the former CIO group found a workable compromise resolving their reluctance to join with each other. The primary obstacles to such mergers were fears that the interests of one group would be submerged by the greater voting strength of the other faction and personal differences among rival leaders. While all state organizations had merged within four years after the initial agreement, greater difficulties were encountered at the city level. In many cases the old AFL city centrals were under the domination of the building trade unions, which still found industrial unionism uncongenial and a threat to their interests in municipal politics.

Directly Affiliated Local Unions Merger of locals directly affiliated with each of the two former federations occasioned few problems, since they considered such arrangements as temporary, pending their assignment to one of the existing national unions or to a new national. New national unions could come into being as organizing committees or national trade councils and were then granted voting status as recognized unions.

Departments The five departments of the AFL were brought intact into the new federation, and an Industrial Union Department (IUD) was created.[10] Former CIO unions automatically became affiliated with the new department, but it was also open to any AFL unions oganized in whole or in part on an industrial basis. The department began with 66 unions, of which 35 were former AFL unions with a membership of more than 2 million workers, while the 31 CIO unions had a membership of about 4 million. The department had its own officers, with Walter Reuther as president and James B. Carey as secretary-treasurer, and with former AFL leaders holding 4 of the 12

[9] Some of the most noteworthy mergers were between the International Brotherhood of Paper Makers (formerly AFL) and the United Paper Workers of America (formerly CIO), between the Upholsterers International Union and the United Furniture Workers (formerly AFL and CIO respectively), between the American Federation of Hosiery Workers (formerly AFL) and the Textile Workers Union of America (formerly CIO), and between the Meat Cutters (formerly AFL) and the Packinghouse Workers (formerly CIO).

In recent years merger activity has increased, but the motivation is to reduce rising operating expenses through consolidation. An important recent merger was that in 1976 between the Amalgamated Clothing Workers of America and the Textile Workers Union of America; the new organization is called the Amalgamated Clothing and Textile Workers Union.

[10] The five former departments were the Building and Construction Trades, the Maritime Trades, the Metal Trades, the Railway Employees, and the Union label and Service Trades. A Public Employees Department was formed in 1974.

vice presidencies. Some of the craft union leaders had been fearful that the IUD would be a power bloc within the merged federation, and there is little doubt that it has increased the bargaining power of the former CIO unions; but the creation of such a body was necessary in order to secure initial CIO acceptance of the merger.

The Convention   The convention, meeting biannually, is the source of power and authority within the AFL–CIO. It frames policy and elects the president, the secretary-treasurer, and 33 vice presidents. George Meany, formerly of the AFL, has been president since the first convention. All these officers together form the Executive Council, the principal governing body between conventions, which meets three times yearly. The Executive Council has the power to make decisions and take action between conventions. There is also an Executive Board, made up of the Executive Council plus one representative from each of the affiliated national unions; each of these, unlike the members of the Executive Council, is chosen individually by the appropriate national union rather than by the convention. The Executive Board acts on matters submitted to it by the president and Executive Council.[11]

Department of Organization   To supervise one of the AFL–CIO's most important functions, to "organize the unorganized," a new Department of Organization was created within the federation. This department is initially responsible for the directly affiliated locals and the organizing committees that are in the process of becoming national unions, and it helps national unions in their organizing campaigns. It has also promoted rival unions to replace nationals expelled from the AFL–CIO for corruption, though in all cases it must respect the jurisdictions and organizational direction of member national unions. Renamed the Department of Organization and Field Services in 1973, this body now plans its organizing activities in closer cooperation with the AFL–CIO regional offices.

Standing Committees   Other functions of the federation are carried out by the 14 standing committees explicitly provided for in the constitution. These include committees on legislation and the Committee on Political Education (COPE), which deals with matters formerly supervised by PAC and LLPE—ethical practices, international affairs, education, and the like. Finally, the federation performs certain staff functions relating to economic research, legal affairs, and publications.

---

[11] Originally the Executive Council had 27 vice presidents, with 17 from former AFL unions and 10 from former CIO unions, roughly in proportion to the affiliated membership. In addition, there was an Executive Committee, consisting of the president, secretary-treasurer, and six vice presidents selected by the Executive Council, with three from AFL and three from CIO unions. The Executive Committee, meeting bimonthly, was to advise the president. It was abolished in 1967. Also in that year, the constitutional requirement that the Executive Board was to meet annually was changed so that now it assembles only when summoned by the president.

Membership Trends

At the time of the merger some observers expressed fears that the AFL–CIO would become a monolithic labor movement dominating the American economy; subsequent events have shown that, on the contrary, the federation lost its forward momentum soon after its formation. By 1972 not only was the federation's total membership below its level of 1956,[12] but 6.6 million workers were in unions and bargaining associations unaffiliated with the AFL–CIO, a number equal to 40 percent of the AFL–CIO membership. Just before the merger, in contrast, about 1.8 million union members were outside both the AFL and the CIO (about 11.5 percent of the combined membership of both federations).

A number of reasons explain the failure of the AFL–CIO to continue its dominant leadership in the American labor movement. The strength of the AFL–CIO had been in industries where employment has not been expanding (mining, construction, and manufacturing) or in which it has actually been contracting with the introduction of automated production processes, such as printing. Although affiliates in trade and public employment began to experience high growth rates, they have formed only a relatively small part of the AFL–CIO membership. Moreover, the federation did not have the political power to repeal adverse labor legislation, such as Section 14(b) of the Taft-Hartley Act. The federation claimed that this section, which permitted states to pass "right-to-work" laws that forbade agreements requiring membership in a labor organization as a condition of employment, had hindered organizational efforts in areas generally hostile to unionism. In 1972, for example, in the 19 states with right-to-work laws (located primarily in southern and midwestern agricultural states in which antiunion attitudes had long been prevalent), union workers comprised only about 15 percent of the nonagricultural labor force, while in other states the percentage of union membership was 31.6.

But the problems of the federation could be said to reflect more fundamentally the difficulties inherent in its organizational structure. National unions, giving primary concern to their own interests, were only secondarily concerned with the overall objectives of the federation. Although the Gompers doctrine of autonomy may have been weakened somewhat in the 1955 merger, the nationals were still the major units of the labor movement. Although a national, especially a small one, could receive certain advantages by affiliating with the federation—among them legislative and informational

---

[12] Department of Labor totals on membership changes in unions affiliated with the AFL–CIO, by two-year periods from 1956 to 1972, show increases in five periods and a loss in three for a net decline of 396,000 workers over the 16 years. See *Directory of National Unions and Employee Associations, 1973*, Table 4, p. 68.

services and protection from raiding—the large nationals with sufficient resources of their own were likely to find the benefits of affiliation minimal.

Loss of Key National Unions Two situations that illustrate this affiliation problem most sharply involved the loss of two of the federation's largest affiliates, the International Brotherhood of Teamsters, Chauffeurs, Warehousemen and Helpers of America (IBT), and the United Automobile Workers of America (UAW). In 1974 these unions ranked first and second in size among all unions, with 2.0 and 1.5 million workers respectively. The Teamsters were expelled by the AFL–CIO in 1957 for corruption following disclosures by the Senate Investigation Committee on Improper Practices of Labor and Management (the McClellan commmittee) and after investigation by the federation's own Ethical Practices Committee.[13]

The disaffiliation of the Automobile Workers came in 1968. Critical of the social and political conservatism of the AFL–CIO leadership in both domestic and foreign policy, President Walter Reuther resigned from the Executive Council in 1967; the union withdrew from the federation the following year. The Teamsters and the Automobile Workers joined together in May 1969 in an Alliance for Labor Action, hoping that they could attract other unions, but the effort was unsuccessful, and the alliance was abandoned in 1971.[14]

The expulsion of the Teamsters was an attempt by the federation to demonstrate that it could eliminate racketeering and corruption from its own ranks without government action. Restrictive legislation was passed anyway, with the Labor Management Reporting and Disclosure (Landrum-Griffin) Act of 1959, which provided for government regulation of the internal affairs of unions. But the AFL–CIO had ample justification for handling the matter of corruption the way it did. Not only did its constitution ban racketeering unions; the federation also had the power, under the codes of ethics drawn up by its Ethical Practices Committee, both to expel a union that would not mend its ways and to charter a "clean" union with the aim of winning over members.

The Teamsters, far from suffering after expulsion, continued to grow. The federation had neither the money nor the will to form a rival union to undermine the Teamsters' dominance in the trucking industry. In one major instance the federation attempted to block Teamster expansion into an unrelated field, the organization of agricultural workers. The Teamsters (who had earlier changed their constitution to include in their jurisdiction all unor-

[13] Also expelled for corruption in 1957 were the Laundry Workers and the Bakers Union. The Distillery Workers union was put on probation. Two other unions which had been investigated by the McClellan committee, the United Textile Workers Union and the Allied Industrial Workers, avoided similar action when several of their officers withdrew under pressure from the federation.

[14] Financial difficulties within the UAW contributed to its demise, as did the death of Walter Reuther—a prime mover in the alliance—in an airplane crash in 1970.

ganized workers in any industry) were in bitter dispute in the early 1970s with the United Farm Workers of America, a union headed by Cesar Chavez that had become affiliated with the AFL–CIO, over representation of lettuce and grape workers in California. After the Western Federation of Teamsters had entered into agreements with large growers, the AFL–CIO in 1973 voted to donate $1.6 million to support striking United Farm Workers.

One result of the ensuing struggle was passage of the California Agricultural Relations Act in 1975. It provided for representation elections and collective bargaining rights for farm workers, who had been excluded from coverage under the National Labor Relations Act. At the time the new law was passed, it was estimated that the Teamsters represented some 55,000 workers under 400 contracts, while the United Farm Workers represented 5,-000 workers under 12 contracts. Although elections were suspended for several months when the board that conducted the balloting ran out of funds, by November 1977 the Farm Workers had won 192 elections and the Teamsters 119. Other unions or "no-union" had been chosen in 44 other elections.

The withdrawal of the United Automobile Workers came about partly because of the re-emergence of craft-industrial union jurisdictional controversies and conflicts over social and political policy reminiscent of the days before the merger. There was friction between the UAW and building trade unions over the assignment of work at automobile plants: should it be within the jurisdiction of the accredited bargaining agent of the firm, or should it be farmed out to independent contractors who would use workers organized in the building trades?

Another important issue in the 1968 disaffiliation was the position of the federation with respect to international labor movements and American foreign policy. International labor affairs in the federation were headed by Jay Lovestone, a former member of the American Communist party who had become a hard-line anticommunist. Until his retirement in 1974, Lovestone, with complete support from George Meany, had opposed relationships of the federation with any foreign labor group that was communist, socialist, or, as charged by some observers, even neutral toward official State Department policy. In this period when the cold war aroused intense emotions, Reuther's advocacy of liberalizing relations with the post-Stalinist Soviet Union and Eastern Europe, cutting back on defense expenditures, expanding economic aid abroad, and encouraging better relations with the International Confederation of Free Trade Unions, found little support within the Executive Council.[15] The leadership of the AFL–CIO, with little internal dissent, has since

---

[15] As Jack Barbash pointed out before the disaffiliation of the UAW: "The relationship of the AFL–CIO to the international labor movement generates more controversy than any other issue except jurisdiction." See his *American Unions: Structure, Government, and Politics* (New York: Random House, 1967), p. 108.

Sidney Lens gives a critical view of the federation's international activities in "Partners: Labor and CIA," *The Progressive*, 39 (February 1975), 35–39.

continued its opposition to affiliation with international organizations that include labor representatives from communist-bloc nations. In 1977 the federation was successful in its campaign to end United States participation in the International Labor Organization (ILO), an agency established under the old League of Nations. The organization is unique in that the delegations of participating nations include representatives of labor, industry, and government. Although the ILO has been preeminent in its collection of statistics concerning wages and working conditions throughout the world, the AFL–CIO leadership argued that it had become a political forum for criticism of American policies.

The AFL–CIO and Civil Rights The principle of autonomy of the national unions affected the federation's role in the civil rights movement that began in the latter 1950s and flourished during the 1960s. Many national unions had long been leaders in the movement for human rights and economic equality for blacks and other minorities. During the depression of the 1930s and throughout World War II, CIO unions in steel, autos, coal, and other industries had recruited workers without regard to race. Other unions, however, had racially discriminatory practices, including segregated locals and restrictions on entry into skilled jobs. One of the conditions of the merger, demanded by the former CIO unions, was to incorporate into the constitution of the AFL–CIO a clear affirmation of the protection of minority rights; the only objection to this demand at the time of the merger came from Michael Quill of the Transport Workers Union (CIO), who held that the antidiscrimination clause was not strong enough.

But the merger did not, in fact, resolve the differing attitudes of the constituent nationals toward racial discrimination. In part the problem was compounded by factors over which the federation and the unions had little control. The general stagnation of business during the late 1950s and early 1960s, plus actual declines in employment in certain industries such as railroads, meant conflicts within the ranks of labor for diminishing job opportunities. The flow of black labor out of southern agriculture into both southern and northern cities further increased competition in the labor market. Under these circumstances, some unions became more interested in protecting the job rights of their members than in enrolling new workers, especially minorities.

Against this background the racial issue in the federation soon broke out in a way that nearly ruptured relations between organized labor and the black community. One of the first moves of the AFL–CIO after the merger was to invite two independent unions, the Brotherhood of Locomotive Firemen and the Brotherhood of Railway Trainmen, to join the federation, even though the constitutions of both organizations permitted racial discrimination. Although admitted to the federation on condition that they eliminate the offending clauses at their next convention, black unionists considered this procedure to be a violation of the AFL–CIO constitution. As other affiliated nationals were known to be continuing discriminatory practices, black unionists asked that those unions be expelled, just like unions found guilty of corrupt practices. President Meany, however, replied that a distinction should be made between corruption and discrimination as grounds for expulsion of nationals. Corruption, he said, "seizes" union leadership and "works down to lower levels by perverting the union's democratic procedures." Expulsion is the only way to convince the membership of domination by corrupt forces. Discrimination, on the other hand, should not be blamed on the leadership, but "represents the wrong-headedness of rank-and-file members." Expulsion would not solve the problem, but would hurt the leaders who fight discrimination. It is better to keep discriminatory unions in the "mainstream" of the labor movement where the leaders can get "broad AFL–CIO support" and the rank-and-file can become educated.[16]

In 1960 black leaders formed the Negro-American Labor Council (NALC) to fight racial discrimination within the labor movement. One of its most prominent members was A. Philip Randolph, who, as head of the virtually all-black Brotherhood of Sleeping Car Porters (BSCP), had long been a spokesman for blacks. Although formation of the NALC led to a flurry of charges and countercharges concerning the role of the federation in promoting the rights of black unionists, open conflict was avoided. Tensions continued to persist, but it became apparent that the AFL–CIO leadership had lobbied intensely for the Civil Rights Act of 1964—including Article VII, which prohibited racial discrimination in employment. Moreover, some civil rights organizations, including the National Association for the Advancement of Colored People, had joined with labor in attempting to repeal Section 14(b) of the Taft-Hartley Act.[17]

The doctrine of autonomy has limited the federation's ability to deal with the prejudice and discrimination that are found primarily in nationals and local unions, and has been an obstacle to the formation of joint organizing drives among black workers in the South and elsewhere. Positive action has come from elsewhere. Under the Taft-Hartley Act, the National Labor Relations Board adopted a new doctrine in 1964 that unions may not be certified to represent workers in collective bargaining with an employer if they refuse to represent workers on the basis of race, and that they may be guilty of an unfair labor practice.[18] In addition, some unions—among them District 1199 of the National Union of Hospital and Health Care Employees, and the Service Employees International Union (AFL–CIO)—have engaged in their

---

[16] Quoted in Jack Barbash, *American Unions*, p. 112.

[17] See Ray Marshall, *The Negro Worker* (New York: Random House, 1967), ch. III, "The Negro and the AFL–CIO."

[18] The case was the *Independent Metal Workers Union, Local No. 1, and Hughes Tool Company,* 56 LRRM 1289 (1964).

own membership drives in occupations having a high percentage of black and other minority workers. And, finally, black workers themselves have formed black caucuses in order to bring about leadership changes in their own unions.

The AFL-CIO and the Bargaining Associations One other aspect of the AFL–CIO's position in the American labor movement is its relationship with those employee associations in the public and nonprivate sectors that have turned toward collective bargaining in the last fifteen years. It was aggressive AFL–CIO affiliates that first provided the breakthrough that led to the upsurge of public sector unionism in the early 1960s. A local affiliate of the American Federation of Teachers (AFT) under Albert Shanker achieved a major victory in New York City in 1961 when it won an election that gave it bargaining rights for about 44,000 teachers in the city; teachers in other cities were soon drawn toward the AFT as the leader for unionization. The American Federation of State, County and Municipal Employees (AFSCME), which had been formed in the 1930s and affiliated originally with the AFL, also initiated a major campaign for organization and recognition of public sector workers in major cities. At the federal level—in addition to the postal unions—the American Federation of Government Employees (AFGE), another original AFL union, made sharp organizational gains after the promulgation of President Kennedy's Executive Order 10988 in 1962. In the period from 1964 to 1974, these three unions reported some of the largest membership increases of any AFL–CIO national unions. Of the 12 national unions with gains of more than 100,000 during the decade, the AFT ranked first, AFSCME second, and AFGE tenth.

In the face of this growth, and the new laws that encouraged it, some of the older types of employee associations among teachers and civil service employees, which had eschewed unionization in the past, were forced to reconsider their policy if they wished to hold their members. One of the largest of these groups, the National Education Association (NEA), which included some 1.5 million schoolteachers throughout the nation, embraced collective bargaining as a basic principle in 1967. Other associations, often limited to civil service employees within a single state, also dropped their former opposition and became certified as collective bargaining agencies. The Civil Service Employees Association of the State of New York, for example, bargains for 200,-000 employees.

In the competition to organize and represent government employees at the state and local level—including sometimes bitter disputes between the AFT and the AFSCME—the employee associations have tended to remain apart from the AFL–CIO or its member unions. Although a few NEA locals have joined with AFT locals in several cities, merger talks in 1973–1974 between the two national organizations failed, apparently on the grounds that the

NEA did not wish to be considered an affiliate of the AFL–CIO. On the other hand, the NEA in 1971 joined with the AFSCME to form the Coalition of American Public Employees (CAPE), a political action and lobbying organization unaffiliated with the AFL–CIO. (CAPE later included, for a brief period, the International Association of Fire Fighters, a federation affiliate, and the independent National Treasury Employees Union.) One of the specific points at issue was the desire for new national legislation that would establish uniform standards for representation, collective bargaining, and impasse procedures at the state and local levels throughout the United States. Such legislation, according both to Jerry Wurf, president of the AFSCME, and to representatives of the NEA, should differ in certain respects from the National Labor Relations Act, which applied to private-sector labor relations.

An underlying problem that keeps the associations apart is the possibility of jurisdictional conflict. If the employee associations were to join the federation, they would find that certain occupational groups could be claimed by existing AFL–CIO craft unions; to resist such challenges they would have to submit to jurisdictional resolution procedures over which they had little knowledge or control. Even the AFSCME, which originally claimed to represent all employees in state and local governments, has fought jurisdictional battles with craft unions in the federation as well as with the American Federation of Teachers. Unless the AFL–CIO is willing to adjust its own organizational structure and modify policies in order to make affiliation attractive to the employee associations, the split between public and private sector unionism seems likely to continue.

SUMMARY

The historical roots of the American labor movement extend back to the years immediately following the Revolution. Although the first unions were small, local, and weak, they exhibited the characteristics of the labor movement to come: by joining together, workers sought to protect work and wage standards from what they believed to be the degrading forces of the market. In the early nineteenth century, workers supported programs, such as producers' cooperatives, that they hoped would lead to economic independence rather than wage-earning dependency. Although these reformist dreams persisted among the leaders of the Knights of Labor in the 1880s, by then workers who had formed craft unions—and even many who had joined the Knights—had accepted as inevitable their wage-earning status in the new industrial system.

The American Federation of Labor, under Samuel Gompers, was organized in 1886 on the basis of the autonomy and exclusive jurisdiction of the national trade unions. AFL leaders believed that unions could survive only if they were based on the solid, job-security interests of the skilled. Because of this form of organization, semiskilled and unskilled workers in the mass production industries were generally left out. Industrial unionism, supported by socialist groups, was generally unsuccessful in the early part of the twentieth century.

It was not until the 1930s that the Congress of Industrial Organization was formed, broke away from the AFL, and unionized the basic industries of the United States. Conflicts over jurisdictional rights between craft and industrial unions eventually ebbed as the AFL leaders recognized that the new unions had come to stay; moreover, the representation voting and certification procedures under the 1935 Wagner Act undermined union claims for exclusive jurisdiction. Merger of the AFL and CIO came in 1955.

Like its predecessor federations, the AFL–CIO rests upon the foundation of the power of the national unions. Their autonomy, however, can pose problems for the AFL–CIO leadership. Demands for the elimination of racketeering or discriminatory racial policies can go unheeded, and the federation's only remedy is expulsion. The loss of two of the largest unions—the Teamsters in 1957 and the United Automobile Workers in 1968—have limited the growth of the federation. With the continuing expansion of bargaining employee associations in the public sector, the number of organized workers unaffiliated with the federation has continued to grow. In 1974 their numbers were 40 percent of the total AFL–CIO membership.

DISCUSSION QUESTIONS

1. How do you account for the fact that most of the first unions in the United States were formed by skilled, rather than unskilled, workers?
2. Contrast what are called the "reformist" objectives of labor organizations with "bread-and-butter" unionism. Do you believe that these two types of objectives are inconsistent with each other?
3. Gompers claimed the national trade union was the form of organization essential to the long-run stability of the labor movement in America. What were his reasons? If the national union was considered so important, what were the functions of the federation?
4. Contrast the organizational structure and the objectives of the Knights of Labor and the American Federation of Labor. What made conflict between the two inevitable?
5. To what factors do you attribute the rise and decline of the Industrial Workers of the World?
6. Why did the conflict between the industrial and craft forms of labor organization, which had been simmering for so long, suddenly erupt in the 1930s with the formation of the CIO? How was the conflict over union structure resolved in 1955 under the constitution of the new AFL–CIO?
7. Do Gompers's early principles concerning the desirability of autonomy of the national union still govern the AFL–CIO? Discuss this question in terms of such issues as racketeering and racial discrimination.
8. What are the advantages and disadvantages to a national union of affiliation with the AFL–CIO?

SELECTED READINGS

For general studies in American labor, see references cited in footnote 1 above. A basic study of national unions is Lloyd Ulman, *The Rise of the National Trade Union* (Cambridge, Mass.: Harvard University Press, 1955). For Gompers and the American Federation of Labor, see Philip Taft, *The A.F. of L. in the Time of Gompers* (New York: Harper, 1957), and his *The A.F. of L. from the Death of Gompers to the Merger* (New York: Harper, 1959). On the industrial-craft union controversy, see James O. Morris, *Conflict Within the AFL: A Study of Craft versus Industrial Unionism, 1901–1938* (Ithaca, N.Y.: Cornell University Press, 1958); Walter Galenson, *The CIO Challenge to the AFL, a History of the American Labor Movement, 1935–1941* (Cambridge, Mass.: Harvard University Press, 1960); and Arthur J. Goldberg, *AFL–CIO Labor United* (New York: McGraw-Hill, 1956).

The special importance of the Knights of Labor is stressed by Norman J. Ware in his *The Labor Movement in the United States, 1860–1895, A Study in Democracy* (New York: Random House, 1964).

On socialists in the American labor movement, see John H. Laslett, *Labor and the Left: A Study of Socialist and Radical Influences in the American Labor Movement, 1881–1924* (New York: Basic Books, 1970). Until the 1930s, violence often characterized attempts of unions to organize. One study is Samuel Yellen, *American Labor Struggles* (New York: Harcourt, Brace, 1936); a more recent one is Sidney Lens, *The Labor Wars: From the Molly Maguires to the Sitdowns* (Garden City, N.Y.: Doubleday, 1973).

On the labor movement and blacks, see Philip Foner, *Organized Labor and the Black Worker, 1619–1973* (New York: Praeger, 1974); Herbert Hill, "Black Dissent in Organized Labor," in J. Boskin and R. Rosenstone, eds., *Seasons in Rebellion: Protest and Radicalism in Recent America* (New York: Holt, Rinehart and Winston, 1972); F. Ray Marshall, *The Negro and Organized Labor* (New York: John Wiley & Sons, 1965); Julius Jacobson, ed., *The Negro and the American Labor Movement* (Garden City, N.Y.: Doubleday, 1968). On women and labor, see Barbara Mayer Wertheimer, *We Were There: The Story of Working Women in America* (New York: Pantheon, 1977).

8

The Organization
of the National Union

Among the various institutional organizations of the labor movement, the national (or international) union is the main center of power and authority. As we have seen, the importance of national unions was recognized by Sylvis as early as the 1850s and by Gompers and other leaders in the AFL; their effectiveness was demonstrated by the fact that they survived both the early attacks by employers and the mass movement of the Knights of Labor. Especially after the turn of the century, their strength increased in comparison with the state and local federations of labor, and they dominated both the AFL and the CIO. Although there have been some attempts to lessen autonomy within the AFL–CIO, the merged organization would be powerless if the nationals, especially the larger ones, were unwilling to work together.

The national union's source of strength is essentially its control, through either its national officers or its chartered locals, of the bargaining with employers on the terms and conditions of employment. The AFL–CIO bargains with employers only in the case of directly affiliated locals that are chartered by the federation rather than by a national union, and state federations of labor and city centrals do not act as bargaining agencies. At times several nationals or their locals will cooperate in negotiating with a common employer or with groups of employers, on either a temporary or a permanent basis, through joint councils such as those found in the construction, printing, and hotel industries, or through some form of coordinated bargaining. But the ultimate authority for participation in such arrangements, for the determination of collective bargaining policy, and hence for approval of the terms of the labor agreement, still resides within the national unions.

NUMBER AND SIZE

In 1974 there were 175 national unions in the United States, 111 of which were affiliated with the AFL–CIO. The size of the nationals in terms of members ranged from the independent Teamsters, the largest with nearly 2 million members, to the Siderographers, an AFL–CIO affiliate, with 18 members. The 10 largest nationals, each with a membership of 550,000 or more, claimed a total of 10 million workers in 1974 , nearly half (46.7%) of the reported 21.6 million union members. These included the independent Teamsters and Automobile Workers and eight AFL–CIO unions: the Steelworkers; Electrical Workers (IBEW); Machinists; Carpenters; Retail Clerks; Laborers; State, County and Municipal Workers; and Service Employees. An additional 10 unions with a membership of 300,000 to 525,000 accounted for another 4 million members. (See Table 8–1.) In short, the 20 largest national unions (11.3% of the 175 total) had nearly two-thirds of the total union membership. Membership has long been concentrated in a relatively few nationals. Although there is some evidence that concentration has been increasing in recent years, the top six national unions have accounted for about a third of all union members since the early 1950s; in 1972 the percentage was 35.1.

Of course the size of a national union is not necessarily a measure of its power, either economically or politically. A national may occupy a highly strategic bargaining position in an industry or firm and yet have relatively few members: a strike of the Flight Engineers International Association, with 4,-000 members, for example, can force a shutdown of major airlines. Yet size does have a decided effect on the government of a union, on the relationship of individual members to their unions and jobs, and on the formulation of bargaining policy. Furthermore, the number of members affects the union's voice and voting strength in the federations on the national, state, and local levels. And the greater revenues from dues in the larger unions result in expanded programs, greater ability to finance organizing campaigns, and more staff support for effective bargaining, particularly with large firms.

Most members of national unions belong to locals that are directly chartered by the nationals. In 1974, there were some 70,000 local unions affiliated with American national unions, of which 5,000 were located outside the United States. A few nationals—primarily in the entertainment industry and the public sector, where activities were confined to a single geographical area—had no locals at all. The recent trend in the total number of local unions has been downward, probably reflecting the consolidation of small locals in the interests of greater administrative efficiency. However, though some large locals may technically encompass tens of thousands of workers, they are usually divided into smaller, sublocal units.

GOVERNMENT OF THE NATIONAL UNION

Each national is organized in accordance with is own constitution and bylaws. Typically there are three primary structural elements: the national of-

Table 8-1

National Unions and Employee Associations Reporting 100,000 Members or More, 1974[a]

Organization	Members	Organization	Members
Unions:		*Unions—Continued*	
Teamsters (Ind.)	1,973,000	Painters	211,000
Automobile Workers		Rubber	191,000
(Ind.)	1,545,000	Iron Workers	182,000
Steelworkers	1,300,000	Retail, Wholesale	180,000
Electrical (IBEW)	991,000	Oil, Chemical	177,000
Machinists	943,000	Fire Fighters	172,000
Carpenters	820,000	Textile Workers	167,000
Retail Clerks	651,000	Electrical (UE) (Ind.)	163,000
Laborers	650,000	Sheet Metal	161,000
State, County	648,000	Transport Workers	150,000
Service Employees	550,000	Bricklayers	148,000
Meat Cutters	525,000	Transit Union	140,000
Communications		Boilermakers	138,000
Workers	499,000	Bakery	134,000
Hotel	452,000	Printing and Graphic	129,000
Teachers	444,000	Maintenance of Way	119,000
Operating Engineers	415,000	Typographical	111,000
Ladies' Garment	405,000	Woodworkers	108,000
Clothing Workers	350,000	Government (NAGE)	
Musicians	330,000	(Ind.)	([b])
Paperworkers	301,000	Graphic Arts	100,000
Government (AFGE)	300,000	Federal Employees	
Electrical (IUE)	298,000	(NFFE) (Ind.)	100,000
Postal Workers	249,000		
Transportation Union	238,000	*Associations:*	
Railway Clerks	235,000	Education Association	1,470,000
Letter Carriers	232,000	Civil Service (NYS)	207,000
Plumbers	228,000	Nurses Association	196,000
Mine Workers (Ind.)	220,000	Police	147,000
		California	106,000

[a] Based on estimates to the U.S. Bureau of Labor Statistics. All unions not identified as independent (Ind.) are affiliated with the AFL–CIO.

[b] Not Available.

Source: U.S. Department of Labor, Bureau of Labor Statistics, *Directory of National Unions and Employee Associations, 1975,* Bulletin 1937 (Washington, D.C.: U.S. Government Printing Office, 1977), p. 65.

ficers and staff, officers of the locals, and the members, known as the rank and file. In addition, a fourth element—the intermediate body, often called the "regional" or "district office" or "joint board"—has become increasingly important. The general convention is the ultimate source of authority within every national.

The Convention

As a legislative body, the convention has the power to lay down policies, elect officers, and amend the constitution. Convention delegates are representatives of the union's membership chosen in accordance with procedures specified by the constitution and bylaws; usually they are elected from the locals, with the number of delegates from each local varying according to its size. Authority flows from the individual members through the local delegates to the convention, which grants to the national officers the power to carry out the will of the majority between conventions.

The planning of each convention and the supervision of its work are usually done by the national officers. They have a major role in the selection of the various committees, such as the important committee on credentials (which certifies that delegates have been properly elected) and the committee on resolutions. The officers also prepare and present statements on the union's goals and collective bargaining strategies for the coming year, and they are likely to be seeking reelection. At the same time, the convention serves as a forum for the delegates to present problems, criticisms of national leadership, or suggestions for new policies. Delegates also informally get together with old friends, exchange views, and in general acquire a wider understanding of the problems of their union, trade, and industry.

Conventions are expensive, and some unions try to minimize costs by holding fewer of them. Nonetheless, most nationals recognize the advantages of conventions as a way of keeping the membership in touch with the union's problems at the national level and of informing the national officers about rank-and-file opinion. About half the nationals hold conventions every year or two years (see Table 8–2). Some unions conduct polls of the entire member-

Table 8–2
Frequency of Conventions, 175 National Unions, 1974

Frequency of Convention	Number of Nationals
Every year or less	41
Every 2 years	45
Every 3 years	19
Every 4 years	37
Every 5 years	25
No conventions[a]	3
Other, or information not available	5
Total	175

[a] These were small, unaffiliated unions with activities in a single area or occupation.

Source: U.S. Department of Labor, *Directory of National Unions and Employee Associations*, 1975 p. 79.

ship, known as the "referendum." In 1972 reports from 171 national unions revealed that the use of the referendum in the election of the president was prescribed in the constitutions of 36 unions, while 135 called for election by the convention. Some unions use referendums as a means of initiating new legislation or for obtaining membership opinions on policy matters.

The National Officers

The officers and the executive board of a national union are its responsible administrators. They carry out the convention's policies, and under certain circumstances they can make decisions on new policy that must be acted upon between conventions. The full-time officers, usually a president and a secretary-treasurer, have responsibility over the day-to-day administration of union affairs, while the executive board, meeting at frequent intervals throughout the year, acts as a board of directors or a parliamentary cabinet. Members of the executive board other than the president and secretary-treasurer usually include the elected vice presidents; others may be appointed. The president, as the foremost figure among the officers, receives the highest salary; by and large, the larger the union, the higher the salary. The president's term of office usually varies from one to five years, the maximum allowed under the Landrum-Griffin Act. For about half of the union presidents the term is three years. National officers tend to be reelected more frequently than officers of locals.

Some national presidents appear to be almost permanent fixtures. John L. Lewis, for example, served as president of the United Mine Workers for 41 years—from 1919 to his voluntary retirement in 1960. In recent years, however, there seems to be more turnover among union presidents. In the decade 1961 to 1971, 133 out of 174 national unions, or nearly three-fourths, changed presidents (see Table 8–3). To a large extent this situation reflected the fact that the leaders who had risen to union presidencies during the great upheaval of the 1930s and 1940s were at last stepping down. In the two-year period from 1969 to 1971, for example, only 3 of the 47 changes in union presidency were the result of election defeats; most of the rest were due to retirement, resignation, or death.[1]

The executive board of a national union is usually designed to give representation to the different interests within the union. The members of the board other than the full-time officers may be elected (or appointed) to represent different geographical areas of the country or they may be identified with different industrial areas with which the union is concerned.

---

[1] See U.S. Department of Labor, *Directory of National Unions and Employee Associations, 1971*, Bulletin 1750 (Washington, D.C.: U.S. Government Printing Office, 1972), p. 59.

Table 8-3
Year in which Presidents of National Unions in 1971 Were First Elected to Office[a]

Year	Total Number of Unions	Total Number of Members (thousands)	Number of AFL–CIO Unions	Number of Unaffiliated Unions
Total	174	20,695	114	60
1934–40	4	174	2	2
1941–45	6	733	5	1
1946–50	6	483	5	1
1951–55	6	1,547	5	1
1956–60	19	1,747	15	4
1961–65	37	4,657	24	13
1966–69	47	5,464	30	17
1970–71	49	5,890	28	21

[a] As reported by national labor unions and supplemented for 1971 by reports of new officers elected. In addition, those unions that merged or became defunct as of December 1971 were excluded. Changes in affiliation were also taken into account.

Source: U.S. Department of Labor, *Directory of National Unions and Employee Associations, 1971*, Bulletin 1750 (Washington, D.C.: U.S. Government Printing Office, 1972), p. 94.

In addition to the full-time officers and executive board, such administrative personnel as regional directors, international representatives, and organizers are usually appointed by the president of the union. The staff functions performed by the national office vary with the size of the union, the role of the national office in collective bargaining, the extent of assistance provided to locals, and the types of social benefits the union tries to promote. In some nationals there are legal staffs, professional economists and statisticians, and extensive publication and educational departments.

The main functions of the national officers relate to organizing new workers, bargaining directly with employers or assisting locals in their bargaining, and administrating union affairs. Not only do the national officers have control of the staff of organizers, but they also plan and direct campaigns, decide on tactics, and determine the jurisdictions within the limits of the constitution and bylaws. The responsibility for the success or failure of every major organizing campaign clearly lies with the national officers, and a president who consistently had to report organizing failures at the regular conventions would be exposed to unfavorable criticism from the membership.

The national officers usually have responsibility for negotiations with employers who bargain on an industrywide basis or who have several plants located in different geographical areas. Furthermore, a national officer or an international representative may participate as an adviser to the local in its bargaining, briefing the members on the phrasing, legality, and effectiveness of proposed clauses of the contract, giving background information on the economics of the firm and the industry, and discussing negotiation tactics, the desirability of bargaining objectives, and attitudes toward employers' counteroffers.

National officers are also responsible for the protection of the rights of members in accordance with the constitution and bylaws, and the judicial processes for adjusting disputes concerning these rights are often under their control. When a union member complains that his treatment by local union officers or other officials has violated his rights, his charges are usually first heard by a local board. Appeals from the decision of that board, however, are often made to the national officers or to some national board established by them.

National officers grant as well as suspend local charters. Suspension may take place when investigation reveals such violations as financial irregularity, collusion of local officers with employers, or acts inconsistent with the policies of the national union as a whole. On occasion a local is placed under direct supervision of the national union—an arrangement known as "trusteeship"—pending a reorganization of its affairs; the problems raised by this aspect of the national officers' functions will be discussed in a later section on union democracy.

Intermediate Bodies

The importance of union organization on the level of districts or regions within the national organization larger than the locals seems to be increasing. This is especially true in those nationals whose national officers wish to exercise greater control over locals, to standardize procedures or policies within a wider area than that of the local, or to promote district organizing campaigns. The intermediate offices may serve simply to extend the power of the national officers, with district leaders appointed by the union president.

Some intermediate organizations have developed in response to pressures from locals for a broader organization to handle their common problems. The organization of "conferences" within the Teamsters, for example, first evolved from attempts to organize "over-the-road" drivers from one city to another. The success of the conference system stemmed from the increasing importance of intercity trucking. It was the Western Conference of Teamsters, first established by Dave Beck in 1937 and finally recognized as part of the official union structure in 1947, that served as Beck's stepping stone to the presidency of the Teamsters in 1953. Jimmy Hoffa rose to president in 1957 from the chairmanship of the increasingly powerful Central States Conference of Teamsters and of the Central States Drivers' Council.

Members of the United Steelworkers of America were given a greater voice in wage negotiations with the introduction of the conference system in 1966; it replaced a Wage Policy Committee, consisting of members from various industries, which drew up a union-wide Wage Policy Statement. Under the new system, conferences for each of the four major industries—steel, containers, aluminum, and copper—were designed to bring more workers into the preparation of wage demands and to give the workers in each industry the right to make their own decisions to strike.

The complexity of union structure may be further increased by other types of subnational organizations—such as departments of skilled workers or professional and office workers—in order to enable these groups to work out special bargaining demands peculiar to their needs. As unions grow in size and acquire a greater diversity of members, the greater becomes the need to give representation to those interests, still coordinating them in order to avoid the loss of bargaining power that a fragmented union structure would entail. Intermediate union bodies can often achieve these results.[2]

Local Unions

The local union is in most cases the basic unit of the national. When workers join a "union," they become members of a specific local. Here they come into contact with fellow unionists, are exposed to union viewpoints, and take part in the discussions of business at the local meeting. Though each local is chartered by the national union and its operation must be in accord with the national constitution, bylaws, and directives, it has its own officers and bylaws and can take independent action on various matters, depending upon the particular national union of which it is a part.

Most local unions have a president, a vice president, a secretary, and a treasurer, besides various standing committees. The officers of smaller unions are likely to perform their union duties after working hours; if they have given up their regular jobs for full-time union work, they usually receive salaries lower than those of national officials and closer to the wages of the rank and file. (The president of one local union received the equivalent of the highest scale in the trade plus one dollar a day.)

Another type of officer, the business agent, or "walking delegate," is found in locals organized by area rather than by plant, such as those in the building and metal trades. As a full-time elected official, the business agent deals directly with employers, keeps a check on wages and employment practices, and refers the workers of his local to jobs. Because of his responsibilities and interests, he is likely to be more important to the welfare of members than the president of the local.

[2] See Arnold R. Weber, "Stability and Change in the Structure of Collective Bargaining," American Assembly, *Challenges to Collective Bargaining* (Englewood Cliffs, N.J.: Prentice-Hall, 1967), pp. 13–36. For the early history of the Teamsters organization, see Robert D. Leiter, "The Relationship between Structure and Policy in the Teamsters Union," *Proceedings of the Tenth Annual Meeting*, Industrial Relations Research Association, New York, September 5–7, 1957, pp. 148–155.

The shop steward is a local union official, usually found in local organizations that cover large plants and therefore need representatives in various departments. A man who holds such a post hears all complaints and grievances of the local's members in his department. He is a full-time worker in the firm, like other members of the rank and file, although, if the employer agrees, he may have a greater degree of freedom to handle grievances and other union problems on company time.

One of the primary functions of the local is participation in collective bargaining. Although the national officers have in recent years had greater control of the bargaining process, the practice varies from industry to industry. In some instances the local's officers, or a special committee, represent the members in bargaining procedures; in negotiations with multiplant firms or on an industrywide basis, a local may send delegates to a special advisory board for the national bargaining committee. Whether the bargaining is local or national, the newly negotiated contract must usually be ratified by the members of a local before its terms can affect them. Even after the two-month strike between the UAW and General Motors in the fall of 1970, disputes over local issues between plant managements and local unions led to a number of additional strikes, some lingering on until the following year.

A second function of the local is control of the grievance procedure, or the handling of disputes between union and management in the interpretation of collective bargaining agreements. A worker who feels that a company action is contrary to the terms of the contract initiates a complaint with the union, and the shop steward, local president, or another union official then attempts to obtain satisfaction from the employer in accordance with some specified procedure of appeal.

The third major function of the local is the conducting of union business and the administration and enforcement of rules and regulations. Locals set dues and initiation fees, within the limitations determined by the nationals, and levy special fees and assessments. Collection of dues is ordinarily a function of the local, but a "checkoff," the collection of union dues by the employer through payroll deductions, is sometimes arranged. In certain craft unions where the objective of the local is to restrict the supply of workers in the trade, initiation fees may be high to discourage new members, but local dues are not generally excessive. Taft estimated that on the whole monthly dues amounted to less than two hours of work.[3] They tend to be lower in the industrial unions, where the locals try to organize as many workers, skilled and semiskilled, as possible. Dues that appear to be relatively high often reflect the costs of special benefits available to members in the form of pensions, retirement centers, or medical and other aid.

[3] Philip Taft, *Structure and Government of Labor Unions* (Cambridge, Mass.: Harvard University Press, 1954), p. 81. Later studies lead to a similar estimate.

Many locals introduce restrictions on membership beyond the eligibility requirements defined by the nationals. Such limitations may refer to race, sex, political views, or citizenship; they are most likely to be found in the skilled craft or trade unions that seek to maintain their economic power by limiting the supply of labor or in those locals that believe that the presence of different groups would lead to dissension and possible disruption. At one time, some union constitutions specifically barred certain types of workers, such as blacks, from membership or placed them in segregated locals. Although formal exclusionary provisions have disappeared, informal discriminatory practices continue. In the craft unions blacks may not be admitted because they are unable to find a sponsor or because apprenticeship opportunities may not be available. Journeyman examinations may be manipulated. Racial discrimination is difficult to eliminate when the national union has no power, or will, to enforce desegregation[4] on a local that has no incentive to change.

UNION POLICY MAKING

Policy making within a union must be appraised in the light of both economic and political considerations. To the extent that a union can exert economic power by affecting the labor supply, wages, and adjustments to changing economic conditions, it is important to know what standards and guides are used in the formulation of policy. A particularly important question is whether the rank and file determine policy and effectively control its application or whether national officers impose their own preferences on members, using the union machinery both to limit opposition and to enhance their own position. From a political viewpoint, the policy issue is more complex than the usual question of the meaning of "union democracy." While the protection of individual workers' rights within the union is important in itself, Congress and the courts have accepted "free collective bargaining" as a matter of public policy and have provided for the legal certification of unions as bargaining agents that firms must legally respect. From such legislation it is only a short step to the view that union affairs should be run in accordance with standards of conduct acceptable to the public, and when such practices as racketeering, extortion, pilferage of funds, and misuse of election machinery are disclosed, the public feels an obligation to impose controls on the

---

[4] Several unions have acted against locals in order to enforce racial-equality provisions of their constitutions. The United Automobile Workers placed a large local in Memphis under receivership for its refusal to desegregate facilities at the local's office, and in another case it expelled a large local at Dallas for its refusal to admit blacks. Other unions that cracked down on southern locals on racial issues were the United Packinghouse Workers (UPWA) and the American Federation of Teachers (AFT). See Ray Marshall, *The Negro Worker* (New York: Random House, 1967), pp. 50–51.

internal operations of unions. In large part, this feeling led to the passage of the Landrum-Griffin Act of 1959. Similarly, when racially discriminatory practices become intolerable to society at large, unions must acquiesce in laws guaranteeing fair employment practices and civil rights, and adjust their actions accordingly.

The Union as a Political Organization

Although for some purposes unions can be viewed as organizations guided by the economic principle of seeking to maximize the income of members through negotiations with employers, the realities are much more complex. Workers in the same union often have interests that differ widely. Skilled workers may believe they should have preferential treatment over the unskilled; older workers may want higher deductions from wages for pensions than younger workers; racial disputes may flare up over seniority provisions and other job rights; members in small-town locals may wish to keep a wage differential to preserve jobs, while a big-city local believes the differential is undercutting theirs. The reconciliation of divergent points of view and the working out of compromises that must be made in order to formulate acceptable programs constitute the political life of unions.

Sometimes strains place a heavy burden on a union's political procedures. But if a union is to be effective in negotiating with employers, its programs, tactics, and strategy must rest fundamentally upon a workable consensus of the members, unimpaired by internal strife.

The process of policy formulation within a union is related to its internal structure. For the individual member, the union's key function is to help him or her in relationships with the employer. If that relationship is more or less satisfactory, the worker may feel little need to attend local meetings, to support union functions, or to be concerned about the activities of regional and national officers, whose connection with the affairs of the local seems remote. But when national officers are involved in collective bargaining negotiations affecting the rank and file, each member has an opportunity to judge the officers at first hand. Such judgment might be harsh if the members believe that they have been "sold out," that their specific interests have been ignored, or that they were kept out on strike longer than necessary because of some officer's objective that was not one of their primary concerns. A dissatisfied membership is always a threat to top union leadership. It may support factionalism within the national, embarrass the leadership by wildcat strikes or work stoppages unauthorized by proper union officials (usually in violation of the no-strike clauses of union-management contacts), or even bolt the national to join a rival union.

Since local officers are usually recruited from the ranks, receive wages close to those of the members, and must be reelected more frequently than the national officers, they are generally responsive to the wishes of the rank and file. The local president tends to see the world in much the same way as his or her constituents. On the other hand, the local leader does not usually wish to become *persona non grata* in the eyes of the national leaders, who can offer helpful advice and who have the ultimate power to revoke the charter of the local and legally to remove its officers and place it under trusteeship if they find violations of the constitution and bylaws. In view of the pressures that can be exercised from both above and below, the local officer must have, or must quickly acquire, considerable political skill in order to survive.

If regional officers are elected by locals in their region, they are in a similar position to that of the leaders of the locals, except that they are one step removed from rank-and-file sentiment. Regional officers motivated by a desire to enhance their own careers may find the office a useful base on which to build a political following. On the other hand, if the regional director is appointed by the national officers, the role is significantly changed: he or she serves as an emissary of the national officers—as their "eyes and ears"—and as a spokesperson for national policy.

National officers, who are concerned with the broader problems of relationships within the federation, with other nationals, and with employers, tend to find themselves insulated from the rank and file. Even those officials who have come up through the ranks may be unconcerned with members' day-to-day problems. Dealing with larger national firms and trade associations and top officials of government, national officers may feel more at ease in the surroundings of the high-salaried managerial class than in local meetings. Their horizons are wider than those of local officials, as they must consider policy proposals advanced by locals in terms of the welfare of the national union as a whole.

Democratic Procedures and Safeguards

The government of a union raises questions concerning the extent to which union policies are sensitive to the wishes of the rank and file. All too often the internal political procedures of a union are characterized by low attendance at meetings, no organized opposition to union leadership, and little turnover of elected officials. Although this pattern of political activity can be interpreted as an indication of a lack of democracy within a union, it does not in itself indicate that union policies are not in accord with members' wishes. For example, membership apathy and the return of some elected officials year after year may reflect satisfaction with their actions and policies. The lack of a two-party system within unions probably reflects, not a failure of democracy, but the fact that unions have one major purpose—to represent workers in bargaining with employers—and that, like other private organizations, they find a split in their ranks over specific programs and policies a source of weakness and ineffectiveness.[5]

Although it is not possible to distinguish by appearances a union that democratically reflects the interests of its members from one where effective control is in the hands of officers who obtain rubber-stamp support from the rank and file, it is possible to determine whether the procedures of government within the union are democratic, whether they are protected from abuse and faithfully followed, and whether there are safeguards for the protection of the rights of dissident union members. Specifically, this procedural test of democracy within a union would require that the union's constitution provide proper procedures for the nomination and election of officers, that the rules be followed in practice, and that the judicial process within the union give protection to members who wish to appeal union rulings against their interests.

Elections   Under the Landrum-Griffin Act of 1959,[6] which established certain standards for democratic procedures within unions, national officers must be elected at least every five years "by secret ballot among members in good standing or at a convention of delegates chosen by secret ballot," local officers at least every three years by secret ballot, and officers of intermediate bodies at least every four years by secret ballot or by representatives who have been elected by secret ballot. Where a union's constitution and bylaws are not in conflict with the law, they will determine the lawful procedure for democratic elections. If a member feels the free-election guarantees have been violated, and if no satisfaction is obtained within a three-month period through the union's appeals procedure, he or she may file a complaint with the Secretary of Labor, who after investigation may bring civil action in court to set aside an illegal election and hold a new one.

The national leadership was overturned in two well-publicized cases arising under this law. One was a 1964 challenge to James B. Carey, president of the International Union of Electrical Workers (IUE) by Paul Jennings, an executive director of the union's New York and New Jersey district. The reported results of the referendum-election showed that Carey had won by 2,200 votes. When an investigation of election irregularities by the Department of Labor revealed that Jennings was the victor by over 23,000 votes, Carey resigned.

The other case involved the United Mine Workers. In a 1969 election Joseph A. Yablonski challenged the union president, W. A. (Tony) Boyle. After

[5] The International Typographical Union is one of the few national unions to have had a long history of an effective two-party system. For a brief summary, see S. M. Lipset, "The Two Party System in the ITU," in Jack Barbash, ed., *Unions and Union Leadership, Their Human Meaning* (New York: Harper, 1959), pp. 149–158.

[6] The Landrum-Griffin Act is discussed in chapter 12.

Yablonski was found murdered, along with his wife and daughter, the Department of Labor discovered widespread violations of election procedures, and conducted a new election. This 1972 contest was won by Arnold Miller, who had replaced Yablonski as the candidate of the rank-and-file reform group, Miners for Democracy.

Judicial Procedure   The internal judicial processes of unions are important in protecting the rights of members from arbitrary action by officers of the union. These processes have sometimes been singled out as an inadequate feature of union government. Problems arise because unions, as voluntary organizations, have the power to fine, penalize, or expel members who do not abide by union rules.[7] Most unions penalize such offenses as slandering officers, aiding competing unions, violating union rules, and engaging in unauthorized strikes. Although the procedure varies from one union to another, most union constitutions provide that a member charged with an offense against the union will be tried before a special board at the local level. Its decision may be appealed to a higher board, with the last step usually being the national convention, where the ruling is final and binding.

Because the appeal machinery is set up by union officers, the charge has been made that the judges in union discipline cases are likely to be the prosecutors as well. Although Taft's study of eight national unions indicated that their judicial process gave satisfactory protection to individual rights,[8] some unions have been highly sensitive to such charges and have organized judiciary systems that seem to be independent and autonomous. A few unions have developed a new approach: an independent appeals review board made up of impartial nonunion members. The Upholsterers' Union adopted such a board in 1953, and the United Automobile Workers set up a Public Review Board in 1957; other unions adopting similar procedures include the United Packinghouse Workers and the American Federation of Teachers.[9] According to the procedure of the UAW, the process of an appeal is as follows:

> Except in cases where direct appeal to the international executive board is specifically permitted by the constitution, a member's complaint against any action, decision, or penalty of his local union must first be passed upon by the membership of his local; if he is dissatisfied with this decision, he may appeal, within thirty days, to the international executive board; if he is still dissatisfied, he may appeal, within an additional thirty days, either to the UAW convention, which meets

---

[7] The Taft-Hartley Act prevents expulsion of a member from a union where union membership is a requirement for employment—that is, in a union shop—except for failure to pay dues.

[8] Taft, *Structure and Government of Labor Unions.*

[9] John Hutchinson, *The Imperfect Union: A History of Corruption in American Trade Unions* (New York: Dutton, 1970), pp. 376–378.

biennially, or to the Public Review Board, but not to both. The decision of the Public Review Board is final and binding.[10]

Under the Landrum-Griffin Act, certain safeguards against improper disciplinary action were provided. The union member may not be "fired, suspended, expelled or otherwise disciplined except for nonpayment of dues" unless he has been "(A) served with written specific charges; (B) given a reasonable time to prepare his defense; (C) afforded a full and fair hearing." The union member may also institute court action against a labor organization for infringement of rights. The worker must first exhaust the union procedures for a hearing, but does not have to wait more than four months before seeking administrative or court relief (Section 101 [4]).

Corruption and Racketeering

The capture and misdirection of certain unions for corrupt ends were, as we have seen, a major concern to the AFL–CIO in the early years of the merger. The exposure of such practices by the Senate Committee on Improper Practices of Labor and Management in the three-year period from 1957 to 1959 was a prime factor leading to the passage of the Landrum-Griffin Act of 1959.

While most unions have been able to prevent the infiltration of criminal elements, the record of unsavory acts in some unions is a long one and raises questions concerning the causes and cures of racketeering as related to the internal government of unions in general.

What are the different forms that corruption and racketeering may take? First, there are the temptations for personal enrichment of union leaders offered by the flow of funds through dues and initiation fees and by the accumulation of assets in pension and other funds. Corrupt union leaders may also indulge in various other practices, from running away with the union treasury to more complex arrangements involving free loans, kickbacks on union purchases, or use of funds for private purposes. Malefactors can cover their acts by taking advantage of membership apathy and of lax enforcement of simple financial checks.[11] The line between illegal and legal acts may be a

---

[10] Quoted in Jack Stieber, *The UAW Public Review Board: An Examination and Evaluation* (Labor and Industrial Relations Center, Michigan State University, 1960–61), Reprint Series No. 35, p. 6.

[11] James R. Hoffa, the former president of the Teamsters, was charged with a number of crimes, including obtaining loans improperly from the union's pension funds, diverting union funds to his personal use, and demanding improper payments from employers. Although Hoffa was found guilty of attempting to bribe a juror and sentenced in 1967, his trial on improper payments resulted in a hung jury. President Richard M. Nixon commuted his sentence in December 1971, with the provision that Hoffa could not hold office until 1980. In July 1975 Hoffa disappeared under suspicious circumstances; he is believed to have been murdered.

tenuous one if corrupt leaders can promote their own pecuniary gain through a high salary and an unlimited expense account. Moreover, corruption can readily spread within a union, not only by emulation, but also by the use of bribes and coercion.

Racketeering, which often goes hand in hand with corrupt practices in a union, refers to the extortion from employers of money or other benefits. Seeking personal enrichment, racketeers turn upon employers and force payment from them by threats of personal violence, strikes, property damage, or wage increases. After World War I several racketeers in the building trades unions in New York City sold "strike insurance" to contractors; they, along with a certain number of employers, were later given court sentences for establishing a monopoly over parts of the industry. In the 1930s William Bioff, who had gained control of the Motion Picture Operators Union, received substantial payoffs from theater owners and Hollywood magnates by threatening to shut down motion picture theaters; in 1941, he and George E. Browne, the union's president, were indicted for extorting $1.5 million. Since World War II extortion tactics have been revealed on the New York Docks, among a variety of Teamsters locals, in the building trades, and in other fields. Evidence disclosed, for example, that New York newspaper publishers had made payoffs in order to maintain deliveries.

It has often been pointed out that, as voluntary associations, unions tend to reflect, for better or worse, the habits and mores of the larger society of which they are a part. Exposures of corruption in government and industry indicate that the problem is not confined to unions. Racketeering as a form of cartelization may even bring stability to a highly competitive industry. There may be other factors involved as well. It is sometimes charged that corruption and racketeering are found predominately among the business type of unions, where leaders are committed solely to the gains of their members by whatever means are necessary. The means are generally legal but there is a temptation to slip into illegal acts, particularly if the union's internal controls are weak. By contrast, social unionists—those who believe that unions should play a role as a democratic counterforce in a society dominated by corporate power—tend to demand exemplary behavior on the part of their officials. (Most racketeering problems have arisen in the former AFL craft unions, while the CIO industrial types have been relatively, although not entirely, free of such charges.) Philip Taft, however, has defended business unionism on the grounds that it cannot be considered the root cause of the problem; many such unions have been untouched by scandals, and they have promoted collective bargaining as "a worthy social objective."[12] The important point is

---

[12] Philip Taft, *Corruption and Racketeering in the Labor Movement*, Bulletin 38, 2nd ed. (Ithaca, N.Y.: New York State School of Industrial and Labor Relations, Cornell University, 1970), p. 23.

that when criminal elements take over a union the casualties are, first, the democratic process within the union and then the interests of the workers themselves.

Discrimination Against Minorities and Women

While the Landrum-Griffin Act attempts to promote democratic procedures in unions, Title VII of the Civil Rights Act of 1964 has implications not only for union procedures but also for the results of union policies, even if democratically determined. Title VII bans discrimination in employment because of race, color, religion, sex, or national origin, for employers of 25 workers or more engaged in an industry in interstate commerce. The law established the Equal Employment Opportunity Commission (EEOC), which receives complaints and tries to settle disputes by persuasion; the more powerful remedy is that any aggrieved parties, and the Attorney General, may bring civil actions in federal court for damages.

Labor organizations are affected by the law in several ways. They cannot discriminate by excluding or expelling individuals from their organization, or from training programs over which they have sole or joint control—Sections 703(c) and 703(d). Unions also must not discriminate in hiring halls or job referrals. They may become subject to Title VII actions if they initiate actions in collective bargaining that are ruled discriminatory. Suits may be filed if unions maintain separate seniority lists designed to prevent women or minorities from acquiring justifiable job rights. In cases where the union discriminates by refusing to represent certain groups in the bargaining process, the remedy is with the National Labor Relations Board and not with the procedures under Title VII. Similarly, the problem of union discrimination against groups claiming that the union leaders and program do not adequately represent their views would come under the requirements of the Landrum-Griffin Act relating to the rights of the union members.

The most successful case so far under Title VII resulted in a massive lump-sum payment of $15 million in 1973 to 13,000 women and 2,000 male minority workers by the American Telephone and Telegraph Company in compensation for discriminatory actions. The company also agreed to give immediate raises to some 36,000 workers and to set goals for greater participation of such groups within the employment structure. The fact that the leading union in the firm, the Communications Workers of America (CWA), had supported the company's position in the dispute indicates the gap that may exist between union policy and public policy on social issues. In a case involving unions as well as employers, the Department of Justice filed charges in 1974 against Trucking Employers, Inc. (a bargaining association of many trucking companies) and the Teamsters and Machinists unions that minorities had been discriminated against in employment and in advancement to better jobs. A consent decree provided for lump-sum payments, improvements in the percentage of minority employment in certain job classifications, and institution of training programs where necessary.

Although unions are essentially voluntary organizations, it is clear that their actions and behavior have implications with respect to social policy, and that the public insists that certain standards be met. Greater regulation and control of internal union affairs seems to be inescapable.

Both blacks and women have tried to make their influence felt in the union

AFFIRMATIVE ACTION PROGRAMS AND THE PHILADELPHIA PLAN

After passage of the Civil Rights Act of 1964, President Lyndon B. Johnson in 1965 issued Executive Order 11246. It required bidders on government contracts to formulate and follow affirmative action programs in order to "ensure that applicants are employed, and that employees are treated during employment, without regard to their race, color, religion, sex or national origin." Charged with administration of the order, the Secretary of Labor established the Office of Federal Contract Compliance (OFCC) to issue guidelines and oversee such contracts. Similar rules apply to federally assisted construction work.

While the OFCC favors voluntary affirmative action programs on an area basis in construction work, this approach does not always produce results. In the Philadelphia area, hearings investigated minority group employment in the construction industry in a five-county region. They revealed that minority representation was 30 percent in unskilled occupations, while in six skilled crafts it was only 1 percent. This imbalance was found to be the result of unions' exclusionary policies. When a voluntary agreement could not be reached, a plan was adopted in 1969. It called for an increase in minority employment over a period of several years in the six skilled crafts—ironworkers, plumbers and pipefitters, steamfitters, electrical workers, sheet-metal workers, and elevator construction workers—in accordance with a specific time schedule.

In a review of the plan after five years, it was found that minority employment in the six crafts had risen to 21 percent of total manhours worked during the year 1973, a level higher than the goal that had been previously set. Nonetheless, the plan had certain limitations. It applied to federally funded projects and not to private construction activities. It had no provisions for the recruitment and training of minority craft workers. Many contractors were not in compliance. And union membership for minorities could not be assured because unions did not fall under the executive order.

On balance, the impact of the plan was beneficial. The plan stimulated voluntary cooperation among contractors, unions, and minorities in other cities to increase minority employment. Where voluntary agreements failed, the federal government has the authority to impose affirmative action programs. That authority has been upheld by the courts.

movement. With low representation in leadership positions, blacks have supported rank-and-file caucuses in the Steelworkers union and the UAW in the hopes of stimulating a greater union militancy on behalf of minority workers. Women trade union members from 58 unions have established a national Coalition of Labor Union Women (CLUW) to work for women's rights within the labor movement.

Centralization and Bureaucracy

One of the clear-cut trends within American national unions has been increasing centralization of decision making at the national level and the decline of autonomy of the local unit. This development underlies much of the discussion of the loss of democracy within national unions.

The factors that have contributed to concentration of power at the top levels of the national unions are related to the development of bargaining strategy and the growth of specialized union services and functions.

Bargaining Strategy A union tends to adapt to the economic pressures and prerequisites of collective bargaining that are governed in large part by the nature of the industry with which it deals. In negotiating with large corporations, especially with those having a number of plants in different areas, a union is likely to find that bargaining solely at the local level weakens its strength because of the duplication of effort at a series of plants; the union's power is enhanced if the bargaining process is centralized at the national level, so that all the resources of the union can be concentrated on the negotiation of one contract covering workers in all plants. Where one or several large corporations set the wage pattern for the industry as a whole, the national's control of the bargaining process is essential in order to secure the best possible terms.

In industries characterized by many small firms, the extent of competition among the firms may be decisive in determining the degree of centralization of the bargaining process. If the competing firms are concentrated in one city, the most effective unit may be a local union that is organized on a similar citywide basis or an area council encompassing various locals within the city. It has already been pointed out that the growth of intermediate bodies, such as district and regional offices and conferences, may arise from the necessity of coordinating bargaining activities in an area wider than a particular city. Industrywide bargaining leads to centralization of bargaining strategy at the national level of the union and, as will be shown later, it is likely to take place in those industries where there are so many employers competing in a national market that a failure to standardize labor costs would lead to wage and price cutting. Agreements that do not completely cover such an industry may, in fact, be disastrous to the union's strength and its members' welfare if low-wage nonunionized employers can undersell the firms that meet the union's demands. The classic example of this situation was the great shift of the textile industry after World War II; after having long dominated New England's industrial structure, it moved to the South, where wages were lower and workers unorganized.

Specialized Services and Functions   Centralized bargaining also offers an opportunity for a union to use specially trained professional negotiators. The national officers are likely to be more skillful in bargaining than those of the local, and the national office can afford the services of staff advisors—lawyers, statisticians, accountants, and economists—to prepare briefs for collective bargaining sessions. The inclusion in collective bargaining agreements of such issues as pensions, supplementary unemployment compensation benefits, job evaluation and time-and-motion studies, and profit-sharing demands that experts participate in the formulation of union bargaining proposals and policy, and locals cannot be expected to hire such experts.

The trend toward long-term contracts covering two, three, or even more years intensified the pressure to employ professionals in preparations for negotiations. A union that makes an error in its forecasts may undermine its position with both the employer and its rank and file. The better the professional advice it receives in analyzing economic trends in the firm and industry, the less likely it is to agree to a contract that will bind its members to an undesirable position in the future.

SUMMARY

The national unions are the key bargaining units for workers in the United States: in 1974 there were 175 of them, of which 111 were affiliated with the AFL–CIO. Many are small in membership; others are large: the ten largest unions had nearly half of the more than 20 million union members in the United States.

Unions are like political organizations in that their ultimate power resides in their members, who usually express their wishes at a convention which members attend or to which they send delegates. Conventions approve policies and elect national officers. Other governmental units of unions include intermediate level organizations and the locals, with their officers.

Union policy formulation reflects the interplay of different interests within the organization. In recent years, both policies and procedures have been subject increasingly to outside public controls. Charges of racketeering and corruption resulted in the Landrum-Griffin Act of 1959, which set standards for union election procedures and safeguards for protecting members' rights. The 1964 Civil Rights Act prohibits discriminatory practices in terms of membership and certain bargaining policies.

In the industrial unions particularly, negotiations with large firms tend to centralize bargaining authority in the hands of the national officers. While this practice increases union effectiveness, it diminishes the participation of the rank and file in the bargaining process.

DISCUSSION QUESTIONS

1. What factors are important in determining union size?
2. The organizational structure of unions is democratic in that the rank and file has the ultimate power to elect officers, determine policies, and amend constitutions and bylaws. Is a trend toward increased powers of national union leaders compatible with democratic controls?
3. What types of safeguards can unions adopt to prevent seizure by racketeering elements?
4. Some unions have been criticized for too much democracy—especially when the rank and file rejects proposed collective bargaining settlements worked out by national leaders with a large firm or firms. Critics argue that national leaders know the economics of the industry and the particular situation better than the rank and file. Do you agree with this criticism? Why or why not?
5. In negotiations with management unions are concerned not only with workers' interests but also with resolving conflicting demands and interests among their own members. In what ways may internal differences of views affect a union's bargaining demands and strategies?
6. The internal judicial procedures established under union constitutions are designed to protect the rights of individual union members. What criticisms have been leveled against these systems? What types of protection for individual rights are provided by the Landrum-Griffin Act?
7. Internal union policies, such as those relating to sex and racial discrimination, have come increasingly under government regulation and supervision. Do you believe such regulation is an invasion of what should properly be considered the internal affairs of a private organization?

SELECTED READINGS

On internal union organization, in addition to Bok and Dunlop, see Jack Barbash, *American Unions: Structure, Government, and Politics* (New York: Random House, 1967); Marten Estey, *The Unions: Structure, Development, and Management,* 2nd ed. (New York: Harcourt Brace Jovanovich, 1976); William M. Leiserson, *American Trade Union Democracy* (New York: Columbia University Press, 1959); and Philip Taft, *The Structure and Government of Labor Unions* (Cambridge, Mass.: Harvard University Press, 1954). A summary of views on democracy in unions is found in Marten S. Estey et al., *Regulating Union Government* (New York: Harper & Row, 1964). On union corruption, see John Hutchinson, *The Imperfect Union: A History of Corruption in American Trade Unions* (New York: E. P. Dutton, 1970). On racial discrimination in unions, in addition to references cited at the end of chapter 7, see Benjamin W. Wolkinson, *Blacks, Unions, and the EEOC* (Lexington, Mass.: D. C. Heath, 1973).

PART THREE

Collective Bargaining and Government Controls

9

Collective Bargaining and Union Policies

THE NATURE OF COLLECTIVE BARGAINING

Collective bargaining is the joint determination and administration of wages and the terms of employment between a union representing the workers and the employer or representatives of a group of employers. It includes both the negotiation of a labor agreement (or contract) in which wages and other conditions and rules are agreed to and the administration and interpretation of those rules in day-to-day problems of the employment relationships between worker and employer. Employer 'recognition' of the union as representative of the workers is a prerequisite to collective bargaining.

From one point of view collective bargaining is a means of settling the question of the price at which workers are employed, while from another viewpoint it is a system of industrial jurisprudence.[1] It is clear that, though both these views are relevant to our understanding of collective bargaining, the first emphasizes economic issues and potential conflict between two parties, while the second stresses the continuous relationships between union and management and the compromises implicit in defining their respective rights and duties. These two perspectives on industrial relations are both pertinent to specific problems. The sale of labor, like that of any commodity, involves agreement over the conditions under which the transaction is to be

[1] There are still other ways of viewing collective bargaining. John R. Commons's approach treats it as a form of industrial government by which the unions place limitations on the arbitrary actions of employers and hence increase the liberty of the individual worker. Related to this approach is Selig Perlman's concept of job control (discussed above, ch. 6), in which collective bargaining amounts to a method of controlling scarce job opportunities through union rules. In contrast, Neil Chamberlain emphasizes that collective bargaining is an instrument of management. His view is that various managerial functions are implicit in a firm, and that collective bargaining is a device whereby these objectives are carried out. This does not mean that the union has control of the managerial functions nor that management has abdicated its functions. See Neil W. Chamberlain, *Collective Bargaining* (New York: McGraw-Hill, 1951), pp. 130ff.

made. Such conditions may be highly complex and detailed, however, and most collective bargaining agreements include decisions about wages and other economic benefits, rules governing such matters as hiring, layoffs, promotion, seniority, work rules, and machinery, and regulations pertaining to the position and role of the union. The complexity of such agreements stems from the complexity of the employee-employer relationship. The amount (including intensity) of work to be performed, the quality of the work, and the conditions under which it is to be performed are all explicitly and exactly stated in the agreements.

The collective bargaining agreement, unlike sales contracts, states the conditions under which a sale is to be made and is not in itself a contract for the sale of labor. In most cases the actual agreement to work is made by the individual worker and the employer, but any action taken by either party—hiring, discharge, promotion, reassignment, and so forth—must be in accord with the labor agreement. Where there is a closed shop or a hiring hall arrangement, the union, by supplying individual workers as requested, acts as an employment agent of the employer, but the employer has the responsibility of making the decision of whether or not to hire.

The phrase "industrial jurisprudence" was first used by Sumner Slichter, who wrote:

> Through the institution of the state, men devise schemes of positive law, construct administrative procedures for carrying them out, and complement both statute law and administrative rule with a system of judicial review. Similarly, laboring men, through unions, formulate policies to which they give expression in the form of shop rules and practices which are embodied in agreements with employers or are accorded less formal recognition and assent by management; shop committees, grievance procedures, and other means are evolved for applying these rules and policies; and rights and duties are claimed and recognized. When labor and management deal with labor relations analytically and systematically after such a fashion, it is proper to refer to the system as "industrial jurisprudence."[2]

Since the end product of collective bargaining is a body of working rules and laws accepted by both labor and management, the industrial "law" governing their relationship is derived from what is essentially the legislative process of negotiating the agreement. This "law" is then administered by the firm and the union. It is interpreted through the judicial process of the grievance procedure: when a worker feels that a rule has been unfairly applied, he or she can appeal, to union and management representatives and finally to a third party, for a decision that is final and binding; not only is the particular

---

[2] Sumner Slichter, *Union Policies and Industrial Management* (Washington: Brookings Institution, 1941), p. 1.

grievance settled, but the decision also becomes a recognized interpretation of the rule in question within the firm. Because contracts have a specified length of life, amendments can be made in the working rules of the enterprise through negotiation of a new contract when the old one expires. When there are no amendments, the old contract is simply renewed.

In the absence of collective bargaining, other procedures must be followed to determine the wages and other conditions of employment and the working rules. In private industry the nonunion employer unilaterally lays down rules, which may be as detailed as contracts negotiated by unions and management in defining occupational wage rates, pension plans, fringe benefits, layoff policies, seniority, and other rights. For governmental employment civil service rules and regulations codify the system of industrial jurisprudence; they can be altered by new legislation or, within limits, by administrative decisions. The essential characteristic of these systems, of course, is that individual workers cannot turn to a union if they feel that their interests are jeopardized. They must either rely on the good will of the employer or of such independent appeals boards as governmental agencies furnish or they must resign, or at least threaten to, and find another job. While it is true that there have always been certain governmental restrictions affecting industrial relations, American unions have strongly supported the procedure of dealing directly with the employer in "free" collective bargaining—that is, "free" from intervention by the government. In part the attitudes of voluntarism on the unions' side and laissez faire on the employers' have been inherited from their past experiences. But the concept of direct negotiation is also a reflection of the unions' emphasis on bread-and-butter objectives rather than on political ones. As we have seen, American unions in earlier times sought such goals as political reform, economic independence, and socialization of the economy. But the dominant objective of Gompers and the AFL unions and of those affiliated with the CIO was business unionism, in which economic gains were attained through collective bargaining.

At the same time it must be recognized that the government has been exerting an increasing influence both on the procedures of collective bargaining and on the determination of the terms and conditions of employment in the private sector. The government has over the years sought to protect the interests of those workers who wish to bargain collectively and the interests of the nonunion worker, the employer, and the public as well. The various laws lay down a complex web of rules within which collective bargaining is carried out, and sometimes take away the power of management and unions to arrange whatever contract provisions they desire. "Free" collective bargaining exists today in the sense that both parties play the game, even though the rules are tighter, but the referee is more watchful, and occasionally may carry the ball.

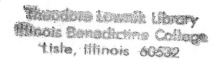

THE STRUCTURE OF COLLECTIVE BARGAINING

Extent

The prevalence of collective bargaining parallels the pattern of union membership, which differs greatly from industry to industry. The number of workers under collective bargaining agreements and the number of union members are not exactly the same, however, because a union may be the bargaining agent of a group of workers not all of whom are members, or because union members may not have obtained collective bargaining in their own shop. Unions may also list as members people who are unemployed or in the armed forces. In 1974, 172 nationals were estimated to have about 22.9 million workers under collective bargaining agreements. If the number of workers under agreements negotiated by other unions and employee associations is added, the estimate rises to approximately 26.2 million,[3] or over a third (37.2%) of the employees in nonagricultural establishments in the United States. The percentages vary greatly by industry (see Table 9–1), ranging from over 75 percent in transportation and contract construction to less than 25 percent in service and trade. By broad industry groups, about 60 percent of all production workers in manufacturing are under agreements, 25 percent in nonmanufacturing, and about one-fifth in government. If employee associations are also included, the ratio within the government sector rises to about 30 percent.[4]

The total number of collective bargaining agreements negotiated by American unions and employee associations in 1974 is estimated at over 200,-000. Some 195,000 agreements were negotiated by 172 national unions, although about 20,000 of these related to members located outside of the United States. The number of agreements negotiated by employee associations is estimated at about 12,500. Some unions negotiate many agreements: nine unions alone accounted for 130,000 agreements, or two-thirds of the total (see Table 9–2). These unions were the Teamsters, Printing and Graphic Union, Electrical Workers (IBEW), Retail Clerks, Operating Engineers, Machinists, Steelworkers, Meat Cutters, and Service Employees.[5] Some agreements cover many workers. In 1973 the Bureau of Labor Statistics reported that 2,237 major private, nonfarm collective bargaining agreements

[3] U.S. Department of Labor, Bureau of Labor Statistics, *Directory of National Unions and Employee Associations, 1975* (Washington, D.C.: U.S. Government Printing Office, 1977), pp. 77–79.

[4] U.S. Department of Labor, Bureau of Labor Statistics, *Directory of National Unions and Employee Associations, 1973* (Washington, D.C.: U.S. Government Printing Office, 1974), p. 81.

[5] U.S. Department of Labor, *Directory, 1975*, p. 79.

Table 9-1

Ranking of 35 Industries and Industrial Divisions by Degree of Union Organization

75 percent and over	25 percent to less than 50 percent
1. Ordnance	18. Printing, publishing
2. Transportation	19. Leather
3. Transportation equipment	20. Rubber
4. Contract construction	21. Furniture
	22. Machinery
50 percent to less than 75 percent	23. Lumber
5. Electrical machinery	24. Chemicals
6. Food and kindred products	25. Electric, gas utilities
7. Primary metals	
8. Mining	Less than 25 percent
9. Telephone and telegraph	26. Nonmanufacturing
10. Paper	27. Government
11. Petroleum	28. Instruments
12. Tobacco manufactures	29. Textile mill products
13. Apparel	30. State government
14. Fabricated metals	31. Local government
15. Manufacturing	32. Service
16. Stone, clay, and glass products	33. Trade
17. Federal Government	34. Agricultural and fishing
	35. Finance

Source: U.S. Department of Labor, Bureau of Labor Statistics, *Directory of National Unions and Employee Associations, 1975,* Bulletin 1937 (Washington, D.C.: U.S. Government Printing Office, 1977), pp. 70–71.

covered 1,000 or more workers each, for a total of 10.2 million workers.[6] In short, for this class of workers 1.4 percent of all agreements covered nearly half of all workers then under collective bargaining arrangements. The relative importance of these large contracts does not appear to have changed significantly in recent years.

Types of Bargaining Arrangements

The variety of bargaining relationships between unions and firms points up the complexity of the factors that must be analyzed. In terms of structure, bargaining for workers may be conducted by a local, a group of locals, the regional or national union, or a group of nationals. On the employer side, a firm may negotiate an agreement with a single union representing all of its workers (or at least those who are organized). An employer may also negotiate sepa-

[6] U.S. Department of Labor, *Wage Calendar, 1973,* Bulletin 1766 (Washington, D.C.: U.S. Government Printing Office, 1973), p. 1.

Table 9-2
Distribution of National Unions by Number of Basic Collective Bargaining Agreements with Employers, 1974[a]

Number of Agreements	All unions		Agreements		AFL-CIO		Unaffiliated	
	Number	Percent	Number	Percent	Unions	Agreements	Unions	Agreements
All unions[b]	172	100.0	194,726	100.0	108	146,589	64	48,137
No agreements[c]	4	2.3	—	—	—	—	4	—
Less than 25	53	30.8	344	.2	16	107	37	237
25 and under 100	25	14.5	1,336	.7	14	798	11	538
100 and under 200	23	13.4	3,126	1.6	19	2,591	4	535
200 and under 300	9	5.2	2,292	1.2	8	2,008	1	284
300 and under 500	11	6.4	4,234	2.2	8	3,231	3	1,003
500 and under 1,000	15	8.7	10,500	5.4	14	9,760	1	740
1,000 and under 2,000	15	8.7	18,889	9.7	14	17,389	1	1,500
2,000 and under 3,000	3	1.7	6,300	3.2	3	6,300	—	—
3,000 and under 5,000	5	2.9	17,750	9.1	4	14,450	1	3,300
5,000 and over	9	5.2	129,955	66.7	8	89,955	1	40,000

[a] The number of basic collective bargaining agreements does not include various supplements or pension, health, and welfare agreements as separate documents.

[b] Includes 36 unions for which the Bureau estimated the number of basic collective bargaining agreements. For 3 unions, the Hotel & Restaurant Employees and Bartenders International Union (AFL–CIO), the Amalgamated Clothing Workers of America (AFL–CIO), and the Pattern Makers League of North America (AFL–CIO), sufficient information was not available on which to base an estimate.

[c] Though 4 unions report an absence of a collective bargaining agreement, this situation is a permanent characteristic of only the National Association of Postal Supervisors (Ind.) and the National League of Postmasters of the United States (Ind.). Both of these unions represent government employees. The National Hockey League Players' Association (Ind.) and the National Football League Players Association (Ind.) usually have such agreements but were without one at the time these data were collected.

Source: U.S. Department of Labor, Bureau of Labor Statistics, *Directory of National Unions and Employee Associations, 1975,* Bulletin 1937 (Washington, D.C.: U.S. Government Printing Office, 1977), p. 78.

rately with several unions that represent different occupational groups and/or different areas. Or employers may join together to conduct multiemployer bargaining with one or several unions.

From a geographical point of view, a common form of agreement includes the workers in one plant of a given firm, which may or may not have plants elsewhere. A second type of agreement is negotiated between the union and the firm to cover several plants owned by the company; if the plants are located in different areas, however, such companywide bargaining usually leads the union to centralize its bargaining at the district, branch, or national level. In some cases, there may be a master agreement that provides for local supplements—negotiations on specific contract items within certain strict guidelines. The General Motors–UAW agreement, for example, provides for such arrangements. Thirdly, in multiemployer bargaining with one union, the geographical area may be local, regional, or nationwide.

Industrywide bargaining is a special case of multiemployer bargaining in that all or a significant percentage of the firms in a particular industry participate in the negotiations; important industries in which such bargaining has been conducted are bituminous coal, clothing, and railroads. Multiemployer agreements covering 1,000 or more workers are more common in nonmanufacturing than in manufacturing industries (see Table 9–3).

Unionwide bargaining should be distinguished from industrywide bargaining. In this relationship, the union first bargains with a leading firm in the industry and then turns to other firms in the same industry to negotiate similar agreements. This "follow-the-leader" practice, or pattern-setting, tends to be found in manufacturing industries where several large producers are dominant. In the automobile industry, the United Automobile Workers generally selects one of the "Big Three" automobile manufacturers—General Motors, Ford, or Chrysler—as its target company. When an agreement is obtained at one, the others accept the new terms in separate agreements. In the rubber industry, the United Rubber Workers of America selects as its target one of the "Big Four"—Goodyear, Firestone, Uniroyal, or Goodrich. In the steel industry, negotiations between the United Steelworkers and United States Steel Corporation had been the pattern-setter for many years, but since 1959 a committee of the major companies has negotiated with the union: the agreement reached is generally accepted with minor modifications by other firms in the industry.

Still another arrangement involves several unions, which cooperate in bargaining with one or more employers. The unions may agree among themselves to adhere to a common bargaining demand yet sign separate agreements, or they may jointly negotiate and sign a single agreement. (The latter practice is less prevalent.) In 1975 only 46 of 1,514 agreements covering 1,000 or more workers were negotiated by two or more AFL–CIO unions, or unions of different affiliations; the number of workers under such agree-

Table 9-3
Employer Unit by Industry (In agreements covering 1,000 workers or more, July 1, 1975)

| Industry | All Agreements | | Single Employer | | | | | | Multiemployer | |
| | | | Total | | Single Plant | | Multiplant | | | |
	Agree-ments	Workers	Agree-ments	Workers	Agree-ments	Workers	Agree-ments	Workers	Agree-ments	Workers
ALL INDUSTRIES	1,514	7,069,750	861	3,829,100	440	1,040,050	421	2,789,050	653	3,240,650
MANUFACTURING	815	3,750,950	661	3,002,750	390	930,850	271	2,071,900	154	748,200
Ordnance, Accessories	12	32,250	12	32,250	—	16,550	4	15,700	—	—
Food, kindred products	105	293,550	61	132,800	37	65,850	24	66,950	44	160,750
Tobacco manufacturing	8	26,350	8	26,350	4	11,000	4	15,350	—	—
Textile mill products	13	38,850	10	23,350	8	19,650	2	3,700	3	15,500
Apparel	50	435,400	11	26,600	1	1,300	10	25,300	39	408,800
Lumber, wood products	6	11,000	3	5,100	2	2,600	1	2,500	3	5,900
Furniture, Fixtures	21	33,450	12	19,150	7	9,300	5	9,850	9	14,300
Paper, allied products	53	101,600	47	87,950	33	50,800	14	37,150	6	13,650
Printing and publishing	23	47,200	5	5,950	4	4,950	1	1,000	18	41,250
Chemicals	47	108,750	47	108,750	40	88,850	7	19,900	—	—
Petroleum refining	13	25,000	12	23,000	3	5,650	9	17,350	1	2,000
Rubber and plastics	19	94,950	19	94,950	11	17,600	8	77,350	—	—
Leather products	14	39,800	7	24,500	4	12,500	3	12,000	7	15,300
Stone, clay, and glass	29	70,750	25	60,650	8	10,900	17	49,750	4	10,100
Primary metals	84	492,000	83	490,950	46	86,300	37	404,650	1	1,050
Fabricated metals	32	85,500	25	68,400	14	27,050	11	41,350	7	17,100
Machinery	90	278,950	88	275,750	59	111,000	29	164,750	2	3,200
Electrical machinery	95	437,550	93	433,650	60	257,550	33	176,100	2	3,900
Transportation equipment	84	1,058,300	79	1,034,800	37	123,800	42	911,000	5	23,500

Instruments	9	20,050	9	20,050	1	3,150	8	16,900	—	—
Miscellaneous Manufacturing	8	19,700	5	7,800	3	4,500	2	3,300	3	11,900
NONMANUFACTURING	699	3,318,800	200	826,350	50	109,200	150	717,150	499	2,492,450
Mining, crude petroleum, and natural gas	13	150,750	11	21,950	8	13,550	3	8,400	2	128,800
Transportation[a]	65	572,750	14	37,850	4	4,750	10	33,100	51	534,900
Communications	65	495,750	63	440,750	4	7,350	59	433,400	2	55,000
Utilities, electric and gas	47	134,100	46	132,850	13	40,250	33	92,600	1	1,250
Wholesale trade	12	22,250	2	2,550	1	1,200	1	1,350	10	19,700
Retail trade	92	298,750	41	120,100	5	9,700	36	110,400	51	178,650
Hotels and restaurants	42	187,900	4	6,000	4	6,000	—	—	38	181,900
Services	70	369,350	13	50,700	7	18,800	6	31,900	57	318,650
Construction	291	1,084,650	5	12,100	3	6,100	2	6,000	286	1,072,550
Miscellaneous Nonmanufacturing	2	2,550	1	1,500	1	1,500	—	—	1	1,050

[a] Excludes railroads and airlines.

Source: U.S. Department of Labor, Bureau of Labor Statistics, *Characteristics of Major Collective Bargaining Agreements, July 1, 1975,* Bulletin 1957 (Washington, D.C.: U.S. Government Printing Office, 1977), p. 12.

ments was about 180,000,[7] or less than 3 percent of the total under such agreements.

Unions may find themselves at a disadvantage in dealing with leading firms. In recent years, the merger movement in American industry has strengthened management's hand not only in its acquisition of greater financial resources but also in its expansion into a variety of product lines. The modern conglomerate, producing for many different product markets, is less vulnerable than a more limited industry when breakdowns halt union negotiations.

One type of union response to the large, multiproduct firm has been the development of coordinated, or coalition, bargaining, first recommended as a major policy by the Industrial Union Department (IUD) of the AFL–CIO in 1961. In this case an alliance of the unions in a particular firm can frame joint demands and form a common front in negotiations. This procedure was used in 1967 in the copper industry; a coalition of 26 unions, headed by the United Steelworkers, successfully won companywide bargaining, in place of negotiations at the local level, for three separate branches of the firms involving copper mining, lead and zinc mining, and metals fabrication. In 1966, 11 unions coordinated their bargaining with General Electric, although each union continued to sign separate agreements with the firm. The automobile workers and the machinists have cooperated in bargaining in the aerospace industries.

DYNAMICS OF THE BARGAINING STRUCTURE

One of the basic factors determining the geographical area of collective bargaining is the union's desire to standardize wages and other terms of the labor contract. As shown by the Webbs's discussion of the common rule and by Commons's analysis of union growth (see chapter 6), standardization eliminates competition and prevents undermining of the desired wage and work standards by lower-paid workers. Within one shop or plant the labor agreement standardizes wages and other factors for all workers within specific occupational grades.[8]

Standardization of rates of pay beyond the confines of a particular plant or

---

[7] U.S. Department of Labor, Bureau of Labor Statistics, *Characteristics of Major Collective Bargaining Agreements, July 1, 1975*, Bulletin 1957 (Washington, D.C.: U.S. Government Printing Office, 1977), p. 11. All large contracts are not included in this study.

[8] One feature of the nonunion shop is that individual workers often do not know what the others are being paid. Each worker is fearful that if wage information were revealed, any favorable arrangements would be lost because other workers would demand similar treatment. In union shops wages are a matter of common knowledge because they are standardized by occupational grade, length of experience, and similar factors.

firm may also be important to the union, however, depending on the areas of competition for specific types of labor and for specific products.[9] The area of labor competition may be local, regional, or national. A traditional example of competition within a local area is found in the construction industry, when contractors bid for local contracts on the one hand and for local labor on the other. If construction workers in the same locality did not have wage uniformity, some employers might obtain contracts at lower costs by hiring non-union or other lower-paid workers and could thus undermine the wage and job standards of contractors who recognized the union. A union can standardize wages locally by bargaining with each contractor separately for identical terms of employment, but, with a large number of contractors and the short duration of many jobs, it is easier for the union to negotiate a single agreement with all employers. Usually this is either a single contract between a local contractors' association and a single trade or a contract between a local building trades council representing all construction trades and a contractor or a contractors' association. In recent years, with the increased mobility of construction workers beyond the confines of a local labor market and with the growth of national contracting firms, these arrangements have become increasingly unsatisfactory; negotiations over certain provisions of contracts, including wages and pension funds, have been shifting to national levels.[10]

The extent of competition in the product market is also a relevant factor. If a firm's product market is relatively insulated from the effects of price changes by other firms, union workers in the firm will have little incentive to push for industrywide bargaining since lower wages elsewhere would not undermine their own standards. Where product competition is regional or nationwide, the union will attempt to extend the area of bargaining to "take wages out of competition." This is especially true where wages are a significant element in the cost of the product and where firms competitively produce the same product. If wages are a small part of total costs, interfirm wage standardization is not important; for example, since in chemicals wages amount to about 15 percent of value added (the value of products less the costs of purchased materials), a difference in wage rates would have only a minor effect on total costs. In bituminous coal, on the other hand, labor costs at one time amounted to about two-thirds of the total cost, so that a 10 per-

[9] Standardization of wages does not necessarily mean exactly the same set of wage rates in each firm under contract. Multiemployer agreements may single out for standardization a particular wage, say the wage for unskilled labor. Where the agreement is signed by a craft union, standardization would be relevant only to the craft workers and not to the other workers in the firms. In the men's clothing industry the basic standardization agreement provides for standardization of labor cost.

[10] See John J. Dunlop, "Structure of Collective Bargaining," in Gerald G. Somers, ed., *The Next Twenty-five Years of Industrial Relations* (Madison, Wis.: Industrial Relations Research Association, 1973), pp. 16–18.

cent wage differential between firms would mean a significant cost differential of about 6.66 percent to the advantage of the low-wage firm.[11]

Where many firms compete within the same national market, as in bituminous coal and clothing, there is a strong tendency to establish industrywide agreements. In textiles, in hosiery, and in shoes, there are relatively high labor costs and many competing firms, but unorganized sections of each industry preclude attempts to secure wage uniformity through multiple bargaining. In industries where a few firms dominate a national market, unionwide bargaining is more likely to be the standard approach to collective bargaining. Sometimes uniformity is modified to give the flexibility desired to meet the special problems of individual firms within the broad pattern of a key wage settlement.[12] Industrywide bargaining has not been widely prevalent in the United States within the manufacturing sector primarily because of its characteristically oligopolistic structure. In 1975, of the 1,514 large contracts involving 1,-000 or more workers, less than 20 percent of the agreements in manufacturing were negotiated with multiple employers. On the other hand, in nonmanufacturing industries, where the firms were smaller and the competition among them greater, 499 of 699, or nearly two-thirds of the large agreements, were of this type (see Table 9–3). There were exceptions: in manufacturing, multiemployer bargaining predominated in the apparel industries, where many firms fight for survival; in nonmanufacturing, single-firm bargaining was the rule in the communications industry, with its relatively few large firms.

Competition from American firms with plants abroad has so far not affected the structure of collective bargaining. Multinational corporations (MNCs), operating in several host countries, have been able to build new plants and shift production from one country to another as the economic situation may dictate. The transfer of production out of the United States to plants abroad, where wages are generally lower, has occurred in various garment, electrical, and nonelectrical machinery industries. To American unions this trend has the same potential for undermining wage and other employment standards as runaway shops in a domestic industry. Even if the MNC sells only in host markets, the American worker may be injured if the output competes with American exports. The problem is compounded if MNC products become imports substituting for domestic production.

The difficulties of attempting to set up American union standards in the

---

[11] Since World War II technological change has reduced the relative importance of labor costs, and hence has decreased the pressure for wage standardization throughout the industry.

[12] The United Automobile Workers at the Studebaker plants in 1954 accepted a wage cut rather than demand an increase following the General Motors pattern, in order to help the company through a period of financial difficulties.

foreign plants of multinational corporations are formidable indeed. Foreign subsidiaries may in fact be organized by unions in the host countries, but foreign labor organizations, such as those in Europe, have different orientations and organizational structures, and function according to a different set of legal institutions. Moreover, accords worked out by unions, foreign governments, and MNCs are not likely to be adjusted to meet the objectives of American labor. Nonetheless, first steps have been taken by some international labor organizations to enable unions in different countries to assemble information and develop policies to protect workers; for example, when workers are engaged in a dispute with an MNC branch in one country, they may be undermined when the MNC shifts production to its divisions in other nations. The International Metalworkers Federation (IMF), to which the United Automobile Workers belongs, and the International Federation of Chemical and General Workers Unions (ICF) have both attempted to coordinate union policies among several countries, but the principal results so far have been information-gathering and not coordination in bargaining.[13]

Tactical considerations affect union attitudes toward collective bargaining. In an industry with many firms, "whipsawing" is a divide-and-conquer policy by which a union seeks a favorable contract from a weak firm and then imposes its terms on the other employers. Firms may desire industrywide bargaining to avoid such a campaign. Unions may also favor multiemployer bargaining to avoid being "whipsawed" by firms, though the danger is usually greater for firms than for unions. A union is more likely to have the power to control its locals and to stand pat until an agreement acceptable to all is negotiated.

Other influences on bargaining agreements may be briefly noted. One is the cost savings to the union that arise from the negotiation of a single multiemployer agreement. Another is the fact that such an agreement reduces the threat of rival unionism. If a union negotiates a contract with an employers' association, it stakes out a legal claim to representation for the jobs controlled by that association. If the claim is "certified" through the election procedure of the National Labor Relations Board, a rival union will find it most difficult to break into the industry and displace the certified union, since so many firms and workers are involved.

The factors that influence the employer's attitude toward multiemployer bargaining are similar to those that motivate the union. In a multifirm industry where labor costs are high and competition intense, an employer may favor industrywide bargaining to stabilize costs of production. Especially in

---

[13] See Stanley H. Ruttenberg, "The Union View of Multinationals: An Interpretation," in Robert J. Flanagan and Arnold R. Weber, eds., *Bargaining Without Boundaries: the Multinational Corporation and International Labor Relations* (Chicago: University of Chicago Press, 1974), pp. 187ff.

confronting a strong local while the competition faces weak ones, an employer may wish to join with other employers in a bargaining association to prevent "whipsawing" tactics. Employers may find that a bargaining association reduces the costs of bargaining and increases its effectiveness. And they can pool their resources to hire the services of more skillful bargaining agents and technical experts that they could not otherwise afford.

Other situations may lead firms to oppose multiemployer bargaining, however, or on occasion even to break away from a bargaining association already established. If firms vary greatly in their costs of production and hence in profitability, for example, a common rate of pay or a uniform change in the rate of pay could not satisfy all employers at the same time. The more efficient and profitable firms would be more willing to pay higher wages or give greater increases in order to obtain better workers, while the less profitable firms might find such courses of action financially disastrous.

GOVERNMENT POLICIES

The National Labor Relations Board affects bargaining by designating the unit in which certification elections are held. We have already indicated that this power, which undermined the idea of exclusive union jurisdiction, can freeze a particular geographical bargaining arrangement involving bargaining with one or many employers. The Labor Management Relations Act leaves the determination of the bargaining unit up to the NLRB, which can designate a unit conforming to the wishes of both parties. Where the matter is in dispute, however, the board must rely on its own discretion, using as criteria such matters as the history of collective bargaining in the particular industry, the nature of the employees' and employers' organizations, and similarity of jobs and wages. The NLRB tends to adapt its decisions to current practices and is not so much an instigator of change as an instrument through which actual practices are expressed.

Specific attempts by government to alter the structure of collective bargaining may come in certain industries in which the government plays a direct role. This has been the case in railroads. More recently it has also been true of the construction industry. In 1969 President Nixon established a Construction Industry Collective Bargaining Commission with the objective of reforming the geographical scope of collective bargaining in the industry. A tripartite board of labor, management, and public members, the commission sought to widen the scope of bargaining so that regional and national interests could prevent what has been called the instability of craft bargaining in local areas. Of special concern was the ability of local unions to escalate wages by outbidding neighboring locals. On March 29, 1971, a further step was taken to prevent a rapid rise in construction wages when Nixon issued Executive Order 11588 setting up the tripartite Construction Industry Stabilization Committee (CISC) with wage-control powers. (The introduction of general wage and price controls for the economy as a whole came later, on August 15, 1971.) The premise of the new arrangement was that reform of the bargaining structure was essential to wage restraint. Eighteen joint labor-management Craft Dispute Boards were established at the national level and were encouraged to help settle local disputes, while the CISC was given power of final review. National organizations of crafts and employers were asked to consolidate agreements on a regional basis. The committee also hoped to reach broader geographical uniformity in other aspects of the labor agreement, especially those relating to pension funds and work rules.[14]

Government intervention to alter bargaining arrangements, unless it helps the parties make changes which they themselves want, can be unsettling and lead to conflict because it is likely to change relative bargaining power. One type of proposal, frequently made but not acted upon, would extend the antitrust laws to prohibit industrywide and unionwide bargaining.[15] Those who favor the proposal argue that such bargaining is injurious to consumer interests because it increases the power of labor and leads to inflationary pressures throughout the entire economy. They also claim that strikes in these situations involve more workers and affect the public more severely than if bargaining were conducted locally. The proposed legislation would limit bargaining either to individual firms or to localities and prevent national unions from coordinating bargaining efforts among them.

Critics of such proposals point out that the existence of monopoly and monopsony power in labor markets does not necessarily accompany industry- or unionwide bargaining. Nor can wage changes be considered a unique cause of inflation. And in any case the government already has the power to protect the public interest in emergency disputes.

Although action on such proposals depends upon political circumstances, the broad historical tendencies in collective bargaining appear to lead in the opposite direction: toward greater centralization of the process, with government intervention at the national level. As the construction industry experience indicates, local bargaining structures may accentuate wage increases as local unions vie with neighboring locals for wage gains. Government inter-

---

[14] See Michael H. Moskow, "New Initiatives in Public Policy for the Construction Industry," *Proceedings of the Twenty-Fourth Annual Winter Meeting* (Industrial Relations Research Association, 1971), pp. 25–32.

[15] Under the present interpretation of such laws, a union may legally pursue its legitimate trade-union objectives by bargaining with employer associations; only an agreement between the union and employers to set the price of a product or to limit competition in the product market would be considered a violation of the laws. There are no limitations on multiemployer bargaining per se.

vention to restrain leapfrogging wages is more easily undertaken nationally with the participation of the national unions themselves.

CONTRACT NEGOTIATIONS AND BARGAINING POWER

Economic Pressure

In economic terms, the bargaining process is akin to any other type of market transaction in which the price of the commodity or service is subject to attempts of each party to gain the advantage. Employers, like any other buyers, seek to obtain a low price; if the union demands too much, they can refuse to buy, while the union can refuse to sell if the terms are not satisfactory.[16] The strike (or lockout) in labor-management negotiations, even if it is only threatened, is part and parcel of the bargaining process. When a contract expires and the parties cannot agree on a new one, a strike may be called on the grounds of "no contract, no work." At other times, both parties may agree to extend the old contract until agreement is reached and to apply the new terms retroactively to the original date of expiration. A contract can sometimes be changed during its life if a "reopening" clause permits negotiations over certain points even though the rest of the contract remains unchanged.[17] Usually such clauses pertain only to wage rates and are found in long-term contracts that allow for adjustments to changed market conditions. One disadvantage of a reopening clause in a long-term contract is that the union's power cannot be brought to bear fully upon the employer when it must abide by the no-strike clause during "reopening" negotiations. A union willing to sign a long-term contract is therefore more likely to seek automatic wage adjustments during the life of the contract. These may take the form of gearing the wage rate to changes in the cost of living (escalator clauses), of an "annual improvement factor," or of a wage increase deferred to some subsequent date.

The power of the strike (or lockout) lies in its ability to impose costs on the

---

[16] A refusal to buy is called a lockout, while a refusal to sell at the offered price is a strike. In actual practice, it is often difficult to determine whether a work stoppage is a strike or a lockout. In its collection of "strike" statistics, the U.S. Bureau of Labor Statistics has dropped the terms "strike" and "lockout" and uses the term "work stoppage" instead.

[17] Sometimes negotiations occur during the course of a contract even where there is no contractual basis for reopening. During the term of the five-year (1950–55) General Motors contract that contained no reopening clause, Walter Reuther successfully sought to reopen the contract in 1952 on the grounds that the Korean situation had outdated the economic situation. Reuther said that the contract should be considered a "living document."

other party. But since any work stoppage is double-edged, each party attempts not only to inflict losses on the other but also to minimize its own costs. Neil Chamberlain has devised the following formal measure of bargaining power.[18]

$$\text{Bargaining power}_A = \frac{B\text{'s cost of disagreeing on } A\text{'s terms}}{B\text{'s cost of agreeing on } A\text{'s terms}}$$

This formula indicates that the more costly it is for B to disagree with A's terms, the greater the bargaining power of A. On the other hand, a relatively high cost of agreement reduces A's bargaining power. B's bargaining power is expressed in terms of A's relative cost of disagreeing and agreeing with B's terms. The strength or weakness of A with respect to B depends on the relative values of the bargaining power ratios.

If B were an employer, the costs of a strike would include those of shutting down and starting up the firm, loss of profits, loss of markets to competitors, and loss of value of perishable inventories or of materials subject to obsolescence. The higher these costs, the greater the union's bargaining power (A); for example, the union's advantage would be greater if a firm is struck during its busy season, when profits are higher and competition keener, rather than during the off season.

Losses to a union during a strike consist of the possible departure of members who have lost wages despite strike benefits and income earned at part-time jobs elsewhere, and the development of factionalism that may lead to modifications of demands. A large strike fund reduces the economic disadvantage and hence decreases the bargaining strength of the employer. On the other hand, the unavailability of part-time job alternatives in the market (for example, during a recession) would increase the disadvantage of workers and increase the employer's bargaining power.

Strike tactics are directed toward enhancing one party's bargaining advantage with respect to the other side. Attempting to keep the plant producing goods, a firm may hire nonunion workers as strikebreakers or use supervisory personnel in plant jobs. It can increase the union's disadvantage by threatening not to rehire strikers or to blacklist them, to evict strikers from company-owned houses, or to cut off the consumer credit available to them from banks sympathetic to the firm. Noneconomic weapons, such as public identification of the union as a minority or obnoxious group acting on principles abhorrent to the prevailing social mores, may also be used.

A union can increase its bargaining advantage by setting up a picket line to prevent the employer from hiring strikebreakers. It may try to promote a boy-

---

[18] Chamberlain, *Collective Bargaining*, pp. 220–221.

cott of the firm's products and thus increase management's cost of disagreeing. A "primary boycott" is conducted by members of the union, and a "secondary boycott" may be organized among individual consumers of the firm's products or among firms who buy, handle, transport, or otherwise deal with the struck employer.

Unions may also increase their advantage by increasing the firm's nonpecuniary costs of disagreement. Attempting to isolate the firm and build an adverse public image of it, the union may charge that it pays substandard wages, is greedy or too rich, or is undemocratic. Noneconomic tactics, however, whether indulged in by unions or firms, serve their purpose only when the opponent actually modifies a position in response to pressure; to the extent that the public automatically discounts the validity of the charges and countercharges in advance, they have no effect on bargaining positions and become ceremonial.

Another formulation, devised by John R. Hicks,[19] assumes that the longer the strike, the greater the cost to each side, and presents relative bargaining power in terms of duration of strike in the form of a graph (see Figure 9-1). Beginning with the wage rate that the employer would pay in the absence of union pressure, OE, the concession curve, EE, represents the amount of additional wages the employer would pay in order to forgo a strike of a given duration. The curve rises but then flattens out because at some high wage the firm would be forced out of business. UV', the union resistance curve, represents the wage below which the union would prefer a strike of the given duration. It slopes downward as the union modifies its demands in the face of a lengthier work stoppage. The curves do not present "historical" information, but rather represent the probable attitudes of union and management at given moments of time. If each party in negotiations sounds out the other position correctly—that is, identifies the shapes of both curves—the new wage will be OP and a strike will be avoided.

Other writers have attempted to define more precisely the factors that govern the outcome in bargaining situations. The assumptions of the different models vary from writer to writer. With union and preference schedules, Allan M. Cartter[20] examines the conditions under which the two parties would share the benefits of an increasing demand for labor, but has little to say about negotiation strategy. Carl Stevens[21] develops a choice model based on avoidance of undesirable alternatives and views the negotiation process as

---

[19] John R. Hicks, *Theory of Wages* (New York: Macmillan, 1932), ch. 7.

[20] Allan M. Cartter, *Theory of Wages and Employment* (Homewood, Ill.: Irwin, 1959), ch. 8.

[21] Carl M. Stevens, *Strategy and Collective Bargaining Negotiations* (New York: McGraw-Hill, 1963).

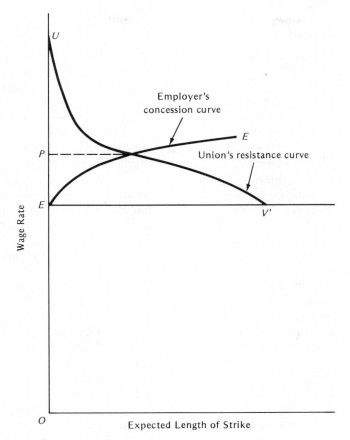

FIGURE 9–1 Hicks's Strike Analysis

attempts to change the opponent's position. Other writers introduce utility evaluation functions of each party, the costs of changing preference functions, and risks and uncertainties concerning the nature of the opponent's objectives.[22] In economic theory, wage indeterminancy, which does not arise under conditions of perfect competition, is possible under bilateral conditions. By contrast, bargaining models attempt to make the outcome theoretically determinate. Admittedly, however, they have no empirical content.

[22] J. Pen, *The Wage Rate Under Collective Bargaining* (Cambridge, Mass.: Harvard University Press, 1959); Richard E. Walton and Robert B. McKersie, *A Behavioral Theory of Labor Negotiations* (New York: McGraw-Hill, 1965); Bevars D. Mabry, *Labor Relations and Collective Bargaining* (New York: Ronald Press, 1966); Orley Ashenfelter and George E. Johnson, "Bargaining Power, Trade Unions, and Industrial Strike Activity," *American Economic Review,* 59 (March 1969), 35–49.

The Political Process

In preparation for bargaining negotiations, each party must determine what its demands will be, appraise its chances of success, and decide what it would be willing to accept. Both parties must arrive at such decisions by means of certain political processes. In the case of labor, if bargaining is in the hands of the local union, demands generally have to be approved by the membership. While the international representatives and the national officers are not likely to have direct control over the formulation of demands, they may have the power to approve or disapprove strike action if it is needed. Agreement must therefore be reached among local members, local leaders, and the international both on what is to be asked and on what minimums will be acceptable—in short, on what can be traded. Since most union constitutions require the negotiators to return to the local for a vote of approval before the final terms of the negotiations are accepted, negotiators must know realistically how much management will give and how little the rank and file will accept.

When the rank and file have confidence in their bargaining representatives and issues have not become emotionally charged, the leaders may easily win votes of approval for what they consider to be the best terms available. In other instances, however, hostile intraunion factions may seek to make political capital out of the failure of negotiators to get the terms they had hoped for.

When the area of contract negotiations is increased to that of the large multiplant employer or to a group of employers, the internal political process of formulating a union's demands becomes more complex. Regional and national officers, because they usually take the leadership in bargaining, must exert a greater control over the nature of the demands as well as over strategy and tactics, while the locals assume an advisory role. There may be prebargaining conferences to which locals send representatives to recommend terms for a new agreement. Such groups may also be called into session during negotiations. The union's bargaining team can report to them and seek their advice and support; sometimes they have delegated authority to approve the final terms of the agreement. Because a union's bargaining strength is dependent upon maintaining a solid front, the national officers face the political task of securing a consensus that will hold even in case of failure at the bargaining table.

Management, except in "one-man firms," faces similar problems of internal politics, although they may not be so obvious to the public as those of the union. Management in the modern corporation is a far cry from the simple line organization, in which the owner delegated broad powers to a foreman. Three different groups within management are immediately concerned with labor relations: those in the line of authority, such as the vice president in charge of operations, the plant superintendent, and the foremen; those in staff functions, such as personnel and industrial relations officers; and those in other managerial areas, such as sales and public relations officers. Conflicts may develop between line and staff as well as between different points in the line—between foremen and the plant superintendent, for example.

The line may have little to do with certain aspects of collective bargaining that have been taken over by the staff functions of the modern personnel department. The line authorities may not be fully or even marginally responsible for such activities as recruitment, training, wage and salary administration, discipline, safety, and health and welfare plans, in addition to union negotiation. At the same time, since the line is responsible for production of goods according to set time schedules and quality standards, it may demand the authority to discipline "loafers," to prevent interdepartmental seniority transfers, or to act in other areas differently from the recommendations of the personnel department. In some situations, for example, the personnel manager may take the view that long-term union-management stability is better for the firm than an attempt to secure some solution to an immediate problem, however vexing to a foreman.

Procedures for reconciling the views of different groups vary from firm to firm. Often a managerial committee, set up on either a permanent or a temporary basis, develops the company's bargaining position. That position may be relatively "firm," and in actual negotiations the company may make a point of refusing to diverge from it.[23] In other cases a management bargaining team may have the authority to sign an agreement that lies within the limits of the prebargaining plan without ratification by higher authorities; if the negotiators cannot settle within those limits, higher management must be consulted for further instructions. Theoretically, the shareholders of the company hold the ultimate decision-making power, but in most cases they are not interested in industrial relations.[24] Usually it is the president, the vice president, or possibly the board of directors who exercises final power of decision.

The diversity of opinions within a firm also increases with the scope of the firm. Managers of plants in a multiplant corporation are likely to face differing local labor market conditions or have differing cost structures; these

---

[23] In extreme cases, this practice is sometimes called "Boulwareism," after Lemuel R. Boulware, former vice president of public and employee relations of General Electric. It has been declared an unfair labor practice by the National Labor Relations Board.

[24] Stockholders may be required to vote on issues requiring long-run commitments by the firm. Pension plans or profit-sharing plans would be likely issues for stockholders' approval before final signing of an agreement is permitted. See Paul V. Johnson, "Decision Making Under Collective Bargaining," *Monthly Labor Review*, 80 (September 1957), 1060.

can lead to disagreements within the firm over the feasibility of a proposed wage objective. Of course, the internalization of conflicting economic objectives characterizes the managerial decision-making process within a firm. By contrast, each firm in an employer bargaining alliance voluntarily gives up some of its independence of action for an anticipated gain, but can nullify its commitment by withdrawal.

THE INSTITUTIONALIZATION OF THE BARGAINING PROCESS

Bargaining Procedures

Although the actual negotiations in any bargaining situation reflect particular circumstances and even the personal characteristics of the negotiators, certain generalizations can be established about the bargaining process as it has developed in American industry. First of all, as bargaining relationships continue between one firm and one union over a period of years, each party comes to accept, respect, and perhaps understand the general orientation of the other, a situation that can result in less acrimony in disputes, less conflict, more orderliness, and more willingness to find out what exactly the other side wants and to deal directly with the problem. Many of the tactics developed from an earlier, more violent day may continue primarily as rituals but have little effect on the outcome of negotiations. However, this institutionalization of collective bargaining does not imply that strikes are "withering away"—an idea we will examine later—because even two parties that are willing to accept and deal with one another may come to no agreement and be forced to resort to the economic pressure of a work stoppage.

Secondly, factual information is now used more frequently in negotiations than it was in the past, and specialists—economists, lawyers, or accountants—are employed more often and in greater numbers. This development tends to make negotiations more formal and technical, and possibly less satisfactory as a means of resolving the real conflicts of interest. When the negotiators are specialists, the rank and file may wonder how and in what ways they are participating in the formulation of the contract under which they are to work. Furthermore, the legal and technical intricacies in the contract may subsequently lead to more problems than are momentarily resolved at the time of negotiation. Nonetheless, the widening scope of collective bargaining to include such technical issues as health and welfare plans, supplementary unemployment compensation, and profit sharing makes the increasing use of specialists inevitable, and their role will undoubtedly continue to grow more important.

A third development is the attempt to avoid crisis-bargaining by referral of knotty issues to "informed neutrals," a term used to describe panels whose members may be either jointly selected by both parties or appointed by governments to hear opposing viewpoints and recommend solutions, or to special labor-management committees. Unlike those fact-finding boards or governmental arbitrators that act to resolve a dispute during negotiations, such panels and committees are designed not to bring an end to an immediate impasse in negotiations, but to provide a "continuous bargaining" procedure that deals with wider and more long-standing issues. Several panels established a number of years ago included the Kaiser Steel Corporation–United Steelworkers Committee on work rules, the panel on automation problems in Armour & Company, and the Presidential Railroad Commission on work rules. The early hopes that use of such panels would spread and provide a reasoned resolution of issues outside the usual pressures of a strike deadline and a possible trial of strength by a work stoppage have not been fulfilled. While the Kaiser Steel committee has been considered successful, the issue of work rules on the railroads was not settled voluntarily but only through compulsory arbitration established by Congress. And a Human Relations Committee, formed after a 116-day steel strike in 1959, came to an end in 1965 when I. W. Abel defeated David McDonald, the incumbent president of the Steelworkers Union; Abel charged, among other things, that the Human Relations Committee had in effect denied to the membership its right to participate in determining the terms and conditions of its employment.[25]

With the institutionalization of collective bargaining, professionals and neutrals may help to define issues, but it should be recognized that they do not eliminate the underlying conflict of economic interests between the two parties, nor can they be expected to. An agreement specifies a period of time during which the workers will relinquish their right to withhold their labor (that is, strike) in return for a particular set of working conditions and wages which the employer agrees to guarantee. The labor agreement spells out the compromises both parties are willing to make in accepting those obligations.

Grievance Procedures

During the life of a contract, disputes between the union and management may arise over the application and interpretation of its clauses. For example, workers may feel that they have been discharged unjustly, or that they have not been promoted to a higher-paying job that they think they deserve on the basis of the seniority clause in the contract. To handle such disputes, over 90

---

[25] For an evaluation of "continuous bargaining" procedures, see Neil W. Chamberlain and Donald E. Cullen, *The Labor Sector*, 2nd ed. (New York: McGraw-Hill, 1971), pp. 213–216.

percent of contracts provide formal grievance procedures by which specific complaints may be jointly reviewed by both parties and resolved without economic threats.

The formal procedure varies from contract to contract but usually consists of several steps by which a grievance, if not settled immediately, is appealed to higher levels of authority within both the unions and management, and finally to a third party who arbitrates the dispute. The initiation of the grievance usually comes from the worker, since management is more likely to act in a way it thinks desirable and let employees complain if they feel unfairly treated.

A worker who has a complaint usually discusses it first with the shop steward, who can determine whether it seems justifiable. If the shop steward feels that the complaint is justified, the issue goes to the foreman. If the foreman does not accept the worker's point of view, the complaint must be appealed to a grievance committee composed of shop stewards and foremen or the chief steward and the labor relations director. This action may require that the worker file a written statement of the grievance with the shop steward and also that the foreman indicate in writing why the complaint was unacceptable. If no satisfactory agreement is obtained at this second level, the grievance goes to a higher appeals board, which may consist of the president of the local and top management of the firm. (Other steps may be included in the formal arrangement, depending upon the complexity of the organization of management and the history of industrial relations within the firm.) A final appeal may generally be made to a "neutral" arbitrator chosen by the two parties. Unlike a mediator, who attempts to bring about agreement between parties by making suggestions for settlements, an arbitrator makes a decision that is final and binding on the two parties.[26] The arbitrator may be selected on an ad hoc basis to handle a particular grievance, or may be retained by the firm, or firms, and the union to serve as permanent umpire.

The effectiveness of grievance procedures within a plant reflects the same factors that underlie effective and responsible collective bargaining. If both sides accept their role in the plant and are willing to understand the position of the other party and live with their respective relationships in a responsible way, the settlement of grievances may be a routine and effective process. At the same time, that process may contribute to the effectiveness of bargaining relationships generally.

The role of the third party can be of vital importance to the effectiveness of the grievance procedure. Labor economists and others have expressed some uneasiness that arbitrators have been used to resolve issues that had best be

---

[26] This is called voluntary arbitration because both parties agree to submit the dispute. Compulsory arbitration refers to that procedure whereby a dispute must be submitted to an arbitrator under penalty of law, whether agreed to or not by one or both parties.

settled by the union and management in direct discussion. It is often easier to let a third party settle the question, and then later "blame" the arbitrator if the decision goes in the wrong direction. Sometimes one party will appeal a losing case to the arbitrator as a face-saving device.

Arbitration awards are open to challenge in the courts if one party believes that the arbitrator, in making the decision, exceeded his or her authority as defined by the labor agreement. In 1960 the Supreme Court ruled that an arbitrator could not "dispense his own brand of industrial justice";[27] he must attempt to resolve a dispute by acting not as a mediator but as an interpreter of specific contract clauses. In contrast to the consensus approach to arbitration, this legalistic approach tended to weaken the position of permanent umpires, who often believed that they could offer suggestions constructive to the long-run interests of both parties.

The more formal, legalistic approach to arbitration has its pitfalls. The grievance procedure can become so time-consuming and costly that workers become resentful and frustrated by delays. Some unions and managements have tried to reform the procedure. One reform, known as "expedited grievance arbitration," is designed to guarantee quick decisions on routine grievances involving questions of fact. (It is recognized that grievances related to the interpretation of contract clauses cannot necessarily be resolved quickly and should be handled according to regular procedures.) Expedited grievance arbitration, adopted by 10 steel companies and the United Steelworkers of America in 1971, successfully reduced a sizable backlog of grievance cases. The U.S. Postal Service and its four major unions introduced a similar system in 1973; it requires that a hearing must be held in 10 days, that the hearing be informal with no filing of briefs, and that a decision must be issued within 48 hours.

SUMMARY

Collective bargaining is the joint determination of wages and other terms of employment between a union and an employer or organization of employers. The bargaining agreement, or contract, becomes the working rules or the "law" of the firm. It is accepted by both parties, modified by subsequent negotiation, and interpreted through a grievance procedure.

---

[27] *United Steelworkers of America* v. *Enterprise Wheel & Car Corp.*, 363 U.S. 593, 597 (1960). This case and two others involving the Steelworkers became known as the "Trilogy cases" and established guidelines for arbitrators and the arbitration process. The other two cases were *United Steelworkers of America* v. *American Manufacturing Company*, 363 U.S. 564 (1960), and *United Steelworkers of America* v. *Warrior and Gulf Navigation Company*, 363 U.S. 574 (1960). In general, the rulings laid down the principle that where the arbitrator lawfully fulfills the proper role, the courts will not overrule the decision.

However, the arbitrator is not free to make decisions, even if supportable by the collective bargaining agreement, if they limit or deny statutory rights of employees as determined under Title VII of the Civil Rights Act of 1964. See *Alexander* v. *Gardner-Denver*, 415 U.S. 36 (1974).

Collective bargaining is more common in some industries than in others. Agreements vary widely as to the number of workers covered. In 1973, 2,237 contracts—about 1.4 percent of the 165,000 agreements for private, nonfarm workers—included 1,000 or more workers each.

In terms of bargaining structure the majority of large contracts are negotiated between a union and a single firm. With companywide bargaining, workers in the various plants of the firm are covered by a single-firm master agreement. Multiemployer bargaining with one union, found at local, regional, and national levels, is termed industrywide bargaining if all the firms are in the same industry. Pattern-setting, or the negotiation of similar contracts with seperate firms in an industry, is found in many oligopolistic industries. Coalition bargaining refers to an agreement of several unions to negotiate a common agreement with a single firm.

A major incentive for unions to extend the area of bargaining is the prevention of lowered wages through competition from other firms. But unions find this difficult in the case of the multinational corporation that develops competitive imports with low-paid foreign labor.

Bargaining power is the extent to which one party can impose its terms on the other. In bargaining tactics, both unions and firms must consider not only the economic situation but also the political process within their own organizations whereby conflicting interests are reconciled. As issues in negotiations become more complex, both parties may have professional assistance in framing bargaining positions.

Grievances concerning the interpretation of contract clauses are handled through fairly standardized procedures that usually include arbitration by third parties. Although sometimes abused, arbitration has generally been considered one of the more satisfactory means of peacefully resolving conflicts in the collective bargaining process.

DISCUSSION QUESTIONS

1. How does a collective bargaining agreement differ from a typical business sales contract?
2. Give examples of various types of work rules dealt with in collective bargaining agreements. How important are they to the worker? to the firm?
3. If you were an employer, under what circumstances would you prefer to bargain with one union representing all of your workers, rather than several unions representing different skills, departments, plants, and/or areas? If you were a national union, under what circumstances would you prefer to bargain with all firms in a given industry, rather than with each firm individually? Explain in each case.
4. Is "pattern-setting" bargaining in industries that are generally oligopolistic consistent with the analysis of oligopolistic pricing discussed in chapter 4? Why or why not?
5. In those competitive industries where labor costs are relatively high, unions seek

to extend unionization to all branches of the industry in order to "take wages out of competition." Is the motivation of equity or economics—or both? Do unions ever make exceptions to the principle of wage equalization? If so, under what circumstances?

6. What are the implications for collective bargaining in the United States of multinational expansion overseas?

7. Under what circumstances do governments presently influence the structure of collective bargaining arrangements?

8. Would the bargaining power of a union be adversely affected if its ability to call, or threaten to call, a strike were limited? Explain.

9. The formulation of a bargaining position within firms often involves a political process. Can you reconcile this with the proposition that firms are profit-maximizers?

10. Grievance procedures involve interpreting, not negotiating, an agreement. Why are such procedures considered to be one of the more important aspects of the collective bargaining process?

SELECTED READINGS

For a systematic discussion of collective bargaining, see John T. Dunlop, *Industrial Relations Systems* (New York: Rinehart & Winston, 1958). For difference aspects of the bargaining process, the following works should be examined: American Assembly, *Challenges to Collective Bargaining* (Englewood Cliffs, N.J.: Prentice-Hall, 1967); William Chernish, *Coalition Bargaining: A Study of Union Tactics and Public Policy* (Philadelphia: University of Pennsylvania Press, 1969); John T. Dunlop and Neil W. Chamberlain, eds., *Frontiers of Collective Bargaining* (New York: Harper & Row, 1967); Robert J. Flanagan and Arnold R. Weber, eds., *Bargaining Without Boundaries: The Multinational Corporation and International Labor Relations* (Chicago: University of Chicago Press, 1974); James J. Healy, ed., *Creative Collective Bargaining* (Englewood Cliffs, N.J.: Prentice-Hall, 1965); Reed C. Richardson, *Collective Bargaining By Objective: A Positive Approach* (Englewood Cliffs, N.J.: Prentice-Hall, 1977); Carl M. Stevens, *Strategy and Collective Bargaining Negotiations* (New York: McGraw-Hill 1963); and Richard E. Walton and Robert B. McKersie, *A Behavioral Theory of Labor Negotiations* (New York: Ronald Press, 1966).

10

Union Objectives in Collective Bargaining

Wages and Wage Supplements

Since a union seeks to participate in the control of those aspects of a firm's labor policy that affect the workers' welfare, there is virtually no limit to the range of policies that, if it is aggressive, it may try to bring into negotiations of the labor contract. One of the trends in collective bargaining since World War II has been the widening range of substantive issues brought into negotiations. No longer does the typical bargaining session deal only with wages and hours; it may include lengthy discussions of pension plans, health and welfare funds, supplementary unemployment benefits, and profit sharing.

The increasing scope of collective bargaining follows logically from the union's concern for its members' welfare. If wage rates are within the province of the union, so are rules involving such issues as the amount of work to be paid for, as defined by work speeds, and the type of tools with which the work is performed. If members wish part of their wages to be paid to them later in the form of pensions, unemployment funds, or medical insurance, the union argues that such objectives also fall logically within the scope of collective bargaining.

For management, however, the widening scope of collective bargaining is more likely to be a cause of alarm because it appears as an invasion by the union into matters previously determined unilaterally. Employers feel that their authority is under unfair attack when unions that have been recognized and dealt with on certain issues raise new issues and brush aside employers' claims that they have sole control and responsibility over these matters. The union challenge to managerial authority and its ever-widening sphere is, however, the essence of labor movements, and always has been.

In this and the following chapter we shall examine some of the important substantive issues in collective bargaining negotiations: wages and hours, union security, seniority, and union work rules. The objective of these chap-

218

ters is to give a measure of understanding of the positions often taken by unions and employers and to indicate the assumptions as well as the implications of the various policies

GENERAL WAGE CHANGES

The issues of wages lies at the economic center of the labor contract. Management does not dispute the fact that wages are subject to negotiation—once it has recognized the union—and public policy, except during periods of war or economic emergency, has granted a substantial freedom to both parties to work out their agreements on wage rates.

Union Demands

When a union that has been recognized by an employer is preparing its wage demands for coming negotiations, it uses certain arguments to determine the change it should hope for. These arguments can be studied quite apart from the broad generalities of "more, more, and more" or from the union's particular bargaining tactics. They can be classified in four categories as changes in the going rate, productivity, profitability, and the cost of living.

The Going Rate In formulating their wage demands many unions simply follow the wage changes that have been obtained by other unions or granted by other firms. Though this policy of following the going wage change seems at first sight simple, direct, and consistent with the basic union philosophy of equal pay for equal work, it is neither a sufficient nor a necessary explanation of union wage policy. It would be consistent with the equal wage principle only if all workers in similar occupations in different firms did receive equal wages. This situation does not generally exist.

There is usually a wide range of wage rates for a particular occupation or skill even in the same local labor market, as a result of differences in job content, market imperfections, and historical factors. When a union demands a wage change that is equal to that obtained by other unions, it is not asking for the same pay for equal work, but only for the maintenance of the existing wage differential. Rarely do all negotiations result in a uniform wage increase. The question arises as to which wage increases elsewhere should serve as the guide to a given union—those by other locals of the same union or by locals of a rival union, those reflected in a national pattern, or a particular increase given by a nonunion employer. While there is no ready answer to this, in large part a union tends to follow the demands of some other local unless faced with special circumstances in its own firm or union. Finally, the policy of following the going rate of wage change is obviously not adequate to explain the decisions of the wage leader—the union that establishes the pattern, if any, that others follow. In short, while a union may claim that it is following others in its wage demands, other factors must be taken into consideration by the union.

Productivity   Unions commonly claim that wages should be increased when workers produce more. The exact cause of the increased output—whether the result of better equipment, more efficient management, or greater worker effort—is considered irrelevant: unions (and the public generally) expect that workers should obtain their fair share of the fruits of industrial progress. Although we discuss later the analysis of wage trends as they relate to productivity, the underlying truth in the argument is that workers' wages are ultimately paid for through the goods and services they produce. But the productivity argument is not easily translated into wage demands by a particular union. There are three difficulties. If the productivity gains can be attributed to only part of the operations covered in the bargaining unit, should wage gains be demanded only for the particular workers involved, or should they be shared among all workers in the bargaining unit? Similarly, if a union deals with employers in different bargaining units, should the union seek higher wages depending upon the extent of the productivity gain in each firm? If productivity gains vary from firm to firm, the productivity argument will be inconsistent with the equal-pay-for-equal-work argument.

A second difficulty has to do with measuring productivity changes in specific jobs, departments, firms, or industries. It is a rare firm where a measure of output is unambiguous, because firms usually produce an array of differentiated services or products, and because quality of output may change. For this reason productivity arguments often turn into arguments concerning profitability.

The third difficulty concerns the fact that, since negotiated wages extend over a period of time, there is no way to know the future course of productivity during the life of a contract. In a short-period contract, say of one year, the changes in productivity are likely to be small. In a contract covering two, three, or more years, the original wage agreement is likely to be increasingly out of date. Catching up on productivity gains at the next negotiations would mean that workers would not be able to use the funds when earned. To avoid this situation, a union could seek an initial wage increase greater than the productivity gain to compensate for the loss at the end of the period, or it could ask for deferred wage increases. The latter course has now become the typical arrangement for long-term contracts. The earliest of such agreements—one reached in 1955 when Ford and General Motors signed with the UAW for a period of three years—introduced an "annual improvement factor" of 2.5 percent or $.06 an hour (whichever was greater). It was not based upon any formula of actual productivity changes but was simply a way of providing automatic upward wage adjustments.

Profitability   Unions sometimes use employers' profits in defining their wage demands. Profits appear to indicate the ability to pay and hence are believed to be a better guide to wage demands than productivity. But profits too can present difficulties. For one thing, profits are defined in accounting terms, and items such as depreciation are subject to different interpretations, and bigger profits do not necessarily mean that a firm has the funds needed to pay higher wages.

More fundamentally, the profitability argument is likely to raise the question of the rate at which a firm will make new investments for plant expansion or improvement. Because funds for capital improvement often come from reinvestment of profits, the ability of the firm to pay higher wages in the future will be diminished if the unions demand more now. There is another contradiction: although it seems reasonable to ask for higher wages when an employer has a highly profitable year, unions do not like to accept wage cuts when firms suffer financial reverses. The argument of profitability can also be inconsistent with the equal-pay principle if competing firms have different profit rates during the same year.

The Cost of Living   A union demand for wage increases to keep pace with rising consumer prices is aimed, of course, at maintaining the existing real wage; it does not lead to any gain in real wages.

A union can be assured of cost-of-living increases by introducing into the contract an "escalator clause" that provides an automatic adjustment of wages in response to changes in some indicator of consumer prices. The Bureau of Labor Statistics Consumer Price Index has often been used as the measure of price changes.[1] A typical clause may relate either point or percentage changes in the index with a wage change of so many cents per hour. Adjustments are made at specified intervals—such as quarterly or semiannually—during the life of the contract, and the total amount of the increase may be "capped" (limited) or "uncapped" (unlimited).

The cost-of-living argument is most frequently used during times of rapid price increases. If a union has signed a two-year contract for a 6 percent wage increase without a cost-of-living clause, for example, a price rise of 0.5 percent

---

[1] Since 1977, this index is designated as the Consumer Price Index (CPI) for Urban Wage Earners and Clerical Workers. It is designed to reflect price changes in the goods and services purchased by an estimated 45 percent of the noninstitutional population of the United States. A second index, the CPI for All Urban Consumers, was introduced in 1978 to give broader coverage of consumers, both workers and others, in metropolitan areas. See U.S. Bureau of labor Statistics, *The Consumer Price Index: Concepts and Content Over the Years*, Report 517 (Washington, D.C.: U.S. Department of Labor, 1977).

per month would wipe out the gain by the end of the first year and cause a real wage loss during the second.

Cost-of-living clauses had been used by certain unions for many years. During the post–World War II period an escalator clause was introduced in the two-year contract between General Motors and the United Automobile Workers in 1948 and in their five-year contract in 1950. Escalator clauses became common during the Korean hostilities, when unions were fearful of inflation: coverage increased from approximately 800,000 workers in September 1950, to 3.5 million workers two years later. The number fell off with the ending of hostilities and the recession of 1954, but rose to 4 million between 1958 and 1960 and then declined again in the early 1960s. With the Vietnam War and the inflation of the 1970s, unions again sought escalator clauses: the number of workers covered rose from 2 to over 5 million between 1966 and 1975, or from 20 to 50 percent of major contract coverage.[2]

Employers' Attitudes

Employers use criteria and arguments similar to those used by unions in reaching decisions about wage changes, and they adopt those that best promote their own interests. A highly profitable employer may argue for the going rate of change against a union demand for a larger increase based on profits. A firm may plead poverty or low productivity when a union points to increases elsewhere. To the union argument for a cost-of-living clause, management may reply that wage increases on whatever grounds cost the firm money, and that to contract for an undetermined wage increase adds an uncertainty to future costs; to protect itself, such a firm may demand some factor to offset the increased uncertainty, such as a smaller negotiated wage increase or a longer-term contract that will reduce the costs resulting from more frequent negotiations.

Other Economic Considerations

In their wage negotiations both unions and management use arguments that often seem contradictory and opportunistic. However, labor economists claim that other and more significant considerations, whether articulated or not, influence bargaining postures. First of all, the *employment effect* entails recognition of the downard slope, from left to right, of the firm's demand for labor: a higher wage may lead to less employment.[3] A union that is demand-

---

[2] See H. M. Douty, *Cost-of-Living Escalator Clauses and Inflation,* prepared for the Council of Wage and Price Stability (Washington, D.C.: U.S. Government Printing Office, August 1975), pp. 11–13.

[3] The relationship between the percentage loss in employment and the percentage increase in wages is the coefficient of elasticity of the demand curve for labor. Other things being equal, the coefficient will be less if (a) the labor cost is small relative to total cost, (b) the demand for the firm's products is less elastic, (c) other factors of production cannot

ing a higher wage may consider the possible adverse effect upon the employment of its members in the firm and at some point cease pressing its demands. If the employment effect is substantial, a union that has its own unemployment benefits plan will also recognize that the cost of outlays for its unemployed members may be a further restraint to demands for increased wages.[4]

A second consideration is the effect of a rise in wages upon the number of members attracted to a union. John Dunlop, who called this the *membership effect*, regards the "membership function" as "the appraisal by the leadership of the amount of labor that will be allied to the union at each wage rate";[5] it may differ from the usual supply curve of labor because various policies, such as those related to apprenticeships or to initiation fees, restrict union affiliation. In general, the more successful the union is in winning higher wages, the greater will be its ability to attract new members. A union that wishes both to open its ranks to all new members and to provide all of them with jobs will not ask for as high a wage as if it were attempting to maximize the wage bill. On the other hand, when a union is pursuing a restrictive membership policy, or when it considers desirable the employment of those members who have greatest seniority, its demands for wage increases can be stronger; the membership-function curve will be relatively inelastic and the wage rate can be pushed further upward.

A union may be mindful of the employment effect in one situation but ignore it in another. In some industries where employment had been shrinking in the face of increasing cheaper imports—among them shoes, apparel, and steel—unions are well aware that their wage demands must be restrained if job losses are to be minimized. But sometimes unions demand wage increases with little regard for adverse employment effects. A restrictive membership policy (often found in the craft unions) can make it possible for the union leadership to disregard those who might want to join the union as it wins higher wages. In coal, the United Mine Workers at one time sought high wages despite the cost of unemployment. While certainly not all of the unemployment problems that eventually developed in the coal fields could be assigned to union wage policy,[6] both unemployment and the later expansion of nonunion coal production forced a revision of union policy.

---

easily be substituted for labor, and (d) the supply of those other factors cannot easily be increased.

[4] John T. Dunlop, *Wage Determination and Trade Unions* (New York: Augustus M. Kelley, Inc., 1950), ch. III.

[5] Ibid., p. 33. See also Allan M. Cartter, *Theory of Wages and Employment* (Homewood, Ill.: Irwin, 1959), ch. 7.

[6] Introduction of strip mining, shifts by consumers (before the oil embargo of 1973) from coal to oil and other fuels as sources of power, and exhaustion of old mines were important factors in the decline of employment in the older coal mining areas.

Political Considerations

As Arthur Ross pointed out in his classic *Trade Union Wage Policy*,[7] a union is basically a political organization that will consider the pressures that develop, or may develop, both within and outside itself. Internal pressures result from the composition of membership, the specific interests of each group, and the nature of the political mechanism by which those interests are expressed. For example, there are the possible conflicts between the older workers who may prefer larger contributions to pension funds and the younger workers who may prefer higher immediate wages. The primary external pressures are the achievements of other union leaders, who may be a factional group within the same national or leaders of a rival union.

Union leaders may sometimes feel politically forced to advocate wage increases higher than they think may be successfully won in order to forestall criticism from political rivals within the union or to justify their position to regional or national leaders in the union hierarchy. Moreover, a nonunion employer may increase wages by an amount that a union leader may feel must be duplicated in order not to lose face with the membership. The pattern of "coercive comparison" among unions and between unions and management is part of the hard political world within which union leaders live. In their struggle for survival, they may feel forced to embark upon a wage policy that will have a substantial employment effect on the members of their union.

THE INTERNAL WAGE STRUCTURE

The relationships among the occupational wage rates of a firm make up what is known as the occupational wage structure. For union members these relationships are important insofar as they define the wage differentials between different jobs and different skills. Problems of adjustments in wage structures often arise, especially in unions representing workers in a variety of occupations. In part these are internal union problems. For example, when skilled workers feel that their interests have been neglected and that the wage differential between them and less skilled workers is too narrow, they may win support from the union leadership for their wage adjustment demands by threatening to withdraw from the union and form a separate skilled workers' union, or by other political maneuvering.

Changes in the occupational wage structure are also of vital importance to management. They may raise the total wage cost to the firm and affect incentive and output per worker. Also, adjustments in rates in response to the im-

[7] Arthur M. Ross, *Trade Union Wage Policy* (Berkeley: University of California Press, 1953).

mediate political pressures within a union may lead to a distorted wage structure that generates new complaints later. As shown in chapter 5, one characteristic of the structured labor market revealed by the complex occupational wage structure of modern industry is its relative insulation from market forces and the extent to which it is determined by administrative decisions alone.

Although attempts have been made to relate internal wage differentials to differences in human capital investments, particularly those specific to the firm, the results have not been successful precisely because the nature of those investments is difficult to measure and evaluate. The fact that subjective factors are involved in estimating job content leads unions to insist that they should participate with management in the determination of the internal wage structure.

Job Evaluation

The problems of determining the criteria that should govern the occupational wage structure, the nature and size of the differentials between one level of skill and another, and the objective yardsticks by which differences in skill can be measured are difficult but not impossible to solve. A graph may be used to indicate the possibilities (see Figure 10–1). Grades of jobs within a firm are marked off on the horizontal axis from lowest to highest degree of skill and the wage rate is measured on the vertical axis. In Figure 10–1(A) the straight line AA' represents equal wage differentials between one level of skill and another, with OP representing the average wage rate of the firm. For a different wage structure for the firm, indicated by BB', the average wage would be the same, but both the individual wage differentials between jobs and the over-all range of the entire structure would be greater than AA'. Other possible wage structures are shown in Figure 10–1(B). Here the relationships are curvilinear, either concave or convex to the horizontal axis— that is, with the amount of differentials between jobs decreasing or increasing respectively as skill increases.[8]

One approach to the problem of setting occupational differentials, *scientific wage determination*, was originally developed in the later years of the nineteenth century by Frederick Taylor, one of the first management consul-

---

[8] The latter curve is drawn to represent the case of equal percentage differentials—that is, where

$$\frac{W_1 - W_0}{W_0} = \frac{W_2 - W_1}{W_1} = \frac{W_3 - W_2}{W_2}$$

W_0, W_1, W_2, and so on, representing wage rates at different occupations arranged by increasing skills. "Relative," or percentage, wage differentials would change if all occupational wages were increased by the same flat number of cents per hour. On the other hand, if the equalities in the formula were to be maintained when the wage level of the plant was raised, then the wage rates would have to be raised by the same percentage.

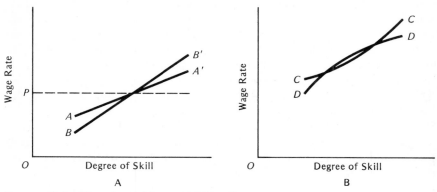

Figure 10-1   Hypothetical Internal Wage Structures

tants. Taylor attempted to bring the advantages of division of labor specifically to the managerial function with respect to workers in a firm, and his principal objective was to determine how each worker could do the job most effectively and be induced to maximum production. Somewhat later, industrial engineers developed the principles for determining job relationships based on skill and other criteria as guides to wage differentials in what is now called *job evaluation*. Though the objectives of job evaluation are essentially different from Taylor's, there are similarities in the analysis of job content that logically precedes the establishment of methods of job performance.[9]

In job evaluation, the criteria by which each job is to be compared with others are determined, and then each job is ranked according to those standards. Later, wage rates are assigned to different classifications. The criteria for measuring the relative difficulty of jobs may include several different factors, such as skill, amount of training required, necessary educational background, extent of responsibility, and amount of physical exertion. In analyzing a job, point values are assigned to various factors in accordance with their relative importance for adequate job performance. Thus a total point value for each job can be obtained. For example, a particular occupation might be evaluated at 280 points out of a theoretical maximum of 400, derived from 50 possible points for each of eight component factors. When every other job is evaluated in terms of the same eight factors, the point scores become an objective basis for comparing relative ranks. For example, if a second job were evaluated at 252 points, or 10 percent less than the first, the wage differential should reflect that fact, although it need not necessarily be 10 percent.

The job evaluation procedure gives a quantitative basis for the classifica-

---

[9] A discussion of scientific wage determination is found in David Belcher, *Wage and Salary Administration* (Englewood Cliffs, N.J.: Prentice-Hall, 1955).

tion of jobs in terms of complexity and for the assignment of economic value to those jobs for which market rates are lacking or not representative. The principal limitations of the procedures lie in the subjectivity of the selection of the factors to be evaluated, the weights (or points) to be given each factor, and the monetary values assigned to points. Different consultants using different systems will arrive at different sets of wage differentials.

For many years unions opposed job evaluation procedures, suspecting that management wished to impose its own subjective standards of the wage structure upon workers under the guise of a pseudoscientific method. Since World War II, however, many unions have come to accept job evaluation as a rational approach to internal wage structure problems, but insist upon reserving their right to protest through the regular grievance procedure any wage changes that result from management's new job evaluations; some unions participate directly in the evaluation process. This change in attitude has resulted both from management's willingness to recognize the subjective elements in job evaluation and to allow the union a voice in its administration and from the union's recognition of the usefulness of such procedures in bringing about wage uniformity for similar work within a large complex firm or among several firms. Unions recognize that unless each job title always entails the same duties, the principle of equal pay for equal work cannot easily be applied.

Job Performance and Incentive Wages

With stopwatches and motion pictures, the details of workers' performances can be observed, timed, and analyzed. Unlike job evaluation, which refers to a comparison of job characteristics, such time-and-motion studies pertain to the establishment of standards of job performance. Their objective is to determine both the actual performance of each worker on each job and the standard for performance of the job. The ultimate goal is to determine the most efficient method of work for the average worker at a speed that he or she can be expected to maintain. In many instances a different location of materials or a different flow of work will save time and increase the output per worker. Once the "best" method of job performance has been determined, the standard of output per unit of time that the average worker should be able to accomplish can be established.

Standards established in this way often become the basis for what is known as an "incentive wage system," a method of payment that induces the worker to meet the established standard of performance and to exceed it where possible. However, the use of such standards does not require an incentive system of payment. The wage rate can be set by the hour, day, or week, irrespective of the rate of output, even when time-and-motion studies are used to determine the amount of work an employee should normally be required to perform; an employee who fails to meet that standard can be fired or transferred.

In order for an incentive system to be a feasible method of wage payment for production workers, certain requirements should be met. The work procedure must be standardized and repetitive. Changes in output must be attributed primarily to changes in workers' efforts[10] and not to other factors, such as changes in equipment, tools, or raw materials. Furthermore, the product must be uniform and not subject to variation in quality or consumer specifications, the output must be measurable, and the unit of time for production should be short. Finally, the materials and the product should not be of such high value that the worker's incentive to higher production can cause high waste or spoilage costs.

An incentive system of wage payment entails the establishment of a standard of production that the average worker under average conditions can attain for each particular job, and the devising of some formula to reward the worker with increased earnings if he or she produces above that standard. Most of the systems used today fall into two categories. In "straight piecework" the wage for the job per some definite unit of time is divided by the number of units of goods that can be produced in that time if the standard is achieved. The quotient is known as the "piece rate." A worker who exceeds the established standard is paid the piece rate for each extra unit produced in addition to the "base rate," which is usually a guaranteed minimum wage per unit of time. The "bonus system" of payment defines an "hour" of work as the production of the standard output. Under a 100 percent bonus plan, for example, when a worker's output is double the standard, he or she is paid for two "hours" of work. In some plans, the "extra" hours are remunerated at only 50 or 75 percent of the base pay.[11]

Workers' attitudes toward incentive methods of payment vary from hostility to complete acceptance. Both unorganized and organized workers have expressed the suspicion that piecework rates can be manipulated to induce the worker to produce more and more without a compensating wage increase. Arguing against a "speed-up," unions have pointed to firms that have induced more production by an incentive wage scheme and then arbitrarily raised the standard of performance so that the wages were cut. Another argument has been that a "pace setter," or an exceptionally fast worker, may create serious tensions within the work group and undermine morale and efficiency. Finally, the argument that increased output is to every employee's benefit loses force when firms that have introduced incentive systems boast of a reduction in employment and lower labor costs as a result of greater effi-

[10] When output is under the control of a group or team of workers, individual incentive systems are sometimes replaced by a group incentive plan.

[11] These are known as "gain-sharing" plans, although some workers may refer to them as "take-away" plans.

ciency; a worker confronted with the prospect of a new incentive system is likely to feel that his job is less secure.

On the other hand, some unions have accepted incentive wage systems, and there is even some evidence of greater acceptance now than formerly.[12] Objective appraisals of jobs by means of time-and-motion studies are clearly necessary in large and growing firms, where wage structures can easily become disorganized and chaotic, and unions have been willing to accept them if proper safeguards are provided. Such controls might include union participation in the studies, bargaining over incentive plans, or the right to protest new rate changes through the grievance procedure. An example of acceptance is to be found in the women's garment industry, where an incentive system not only proved feasible but also helped to assure the stabilization of labor costs that both unions and employers have tried to achieve throughout the industry; much of the job analysis in this system was done by the union.

WAGE SUPPLEMENTS

Union policy also seeks to increase indirect types of monetary payments. These supplementary wage payments, or fringe benefits, include shift differentials, paid holidays and vacations, group health insurance, private insurance programs, private pensions, supplementary unemployment payments, and various forms of profit sharing. The growth of supplements in union agreements began during World War II, when the National War Labor Board, though placing a ceiling on wage increases, did allow bargaining over fringe benefits. After the war, the National Labor Relations Board, which contended in the Inland Steel case that supplementary benefits were legitimate bargaining issues, was upheld by the Supreme Court in 1949. After the steel strike of the same year, conducted to force acceptance of a favorable report by a presidential fact-finding board, the big steel companies agreed to union bargaining over pensions, life insurance, temporary disability payments, and hospital and surgical benefits. This success established a pattern that was quickly followed by the United Automobile Workers and other unions.

Since then supplementary benefits have grown phenomenally. The cost of fringe benefits is a significant part of a firm's total wage bill. In 1959 an employer's expenditures for supplementary benefits amounted to 18 percent of the compensation of production workers in manufacturing; by 1970 it had arisen to 24 percent.[13] (These costs include employers' matching Social Secu-

---

[12] To the extent that automation is introduced in industry, the individual worker's control over the rate of output is reduced and the incentive system becomes inapplicable for the individual; an incentive plan can often be devised however for a group, or team, of workers.

[13] George Rubin, "Major Collective Bargaining Developments—A Quarter Century Review," *Current Wage Developments* (February 1974), 47.

rity taxes and the tax payments under state unemployment compensation laws.)

Estimates for all employees in the private nonfarm sector show a slightly lower percentage. In 1972 it was 19.5 percent, averaging $1.02 cents out of a total compensation per hour of $5.23. As shown in Table 10–1, the greatest amount of the supplementary pay (36 cents) went for the employers' contribution to retirement plans, while 29 cents went for vacations and holidays, and 24 cents for insurance and health programs.

Table 10-1
Expenditures for Employee Compensation, 1966 and 1972
(In dollars per work hour)

Employee Group and Compensation Item	1966	1972	Percent Change
ALL EMPLOYEES			
Total compensation	$3.44	$5.23	52
Pay for working time	2.85	4.21	48
Compensation beyond pay for working time	.59	1.02	73
Pay for leave[a]	.18	.29	61
Vacations	.11	.17	55
Holidays	.07	.11	57
Employer expenditures for retirement programs	.20	.36	80
Social security	.11	.19	73
Private retirement plans	.09	.17	89
Employer expenditures for insurance and health benefit programs	.12	.24	100
Life, accident, and health insurance	.07	.16	129
Sick leave	.02	.04	(*)
Workers' compensation	.03	.05	(*)
Other[b]	.09	.13	(*)
Office employees			
Total compensation	4.51	6.71	49
Pay for working time	3.69	5.34	45
Compensation beyond pay for working time	.82	1.37	67
Pay for leave[a]	.27	.43	59
Vacations	.16	.26	63
Holidays	.10	.16	60
Employer expenditures for retirement programs	.26	.48	85
Social Security	.12	.21	75
Private retirement plans	.14	.27	93
Employer expenditures for insurance and health benefit programs	.13	.28	115

Employee Group and Compensation Item	1966	1972	Percent Change
Life, accident, and health insurance	.08	.18	125
Sick Leave	.04	.07	(*)
Workers' compensation	.01	.02	(*)
Other[b]	.16	.18	(*)
Nonoffice employees			
Total compensation	2.98	4.45	49
Pay for working time	2.50	3.62	45
Compensation beyond pay for working time	.48	.83	73
Pay for leave[a]	.14	.22	57
Vacations	.08	.13	63
Holidays	.05	.08	60
Employer expenditures for retirement programs	.16	.30	88
Social security	.10	.18	80
Private retirement plans	.06	.12	100
Employer expenditures for insurance and health benefit programs	.12	.23	92
Life, accident, and health insurance	.07	.14	100
Sick leave	.01	.02	(*)
Workers' compensation	.04	.06	(*)
Other[b]	.06	.08	(*)

[a] Excludes paid sick leave. Includes civic and personal leave and certain payments to funds for leave not shown separately.

[b] Includes expenditures for unemployment benefit programs, savings and thrift plans, and nonproduction bonuses.

NOTE: Because of rounding, sums of individual items may not equal totals. Asterisk (*) indicates items for which percent change was not computed due to the effects of rounding.

Source: Paul L. Scheible, "Changes in Employee Compensation, 1966 to 1972," Monthly Labor Review, 98 (March 1975), 11.

Holidays and Vacations

In terms of union motivations, a number of wage supplements are an expression of the workers' desire to take part of their economic gains in the form of leisure time. In addition to the attempts to shorten the workday or workweek (discussed in the following chapter), unions seek paid vacations and paid holidays that shorten the working year.[14] Prior to the mid-1930s these

---

[14] A differential in the wage rate for work on the night shift also reflects workers' leisure-time preferences. In this case, the differential compensates for the greater desirability of free hours at night. Another example is call-in pay, which is paid to a worker "called in" to work during nonscheduled hours. Usually a minimum of a certain number of hours of pay

Table 10-2
Paid Holidays by Industry, 1974

Industry	Number of Paid Holidays
Automobile manufacturing	12 or 13[a]
Aerospace	12
Aluminum	10[b]
Apparel	8 or 9
Coal mining	
Bituminous	9
Anthracite	8
Electrical equipment	10
Longshore	
East Coast	13
West Coast	5
Lumber (West Coast)	10
Meatpacking	10
Petroleum refining	9
Postal service	9
Pulp and paper (West Coast)	10
Railroads	9
Rubber	10
Steel	9
Telephone communications	9
Tobacco	10
Trucking[c]	9 to 14[b]

[a] Depending on the number required to give employees unbroken paid time off from day before Christmas through New Year's Day. Employees also receive holiday pay for a designated Sunday in December.
[b] By 1975.
[c] Number of holidays varies by area.

Source: George Rubin, "Major Collective Bargaining Developments," *Current Wage Developments* (February 1974), 49–50.

benefits were rare for the nonsalaried worker. Now almost all unionized production workers receive paid holidays. Some of the arrangements prevailing in 1974 in major American industries are shown in Table 10–2.

Paid vacations have also become firmly established features of labor-management agreements. In 1935 only some 10 percent of industrial workers had paid vacation provisions. By 1940 the total had risen to about 50 percent, and

---

is offered, at a premium rate, even though the actual work may be performed in less time. Pay for "reporting time" is another fringe benefit based on the principle of extra pay for interruption of leisure; this payment for a specified number of hours of work is made to the employee who is required to report for work but who finds upon arrival that there is no work to do.

by 1952 to 90 percent of those under major collective bargaining agreements.[15] An innovative development was the extended, or sabbatical, vacation plan, which was first introduced in an agreement between the United Steelworkers and the American Can Company in 1962 and extended to the steel industry in the following year. The plan now provides for extended vacations every fifth year with a duration of 13 weeks for those in the upper half of the seniority list and 3 weeks for junior employees. Although this plan has attracted considerable attention, many industries do not find it feasible because of scheduling and production problems.

Insurance Programs

Union demands for health insurance, other insurance, and various welfare plans reflect a desire to forgo wage payments in order to buy health and welfare benefits at lower costs under group plans. Although a few unions had their own programs before World War II, most workers and their families had no protection against the uneven incidence of sickness and disease and the high costs of medical care. A new approach came in the 1946 negotiations of the United Mine Workers with Secretary of the Interior Julius A. Krug, who was then administrator of the soft coal mines that had been seized by the government under the War Labor Disputes Act. The agreement provided a health and welfare program, including a welfare and retirement fund and a medical and hospital fund, to be financed by a five-cent royalty on each ton of coal mined. The funds were to be administered by three trustees, one from the union, one from the industry, and a neutral. While the later NLRB ruling—which made health and welfare a mandatory bargaining issue—helped pave the way for the adoption of such programs in other industries, an additional factor was the defeat of organized labor's attempt to secure passage of a national health system. As it turned out, it was collective bargaining that gave direction to the development of health and welfare programs.[16]

Most employees, whether unionized or not, now have some form of health and welfare insurance. In 1970, the percentage of all employees, both public and private, was 80.2 for hospitalization insurance, 79.2 for surgical insurance, 71.1 for regular medical insurance, and 69.4 for life insurance and death benefits.[17] The percentage of workers covered by such plans is higher for those in unionized establishments. Under negotiated plans in private in-

---

[15] Rubin, "Major Collective Bargaining Developments," p. 50.

[16] For background on these issues see Raymond Munts, *Bargaining for Health: Labor Unions, Health Insurance, and Medical Care* (Madison, Wis.: University of Wisconsin Press, 1967), part I.

[17] Rubin, "Major Collective Bargaining Agreements," p. 51.

dustry 16.4 percent of workers were covered, or 93 percent of those under collective bargaining agreements in 1972.[18]

Health and welfare plans raise issues that differ from the wage objectives of unions. One question concerns whether the plan is to be contributory, with workers sharing part of the cost, or noncontributory, with the employer bearing the entire cost. The cost may be allocated on a payroll basis, in terms of so many cents per hour, or it may be dependent upon the level of benefits, with the employer usually paying whatever amount is required to obtain the benefits specified by the contract. In plans negotiated with large companies and in multiemployer agreements, the tendency seems to be toward noncontributory arrangements. Tax laws can be an important factor. Savings are made when employers pay the costs, because contributory payments are taxable under the rules of the Internal Revenue Service, while employers' payments are considered costs.

Other questions concern coverage—should workers' dependents also be covered?—and the fact that benefits per dollar which workers receive vary because medical costs differ in different localities. The fundamental problem in these respects is that in the bargaining between unions and management the benefits are not furnished by either party. The price agreed to is usually the price to be paid to intermediaries, such as Blue Cross/Blue Shield or private insurance agencies, not directly to the providers of the medical and hospital services. With the costs of such benefits rising more rapidly than the general cost of living, unions have found themselves winning gains at the bargaining table that evaporate as medical charges continue to climb.

Some unions have pioneered in promoting community health plans on the grounds that direct purchase of medical and other services can control the quality of the benefits paid for under collective bargaining. One of the most successful of such plans has been the Kaiser Foundation Health Plan on the West Coast. The United Steelworkers found that the prepayment, group practice community plan, first negotiated with Kaiser Steel in 1949, covered a higher percentage of insurable costs at a lower price. The key to savings resulting from the prepayment approach is reform of the delivery system of health services; the providers (physicians and hospitals) have an incentive to reduce costs and prevent unnecessary operations, and expenses are not passed on automatically to insurance carriers and thence to the bargaining table. The federal government has also entered the field of medical services, most recently in 1973 with the establishment of programs for Health Maintenance

[18] Richard Greene, "Unions Report Slow Rise in Health, Insurance, and Pension Coverage," *Monthly Labor Review*, 98 (January 1975), 67–70. Both payments and the incidence of such programs positively related to average hourly earnings, establishment size, and union status. See the econometric study of William R. Bailey and Albert E. Schwenk, "Employer Expenditures for Private Retirement and Insurance Plans," *Monthly Labor Review*, 95 (July 1972), 15–19.

Organizations (HMOs), experimental prepaid community health plans. One provision of the enabling act was that employers with 25 or more employees who have health benefit plans must offer a qualifying HMO, if one is available, to their workers as an alternative. There has been little experience under these provisions so far; the number of HMOs that qualify has been disappointingly small because of lack of funding, and their costs have been relatively high because of the many types of services mandated by the legislation.[19]

Unions have favored the reform of health care delivery systems through encouragement of HMOs as well as the passage of a national health security law that would make health care available to all. With respect to the 1973 legislation, however, some unions have contended that the provision requiring the employer to offer HMO choices directly to employees violates the NLRB principle that health and welfare demands must be subject to collective bargaining.

Pension Plans

With respect to pension plans in collective bargaining, several issues became matters of national debate in the early 1970s. Although most negotiated plans were funded, others had established no reserves and paid pensions out of current revenues—a practice no longer legal. In those cases, it was to the advantage of the employer to make the requirements for receiving a pension so restrictive—by requiring a lengthy period of continuous service, for example—that few if any workers would qualify. Other plans, inadequately funded, sometimes led to disappointment. Experience with plant shutdowns, moreover, showed a number of unions that negotiated benefits even for workers already retired could not be guaranteed.[20] The case of the deficit in the pension fund in the 1964 closing of the Studebaker plant in Indiana was a painful example.

For funded plans a major concern of workers is whether the pension is vested—that is, whether the funds contributed by the employer are payable at retirement even though the worker might no longer be working under the plan. In nonvested plans, rights to pensions are forfeited if workers leave the employ of a firm; in other plans workers lose their rights if they have worked less than a specified number of years (sometimes as high as 20) or have not attained a specific age, such as 50. An additional issue is the portability of a

---

[19] Paul Starr, "The Undelivered Health System," *The Public Interest,* 42 (Winter 1976), 66–85. See papers by Betty G. Lall and Don Vial on "Health and Collective Bargaining," in *Proceedings of the Twenty-Seventh Annual Winter Meeting, Industrial Relations Research Association,* December 28–29, 1974, pp. 9–29.

[20] Deficits can technically arise in funds of nonbankrupt firms during periods when the value of investments, such as stocks, is declining.

pension: whether a worker can transfer pension rights to a new employer. Unions and employers have generally been reluctant to press for portability on the grounds that plans are built exclusively for the benefit of those in a firm. In multiemployer bargaining, however, where a pension fund is established for workers in a group of firms—such as construction or services—workers can move freely among the participating firms without loss of pension rights.

Restrictive eligibility requirements for pensions and inadequate vesting and portability rights, of course, can deny to workers a return on that part of their wages which had presumably been allocated for their retirement. Although in 1973 some 50,000 pension plans, both negotiated and employer-initiated, covered 28 million workers (nearly half the private nonfarm work force),[21] workers with high turnover rates are not likely to benefit; these are workers in service industries and trade, women, and those with lower wages. At the same time, pension funds have become one of the most significant sources of capital for the American economy. In 1973 their total assets were $179 billion and their net increase per year was around $9 billion. Managed by bank trust departments and insurance companies, these funds, invested in the stock of major corporations, have given their managers positions of substantial influence. A handful of large banks control a major share of these assets; it is ironic that attempts to aid workers in their old age through private pensions have also contributed to the concentration of economic power.

In view of the social implications of pension plans, the federal government has attempted to exercise certain controls. The 1958 Welfare and Pension Plans Disclosure Act provided for disclosure of the finances of private pension funds in the hope of preventing misuse of funds for illegal purposes. In 1974 the Employee Retirement Income Security Act (ERISA) was passed, having as its major goal the introduction of requirements for funding and for vesting. The law requires that employers must build eventually a fund sufficient to pay pensions for future and present employees. Among the options now allowed for vesting are 100 percent vesting after 10 years of service, and a procedure for gradually increasing vested rights, beginning with 25 percent after five years of service and reaching 100 percent after 15 years of service. The act provides for modest beginnings in the insurance of funds against termination of a plan. In the case of portability, the act allows what are called "tax-free rollovers"—the shifting of funds (if agreed to by the original employer) to another pension plan without tax liability.

---

[21] See Peter Henle and Raymond Schmitt, "Pension Reform: The Long, Hard Road to Enactment," *Monthly Labor Review*, 97 (November 1974), 3–12.

Profit Sharing

A final type of wage supplement is profit sharing. According to an agreed-upon plan, some fixed proportion of the profits—usually from 5 to 25 percent—is distributed to workers. With a "deferred payment" plan, the sum set aside each year is most likely to be used for the purchase, often by the firm itself, of retirement pensions that are later allocated to workers in accordance with their earnings. A "cash bonus" plan provides annual or periodic payments to the work force on the basis of a formula generally related to workers' earnings or seniority. A few plans provide for distribution of stock in the firm to workers, but they are not common.

One aspect of the profit sharing that appeals to a management is that the work force may come to recognize that greater productivity can benefit the workers. In contrast to many incentive wage plans, where workers are likely to feel that they are working against each other and against management, profit sharing on a company basis can lead to greater cooperation in the achievement of common goals.

Although formerly considered a scheme to reduce workers' temptation to join a union, profit sharing is now more likely to be supported by unions, and in 1961 the United Automobile Workers and American Motors introduced such a plan in their three-year contract. Undoubtedly in those bargaining situations in which each side distrusts the other, profit sharing may be viewed with suspicion. But where management takes the union into its confidence, and where the union stands ready to view managerial problems realistically and sympathetically, a system combining group incentives with profit sharing may be more effectively introduced. The Scanlon Plan is an example of a successful arrangement that links labor-saving efforts by workers to profits.[22] In this system a standard ratio of labor cost to value of output is established, and any savings that result from relatively lower labor costs are distributed to all the workers in proportion to their wages.

The value of profit-sharing plans is limited in several ways. The extent of profits in a firm is dependent upon many factors other than worker efficiency: because of poor location, changing consumer tastes, development of new competition, financial restraints, or poor management, a firm may not have profits to share. With profit sharing workers may feel that their wages are lower than they otherwise would be and that a variable "extra" return for their labor in the form of a bonus is not a satisfactory compensation for the

---

[22] Named after Joseph N. Scanlon, an official of the United Steelworkers of America and later a member of the Industrial Relations Section at the Massachusetts Institute of Technology until his death in 1956. See Frederick G. Lesieur, ed., *The Scanlon Plan. A Frontier in Labor-Management Cooperation* (Cambridge, Mass.: Technology Press of Massachusetts Institute of Technology, and New York, John Wiley, 1959), pp. 21ff.

certainty of a fixed wage. It is also doubtful whether a large firm can secure the support of increased worker effort as readily as a smaller firm.

SUMMARY

The fundamental issue in collective bargaining is the price of labor. The main interest in most negotiations concerns wages as such, and more particularly the change in the general level of wages. Among the arguments that both employers and unions consider in deciding upon their negotiating position is the going rate—pay for similar work in the market. Estimations of the going rate can vary, however, because even in local markets there may be a range in occupational wage rates. If it is to their advantage, employers or unions may point to national wage levels as indicators of the going rate. Another argument for a wage change, the productivity argument, is also frequently ambiguous because of difficulties in measurement. Unions sometimes use high profits as an argument for a wage increase, but are not necessarily deterred from asking for an increase when profits are low. Cost-of-living increases invariably produce demands by unions for wage hikes. Escalator clauses that provide for automatic wage adjustments in accordance with changes in some recognized index have been used successfully in many contracts.

In negotiations, unions may be concerned with the "employment effect" of a wage change, especially when severe loss of employment may result from a wage increase. Both unions and employers also consider the internal, or political, effects of negotiated wages upon the various interest groups within their organizations.

The internal wage structure that defines wage differentials between different jobs in a firm is of considerable importance to both unions and management. Various job evaluation systems used in trying to provide objective criteria for establishing such differentials are subject to collective bargaining. Unions may support incentive wage systems, which tie wages to job performance, if they believe the controls are adequate to prevent arbitrary speed-ups.

Fringe benefits, or wage supplements, have grown in recent years more rapidly than wages. Paid holidays, paid vacations, and the extended vacation are ways by which workers can shorten their work year; hence these arrangements reflect the income effect of rising wages in terms of the work/leisure trade-off. Demands for various welfare plans and health insurance have been labor's responses to the high price of medical care. One major problem in such plans is the fact that the agreement reached in collective bargaining relates to intermediaries, such as insurance companies, and not to the final providers of medical services. To avoid escalation of medical costs, a few unions, together with managements, have experimented in the direct purchase of medical services through community health centers. Pensions are a popular wage supplement. Before 1974 pension plans had sometimes been nonfunded, noninsured, and most often not vested, with the result that gains at the bargaining table could disappear for a worker who left the firm. Profit-sharing plans enable the worker to participate in a firm's profits; they are often designed to give workers an incentive toward greater productivity.

DISCUSSION QUESTIONS

1. In formulating wage demands, unions may use arguments related to the going rate, productivity, profits, or changes in the cost of living. Which, if any, do you believe should be controlling in all circumstances? Explain.
2. Do unions consider the elasticity of the demand curve for labor in their wage demands? Explain in terms of the analysis of employment and membership effects.
3. As a political organization a union must be responsive to various interest groups, both internal and external—in Ross's term, the "orbit of coercive comparison." Show how this aspect of unions affects the formulation of wage demands.
4. Escalator clauses and deferred wage increases characterize many long-term contracts. What are their advantages and disadvantages from the viewpoints of labor, employers, and the general public?
5. If workers are not employed on piecework, their contribution to the output of the firm cannot be easily identified. What procedures may firms follow to assess a worker's job performance? Do difficulties in measuring a worker's output invalidate the theory of labor demand in terms of the marginal product?
6. What is an incentive wage system, and under what circumstances is it most effectively applied?
7. Discuss the proposition that the growth of wage supplements in the American economy reflects the income effects of wage increases.
8. Criticisms of vesting and of portability of pension plans led to passage of the Employment Retirement Income Security Act of 1974. What were the criticisms and what remedies were provided by the act?

SELECTED READINGS

On union wage policies, basic references include: John T. Dunlop, *Wage Determination and Trade Unions* (New York: Augustus Kelley, 1950); John T. Dunlop, ed., *The Theory of Wage Determination* (New York: St. Martin's, 1957); Joseph W. Garbarino, *Wage Policy and Long-Term Contracts* (Washington, D.C.: Brookings Institution, 1962); Arthur M. Ross, *Trade Union Wage Policy* (Berkeley: University of California Press, 1953; George W. Taylor and Frank C. Pierson, eds., *New Concepts in Wage Determination* (New York: McGraw-Hill, 1957); and Lloyd G. Reynolds and Cynthia H. Taft, *The Evolution of Wage Structure* (New Haven: Yale University Press, 1956). On the Dunlop-Ross controversy on union wage policy, see Daniel J. B. Mitchell, "Union Wage Policies: The Ross-Dunlop Debate Reopened," *Industrial Relations* 11 (February 1972), 46–61. Standard works on the management side of wage policy include Paul Pigors and Charles A. Myers, *Personnel Administration*, rev. ed. (New York: McGraw-Hill, 1969); and Sumner H. Slichter, James J.

Healy, and E. Robert Livernash, *The Impact of Collective Bargaining on Management* (Washington, D.C.: Brookings Institution, 1960). On problems of work measurement, see Norman A. Dudley, *Work Measurement: Some Research Studies* (New York; St. Martin's, 1968).

While general studies of fringe benefits are relatively few, the literature on pension plans has been growing rapidly. A few studies are: H. Robert Bartell, Jr., and Elizabeth T. Simpson, *Pension Funds of Multiemployer Industrial Groups, Unions, and Nonprofit Organizations*, National Bureau of Economic Research (New York: Columbia University Press, 1968); Merton C. Bernstein, *The Future of Private Pensions* (New York: Free Press, 1964); William C. Greenough and Francis P. King, *Pension Plans and Public Policy* (New York: Columbia University Press, 1976); Ralph Nader and Kate Blackwell, *You and Your Pension* (New York: Grossman, 1973); Alfred M. Skolnik, "Private Pension Plans, 1950–74," *Social Security Bulletin,* 39 (June 1976), 3–17; and Robert Tilove, *Public Employee Pension Funds* (New York: Columbia University Press, 1976).

11

Union Objectives in Collective Bargaining

Hours of Work, Security, Seniority, and Work Rules

Having examined union objectives regarding wages and fringe benefits, we shall now discuss other matters dealt with in collective bargaining: hours of work, union security, seniority, and work rules.

HOURS OF WORK

Controversies and Public Policies

Over the years unions have taken a generally consistent stand in favor of shorter hours of work, both per day and per week. Different arguments have been used in different periods. In the 1820s unions stressed the argument of citizenship, when work from "sun to sun" six days a week was held to keep the workingman too busy to give him an opportunity to exercise his political rights. Shorter hours were also supported on the grounds of health and decency, especially for women and children. During the Civil War the eight-hour-day agitation was based on the idea that a reduced supply of labor would raise wages. Later Samuel Gompers and the American Federation of Labor used the "lump-of-labor" assumption—that is, the implication that at any one time there is a fixed amount of work to be performed—to argue that unemployment could be reduced by decreasing the amount of work shared by each individual worker.[1] More recently, the positive note of more leisure activities for workers has been emphasized.

[1] Gompers's oft-quoted statement in 1887 was: "So long as there is one man who seeks employment and cannot obtain it, the hours of labor are too long."

Some of these arguments are still used by unions in one way or another today, depending upon the prevailing economic conditions. In 1962 the unemployment issue was dramatized in New York City by a strike by Local 3 of the International Brotherhood of Electrical Workers for a workweek of 20 hours; the final settlement scheduled a 25-hour week, still one of the shortest among union contracts. Although AFL–CIO leaders did not push for shorter scheduled workweeks during the 1974–1975 recession as they had during the early 1960s, a few union leaders are now making the case for an eight-hour day and a four-day workweek. The stress and fatigue of prolonged periods of work are still issues for unions in certain situations. One union objection to the 40-hour, four-day week proposal of certain managements is the fatigue factor in a 10-hour workday. Similar grounds are invoked in union criticisms of compulsory overtime.

Employers often view union demands for shorter hours as attempts to reduce output, raise costs, and lower profits. Actually, this view neglects the role of productivity, at least in the long run. Historically, the decline in weekly hours of work has been accompanied by a rise in income not only per hour of work but also per week. The underlying explanation is not that reduced hours have led to reduced income but, on the contrary, that increased income has led to shorter hours. The choice to increase leisure time rather than consumption as a benefit of increased productivity, the possibility of which was discussed in the analysis of hours of work in chapter 3, seems to be precisely the one that the American worker has made.

In manufacturing, about 60 hours constituted the usual workweek in the 1890s. The average had fallen to about 55 by World War I, and to 50 during the prosperous 1920s, principally as a result of a shift from the six- to the five-and-a-half and then to the five-day week. The workday tended to average 10 hours before World War I, but during the 1920s the eight-hour day was achieved in many industries. During the Great Depression of the 1930s declines in business activity, unemployment, the idea of work sharing, and shifts in public attitudes toward national legislation on hours of work supported the change to the eight-hour day and the five-day week that caused the average workweek to fall to 40 hours.

The first national law regarding hours of work was the Fair Labor Standards Act, passed in 1938, which required that overtime rates of time and a half be paid for work in excess of 44 hours during the first year after passage of the law, of 42 hours during the second year, and of 40 hours thereafter. Exceptions to this provision were made for agriculture and several other activities, and firms in intrastate commerce were of course excluded. The act did not set absolute maximum hours, and workers could work as long as they wished if employers were willing to hire them and pay their overtime wages. Although the hours provisions of the 1938 law have remained unchanged, the coverage of the act has increased. The 1974 amendments brought an estimated additional 7.4 million workers under its provisions.[2]

While the actual average number of hours of work have varied with changes in business activity and with periods of war and peace, scheduled hours of work per week in manufacturing have remained remarkably constant since World War II, ranging on the average from 39.1 to 41.3 between 1947 and 1970. (Long-run declines in the overall average number of weekly hours of work for the total private economy reflect the downward trend in weekly hours in the trade and service industries, where increasing amounts of part-time labor have been employed.) The 40-hour week consisting of five days of eight hours each has become well fixed in most labor agreements. Many agreements call for overtime payments in excess of eight hours a day; usually "pyramiding" of overtime is prohibited—that is, weekly overtime is not to be paid on daily overtime payments already made.

Current Issues in Hours of Work

The problems of reconciling the interests and preferences of workers in their hours of work with management's interests in production underlie several current issues. One is a proposal for the introduction of a four-day work-week with a daily schedule of 10 hours. Introduced by a few employers in the early 1970s, the scheme was heralded as a major social invention that would enhance productivity simply by rearranging the traditional 40 hours of the workweek. It was held that workers would benefit from a three-day weekend; they could devote more time to attending to their personal affairs, to leisure activities, and to the enjoyment of their income. From such gains, workers would have higher morale, be more efficient in their productive efforts, be absent less (because the loss of one day's work would take a bigger bite from the paycheck), and be less apt to quit. All of these factors, according to Riva Poor, a leading advocate of the plan, would lower labor costs.[3]

The plan has met with only limited success—about 2 percent of the full-time workers of American firms are estimated to be working on rearranged schedules of four- or three-day weeks—and unions are not enthusiastic about it. One reason is that the 10-hour day increases work fatigue and places a hardship on those whose personal daily routines cannot be postponed until

---

[2] It is estimated that in 1974, 57 million out of 77 million wage and salary earners in the United States, or approximately three out of four, were subject to the act's overtime provisions. The groups now excluded are administrative and professional workers, agricultural workers, outside salespersons working on a commission basis, drivers engaged in over-the-road trucking, hospital workers, and employees of airlines, railroads, hotels, and motels. Peyton Elder, "The 1974 Amendments to the Federal Minimum Wage Law," *Monthly Labor Review*, 97 (July 1974), 33–37.

[3] Riva Poor, ed., *4 Days, 40 Hours and Other Forms of the Rearranged Workweek* (New York: New American Library, 1973), pp. 26–27.

the weekend—for example, women who rely on child-care centers that are not open for the extended hours. Experience so far indicates that absenteeism has not been reduced by the introduction of the four-day week. A further question appears to be whether the presumed gains of greater worker efficiency that result from the longer weekend might be lost as workers use extra days to moonlight. There is some evidence that a higher percentage of those on shorter workweek schedules find second (and even third) jobs.

Less rigid than the 40-hour, four-day week is the proposal for flexible work schedules. Called "flexitime," this innovation permits individuals to adjust their daily work schedules to fit their own needs.[4] Some workers may wish to begin work earlier in the day and leave earlier, while others may prefer later daily hours. Usually a "core time" of four to six hours during the day is established during which everyone is expected to work. To some employers who have already introduced such plans, flexitime can improve worker productivity, reduce absenteeism, and lead employees to become more responsible for the work they perform.

The extent to which flexitime is feasible depends upon the nature of the work involved. It appears to be more successfully introduced among managerial, professional, and clerical workers than among blue-collar workers where production requirements allow less scope for individual worker preferences. Moreover, some firms have found that administration costs are increased and some productivity lost because support services are not available at the less popular hours. Laws, both state and federal, concerning overtime payments may also lessen the attractiveness of such plans: so far legislative attempts in Congress to modify overtime requirements of the Fair Labor Standards Act, as well as for federal employees, have not been successful.

In general unions have not been enthusiastic about flexitime proposals. In keeping with their traditional bargaining objectives, they have emphasized shortening the work period with no reduction in pay rather than making adjustments which assume that total hours and wages are fixed. Attempts to increase vacation time and the number of paid holidays, or to introduce sabbatical leaves, indicate that a "flexiyear," or what might be called, albeit clumsily, a "flexiworklife," would be more appealing to them than rescheduling daily or weekly work.

A second current issue concerns compulsory overtime. This is an arrangement whereby the employer has the right to order overtime work and impose penalties on those who refuse. Under some collective bargaining agreements such penalties may involve denial of eligibility to work overtime at other

---

[4] Alvar O. Elbing, Herman Gadon, and John R. H. Gordon, "Flexible Working Hours: It's About Time," *Harvard Business Review*, 52 (January–February 1974), 1–6; John D. Owen "Flexitime: Some Problems and Solutions," *Industrial and Labor Relations Review*, 30 (January 1977), 152–160; and "Special Flexitime Reports," articles in *Monthly Labor Review*, 100 (February 1977), 62–74.

times, or even discharge. To employers, the power to require overtime work, even at 1.5 times the wage rate, may be preferable to hiring additional workers. The company would not have to bear the costs of hiring and training a different work force to meet unexpected or temporary demands for increased production. Moreover, the labor cost of the overtime is likely to be considerably less than that indicated by the wage rate of time and a half because of the importance of fringes, or indirect labor costs. As the latter have increased relative to the wage rate, the incidence of overtime pay has been relatively diminished.

Unions recognize that some workers are more eager than others to work overtime; they try to find some way to insure that the rights of all workers to participate in overtime are respected. At the same time, however, unions see the possibility that in periods of high unemployment, or when the work force is decreasing through the impact of automation and technological change, a firm may concentrate more and more production among fewer workers through overtime while it lays off or discharges others. To preserve job opportunities, some unions have sought to limit, and even prohibit, overtime work.[5] During the recession of the early 1960s, the AFL–CIO advanced, and President Lyndon B. Johnson briefly supported, a plan to amend the Fair Labor Standards Act to increase the rate of overtime pay from time and a half to double time. The proposal died in the face of strong adverse reaction by business and the business upturn that came with American involvement in the Vietnam War. During the early 1970s the principal union bargaining objective in such industries as automobiles was curtailment of compulsory overtime. Both fatigue and share-the-work motives were involved.[6] In 1973 the United Automobile Workers won the concession from the automobile makers that workers had the right to refuse overtime work beyond a certain number of hours under certain circumstances.

UNION SECURITY

Union security is provided by those labor contract clauses that protect and strengthen the union as a bargaining agent within a firm. The most important

[5] See Frederic Meyers, "The Economics of Overtime," in Clyde E. Dankert, Floyd C. Mann, and Herbert R. Northrup, eds., *Hours of Work*, Industrial Relations Research Association Publication No. 32 (New York: Harper & Row, 1965), pp. 95–110, for an analysis of "overtime unemployment"—that is, the inability to secure extra work because of union rules—as preferable to actual unemployment.

[6] In testimony before the Michigan Occupational Safety Standards Commission in 1969, female employees in auto and packing industries described the fatigue and exhaustion of women required to work 69, and even 84, hours a week. See Raymond Munts and David C. Rice, "Women Workers: Protection or Equality?" *Industrial and Labor Relations Review*, 24 (October 1970), 3–13.

of such clauses define the "shop" in terms of the firm's hiring policy and the relationship of workers to the union. Another union security provision is the checkoff. We shall consider first the six types of shops, then the checkoff, and finally arguments for and against such provisions.

Types of Shop

1. The "open shop" has several meanings. In an *open shop with union recognition* an employer may hire and fire workers irrespective of whether they belong to the union that has been recognized as their exclusive bargaining agent. In a true *open shop without union recognition* there is no discrimination in hiring or firing because of union affiliation even though the firm has not recognized the union. This type of shop should not be confused with what unionists have often called an *antiunion open shop*—namely, a closed nonunion shop in which the employer does not recognize the union, hires only nonunion workers, and fires any workers who join the union. Such discrimination in hiring and firing is illegal under federal law, while the open shop with or without union recognition is legal.

2. A *union shop* arrangement allows the employer to hire nonunion as well as union labor but requires that new employees shall join the union within a specified period of time as a condition of continued employment. Under the present law, the minimum time before the worker must join the union is 30 days (except in the construction industry, where the minimum can be seven days). The union shop was declared legal under the Taft-Hartley Act, though the act as passed in 1947 specified that a union could not request a union shop unless a majority of the workers in the bargaining unit[7] voted in favor of it in a special election conducted by National Labor Relations Board. This qualification was eliminated in the Taft-Hartley Act amendment of 1951 after it became clear that workers overwhelmingly supported the union shop in nearly all elections.[8]

The revised law included two other clauses relating to the union shop. One provision—Sections 8(a) (3) and 8(b)(2)—states that a worker may not be expelled from the union except for nonpayment of dues. Thus employees are protected from losing their jobs because of expulsion from the union for such reasons as violation of the union constitution and bylaws. The other provision—Section 14(b)—grants more restrictive laws of state governments prec-

---

[7] A majority of those voting was not enough.
[8] From 1947 to October 22, 1951, when the amendment was effective, the NLRB conducted 46,119 elections, and of these the union shop was authorized in 44,795 polls, or 91.1 percent of the cases. The proportion of the 5,547,478 workers voting who cast votes in favor of the union shop was 92.2 percent. They represented 77.5 percent of the employees eligible to vote. National Labor Relations Board, *Sixteenth Annual Report, for Fiscal Year Ending June 30, 1951* (Washington, D.C.: Government Printing Office, 1951), p. 301.

edence over federal law, so that any state prohibition of the union shop affects firms in interstate as well as in intrastate commerce. At the present time, 19 states have "right-to-work" laws that outlaw the union shop as well as the closed shop.[9]

In a *modified union shop* employees who do not wish to become union members when the agreement goes into effect may keep their nonunion status, although all new employees are required to join the union. This modification is used when there is a small but vocal group of employees with strong antiunion feelings.

3. The *maintenance-of-membership shop* is similar to the modified union shop, except that an "escape period" is allowed at the beginning of the life of the contract, during which those who want to withdraw from the union may do so. Those who do elect to join the union are required to maintain their membership in good standing as a condition of employment. The maintenance-of-membership shop was introduced during World War II by the National War Labor Board as a compromise between advocates of the union shop and those employers who did not want unions to consolidate their foothold in plants under the temporary conditions of a war emergency.

4. An *agency shop* is somewhat different from either the modified union or maintenance-of-membership shop. It requires that workers in a plant must either join or pay a fee to the union as a condition of continued employment. This is justified on the grounds that any expenses in negotiations incurred by the union as the exclusive bargaining agent for all workers should be borne by all workers. It is directed towards eliminating the "free riders" who gain benefits without sharing in the costs. The distinction between paying a fee and paying dues as a union member is rather finely drawn, but presumably it enables nonunionists to pay their share without considering themselves union members.

5. In the *preferential shop* the employer gave preference in hiring to union members. Declared illegal under the Taft-Hartley Act, the preferential shop was first devised as an answer to the problem of union security in the men's garment industry in an agreement that ended a lengthy strike in Chicago in 1911. Under its terms the union became in essence the labor recruiting agency for the employer as long as unemployed members were available. When no more unionists were available, the employer could hire additional workers through other channels, and at times the union would issue temporary work permits to nonunionists. The preferential-shop clause usually provided that in times of layoff nonunionists would be discharged before unionists.

---

[9] These are primarily agricultural states in the South and Midwest: Alabama, Arizona, Arkansas, Florida, Georgia, Iowa, Kansas, Mississippi, Nebraska, Nevada, North Carolina, North Dakota, South Carolina, South Dakota, Tennessee, Texas, Utah, Virginia, and Wyoming.

6. In the *closed shop* all workers hired had to be members of the union. Declared illegal under the Taft-Hartley Act, the Railway Labor Act, and the "right-to-work" laws of various states, the closed shop provided an old and most effective type of union security because the union became the sole labor recruiting agency. Unions in the construction trades, those in the maritime, longshore, printing, and amusement industries, and craft unions generally favored the closed shop as an efficient way of controlling the supply of labor and regularizing its use. Employers often accepted the closed shop in order to be assured a supply of skilled labor: a request to the union's business agent was all that was necessary when a crew of people were needed for a particular job.

The impact of the ban in the Taft-Hartley Act was substantial in those industries where closed shops had long been in effect. Some unions fought bitterly to preserve their controls. The International Typographical Union struck in several cities, for example, as did the West Coast longshoremen, but their efforts were unsuccessful.

In certain industries institutional arrangements that are of questionable legality have often maintained the advantages of the closed shop to both unions and employers in the years since the bill was passed. In the construction trades, for example, the provision that workers should join the union after 30 days was found to be inapplicable because jobs were generally of shorter duration. Employers continued to rely on the union for referral of workers on the basis of such criteria as seniority, competence, and experience—a procedure that in effect gave priority to union members. Partial recognition of the economic justification of these practices came in 1959, when an amendment to the Taft-Hartley Act, passed as Section 8(f) of the Landrum-Griffin Act of 1959, permitted unions in the construction industry to make referrals of workers for employment and to require their joining the union after seven days of employment.

The Checkoff

As a union security device, the checkoff eliminates the risk of union members dropping out of unions for nonpayment of dues: it requires employers to deduct dues from wages before distributing paychecks. The system simplifies the collection of dues and in most instances shifts the cost of collection to the employer. Under Section 302 of the Taft-Hartley Act, the checkoff is lawful only if the worker gives written authorization for it to the employer.

The checkoff is popular. A survey of 1,514 major labor agreements in 1975 showed that 81.1 percent of the contracts contained checkoff clauses; such agreements covered some 5.8 million workers, or 81.9 percent of the 7 million workers under these major agreements.

Controversies over Union Security

Union security has been a controversial issue in bargaining negotiations between unions and management and in formulating public policy at both the federal and state levels. Unions have fought for security primarily on the grounds of survival, justifying their demands with the claim that unsympathetic employers could readily undermine them by hiring nonunionists and firing union members. They have argued that in countries where employer opposition to unions has been moderate or nonexistent, labor has been less inclined to demand union security clauses. On the other hand, some employers are unwilling to concede that a union should be a permanent institution, and regard security clauses as monopolistic devices to compel them to be a party in forcing unwilling workers into unions.

While the facts cannot resolve the policy question of union security, it does seem questionable whether the legal ban on the closed shop has seriously hindered unions in maintaining themselves in the face of employer opposition. At the same time there is some indication that bans on union shops in "right-to-work" states have slowed union growth in unorganized sectors of the labor force.[10]

A second element in the union shop controversy is the difference in attitudes of management and the union toward the nonunion worker. Especially in the craft unions, members may refuse to work beside nonmembers, since skilled workers believe that they have a stake in their trade and in high standards of job performance and that the union has been the means by which those standards have been upheld. Nonunion workers, they argue, do not appreciate the long history of struggle for job standards and may undermine standards, downgrade their job status, and impair the reputation of the trade by accepting different terms of employment. Bringing them into the union will protect their own interests as well as those of the present members.

Another argument often advanced, especially for the union shop among industrial workers, is that since the union secures benefits that are applicable to all workers in its bargaining unit, not just to union members, nonmembers should not be given a "free ride." They should contribute to the cost of the administration and to the formulation of bargaining policy by the entire union membership.

Employers, on the other hand, argue that the "right" of a worker to remain nonunionized should be respected, and that a union is not a "government" that can demand the payment of a "tax" in the form of dues. On the question

[10] See Harold W. Davey, "The Operational Impact of the Taft-Hartley Act upon Collective Bargaining Relationships," in Davey et al., *New Dimensions in Collective Bargaining* (New York: Harper, 1959), p. 183.

Table 11-1
Union Security Provisions in Agreements Covering 1,000 Workers or More,
July 1, 1975

	Agreements		Workers	
Type of Shop	Number	Percent	Number	Percent
Union shop	975	62.4	4,441,350	62.8
Modified union shop	93	6.1	313,650	4.4
Agency shop	89	5.9	492,250	7.0
Maintenance-of-membership	51	3.4	153,700	2.2
Combinations of above	73	4.8	792,650	11.2
Sole bargaining[a]	263	17.4	876,150	12.4
Total	1,514	100.0	7,069,750	100.0

[a] Union is exclusive bargaining agent for both union and nonunion employees, but union membership is not required as a condition of employment.

Source: Adapted from U.S. Department of Labor, Bureau of Labor Statistics, *Characteristics of Major Collective Bargaining Agreements, July 1, 1975,* Bulletin 1957 (Washington, D.C.: U.S. Government Printing Office, 1977), pp. 16–17.

of work standards, employers criticize union controls as restrictive and out-moded and point out that more efficient productive processes can often be introduced only where the union does not control the labor supply.

Most major union agreements contain union security provisions; in 1975 over two-thirds of the workers were employed under union shop or modified union shop clauses (see Table 11–1). The percentage of workers who had no formal union security contract provisions—listed as "sole bargaining"—was 12.4; 7.0 percent worked under the agency shop arrangement; the remainder were under maintenance-of-membership agreements, combinations of clauses, or clauses that provided for negotiations at the local level. Since World War II, significant changes have included the virtual disappearance of the closed shop, which in 1946 (before the impact of the Taft-Hartley amendments) covered a third of the workers under major collective bargaining agreements, and a decline in maintenance-of-membership shops, which had been introduced during the war as unions won union shop arrangements. The percentage of workers in shops with no formal security clauses also steadily dropped after 1946, when about a fourth of the workers had no such protection.[11]

SENIORITY

Among the administrative rules of the structured labor market that most unions insist upon is the principle of seniority, whereby length of service is a

[11] For a breakdown of the earlier types of shops see "Union Security Provisions in Major Union Contracts," *Monthly Labor Review,* 82 (December 1959), 1349.

guide to the allocation of job opportunities and other benefits within a firm. Unions have generally taken the position that workers who have worked longest for a firm should be favored in one way or another, and many employers have also come to accept this general principle. Yet the extent and types of advantages to be granted on the basis of seniority are often bitterly disputed. The manner in which the principle is interpreted can have significant repercussions on the welfare of the worker, the efficiency of managerial operations, and, as revealed by the growing number of cases involving Title VII of the Civil Rights Act, on minorities and women, who have been denied access to job rights by discriminatory seniority systems.

Some writers distinguish two types of contractual clauses to which the seniority principle is applied. A commonly accepted type is "benefit-seniority," which determines the extent to which a worker can participate in fringe benefits. The number of weeks of paid vacation, the number of holidays, pension rights, and similar benefits may be allocated on the basis of workers' accrued seniority as determined by years of continuous service with a firm. More controversial is "competitive-status seniority"[12]—the use of length of service to determine who is to be promoted, who can compete for other jobs within the department, plant, or firm, who is last to be laid off, or who is first to be rehired after a layoff. Benefit-seniority has been viewed by workers, unions, and management generally as a practical and equitable guide to the allocation of supplementary benefits that have become increasingly important in the last several decades. In competitive-status seniority, different rules within the same firm may be applied to layoffs as compared with promotion. In some industries seniority clauses may not be relevant, such as construction, in which skilled workers are employed for short periods of time. In these cases, however, the union is likely to apply the seniority principle when assigning workers to jobs: those out of work the longest become the first in line for new jobs. In the maritime industries on both the Atlantic and Pacific coasts industrywide seniority governs new hires.

Approaches to Seniority

In regard to seniority as it governs personnel reassignments, unions tend to emphasize length of service, or "straight seniority," while management, in its concern for low-cost operation, is more likely to stress ability. Seeking a free hand to exercise its judgment in determining ability, management may feel that the worker who has been with the company longest should not necessarily be promoted to a higher-paying job as a reward for service.[13]

[12] These terms were first used in Sumner H. Slichter, James J. Healy, and E. Robert Livernash, *The Impact of Collective Bargaining on Management* (Washington, D.C.: Brookings Institution, 1960), p. 106.

[13] Another type of seniority is "superseniority," or greater protection than is indicated by length of service. It is sometimes given to shop stewards and union officials who might

Various compromises between the union and management viewpoints on seniority have been reached. Some have provided that "modified seniority," a combination of efficiency and length of service, should govern promotions. The union has sometimes participated in the determination of the exact definition of "efficiency." Contract clauses may give "due reference to seniority and ability," provide for seniority to govern where ability is "substantially" (or "relatively") equal, or state that ability shall be controlling only where length of service is equal. Under any seniority clause the union can initiate a grievance if it disputes management's action.

Management has been willing to accede to union demands for consideration of seniority, within limits, for several reasons. First, some correlation between length of service and efficiency certainly exists: the person who has worked in a firm for years has acquired knowledge and experience that a newer worker cannot offer. (Of course this consideration is not necessarily relevant to certain types of jobs, such as those requiring youth, sheer physical labor, or dexterity.) Secondly, many firms want to encourage personal loyalty in their employees in the hope of promoting a stable labor force and reducing the costs of high turnover; rewards for seniority can accomplish this, whether or not a firm is unionized. Finally, a rule or set of rules regarding seniority helps to simplify and standardize administrative decisions on personnel, so that, instead of being held personally responsible for bypassing one worker in promoting another, a foreman or departmental supervisor can "go by the book."

Seniority as a Controversial Issue Within Unions

In some ways seniority policies raise more controversy within unions than between unions and management. The security of any worker is affected by the precise way in which the rules for promotion, demotion, transfer, and layoffs are framed and interpreted. When "straight seniority" is applied to a whole plant, a vacancy is always filled by the employee at the next lowest grade who has the longest record of service if he or she is capable of performing the work required, irrespective of the department in which the worker is employed. Departmental seniority, on the other hand, assigns the job to the worker with the greatest seniority within the department, even if outranked by another employee elsewhere in the plant. One advantage of plant seniority is that long-service workers may remain secure even when the number of employees in their departments are being reduced, since they can replace em-

---

otherwise lose their jobs during a layoff and whose loss would undermine the existence of the union.

ployees with less seniority in other departments. On the other hand, the workers in a department where employment is relatively stable during times of layoff will favor departmental seniority. As a compromise, some seniority schemes provide for a combination of plant seniority at lower-ranked jobs and departmental seniority at higher-paid ones. In some instances there have been developed citywide seniority plans among the plants of a specific firm.

A particular seniority problem arises during mergers or consolidations of plant forces. For example, in one firm that wished to close one of its plants and use only its two more modern plants (one located within the same commuting area as the old plant and the other in an out-of-the-way town), the workers in the plant that was to close had accumulated much more seniority than those in the two newer locations. After several months of impassioned oratory in union meetings, a solution to the problems this move presented was worked out by the representatives of the locals and accepted without change by the management. It provided that workers from the closed plant would maintain their seniority if they transferred to the plant to which their particular jobs had been reassigned. Workers who did not want to follow their work to the more inconvenient location could take work at the other plant but would lose their claims to seniority for six months; if they were still employed at the end of that period, their full seniority rights would be restored. Fortunately an increase in business and a high enough rate of resignations during the six months enabled everyone who wished to remain with the firm to keep the accumulated seniority.

It is not always so easy. Another union-management solution to the consolidation of seniority lists—in this case resulting from the merger of two distilleries—was overturned by the National Labor Relations Board on the grounds that the union had failed fairly to represent the workers in the smaller of the two firms. Although before the merger the two firms had been organized by the same union (under separate contracts), the larger local had been able to override the seniority list of the smaller firm, claiming that the seniority of its workers should begin with the date of the merger. Although management accepted this arrangement, the NLRB found that both the union and management had committed an unfair labor practice, and ruled that the lists should be "dove-tailed."[14]

From the point of view of the economy as a whole, the impact of seniority on the efficiency of labor allocation has been the subject of much inconclusive debate. Within a firm, management may believe that seniority prevents the assignment of personnel in the interests of greater flexibility and productivity. To workers who are likely to place a high value on job security, senior-

[14] *Barton Brands, Ltd.* and *Distillery Workers, Local 23* and *Edward Humes*, 213 NLRB No. 71, October 8, 1974. See discussion in *Monthly Labor Review*, 98 (January 1975), 79–80.

ity means that the freedom from fear of arbitrary and capricious job assignments that comes from establishing systematic guidelines can lead to gains in worker morale and efficiency. Another argument is that seniority reduces labor mobility among firms and hence limits efficiency in labor allocation. A rebuttal is that those who have greater seniority tend to be older workers, who would be less inclined to move from employer to employer in any event. And in the structuring of labor markets, as shown earlier, stability of the labor force can result in considerable savings to a firm, both in recruitment costs and in resources invested in worker training and development.

Seniority and Equal Employment Opportunity

With the passage in 1964 of Title VII of the Civil Rights Act, and with other regulations designed to curb racial and sex discrimination, seniority systems have become the object of new criticisms. It is ironic that the union movement, which played a vital role in the passage of civil rights legislation, should find its achievement of job protection through seniority rights being challenged as violating the rights of minorities and women. The problem arises in two connections. One is the role of seniority in establishing ladders of promotion within a firm; the other is its role in determining the order of layoffs.

In promotions, few seniority systems are now openly discriminatory. In the past there were arrangements whereby separate ladders for blacks and whites were set up in the same firm in order to preserve higher-paying positions for whites and to prevent blacks from transferring from shorter promotional ladders regardless of seniority accumulations. Even where promotional ladders are not designed to discriminate, however, seniority systems may still effectively deny open access to better jobs. If blacks or women are concentrated in specific departments or occupations, and if promotional ladders reach a dead end in those departments or occupations, a system can be discriminatory in practice.

Whether such systems, even though established in accordance with lawful collective bargaining procedures, violate an individual's right of equal access to employment opportunities, as guaranteed by Title VII, is a matter of court decision. In several instances the government has obtained consent decrees under which firms have agreed to eliminate discrimination and compensate the victims. In one of the most celebrated of these cases, the 1973 judgment against AT&T (discussed in chapter 8), the company not only made remedial wage adjustments of $38 million but also changed its seniority system. The consent decree in this case eliminated separate departmental or unit promotional ladders because they had led to sex and racial segregation; for the purpose of determining promotions and job transfers, it established length of service within the operating (Bell) company. The Communications Workers of America, which had major bargaining agreements with Bell companies, did not participate in the negotiations that led to the settlement; in fact the union unsuccessfully attempted to block the new arrangements in court on the grounds that they infringed on its bargaining rights.[15]

In general, the Supreme Court has shown little disposition to outlaw a collective bargaining arrangement if there had been "no intent to discriminate" when such a system was formulated. In a 1977 case involving a trucking concern and the Teamsters, the Court also refused to ban a discrimination seniority system that had been established prior to the passage of the Civil Rights Act in 1964. If an individual, however, could prove having been denied a job in violation of Title VII, the Court has generally been willing to grant additional seniority retroactive to the date of the job denial.[16]

In terms of layoffs, seniority rules can contribute to discrimination against minorities and women. Workers with the least seniority are the first to be laid off during business downturns and the last to be rehired during business upswings. If there was an initial imbalance in hiring minorities and women, it is the whites and males who gain the job protection of seniority and the blacks and women who bear the brunt of periodic job losses; in effect they are denied the opportunity to gain sufficient seniority for job security. Affirmative action programs, negotiated by the Equal Employment Opportunities Commission with specific firms under the Civil Rights Act and other federal regulations, apply to the hiring and promotion of workers, not to layoff policies.[17] During recessions, such as that of 1974–1975, seniority rules that apply to layoffs may have the unintended effect of negating affirmative action programs.

The conflict between union-management negotiated seniority rules and civil rights regulations has led to a number of court decisions. In one case involving the Jersey Central Power and Light Company and local unions of the International Brotherhood of Electrical Workers, the company asked for a judgment by the federal courts with respect to a conflict on layoffs: its bargaining agreement required the application of seniority rule, while its conciliation agreement with the EEOC required protection of minorities. In this case, the district court ruled that the conciliation agreement had priority, but

---

[15] See Phyllis A. Wallace, ed., *Equal Employment Opportunity and the AT&T Case* (Cambridge, Mass: MIT Press, 1976), pp. 275–276.

[16] See U.S. Supreme Court, *Alexander v. Gardner-Denver Co.*, 415 U.S. 36 (1974), and *Franks et al.* v. *Bowmen Transportation Co. Inc.*, 44 U.S.L.W. 4356 (U.S. Mar. 24, 1976). The practice is to devise some method of taking into consideration layoffs that occurred during the period when the worker was denied employment.

[17] Affirmative action programs are required of all prime contractors and subcontractors who supply goods and services, both defense and civilian, to the federal government. Although certain employment responsibilities of federal contractors go back to the administration of Franklin D. Roosevelt, present regulations stem from Executive Order 11246, issued by President Lyndon B. Johnson in September 1965, as later amended, and Labor Department Order No. 4, issued in January 1970.

the circuit court, in a reversal, held that the collective bargaining agreement was paramount; in 1976 the Supreme Court upheld the circuit court decision (*Franks* v. *Bowmen*).[18] In this decision the Court also reaffirmed its position that the calculation of length of service should take into account any past discrimination concerning employment. This decision preserved the integrity of seniority systems, if established on a nondiscriminatory basis, but did not of course eliminate their de facto discriminatory impact during recessions.

"Inverse seniority" has been suggested as a way of resolving the conflict between equal opportunity goals and the preservation of seniority rights. This simply means that the worker with greatest seniority is laid off first. It becomes a practicable alternative, however, only when the agreement provides for income maintenance of the laid-off worker through a program such as supplementary unemployment benefits, and when the layoff is short. Under such circumstances, more senior workers can enjoy a layoff as a vacation with full pay, or nearly full pay, with their job rights unimpaired; the workers most recently hired in accordance with affirmative action programs can continue to work and gain additional seniority; and management will not be forced to make the types of job reassignments often required by layoff seniority rules when one worker with greater length of service displaces another one down the promotion ladder.[19] Although some firms and unions have found inverse seniority a workable policy, the fact that most workers do not benefit from income maintenance schemes limits its usefulness in cases involving equal employment opportunity.

WORK RULES

Work rules regulate the individual worker's rate of output. They may take the form of direct controls, limitations on methods of production, or requirements for a work force larger than that actually necessary. Work practices have been the source of persistent controversy, especially in such fields as railroads, construction, and printing. Management often denounces work rules as hindrances to increased productivity and economic growth, while unions insist on them to provide job security and prevent speed-ups, deterioration of work standards, and arbitrary managerial actions. The complex issues involve basic differences in philosophy between unions and management. Among the

[18] For the background of this case see "Significant Decisions in Labor Cases," *Monthly Labor Review*, 98 (February 1975), 77–78.

[19] Conventional layoffs on the basis of plantwide seniority can lead to a considerable reshuffling of jobs that is costly and time-consuming. In one company that later shifted to inverse seniority, the average number of "bumps" per layoff was 3.5, and in one case as high as 15. See Robert T. Lund, Dennis C. Bumstead, and Sheldon Friedman, "Inverse Seniority: Timely Answer to the Layoff Dilemma?" *Harvard Business Review*, 53 (September-October 1975), 65–72.

operating brotherhoods on the railroads, work-rule changes have been at the bottom of most disputes since the end of World War II; local work rules were also basic to the 1959 steel strike that lasted 116 days.

Types of Work Rules

Direct Output Controls Output may be limited directly by a rule that determines the rate of speed at which machines are to be operated, or by a regulation such as the longshoremen's limit on the number of pounds in sling loads. Less apparently direct are "make-work" policies that require that work be done over again even when it is unnecessary. In the printing industry, for example, a "bogus rule" of the International Typographical Union required that when a plate or papier-mâché matrix is obtained from an outside source, the copy must be reset within a certain period of time by union members who would otherwise have less work to perform. Make-work policies are obviously expensive to the firm, since the workers' additional time must be paid for even if the output of salable services is not increased. Certain other output controls may be established on the grounds of health and safety (for example, the rate of operation of punch pressers), or of quality (for example, the number, of bricks laid per hour).

Limitations on Methods of Production Union policies sometimes specify the quality or amount of equipment that must be used. The painters' union, for example, might require brushes of certain widths and prohibit spray guns for certain types of work. A textile union might prescribe the maximum number of looms to be tended by an individual, and longshoremen might try to prevent containerization of goods. Opposition to new and faster machines also falls within the same category.

Unnecessary Labor A final type of union policy is concerned with the number of persons to be employed on a job. The firemen's union has stressed the need for a fireman on diesel engines, and the musicians' union asks for stand-by musicians when recorded music is being used.

The Economics of Work Rules

Certain types of work rules, even though they reduce output or increase the labor per unit, can often be justified to the general public's satisfaction. Limitations based on considerations of health and safety generally fall within this category. Similarly, rules that set limits on the intensity of work or on the amount of effort expended by the worker reflect an accepted rationale. Neither of these justifications, however, leads to automatic determination of the precise degree of restriction that a union should practice. Such matters as the number of looms for which a loomtender should be responsible are settled primarily in collective bargaining, since the intensity of the loomtender's work is as much a bargainable issue as are wages. Similarly, the size of sling loads on the docks is to some extent a matter simply of health and safety, but there is no reason why the standard cannot be set in the bargaining process.

Other grounds for work rules often seem less justifiable to the public. But unions feel that protecting their members' interests is reason enough for work rules, however restrictive, especially in the face of threatened unemployment. An emphasis on the job security provided by work rules is usually found in declining industries. The fact that the railroad operating brotherhoods stress work rules much more than do the railroad shop unions, for example, points up the greater insecurity of the operating personnel because of the industry's declining employment and the lack of adequate alternative job opportunities for their skills: a brakeman would have less opportunity to transfer his skills to another industry than would a machinist in a railroad shop. Emphasis on work rules to provide extra jobs is found in those industries marked by casual and intermittent employment with a large floating supply of labor. The parceling out of jobs to secure the most employment from available work is considered the prime objective of such unions as the longshoremen's and the musicians.' The ability of a union to win work rule protections in bargaining is affected by the nature of the industry. If its members offer a service that is valuable only at a particular time and if the labor costs of rendering the service are relatively small, the union will be in an especially strong bargaining position. Both of these conditions have been true in the case of the longshoremen, the locomotive engineers and other railroad operating brotherhoods, and such unions in the amusement and entertainment industries as those of the musicians and stagehands. In the printing industry, especially newspapers, the printers hold a strategic position because of lack of satisfactory alternative news and advertising media.

Union Adjustments

Even unions that have a strategic position in a particular industry may eventually find, however, that changes in technology or in consumers' preferences for goods can erode a seemingly impervious bargaining position. Truck and automobile competition has already undermined the power of the railroad brotherhoods, for example. Though technological changes in work methods or in types of labor required may be temporarily thwarted by union action, they are not likely to be permanently halted. Competition from new and nonunion firms may make the preservation of older ways of production by means of work rules completely impractical.

Taking the long view, several unions have successfully accommodated themselves to the inevitable technological changes that threatened the jobs and skills of their members. For example, in the late nineteenth century several factors reduced the impact of linotype machines on the employment of printers who had been setting type by hand. The demand for newspapers increased so much that higher productivity did not result in unemployment. Moreover, the old International Typographical Union instituted programs of training printers to use the new machines so that the transition could be accomplished with a minimal disruption of the work force. Furthermore, since the linotype operator was a skilled worker, no loss of wages occurred in the shift from one occupation to another.

A post–World War II example of union-management negotiations to adjust work rules to changing technology was the 1960 West Coast mechanization and modernization agreement between the International Longshoremen's and Warehousemen's Union and the Pacific Maritime Association. This five-and-a-half-year agreement, negotiated after long preparations, provided that the employers would contribute $5 million annually to a fund for the exclusive use of "fully registered" longshoremen—that is, those who are given first preference for jobs—at the time the agreement was signed. "Partially registered" men, who are entitled to any work not claimed by the first, had no right to the benefits of the fund but were granted all the other rights provided by contract. From one part of the fund, the fully registered worker could receive benefits for voluntary early retirement at age 62, or for compulsory retirement if job opportunities should decline. If he did not retire early, he was to receive a lump-sum payment at age 65. Another part of the fund was set aside for a wage guarantee if weekly earnings were less than a stated minimum.

In exchange for the benefits under this system, the union agreed to relax certain work rules governing loading operations. Under specified circumstances and with appropriate safeguards for safety and prohibition of speedup, loads could be increased and work forces reduced. The underlying theory of the agreement was that work rules, built up by the union, were sold, with the proceeds used to give economic security to those fully registered workers who would be most likely to suffer from layoffs or reduced earnings from technological change. The agreement yielded substantial productivity gains and was renewed, with a few modifications, for another five years in 1966. Despite a strike in 1971 and 1972, the arrangement has continued to be a satisfactory resolution of the union's concerns for job security and safety and employers' desires for a free hand to introduce technological improvements.[20]

Similar agreements exist in other industries. In 1974 New York Local 6 of the International Typographical Union, faced with automation and elec-

[20] On the difficulties of the 1972 wage settlement before the Pay Board under Phase II, specifically relating to wage control exemptions on grounds of productivity, see Wayne L. Horvitz and Peter Tchirkow, "Productivity, Collective Bargaining and Wage Control," in Gerald Somers et al., eds., Collective Bargaining and Productivity (Madison, Wis.: Industrial Relations Research Association, 1975), pp. 155–163.

tronic typesetting machines that threatened its occupational existence, negotiated a 10-year contract with *The New York Times* and *New York Daily News* which gave the publishers the freedom to introduce new equipment and to determine unilaterally the number of workers needed. For this abandonment of work rules that had been zealously protected for many decades, the employers agreed to give 1,400 regular printers and nearly 400 full-time substitutes virtual lifetime security in their jobs, with bonuses and extra payments if they retired or moved elsewhere. Among the innovations was a paid six-month sabbatical leave for each printer during the 10 years of the contract. The reason for the exceptional length of the contract was the union's fear that as automation continued to erode its power, a shorter contract would make it possible for the employers to alter the guarantees unfavorably. The average age of the printers was 56.[21]

Negotiations aimed at increasing labor productivity that result in the withdrawal of work rules in exchange for specific guarantees of job security and other benefits have sometimes been called "productivity bargaining." The term was first used in 1960 to describe Esso's modernization of employment practices at its Fawley refinery in Great Britain, where outmoded work arrangements had proven costly. Although a number of British firms initiated similar agreements during the 1960s, the concept lost its attractiveness by the early 1970s. Apparently this came about because of union suspicions that management was acquiring greater authority in the work place, especially when unemployment was high, and because of limitations on possible monetary gains imposed by government incomes policies.[22]

Productivity bargaining may be limited in its applications in any case; in some industries, particularly mass production industries, there are few work rules that could be bargained at a price high enough for management to guarantee security of job and income. Moreover, such a "sale" would be only a one-time affair. One of the reasons that the Pacific Coast longshore arrangement was successful was that after the initial change in work rules, the agreement provided that the impact of technological changes would be continuously negotiated.

SUMMARY

Unions have used several arguments in favor of shorter hours of work per week or per day. One of the oldest was that workers needed time (and energy) to exercise their broad political rights as citizens. Others stressed the fatigue

[21] For an analysis of the contract and its background see article by A. H. Raskin in *The New York Times* (July 29, 1974), pp. 12–13.

[22] The British experience is discussed in Allan Flanders, *The Fawley Productivity Agreements* (London: Faber and Faber, 1964) and in R. B. McKersie and L. C. Hunter, *Pay, Productivity and Collective Bargaining* (London: Macmillan, 1973). See also Laurence C. Hunter, "Productivity Bargaining Abroad: An Evaluation," in Gerald Somers et al, eds., *Collective Bargaining*, pp. 170–175.

from overwork that contributed to injury and disease, wage increases that would be possible if the supply of labor (in hours) were reduced, the desirability of spreading the work during times of unemployment, and a desire for leisure time. Employers have usually countered with the claim that shorter hours boost costs and lead to less employment. Since the passage of the Fair Labor Standards Act of 1938, the scheduled workweek has remained remarkably constant at 40 hours. A recent proposal for a four-day week of 10 hours each day has found favor in only a few concerns.

A more controversial issue in collective bargaining is the union demand for union security. Under Section 14(b) of the Taft Hartley Act, some 19 states have passed laws prohibiting the union shop, under which workers are required to join a union within a specific period of time. Unions argue that workers should support the union shop because the union bargains for union and nonunion workers alike. Employers often counter with the claim that individual workers should be free to join or not as they see fit. In 1972 most workers under agreements covering 1,000 or more workers were employed under some type of union security provisions.

Seniority provisions are found in most contracts. Managerial opposition is usually based on the desire to use efficiency as a basis for rewards. Seniority rules may conflict with affirmative action programs, especially during layoffs. Courts have generally upheld seniority provisions if established on a nondiscriminatory basis.

Work rules laid down by unions to govern work speeds, output, and methods of production are often criticized on the grounds that they limit productivity. The question essentially is the issue of how much work is to be performed at specified pay levels, and hence becomes a matter of bargaining. "Productivity bargaining"—the trading of restrictive regulations in exchange for guaranteed wages or retirement benefits—has been used in a few areas to resolve this type of conflict.

DISCUSSION QUESTIONS

1. What are the arguments for and against the four-day week with a 10-hour day? with an 8-hour day? Discuss in terms of the effects on wages, worker preferences, and the employer's labor costs.
2. During times of high unemployment, unions often seek shorter work hours. Is this desirable on economic grounds? on grounds of equity?
3. What types of union security arrangements are currently outlawed in the United States?
4. The closed shop was usually found in industries where the unions recruited workers for employers. Has the practice been entirely eliminated?
5. What are the advantages and disadvantages of the union shop from the point of view of the worker—union and nonunion—and of the employer?
6. Some writers point to a conflict between the principle of seniority and efficiency in

plant operations, yet seniority is generally a minor issue in disputes between firms and unions. Under what circumstances might employers find that the principle works in their interests?
7. Do you believe that seniority provisions in labor agreements should be modified or eliminated if their effect is to discriminate against women or minorities? Why or why not?
8. What is "productivity bargaining"? How satisfactory do you think it is in solving problems of restrictive work rules?

SELECTED READINGS

On nonwage issues in collective bargaining, see Sumner H. Slichter, James J. Healy, and E. Robert Livernash, *The Impact of Collective Bargaining on Management* (Washington, D.C.: Brookings Institution, 1960). Analyses of case studies are useful in pointing the various implications of particular disputes: see, for example, Sterling H. Schoen and Raymond L. Hilgert, *Cases in Collective Bargaining and Industrial Relations: A Decisional Approach,* 3rd ed. (Homewood, Ill.: Irwin, 1978). For a general statement, see Allan Flanders, *Management and Unions, The Theory and Reform of Industrial Relations* (London: Faber and Faber, 1970).

On several issues raised in this chapter, see Riva Poor, ed., *4 Days, 40 Hours and Other Forms of the Rearranged Workweek* (New York: New American Library, 1973); Thomas R. Haggard, *Compulsory Unionism, the NLRB, and the Courts: A Legal Analysis of Union Security Agreements* (Philadelphia: Wharton School, Industrial Research Unit, 1977); Phyllis A. Wallace, ed., *Equal Employment Opportunity and the AT&T Case* (Cambridge, Mass.: M.I.T. Press, 1976); Joseph Goldberg et al., *Collective Bargaining and Productivity* (Madison, Wis.: Industrial Relations Research Association, 1975).

12

Government Control
of Labor Relations

A system of laws and rules, backed by the ultimate power of the state, defines the rights, duties, and liberties of workers, unions, and employers. This system not only establishes the broad framework of the social, economic, and political environment within which unions function, but also directly affects the substance of their actions. This chapter will review the development of law in the United States, especially at the level of the federal government, in its relationship to unions, agreements, and collective bargaining procedures.

LAW AND THE LABOR MARKET

Whether an economic system provides for slavery, for a free labor market with free contracts, or for some other procedure for the allocation of labor and resources, it sets the rules, establishes the procedures to be followed in settlement of disputes over legal interpretations, and defines the penalties for infraction.

A *free wage earner* is a worker who may of his or her own volition sell labor services to a buyer upon conditions acceptable to both seller and buyer, and who may terminate such sale—that is, resign—freely. The conditions of the sale may be limited by governmental restrictions as to hours, conditions of work, and wages, but the essence of the free contract is the freedom to work and to quit. Even if a worker who has resigned owes money to the employer, the debt can be collected as "damages," but the worker cannot be forced by law to pay for it with labor. The importance of this distinction can be seen by comparing it with various types of other economic situations the essential condition of which is that the worker is under a legal obligation to work.

The most extreme form of unfree labor was *slavery*, where the worker was born to the position of servility and was solely an instrument or tool of the owner. *Serfdom*, which was primarily a European institution during the Middle Ages, was distinguished from slavery principally in that serfs had a measure of freedom to work for themselves and could not be sold or forced from the land.

The *apprenticeship* agreement, found in Elizabethan days in England and in colonial America, and the *indenture* system are examples of master-servant relationships that differed from slavery and serfdom because of the existence of a contract between both parties, though they sometimes involved a measure of involuntary servitude. The apprenticeship agreement specified a certain number of years, usually four to seven, during which the servant would work for the master and in turn be taught a trade and given food and lodging; at the end of that period the apprentice would be free of any obligations. Under the indenture system the worker agreed to work for a specified number of years for the master, but without the goal of learning a trade. *Redemptioners* were those in colonial America who signed indentures to pay for passage from the Old World to the New.

Other types of unfree labor are *peonage* and *contract labor*. Peonage was found generally in plantation systems in Spanish colonial America. Peons received advances of food, clothing, and shelter, and the value of the work they performed during the season was later applied toward their cost. Since peons were never out of debt, they were compelled to continue to work for the master. In the contract labor system, found well into the twentieth century, particularly in colonial areas of southeastern Asia, the worker who contracted for employment for a specified period of time—say, five years—was guaranteed employment for that time and in turn had to continue to work for the same employer.

In each system of unfree labor the compulsion to work was enforced by the authority of the state. A peon, a contract worker, or an indentured servant, as well as a slave or a serf, who decided to leave the job or run away would be treated as a fugitive of the law, subject to criminal penalties if caught, and forced to work out the obligation.

In the United States various forms of unfree labor persisted well into the twentieth century. In colonial days, slavery and indenture were important in the control and recruitment of labor. The Dutch first landed blacks at Jamestown in 1619 under a form of servitude that preceded the statutory recognition of slavery. All or nearly all of the English mainland colonies provided for the institution of slavery—Massachusetts in 1641, Connecticut in 1650, Virginia in 1661, and later other colonies. Not only were blacks enslaved, but also Indians, Jews, Moors, and Turks. By 1800 there were nearly 900,000 slaves in the United States, or one-sixth of the population of 5.3 million. By 1860 the slave population had risen to nearly 4 million, although the ratio to the total population had fallen to one-eighth.

Indentured labor and similar forms of master-servant relationships lasted ·oughly from 1619 to 1819. Before the American Revolution it appeared that in some colonies, such as Pennsylvania, the proportion of new immigrants who were redemptioners was increasing, but after the Revolution the unfavorable competition with black slaves in the South and with free labor in the North led to the decline of the indenture system. The Massachusetts Supreme Court outlawed slavery in 1783 on the grounds that it was inconsistent with the state's bill of rights that all men were "free and equal." In 1808, following the lead of Great Britain a year earlier, Congress prohibited foreign trade in slaves, and all forms of involuntary servitude, except those as punishments for crime, were abolished by the Thirteenth Amendment to the Constitution in 1865.[1]

A variety of practices involving compulsory labor led the United States Congress in 1875 to pass several laws clearly defining involuntary servitude. Peonage had developed in certain instances where employers granted advances of transportation, food, and lodging to workers who were thereupon prohibited from quitting because of indebtedness. The vagrancy laws were also misused by employers. An unemployed worker who had been arrested for vagrancy, for example, might subsequently be released to an employer who would advance the money for the fine if it were paid back by work. Once the fine was "worked out," the person might again be released and perhaps later rearrested for vagrancy. Another way by which the Thirteenth Amendment was evaded involved the claim of fraud. A law in Mississippi, for example, stated that a refusal to perform an act or service required by contract was prima facie evidence of intent to injure or defraud the employer. But this and similar state laws were ruled unconstitutional by the United States Supreme Court on the grounds that they were attempts to circumvent the 1875 law and the Thirteenth Amendment. Merchant seamen were excluded from the protections of the laws outlawing involuntary servitude until the LaFollette Seamen's Act of 1915, which prohibited arrest and imprisonment for desertion, payment of wages in advance, or payments to persons for recruitment of sailors, a practice that included shanghaiing in its more violent forms.

The present governmental approach to employer-employee relationships is based on the legal concept of "free labor"—that work will be performed only when it is mutually agreeable to employee and employer to have it performed, that the worker cannot be required to work if it is not in his or her interest to do so, and that a worker who does violate a labor agreement can be held accountable for damages but not forced to work. This freedom to quit, however, can be limited by the government in the interests of preserving the peace or the security, health, or safety of its citizens during emergencies. But

---

[1] Amendment XIII of the Constitution reads: "Section 1. Neither slavery nor involuntary servitude, except as a punishment for crime, whereof the party shall have been duly convicted, shall exist within the United States, or any place subject to their jurisdiction. "Section 2. Congress shall have power to enforce this article by appropriate legislation."

the degree to which this limitation can or should be imposed is subject to dispute, as we shall see later.

THE RIGHT TO ORGANIZE

Full legal protection of the "right" of free workers to organize unions came slowly in the United States. In the early nineteenth century employers were in no way obliged to allow the formation of unions or to respect their demands. Indeed, it was doubtful whether even the act of forming a union was legal under the conspiracy doctrine as it was then applied. Later, workers were legally permitted to associate with each other in unions, but employers had no legal duty to recognize or deal with them. Workers did not attain the "right" to unionize until the 1930s, when laws commanded employers to recognize and bargain with them.

The Conspiracy Doctrine

The first question of the legality of trade unions arose in the Philadelphia cordwainers' case in 1806. Since no statutes governing unions existed at that time, the question arose of the applicability of the "conspiracy doctrine" adopted by the British courts to the settlement of American disputes. The conspiracy doctrine, which had developed as early as the fourteenth century and had been incorporated into English statutes, declared certain acts unlawful when committed by a group of persons acting in concert, even though the same acts were lawful when performed separately by individuals. The cordwainers' case was debated by well-known lawyers of the day because the issue was related directly to the political conflict between proponents of greater state power and proponents of greater rights for individuals. The latter were defeated when the jury accepted the judge's instruction: "A combination of workmen to raise their wages may be considered in a twofold point of view: one is to benefit themselves. . . . The other is to injure those who do not join the society. The rule of law condemns both."[2]

There were other cases, but the period of conspiracy charges against unions was brought to an end by the *Commonwealth* v. *Hunt* decision in Massachusetts in 1842, a case also involving shoe workers. Chief Justice Shaw of the state's supreme court held that labor organizations as such were lawful, that the closed shop was a lawful union objective, and that strikes were also legal provided that they were conducted in a peaceful manner. Although this decision was not binding on courts in other states, for all practical purposes it laid

---

[2] For a readable account of the trial see Elias Lieberman, *Unions Before the Bar* (New York: Harper, 1950), ch. 2.

to rest the doctrine that unions were not lawful organizations per se. Other courts did not necessarily follow the view that the closed shop was a lawful objective; in fact, there were differences among judges about just which objectives of unions were lawful or unlawful and about the legality of the means they employed.

The Labor Injunction

An injunction is a court order commanding persons to do, or not to do, certain acts; it is issued by a court of equity to protect property from irreparable damage when other legal remedies are inadequate. The usual remedy for injury to property is a damage suit, but if the loss can never be compensated adequately, or if the offenders are too numerous or impecunious, an injunction can be justifiably used to stop the action before it begins.

Since the injunction must be obeyed under penalty of contempt of court even before there is a legal resolution of the issue in dispute, it is recognized to be a powerful weapon, and certain controls have been placed on its use. The person who requests the injunction must come into court with "clean hands"—that is, without complicity in the dispute—and must indicate that the injunction does not impose a greater loss on others than the petitioner would suffer if the act were committed.

The use of injunctions in labor disputes is almost entirely an American development. Typically, an employer faced with a strike by employees would ask a judge to issue an injunction ordering the union officers to "cease and desist" from certain acts, on the grounds that the employer's property was being injured. It was not necessary to show that physical property was being damaged, or likely to be damaged, for under a broadening interpretation developed during the 1880s, property rights could include the right to do business, to make profits, and to preserve such intangibles as good will. A judge could grant a temporary restraining order based solely on the affidavits presented by the employer in support of the request; a later hearing in which both sides presented their viewpoints would determine whether the order was to be continued; and eventually a trial would decide whether the injunction would be permanent. In most cases, however, the original court order ended the matter, since any action on labor's part was prohibited and punishable by the judge for contempt. Once a strike had been stopped and the workers had returned to work, the final decision on the injunction seemed unimportant: the strike was lost and the enthusiasm gone.

The use of the labor injunction, which began in the 1880s, continued without effective limitations until the 1930s. At first there was some doubt about whether strikes could be enjoined by labor injunctions in federal courts, since the prohibition of quitting would be in violation of the Thirteenth Amendment. The Supreme Court ruled in 1894 that an injunction may not be used if the effect is to prevent resignations, but in the following year the Court upheld the use of the injunction in the Debs case.[3] In 1897 the Court upheld the "blanket injunction," which prohibited from engaging in certain acts any persons "whomsoever," whether or not they had been notified of the injunction.

Restraint of Trade

The common-law doctrine of restraint of trade declares that trade should be free, unhindered by any restraints on individual workers' right to sell their labor for whatever price they wish or on the employers' right to buy labor at whatever price they wish. During the nineteenth century this doctrine was applied to labor cases generally in connection with the determination of whether the "ends" of union activity were lawful. If the judge ruled that a union was attempting to restrain trade, its objectivies were considered illegal and hence its actions could also be ruled illegal. If, on the other hand, a striking union was attempting only to better the position of its members, a judge could rule that since its primary objective was lawful, the incidental effect of restraint of trade did not make the action unlawful.

The Sherman Anti-Trust Act of 1890 stated flatly that "every contract, combination in the form of trust or otherwise, or conspiracy, in restraint of trade among the several States, or with foreign nations is illegal." The act provided three types of penalties: fine and imprisonment, an injunction that could be obtained by the United States Attorney General in a federal court, and a damage suit initiated by any party injured by the illegal restraint for an amount three times the value of the damage. Although the best evidence indicates that the intent of Congress was to control business monopolies and not unions, the act was applied against unions in seven cases in 1893 and 1894. Six of these were railroad disputes, and one judge expressed an opinion that the act made illegal every railroad strike that affected interstate commerce.

The most famous application of the Sherman Act was in the Danbury hatters' case. A suit for triple damages was brought by Loewe, a manufacturer of hats in Danbury, Connecticut, against the union that had first struck to secure union recognition and, failing that, had initiated a national boycott against Loewe's hats. The case was in the courts for 14 years, twice before the United States Supreme Court,[4] and ended with a payment of $234,000 by the union, with financial assistance from the American Federation of Labor. In the first case to reach the Supreme Court, the union's secondary boycott was ruled in violation of the Sherman Act. In the second case, which consid-

---

[3] *In re Debs*, 158 U.S. 564 (1895).
[4] *Loewe v. Lawlor*, 208 U.S. 274 (1908) and *Lawlor v. Loewe*, 235 U.S. 522 (1915).

ered the question of the liability of union members for payment of the damages, the Court held that the members were individually liable as long as they had paid dues and delegated their authority to their officers. Although many of the members were not even aware that the boycott had been initiated, the homes of all members had been attached as security for the amount of damages.

Between the first Danbury decision and the passage of the Clayton Act in 1914, some court decisions came close to the extreme position of outlawing strikes in interstate commerce. Judge Dayton, in *Hitchman Coal and Coke Co.* v. *Mitchell*, ruled that the United Mine Workers was an illegal combination, but his decision was reversed by the circuit court, and on appeal to the Supreme Court, the decision went against the union but did not include reference to the Sherman Act or to the unlawfulness of the union. In the Buck Stove and Range case, the AFL was enjoined from placing the name of that company on its "Don't Patronize" list on grounds similar to those for the ruling in the Danbury hatters' case: the list was considered a secondary boycott in violation of the Sherman Act.

First Attempts to Protect Union Activity

After 1890 the impact of the growing use of the injunction in labor disputes and the heavy blows under the Sherman Anti-Trust Act seemed to indicate that the weight of the government was being used to crush the union movement in the United States. The principal source of the opposition to unions, however, was the courts, which tended to emphasize the inviolability of free, individual bargaining.

The first attempts to grant workers a "right" to organize (in contrast to the unprotected "liberty") occurred in 14 states before World War I. An Indiana law of 1893, for example, declared that it was unlawful to prevent employees from joining any lawful labor oganization, to coerce or to discharge them, or to secure a pledge from them not to become union members; a fine of $100 and six months imprisonment were the penalties. Similar provisions were written into laws in other states. In Congress the same point of view found legislative expression in the Erdman Act of 1898. Directed toward establishing procedures for settling labor disputes in railroads, this act was based on the assumption that in order for management and labor to work out peaceful solutions to their conflicts, the union had to be recognized by the employer as a legitimate and legal entity for purposes of collective bargaining. Section 10 stated that no employer should threaten any employee with loss of employment or discriminate against him because of union membership.

The Erdman Act was appealed to the courts, and in 1908, in *Adair* v. *United States*,[5] the Supreme Court held Section 10 unconstitutional as "an

[5] 208 U.S. 161 (1908).

invasion of the personal liberty, as well as of property," guaranteed by the Fifth Amendment's statement that no person shall "be deprived of life, liberty, or property, without due process of law. . . ." Said the Court: workers and employers have equal rights in determining the terms of employment, and the right of a worker to quit is equal to the right of an employer to fire. "Any legislation that disturbs that equality is an arbitrary interference with the liberty of contract which no government can legally justify in a free land."

The same line of argument was followed in the *Coppage* v. *Kansas* case of 1915,[6] in which the Supreme Court ruled that a state law forbidding the "yellow-dog" contract was unconstitutional on the grounds that it violated the clause of the Fourteenth Amendment prohibiting a state government from depriving any person "of life, liberty, or property without due process of law." (A "yellow-dog" contract was an agreement made by a worker that as a condition of employment he would not join a union.) In the *Hitchman Coal and Coke Compnay* v. *Mitchell* case in 1917[7] the Court upheld an injunction against the United Mine Workers who had attempted to organize West Virginia miners who had signed "yellow-dog" contracts, on the grounds that the union was attempting to induce a breach of contract.

The position of the Court did not go unchallenged. The basic reliance on the concept of "due process of law" was questioned on the grounds that "due process" referred only to the proper procedures of Congress or of a state legislature. But the Court held to a *substantive* interpretation of the due process clause, contending that certain basic rights were embodied in the Constitution and could not be altered by any legislative body. The majority of Supreme Court justices did not believe that the right of workers to organize was among them.

A major factor in the gradual shift of public opinion toward support of a change in governmental policy was the famous report of the United States Commission on Industrial Relations in 1914. Authorized by Congress two years earlier, the commission conducted hearings on labor unrest, and as Perlman points out, "for the first time in the history of the United States the employing class seemed to be arrayed as a defendant before the bar of public opinion."[8] The commission firmly supported trade unionism and collective bargaining as desirable and effective remedies for labor unrest and violence.

In essence the philosophy of the Clayton Act, passed by Congress in 1914 and hailed by Gompers as labor's Magna Carta, was to create basic union rights and to give protection to those that were reasonable, just as the Supreme Court in its famous "rule of reason" decision in 1911 had stated that

---

[6] 236 U.S. 1 (1915).
[7] 245 U.S. 229 (1917).
[8] Selig Perlman, *A History of Trade Unionism in the United States* (New York: Macmillan, 1937), p. 228.

reasonable restraints of trade by business firms were lawful under the Sherman Act.[9] It laid down two provisions to protect the legitimate activities of labor from prosecution under the antitrust laws and injunctions. Section 6 declared that the "labor of a human being is not a commodity or article of commerce" and stated that the antitrust laws could in no way forbid unions' existence or their operations as labor organizations in carrying out their legitimate objective. Section 20 specified the procedure concerning the issuance of injunctions and prohibited their use in any dispute between employer and employees over the terms and conditions of work. The act further specified as legitimate such activities as ceasing to work, payment of strike benefits, and peaceful assembly.

Although the intent of Congress in passing the Clayton Act was absolutely clear, the Supreme Court reinterpreted its provisions in such a way that the new law had little effect. The case of *Duplex Printing Press Co.* v. *Deering* involved an injunction obtained by a firm against a union for refusing to install presses because the firm had initiated an open-shop policy;[10] the injunction was upheld on the grounds that the union's action constituted an unlawful secondary boycott and that the Clayton Act gave protection only to a union in dispute with its own employer. The Court said: "By no fair or permissible construction can it [the Clayton Act] be taken as authorizing any activity otherwise unlawful, or enabling a normally lawful organization to become a cloak for an illegal combination in restraint of trade as defined by the antitrust laws."

Several other cases indicated that the Court would accept no modification of its previous views on union activity. In the American Steel Foundries decision,[11] picketing was held to be unlawful intimidation if more than one picket was established at each factory gate. In the first of the two Coronado cases,[12] the Court again held that unions were suable as an entity under the Sherman Act and, if convicted, would have to pay triple damages from their treasuries; in the second case, a union attempt to stop production and shipment of non-union coal was declared illegal because it interfered with interstate commerce.

[9] The Supreme Court enunciated this doctrine in 1911 when it broke up the American Tobacco Company and Standard Oil into a number of separate companies on the grounds that only *unreasonable* restraints of trade were illegal.

[10] 254 U.S. 443 (1921). The Clayton Act added a fourth remedy for illegal restraints of trade by providing that the injured party could secure injunctive relief.

[11] *American Steel Foundries* v. *Tri-City Central Trades Council*, 257 U.S. 184 (1921). In *Truax* v. *Corrigan*, 257 U.S. 312 (1921), the Court invalidated an Arizona anti-injunction law. Altogether, some nine states had such statutes, a number of them in the Clayton Act pattern.

[12] *Coronado Coal and Coke Co.* v. *United Mine Workers*, 259 U.S. 344 (1922), and 268 U.S. 295 (1925).

Full Legal Protection of Union Activity

A new attempt by Congress to protect the right of railroad workers to organize came with the passage of the Railway Labor Act of 1926. Following the disastrous shopmen's strike of 1922 and general unrest among railroad workers, the new act laid down basic principles of resolving disputes, declaring that collective bargaining was to be promoted as the best way of enabling unions and the carriers to work out their own problems. Thus, nearly 30 years after the Erdman Act had been passed, Congress again enacted into law the provision that workers should be free to choose representatives of their own without interference from employers. In 1930 the Supreme Court for the first time gave judicial support to a legally protected right for labor when it unanimously upheld the act. Its doctrine now was that "collective bargaining would be a mockery if representation were made futile by interference with freedom of choice."[13] The fact that the legislation concerned an industry under national regulation and that both management and unions helped to work out the details of the act in the first place contributed to the change in viewpoint.

The decision enabled Congress to grant the same protection to labor in other industries by means of the Norris-LaGuardia Act, signed into law by President Herbert Hoover in 1932. Its preamble stated that it was official public policy to give the worker "full freedom of association . . . free from interference . . . for the purpose of collective bargaining." Unionization and other activities were legally protected by specifying acts that were not to be enjoined in federal courts. Section 13 tried to avoid the limitations of the Clayton Act by defining a labor dispute to include any controversy over the terms and conditions of employment, "regardless of whether or not the disputants stand in the proximate relation of employer and employee"—thus protecting secondary as well as primary boycotts.

The official title of the law, the Federal Anti-Injunction Act, indicates its primary objective, and among the procedural restrictions it established were the five-day limitation on temporary restraining orders and the requirement that a company seeking such an order must post bond for payment of damages if the union should be wrongfully harmed. Before an injunction could be granted, the employer must have sought a damage suit first or must be able to show why it could not be successful, and the firm must have fulfilled its own obligations by not violating an agreement and having tried bargaining; furthermore, the police must have stated that they were not able to furnish protection.

[13] *Texas and New Orleans Railroad Co.* v. *Brotherhood of Railway and Steamship Clerks*, 281 U.S. 548 (1930).

The Norris-LaGuardia Act (as the law is usually known), upheld by the courts, laid the basis for new interpretations of the antitrust laws. In the Apex decision,[14] the Supreme Court declared that unions were subject to the antitrust laws if they attempted to fix prices and monopolize product markets, either by themselves or in combination with employers. However, although the union in the Apex case had engaged in a sitdown strike, destroyed property, and stopped production of goods that entered interstate commerce, the Court found no evidence of attempts to fix prices and stated that the firm could not sue for triple damages under the Sherman Act, though it could sue for damages in state courts.

A similar restriction on the applicability of the Sherman Act came in the Hutcheson decision of 1941,[15] in which the Supreme Court held that picketing and a boycott in a case involving a jurisdictional dispute were not enjoinable under the immunities of the Clayton and Norris-LaGuardia acts and therefore were not subject to the Sherman Act. But in 1945 the Court ruled that a collaboration of a union and several employers to fix the price of electrical products by banning the sale of goods produced outside the New York City area was illegal monopolization under the Sherman Act.[16] As seen by the Court, union actions to benefit members were lawful even when strikes or boycotts restrained interstate trade; they were unlawful only if the objective was to affect the product price directly or with employer collusion.

The Norris-LaGuardia Act did not provide the means to implement its stated policy of encouraging collective bargaining except by limitation of the injunction procedure. But during Franklin Roosevelt's New Deal administration, new legislation transformed policy into effective legislation. The first such law, the National Industrial Recovery Act (NIRA) of 1933, had as its primary objective the promotion of economic recovery by allowing firms in various industries to join together to establish codes of fair practices, after approval by the head of the National Recovery Administration (NRA). Usually such codes included price-fixing provisions, limitations on hours of work, and similar agreements to eliminate "ruinous price cutting." Antitrust laws were suspended in order to allow these agreements to take place legally.

To make the act palatable to labor, Section 7(a) was added. This famous clause, which stated that employees should have the right to organize and bargain collectively with their employers through representatives of their own choosing, was regarded as a new Magna Carta for labor, and an organizing boom soon got under way throughout the nation.

But the 7(a) clause left much to be desired. No government machinery existed to guarantee that these new-found rights of workers were duly respected.

[14] *Apex Hosiery Co.* v. *Leader,* 310 U.S. 469 (1940).
[15] *U.S.* v. *Hutcheson,* 312 U.S. 219 (1941).
[16] *Allen Bradley Co.* v. *Local #3, Brotherhood of Electrical Workers,* 325 U.S. 797 (1945).

To remedy this situation, President Roosevelt's executive order of August 1933 created a National Labor Board to interpret the clause. But this tripartite board of representatives of labor, management, and the public was never certain whether its major purpose was to settle disputes or to enforce the law, and its enforcement powers were never clear. Since lawyers for the board had doubts about whether the act itself would be upheld in the courts, the board was reluctant to prosecute recalcitrant employers to the point of bringing them into court. Its powers were quickly challenged by refusals of some employers to cooperate, and the board finally gave way to the National Labor Relations Board, whose three members were to "effectuate the policy of the NIRA." Created by President Roosevelt under Public Resolution No. 44, which was passed by Congress in 1934, this board was not to be representative of the interests of labor, management, and the public; it was empowered to enforce the law by investigating complaints, issuing orders, and conducting representation elections. But it was no more successful than its predecessor, and the whole experiment came to an end in 1935, when the Supreme Court ruled that the NIRA was unconstitutional on the grounds of an undue delegation of governmental powers to private parties.

The National Labor Relations Act, known as the Wagner Act, was enacted in 1935, shortly after the demise of Section 7(a). In April 1937 it was declared constitutional by a Supreme Court vote of 5 to 4, in *NLRB* v. *Jones & Laughlin Steel Corporation* and four other cases. The Court fully upheld the act, accepting the grounds laid down carefully by Congress in Section 1 that refusal to bargain and denial of the right to organize was a cause of unrest and of the strikes that burdened and disrupted commerce among states. The Court found no violation of either the procedural or substantive interpretation of the "due process" clause of the Fifth Amendment. The majority decision read:

> The Act does not compel agreements between employers and employees. . . . It does not prevent the employer "from refusing to make a collective contract and hiring individuals on whatever terms" the employer "may by unilateral action determine." . . . The theory of the Act is that free opportunity for negotiation with accredited representatives of employees is likely to promote industrial peace and may bring about the adjustments and agreements which the Act in itself does not attempt to compel.[17]

The cases of *Adair* v. *United States* and of *Coppage* v. *Kansas* were considered inapplicable to the act

The court had correctly phrased the essence of the spirit of the Wagner

[17] 301 U.S. 1 (1937). The other four cases were *Associated Press* v. *NLRB*, 301 U.S. 103; *NLRB* v. *Friedman-Marks Clothing Co.*, 301 U.S. 58; *NLRB* v. *Fruehauf Trailer Co.*, 301 U.S. 49; *Washington V. & M. Coach Co.* v. *NLRB*, 301 U.S. 142.

Act: that free collective bargaining between "accredited" representatives of employees and employers is "likely" to promote industrial peace. The law did not require that an agreement be obtained, but only that collective bargaining be attempted without intimidation and coercion of employees who were exercising their rights to join a union.

The new rights of workers were stated in Section 7. The phraseology came from the Norris-LaGuardia Act, and the number was carried over from the 7(a) clause of the NIRA. The new approach of the Wagner Act, designed to overcome the inadequacies of the labor program of the 1933–1935 period, was outlined in Section 8, which specifically listed five practices of employers that would deny those rights.[18] The first clause dealt with general interference with the rights of workers as stated in Section 7, and covered such antiunion activities as the use of professional spies, bribery, violence, and strikebreaking. The second unfair practice was domination of a union, which, as interpreted by the NLRB, consisted not only of setting up a union, making financial contributions to its treasury, or paying of union officials, but also of stating a preference for one of two or more unions competing for recognition. Thirdly, in regard to discrimination in the hiring or firing of workers in order to encourage or discourage union membership, the act sought to remove the fear of "discharge for union activity"; in cases of violation, the NLRB could order reinstatement of the fired worker with back wages. The fourth unfair practice listed was the discharging of or any discrimination against a worker who testified before the board. The fifth section declared unfair an employer's refusal to bargain in good faith with the accredited representatives of the employees. This provision did not require that an agreement be reached with the union; as the Court had said, collective bargaining was *likely* to reduce strikes but provided no guarantee that disputes would cease. Administration of the act was in the hands of the three members of the National Labor Relations Board and their staffs in Washington and in the regional offices. In unfair labor practice cases the board acted on the basis of complaints of violation from workers and unions.

To determine whether a majority of workers in a plant wished to be represented by a union, the act provided for representation elections to be conducted by the National Labor Relations Board. The board had the power to determine the appropriate bargaining unit, call elections, prepare the ballot, conduct the voting (holding runoff elections if necessary), and certify to the employer the union representing the majority of workers. The employer was then required to bargain collectively with that union.

---

[18] These five unfair labor practices were generally referred to as "eight-one, eight-two," and so forth.

THE DEVELOPMENT OF RESTRICTIVE LEGISLATION

The culmination of the movement to secure and protect labor's right to organize—the Wagner Act—effected a revolution in the position of the worker in the American economy. It is not surprising that the act became one of the most controversial pieces of New Deal legislation; it was attacked almost continuously until its revision in 1947. Before it was upheld constitutionally in 1937, corporation lawyers advised their clients to ignore the law on the ground that the Supreme Court would invalidate it. Even after the 1937 decision some employers continued to fight the act in the courts, while in Congress bills were regularly introduced to amend it. The opposition centered around a number of issues: the act was considered to be biased against the employer, to limit employers' free speech, and to omit discussions of unions' unfair labor practices. During jurisdictional disputes complaints came from both employers and from AFL leaders who were concerned about the designation of industrial bargaining units.

In many respects the attacks were unjustified. If the government had not imposed certain duties on the employers, it is obvious that the "right" to organize could not have been protected. The act was necessarily one-sided, just as the Sherman Act was one-sided against those who restrained trade. The National Labor Relations Board was, as some charged, "prosecutor, judge and jury," but no more so than such other administrative boards as the Interstate Commerce Commission, established in 1887, and the Federal Trade Commission, established in 1914, which the American public had accepted. Nonetheless, the basic question of whether free collective bargaining would prove effective as a tolerable means of settling industrial disputes and at the same time be consistent with rights of others, including the general public, still remained unanswered.

The first concrete reaction to the Wagner Act came with the passage of state laws designed to supplement it (intrastate commerce was outside its jurisdiction). They revealed a growing conservative trend, especially during the 1940s. This legislation included, first, a lifting of certain controls over employer activities, such as his right to express a preference for a particular labor organization or to petition for an election among employees. Secondly, unfair practices by unions were designated. A Massachusetts law as early as 1937 declared a sit-down strike unfair, and other acts prohibited secondary boycotts, closed shops (except under certain conditions), strikes without a majority vote, breaking of contract, and use of coercion. In a third area of regulation, procedures for dispute settlements were prescribed. For example, a Minnesota law required 30-day strike notices in industries that affected the public interest. Finally, some states imposed controls on the internal affairs of unions, such as registration of organizers and regulation of election procedures, dues payments, and tenure of officials.

Nationally this trend had little effect prior to 1947. The War Labor Disputes Act of 1943 (known as the Smith-Connolly Act), which was passed over President Roosevelt's veto, gave legislative support to the National War Labor Board, which had been set up to resolve labor-management disputes, to prevent the disruption of war production by strikes, and to provide for plant seizures to enforce the board's decision. But it went on to impose controls on labor organizations by requiring that a majority of the workers had to approve any strike in a vote to be conducted by the National Labor Relations Board, and that a cooling-off period of 30 days had to take place before the strike, if approved, could occur. It also prohibited the use of union funds for political purposes.

The Taft-Hartley Act

The movement to limit unions' rights and activities came to a head in 1947 when the 80th Congress passed the Labor-Management Relations Act, known as the Taft-Hartley Act, over the veto of President Harry Truman.

The philosophy of the act was expressed in Section 1, which stated that industrial strife that burdens interstate commerce can be minimized among employers, employees, and unions if "each recognize under law one another's legitimate rights" and all recognize that no one has any right to "jeopardize the public health, safety, or interest." The purpose of the act was defined as the prescription of the "legitimate rights" of all parties, prevention of interference with those rights, protection of the "rights of individual employees in their relations with labor organizations," prevention of "practices inimical to the general welfare," and protection of the "rights of the public." The body of the act was divided into five main parts, or titles, the first of which consisted of amendments to the National Labor Relations Act that affected both the substance and the procedures of the previous law.

Section 7 of the Wagner Act, which had laid down the basic right of workers to organize unions of their own choosing, was expanded to include the right of workers to refrain from joining and participating in such activities. The five unfair labor practices of the Wagner Act were left more or less unmodified and were listed together in Section 8(a), but the new Section 8(b) listed six unfair labor practices of labor organizations. (A seventh was later added by the Landrum-Griffin Act.) These gave protection to the rights of employers and of nonunion workers. (The amended Sections 7 and 8 are presented in the appendix following this chapter.)

First, in 8(b)(1) interference by unions with the rights of individual workers was generally prohibited. Section 8(b)(2), the "anti–closed shop provision," declared that it was unfair for a union to demand that an employer discriminate in the hiring and firing of workers according to union affiliation except under a lawful union shop agreement.[19] Section 8(b)(3), a parallel section to 8(a)(5), stated that a union's refusal to bargain collectively was an unfair labor practice.

The complex Section 8(b)(4) listed certain types of unfair strikes and boycotts. The first of its four subsections outlawed secondary boycotts in general, and the next two prohibited strikes or secondary boycotts to force any other employer to recognize an uncertified union. The fourth subsection, by declaring as unfair any strikes or secondary boycotts to force an employer to assign work to a particular group of workers, outlawed jurisdictional strikes.

The fifth unfair practice of labor organizations specified by the act was the requirement of "excessive or discriminatory" fees under various forms of union security arrangements, and the sixth was forcing an employer to pay "for services which are not performed or not to be performed." Finally, in 8(b)(7), added later, picketing to organize workers or force union recognition was an unfair practice if an employer has recognized another union, if it was within 12 months after a representation election, or if the union did not file a request for such an election within 30 days.

A "free-speech" amendment, Section 8(c), provided that expression of opinion should not be considered an unfair labor practice if it contained "no threat of reprisal or force or promise of benefit."

The procedure for certification of unions as accredited bargaining agents was also modified in the Taft-Hartley Act. In determining the appropriate bargaining unit, the NLRB could not include professional among nonprofessional employees unless the former voted agreement; nor could it deny a craft-unit designation, unless the craft workers voted opposition. Guards, watchmen, and other workers who protect the employer's property had to form separate unions, which could be certified only on the condition that they did not admit other employees and were not affiliated with other unions. No foreman or "individual employed as a supervisor" could be included in a bargaining unit; this restriction denied to foremen's unions the legal protection formerly granted by the Wagner Act and upheld by the Supreme Court. The new law also specified that an election leading to certification would be binding on the employer for a 12-month period, that the union had to file financial and other information concerning its organization prior to an election, that elections leading to the decertification of a union could be held, and that an employer as well as employees could petition for an election or for decertification.

---

[19] The law also amended Section 8(a)(3) so that it is an unfair labor practice for the employer to discriminate in hiring and firing of employees because of a union agreement, except under the conditions allowed by the act. According to the new 8(a)(3), the employer shall not discriminate against an employee for nonmembership if the union is not open to any employee on the same terms applicable to other members or if membership was denied or terminated for reasons other than failure to pay dues.

Among the changes in the administration and enforcement of the law were the increase in the size of the National Labor Relations Board from three to five members and the creation of the position of General Counsel. The General Counsel, who had control over attorneys other than administrative law judges (originally called trial examiners) and the regional officers, was granted the important power to investigate charges of unfair labor practices, to seek federal injunctions where necessary, and to issue and prosecute complaints before the board. His independence was designed to avoid the earlier charge that the board was prosecutor, judge, and jury by making him the prosecutor.

The most important addition to the normal procedure for handling unfair labor practices under the amended act was that the General Counsel was permitted to petition in the federal courts for an injunction to halt an unfair labor practice of either employer or union. The permissive injunction procedure was presented in detail in Section 10(j), while under Section 10(l) the injunction became mandatory for illegal strikes and secondary boycotts, which were prohibited in Section 8(b)(4), paragraphs A, B, or C. Not only was the General Counsel required to petition for injunctive relief of such violations, but he had to give them priority over all other cases.

In a miscellaneous group of new provisions under Title III,[20] Section 301 provided for suits by and against unions for violation of contracts. In such suits, however, individual union members and their assets were exempted from liability in any monetary judgments against the union. In Section 302 payments by employers to union representatives were prohibited except in such specified situations as joint management of trust funds or the checkoff, where safeguards were carefully spelled out. Section 303 authorized suits by injured parties to recover damages resulting from unlawful strikes and boycotts. Section 304 amended the Federal Corrupt Practices Act of 1925 to make unlawful any political contributions by a labor organization, thus replacing the restriction of the Smith-Connolly Act with a similar provision applicable in peacetime.[21] Section 305 banned strikes of employees of the federal government.

The Taft-Hartley Act provided a highly complex and detailed system for regulating unions and collective bargaining in the United States. Though critics charged that it was excessively legalistic, its supporters defended the new controls over unions and argued that it brought a better balance in bargaining power between labor and management. In its immediate impact, the act proved to be not so drastic in limiting union actions as its foes had feared.

[20] Title II, discussed in the next chapter, established machinery to handle national emergency disputes. Title IV created a joint congressional study committee on labor relations. Title V contained definitions.

[21] Under the Federal Election Campaign Act of 1971 union political funds are legal if collected separately from dues and if members are properly informed as to their use and not subject to reprisal.

Established bargaining procedures in most major industries were little affected. As to unfair labor practices by unions, the number of violations has been fewer than those of employers; the most frequent complaints have involved mass picketing and violations of individual rights under 8(b)(1). Charges under 8(b)(2) were more important soon after passage of the act as they were directed against existing closed shop arrangements. But relatively few actions have been taken against unions in connection with 8(b)(3), the refusal to bargain; Section 8(b)(5), relating to excessive union fees; and 8(b)(6), the antifeatherbedding provision. (In the case of antifeatherbedding, it soon became apparent that charges could not be upheld if work was performed, whether "necessary" or not.)

Far more controversial have been the provisions concerning secondary boycotts in Section 8(b)(4) and the 8(b)(7) prohibition of picketing in such disputes. The justification for the ban on secondary boycotts was that innocent third parties, or "neutrals" should be protected from a strike when an employer and employees are not disputing the terms and conditions of their employment. However, this section of the law has raised questions of interpretation that have not been satisfactorily resolved. Take the case of a struck producer of goods who farms out work to another employer in order to avoid the economic pressures of the strike; under present interpretation of the law, the employees of the second firm can support the striking workers by striking themselves only if it can be proved that their employer is an "ally" of the first employer. Such proof may be difficult to obtain.[22]

One attempt to circumvent the secondary boycott provision was introduced by the Teamsters union in the 1950s in a "hot cargo" clause written into their contracts with trucking firms. This clause gave the union the freedom not to handle goods shipped by a nonunion firm where a strike was in process ("hot cargo"); if forced to carry such goods, the union could argue that its contractual rights were violated. The Supreme Court ruled that the clause violated the law, and Congress later specifically outlawed the practice in Section 8(e) of Landrum-Griffin Act.

One major effort by unions to modify secondary boycott provisions came with passage by Congress of the Common Situs (common-site picketing) bill in 1975. Desired primarily by the building trades unions, the law was designed to permit picketing at a job site even if several contractors, both union and nonunion, were engaged in a construction project at the same location. In an earlier legal interpretation, the Supreme Court had stated that at such

---

[22] In one case involving a television station and a newspaper in the same area, both owned by the same parent corporation, the court upheld an NLRB ruling that the two divisions were separate "persons." An attempt by strikers at the television station to win support by a work shutdown at the paper was therefore considered to be a violation of 8(b)(4); *AFTRA, Washington-Baltimore Local* v. *NLRB*, 462 F.2d 887 (1972).

sites where there was a labor dispute involving union employers, the non-union employers could have a "reserved gate" at which no picketing would be allowed. Although the 1975 remedial legislation had been supported initially by the administration, President Gerald R. Ford unexpectedly vetoed the bill after passage. Secretary of Labor John T. Dunlop, who had been the bill's chief architect, resigned from the cabinet in protest shortly thereafter.

One of the most serious charges against the Taft-Hartley Act from the worker's viewpoint has been that it has hindered unionization. Although total union membership rose in the years immediately following its passage in 1947, relatively little expansion occurred in certain geographical areas, especially the South and Southwest. Moreover, in recent years, when workers in newer industries and occupations sought representation through unions, frustration increased as employers appeared to be able to deny them the rights to join unions and bargain collectively. Legal limitations on union policies, administrative delays that hampered organizing efforts, and lack of effective penalties in the act strengthened the hand of antiunion employers.[23]

There have been several minor reforms. One change concerned a provision of the Taft-Hartley amendments that had disenfranchised "economic strikers"—that is, workers on strike over issues arising from a bargaining impasse. Such workers could not vote in elections, even though workers on strike over an unfair labor practice of the employer did not lose their voting rights. In the case of an employer who replaced workers striking over an economic issue with strikebreakers, this provision made it legal to call for a union decertification election and bar the striking workers from voting. Although the tactic was not widely used, the law was changed in 1959 to outlaw it. Under Section 9(c)(3) "economic strikers" maintain their rights to vote during the first twelve months of a strike.

There have also been several extensions of the act to cover certain groups of workers previously excluded. In 1974 the law was amended to permit employees of private nonprofit hospitals to have union representation and collective bargaining. (This class of employees had been excluded originally by a clause inserted during congressional debate over the Taft-Hartley amendments in 1947.[24]) In addition, in 1970 and 1971 the National Labor Relations

---

[23] This situation, it must be pointed out, was in fact what the Taft-Hartley amendments were designed to accomplish. See Frank McCulloch and Tim Bornstein, *The National Labor Relations Board* (New York: Praeger, 1974); Joseph P. Goldberg, "The Law and Practice of Collective Bargaining," in Goldberg et al., eds., *Federal Policies and Worker Status since the Thirties* (Madison, Wis.: Industrial Relations and Research Association, 1976), pp. 30, 33ff.

[24] The 1947 exclusion had the effect of abruptly stopping an organizing movement by the American Nurses' Association that had just begun. See Robert T. Woodworth and Richard B. Peterson, *Collective Negotiation for Public and Professional Employees*

Board changed its earlier position and gave protection to workers in private nonprofit institutions of higher learning who worked to form unions and bargain collectively, at first with respect to nonfaculty personnel and then to faculty members. Until that time, these workers had been explicitly excluded, not by law but by a deliberate decision—then legally permissible—on the part of the NLRB to refuse to assert its authority in such cases. The new administrative ruling, upheld in the courts, set off a small wave of organizing efforts among a number of private nonprofit colleges and universities, especially in the North. (Collective bargaining by faculties of public colleges and universities is subject to state legislation.)

Irrespective of coverage, however, worker dissatisfaction with representation election procedures and with unsatisfactory resolution of unfair labor practices by employers mounted during the 1970s and led to proposals for reform. In the congressional oversight hearings on the act in 1975–1976, the delays in negotiation of first contracts and the long procedures involved in handling unfair labor practices revealed how inadequately the law was being applied in many instances.[25] Although not passed at the time, a Labor Law Reform bill, introduced in Congress in 1977 and supported by President Jimmy Carter, was designed to strengthen the National Labor Relations Board and provide new sanctions against violators of the act.

One of the issues has been the increasing workload of the board, which has caused delays in handling both representation and unfair labor practice cases. The total number of cases before the board rose from 21,000 in 1960, to 33,-000 in 1970, to 49,000 in 1976; of these about 18,000 were pending at year's end. In contested representation cases carried to the board, the time elapsed between the initial petition and the actual election reached an average of 275 days. A charge of an unfair labor practice brought before the board required about a year for final disposition. If the case were taken to a court of appeals, the time required from the date of complaint to settlement averaged two years. Under such conditions, employers who want to resist unionization often find that the delays work in their favor, and plan their tactics accord-

---

(Glenview, Ill.: Scott Foresman, 1969), ch.7. Coverage now includes private nonprofit hospitals and all other health care institutions, such as health maintenance organizations, clinics, and nursing homes. Federal, state, and municipal health care institutions fall outside the jurisdiction of the act; proprietary hospitals had already been covered. The 1974 amendment also specified certain restrictions of union actions at health care institutions, including a new unfair labor practice of striking or picketing without first giving a 10-day notice.

[25] Some employers have been able to hold off unionization for years. In the case of J.P. Stevens & Co., a textile firm with 44,000 workers in 85 plants located mostly in North Carolina and South Carolina, the company in 1977 had still been able to refuse to negotiate with the union. The NLRB had found it guilty of violating the law in 15 separate cases since 1965. The board's action had been upheld by the federal appeals courts eight times and by the Supreme Court three times.

ingly.[26] Postponement of elections because contested issues are being appealed to the NLRB or to the courts may discourage workers so that they lose interest in unionization. During delays in settling unfair labor practices, an employer can with impunity refuse to bargain, and can initiate actions that are known to be violative of the act. For example, if a firm fires unionists in order to stop an organizing effort, the union's campaign may have lost its effectiveness by the time the company is ordered to cease the practice; the firm may believe that the penalties imposed are so light that its actions were well worth the cost.

One of the criticisms of the Taft-Hartley Act has been the inadequacy of remedies for workers adversely affected by unfair labor practices. In the case of violations of 8(a)(3)—the discharge of workers for union activity, an unfair labor practice most frequently reported—the usual remedy is reinstatement of the worker with back pay; but many workers, if finally reinstated to previous jobs, do not return because they fear some form of company retaliation.[27] The increasing number of charges of violation of 8(a)(5), the refusal to bargain, also point to the lack of adequate remedies under the act. Evidence of refusal to bargain currently has several interpretations: refusing to bargain altogether, bargaining but refusing to consider any alternative proposals, and so-called "surface bargaining," or going through the motions without intending to reach an agreement. Even if the bargaining is in good faith, impasses can of course occur and strikes ensue; this is considered part of the test of economic pressure that is characteristic of collective bargaining. But it is not consistent with the principle of collective bargaining if the employer will not bargain with the union over wages, hours, and conditions of employment as mandated by the act. The NLRB's remedy for such a violation is to issue a cease-and-desist order; if not obeyed the board must then seek enforcement from a court of appeals, a process that usually leads to further delay. Injunctive relief, although required when unions are charged with unfair labor charges involving secondary boycott, is optional when charges of unfair labor practices are made against employers; the record reveals that the General Counsel has rarely invoked it in cases of 8(a)(5). A penalty of financial reparations to be paid to workers by an employer guilty of a violation of this section

[26] Most of the cases involving unfair labor practices under the law, however, are resolved at the earliest stages of the legal process. Even of those cases that reach the NLRB, a large percentage are disposed of without formal action by the board. In 1974, of 27,016 unfair labor practice cases, 85.8% were closed before formal action; of 13,542 representation cases, 82.9% were closed before a hearing was required. See statistical analysis of cases of the National Labor Relations Board, 1936–1974 in U.S. Department of Labor, *Handbook of Labor Statistics, 1975—Reference Edition*, Bulletin 1865 (Washington, D.C.: Superintendent of Documents, 1975), pp. 422–423.

[27] See Lee Aspin, "Legal Remedies Under the NLRA: Remedies Under 8(a)(3)," *Proceedings* of the Twenty-Third Annual Winter Meeting, Industrial Relations Research Association, pp. 264–272.

was recommended in President Carter's 1977 Labor Law Reform message.[28]

The free-speech provision, Section 8(c), has also presented difficulties in interpretation because of the fine line between free speech and antiunion statements that threaten or coerce. Nonetheless, the board has at times not considered it a violation if, immediately before an NLRB election, employers give an "economic forecast" to the effect that the plant will close down if workers accept the union, if they appeal to racial prejudice, or if they require that employees, on company time, listen to antiunion speeches but deny union organizers a chance to address workers.

The Landrum-Griffin Act

The Labor-Management Reporting and Disclosure Act of 1959, known as the Landrum-Griffin Act, was passed after several years of public hearings held by the McClellan Senate investigating committee on union corruption and racketeering. The primary objective of the act was to eliminate the "unethical and improper practices of labor organizations, employers, labor relations consultants, and their officers and representatives" that "distort and defeat the policies" of the Taft-Hartley Act and hamper the free flow of interstate commerce. The act also included in Title VII the amendments to the Taft-Hartley Act that have already been considered.

The basic assumption of the act was that the evils of corruption in the union movement stemmed from undemocratic practices within unions. If the internal affairs of unions were conducted in accordance with certain minimum standards for democratic procedures, members would be able to "clean their own houses." The required filing of financial information by unions, employers, and labor consultants might give evidence of criminal offenses that could lead to governmental remedial action.

Title I enacted a "bill of rights" for union members and provided for its enforcement through the courts by actions brought by the workers who had been denied such rights. Included were the right to participate in nominations and elections, to attend and participate in union meetings, and to vote by secret ballot on increases in dues, initiation fees, or other assessments. The act recognized the necessity of rules concerning the responsibility of the individual union member to the organization in order for it to carry out its legal and contractual responsibilities, and of disciplinary action against members who violate those rules, but it set up minimum safeguards on the unions' judicial procedures. A maximum four-month period was declared necessary to "exhaust reasonable hearing procedures" before a member could sue the union for violation of rights. The act also provided that any employee under a

---

[28] A similar type of remedy had been recommended previously by the National Labor Relations Board in *Ex-Cell-O Corp.*, 185 NLRB 107–108 (1970).

contract negotiated by the union had a right to obtain a copy of the collective bargaining agreement.

The requirements for minimum democratic election procedures in unions are stated in Title IV. National unions must hold elections of officers "not less often" than once every five years; intermediate bodies, such as joint boards and councils, every four years; and local unions, every three years. In all three cases elections must be conducted by secret ballot of members in good standing. National elections can also take place at a convention of delegates chosen by secret ballot. The act provides that unions shall not interfere with the right of any candidate to run for union office, that safeguards must be provided for a fair election—including the right of any candidate to have "an observer at the polls and at the counting of ballots"—and that no union funds shall be used to promote the candidacy or election of any individual. Constitutions must be brought into conformity with the minimum requirements; thereafter, the constitution and bylaws determine the rules of election procedures that are enforceable in the courts. Penalties for violation of the election requirements are that the election may be declared null and void and that the Secretary of Labor may supervise a new election.

Title II requires comprehensive and detailed reports from labor organizations of such provisions as election procedures, membership requirements, dues and fees, and annual financial reports. These requirements take the place of the Taft-Hartley filing provisions and are mandatory for all labor organizations, irrespective of whether they wish to use the protections of the Taft-Hartley Act.

Title III deals with "trusteeships"—suspensions of the autonomy of a labor organization by its parent body. The law defines the proper purposes of such actions and limits the period of trusteeship to 18 months unless exceptional circumstances are found.

Union officers and union employees (except clerical and custodial workers) are required to report any financial transactions with employers, their agents, or their consultants with whom the union does business (except as a bona fide employee), and employers and labor consultants are also required to report such transactions. Heavy penalties of fines and imprisonment are imposed for violation.

Other safeguards are contained in Titles V and VI. The bonding of union officials who handle union funds is required. A union cannot make loans to its officials in excess of $2,000, nor can it pay the fine of any officer convicted of a willful violation of the act. No person shall serve as a union officer or official, or as a labor relations consultant to an employer, who has been convicted of a felony or has served any part of a prison term under such a conviction during the previous five years. (A similar provision involving membership in the Communist party was later held unconstitutional.) Embezzlement of union funds and extortionate picketing are made federal crimes.

Evaluations of the impact of the Landrum-Griffin Act indicate that in general the problems of corruption and undemocratic procedures in unions were not as widespread and endemic as some legislators had assumed.[29] Investigations made by the Office of Labor-Management Services Administration (formerly the Bureau of Labor-Management Reports)—an agency of the Department of Labor—indicate that most complaints have been minor and not actionable. Many union constitutions were amended in the early years after the act was passed in order to comply with new requirements. However, the number of trusteeships, through which a national could directly control a recalcitrant local, dropped sharply. Also, as noted earlier, in several significant cases, governmental intervention in election procedures produced far-reaching results; these included the 1965 election of the International Union of Electrical Workers and the 1972 election of the United Mine Workers.

Probably most observers believe that the internal balance of power within unions has not been significantly affected by the Landrum-Griffin Act.[30] By establishing democratic procedures, its framers hoped to provide effective democratic controls. But if the membership of a union is generally apathetic except during times of contract negotiations or of strikes, the best procedures cannot guarantee a truly democratic organization.

SUMMARY

The rights, duties, and liberties of workers, unions, and employers are defined by the laws and rules of any economic system. The essence of a free labor market is the freedom of an individual to work or to quit work without being forced by law to work if he or she does not desire to do so. Slavery, serfdom, indentured labor, peonage, and contract labor are various forms of nonfree, or forced, labor. In the United States, all types of involuntary servitude, except as punishment for crime, were abolished in 1865 by the Thirteenth Amendment to the Constitution.

American workers did not win the right to form unions until the twentieth century. In the early nineteenth century, some unions were declared illegal under the common-law doctrine of criminal conspiracy. This position was generally abandoned after the *Commonwealth of Massachusetts* v. *Hunt* decision in 1842, which ruled that unions as such were lawful. But employers

---

[29] See, for example, Philip Taft, *The Rights of Union Members and the Government* (Westport, Conn.: Greenwood Press, 1975), pp. 271–285; Joseph P. Goldberg, "The Law and Practice of Collective Bargaining," pp. 30–33.

[30] Benson Soffer expressed this attitude in his analysis "Collective Bargaining and Federal Regulation of Union Government," in Martin Estey, Philip Taft, Martin Wagner, eds., *Regulating Union Government* (New York: Harper & Row, 1964). John T. Dunlop, however, has taken the position that the rank and file has acquired greater power, with adverse effects on the stability of collective bargaining relationships; this change stems from the "exaggerated views of union democracy expressed in the spirit of the Landrum-Griffin Act." See "The Social Utility of Collective Bargaining," in Lloyd Ulman, ed., *Challenges to Collective Bargaining* (Englewood Cliffs, N.J.: Prentice-Hall, 1967), p. 179.

were still under no obligation to allow unions among their employees or to bargain with them. Employers could obtain injunctions from the courts, both state and federal, to prohibit union activities on grounds that such activities impaired their property rights.

The common-law doctrine of restraint of trade, as well as the Sherman Anti-Trust Act of 1890, also furnished grounds for declaring certain union actions illegal. The Clayton Act of 1914 attempted to protect union activity, but the U.S. Supreme Court soon denied its constitutionality when unions, in its opinion, restrained trade.

Because the existence of a legal right requires that others have the duty to respect it, the right to organize came only when the courts agreed to recognize as constitutional those laws that imposed duties on employers not to interfere with union activities and to bargain collectively. The first such law ruled constitutional by the U.S. Supreme Court was the Railway Labor Act of 1926. The precedent was followed in decisions concerning the Federal Anti-Injunction Act of 1932 and the National Labor Relations Act (Wagner Act) of 1935.

The National Labor Relations Act, as amended, governs labor relations in the private sector today. To protect the right of workers to form unions, the act defines specific unfair labor practices of employers that would deny those rights. As amended by the Labor-Management Relations Act (Taft-Hartley Act) of 1947, the law also designates specific unfair labor practices of unions in order to protect certain rights of nonunion workers and of employers. To certify unions to employers for collective bargaining, the law provides for representation elections conducted by the National Labor Relations Board. The law also spells out the procedures and rights of parties in the collective bargaining process. The Labor-Management Reporting and Disclosure Act (Landrum-Griffin Act), passed in 1959, specifies the rights of workers as union members and provides rules for democratic procedures within unions.

DISCUSSION QUESTIONS

1. What is the constitutional basis of the free labor market in the United States? Can rights of workers be limited despite constitutional guarantees?
2. In the years before the labor legislation of the 1930s, what legal doctrines were used to restrict workers' attempts to form unions of their own choosing?
3. One of the first attempts to give legal protection to union activity came with the Clayton Act of 1914. What did it provide, and how was it modified in the courts?
4. Contrast the objectives of the Wagner and the Taft-Hartley acts. What Taft-Hartley provisions do you believe especially reflect differences in philosophy?
5. Would union membership have increased as rapidly as it did in the 1930s without the Wagner Act? Would membership have increased more rapidly in the 1950s if the Taft-Hartley Act had not been passed?
6. What are the specific issues in recent proposals for labor law reform?

SELECTED READINGS

For the general development of labor law, see Felix Frankfurter and Nathan Greene, *The Labor Injunction* (New York: Macmillan, 1930); Irving Bernstein, *The New Deal Collective Bargaining Policy* (Berkeley: University of California Press, 1950); and Harry C. Millis and Emily C. Brown, *From the Wagner Act to Taft-Hartley* (Chicago: University of Chicago Press, 1950).

The following studies are useful on the general nature of labor law and its applications: Archibald Cox, *Law and the National Labor Policy* (Los Angeles: Institute of Industrial Relations, University of California at Los Angeles, 1960): A. Howard Myers and David P. Twomey, *Labor Law and Legislation*, 5th ed. (Cincinnati: South-Western, 1975); Philip Ross, *The Government as a Source of Union Power: The Role of Public Policy in Collective Bargaining* (Providence: Brown University Press, 1965); Joseph Shister, Benjamin Aaron, and Clyde W. Summers, eds., *Public Policy and Collective Bargaining* (New York: Harper & Row, 1962); and Harvey H. Wellington, *Labor and the Legal Process* (New Haven: Yale University Press, 1968). On the NLRB, see Frank McCulloch and Tim Bornstein, *The National Labor Relations Board* (New York: Praeger, 1974).

APPENDIX

Sections 7 and 8 of the National Labor Relations Act (Wagner Act), July 5, 1935, C. 372, 49 Stat. 452. as Amended by Title I of the Labor Management Relations Act of 1947 (Taft-Hartley Act) June 23, 1947, C. 120, Title I, 101, 61 Stat. 140, and by the Labor-Management Reporting and Disclosure Act (Landrum-Griffin Act), September 14, 1959, C. 158, 73 Stat. 519.

Section 7 Employees shall have the right to self-organization, to form, join, or assist labor organizations, to bargain collectively through representatives of their choosing, and to engage in other concerted activities for the purpose of collective bargaining or other mutual aid or protection, and shall also have the right to refrain from any or all of such activities except to the extent that such right may be affected by an agreement requiring membership in a labor organization as a condition or employment as authorized in section 8 (a) (3).

Section 8 (a) It shall be an unfair labor practice for an employer—
(1) to interfere with, restrain, or coerce employees in the exercise of the rights guaranteed in section 7;

(2) to dominate or interfere with the formation or administration of any labor organization or contribute financial or other support to it: Provided, That subject to rules and regulations made and published by the Board pursuant to section 6, an employer shall not be prohibited from permitting employees to confer with him during working hours without loss of time or pay;

(3) by discrimination in regard to hire or tenure of employment or any term or condition of employment to encourage or discourage membership in any labor organization: *Provided,* That nothing in this Act, or in any other statute of the United States, shall preclude an employer from making an agreement with a labor organization (not established, maintained, or assisted by any action defined in section 8 (a) of this Act as an unfair labor practice) to require as a condition of employment membership therein on or after the thirtieth day following the beginning of such employment or the effective date of such agreement, whichever is the later, (i) if such labor organization is the representative of the employees as provided in section 9 (a), in the appropriate collective-bargaining unit covered by such agreement when made; and (ii), if, following the most recent election held as provided in section 9 (e) the Board shall have certified that at least a majority of the employees eligible to vote in such election have voted to authorize such labor organization to make such an agreement: *Provided further,* That no employer shall justify any discrimination against an employee for nonmembership in a labor organization (A) if he has reasonable grounds for believing that such membership was not available to the employee on the same terms and conditions generally applicable to other members, or (B) if he has reasonable grounds for believing that membership was denied or terminated for reasons other than the failure of the employee to tender the periodic dues and the initiation fees uniformly required as a condition of acquiring or retaining membership;

(4) to discharge or otherwise discriminate against an employee because he has filed charges or given testimony under this Act;

(5) to refuse to bargain collectively with the representatives of his employees, subject to the provisions of section 9 (a).

(b) It shall be an unfair labor practice for a labor organization or its agents—

(1) to restrain or coerce (A) employees in the exercise of the rights guaranteed in section 7: *Provided,* That this paragraph shall not impair the right of a labor organization to prescribe its own rules with respect to the acquisition or retention of membership therein; or (B) an employer in the selection of his representatives for the purposes of collective bargaining or the adjustment of grievances;

(2) to cause or attempt to cause an employer to discriminate against an employee in violation of subsection (a) (3) or to discriminate against an employee with respect to whom membership in such organization has been denied or terminated on some ground other than his failure to tender the periodic dues and the initiation fees uniformly required as a condition of acquiring or retaining membership;

(3) to refuse to bargain collectively with an employer, provided it is the representative of his employees subject to the provisions of section 9 (a);

(4) (i) to engage in, or to induce or encourage any individual employed by any person engaged in commerce or in an industry affecting commerce to engage in, a strike or a refusal in the course of his employment to use, manufacture, process, trans-

port, or otherwise handle or work on any goods, articles, materials, or commodities or to perform any services; or (ii) to threaten, coerce, or restrain any person engaged in commerce or in an industry affecting commerce, where in either case an object thereof is:

(A) forcing or requiring any employer or self-employed person to join any labor or employer organization or to enter into any agreement which is prohibited by section 8(e);

(B) forcing or requiring any person to cease using, selling, handling, transporting, or otherwise dealing in the products of any other producer, processor, or manufacturer, or to cease doing business with any other person, or forcing or requiring any other employer to recognize or bargain with a labor organization as the representative of his employees unless such labor organization has been certified as the representative of such employees under the provisions of section 9: *Provided,* That nothing contained in this clause (b) shall be construed to make unlawful, where not otherwise unlawful, any primary strike or primary picketing;

(C) forcing or requiring any employer to recognize or bargain with a particular labor organization as the representative of his employees if another labor organization has been certified as the representative of such employees under the provision of section 9;

(D) forcing or requiring any employer to assign particular work to employees in a particular labor organization or in a particular trade, craft, or class rather than to employees in another labor organization or in another trade, craft, or class, unless such employer is failing to conform to an order or certification of the Board determining the bargaining representative for employees performing such work: *Provided,* That nothing contained in this subsection (b) shall be construed to make unlawful a refusal by any person to enter upon the premises of any employer (other than his own employer), if the employees of such employer are engaged in a strike ratified or approved by a representative of such employees whom such employer is required to recognize under this Act; *Providing further,* That for the purposes of this paragraph (4) only, nothing contained in such paragraph shall be construed to prohibit publicity, other than picketing, for the purpose of truthfully advising the public, including consumers and members of a labor organization, that a product or products are produced by an employer with whom the labor organization has a primary dispute and are distributed by another employer, as long as such publicity does not have an effect of inducing any individual employed by any person other than the primary employer in the course of his employment to refuse to pick up, deliver, or transport any goods, or not to perform any services, at the establishment of the employer engaged in such distribution.

(5) to require of employees covered by an agreement authorized under subsection (a) (3) the payment, as a condition precedent to becoming a member of such organization, of a fee in an amount which the Board finds excessive or discriminatory under all the circumstances. In making such a finding, the Board shall consider, among other relevant factors, the practices and customs of labor organizations in the particular industry, and the wages currently paid to the employees affected;

(6) to cause or attempt to cause an employer to pay or deliver or agree to pay or de-

liver any money or other thing of value, in the nature of an exaction, for services which are not performed or not to be performed; and

(7) to picket or cause to be picketed, or threaten to picket or cause to be picketed, any employer where an object thereof is forcing or requiring an employer to recognize or bargain with a labor organization as the representative of his employees, or forcing or requiring the employees of an employer to accept or select such labor organization as their collective bargaining representative, unless such labor organization is currently certified as the representative of such employees:

(A) where the employer has lawfully recognized in accordance with this Act any other labor organization and a question concerning representation may not appropriately be raised under section 9(c) of this Act,

(B) where within the preceding twelve months a valid election under section 9(c) of this Act has been conducted, or

(C) where such picketing has been conducted without a petition under section 9(c) being filed within a reasonable period of time not to exceed thirty days from the commencement of such picketing: *Provided,* That when such a petition has been filed the Board shall forthwith, without regard to the provisions of section 9(c) (1) or the absence of a showing of a substantial interest on the part of the labor organization, direct an election in such unit as the Board finds to be appropriate and shall certify the results thereof: *Provided further,* That nothing in this subparagraph (C) shall be construed to prohibit any picketing or other publicity for the purpose of truthfully advising the public (including consumers) that an employer does not employ members of, or have a contract with, a labor organization, unless an effect of such picketing is to induce any individual employed by any other person in the course of his employment, not to pick up, deliver or transport any goods or not to perform any services.

Nothing in this paragraph (7) shall be construed to permit any act which would otherwise be an unfair labor practice under this section 8(b).

(c) The expressing of any view, argument, or opinion, or the dissemination thereof, whether in written, printed, graphic, or visual form, shall not constitute or be evidence of an unfair labor practice under any of the provisions of this Act, if such expression contains no threat of reprisal or force or promise of benefit.

(d) For the purpose of this section, to bargain collectively is the performance of the mutual obligation of the employer and the representative of the employees to meet at reasonable times and confer in good faith with respect to wages, hours, and other terms and conditions of employment, or the negotiation of an agreement, or any question arising thereunder, and the execution of a written contract incorporating any agreement reached if requested by either party, but such obligation does not compel either party to agree to a proposal or require the making of a concession: *Provided,* That where there is in effect a collective-bargaining contract covering employees in an industry affecting commerce, the duty to bargain collectively shall also mean that no party to such contract shall terminate or modify such contract, unless the party desiring such termination or modification—

(1) serves a written notice upon the other party to the contract of the proposed termination or modification sixty days prior to the expiration date thereof, or in the event such contract contains no expiration date, sixty days prior to the time it is proposed to make such termination or modification;

(2) offers to meet and confer with the other party for the purpose of negotiating a new contract or a contract containing the proposed modifications;

(3) notifies the Federal Mediation and Conciliation Service within thirty days after such notice of the existence of a dispute, and simultaneously therewith notifies any State or Territorial agency established to mediate and conciliate disputes within the State or Territory where the dispute occurred, provided no agreement has been reached by that time; and

(4) continues in full force and effect, without resorting to strike or lock-out, all the terms and conditions of the existing contract for a period of sixty days after such notice is given or until the expiration date of such contract, whichever occurs later: The duties imposed upon employers, employees, and labor organizations by paragraphs (2), (3) and (4) shall become inapplicable upon an intervening certification of the Board, under which the labor organization or individual, which is a party to the contract, has been superseded as or ceased to be the representative of the employees subject to the provisions of section 9 (a), and the duties so imposed shall not be construed as requiring either party to discuss or agree to any modification of the terms and conditions contained in a contract for a fixed period, if such modification is to become effective before such terms and conditions can be reopened under the provisions of the contract. Any employee who engages in a strike within the sixty-day period specified in this subsection shall lose his status as an employee of the employer engaged in the particular labor dispute, for the purposes of sections 8, 9, and 10 of this Act, as amended, but such loss of status for such employee shall terminate if and when he is reemployed by such employer.

(e) It shall be an unfair labor practice for any labor organization and any employer to enter into any contract or agreement, express or implied, whereby such employer ceases or refrains or agrees to cease or refrain from handling, using, selling, transporting or otherwise dealing in any of the products of any other employer, or to cease doing business with any other person, and any contract or agreement entered into heretofore or hereafter containing such an agreement shall be to such extent unenforcible and void: *Provided*, That nothing in this subsection (e) shall apply to an agreement between a labor organization and an employer in the construction industry relating to the contracting or subcontracting of work to be done at the site of the construction, alteration, painting, or repair of a building, structure, or other work: *Provided further*, That for, the purposes of this subsection (e) and section 8(b) (4) (B) the terms "any employer," "any person engaged in commerce or an industry affecting commerce," and "any person" when used in relation to the terms "any other producer, processor, or manufacturer," "any other employer," or "any other person" shall not include persons in the relation of a jobber, manufacturer, contractor, or subcontractor working on the goods or premises of the jobber or manufacturer or performing parts of an integrated process of production in the apparel and clothing industry: *Provided further*, That nothing in this Act shall prohibit the enforcement of any agreement which is within the foregoing exception.

It shall not be an unfair labor practice under subsections (a) and (b) of this section for an employer engaged primarily in the building and construction industry to make an agreement covering employees engaged (or who, upon their employment, will be engaged) in the building and construction industry with a labor organization of which building and construction employees are members (not established, maintained, or assisted by any action defined in section 8(a) of this Act as an unfair labor practice) because (1) the majority status of such labor organization has not been established under the provisions of section 9 of this Act prior to the making of such agreement, or (2) such agreement requires as a condition of employment, membership in such labor organization after the seventh day following the beginning of such employment or the effective date of the agreement, whichever is later, or (3) such agreement requires the employer to notify such labor organization of opportunities for employment with such employer, or gives such labor organization an opportunity to refer qualified applicants for such employment, or (4) such agreement specifies minimum training or experience qualifications for employment or provides for priority in opportunities for employment based upon length of service with such employer, in the industry or in the particular geographical area: *Provided,* That nothing in this subsection shall set aside the final proviso to section 8(a) (3) of this Act: *Provided further,* That any agreement which would be invalid, but for clause (1) of this subsection, shall not be a bar to a petition filed pursuant to section 9 (c) or 9 (e).

13

Strikes and the Public Interest

The theory of free collective bargaining assumes that if both parties to a dispute are unable to agree peacefully, a test of economic strength by strike or lockout will resolve the issue. Collective bargaining is predicated on the recognition by an individual or group of the existence and rights of other individuals and groups—the fundamental assumption of a pluralistic society—and on the corollary recognition that each group and individual must at times compromise and adjust its position to others in the face of the economic pressures of the marketplace.

STRIKE BEHAVIOR IN THE UNITED STATES

Although, as already noted, strikes (and lockouts) are an integral part of the collective bargaining system, 4,000 or 5,000 strikes a year are still a relatively small number in comparison with the 180,000 or more contracts in existence. Except in several exceptional years, the severity of strikes in terms of days lost has not been excessive: less than 0.3 percent of the estimated working time of all workers per year was lost by strikes from 1951 to 1975—except in 1952, when the rate rose to 0.57 percent; in 1959, when it was 0.61 percent; and in 1970, when the rate was 0.37 percent.

Three measures of work stoppages[1] in the United States have been generally accepted: the number of strikes, the number of workers involved in strikes, and the number of man-days lost by strikes (that is, the number of strikers times the length of the strike in days). The data indicate a wide range in strike activity; relatively few years are characterized by a large number of strikes, while most years are peaceful. From 1890 to World War II (with the exception of 1906–1915 inclusive, when no data were available), the peak

[1] All such data are prepared by the U.S. Department of Labor. Because both strikes and lockouts are included, the department prefers the term "work stoppages."

years in the number of strikes were 1903, with 3,648 recorded strikes; 1917, with 4,450; 1937, with 4,749; and 1941, with 4,288. The lowest number of strikes per year was in the period 1927–1932, when fewer than 1,000 strikes took place annually. Near the end of World War II strikes increased again in a wave that began in 1944 and extended through 1955; in that 12-year period the number of strikes rose above 4,500 for each of the three years from 1944 to 1946 and for each of the four years from 1950 to 1953. A peak occurred in 1952, when 5,117 strikes were recorded. Since 1955 the total was fewer than 4,000 until the mid-1960s, when the number began to increase fairly steadily, reaching an all-time peak of 6,074 in 1974. (See Table 13–1.)

Strikes are associated with changes in business conditions. The number increases with improving business activity, rising prices, and falling unemployment; it declines during periods of depressed conditions.[2] The data reveal that there is a close association of strikes with the booms of wars and immediate postwar periods, such as after World War II (during the war the National War Labor Board was effective in reducing strike activity), the Korean conflict, and the Vietnam War. The end of wage and price controls in 1974 (and the anticipation of their ending) undoubtedly led to the large number of strikes as workers attempted to catch up with consumer price rises. In addition, a strike wave may occur when new collective bargaining relationships are extended into new fields, because employers are reluctant to change over from previous patterns of individual negotiation with their employees. Such a break with past behavior took place in the 1930s—especially 1937—when strikes shot up sharply; a similar situation developed with the expansion of unionization into the public sector in the 1960s and early 1970s.

In terms of the number of workers involved in strikes, two years during the twentieth century stand out as exceptional: 1919, when 4,160,000 workers went out on strike, and 1946, when the total reached 4,600,000. Both of these peaks came immediately after the nation's involvement in long wars, with the release of pent-up tensions from under wartime controls. In only five other years has the number of workers involved in strikes risen over 3 million: 1945, 1949, 1952, 1970, and 1971. The trend in the percentage of employed workers involved in strikes has been downward since 1946, when it was 10.5. The percentage has been less than 5.0 in the last two decades.

The number of man-days lost by strikes has also shown great variation from year to year. Again, 1946—when 116 million working days were lost—looms as the year of the biggest strikes in modern United States history (these statistics go back only to 1927). In only three other years was the lost time as much as even half that amount: in 1959, 69 million man-days (40 percent of which resulted from the long steel strike of that year); in 1952, 59.1 million

---

[2] For a study of factors influencing the incidence of strikes over time see Orley Ashenfelter and George E. Johnson, "Bargaining Theory, Trade Unions, and Industrial Strike Activity," *American Economic Review*, 59 (March 1969), 35–49.

Table 13-1
Work Stoppages in the United States, 1945–1975[a]

Year	Work Stoppages		Workers Involved[b]		Man-Days Idle During Year		
	Number	Average Duration (calendar days)[c]	Number (thou- sands)	Percent of Total Employed	Number (thou- sands)	Percent Esti- mated Working Time of all Workers	Per Worker Involved
1945	4,750	9.9	3,470	8.2	38,000	.47	11.0
1946	4,985	24.2	4,600	10.5	116,000	1.43	25.2
1947	3,693	25.6	2,170	4.7	34,600	.41	15.9
1948	3,419	21.8	1,960	4.2	34,100	.37	17.4
1949	3,606	22.5	3,030	6.7	50,500	.59	16.7
1950	4,843	19.2	2,410	5.1	38,800	.44	16.1
1951	4,737	17.4	2,220	4.5	22,900	.23	10.3
1952	5,117	19.6	3,540	7.3	59,100	.57	16.7
1953	5,091	20.3	2,400	4.7	28,300	.26	11.8
1954	3,468	22.5	1,530	3.1	22,600	.21	14.7
1955	4,320	18.5	2,650	5.2	28,200	.26	10.7
1956	3,825	18.9	1,900	3.6	33,100	.29	17.4
1957	3,673	19.2	1,390	2.6	16,500	.14	11.4
1958	3,694	19.7	2,060	3.9	23,900	.22	11.6
1959	3,708	24.6	1,880	3.3	69,000	.61	36.7
1960	3,333	23.7	1,320	2.4	19,100	.14	14.5
1961	3,367	23.7	1,450	2.6	16,300	.11	11.2
1962	3,614	24.6	1,230	2.2	18,600	.13	15.0
1963	3,362	23.0	941	1.1	16,100	.11	17.1
1964	3,655	22.9	1,640	2.7	22,900	.15	14.0
1965	3,963	25.0	1,550	2.5	23,300	.15	15.1
1966	4,405	22.2	1,960	3.0	25,400	.15	12.9
1967	4,595	22.8	2,870	4.3	42,100	.25	14.7
1968	5,045	24.5	2,649	3.8	49,018	.28	18.5
1969	5,700	22.5	2,481	3.5	42,869	.24	17.3
1970	5,716	25.0	3,305	4.7	66,414	.37	20.1
1971	5,138	27.0	3,280	4.6	47,589	.26	14.5
1972	5,010	24.0	1,714	2.3	27,066	.15	15.8
1973	5,353	24.0	2,251	2.9	27,948	.14	12.4
1974	6,074	27.1	2,778	3.4	47,991	.24	17.3
1975	5,031	26.8	1,746	2.2	31,237	.16	17.9

[a] The number of stoppages and workers relate to those beginning in the year; average duration, to those ending in the year. Man-days of idleness include all stoppages in effect.

[b] Workers are counted more than once if they were involved in more than one stoppage during the year.

[c] Figures are simple averages; each stoppage is given equal weight regardless of its size.

Source: U.S. Department of Labor.

(20.4 percent due to that year's steel strike); and in 1970, 66.4 million (26.9 percent attributable to the strike at General Motors). In the period since World War II the average number of man-days lost per worker involved has ranged from a minimum of 10.3 days in 1951 to 36.7 days in 1959.

These statistics do not, of course, indicate the extent of the loss that any specific strike may cause strikers, other workers, management, or the public. A strike in one industry may cause layoffs and lost time in others that are not included directly in the statistics. Also, the average number of strikes in the United States, although seemingly low, has been higher than that in most other countries.[3] On the other hand, the estimated number of man-days lost because of strikes may overstate the problem. A high rate of production before an anticipated strike may indicate that the workers would not have worked full time if the strike had been called off. In a seasonal or cyclical industry, where employment is shiftable, a strike may merely affect the distribution of work over a period of time and not reduce total employment and output.

Several factors tend to limit strike activity. One is the spread and general success of the institution of collective bargaining itself, which has provided the possibility for peaceful resolution of disputes over wages and the terms of employment, in a manner as envisioned by those who advocated the passage of the National Labor Relations Act in the 1930s. Management has not only come to accept collective bargaining but also found that it can be useful for promoting a stable work force. Secondly, automation of production processes in various industries has undermined labor's use of the strike weapon. In electric utilities, oil refining, long-line telephones, printing, and chemicals—among other industries—a relatively few supervisory and technical personnel can often keep firms in operation during strikes. Thirdly, government controls of strikes have been increasing. The National Labor Relations Act, which stimulated the growth of collective bargaining, sharply reduced labor's use of the strike for union recognition by providing for representation elections. As amended, the act has made illegal the jurisdictional strike (in which a union attempts to force an employer to assign work to its members) and the secondary boycott (in which a strike may be called against third parties). Arbitration of interpretations of "rights" in union agreements has virtually ended grievance strikes, and no-strike clauses have made union leaders the enemy of wildcat strikes in view of their liability for penalties under the Taft-Hartley Act. The fact that all strikes are illegal among federal employees and, with only a few exceptions, among state and local government employees means that with the continued growth of public-sector employment an increasing proportion of American workers is denied all rights to strike.

[3] Arthur M. Ross and Paul T. Hartman, *Changing Patterns of Industrial Conflict* (New York: John Wiley, 1960), p. 31.

These factors, either singly or in combination, do not mean that all strikes will "wither away" in the future. The rising trend in strike activity since the early 1960s gives empirical evidence for the contrary view. A prerequisite of "free" collective bargaining is the availability of the strike and lockout as tools for economic pressure. Automated production lines may simply change the nature of unions' bargaining tactics. And, despite laws to the contrary, workers who feel that they have no alternative will support illegal strikes, as they have on many occasions.

THE PUBLIC INTEREST IN PRIVATE-SECTOR STRIKES

Three factors influence how seriously a strike in the private sector will affect the public: the type of industry, the relative number of workers involved, and the strike's timing and duration. As to the type of industry, a strike has less effect on the public if it stops production of goods that are storable or nonessential to the consumer's or the nation's survival. On the other hand, in industries whose products are perishable (such as milk), essential to daily life (such as electricity or gas for heating and cooking), or vital to national survival (such as missiles), strikes can have an immediate detrimental impact on the welfare of the public.

Disregarding other factors, a work dispute involving a relatively small number of workers is likely to be less burdensome to the public than a "large" strike. A work stoppage by employees of a restaurant in a large city would hardly be felt, for example; but when the dominant plant in a community is shut down, the loss of the weekly payroll can hurt merchants, suppliers, loan collections of financial institutions, and even the flow of tax funds to the community. Similarly, an industrywide strike can have greater repercussions upon the economy as a whole than can one in a single firm.

The longer a strike continues, the greater will be its effect upon the public. A strike that cuts off the flow of storable products will not have an effect upon consumers until inventories are depleted and begin to be in short supply. In such industries as rubber, where inventories may be high at the beginning of the strike, the public may not be inconvenienced for several weeks or months.

Types of Government Intervention

When the public fears that its interests are affected, or about to be affected, by a strike, some form of government intervention is usually demanded. In earlier days strikes were "broken" by troops or by injunctions or other court actions. But with the recognition of the legitimacy of unions, of the process of collective bargaining, and of strikes as a part of that process, the problem arose of protecting the public interest and collective bargaining rights at the same time. Several types of government intervention to bring about an end to a strike have proved to be consistent with the voluntary resolution of a dispute by both parties under collective bargaining.

In *conciliation* a governmental representative or third party enters a dispute simply to keep both parties negotiating with each other. In *mediation* a third party not only attempts to keep both sides negotiating, but also advances possible solutions to the controversy. The mediator may introduce compromises that opposing factions had not considered or had been unwilling to advance. In both conciliation and mediation the contending parties are under no compulsion to agree. Both types of intervention are consistent with "free collective bargaining," but they do not guarantee settlement.

Voluntary arbitration, a third type of intervention, involves submission of a dispute to a third party who makes a decision—known as an "award"—binding on the two parties. The two parties are not required to submit their dispute for arbitration, but if they voluntarily elect to do so, they are required to accept and abide by the decision of the arbitrator. As we have seen earlier, voluntary arbitration is most often used in the settlement of grievances. Although the procedure is consistent with collective bargaining, it is used less frequently in settling contract disputes, since both unions and management are usually reluctant to submit to a third party matters that so substantially affect their own economic interests.

A fourth type of governmental intervention, also in accord with the premise of voluntary agreement, is *fact-finding with recommendations*, sometimes called *compulsory investigation*. Both parties are required to submit their dispute to a third party who, after hearings, offers recommendations for a fair settlement. The effectiveness of fact-finding lies in the strength of public opinion to force acceptance of the proposed terms of agreement, and the procedures are designed to build up public pressures on both parties to sign. The third party is usually a person, or a panel of individuals, widely respected as fair, knowledgeable, and impartial. The hearings are made public, and the final recommendations are usually given publicity as a reasonable compromise that any fair-minded person would accept.

On some occasions governmental intervention in labor disputes occurs without the consent of both parties to the terms of settlement. In *compulsory arbitration* both labor and management are required not only to submit their dispute to a third party, but also to abide by the final decision. This is known as "interest arbitration" in that the economic interests of both parties are determined by an outsider. Although the arbitration board may be composed of disinterested and impartial members, either or both parties may feel that the decision is not fair and that they are being forced to accept it against their will. When decisions concerning their economic interests are enforced without the consent of those concerned, any of several reactions can weaken the effectiveness of the law. Strikes (or lockouts) that occur despite a law forbid-

VOLUNTARY ARBITRATION AND ECONOMIC INTERESTS

In 1973, the United Steelworkers of America and the ten basic companies that make up the coordinated committee for the industry agreed to an innovative Experimental Negotiating Agreement (ENA), which provided for voluntary arbitration of any contract differences over the terms and conditions of employment after their three-year agreement expired. The use of arbitration to resolve conflicts over economic interests, unlike arbitration of grievances involving interpretation of rights under existing contracts, is relatively unusual because it places bread-and-butter questions in the lap of third parties.

Worked out one year before the existing contract expired in 1974, ENA gave each worker a one-time bonus of $150 when the contract ended, continued the escalator clause for the new three-year contract, and provided for a general wage increase of 3 percent for each year of the new contract. Any unresolved issues on new terms would go to arbitration so that a strike was precluded. The agreement attempted to avoid the previous jockeying for better negotiating positions that had cost the industry in prenegotiating inventory buildups and lengthy strikes (such as the one in 1959); many customers had sought foreign sources or switched to other materials, with subsequent loss of employment and greater payments by the industry for supplementary unemployment compensation. Contributing to ENA was an earlier agreement between the union and the steel companies to establish employment security and plant productivity committees that would lower costs and yet protect jobs.

The no-strike agreement became an issue in the 1977 election contest for union president. The challenger, Edward Sadlowski, the insurgent director of the union's Chicago-Gary district, argued that the agreement worked to the detriment of the rank and file because it placed too much power in the hands of the union's administration. Lloyd McBride, who had the backing of the retiring union president, I. W. Abel (the negotiator of the original ENA), won the election with some 58 percent of the votes. Later, contract talks were conducted with the steel operators, as they had been three years earlier in 1974, and both parties agreed to continue the standby arbitration procedure until 1980.

---

ding them are difficult to prevent. If employees are jailed for refusing to work under terms of which they disapprove, the political repercussions in a democratic society can be serious (except perhaps under such exceptional circumstances as wartime emergencies, when the existence of the nation is menaced, or in industries where the public has already accepted the idea of governmental controls). The parties to the dispute may seek political control over the selection of arbitrators in order to secure greater likelihood of favorable decisions. Compulsory arbitration thus tends to politicize labor disputes, and the economic conflicts of the picket line are likely to become battles for ballots and public opinion.

Moreover, the system tends to undermine collective bargaining. Even before the procedures begin, each party in the dispute tends to overstate its case and to underestimate the value of concession and agreement. A union, for example, may not see why it should scale down its demands to what it believes the employer might reasonably be expected to accept if there is the possibility that the arbitrator might award more.

Another type of control of strikes and lockouts that is not based on the theory of free collective bargaining is *seizure*; here the government takes possession of a firm in which a labor dispute is taking place. Forbidding strikes, it runs the plant under the contract already in existence until a new agreement between the union and employer has been negotiated. Usually the management employees continue to act as agents for the government in day-to-day operating decisions, but questions obviously arise about the locus of decision-making power and the distribution of profits. The principal advantage of seizure is that, since workers are likely to be unwilling to strike against the government, production can be resumed. The principal disadvantage is that seizure prevents the full economic power of the strike from being brought to bear upon both parties, and hence can affect the outcome: though continued negotiations can take place under seizure, neither side is compelled to compromise because the effective economic pressure of loss of income is lacking.

Historical Review of Government Intervention

Each of the types of government intervention discussed has been used in the United States. Let us look first at the railroads, where the first federal recognition of the need for formal intervention appeared with the Arbitration Act of 1888. It provided for voluntary arbitration of disputes and was strenghtened, after the Pullman strike of 1894, when Congress passed the Erdman Act. This act attempted to promote collective bargaining and at the same time set up machinery for mediation and voluntary arbitration of railroad disputes by the commissioner of the Bureau of Labor Statistics and the chairman of the Interstate Commerce Commission. In World War I the federal government took over the railroads during a strike and bargained with the workers about the terms and conditions of employment. After the war the Esch-Cummins Act of 1920 established a tripartite Railway Labor Board of nine members to investigate and aid in the settlement of labor disputes by mediation and arbitration; when this act proved to be unwieldy, it gave way to the Railway Labor Act of 1926.

As amended in 1934, 1936, 1951, and 1966, the Railway Labor Act authorizes two boards. The National Railroad Adjustment Board, composed of 36 members, half from the railroads and half from the unions, arbitrates grievances arising from interpretation of contracts; it may use outside referees when deadlocks must be broken. Since the unsettled grievances between unions and railroads must be referred to the board, the provision can be classified as a form of compulsory arbitration.[4] The second agency, the National Mediation Board, consists of three persons, appointed by the president, who attempt to mediate disputes about changes in the terms and conditions of employment. If its proposals fail to promote an agreement, the board can offer its services for voluntary arbitration. If these services are refused, the act provides for an Emergency Board, appointed by the president, to investigate the dispute and report its recommendations to him within 30 days. The president in turn can then report the results of the fact-finding to Congress. From the beginning of the dispute until 30 days after the Emergency Board reports to the president, strikes or lockouts are prohibited.

This fact-finding procedure was considered highly successful in preventing disputes until World War II. Since then, the system has tended to break down, and some labor economists have urged that the special legislation for railroads should be repealed. One aspect of the "crisis" of public policy on the railroads was the growing realization after World War II that the statutory procedure could stifle negotiations between the parties. Both labor and management were showing an increased reluctance to bargain with each other by pushing the issue through every step in the fact-finding procedure. In fact, several new though unofficial steps were added. During World War II the unions began the practice of appealing the recommendations of an Emergency Board to President Roosevelt, who often negotiated more favorable settlements. In several cases, even his proposals were turned down, and FDR resorted to seizure in order to maintain service on the railroads. President Truman also utilized the weapon of seizure in three railroad cases in 1950 and 1951.

During the 1950s and 1960s it became increasingly plain that the fact-finding Emergency Board procedures were not resolving disputes, and that the public was not willing to allow strikes to occur at will. Spurred by a lengthy dispute over work rules and charges of featherbedding, as well as an accumulation of grievance cases, President Eisenhower established a Presidential Railroad Commission in 1960 to resolve the impasse. In 1961, President Kennedy set up two special boards, the Railroad Marine Commission and the Railroad Lighter Captains Commission, to deal with labor disputes concerning New York Harbor carriers. In all three cases, the regular procedures of the Railway Labor Act had been exhausted, and in all three the unions rejected the final recommendations.

With the failure of these expediencies, the Congress has intervened with ad hoc legislation requiring compulsory arbitration. The first such act, passed

[4] The sting of compulsory arbitration was removed at the time the bill was originally prepared because most of the bill was written by the railroads and the unions themselves.

The airlines, included under the Railway Labor Act since 1936, have separate boards of adjustments for handling grievance procedures.

in 1963, established a tripartite arbitration board to make a final and binding award on the use of firemen and other train and yard crews. Congress intervened again in four other disputes, sometimes solely to extend the time limit during which further negotiations could continue without strikes.[5]

While it is clear that these procedures can undermine voluntary settlements—one party may hold out for the possibility of better terms at the next step of governmental intervention—it is also true that serious substantive problems have plagued labor relations on the railroads. The railroads have suffered since the 1920s from the competition on the part of motor vehicles, commercial aviation, pipelines, trucks, and buses. The decline of employment on class I line-haul railroads was calamitous, with jobs dropping by nearly 53 percent, from over 1.2 million in 1950 to fewer than 600,000 in 1969. Particularly hard hit were telegraphers, and Pullman conductors—the last group in one case reporting a drop of almost three-fourths in 14 years.[6] With little opportunity for alternative employment, railroad workers had only their unions to rely on for job and income security. Although they were able to win some gains, primarily through delaying actions, the institution of collective bargaining by itself could not resolve the economics of an industry facing severe contraction.

The issue of public rights in labor disputes in areas other than railroads was first recognized by legislation creating the United States Conciliation Service in the Department of Labor in 1917. This quasi-independent agency consisted of experienced persons whose services as conciliators, mediators, or arbitrators in the settlement of disputes were available when requested. The Taft-Hartley Act provided for the transfer of the agency from the Labor Department to independent status as the Federal Mediation and Conciliation Service. The act also required that the service's aid be used during negotiations prior to the ending of contracts and during disputes that lead to national emergencies.

Fact-finding as a form of governmental intervention has had a lengthy history in the United States, even apart from its use on the railroads. The first fact-finding board appointed by executive order of the president was the Anthracite Coal Commission established by President Theodore Roosevelt in October 1902; a number of similar boards were established by executive order under Wilson, Franklin Roosevelt, and Truman. Ad hoc fact-finding boards have been used to end disputes in steel, coal, and automobiles. Fact-finding

---

[5] See U.S. Department of Labor, *Handling of Rail Disputes Under the Railway Labor Act, 1950–69*, Bulletin 1753 (Washington, D.C.: U.S. Government Printing Office, 1972), pp. 20–22. For a general review, see Donald E. Cullen, *National Emergency Strikes* (Ithaca, N.Y.: Cornell University Press, 1968).

[6] U.S. Department of Labor, *Handling of Rail Disputes*, p. 5. Of seven major occupational classifications in the two decades from 1950 to 1969, declines were reported in all but one, "executives, officials, and staff assistances"; their numbers increased by 6.4 percent—a fact stressed by the unions.

has also been appealing as a remedy for labor conflict in industries of a special emergency character. Atomic energy plants, for example, were natural candidates for emergency action to prevent labor unrest and strikes, and an Atomic Energy Labor Relations Panel, appointed by President Truman in 1949, relied primarily on mediation and fact-finding in the disputes that came before it, although it was empowered to use almost any remedy it saw fit if the circumstances warranted it. In 1961 President Kennedy set up an eleven-member Missile Sites Labor Commission for labor disputes at missile bases.

Presidential seizures of strikebound or strike-threatened industries have also occurred. President Wilson made three seizures, and President Franklin Roosevelt made three during the defense period prior to our involvement in World War II. During that war, 46 seizures were ordered under the authority of the War Labor Disputes Act, and after the war President Truman used the procedure 11 times.[7] Seizures worked most effectively during wartime, when patriotism led most workers and managements to accept governmental direction. Except in periods of serious war emergencies, seizure raises certain uncertainties in terms of its legality and its effectiveness as a solution to a collective bargaining impasse. When the Supreme Court declared the 1952 steel seizure unconstitutional, the rationale of its decision was that Congress, not the president, had the power to seize on the grounds of the right of eminent domain, and that Congress had already provided for a specific procedure to be followed in national emergency disputes under Title II of the Taft-Hartley Act.[8] Since the government may be put under "heavy pressure" to "determine the substantive issues" of the dispute, with all the resulting headaches and political repercussions if the decision is considered contrary to the best interests of one party or the other, seizure may not be successful as a means of forcing both parties to arrive at some mutually satisfactory arrangement.

American legislation for compulsory arbitration has been limited primarily to a few state laws and to the special circumstances of World War II. In the latter instance, both unions and managements supported the authority of the National War Labor Board to make substantive determinations of the content of collective bargaining agreements; unions gave up the right to strike with no-strike pledges. Even so, as we have seen, some seizures were made to enforce the decisions and prevent strikes.[9] The first state law to provide for compulsory arbitration was passed in Kansas in 1917, but it was declared unconstitutional by the Supreme Court in 1923.[10] New laws were passed in

---

[7] These included seizures in oil, coal, steel, and meat packing, and three seizures of Class I railroads. See Edwin E. Witte, "Industrial Conflict in Periods of National Emergency," in Arthur Kornhauser, et al., eds., *Industrial Conflict* (New York: McGraw-Hill, 1954), pp. 431 ff.

[8] *Youngstown Sheet & Tube Co.* v. *Sawyer*, 343 U.S. 579 (1952).

[9] In all, 26 seizures were directed toward the prevention of walkouts, and 20 to prevent noncompliance by the employer.

[10] *Wolff Packing Co.* v. *Court of Industrial Relations*, 262 U.S. 522 (1923).

seven states after World War II to provide for compulsory arbitration in public utilities, but these too have a dubious legal status as a result of an adverse decision of the Supreme Court in 1951.[11]

Title II of the Taft-Hartley Act

The Taft-Hartley Act of 1947 established under Title II a set of procedures to end disputes that "will, if permitted to occur or to continue, imperil the national health and safety."[12] When any such dispute occurs, the procedures provide, first, for the appointment of a board of inquiry by the president. The board holds hearings and reports back on the issues of the dispute, but it does *not* make any recommendations for settlement. If the strike affects an entire industry or a substantial part of it, or if it imperils the national health or safety, the president then directs the attorney general to petition a district court for an 80-day injunction against the strike or lockout. During that time the Federal Mediation and Conciliation Service can intervene to assist in the settlement of differences. At the end of 60 days from the time the injunction is obtained, the board of inquiry reports on the last offer made by the employer, and within the following 15 days the National Labor Relations Board takes a secret ballot of the employees to see whether they accept it or not. The results must be certified within five days. At this point the injunction is discharged and the president submits a report to Congress.

Essentially, this procedure enforces an 80-day cooling-off-period by means of a federal injunction. The board of inquiry makes no recommendations, as it would in fact-finding. Conciliation and mediation are provided, but Title II explicitly rejects compulsory arbitration. The vote on the employers' "last offer" carries with it neither a mandate for the employer to change the offer if it is not accepted nor a mandate for the union to accept it if the members so vote.

The concept of the cooling-off period was developed to protect the public's interest in production and to give more time to both parties to settle their dispute. In the 34 cases in which Title II was invoked from 1947 to 1977, the procedure generally provided immediate protection, although several disputes were settled before the injunction was invoked. However, in nine cases the injunction apparently simply postponed the strike, which erupted after the 80-day period was over. (See Table 13–2.)

The principal objection to Title II is that the procedure is so rigid that the parties can plan their strategy around it. As a result, it delays rather than promotes bargaining. There is no reason, for example, to bargain seriously before

---

[11] *Amalgamated Association of Street, Electric Railway and Motor Coach Employees of America, Division 998 et al.* v. *Wisconsin Employment Relations Board,* 340 U.S. 383 (1951).

[12] Strikes under the Railway Labor Act are excluded.

Table 13-2
Strikes and Settlements in National Emergency Disputes, 1947–1977

Strikes and Settlements	Number of Disputes	Number of Workers[a] (thousands)
Total disputes	34	2,144.8
Strikes—total	29	1,800.0
Before 80-day injunction	18	1,384.1
After 80-day injunction	2[b]	73.0
Before and after 80-day injunction	· 7	259.7
No injunction issued	2[c]	83.2
Settlements—total	34	2,144.8
Settlements without strike	5[d]	344.8
Settlements after strike	29	1,800.0
Within 80-day injunction period	14	1,316.7
After 80-day injunction period	13	400.1
Without strike	4	67.4
After strike	9[b]	332.7
No injunction issued	2[c]	83.2

[a] The number of workers refers to those in the bargaining unit or to those directly involved in the strike.

[b] One stoppage involved 6 maritime unions and the International Longshoremen's and Warehousemen's Union on the Atlantic, Gulf, and Pacific coasts and the Great Lakes. Settlements were reached for the Atlantic and Gulf Coast and the Great Lakes during or immediately after the injunction period. The ILWU and several maritime unions struck on the Pacific Coast after the injunction had expired.

[c] An injunction was not requested in the 1948 meat packing dispute and a request for an injunction in the 1971 Chicago grain elevator dispute was denied by the district court.

[d] Injunctions were not issued in 3 of the 5 cases.

Source: U.S. Department of Labor

the vote of the membership on the employers' last offer; on the contrary, there is every reason for workers to demonstrate their solidarity by voting down the offer, as they have done in nearly every case.

Another limitation of the procedure is that the boards of inquiry do not have the right to make recommendations for settlement. Such an addition to the present provisions could be desirable. But there is no reason why Title II cannot be made more flexible in other ways. The Federal Mediation and Conciliation Service could be brought into the negotiation before the positions taken by the two parties had hardened and been expressed publicly before the board of inquiry. It has also been argued that the number of weapons the government can use in a dispute should be increased (say, to include seizure) and that the rigidity of a fixed procedure should be discarded. Such changes would serve to create an atmosphere of uncertainty in which neither unions nor management would be able to predict the line of action that the government would take, and they would therefore presumably be more likely to settle beforehand in order to avoid unfavorable situations.

Although certain changes in dispute procedures were recommended by the Nixon administration in 1970, none was passed, in part because strike activity in the private sector was at a low ebb. The period of the big "national emergency strike," which began immediately after World War II and which helped to create the atmosphere for the passage of the Taft-Hartley Act, appeared to be over. Of the 34 disputes in which Title II was invoked during the 30 years from 1947 to 1977, half occurred before 1960. These 17 disputes, moreover, involved over 1.5 million workers, or 84.5 percent of the total strikers in all 34 cases.[13] Not only has the incidence of emergency disputes declined, but many analysts have questioned whether these disputes were in fact true emergencies, and whether they could not have been resolved more satisfactorily through collective bargaining without Title II intervention.[14] Similar questions arose in connection with the coal strike of 1977–1978. Although President Carter invoked Title II procedures after the strike of some 180,000 miners had lasted for three months, a temporary restraining order issued in March 1978 did not prove helpful. Strikers generally ignored it, and the government did not seriously enforce it. The order expired in less than two weeks, and a settlement between the union and the operators came shortly afterward.

LABOR DISPUTES IN THE PUBLIC SECTOR

As the 1930s and 1940s were the period when unionism and collective bargaining finally became established in the mass production industries in the private sector of the United States, so the 1960s and 1970s saw a similar transformation of labor relations in the public sector. At the end of the 1950s few believed that public workers should have any say in the terms and conditions of their employment; since then the dramatic growth of unionization and increasing acceptance of collective bargaining indicate a revolution in public attitudes that is still occurring.

The underlying structural change in government employment, especially at the state and local level, has been the crucial factor. Faced with rapidly mounting problems in metropolitan areas, cities tried to provide services for a changing population—including desegregated education and welfare—while coping with the erosion of their tax base through the suburbanization of industry. The number of employees at all levels of government rose from 8.3

[13] See U.S. Department of Labor, Summary Report, *National Emergency Disputes Under the Labor-Management Relations (Taft-Hartley) Act, 1947–72,* Table I.
[14] See, for example, Benjamin Aaron, "Collective Bargaining Where Strikes are Not Tolerated," in Richard L. Rowan, ed., *Collective Bargaining: Survival in the '70's?* (Philadelphia: University of Pennsylvania Press, 1972), pp. 129–153.

million in 1960 to nearly 15 million in 1975, but most of this increase was at the state and local level, where the number doubled from 6 million to 12 million.

Former methods of labor recruitment, salary determination, and administration of work rules were inadequate to meet these new strains, and produced a number of inequities and inconsistencies in work rules and job relationships. Securing wage changes through the legislative process often meant delays and a widening of the gap between private- and public-sector wage levels; as consumer prices rose in the late 1960s, the dissatisfaction of public employees was exacerbated. The right to collective bargaining, established in law for private-sector workers, was largely denied as a channel of communication between government employees and management. Strikes by government workers were illegal. These facts only accentuated the belief that public employees—who in 1975 accounted for one out of every five (19.2 percent) of the nonagricultural workers in the United States—were being treated unfairly.

Under these circumstances it is not surprising that government workers sought collective bargaining in order to better their wages and working conditions, and also the right to strike if necessary. Despite their illegality, strikes in the public sector rose sharply beginning in the latter 1960s, reaching a level in the early 1970s that would have been unbelievable a decade before (see Table 13–3). Strikes have occurred at all levels of government, and strikers have come from all major occupational groups—police, firefighters, teachers, production and maintenance employees, and hospital workers. Nonetheless, in proportion to the number of employees, there have been far fewer strikes among government workers than among nonagricultural employees. In the four years from 1970 through 1973, an average of 1.6 percent of government workers were involved in work stoppages, in contrast to 4.1 percent for all nonagricultural employees; man-days of idleness per striker averaged 8.0 in the public sector but 16.2 for all.

Changes in Attitude

It has been recognized that employment relationships in the public sector have certain features that require policies with respect to unions, collective bargaining, and strikes that are different from those in private industry. The Taft-Hartley Act, for example, explicitly excludes from its coverage the United States government, any of its wholly owned corporations, states, and their political subdivisions. A government as an employer stands on a different legal footing by virtue of its sovereignty. In the United States, the concept of absolute sovereignty would deny as a matter of principle attempts by a government's employees to organize and influence through collective bargaining or strikes the terms of employment that are laid down administratively by the

Table 13-3
Government Work Stoppages[a] in the United States, 1960–1975

| Year | Number | Workers Involved (*thousands*) | Man-Days Idle | | Percent of Total Man-Days Idle[b] |
			Thousands	*Per Worker*	
1960	36	28.6	58.4	2.0	c
1961	28	6.6	.15.3	2.3	c
1962	28	31.1	79.1	2.5	c
1963	29	4.8	15.4	3.2	c
1964	41	22.7	70.8	3.1	c
1965	42	11.9	146.0	12.3	0.6
1966	142	105.0	455.0	4.3	1.8
1967	181	132.0	1,250.0	9.5	3.0
1968	254	201.8	2,545.2	12.6	5.2
1969	409	159.8	740.1	4.6	1.7
1970	412	333.5	2,023.3	6.1	3.0
1971	329	152.6	901.4	5.9	1.9
1972	375	142.1	1,257.3	8.8	4.6
1973	387	196.4	2,303.9	11.3	8.2
1974	384	160.8	1,404.2	8.7	2.9
1975	478	318.5	2,204.4	6.9	7.1

[a] For definitions see Table 13–1.
[b] See Table 13–1.
[c] Less than 0.5 percent.
Source: U.S. Department of Labor

authority delegated by the appropriate legislative body. In this view, workers dissatisfied with their wages, hours, seniority rights, or any other conditions of work have the option only of quitting. Civil service regulations, although designed to eliminate patronage, are an example of unilaterally determined sets of rules to control hiring, firing, promotion, wages, and other aspects of work relationships.

In practice, most governments have accepted limitations on their sovereign powers. Two factors have led to these modifications: the difficulty of recruiting workers from the private sector where certain unionization rights had been attained, and community pressures in areas where organized labor was strong. The federal government permitted unionization of postal workers with the Lloyd–La Follette Act of 1912 and gave them the right to petition Congress for improvements in wages and conditions of work. Over many years, the federal government has also accepted collective bargaining with printers in the Government Printing Office and with various craft and blue-collar workers in navy yards and other industrial establishments. At the local level governments have on occasion recognized and voluntarily dealt with unions long before legislation authorized them to do so. In the World War I period unions had been formed among firefighters, teachers, hospital workers, and other employee groups. The American Federation of Teachers, formed in 1916, won a number of victories during World War I.

What distinguishes the present period of rapid union growth in the public sector from earlier years is the willingness of the federal government and some state governments to encourage unionization and collective bargaining. At the federal level, Executive Order 10988, issued by President Kennedy in 1962, gave civil service employees the right to organize (or refrain from organizing) and to bargain collectively within certain narrowly prescribed limits. The order preserved management authority on such key matters as promotion, transfers, discharges, annual leaves, introduction of methods of operation, and designation of appropriate bargaining units. Salaries and benefits were excluded from bargaining. At first, grievance procedures terminated in "advisory" arbitration, with the power of final decision residing in the head of the agency. This procedure was later revised, and under Executive Order 11491, issued by President Nixon in 1969 (and further amended in 1971) grievances can go to final arbitration. A Federal Labor Relations Council was established to unify and clarify basic labor policies. With respect to a bargaining impasse, the Federal Mediation and Conciliation Service is authorized to assist in resolution, and in event of failure the issue can be taken to a Federal Service Impasses Panel, an agency consisting of three members within the Council, appointed by the president, with broad powers including recommendations for arbitration or third-party fact-finding.[15]

However modest, these changes nonetheless represent a fundamental shift in the attitudes of the federal government toward unionization. While it is important to recognize that an executive order does not have the standing of federal law and that an order can be rescinded as easily as it can be issued, there is every indication that the new attitudes will persist.

At the local level, one of the first breakthroughs in the encouragement of unionism came in New York City with an executive order issued in 1958 by Mayor Robert F. Wagner. The response came quickly, with the organization of some 44,000 public school teachers and recognition of the United Federation of Teachers (an affiliate of the American Federation of Teachers) as bargaining agent. After Executive Order 10988 in 1962, other state and local employees sought legislative support for unionization. By 1966 six states had comprehensive collective bargaining statutes; the number had risen to 21 by 1970. The picture is complex, as some states oppose any limitation on the principle of absolute sovereignty. Others allow unionization and give the right to "meet and confer" with the agency, but prohibit collective bargaining. In other instances, special occupations are given rights that are denied to

[15] For an analysis of these provisions, see Michael H. Moskow, J. Joseph Loewenberg, and Edward Clifford Koziara, *Collective Bargaining in Public Employment* (New York: Random House, 1970), pp. 38 ff.

others: often police officers and firefighters are excluded, and sometimes teachers.[16]

Most states prohibit strikes by public employees on the grounds that the use of force for the purpose of influencing governmental decisions is inconsistent with the government's sovereignty. (At the federal level, the Taft-Hartley Act in its only reference to public sector employees—in Section 305—bans all strikes of federal workers.) Yet the legislatures of Hawaii and Pennsylvania have passed legislation upholding the right to strike in impasse procedures. In Montana also, the courts have upheld the right to strike under specific conditions. In New York state, however, the 1947 Condon-Wadlin Act provided punitive penalties against a striker who was rehired—no wage increase for three years and no civil service tenure rights for five years. Superseded in 1967 by the Public Employees Fair Employment Act (known as the Taylor Act after Professor George Taylor, who headed a special commission to revise bargaining procedures), the ban against strikes was continued but the penalties were lightened: a striking union could be decertified, or its dues checkoff rights withdrawn.

Nature of Labor Relations in the Public Sector

Labor relations in the public sector are characterized by a complex, fragmented structure of managerial authority. This stems from the principle of the separation of powers between the legislative and executive branches of government, and the theory of checks and balances. As already noted, authority for collective bargaining at the federal level is in the hands of the executive branch; at the state level the practice varies. Under the Taylor Act in New York, the authority is vested in the executive. In some states the power is in the legislature, which must therefore approve contracts. For teachers, the bargaining authority typically resides with school boards, which may delegate actual negotiations to superintendents or their representatives. One of the complaints of many mayors and city councils is that they have little or no power to institute the labor policies that they believe would best represent the wishes of the citizens who elected them.[17] The fragmentation of government authority among appointed heads of fire and police departments, building

---

[16] For an analysis of state legislation see Robert D. Helsby and Thomas E. Joyner, *Collective Bargaining in Government* (Englewood Cliffs, N.J.: Prentice-Hall, 1972); Joel Seidman, "State Legislation on Collective Bargaining by Public Employees," *Labor Law Journal*, 22 (January 1971), 13–22. A brief description of state statutes is found in "Changing Policies in Public Employees Labor Relations," *Monthly Labor Review*, 93 (July 1970), 8–9.

[17] See statement of Henry W. Maier, Mayor of Milwaukee, "Collective Bargaining and the Municipal Employer," in Sam Zagoria, ed., *Public Workers and Public Unions* (Englewood Cliffs, N.J.: Prentice-Hall, 1972), pp. 53–62.

service agencies, transit systems, hospitals, and heads of bureaus and commissions often results in delays, frustration among both employees and agencies, and whipsawing because negotiated rights and benefits can vary
considerably within a single municipality.

Because the fragmented structure of government makes it difficult to identify who is the employer with the final authority, collective bargaining in the
public sector has been termed multilateral rather than bilateral (as it is the
private sector).[18] In a private firm, those who negotiate with the union are
able to make definite decisions about the terms of an agreement, or at least
quickly reach those in the chain of command who have that power. In the
case of the railroads and in some other instances there may be third-party intervention, or multilateralism, as already noted, but such participation generally occurs at a later stage in negotiations. But the public sector is affected
by the political nature of government decision-making. Elected public employers have a responsibility to their constituents. Special-interest groups may
subject them to intense pressure in negotiations. Appointed public employers
may have more freedom of action, but its extent will depend on the terms of
their appointment and on the amount of pressure applied by the elected officials who appointed them. Employees too can exercise political influence because they are part of the constituency of elected officials. Multilateralism
makes it possible for citizens, interest groups, and elected officials to affect
contract negotiations.

Public-sector bargaining operates under a set of economic constraints different from those faced in private industry. In the latter case, an employer's
power to grant concessions to union demands is restricted by the market for
the firm's products. Price increases to cover higher wages may lead to diminishing sales and lower profits as consumers turn to competitors or to substitute products. The employer may also try to reduce costs by substituting
capital for labor. In short, the private-sector market mechanism provides economic incentives to the employer to check wage increases and counter union
demands. A different mechanism operates at the state and local level. (At the
federal level, as noted earlier, wage scales are not bargainable.) Here the employer faces the political problem of attempting to obtain approval of a larger
budget in order to cover the increased labor costs. As the funds must come
eventually from higher taxes, the public has to accept the desirability of the
services performed as weighed against their added costs. Because tax increases
will not necessarily fall on those who are the chief consumers of the services,
the balancing of demand and cost is "political" in the sense that there must

---

[18] See Kenneth McLennan and Michael H. Moskow in "Multilateral Bargaining in the
Public Sector," *Proceedings* of the Industrial Relations Research Association, 1969, pp.
31–40. The concept is elaborated in Moskow, Loewenberg, and Koziara, *Collective Bargaining*, ch. 8.

be an accommodation among the various interest groups of the community, both as consumers and as taxpayers, before an outlay is approved.

It is sometimes claimed that this political mechanism does not offer restraints to wage increases as effective as those of the private market. The specific argument is that the demand for government services is relatively inelastic because the services are essential and because governments prevent competition from the private sector. With inelastic demands for their services, unions are in the position of being able to win higher wages than they would otherwise obtain.[19]

But this assessment is incomplete. It is true that the public may sometimes tolerate exceptional salary increases for special groups if the services they furnish are strongly desired—that is, if demands are highly inelastic—and if the impact on aggregate expenditures is small. But taxpayer revolts, or threats of revolt, offer a counterforce to union demands that can be effective and severe. Even the question of need is a political one, and some taxpayer groups can be in a position to deny funds for services which others believe are essential. One of the complicating elements in the political mechanism, especially in cities, is the lack of a close relationship between the services performed by the local government and the sources of taxes. As cities are still subdivisions of the state, their taxing authority operates only within the limits set by state legislatures. Because many state legislatures are dominated by interests unsympathetic to urban problems, a local city union may find that the final veto power on its wage demands lies in the hands of those who not only are not consumers of local services but are even antagonistic to those who are.[20]

The diverse influences that affect wage determination in the public sector lead to conflicting patterns of public/private wage differentials. Empirical studies, most of which were initiated in the 1970s, show, for example, that unions among teachers have had only a small influence on wages.[21] Compar-

[19] This argument has been made by Harry H. Wellington and Ralph K. Winter, "The Limits of Collective Bargaining in Public Employment," *The Unions and the Cities* (Washington, D.C.: Brookings Institution, 1971), pp. 7–32.

[20] In the 1975 financial crisis of New York City, where large-scale renegotiations of city indebtedness were required in order to forestall bankruptcy, the effective decision-making power in labor negotiations went into the hands of the financial community, which insisted upon certain cost limitations before refinancing. A State Emergency Financial Control Board for New York City was set up with the authority even to override negotiated contracts. Three of the seven members of the board were drawn from the business community. Moreover the federal government gained a voice in labor negotiations in 1976 as a condition for its loan of nearly $3 billion to bail out the city.

[21] For one of the first econometric studies, see Hirshel Kasper, "The Impact of Collective Bargaining on Public School Teachers' Salaries," *Industrial and Labor Relations Review*, 24 (October 1970), 57–72. Another that finds practically no influence of unionization on wages is that of Donald E. Frey, "Wage Determination in Public Schools and the Effects of Unionization," in Daniel S. Hamermesh, ed., *Labor in the Public and Nonprofit Sectors* (Princeton, N.J.: Princeton University Press, 1975), pp. 183–219.

ing wages in other government occupations with union wages in the private sector, Daniel S. Hamermesh found an advantage for one group of workers (bus drivers) but no difference for two other groups of occupations.[22] On the other hand, some investigators have concluded that the political process tends to produce higher wages when governments seek to establish comparability with the private sector.[23] As there usually is a range of private-sector wages for a particular occupation, governments are more likely to choose a standard from the higher end of the range, for several reasons. To be consistent with policy encouraging unionization in the private sector, governments will designate the higher union rate as the going rate of pay. Where a government sets a uniform occupational wage rate to be applied to several different communities, it will often take the highest community wage rate as its guide in order to avoid recruitment difficulties at that location, even though the market rate is lower elsewhere. And low private-sector wage levels may be inappropriate as guides for public policy if they are discriminatory in terms of sex or race.

In summary, the determination of wages in the public sector involves considerations of equity as well as efficiency. This means that even the criterion that public wages should be equal to—or above, or even below—private-sector wages is a value judgment that can be arrived at only through the political process.

Impasse Procedures

Historically, one value judgment that the public has agreed upon is that strikes of public employees should be declared illegal. The grounds are twofold: strikes challenge the decision-making procedures of the community (that is, they undermine sovereignty), and strikes disrupt the flow of services essential to the health, safety, and welfare of community members. These views have been somewhat modified recently in certain localities because it has become obvious that, despite their illegality, strikes have occurred if workers believe strongly enough that their grievances are not being taken seriously. Employees may use other ways to indicate dissatisfaction: mass sick calls (known among policemen as the "blue flu") and slowdowns in work performance. Moreover, the public has discovered that some strikes, such as those of schoolteachers, do not cripple a community even though they do create inconvenience. Finally, a few jurisdictions have legalized the strike, at least in certain less essential occupations, as the most satisfactory way to resolve an

---

[22] Hamermesh, *Labor in the Public and Nonprofit Sectors,* pp. 227–255.

[23] Walter Fogel and David Lewin, "Wage Determination in the Public Sector," *Industrial and Labor Relations Review,* 27 (April 1974), 410–431. Their analysis applies primarily to federal employees.

impasse. What the public, in its sovereign capacity, can make illegal, it can if it chooses declare legal.

No community, however, wants to see its public services disrupted by strikes: those services are by definition performed in the public interest. In searching for alternatives to the strike in labor disputes, the hope is that some appeals procedure may be established that enables impasses between employees and the public to be resolved in such a way that the terms and conditions of work are in fact mutually acceptable to both sides. Such procedures require third-party intervention. The types of intervention are those already described for the private sector: conciliation, mediation, voluntary arbitration, fact-finding, and compulsory arbitration. The premise of appeals machinery is that, as direct negotiations between both parties brings the most satisfactory settlement, the steps in the procedure should be arranged to prod the parties with increasing pressure toward a voluntary agreement. For this reason mediation usually comes first, followed by fact-finding, with voluntary arbitration as an alternative. Interest arbitration becomes the last step when all else fails.

Among the first questions raised by an appeals procedure is how the intervener will be chosen, whether as mediator, fact-finder, or arbitrator. In private-sector intervention, the third party may be drawn from the government. But in public-sector cases, where the government is one of the parties, the question is whether a governmental third party would prejudice the case. In some instances state and local governments have been critical even of mediators drawn from the Federal Mediation and Conciliation Service. Although both parties have adjusted to this problem in most states, the issue is compounded by the general shortage of experienced "neutrals"—people who have been engaged in either private- or public-sector mediation and arbitration. Moreover, because of statutory deadlines on budgets, public-sector demands for interveners are likely to be concentrated seasonally, aggravating the shortage.

A more fundamental aspect of impasse procedures in the public sector involves the delegation of authority to make recommendations or even decisions to a third party who is not part of the established decision-making apparatus. For example, can the intervener commit a government to an increase in wages if this means a deficit or higher taxes? Under what limitations does the third party attempt a resolution of the impasse, and who sets forth those limitations? This issue may be resolved by requiring, in the case of either voluntary or compulsory arbitration, that the appropriate legislative body—whether school board or school committee, city council, or even state legislature—agree to the proceedings in advance, or by requiring that interveners give weight to the financial ability of the agency to meet the costs. A similar problem arises with respect to work rules and other nonwage aspects of employment. Should regulations established by law be modified if an arbitrator believes that it is desirable to do so to settle a dispute? Some laws setting up dispute procedures explicitly designate areas in which the arbitrator's decision can modify existing regulations, and indicate others that are reserved exclusively as inherent managerial rights (for example, the right to appoint, promote, and assign police officers).

Impasse procedures have been criticized on the grounds that instead of promoting voluntary agreement among both parties they have the opposite tendency of discouraging good-faith bargaining. As long as one party believes there are possibilities of better terms at the next stage of the process, he has no incentive to modify his position. This is known as the "chilling effect." It has been in evidence in the appeals mechanism for the railroads. Although experience in the public sector is perhaps too recent to give an adequate test of the theory, there are some indications that the number of requests for arbitration are not so high, relative to the number of negotiations, as some had expected. The costs of arbitration, including the fees of lawyers and others, are generally paid by both sides, and can thus be a deterrent.

A new form of compulsory arbitration has been introduced in a number of states in order to make arbitration less attractive and encourage earlier settlement by the parties on a voluntary basis. Called "final-offer arbitration," this procedure gives the arbitrator only the choice between the last offer of the union and last offer of the employer. Compromise and split decisions are ruled out. In one modification of final-offer arbitration, the arbitrator may choose among the specific items of the terms proposed by each side; the more usual form is that the entire package proposed by one side or the other must be selected.

One criticism of this approach is that the arbitrator is placed in an untenable position, especially if the last offers are not significantly different from the original positions. Under such circumstances an award, as one arbitrator pointed out, could be destructive of good bargaining relationships.[24]

SUMMARY

Strikes and the possibility of strikes are inherent in a system of collective bargaining. The option of refusing to sell labor services if wages and conditions of work are not satisfactory is fundamental to free labor markets. By most measures—the number of strikes, number of workers involved, and man-days lost—strikes in the United States over the last several decades have

[24] See Arnold M. Zack, "Impasses, Strikes, and Resolutions," in Zagoria, ed., *Public Workers and Public Unions*, p. 120. For a review of experience, which is necessarily limited, see Charles M. Remus, "Legislated Interest Arbitration," *Proceedings* of the Industrial Relations Research Association, 1974, pp. 307–314; Fred Witney, "Final-Offer Arbitration: The Indianapolis Experience," *Monthly Labor Review*, 96 (May 1973), 20–25; James L. Stern, "Final Offer Arbitration—Initial Experience in Wisconsin," *Monthly Labor Review*, 97 (September 1974), 39–43.

not been excessive. For example, from 1951 to 1975 the percentage of estimated working time lost because of strikes was less than 0.3, except in three different years. The worst year in recent history was 1946, when over 10 percent of employed workers were involved in work stoppages and the time lost by strikes was 1.43 percent.

Among the reasons why strikes are not excessive is, first, that legislation provides for representation elections and union certification to employers so that "union-recognition" strikes have been greatly reduced. Second, in certain industries automated production processes make it difficult for strikers to stop production completely. Finally, the increasing number of governmental controls of strikes—such as laws against jurisdictional disputes and strikes of government workers—has undoubtedly had an effect, although the illegal strike still exists.

Even if strike activity is low, a strike may generate strong public opposition. The public may feel adversely affected in a case where there is disruption of essential services, where other workers suffer loss of work, or where national security, health, and safety may be impaired. The forms of government intervention range from conciliation and mediation to more formal procedures that involve fact-finding, voluntary arbitration, and compulsory arbitration. All types have been used in attempting to resolve labor disputes in the United States. Under Title II of the Taft-Hartley Act, the federal government has the power to halt for 80 days a strike that imperils national health and safety.

In the public sector, with its recent upsurge in unionism, the rise in strike activity has posed new problems. The fragmented nature of governmental authority and the fact that economic constraints depend on taxes and the political process differentiate the public from the private sector. In addition, the resolution of impasses by third parties raises questions concerning the limits to the authority a government can give to an "outsider" in making decisions that may impose financial burdens. Impasse procedures requiring that a dispute be taken through numerous steps leading to final and binding arbitration have been criticized on the grounds that they may discourage bargaining in good faith if one party believes that there are greater possibilities for better terms at the next stage of the process. One innnovation that attempts to remedy this disadvantage is final-offer arbitration, in which the arbitrator has only the option of selecting the last offer of the union or the last offer of the employer.

DISCUSSION QUESTIONS

1. What have been the periods of high strike activity in the United States, and what explanations can you give for them?
2. What criteria do you believe should determine whether a strike in the private sector adversely affects the "public interest"?

3. What is the distinction between voluntary arbitration of rights and voluntary arbitration of interests? Is the difference important to unions and to managements? Explain.

4. Discuss whether each of the following forms of government intervention in labor disputes in the private sector is consistent with the principles of free collective bargaining: (a) mediation; (b) fact-finding; (c) the emergency provisions of Title II of the Taft-Hartley Act; (d) compulsory arbitration.

5. Collective bargaining in the public sector has been termed multilateral to distinguish it from the typical bilateral relationships of the private sector. Why is this so? Is the public affected adversely because of this difference?

6. Should workers in public employment—federal, state, and local—have the same rights as workers in the private sector, including the right to form unions and to strike?

7. It is said that because governments do not sell their products and services in markets, they are under no economic restraint to check wage increases demanded by public unions. Is this true?

8. What are the arguments for introducing final-offer arbitration into the impasse procedures of labor disputes in the public sector? What are the arguments against?

SELECTED READINGS

For a theory of the long-run tendency for strikes to decline with industrialization, see Arthur M. Ross and Paul T. Hartman, *Changing Patterns of Industrial Conflict* (New York: John Wiley & Sons, 1960). On government intervention in private sector disputes, see Donald E. Cullen, National Emergency Strikes (Ithaca, N.Y.: New York State School of Industrial and Labor Relations, Cornell University, 1968); Herbert R. Northrup, *Compulsory Arbitration and Government Intervention in Labor Disputes* (Washington, D.C.: Labor Policy Association, 1966); and Herbert R. Northrup and Gordon F. Bloom, *Government and Labor* (Homewood, Ill.: Irwin, 1963). Well worth reading for insights into the role of arbitrators is Brook I. Landis, *Value Judgments in Arbitration: A Case Study of Saul Wallen* (Ithaca, N.Y.: New York State School of Industrial and Labor Relations, Cornell University, 1977). For a general reference to arbitration, see Frank Elkouri and Edna Osper Elkouri, *How Arbitration Works*, 3rd ed. (Washington, D.C.: Bureau of National Affairs, 1973).

Unionism and strikes in the public sector have been the subject of many recent studies. See A. Lawrence Chickering, ed., *Public Employee Unions: A Study of the Crisis in Public Sector Labor Relations* (San Francisco: Institute for Contemporary Studies, 1976); Ralph J. Flynn, *Public Work, Public Workers* (Washington, D.C.: New Republic Book Co., 1975); Robert D. Helsby and Thomas E. Joyner, *Collective Bargaining in Government* (Englewood Cliffs, N.J.: Prentice-Hall, 1972); Daniel S. Hamermesh, ed., *Labor in the Public and Nonprofit Sectors* (Princeton, N.J.: Princeton University Press, 1975); Michael H. Moskow, J. Joseph Loewenberg, and Edward Clifford Koziara, *Collective Bargaining in Public Employment* (New York: Random House, 1970); Murray S. Nesbitt, *Labor Relations in the Federal Government Service* (Washington, D.C.: Bureau of National Affairs, 1976); Harry H. Wellington and Ralph K. Winter, *The Unions and the Cities* (Washington, D.C.: Brookings Institution, 1971); and Sam Zagoria, ed., *Public Workers and Public Unions* (Englewood Cliffs, N.J.: Prentice-Hall, 1972).

PART FOUR

Wages, Unemployment, and Economic Security

14

Wage Structures

The analysis of wages proceeds along two lines. One is the comparison of the wages paid one group of workers with those paid another; the other is the study of wage movements in the economy as a whole. The latter analysis is reserved for the following chapter; here we shall examine wage structures— the relationships of wages among selected categories of workers. The concept of a wage structure refers to the wage differential between groups and can be expressed either in ratios (or percentages) or in absolute dollar amounts, each being relevant for certain analytic purposes. In this chapter we shall review several of the many different wage structures: occupational wage structures in terms of both skill and area, wage structures according to industry, and wage differentials in terms of unionization, sex, and race.

Analysis of wage structures poses certain problems in regard to empirical information and research objectives. Statistical data can be ambiguous.[1] One wage structure affects another: for example, different proportions of black and white workers in various occupations (that is, the racial wage structure) can affect the occupational wage structure; it is not always easy to disassociate one from the other because relevant wage data are often lacking. In some studies wage differentials are estimated with econometric models that predict what wages would be under differing sets of circumstances in which specific variables are controlled. The differences are hypothetical. These techniques are perfectly admissible, but the results should be recognized as tentative and dependent upon both the types of data used and the variables included in the predictive model. Although we will review some of these studies, the objective of this chapter is to examine the extent to which the structured labor market influences competitive forces in determining wages. We will be concerned with different wage structures, changes in these structures, and the reasons for the changes.

---

[1] See Appendix to chapter 15 for definitions of wages and a brief description of the major sources of data.

OCCUPATIONAL WAGE DIFFERENTIALS

The occupational wage structure is basic. According to the competitive model, in the long run wages by occupations reflect the training and other costs incurred by individual workers that must be paid for by firms wishing to employ them. If the wages were not commensurate with these human investment costs, workers would not enter the occupations. On the other hand, firms would not employ a worker in any particular occupation unless the worker's productivity—that is, the marginal revenue product—justified the payment. In the long run, therefore, the wage paid to a worker would equal the (marginal) productivity of workers in that occupational category and also the costs incurred by workers who prepared for it. In the short run, an increasing or decreasing demand for a particular type of labor could cause the wage to be higher or lower than costs; but such a disequilibrium would motivate workers either to enter the field or leave it and eventually restore the equality between earnings and costs.

Comparisons Among Groups

There are sizable differences in earnings by broad occupational groups, as seen in Table 14–1, which presents the median annual earnings of year-round, full-time male workers. In both 1962 and 1972, it should be noted first that earnings of farmers and farm laborers were considerably below nonfarm occupational earnings. Secondly, the range in the earnings of nonfarm occupations increased between 1962 to 1972. Professional, technical, and related workers received incomes that were 74.1 percent above those of nonfarm laborers in 1962 but 81.1 percent higher in 1972. Significant gains in relative standings were also made by nonfarm managers and salesworkers. Only craftsmen and operatives dropped slightly in terms of the percentage wage differential, although the absolute differential increased.

Although Table 14–2 covers a slightly different group of employed males, it shows the median years of education by occupational groups. In 1962 the range was from 8.3 to 16.4 years and in 1972 from 8.9 to 16.5 years. The correlation between years of education and median income is positive although not perfect. Professional workers had the most education and received the highest earnings in each period. Laborers, with less schooling, had low earnings. However, clerical workers, though they had more years of schooling, earned less than craftsmen. Rank correlations of median years of education and median earnings, when calculated for the eight nonagricultural occupational groups, are high, with coefficients of 0.83 for 1962 and 0.93 for 1972.

Rates of change in occupational earnings between 1962 and 1972 indicate

Table 14-1
Median Annual Earnings of Males by Occupations, 1962 and 1972[a]

Occupational Group	1962	Index (Common Labor=100.0)	1972	Index (Common Labor=100.0)	Percent Change 1962-1972
All occupations	$5,754		$10,202		77.3
Professional, technical and kindred	7,621	174.1	13,542	181.1	77.7
Managers, proprietors (nonfarm)	6,907	157.8	13,486	180.4	95.3
Farmers and farm managers	2,490	56.9	5,060	67.7	103.2
Clerical and kindred	5,613	128.2	9,716	129.9	73.1
Salesworkers	6,225	142.2	11.610	155.3	86.5
Craftsmen and foremen	6,249	142.8	10,413	139.3	66.6
Operatives	5,335	121.9	8,747	117.0	64.0
Service workers, except private household	4,386	100.2	7,630	102.0	74.0
Farm laborers and foremen	1,881	43.0	4,615	61.7	145.3
Laborers, except farm and mine	4,377	100.0	7,477	100.0	70.8

[a] Earnings are for year-round full-time workers; covers persons 14 years old and over as of March of following year.

Source: U.S. Department of Commerce, *Statistical Abstract of the United States,* 1974.

Table 14-2
Median Years of School Completed by the Employed Males[a] in the Civilian Labor Force by Occupational Group, March 1962 and March 1972

Occupational Group	March 1962 Years	March 1962 Rank	March 1972 Years	March 1972 Rank	Percent Change %	Percent Change Rank
All occupational groups	12.1	—	12.5	—	3.3	—
Professional, technical and kindred	16.4	1	16.5	1	0.6	10
Managers, proprietors	12.5	3.5	12.9	3	3.2	7
Farmers and farm managers	8.8	9	11.2	8	27.3	1
Clerical and kindred	12.5	3.5	12.6	4	.8	9
Salesworkers	12.7	2	13.0	2	2.4	8
Craftsmen and foreman	11.2	5	12.2	5	8.9	5
Operatives	10.2	7	11.9	7	16.7	4
Service workers, including private household	10.3	6	12.1	6	17.5	3
Farm laborers and foremen	8.3	10	8.9	10	7.2	6
Laborers, except farm and mine	8.9	8	11.1	9	24.7	2

[a] Males 18 years of age and over. Not precisely comparable with Table 14-1.

Source: U.S. Department of Labor, *Handbook of Labor Statistics 1975,* Reference Edition.

that the operation of demand shifts can lead to changes in earnings unrelated to educational investment. If the agricultural sector is excluded, those workers whose education increased most over the ten-year period—nonfarm laborers, service workers, operatives, and craftsmen—were those whose relative income levels slipped. Professional, managerial, and sales workers gained in income relative to the others; yet their educational investments increased the least. What caused this deterioration in the position of blue-collar, service, and lower-paid clerical workers? Certainly it was not unwillingness to invest in further education. The investment was made, but it did not pay off when earnings are compared with those of white-collar workers. The reasons appear to be twofold: on the one hand, an increasing demand for professional, technical, and similar workers that brought higher wages (marginal revenue products); and secondly, the increasing pace of technological change and automation that reduced the demand for blue-collar workers.[2]

Let us next examine the occupational wage differentials between skilled and unskilled labor. Because Table 14–3 uses establishment data, information on the personal characteristics of workers is not available. Nevertheless, the data reveal a long-term contraction in the skilled-unskilled wage structure.

During the 40-year period from 1907 to 1947, the relative differential was cut in half. Skilled workers received twice as much as the unskilled in 1907, but after World War II the ratio was reduced by half—a decline of about 1 percent a year. Some cyclical variations in the differential are revealed in the rapid narrowing during World War I and the widening during the depression of the 1930s.

Information concerning wage differentials in the construction industry yields similar conclusions. A long-run decline reduced the ratio of wages of journeymen to those of laborers and helpers from 196 in 1907 to 152 in 1947—nearly a 50 percent drop in the relative gap, similar to that of manufacturing wages. On the other hand, the absolute gap between the two levels of wages increased from $0.21 to $0.70 an hour. The construction wage series also showed sensitivity to the business cycle, with the spread widening in periods of depression and narrowing in times of prosperity. In these cyclical movements unskilled workers' wages showed greater sensitivity than those of skilled workers.

As to occupational wage differentials since 1947, data of the Bureau of Labor Statistics indicate a continuation of the trend toward narrower relative differentials for a few years, and then a stabilization that has persisted until

---

[2] Undoubtedly the increasing spread between the earnings of blue-collar and white-collar workers was responsible for the phenomenon known in the early 1970s as the "blue-collar blues." The squeeze on incomes was compounded by the inflation that began in the late 1960s. See Jerome M. Rosow, "The Problems of Lower-Middle-Income Workers," Sar A. Levitan, ed., *Blue Collar Workers: A Symposium on Middle America* (New York: McGraw-Hill, 1971), pp. 76–94.

Table 14-3
Wage Differentials of Skilled and Unskilled Labor, 1907–1947

Year	Ratio of Median Skilled to Unskilled	Range of Middle Half
1907	205	180–280
1918–1919	175	150–225
1931–1932	180	160–220
1937–1940	165	150–190
1945–1947	155	145–170

Source: These data are drawn from one of the first major studies of wage structures, Harry Ober's "Occupational Wage Differentials, 1907–1947," in *Trends in Wage Differentials, 1907–1947*, Serial No. R 1932, from *Monthly Labor Review*, April, June, and August, 1948.

the present. The relative spread of occupational wage rates in manufacturing declined to 37 percent between the medians of skilled and unskilled by 1952–1953, a level maintained through 1974. In the building construction industry from 1947 to 1973 the relative spread in average wages for journeymen as compared to laborers and helpers behaved in a similar fashion. The long-run decline continued through the 1950s, stabilizing at about 32 percent beginning in the mid-1960s. The absolute differential had increased to $1.96 by 1973.[3]

Causes of Changes

Why have these differentials narrowed during the first half of the twentieth century? Why have they behaved in a sort of accordion fashion with the business cycle? And why has this wage structure now apparently been stabilized?

First, the long-run, secular decline in the wage of the skilled worker relative to the wage of the unskilled from 1907 to the Korean War period was a response to shifts in the underlying supply and demand forces in the labor market. The tide of "new" immigration, from 1890 to 1914—which consisted to a great extent of unskilled laborers—was halted by World War I and the postwar immigration acts; this had the effect of raising the price of unskilled labor in relation to skilled workers. The greater willingness of society to bear the costs of public education through taxation has contributed to an increase of better-trained workers. Underlying that willingness were two other factors:

[3] The occupational differential in manufacturing for the years through 1967 are found in Donald J. Blackmore, "Occupational Wage Relationships in Metropolitan Areas," *Monthly Labor Review*, 91 (December 1968), 36. The unpublished series since 1967 has been calculated from the Bureau's regular area wage surveys of metropolitan areas. The data for construction workers appear in Arthur Rose, "Wage Differentials in the Building Trades," *Monthly Labor Review*, 92 (October 1969), 14–17, and in Martin E. Personick, "Wage Differentials between Skilled and Unskilled Building Trades," *Monthly Labor Review*, 97 (October 1974), 64–66.

the rising income level that made such expenditures possible without encroaching on basic necessities, and the changing nature of job opportunities. The demand for unskilled labor was reduced by shifts in the industrial composition of employment, the decreasing proportion of workers in agriculture, and the continuing process of mechanization in manufacturing and mining. In addition, the increasing importance of the industrial union after the 1930s, with its concern for the semiskilled worker in mass production industries and its lesser sensitivity to the interests of skilled workers, meant further pressure to narrow the spread in wage rates. (The influence of unions on long-run trends has not been conclusively demonstrated, however; the decline in the differential had begun long before industrial unions gained strength after 1935, and the decline in the skilled-unskilled differential in the construction trades kept pace with the decline in manufacturing, even though no industrial unions were involved.)

Although the hypothesis cannot be tested satisfactorily, changes in the American public's willingness to support a variety of welfare measures designed to boost the incomes of those at the lower end of the income scale undoubtedly resulted in a sharp upward revision of tolerable minimum wage levels, or what Reder has called the "social minimum hourly wage rate" (SM).[4] Essentially the rate of pay below which no one will accept or be offered a job, the SM was strengthened by the passage of minimum wage laws and unemployment insurance payments.

The accordion movement of the age structure during business cycles results from the fact that the wages of the unskilled tend to be more flexible than those of the skilled. During times of reduced economic activity, a firm is more inclined to retain its skilled labor force than its unskilled workers. The greater competition for jobs among the unemployed unskilled lowers relative wages, while the semiskilled and the skilled workers, being less market-oriented, tend to be insulated from short-run changes in labor demand.[5] During boom times, the reverse process occurs and the wages for the less-skilled rise as firms compete for labor at the job-entry levels.

The underlying reasons for the stabilization of wage differentials between skilled and unskilled workers since the mid-1950s are less clear. There have been several diverse trends. On the one hand, the increase in the average level of education during this period may have exerted downward pressure on wage differentials in that more and more workers acquired the credentials that fitted them for many jobs. On the other hand, there was an acceleration of the migration of less-trained workers, especially in the 1960s, from rural areas of the South to urban areas in both South and North. These additional supplies of unskilled labor would counter the trend toward a narrowing of wage differ-

---

[4] M. N. Reder, "The Theory of Occupational Wage Differentials," *American Economic Review*, 45 (December 1955), 839.
[5] Ibid., pp. 836ff.

entials. In a number of industrial unions, moreover, skilled workers began to voice dissatisfaction with their declining wage differentials and won special advantages by threatening to establish separate craft unions.

GEOGRAPHICAL WAGE STRUCTURES

National averages of occupational wages should not be interpreted to mean that similar differentials and trends are necessarily found everywhere. In this section we examine the occupational wage structure by geographical area: first, the urban-rural differential; secondly, metropolitan differences; and, third, regional differentials.

The Urban-Rural Differential

That earnings are lower in rural areas than in urban communities have been, and still is, characteristic of most economies throughout the world. The substantial differential in earnings partly explains the flow of labor from rural to urban areas, especially when it is linked to the expansion of job opportunities in urban areas and their contraction in agriculture.[6]

The basic reasons for the urban-rural differential are, first, that productivities of agricultural workers are less than those of employees in manufacturing and the service industries and, second, that the supplies or labor in rural areas tend to remain relatively large because birth rates are higher. Third, although the flow of labor from rural to urban areas is one of the dominant characteristics of the American economy, it has not been sufficient to wipe out the differential. One reason is the perversity of response in the supply of labor. Migration out of agriculture is adversely affected by the low incomes earned in agriculture: the lower the income, the more difficult it is to acquire the cash outlays to move. In addition, those that do migrate find that their education and experience do not often enable them to compete satisfactorily for jobs in urban markets. Unemployment in central cities and discrimination against blacks and other minority groups discourage urban migration and, as studies have shown, induce a substantial proportion of in-migrants to return to rural areas when their expectations of higher nonfarm earnings have not been realized.[7]

[6] The definition of "rural" in this connection refers to the rural farm population, which in the United States declined from over 30 million to 9.7 million in the period from 1940 to 1970. The rural nonfarm population has grown over this same period. See Ray Marshall, *Rural Workers in Rural Labor Markets* (Salt Lake City: Olympus Publishing Co., 1974), chs. 1–3.

[7] See Dale S. Hathaway and Brian B. Perkins, "Occupational Mobility and Migration from Agriculture," in *Rural Poverty in the United States*, President's National Advisory Commission on Rural Poverty (Washington, D.C.: U.S. Government Printing Office, 1968).

Nonetheless, the attractions of the urban area cannot be denied. In general, both earnings and occupational wage rates increase with the size of the community. The more populated areas can provide greater specialization of services and, as Adam Smith pointed out long ago, the larger the market the greater the division of labor and the higher the productivity per worker. Moreover, economies of scale are possible in areas where firms can serve larger markets and where labor supplies of special skills are available. To workers the more urbanized areas offer more and higher-paying alternative job opportunities. In a small community, where job opportunities are few and pay is low, workers who want to remain there have little choice but to accept what is available.

Metropolitan Differentials

Gross average hourly earnings vary widely among large metropolitan areas. For example, in 1973 the average wage of all factory workers in the Detroit area was $5.58. In the New York City area, on the other hand, the average of $4.04 was not only a fourth less than Detroit's but also less than the average of $4.20 in the Atlanta area and the national average of $4.08. But averages reflect a variety of influences, among them the extent of unionization; the composition of industry, with different skills required; and the composition of the labor force, with differing degrees of wage differentials according to race and sex.

If one compares rates of pay for comparable work, a somewhat different picture emerges. Using data for 1968–1969, the Bureau of Labor Statistics has devised wage indices of three sets of standardized occupations for a number of metropolitan areas. As shown in Table 14–4, covering 22 areas, the index of pay for office clerical jobs ranged from a low of 93 in Minneapolis to a high of 115 in Detroit, the index for skilled maintenance workers ranged from 92 in Dallas to 115 in Detroit, and the index for unskilled plant occupations ranged from 81 in Houston to 125 in the San Francisco–Oakland area. While the New York–Northeastern New Jersey area was below Detroit in terms of its pay indices for the three groups, it ranked above Atlanta in each category.

Although it is sometimes believed that money wage differences can be explained by cost-of-living differences, a comparison of wages with the budget costs of urban families in various metropolitan areas shows that this does not hold.[8] The intermediate budget for a family of four in the spring of 1970 cost $10,664 nationally, but the range among the 22 metropolitan areas in Table

---

[8] Budgetary cost studies are not wholly satisfactory as indicators of relative living costs, but they are the only available method for estimating intercity differences. For methodology see U.S. Department of Labor, *3 Budgets for an Urban Family of Four Persons, 1969–70*, Supplement to Bulletin 1570–5 (1972).

14–4 was from an index of 91 in Atlanta and Dallas to 112 in the Boston and New York–Northeastern New Jersey areas. Although some of the southern cities gain in terms of lowered budget costs, the unskilled wage disadvantage was a real one. In Detroit, where the budget cost was slightly below the national average, the real wage differential was clearly substantial.

One explanation of metropolitan real wage differentials is similar to that of occupational wage differences among industries (see "Interindustry Wage Structures," below). In areas with high-wage industries, other occupations

Table 14–4

Relative Pay Levels for Certain Occupational Groups[a] and Indices of Comparative Living Costs, 22 Metropolitan Areas, 1968–1970

Area	Office Clerical[b]	Skilled Maintenance[b]	Unskilled Plant[b]	Costs of Budget[c]
Northeast				
Boston	96	96	95	112
Buffalo	100	96	106	107
New York–Northeastern N.J.	104	100	107	112
Philadelphia	96	97	102	102
Pittsburgh	101	99	106	96
North Central				
Chicago–Northwestern Ind.	104	106	107	104
Cincinnati	97	98	103	97
Cleveland	102	104	111	104
Detroit	115	115	123	99
Indianapolis	99	105	101	103
Milwaukee	99	107	111	107
Minneapolis	93	104	108	101
St. Louis	98	105	105	100
South				
Atlanta	100	97	83	91
Baltimore	98	100	93	98
Dallas	94	92	83	93
Houston	99	97	81	91
Washington, D.C.	102	98	86	103
West				
Denver	97	98	98	97
Los Angeles–Long Beach	111	106	113	102
San Francisco–Oakland	109	114	125	108
Seattle	107	106	118	105

[a] The indices relate to the average weekly salary of 20 office jobs, average straight-time earnings of eight skilled maintenance jobs, and two unskilled plant jobs weighted by employment in all industries in each area, 1968–1969.

[b] 100 equals the average of the pay levels of 229 metropolitan areas.

[c] 100 equals the annual cost of an intermediate budget of a four-person urban family in 1969–1970.

Source: U.S. Department of Labor.

tend also to offer higher-than-average rates of pay. In short, the effects of high wages in one labor area extend beyond the confines of the single industry: not only are the average *earnings* of the factory worker affected by the prevalence of high-wage industries, but the *rates* within the various industries are also influenced. Occupational wages do not unilaterally determine metropolitan wage structures.

One must further consider not only the industry mix in one given market but also the nature of the industrial demands and the relative supplies of labor in surrounding areas. For example, in the main industrial belt of the United States, stretching from the New York–New Jersey area through Pennsylvania, Ohio, and lower Michigan to northern Indiana and Chicago, the prevalence of high-wage metalworking industries tends to influence the entire level of wages. On the other hand, Memphis and Atlanta have low wages, not only because the predominant industries are low-paying, but also because they are located in states that are primarily agricultural, with low productivities and excessive supplies of unskilled labor.

Regional Differentials

Regional wage differences can be estimated using differentials by metropolitan areas. Early studies of manufacturing industries by the Bureau of Labor Statistics revealed a wage level in the South about 15 percent below that of the Northeast and Midwest in the period from before World War I to just after World War II; this dropped to around 25 percent below the other two regions during the depression of the 1930s. Higher wages in the Far West fell from 30 percent above those in the Northeast to 15 percent in the same period. The studies also showed that, as expected, the southern wage differential was greater for the unskilled than for skilled workers.[9]

More recent studies give some indication that the differentials are narrowing. In the late 1960s, according to one study covering more occupations,[10] the wage gap was still large for southern unskilled workers but had shrunk for clerical and skilled maintenance workers and was minimal for those in professional and administrative occupations (see Table 14–5). For the West, the differential with the North Central states had been eliminated for two of the five broad occupational categories and greatly reduced for the other three.

As indicated above, a prime cause of the low southern wage differential is that the excess supply of labor in rural areas, fed by the contraction of jobs in agriculture as well as by a high birth rate, exerts downward pressures on the wage structures of southern cities. The impact is naturally greatest on the

[9] U.S. Department of Labor, Bureau of Labor Statistics, *Trends in Wage Differentials, 1907–1947*, Serial No. R 1932, Reprint from *Monthly Labor Review*, 66 (April 1948), 2ff.
[10] Harry F. Zeman, "Regional Pay Differentials in White-Collar Occupations," *Monthly Labor Review*, 94 (January 1971), 53ff.

Table 14–5
Regional Pay Differences by Major Occupational Groups, 1968–1969

Groups of Occupations	United States	Northeast	South	North Central	West
Unskilled plant	100	102	80	109	109
Clerical	100	101	96	100	105
Skilled maintenance	100	95	94	105	106
Technical support	100	101	97	101	101
Professional and administrative	100	101	99	99	102

Source: Harry F. Zeman, "Regional Pay Differentials in White-Collar Occupations," *Monthly Labor Review*, 94 (January 1971), 53.

wage rates of unskilled workers. But as industry expands in the South, the demands for skilled and professional workers can be met only at higher wages. In the professional market, where workers often compete nationally, the wage differentials are slight.

Two other factors that cannot be neglected in explaining the North-South wage differential are the effects of unionization and race. Among unionized white workers, the regional wage differential—adjusted for age, education, and major occupation—was shown in a recent study to be less than 8 percent between the East North Central states on the one hand and the East and West South Central states (i.e., the Deep South) on the other. A similar differential existed with respect to the white male unionized workers in New England. For the South Atlantic states, wages were lower by only 2.6 percent. For nonunion white male workers, however, the differential ran to around 15 percent in the Deep South and 10 percent in the South Atlantic states. For black male workers, the differential between the East North Central states and the South was far greater. For unionized blacks it ranged from 14 to 18 percent, for nonunionized from 20 to 28.9 percent.[11]

INTERINDUSTRY WAGE STRUCTURES

Wages vary considerably among industries. As shown in Table 14–6, gross average hourly earnings of production workers in manufacturing averaged $5.19 in 1976, but the range was from $3.44 in leather and leather products to $7.14 in petroleum refining; this was a spread of $3.70 per hour, or from 33.7 percent below the average to 37.6 percent above. These differentials understate the range within industries. For example, workers in apparel—a low-

[11] Paul M. Ryscavage, "Measuring Union-Nonunion Earnings Differences," *Monthly Labor Review*, 97 (December 1974), 3–9. This econometric study uses data from the May 1973 Current Population Survey reported as "usual earnings." The differentials are calculated from Table 4, p. 7.

paying industry—had average earnings 15 percent less than the industry average if employed in men's and boy's work clothing, but 25 percent higher if employed in men's and boy's suits. Wide spreads in earnings are found in nonmanufacturing industries, too; in 1976 contract construction paid an average of $7.68 per hour while retail trade establishments paid $3.55 to non-supervisory workers.

What causes these differences in wages? Clearly, industrial wage structures can be explained by other types of wage structures. An industry using primarily unskilled labor will have a lower average than one using more skilled labor. The composition of an industry's labor force by race, sex, and regional location may explain part of the differential.

An underlying long-run cause of interindustry wage differentials is labor

Table 14-6
Average Hourly Earnings of Production Workers in Manufacturing, Annual Average, 1976

Major Industry Group	Annual Average
All Manufacturing	$5.19
Durable goods	5.55
Ordnance and accessories	5.72
Lumber and wood products, except furniture	4.71
Furniture and fixtures	3.98
Stone, clay, and glass products	5.29
Primary metal industries	6.80
Fabricated metal products	5.43
Machinery	5.76
Electrical equipment and supplies	4.91
Transportation equipment	6.54
Instruments and related products	4.87
Miscellaneous manufacturing industries	4.01
Nondurable goods	4.68
Food and kindred products	4.96
Tobacco manufactures	4.91
Textile mill products	3.67
Apparel and related products	3.41
Paper and allied products	5.43
Printing, publishing, and allied industries	5.69
Chemicals and allied products	5.87
Petroleum refining and related industries	7.14
Rubber and miscellaneous plastic products	4.62
Leather and leather products	3.44

Source: "Current Labor Statistics: Establishment Data," *Monthly Labor Review*, 100 (December 1977), 94.

productivity. Differences in productivity among industries are related to the differing amounts of capital invested per worker and to differing rates of technological change. But physical production functions alone cannot explain wage differences. Other factors that influence prices and wages are the extent to which firms in an industry can exercise market power over product prices, changes in the demand for the products of industries, the extent of local competition by other industries for workers in the labor market, and union wage and employment policies.

If one were to accept the competitive model of labor markets, interindustry wage differentials in the long run should reflect only the mix of occupations by skill within the various industries.[12] The amount of capital employed per worker would have no effect upon an industry's relative wage except insofar as it affected the composition of labor employed in terms of skill. The argument is that the labor supply of each occupation would be perfectly elastic at a wage equalizing the rate of return on human capital investments with those of other occupations. Under the competitive hypothesis, the firm (and industry) would adjust its employment of each skilled group to bring marginal productivities into equilibrium with wage rates. Differences in regional wages would be consistent with the competitive hypothesis if they reflected differing costs of living.

In the short-run competitive model, industrial wage differences would reflect changes in demands for output in product markets. Industries faced with expanding demands would pay higher wages in order to attract more workers; firms faced with declining demands for their output would cut back production, and the relative wages of their workers would fall. Wage differences by industry would serve to allocate labor supplies among industries in response to the ultimate demands of consumers for goods and services. In those industries characterized by technological advances—either in the form of lowered costs of production for old products or the creation of new products—the competitive hypothesis assumes that firms would be able to pay higher wages to attract workers, and that other industries would be forced to raise wages in order to retain needed workers: thus gains from productivity changes could not be captured for long by any specific industry but would be diffused throughout the economy.

Although investigations of interindustrial wage structures have varied in their conclusions, the weight of evidence indicates that the applicability of the competitive model is limited. In the case of the relationship between occupational wages and interindustry wage differences, cause and effect are not readily distinguishable. For example, Rees and Hamilton point to an increase

---

[12] One of the best statements of the competitive hypothesis is that of Melvin W. Reder, "Wage Differentials: Theory and Measurement," in *Aspects of Labor Economics* (New York: National Bureau of Economic Research, 1962), pp. 257–299.

Table 14-7
Indices of Straight-time Earnings for Selected Occupations by Major Industry
Divisions, February 1974

Industry Division	Occupations			
	Office Clerical	Electronic Data Processing	Skilled Maintenance	Unskilled Plant
All industries	100	100	100	100
Manufacturing	104	103	98	107
Nonmanufacturing	98	98	(^{a})	98
Public utilities	118	110	(^{a})	132
Wholesale trade	101	99	(^{a})	100
Retail trade	91	97	(^{a})	87
Finance	91	94	(^{a})	(^{a})
Services	98	97	(^{a})	78

^{a} Data are insufficient to meet publication criteria.

Source: U.S. Department of Labor, *Area Wage Surveys, Metropolitan Areas, United States and Regional Summaries, 1973–74*, Bulletin 1795–29 (Washington, D.C.: U.S. Government Printing Office, May 1976), pp. 4–5.

in the variability of interindustry wage structures in times of slack economic activity and to a narrowing of differentials in times of low unemployment.[13] Differentials contracted during the period from the Great Depression to the Korean War in the early 1950s. Although the authors note the influence of unions in limiting wage dispersion, they also show how the contraction of the skilled/unskilled wage differential, which occurred under these conditions, helped to explain changes in industrial wage relationships.

On the other hand, there can be little doubt that industry wage structures influence occupational wages. Clerical workers, for example, are likely to receive higher wages in manufacturing firms than in nonmanufacturing industries, such as finance (see Table 14–7). Typists in a factory are paid more, not because they are more efficient than their counterparts in an insurance firm or because the conditions of work are less attractive, but because their wages tend to be established at levels consistent with the generally higher wages and productivity of the proportionately larger numbers of production workers. A similar influence of industry on occupational wages can be found for other occupations.

Industrial wage structures do not seem to be responsive to shifts in the demand for labor, at least in the short run. In fact, numerous studies show that there is significant stability in interindustry wage relationships even over long periods of time. In certain cases, however, employment growth with higher wages and employment decline with falling wages lend support to the com-

[13] Albert Rees and Mary T. Hamilton, "Postwar Movements of Wage Levels and Unit Labor Costs," *The Journal of Law and Economics* (October 1963), 50–56.

petitive model. An outstanding example of the former was the growth of employment in the automobile industry in the 1920s, when high wages attracted many workers from rural areas in Michigan and elsewhere to Detroit and other automobile centers. An example of the second case has been the downward drift of wages paid New England textile workers after World War II, when the industry shifted its base to the South. Yet other examples of contrary movements can easily be found. Despite the contraction of employment in mining industries, for example, wages have risen more rapidly than in manufacturing. In bituminous coal mining, affected sharply by contracting markets for coal in the early 1970s, the relative position of coal miners' wages was nearly the same as in 1960—about 43 to 45 percent higher than the average manufacturing wage.

A number of studies designed to examine systematically the relationships between wages and employment changes by industry have tended to support the conclusion that on balance the allocative function in labor markets has been fulfilled by job vacancies rather than by wage flexibility.[14] Workers tend to seek out jobs that are open, and do not offer themselves at lower wages if the jobs are already filled. The stability of the interindustry wage structure apparently stems also in part from the fact that wages are strongly influenced by the inertia of the administered wage-setting process within firms of the same industry and by the pattern-following behavior of industries. The pressure by unions for wage standardization within a firm or industry and the competition among unions to win wage increases similar to or better than those of others also strengthen the tendency toward wage structure stability.

UNION-NONUNION WAGE DIFFERENTIALS

Statistical investigations of union versus nonunion wages do not lead to unequivocal answers about the effects of unions on wages. Because many factors are operating in labor markets, the isolation of any one variable is difficult. Several examples illustrate this point.

1. Unions may take credit for a wage increase that would have occurred in any case. Because of the institutional characteristics of the labor agreement, it is the timing of the wage change rather than the amount that the unions may affect.

[14] One of the most comprehensive analyses of these relationships in a number of countries was conducted by the Expert Group for the Organization for Economic Co-operation and Development. See P. de Wolff, Chairman, *Wages and Labour Mobility* (Paris: OECD, 1965). E. Robert Livernash presents a review of this and other studies in "Wages and Benefits," in Woodrow L. Ginsburg et al., *A Review of Industrial Relations Research* (Madison, Wis.: Industrial Relations Research Association, 1970), vol. 1; see esp. pp. 105–114.

2. Wage differentials between union and nonunion workers may reflect other causes than union membership. Union workers may have greater productivity as the result of more education, ability, or training. Unionized firms may be more efficient, located in higher wage areas and regions, and powerful enough in product markets to pass on wage increases to consumers.
3. Nonunion employers may feel that the best way to ward off threats of unionization is to keep wages and other work standards in line with those in union shops. When demand for labor is high, they may have to raise wages to compete with higher-paying union employers. Therefore, even with no differentials between union and nonunion wages, it could not be concluded that unions did not influence wages.

Statistical investigations of union-nonunion wage differentials are generally of two types. One involves the comparison of changes in union and nonunion wages over periods of time; the other is cross-sectional, attempting to explain differences at a particular moment.

Many of the early studies were of the first type. In a pioneering comparison of average hourly earnings among workers in several nonunion and union industries from 1890 to 1926, Paul H. Douglas concluded that union members gained appreciably when their organizations were first formed but that eventually their wages rose no faster than those of nonunion workers.[15] In later reexaminations of these trends using other statistical techniques, Arthur M. Ross claimed that unions did not lose their ability to make relative gains, and that in fact they continued to do so through the World War II period.[16]

Harold M. Levinson showed that the economic conditions prevailing in a specific period made significant differences. Using data from World War I to the early post–World War II period, Levinson argued that these movements indicated that union power to influence wages was conditioned by three factors—the level of employment within the economy, governmental action, and sympathetic pressure from nonunion employers. Under conditions of full employment, the high demand for labor pulls up the level of both union and nonunion wages, while with declining employment the unions' efforts to prevent wages from falling lead to a favorable differential. Through minimum wage legislation or encouragement of the right to organize, the government acts to raise both union and nonunion wages and hence tends to cause similar rates of change in wages. Levinson regards this factor as part of the explanation for the small differential from 1933 to 1941. The government may pursue different policies, however: for example, during the 1920s, when it neither

---

[15] Paul H. Douglas, *Real Wages in the United States, 1890–1926* (Boston: Houghton Mifflin, 1930).

[16] Arthur M. Ross, *Trade Union Wage Policy* (Berkeley: University of California Press, 1950), Ch. VI. This study appeared earlier as "The Influence of Unionism upon Earnings," *The Quarterly Journal of Economics*, 62 (February 1948), 263–86.

supported wage legislation nor encouraged collective bargaining, nonunion wages definitely lagged behind union levels. The extent to which nonunion employers exert sympathetic pressure to minimize the union-nonunion wage differential will, according to Levinson, be greater (and hence minimize the differential) when the level of employment is high and when government action is favorable to workers.[17]

After 1950 an increasing number of studies dealt with the influence of unions in particular industries or groups of industries, including steel, coal, garments, and construction. A number of them attempted to eliminate the possibility that other variables could in fact explain the gains apparently attributable to unionization. Most often cross-sectional in nature, these studies essentially relied on a comparison of wages paid in unionized cities with those in nonunionized cities, after making adjustments for certain selected variables such as race and sex composition, skill-mix, and incentive wage systems. In a review of 12 of these specific studies, as well as a number of economywide studies, H. G. Lewis concluded that the range of the influence of unions on wages was very large but that the average was modest. His principal conclusion was that the effect varied with changes in the economic conditions of the economy as a whole. During the Depression, in 1931–1933, the average wage effect of unionism in comparison with nonunion labor was 25 percent; as the economy turned upward, the effect was reduced to 10–20 percent by the beginning of World War II, and to 0–5 percent by the postwar period of 1945–1949. For 1957–1958 Lewis estimated the union wage effect at from 10 to 15 percent.[18]

Other studies, using different data and estimation techniques, have arrived at other conclusions. While Leonard W. Weiss found Lewis's estimates for the late 1950s high, more recent investigations indicate that they were too low. For 1967, Michael J. Boskin arrived at a union-nonunion differential of 15 percent for craft and kindred workers and operatives and 25 percent for laborers. Using data on "usual" hourly earnings for 1973, Paul M. Ryscavage estimated that organized craftsmen received 20 to 25 percent more than nonunion workers with similar characteristics, workers in transportation equipment operative occupations 40 percent more, and women in clerical, operative, and service jobs from 20 to 25 percent more. The variables that Ryscavage attempted to account for in his econometric model related to age, race, sex, education, region, and occupation.[19]

[17] Harold M. Levinson, *Unionism, Wage Trends and Income Distribution, 1914–1947,* Michigan Business Studies, Vol. X, No. 4 (Ann Arbor: University of Michigan Press, 1951).
[18] H. G. Lewis, *Unionism and Relative Wages in the United States: An Empirical Inquiry* (Chicago: University of Chicago Press, 1963). Lewis reviews the 12 specific studies in ch. 3 and economywide studies in ch. 4.
[19] Weiss estimated union power at 8 to 15 percent for craftsmen and 6 to 8 percent for operatives. See his "Concentration and Labor Earnings," *American Economic Review,* 56

Concentration Versus Competition

One important aspect of measuring union strength has been the relationship between the union's ability to raise wages and the employer's power in product markets. The issue, which first arose in the 1950s, was whether unionized workers in monopolistic and oligopolistic industries were able to gain an advantage over workers in competitive industries in periods of less than full employment. Although some analysts were concerned primarily with problems of cost-push inflation (a subject reviewed in the next chapter), a number of studies indicated that, with respect to the interindustry wage structure, wage changes were associated positively with a higher incidence of monopoly (as measured by concentration ratios), higher profits, and a greater degree of unionization. These results have not been wholly accepted by all writers, however, in part because it is difficult to separate out the independent effects of these three variables. Weiss, in fact, has concluded from his own investigation that unions have not been able to win exceptional wages at the expense of profits in the highly concentrated industries; rather he finds that such industries employ workers whose personal characteristics more than adequately account for their wage differentials.[20]

Nonetheless, the relationships between product and labor market structures and the degree of unionization with wages and wage changes become more apparent, if more complex, when specific industries and industry groups are analyzed in detail. An early study by William G. Bowen covering the post–World War II period (1947 to 1959) concluded that wages in industries characterized by both high concentration ratios and high degrees of unionization tended to rise more rapidly than in low-concentrated and low-unionized industries, irrespective of general employment conditions.[21] Other studies have corroborated the importance of profits as a variable influencing wage changes in specific industries, but the fact that a wage settlement in one industry may become a pattern followed by unions and managements in other industries requires more than the monopolistic power of certain firms in product markets. The extent of "spillover effect" from a wage change in one in-

(March 1966), 96–117, and his "Concentration and Labor Earnings: Reply," *American Economic Review,* 63 (March 1968), 181–184. Michael J. Boskin, "Unions and Relative Real Wages," *American Economic Review,* 62 (June 1972), 466–472. Paul M. Ryscavage, "Measuring Union-Nonunion Earnings Differences," *Monthly Labor Review,* 97 (December 1974), 3–9. Other support for the higher estimates is found in Frank P Stafford, "Concentration and Labor Earnings: Comment," *American Economic Review,* 58 (March 1968), 174–181, and Adrian W. Throop, "The Union-Nonunion Wage Differential and Cost-Push Inflation," ibid., pp. 79–99.

[20] Weiss, "Concentration and Labor Earnings." Lewis also minimizes the effect of concentration ratios on the union wage structure in his *Unionism and Relative Wages,* ch. 9.

[21] William G. Bowen, *Wage Behavior in the Postwar Period, An Empirical Analysis* (Princeton, N.J.: Industrial Relations Section, 1960), ch. 5.

dustry to other industries depends upon several other factors as well, such as the degree of interunion rivalry and economic constraints faced by the other industries. During the 1950s, the importance of interunion competition—especially in the heavy industries such as steel, automobiles, and rubber—seemed to indicate that wage determination was interdependent; once a wage decision was established in one industry, the other unions and managements in the key group of industries followed the pattern with wage and price increases.[22] Later, as the major unions developed their own cycles of three-year contracts with termination dates that did not coincide, the significance of specific "wage rounds" for major industries in a given year diminished. Although this did not necessarily mean that spillover effects had ceased, it did mean that they were less identifiable.

The market structure of specific industries influences how effectively unions can raise wages.[23] As shown in studies of steel, autos, tires, and other concentrated industries operating in national markets and organized by a single union, there is a strong tendency toward uniformity of wage changes among all firms within an industry. Over periods of time, however, deviations occur when firms with somewhat different products and product markets, or with plants located in less competitive areas, are forced to adjust to changing economic conditions. The power of unions is more limited in industries that are competitive on a national basis. In such industries as textiles, shoes, and apparel, where there are relatively more firms than in the concentrated industries, and where new firms can enter more easily because of lower capital costs, unions are more exposed to having their wage scales undercut by nonunion labor. As E. Robert Livernash has pointed out with respect to the shoe industry, which is about half organized, "wage costs are a strategic competitive cost because raw material prices are governed by auction markets and technology is highly standardized. . . . Union companies commit suicide if they move significantly ahead of nonunion wage levels."[24]

In industries where the product market is local but monopolistic, like public utilities, newspapers, and ship repair installations, union power is en-

---

[22] Among those who have examined industry structure and wages are Otto Eckstein and Thomas A. Wilson, who analyzed wage rounds in "The Determination of Money Wages in American Industry," *The Quarterly Journal of Economics*, 26 (August 1962), 379–414. Eckstein made some modifications in his "Money Wage Determination Revisited," *Review of Economic Studies*, 35 (April 1968), especially 139–141.

[23] An analytical framework for evaluating different market structures, and the one used here, was first presented by Martin Segal in "The Relation between Union Wage Impact and Market Structure," *Quarterly Journal of Economics*, 78 (February 1964), 96–114. A somewhat different approach is used by Harold M. Levinson in his analysis of six West Coast industries. See his *Determining Forces in Collective Wage Bargaining* (New York: John Wiley & Sons, 1966). See also Albert Schwenk, *The Influence of Selected Industry Characteristics on Negotiated Settlements*, BLS Staff Paper 5 (Washington, D.C.: U.S. Government Printing Office, 1971).

[24] Livernash, "Wages and Benefits," p. 99.

hanced because there are few alternatives for firms who wish to avoid union demands. State and municipal governments also fall into this category. The situation is different in local industries that are highly competitive and where union power is limited, as is the case with retail establishments, although to the extent that the union can organize not only existing firms in the industry but also new ones, it will be in a better position to influence wages. In the construction industry in recent years, unions have had difficulty in maintaining control as some national firms with a policy of employing nonunion labor have attempted to "invade" local areas that had previously been well organized. Such competition can limit wage gains. The possible entry of new, unorganized firms is a significant element in industry market structures as far as union wage policies are concerned. As Levinson has shown in the case of the trucking industry—an industry that at first would appear to be a highly competitive one, thereby restraining union power—it was the strategic control of long-distance trucking by the Teamsters' union in key cities that effectively prohibited new entrants and enabled the union to win higher wages.[25]

Unions and Resource Allocation

Since the earliest studies of the competitive economy, many experts have held that unions are powerless to improve the economic lot of workers as a class. As we have seen, a common belief was that, although workers associated with a particular union could gain a position superior to that which they would have received from competition in the marketplace, other workers would be hurt.

The basic assumption of this position was that full and perfect competition characterized or was a reasonable facsimile of the workings of the nonunion economy. Since the competitive model implies that resources are allocated in such a way that consumers obtain the greatest benefits, any union interference with the mechanism would prevent maximization of economic welfare. A union that affected the demand for its products would presumably be interfering least with the competitive market system. As long as it influenced voluntarily the scale of preferences of the buying public, its actions would be no different from those of any advertiser. On the other hand, prevention of more profitable changes in the combination of factors of production within the firm would presumably cause an economically less desirable allocation of resources than would otherwise occur. Similarly, controls over the supply of labor restrict its natural flow among occupations in accordance with workers' estimations of their work preferences, costs, and rates of remuneration. Union power to raise wages either directly or by monopolizing a firm's labor supply would also have an undesirable effect: the higher wage rate would cause a loss

[25] Levinson, *Determining Forces*, ch. VI.

of employment—the extent of which would depend upon the elasticity of the demand for labor—and the wage gain to the employed workers would be immediately offset by the losses to those who became unemployed or were forced to work part-time.

Moreover, it has been argued, union action can have a second adverse effect upon the economy as a whole. With less labor employed, production will decrease and the total welfare of society will be reduced. If the unemployed workers transfer to other (nonunion) markets, wages in those markets will be reduced and the output of nonunionized industries will increase. But those effects will only partly compensate for the original loss of output, because a union-enforced wage differential results in a difference between the marginal-revenue products of the two markets, and the difference is society's loss.

This approach to the influence of unions has found a number of champions among modern economic theorists. One now classic statement is that of Henry C. Simons, who regards an effective union as a monopoly that enforces its position by coercion in strikes or threats of strikes or by control of the labor supply.[26] The power to raise wages by these means creates a distortion in union versus nonunion wage structures and hence a less than optimal allocation of resources.[27] Albert Rees attempted to estimate the cost of union-induced resource distortion in terms of the gross national product.[28] The conclusion of this point of view is that the labor force as a whole does not gain, that unions may shift a part of the income stream to their members but only at the expense of other workers and of consumers. There would be no effective way for unions to tap the returns on capital by reducing the rate of interest and profits except at the cost of inflation or depression resulting from mass unemployment.[29]

[26] Henry C. Simons, "Some Reflections on Syndicalism," *The Journal of Political Economy*, 52 (March 1944), 7, 8, 22.

[27] For a discussion of these points, see articles in Philip D. Bradley, ed., *The Public Stake in Union Power* (Charlottesville: University of Virginia Press, 1959), and David McCord Wright, ed., *The Impact of the Union* (New York: Harcourt, Brace, 1951).

[28] Albert Rees, "The Effects of Unions on Resource Allocation," *Journal of Law and Economics*, 6 (October 1963), 69–78. His estimate of welfare loss was 0.14 percent of GNP. He has subsequently stated that this estimate is now too low. See his *The Economics of Work and Pay* (New York: Harper & Row, 1973), pp. 160–161.
Estimates such as these are based on assumptions concerning elasticities of the aggregate demands for union and nonunion sectors, perfect factor mobility between sectors, full employment, and competition in all markets, except the union sector. The estimates bear the further burden that they cannot be tested scientifically.

[29] A statement of this position is found in C. E. Lindblom, *Unions and Capitalism* (New Haven: Yale University Press, 1949), where it is argued that if unions raise wages, capitalists will in turn raise prices (cost-push inflation) to protect their profits. However, the increase in product prices can go only as far as the monetary authorities are willing to expand the monetary supply. If they are limited in their ability to do so—for example, by an outward flow of gold—a higher price level could not be maintained. Under these circumstances, when a wage increase would definitely begin to encroach on profit levels, new investment would be cut short and the economy would enter a period of recession. Ac-

However, a deductive approach to the question of whether unions raise wages and cause less than optimal allocations of resources need not lead unequivocally to the Simons-Rees conclusion. Other writers, notably both the older and newer bargaining theorists, question the assumption that wages would be at competitive levels without unions. By pointing to the limitations of competition in the labor market, they show that a union may raise wages without an adverse employment effect. They present several different possibilities.

1. As shown above in chapter 4, imperfections in the product market in the form of oligopoly will cause the demand curve for labor to be discontinuous, so that a wage increase obtained by a union will not be accompanied by a decline in employment.
2. Monopsony in the labor market, which results in an upward-sloping labor supply curve, can be offset by union action without an employment loss. If the supply curve is flattened when a union establishes a wage at which the firm can hire additional workers without a change, an increase may even be accompanied by growth in employment.
3. The "shock effect" of a union-negotiated wage increase upon the employer may lead to improvements in labor productivity through better management, more efficient organization, or newly introduced technology. The implication of this situation is that management had not been taking advantage of already existing opportunities for more efficient modes of production.
4. Through their insistence on equal pay for equal work, unions may promote a better allocation of resources within the economy by eliminating, or at least reducing, wage discrimination by area, race, and sex.[30]

In summary, the basic question in considering union power is whether or not the "natural" or nonunion economy is one in which the clean wind of competition blows throughout every nook and cranny at all times. If it does, then union action could be viewed as monopolistically affecting the terms and conditions of employment. But the American economy even without unions cannot be viewed as competitive. In a world of monopolistic and monopsonistic arrangements, and discriminatory tactics, unions can exert a positive effect, and the charge of resource misallocation is unproven.

---

cording to Lindblom, profits in an otherwise free economy could not be appropriated by union action without bringing inflation and/or depression upon themselves and fellow workers.

[30]According to an econometric study by Orley Ashenfelter, unionization has led to an overall wage gain for black males of 3.4 percent. See his "Discrimination and Trade Unions," in Ashenfelter and Rees, *Discrimination in Labor Markets* (Princeton, N.J.: Princeton University Press, 1973), pp. 108–109.

WAGE DIFFERENTIALS BY SEX

That the natural, nonunionized economy is not best explained by the competitive model receives further substantiation with a consideration of the role of discrimination in American labor markets. In a special summary in 1973, the Council of Economic Advisers pointed out that for all women aged 14 and over who worked in 1971, the median annual earnings were 40 percent of the median annual earnings of men.[31] Because of the greater incidence of part-time work among women, the percentage rises to 60 if only earnings of full-year, full-time workers are compared. The percentage rises somewhat further (to 66) if women's earnings are statistically adjusted to compensate for the fact that even "fully" employed women work fewer hours than men. Lower earnings for women was one of the basic characteristics of the American economy, and the differential showed no signs of disappearing: the percentage was lower in 1971 than it had been in 1956. The differential for full-time women workers characterizes all major occupational groups, ranging from 42.1 percent for sales workers to 66.4 percent for professional and technical workers. (See Table 14–8.)

On a finer occupational breakdown of 423 occupations for men and 391 for women, another analysis of data from the 1970 census (referring to 1969 median earnings for full- and part-time workers) disclosed that earnings were higher for men than women in every occupation except public kindergarten teaching. Moreover, the average earnings of women in the top decile of occupations were about half the earnings of the top decile of occupations for men. Earnings in the *lower half* of women's occupations fell in the earnings range of the *lowest decile* of male occupations.[32]

There are two approaches in explaining the differentials in earnings between men and women. The first focuses on occupational discrimination—the concentration of female employment in low-paying occupations. The second deals with wage differences between females and males in the same occupation.

Occupational Discrimination

According to the first approach, the earnings of women on the average would be less than men's, even if the wages paid in each specific occupation

---

[31] *Economic Report of the President*, transmitted to Congress January 1973 (Washington, D.C.: U.S. Government Printing Office, 1973), p. 103.

Most data on earnings by sex and race are reported through household surveys, while earnings data for specific jobs and occupations usually come from firms. The latter do not ordinarily report the personal characteristics of the workers in those occupations.

[32] Dixie Sommers, "Occupational Rankings for Men and Women by Earnings," *Monthly Labor Review*, 97 (August 1974), 47–48.

Table 14-8
Ratio of Total Money Earnings of Civilian Women Workers to Earnings of Civilian Men Workers, Selected Years, 1956–1971

Occupational Group	Actual Ratios					Adjusted Ratios[a]	
	1956	1960	1965	1969	1971	1969	1971
Total[b]	63.3	60.7	59.9	58.9	59.5	65.9	66.1
Professional and technical workers	62.4	61.3	65.2	62.2	66.4	67.9	72.4
Teachers, primary and secondary schools	([c])	75.6	79.9	72.4	82.0	([c])	([c])
Managers, officials, and proprietors	59.1	52.9	53.2	53.1	53.0	57.2	56.8
Clerical workers	71.7	67.6	67.2	65.0	62.4	70.0	66.9
Sales workers	41.8	40.9	40.5	40.2	42.1	45.7	47.4
Craftsmen and foreman	([d])	([d])	56.7	56.7	56.4	60.8	60.2
Operatives	62.1	59.4	56.6	58.7	60.5	65.4	66.6
Service workers excluding private household workers	55.4	57.2	55.4	57.4	58.5	62.5	63.2

[a] Adjusted for differences in average full-time hours worked since full-time hours for women are typically less than full-time hours for men.
[b] Total includes occupational groups not shown separately.
[c] Not available.
[d] Base too small to be statistically significant.
Note.—Data relate to civilian workers who are employed full-time, year-round. Data for 1956 include salaried workers only, while data for later years include both salaried and self-employed workers.
Source: Economic Report of the President, transmitted to Congress January 1973, p. 104.

were the same as men's, simply because women have traditionally been segregated in low-paying occupations. It is argued that individuals of both sexes are conditioned from earliest years to believe that certain jobs are fitted for women—such as nursing, public school teaching, and clerical jobs—and that others are not—such as engineering or construction trades.[33] Discriminatory and exclusionary hiring preferences in employment strengthen occupational segregation by sex and create barriers to the mobility of women into typically male occupations. The consequence is the "crowding" of women into specific occupations identified as "women's work." With resulting declines in marginal productivity, wages in these fields are forced downward.

Occupational differentiation by sex is clearly a fact of American labor markets. By major occupational group, women in 1974 comprised 98 percent of

[33] As Blanche Fitzpatrick has pointed out, the taxpayer's dollars are inefficiently spent on education to the extent that the school system directs girls to low-paying careers. See her *Women's Inferior Education: An Economic Analysis* (New York: Praeger, 1976).

the private household workers, 78 percent of clerical workers, and 59 percent of service workers other than private household, even though they totaled 39 percent of employment in all occupations.[34] They were underrepresented in such major groups as craft workers (4%), transport equipment operatives (5%), nonfarm laborers (8%), and managers and administrators, except farm (18%). Although about proportionately represented in the professional and technical occupations (40%), sales (42%), and operatives other than transport (39%), women were in the lower-paid occupations within these broad categories. In the professional and technical occupations, for example, while about 70 percent of the teachers in colleges and universities are men, about 70 percent of the teachers in elementary and secondary schools, where wages are lower, are women. Despite the recent drive for women's rights, the degree of overrepresentation in occupations stereotyped for women appears actually to have increased. Although recently there have been a few breakthroughs of women into male occupations, most of the higher-paying jobs remain "male-intensive."[35]

Other Discrimination

The second approach is to examine wage differentials for specific occupations. This can be done in two ways. One is to look at the wages paid women who perform the same job as men in the same firm. If narrowly enough defined, such wage discrimination may often be fairly small.[36] The second and

[34] See U.S. Department of Labor, *U.S. Working Women, a Chartbook,* Bulletin 1880 (Washington, D.C.: U.S. Government Printing Office, 1975), p. 9.

[35] See Elizabeth Waldman and Beverly J. McEaddy, "Where Women Work—An Analysis by Industry and Occupation," *Monthly Labor Review,* 97 (May 1974), 3–13; and Barbara R. Bergman and Irma Adelman, "The 1973 Report of the President's Council of Economic Advisers: The Economic Role of Women," *American Economic Review,* 63 (September 1973), 510–511.

One breakthrough has been among school bus drivers: in 1940 less than 1 percent were women, in 1970, 37 percent. It should be noted, however, that the work is part-time, part-year, and low-paid.

[36] A study of average earnings of men and women in 10 specific occupational classifications in 85 metropolitan areas in 1969–1970 showed that the average wage differential between men and women was 18 percent, ranging from 8 percent for messengers to 34 percent for order clerks. For firms employing only one sex in an occupation, the male advantage rose to 22 percent; where firms employed both, the differential dropped to 11 percent. When male and female wages within the same establishment are compared, the median percentage differential ranged from 9 (for order clerks) to −1 for tabulating-machine operators, Class B and C. For six of the occupations, the range was 2 percent or less.

Not taken into account in this study is that some wage differences may reflect length-of-service wage increases as well as somewhat different duties in job descriptions.

How detailed a job description must be in order to establish comparability of pay becomes a highly relevant issue in attempts to enforce the sex-wage discrimination of the Equal Pay Act. See John E. Buckley, "Pay Differentials between Men and Women in the Same Job," *Monthly Labor Review,* 94 (November 1971), 36–39.

more widely used approach is to compare the characteristics for each group of workers, men and women, with their earnings. The assumption here is that such characteristics as age, education, work experience, and health have a causal relationship with earnings because of their effects on worker productivity. If women workers have the same amount of training and background (that is, human capital investment) as men yet receive lower wages, then there is wage discrimination. A number of studies that use this procedure have found, not unexpectedly, that discrimination is substantial. Estimates of the degree of discriminations using this method, however, will vary with the fineness of the occupational classification on the one hand and the particular set of explanatory variables on the other. The Council of Economic Advisers in its special report on women estimated the differential to be on the order of 20 percent; others give an even higher estimate.[37]

One difficulty in estimating wage discrimination by this method arises from the problems of evaluating work experience. One aspect of the pattern of female labor force participation is the interruption of outside work as the result of marriage and bearing and rearing children. Because of the possibility of such interruptions, it is argued that employers are less inclined to make the specific human capital investments that would otherwise improve women's economic position, whether or not the expectation is fulfilled. With less on-the-job training, promotion is slower and opportunities for the best jobs sharply restricted. A similar argument is that women's higher quit rates mean higher turnover costs to employers. The latter then have further reason to exclude women from jobs that require investments in the form of training.

These arguments, however, are not wholly satisfactory. It is true that women tend either to be employed in secondary labor markets or concentrated in those occupations of primary markets where promotional ladders are short in terms of the possibility of advancement to higher incomes. Under such circumstances one would expect higher turnover rates: that is, it is not because the worker is a woman that the turnover rate is high, but rather the turnover rate is high because of the nature of the jobs that women are typically forced to take. When women are found in predominately male jobs, their wages are relatively higher than in the case of women in occupations typically filled by women. Similarly, where men are employed in jobs that are typically staffed by women, their wages are lower than those of men in other occupations.[38]

---

[37] *Economic Report of the President, 1973*, p. 106. Ronald Oaxaca estimates that most of the sex differential in wages (by broad occupational groups) is explainable by sex discrimination—74 percent in the case of white women and 92 percent in the case of black women. If all sex discrimination were eliminated, he estimates that a small differential would remain of the magnitude of about 14 percent for whites and 4 percent for blacks. See his "Sex Discrimination in Wages," in Ashenfelter and Rees, *Discrimination in Labor Markets*, pp. 146–147.

[38] Sommers, "Occupational Rankings," pp. 48–49.

WAGE DIFFERENTIALS BY RACE

For black workers wage differentials have been substantial and pervasive in nearly all labor markets. As shown in Table 14–9, median annual earnings of black males in 1972 were about a third below those of white males, and the earnings of black females were slightly below those of white females. If only the earnings of full-year, full-time workers are compared, the gap is reduced somewhat for males, to a ratio of 69 percent, while it widens for women; this is because of the greater degree of part-time work among black males as compared with white males, and among white females as compared with black females.

Black males earn less than white males in every major occupational category. Among females, blacks have a positive differential for two groups, private household and other service occupations—two of the lower-paying categories; among the other reported comparisons the differential is negative but small. For example, among professional, technical, and similar workers, black women earned 92 percent as much as white women in 1972. Nonetheless, black women, like whites, faced the sex discrimination already referred to. In comparison with white males, black and white women had earnings of only 49 and 57 percent respectively; in comparison with black males, their respective earnings stood at 70.5 and 82.2 percent.

The principal reason for the lower earnings of blacks is their concentration in lower-paying occupations. As shown in Table 14–10, the 8 million black workers in 1973 were 9.5 percent of the 84.4 million employed, but they held only 5.7 percent of the white-collar jobs. They were overrepresented in blue-collar and service industry employment—11.4 and 19.1 percent respectively. In other words, half (49.9%) of the white workers but only a little over a quarter (28.6%) of the blacks had white-collar jobs.

Within each of the major occupational groups, blacks were in less desirable positions. In blue-collar occupations, for example, blacks were less than proportionally represented among carpenters (4.5%) and metal craft workers (5.6%) but heavily represented among transport equipment operatives (14.2%) and nonfarm laborers (19.0%).

Employment distribution as the major factor in wage differentials by race can be explained in part by the limited human capital investment in educating and training blacks. The legacy of centuries of slavery, during which any education was usually legally prohibited, persisted well into the second half of the present century in the form of discrimination against education for blacks. As Richard B. Freeman points out, educational discrimination not only lowers human capital but prevents the development of black professional and managerial supply that could compete with white employers and

Table 14-9
Median Earnings of Civilians 14 Years Old and Over, by Race, Occupation of Longest Job, Work Experience, and Sex, 1972

Occupation	Men		Women		Ratio: Negro and Other Races to White	
	Negro and Other Races*	White	Negro and Other Races*	White	Men	Women
ALL WORKERS						
Total, with earnings	$5,405	$8,332	$3,042	$3,190	0.65	0.95
Professional, technical, and kindred workers	7,946	12,339	7,181	6,307	0.64	1.14
Managers and administrators, except farm	9,141	12,825	6,479	5,531	0.71	1.17
Farmers and farm managers	(*)	4,258	(*)	1,614	(*)	(*)
Clerical and kindred workers	7,248	8,272	4,160	4,294	0.88	0.97
Sales workers	3,201	8,304	2,114	1,609	0.39	1.31
Craft and kindred workers	7,229	9,340	(*)	3,906	0.77	(*)
Operatives, including transport workers	5,940	7,359	3,535	3,418	0.81	1.03
Private household workers	(*)	(*)	1,083	349	(*)	3.10
Service workers, except private household	4,427	4,226	2,831	1,693	1.05	1.67
Farm laborers and supervisors	1,332	1,141	394	417	1.17	0.94
Laborers, except farm	3,959	2,900	(*)	1,580	1.37	(*)

YEAR-ROUND FULL-TIME WORKERS

Total, with earnings	$7,301	$10,593	$5,147	$5,998	0.69	0.86
Professional, technical, and kindred workers	9,467	13,726	8,003	8,776	0.69	0.92
Managers and administrators, except farm	9,964	13,614	(ᵃ)	6,976	0.73	(ᵃ)
Farmers and farm managers	(ᵃ)	5,173	(ᵃ)	3,022	(ᵃ)	(ᵃ)
Clerical and kindred workers	8,194	9,931	5,963	6,061	0.83	0.98
Sales workers	(ᵃ)	11,674	(ᵃ)	4,473	(ᵃ)	(ᵃ)
Craft and kindred workers	8,488	10,553	(ᵃ)	5,536	0.80	(ᵃ)
Operatives, including transport workers	7,085	9,025	4,696	5,076	0.79	0.93
Private household workers	(ᵃ)	(ᵃ)	2,364	2,253	(ᵃ)	1.05
Service workers, except private household	6,172	8,019	4,522	4,454	0.77	1.02
Farm laborers and supervisors	(ᵃ)	4,794	(ᵃ)	(ᵃ)	(ᵃ)	(ᵃ)
Laborers, except farm	5,910	7,819	(ᵃ)	4,637	0.76	(ᵃ)

ᵃ Base too small for figures to be shown.

* Note: "Negro" and "Black" are often used interchangeably by the Bureau of the Census. Technically, about 90 percent of the population of "Negro and Other Races" is black.

Source: Bureau of the Census, U.S. Department of Commerce, The Social and Economic Status of the Black Population in the United States, 1973, Special Studies Series P–23, No. 48, issued July 1974, p. 59.

Table 14-10

Occupations of the Employed Population by Race, 1973
(Numbers in thousands)

Occupation	Total	Negro and Other Races	White	Percent Negro and Other Races of Total
Total employed	84,409	8,061	75,278	9.5
White-collar workers	40,386	2,302	37,545	5.7
Professional and technical	11,777	684	10,876	5.8
Engineers	1,094	15	1,053	1.4
Medical and other health	1,939	124	1,754	6.4
Teachers, except college	2,916	253	2,644	8.7
Other professional and technical	5,828	291	5,426	5.0
Managers and administrators, except farm	8,644	280	8,270	3.2
Salaried workers	6,815	202	6,548	3.0
Self-employed	1,829	78	1,722	4.3
Sales workers	5,415	167	5,207	3.1
Retail trade	3,074	123	2,921	4.0
Other industries	2,342	44	2,286	1.9
Clerical workers	14,548	1,171	13,192	8.0
Stenographers, typists, and secretaries	4,206	269	3,880	6.4
Other clerical workers	10,342	902	9,313	8.7
Blue-collar workers	29,869	3,411	26,147	11.4
Craft and kindred workers	11,288	713	10,479	6.3
Carpenters	1,078	49	1,018	4.5
Construction craft workers, except carpenters	2,357	185	2,152	7.8
Mechanics and repairers	2,903	170	2,702	5.9
Metal craft workers	1,159	65	1,086	5.6
Blue-collar supervisors, n.e.c.	1,460	87	1,364	6.0
All other craft workers	2,333	158	2,157	6.8
Operatives, except transport	10,972	1,410	9,425	12.9
Transport equipment operatives	3,297	467	2,814	14.2
Drivers and delivery workers	2,798	370	2,416	13.2
All other	498	98	398	19.7
Nonfarm laborers	4,312	821	3,429	19.0
Construction	854	178	665	20.8
Manufacturing	1,100	230	859	20.9
Other industries	2,358	413	1,905	17.5
Service workers	11,128	2,130	8,814	19.1
Private household	1,353	509	833	37.6
Service workers, except private household	9,775	1,621	7,981	16.6
Cleaning service workers	2,076	577	1,470	27.8
Food service workers	3,402	401	2,907	11.8
Health service workers	1,596	352	1,225	22.1
Personal service workers	1,543	177	1,346	11.5
Protective service workers	1,158	115	1,033	9.9
Farm workers	3,027	219	2,772	7.2
Farmers and farm managers	1,664	51	1,602	3.1
Farm laborers and supervisors	1,363	168	1,170	12.3

Source: Bureau of the Census, U.S. Department of Commerce, *The Social and Economic Status of the Black Population in the United States, 1973*, Special Studies Series P–23, No. 48, issued July 1974, p. 56.

utilize other black workers more efficiently.[39] Entrenched racism in a social and political system can operate not only directly in limiting educational investments through inadequate schools, fewer teachers, and lower-quality facilities, but also indirectly in the refusal to hire blacks for better jobs in governmental and other employment, in discrimination by employers and craft unions in admittance to job training and apprenticeship programs, and in pressures and "extra-market costs" on organizations that do not discriminate. The effect is a vicious circle of justification—for limited education because there are no good jobs for blacks, and for denial of entry into good jobs because blacks lack education.

Attempts to break the circle of discrimination included the unanimous Supreme Court decision that struck down segregated schools (*Brown* v. *Board of Education*, 1954), the civil rights movement in the years that followed, and massive federal intervention with its culmination in the Civil Rights Act of 1964. In addition, the movement of blacks out of the rural South into cities, both South and North, brought youth into better educational systems and widened economic opportunities. The resulting gains in the level of schooling for blacks were dramatic. The median number of years of schooling for black males in 1952 was 7.2, compared to 10.8 for whites; by 1971 the figures were 11.4 and 12.5 respectively. For females, the median educational level of blacks rose from 8.1 to 12.1 years during the same period; for whites the level went from 12.1 to 12.5[40]

The 1960s witnessed significant occupational shifts for both black men and women. In professional occupations the proportion of black male employment more than doubled between 1962 and 1974 in fields such as accounting and medicine, although there was still underrepresentation: only in the category of social work did they account for more than 10 percent of all men in the occupation.[41] In clerical jobs, the proportion of black men also rose: black mail carriers increased from 8 to 13 percent, and black office machine operators from 8 to 14 percent of the respective job totals. Advancement has also occurred in certain skilled crafts. Black women have achieved

[39] Richard B. Freeman, "Decline of Labor Market Discrimination and Economic Analysis," Papers and Proceedings, *American Economic Review*, 63 (May 1973), 284–285.

Finis Welch points out the long struggle to overcome the educational deficiencies among southern blacks—beginning from the time of emancipation when no slave legally could have been schooled—and shows how those gaps persisted well into the twentieth century. See his "Education and Racial Discrimination," in Ashenfelter and Rees, *Discrimination in Labor Markets*, esp. pp. 51 ff.

[40] Council of Economic Advisers, *Economic Report of the President, 1974* (Washington, D.C.: U.S. Government Printing Office, 1974), p. 151.

[41] The term "black" as used here refers to census data that in fact includes "Negroes and other races." Of the total nonwhite group, 90% on the average are blacks. The actual percentage differs among occupational groups, however. Among male professional and technical workers about 68% of the "other-than-white" workers are blacks. See Stuart H. Garfinkle, "Occupations of Women and Black Workers, 1962–1974," *Monthly Labor Review*, 98 (November 1975), 34, footnote 1.

entry into higher-paying professional occupations, as well as in the clerical field.[42]

The effects of these changes have been to improve the relative wages of black men and women. As reported by the Council of Economic Advisers, the median wage and salary income of black males has increased since World War II at an annual rate of 3.2 percent in comparison with 2.6 percent for white males; among women the annual rate of increase was 4.9 percent for blacks and 1.7 percent for whites.[43] Nonetheless, the wage differentials are still significantly large, especially for men in the older age groups.

Moreover, wage differentials reflect the general cyclical movements of general business activity in the economy as a whole. Gains by blacks in getting better jobs and moving up more desirable ladders of promotion are wiped out by cyclical downturns. Because breakthroughs to good jobs have been recent, blacks have less seniority and less immunity to layoff in times of recession. Increased human capital investment does not provide invulnerability; in the recession of 1969–1971, and again after 1974, unemployment affected blacks more than whites. A long period of expansion of the economy, similar to that of the Vietnam War period of the 1960s, would be necessary to insure a permanent conversion of educational gains into better jobs.[44]

SUMMARY

Wage structures refer to the wage differentials between groups of workers. Their existence is undeniable although the size of differentials depends on the statistical techniques used to measure them. And explanations of differentials are often controversial.

Some economists consider occupational differentials to be basic to all others and point to differences in human capital investments as the relevant cause. But other factors are clearly important. There are the short-run, changing conditions of demand and supply that can affect differentials between skilled and unskilled and blue- and white-collar workers in a manner inconsistent with human investments. The industry of employment also affects occupational differentials. The interaction of market and institutional

---

[42] Ibid., pp. 29 ff. On the basis of an occupational status index constructed for whites and for minority workers for census years from 1910 to 1960, it appears that despite some gains during World War II, the difference in relative occupational status between whites and minority workers was as great in 1960 as it had been 50 years before. Significant gains, however, were indicated for the decade from 1960 to 1970, although they were primarily among the younger and better educated minority workers. See *Manpower Report of the President,* April 1974 (Washington, D.C.: U.S. Government Printing Office, 1974), pp. 107–108 and 123–124.

[43] *Economic Report of the President, 1974,* p. 151.

[44] Bernard E. Anderson and Phyllis A. Wallace, "Public Policy and Black Economic Progress: A Review of the Evidence," *Papers and Proceedings, American Economic Review,* 65 (May 1975), 47–52.

forces, the effects of unionism, and discrimination by sex and race make it difficult to separate out the various causal relationships.

Nonetheless, certain long-run trends have been established. The downward trend in the wage differential between skilled and unskilled workers that began early in this century appears to have been halted since the 1950s. The North-South regional differential appears to have narrowed in recent years for skilled workers but still remains substantial for the unskilled. There has been stability in interindustry wage relationships over long periods of time, attributed by some to the inertia of the administered wage-setting process within firms.

The union-nonunion differential varies cyclically, widening during recessions and narrowing during booms. Some estimates of the size of the union wage effect are in the 10 to 15 percent range for the 1950s; more recent estimates are higher. Although conclusions from various studies are by no means uniform, there are good grounds for the conclusion that unionization has a greater effect on wages in industries that are comparatively profitable. These are often the more concentrated industries with market power.

Wage differentials by sex are substantial and do not appear to be narrowing. Part of the explanation is occupational discrimination, since women are concentrated in lower-paying occupations. But there is also wage discrimination, with women paid less than men for doing the same work.

In the case of racial discrimination, there is again the overcrowding effect; blacks, forced into lower-paying jobs, have earnings that fall below those of whites. Moreover, the lower earnings of blacks reflect a long history of discrimination in terms of inadequate human capital investment.

DISCUSSION QUESTIONS

1. What have been the long-run trends in the skilled-unskilled wage differentials in the United States? How do you account for these trends?
2. How do you explain the persistence of wage differentials between urban and rural areas, and between large cities and small ones? Do you expect these differences to disappear eventually? Why or why not?
3. Industrial wage differentials are subject to cyclical variations, yet are relatively stable in the long run. Why is this so?
4. Why do wages paid to workers in the same occupation vary from one industry to another?
5. What are the principal approaches used to estimate union/nonunion wage differentials? What are the limitations of each approach?
6. Show how the nature of the product market—whether monopolistic or competitive, national or local—can affect the power of a union to obtain wage advantages.
7. A long-time controversy concerns the impact of unions on the allocation of labor

resources in a market economy. What do you consider to be the significant arguments, both pro and con, on this issue?

8. Discuss what is meant by the statement that the sex wage differential is better explained by employment discrimination than by wage discrimination. What is the evidence?

9. Wage differentials by race appear to vary cyclically. How do you explain this?

SELECTED READINGS

For basic studies of wage structures, see J.L. Meij, ed., *Internal Wage Structure* (Amsterdam: North-Holland Publishing Co., 1963); Frank E. Pierson and George W. Taylor, *New Concepts in Wage Determination* (New York: McGraw-Hill, 1957); Melvin W. Reder, "Wage Differentials: Theory and Measurement," *Aspects of Labor Economics* (Princeton, N.J.: Princeton University Press, National Bureau of Economic Research, 1962); and Lloyd G. Reynolds and Cynthia H. Taft, *The Evolution of Wage Structure* (New Haven: Yale University Press, 1956). One summary of research on wage differentials is presented by E. Robert Livernash in "Wages and Benefits," Woodrow L. Ginsburg et al., *A Review of Industrial Relations Research*, vol. 1 (Madison, Wis.: Industrial Relations Research Association, 1970); another is Jacob Mincer, "The Distribution of Labor Incomes: A Survey with Special Reference to the Human Capital Approach," *Journal of Economic Literature*, 8 (March 1970), 1–26.

On the effect of unions on wage differentials, see Harold M. Levinson, *Determining Forces in Collective Wage Bargaining* (New York: John Wiley & Sons), 1960, and the comprehensive study of H. Gregg Lewis, *Unionism and Relative Wages* (Chicago: University of Chicago Press, 1963).

For different approaches to sex and race wage structures, see Orley Ashenfelter and Albert Rees, *Discrimination in Labor Markets* (Princeton, N.J.: Princeton University Press, 1973); Blanche Fitzpatrick, *Women's Inferior Education: An Economic Analysis* (New York: Praeger, 1976); Cynthia B. Lloyd, ed., *Sex, Discrimination, and the Division of Labor* (New York: Columbia University Press, 1975); and Ray Marshall, "The Economics of Racial Discrimination: A Survey," *Journal of Economic Literature*, 12 (September 1974), 849–871.

15

Wages, Productivity, and the Price Level

In this chapter we are concerned with the general level of wages, in both the long run and the short run. Over a long period of time in the United States there has been a significant increase in real wages—one of the outstanding facts of the American economy. This rise has reflected improvements in the productivity of labor made possible in part through investments in the capital with which labor works as well as human investments in skill and knowledge.

Yet the rise in workers' real wages has appeared to be slower in recent years. Inflation has eaten away the gains in money wages. And what causes inflation? Some argue that if money wages are pushed upward more rapidly than productivity, labor costs will rise and lead to rising price levels which undermine real wage gains unless there are restraints on the level of aggregate demand within the economy. Experience with inflation in the last decade has forced a closer examination of these views of the relationships between wages, productivity, and the price level.

In this chapter we shall look first at the historical record of wage and productivity changes, then at the theory of money wages and prices as represented by the Phillips curve, and finally at the American experience with incomes policies. These policies, during the Kennedy-Johnson years and the Nixon administration, were attempts to control wages and prices in accordance with productivity trends in order to achieve price level stability.

HISTORICAL TRENDS IN REAL EARNINGS

One of the major characteristics of the American economy has been the substantial and continuing rise in real wages.[1] While limitations of information hinder the precise measurement of wage trends, there is little doubt that

---

[1] See Appendix following this chapter for definitions of wages and problems of their statistical measurement.

workers in the United States have experienced a remarkable increase in income. Data on wages, costs of living, and hours of work are available as far back as 1840, although in the earlier part of that period statistics on certain relevant matters, especially on the prices of goods bought by wage earners, are sketchy and incomplete.

1840–1860

During the two decades prior to the Civil War, when industrialization in the United States was just beginning, there was a clear upward trend in the real wages of factory workers. Although agricultural earnings undoubtedly tended to hold down the level of wages in manufacturing, nominal hourly earnings rose by 25.6 percent and "real" average hourly earnings by 22.7 percent,[2] or by about 10.9 percent per decade. (See Table 15–1 for a summary of changes by decades, 1840 to 1969.)

1860–1890

During the dramatic changes of the Civil War, the long depression of the 1870s, and the social upheavals of the 1880s, real wages of factory workers varied considerably but finally rose rapidly. In the inflationary period of the Civil War, price increases outran rises in monetary wages, but after 1865 real wages more than regained their losses. They were stabilized during the depression of the 1870s and then shot forward during the decade of the 1880s.

For the entire 30-year period real hourly average earnings in manufacturing increased by 64.5 percent, while real daily wages and real annual earnings in manufacturing rose by about 50 percent. The monetary daily wage rose from about $1.00 in 1860 to $1.50 in 1890, and the average annual wage from "just under $300 in 1860 to just over $425 in 1890."[3] Since the index of living costs at the two terminal dates was about the same, these figures approximate the real wage change. A decline in the daily hours of work of about 7 percent brought the average to about 10 hours in 1890, accounting for the slower rise in real weekly earnings as compared with real hourly earnings. Not all of the increase in earnings can be attributed to a rise in wage rates, however: it is estimated that "a fifth of the increase of wages and earnings may

[2] See references in Witt Bowden, "Trends in Wages and Hours," in W. S. Woytinsky et al., *Employment and Wages in the United States* (New York: Twentieth Century Fund, 1953), pp. 46–47.

[3] Clarence D. Long, *Wages and Earnings in the United States, 1860–1890*, A Study by the National Bureau of Economic Research (Princeton, N.J.: Princeton University Press, 1960), p. 109.

Table 15-1
Change in Real Average Hourly Earnings in Manufacturing, by Decades, 1840–1969

1840–1850	10.9 percent[a]
1850–1860	10.9 percent[a]
1860–1870	8.5 percent
1870–1880	14.9 percent
1880–1890	31.9 percent
1889–1899	12.2 percent
1899–1909	16.4 percent
1909–1919	35.1 percent
1919–1929	19.8 percent
1929–1939	38.0 percent
1939–1949	29.1 percent
1949–1959	29.7 percent
1959–1969	16.7 percent

[a] Based on assumption of constant decennial rate of change for the period 1840 to 1860.

Sources: Calculated from data in W. S. Woytinsky et al., *Employment and Wages in the United States* (New York: Twentieth Century Fund, 1953), p. 46; Clarence D. Long, *Wages and Earnings in the United States, 1860–1890*, A Study by the National Bureau of Economic Research (Princeton, N.J.: Princeton University Press, 1960), p. 153; Solomon Fabicant, *Basic Facts on Productivity Change*, Occasional Paper No. 63 (National Bureau of Economic Research, 1958), Table C, p. 48; and statistics from the *Monthly Labor Review*.

have been due to the relative shift of workers from low-wage soft goods industries to high-wage hard goods industries."[4]

1890–1914

There is some question as to the behavior of real wages from 1890 to 1914. At one time it was held that they did not rise. According to Paul H. Douglas, real average hourly earnings in manufacturing increased slightly from 1890 until 1894 and then barely held their own until World War I.[5] Real average weekly earnings, in fact, were four or five points lower in 1914 than they had been at the beginning of the 1890s, because of the decrease in hours of work per week to 55.2 in 1914. The factors cited by Douglas to explain this trend were the rapid increase in the flow of immigrants to the United States, especially during the first decade of the twentieth century; the closing of the frontier, which forced additional labor supplies into the cities; and a falling off in the rate of technological change.

A revision of this point of view was later presented by Albert Rees, whose new evidence was essentially a recalculation of an index of cost-of-living

[4] Ibid., p. 110.
[5] Paul H. Douglas, *Real Wages in the United States* (Boston: Houghton Mifflin, 1930).

changes.[6] Since his index did not rise as rapidly as Douglas's, Rees estimated a rise in real hourly earnings of 40 percent for factory workers during the 24-year period. Furthermore, he believed that the gain occurred fairly continuously throughout the period, rather than being concentrated in the very early years. Real average daily earnings also rose, but somewhat less rapidly, as hours declined. Rees calculated that the wage earner in manufacturing accepted on the average about 77 percent of his gain in goods and services and 23 percent in leisure.[7]

1914-1929

For the period since 1914 there is greater agreement on trends in wages and prices, since various series of data compiled by the United States Bureau of Labor Statistics (BLS) are available. In 1914 average hourly earnings for production workers in manufacturing were about $0.22, weekly hours were 49.4, and average weekly earnings were $10.92. The inflation during World War I caused hourly earnings to mount to $0.48 by 1919, and weekly earnings to $21.84. The rise in living costs, however, wiped out a large part, though not all, of the monetary wage gains, with the result that real hourly wages in the war period increased by about one-fourth. From 1919 to 1929, the last boom year prior to the Great Depression of the 1930s, average weekly earnings rose to $25 as hours of work continued to decline to 44.2 per week. Because of relative stability in the price level, these gains produced increases in real income. Nevertheless, the actual rise in hourly earnings in the 10-year period from 1919 to 1929 was only 20 percent, less than that of the five years of World War I.

1929-1959

The next 10 years of depression and moderate business recovery were marked by a fall in monetary hourly earnings that lasted until 1933; they failed to return to the 1929 level until 1936 (see Table 15-2). By 1939 the hourly earnings of $0.63 were above the 1929 level, but, because hours of work had slipped to 37.7, weekly earnings were only $23.64, less than those in 1929. Real hourly earnings, however, rose in every year during the depression from 1929 to 1939 except in 1932, when the price level declined less rapidly than wages. By 1939 they had increased by 38 percent in the decade, more than in any of the 10-year periods from 1840 to 1959.

World War II brought a new era of rising wages and prices. Despite the governmental controls imposed after 1942, monetary wages climbed sharply

[6] Albert Rees, *Real Wages in Manufacturing, 1890-1914*, A Study by the National Bureau of Economic Research (Princeton, N.J.: Princeton University Press, 1961), ch. 2.
[7] Ibid., pp. 121ff.

Table 15-2
Average Earnings and Hours of Manufacturing Production Workers in the United States, 1930–1977

Year	Average Weekly Earnings	Average Weekly Hours	Average Hourly Earnings
1930	$ 23.00	42.1	$0.546
1931	20.64	40.5	0.509
1932	16.89	38.3	0.441
1933	16.65	38.1	0.437
1934	18.20	34.6	0.526
1935	19.91	36.6	0.544
1936	21.56	39.2	0.550
1937	23.82	38.6	0.617
1938	22.07	35.6	0.620
1939	23.64	37.7	0.627
1940	24.96	38.1	0.655
1941	29.48	40.6	0.726
1942	36.68	43.1	0.851
1943	43.07	45.0	0.957
1944	45.70	45.2	1.011
1945	44.20	43.5	1.016
1946	43.32	40.3	1.075
1947	49.17	40.4	1.217
1948	53.12	40.0	1.328
1949	53.88	39.1	1.378
1950	58.32	40.5	1.440
1951	63.34	40.6	1.56
1952	67.16	40.7	1.65
1953	70.47	40.5	1.74
1954	70.49	39.6	1.78
1955	75.70	40.7	1.86
1956	78.78	40.4	1.95
1957	81.59	39.8	2.05
1958	82.71	39.2	2.11
1959	88.26	40.3	2.19
1960	89.72	39.7	2.26
1961	92.34	39.8	2.32
1962	96.56	40.4	2.39
1963	99.63	40.5	2.46
1964	102.97	40.7	2.53
1965	107.53	41.2	2.61
1966	112.34	41.3	2.72
1967	114.90	40.6	2.83
1968	122.51	40.7	3.01
1969	129.51	40.6	3.19
1970	133.73	39.8	3.36

Continued

Year	Average Weekly Earnings	Average Weekly Hours	Average Hourly Earnings
1970	133.73	39.8	3.36
1971	142.44	39.9	3.57
1972	154.69	40.6	3.81
1973	166.06	40.7	4.08
1974	176.40	40.0	4.41
1975	189.51	39.9	4.81
1976	207.60	40.1	5.19
1977	226.89	40.3	5.63

Source: U.S. Department of Labor, Bureau of Labor Statistics, *Handbook of Labor Statistics 1975—Reference Edition*, and current issues of *Monthly Labor Review*.

during the war period. This resulted in part from the increase in wage rates and in part from the increase in overtime work, the shifting of workers from civilian jobs to higher-paying war industries, and the upgrading of workers to higher-paying occupations. After the war average money earnings did not continue to rise, despite a general rise in wage rates, because the industrial demobilization brought an end to overtime work and caused the wartime shifts to be reversed. These factors, together with the rapid rise of the consumer price level with decontrol after World War II, resulted in a fall in real average hourly earnings from 1944 to 1948. Real net spendable earnings [8] also declined after 1944 and did not regain that level until 10 or 11 years later (see Table 15–3). Nonetheless, in the entire 10-year span after 1939, monetary earnings more than doubled, from $0.63 to $1.38 per hour; similarly, weekly earnings rose from $23.64 to $53.88. Real hourly earnings increased by 29 percent—a greater gain than that during the 1919–1929 period but less than that of the Depression years—and real weekly earnings rose by 32.4 percent. Because of a change in income-tax laws, however, the real net spendable earnings for a worker with no dependents rose by only 17.8 percent. A worker with three dependents, on the other hand, realized a gain in real take-home pay of about 32.0 percent per week.

From 1949 to 1959 hourly earnings continued to climb, reaching $2.19 in the latter year, while average weekly earnings totaled $88.26. A price rise of about 24 percent reduced the real income gain to 29.7 percent for average hourly earnings, about the same amount of change as had occurred in the previous decade of the war period.

Real weekly earnings increased by one-third—more than hourly earnings because the recession in 1949 reduced hours of work. Net real spendable earnings rose 24.5 percent for a worker with no dependents and 22.6 percent for a worker with three dependents.

---

[8] See Appendix following this chapter for definition.

Table 15-3

Gross and Spendable Average Weekly Earnings of Production Workers in Manufacturing, 1939–1977

| Year | Gross Average Weekly Earnings | | Spendable Average Weekly Earnings | | | |
| | | | Worker with No Dependents | | Worker with Three Dependents | |
	Current Dollars	1967 Dollars	Current Dollars	1967 Dollars	Current Dollars	1967 Dollars
1939	$ 23.64	$ 56.83	$ 23.37	$ 56.18	$ 23.40	$ 56.25
1940	24.96	59.43	24.46	58.24	24.71	58.83
1941	29.48	66.85	27.96	63.40	29.19	66.19
1942	36.68	75.16	31.80	65.16	36.31	74.41
1943	43.07	83.15	35.95	69.40	41.33	79.79
1944	45.70	86.72	37.99	72.09	43.76	83.04
1945	44.20	82.00	36.82	68.31	42.59	79.02
1946	43.32	74.05	37.31	63.78	42.79	73.15
1947	49.17	73.50	42.10	62.93	47.58	71.12
1948	53.12	73.68	46.57	64.59	52.31	72.55
1949	53.88	75.46	47.21	66.12	52.95	74.16
1950	58.32	80.89	50.26	69.71	56.36	78.17
1951	63.34	81.41	52.97	68.08	60.18	77.35
1952	67.16	84.48	55.04	69.23	62.98	79.22
1953	70.47	87.98	57.59	71.90	65.60	81.90
1954	70.49	87.57	58.45	72.61	65.65	81.55
1955	75.70	94.39	62.51	77.94	69.79	87.02
1956	78.78	96.78	64.92	79.75	72.25	88.76
1957	81.59	96.79	66.93	79.40	74.31	88.15
1958	82.71	95.51	67.82	78.31	75.23	86.87
1959	88.26	101.10	71.89	82.35	79.40	90.95
1960	89.72	101.15	72.57	81.82	80.11	90.32
1961	92.34	103.06	74.60	83.26	82.18	91.72
1962	96.56	106.58	77.86	85.94	85.53	94.40
1963	99.63	108.65	79.82	87.04	87.58	95.51
1964	102.97	110.84	84.40	90.85	92.18	99.22
1965	107.53	113.79	89.08	94.26	96.78	102.41
1966	112.34	115.58	91.57	94.21	99.45	102.31
1967	114.90	114.90	93.28	93.28	101.26	101.26
1968	122.51	117.57	97.70	93.76	106.75	102.45
1969	129.51	117.95	101.90	92.81	111.44	101.49
1970	133.73	114.99	106.62	91.68	115.90	99.66
1971	142.44	117.43	114.97	94.78	124.24	102.42
1972	154.69	123.46	125.32	100.02	135.56	108.19
1973	166.06	124.76	132.29	99.39	143.20	107.59
1974	176.40	119.43	139.90	94.72	151.25	102.40
1975	189.51	117.56	150.71	93.49	165.33	102.56
1976	207.60	121.76	166.55	97.68	180.03	105.59
1977	226.89	125.01	182.37	100.48	198.55	109.39

Source: U.S. Department of Labor, Bureau of Labor Statistics, *Handbook of Labor Statistics 1975—Reference Edition,* and current issues of *Monthly Labor Review.*

1959–Present

The last two decades have seen an early period of economic stagnation; a period of recovery, sparked first by a major tax cut and then by the Vietnam War, during which an inflationary spiral got underway; and finally a minor recession in 1970–1971 and a major one in 1975. For the decade to 1969, as the economy rebounded under rising war expenditures, average hourly earnings of production workers rose by 45.7 percent. But, as indicated in chapter 14, manufacturing workers lost ground compared to professional, sales, and managerial workers. Moreover, as inflation gained momentum, the real average hourly wage for production workers was kept to a 15.8 percent increase for 1959–1969, or a little more than half the gain of each of the two previous decades and the lowest since the first decade of the present century. In terms of net real spendable weekly earnings, the worker with no dependents gained only 12.7 percent, and the worker with three dependents only 11.6 percent.

Since 1969, the acceleration of inflation during the early 1970s, wage controls in 1971–1973, and periods of unemployment have also held down the rate of wage increases. During the eight years from 1969 to 1977, although the average hourly wage of the worker in manufacturing increased from $3.19 to $5.63, or 76.5 percent, the real wage rose by only 6.8 percent because of escalating prices. The real, net take-home pay per week increased by 8.3 percent for the worker with no dependents and 7.8 percent for the worker with three dependents.

Whether the slowdown in the rate of improvement of the worker's position since 1959 is a temporary departure from long-run trends or represents some more basic change in the structure of the American economy remains unresolved. Three forces are involved in the trend of workers' wages within the economy as a whole. Most fundamental from the point of view of long-run trends is the productivity of the factors of production and how that productivity is shared among them. Second is the importance of short-run changes in price levels and their impact upon labor income. Third is the rate of utilization of the productive resources of a nation. The first two forces are emphasized in this chapter; the last in the next two.

HISTORICAL TRENDS IN LABOR PRODUCTIVITY[9]

Underlying the long-run rise in real hourly earnings in the United States has been the increasing productivity of the worker. With a greater hourly or daily output of goods, the worker can receive more income without adversely affecting the employer's labor costs of production.

From the long-run point of view, the improvement in labor productivity

[9] See Appendix following this chapter for definitions.

reflects three basic developments. First, increased capital per worker has raised both average and marginal productivities of the labor force. Secondly, technological changes have improved the efficiency of the combination of capital and labor in the production of goods. Finally, the quality of labor has been improved through training, upgrading, and education; in other words, there has been an increased investment in human capital.

The difficulties in disentangling these factors result in complex problems of measurement. The first major empirical study of the American production function, based on the theory of marginal productivity, was made by Douglas in 1934.[10] He found that an increase of 1.0 percent in the amount of labor would raise output by about 0.75 percent, while an increase of 1.0 percent in capital would increase output by about 0.25 percent. Believing that payments to the factors of labor and capital tended to approximate their respective marginal productivities, Douglas argued that his data not only supported the fact of division of the national income by returns to capital and labor in approximately the three-to-one ratio, but justified the conclusion that increased amounts of capital had led to higher outputs per man-hour of labor.

Other writers have pointed to the importance of technological change as a cause of increased output per man-hour. In a 1961 study of productivity in the United States, John W. Kendrick attempted to isolate these factors.[11] His findings about the rates of productivity changes since 1889 were conveniently summarized by Fabricant:

> Over the seventy-year period since 1889—the period which has been examined most closely and for which presently available statistics are most adequate—the rate of increase in productivity has been as follows:
>
> Physical output per manhour in the private economy has grown at an average rate that appears to be about 2.4 percent per annum. Comparing output with a measure of labor input in which a highly paid manhour of work counts for proportionately more than a low-wage manhour yields a measure of productivity for the private economy that grew as a significantly smaller rate—about 2.0 percent per annum.
>
> A measure of productivity for the private economy that compares output not only with labor input (determined as before) but also with tangible capital, each weighted by the market value of its services, grew still less rapidly—about 1.7 percent per annum.
>
> All these indexes of productivity in the private economy rose somewhat more rapidly than the corresponding indexes for the economy as a whole, including government, when the usual measurements of government output and input are utilized. For the total including government, productivity rose about 1.5 percent per annum.[12]

[10] Paul H. Douglas, *The Theory of Wages* (New York: Macmillan, 1934).
[11] John W. Kendrick, *Productivity Trends in the United States*, A Study by the National Bureau of Economic Research (Princeton, N.J.: Princeton University Press, 1961).
[12] "Basic Facts on Productivity Change," an introduction by Solomon Fabricant, Ibid., pp. xxxviii–xxxix.

In this study the increase in labor productivity of 2.4 percent per year is a comparison of output and the amount of labor for the private economy—that is, it does not include the government sector. Kendrick estimates that greater skills of the work force account for part of this rise. The rate would be 2 percent if higher-paid labor were counted as proportionately more units of lower-paid labor. The inclusion of capital as an added input of resources further reduces the annual rate of productivity increase to 1.7 percent, reflecting the fact that the productivities of both capital and labor in combination have risen, exclusive of their relative proportions.[13] Since the rise in "capital productivity"—that is, the output per unit of capital input—is less than labor's productivity (about 1 percent, as compared with 2 percent for labor), the combined effect must be somewhere between those figures (in this case, 1.7 percent). The widening of the concept of the measure of productivity to include government inputs and outputs lowers the rate of technological gain still further—not because government is inefficient, but because services cannot be readily produced with less labor.

Among later studies of productivity in the American economy, those of Edward F. Denison also pointed to the importance of improvements in capital, both physical and human, in raising the national growth rates.[14] The average annual growth rate from 1929 to 1969 was 3.3 percent of the total national income. Denison found that 1.81 percentage points, or over half, resulted from the growth of total factor input; the remaining 1.52 points was the rate of increase in output per unit of input. Of the growth of labor inputs—averaging a rate of 1.31—0.41, or nearly a third, represented the contribution of education in enhancing the skills and versatility of the work force. Increased capital inputs were the source of 0.50 points in the growth rate. Advances in technology and knowledge contributed 60 percent to the rise in productivity of all factors. Other influences were improvements in resource allocation and economics of scale.

Denison found considerable variation in the sources of economic growth by subperiods. For the growth of total actual national income, the breakdown by annual rates of change in total inputs and in productivity is shown at the top of page 365.[15] While the data indicate that the high growth rates of

---

[13] The method by which Kendrick converts capital into units of labor in order to calculate this productivity index is, in essence, to estimate the change in capital stock, to calculate a base period rate of return, and to divide the return on capital by the wage rate. For details, see Kendrick, *Productivity Trends*, pp. 34–36 and 51–54. Objections to this procedure are expressed in Stanley H. Ruttenburg, "Director's Comment," Ibid., pp. 224–227.

[14] Denison's first study was *The Source of Economic Growth in the United States and the Alternatives before Us* (Washington, D.C.: Committee for Economic Development, 1962). The data here are taken from *Accounting for United States Economic Growth, 1929–1969* (Washington, D.C.: Brookings Institution, 1974), Table 9–4, p. 127.

[15] Denison, *Accounting for United States Economic Growth*, p. 138.

Period	Growth	Total Factor Input	Output per Unit of Input
1929–1941	2.34	1.26	1.08
1941–1948	3.44	1.92	1.52
1948–1953	4.54	2.95	1.59
1953–1964	3.23	1.30	1.93
1964–1969	4.54	3.08	1.46

national income immediately after World War II and during the 1960s were the result primarily of substantial increases in the inputs of labor and capital, there was a significant drop in productivity during the period from 1964 to 1969. At the time, it appeared that this stemmed from cyclical influences. With the beginning of the recession in 1969, there was a decline in the "intensity of demand," as Denison termed it, which had the effect of causing productivity to fall. The reason is that during prosperity, when capital equipment and labor are more efficiently employed, productivity tends to increase, but during recessions, when capital equipment and labor are not used at capacity, productivity tends to decline or to rise less rapidly.

Since the 1960s there has been striking evidence of a continuing slowdown in productivity. The Council of Economic Advisers in 1977 estimated that the rate of productivity growth in the private sector of the American economy from 1966 to 1976 was only about two-thirds of the growth rate from 1948 to 1966. They attributed the slowdown to a lower growth rate of capital investment per worker, to the entrance of a large number of inexperienced workers into the labor force, and to greater employment in service industries, where productivity gains are less easily achieved.[16] An additional factor is that productivity in industries that are highly dependent upon scarce natural resources will also decline as output is expanded. Although it has not yet been fully established, there is evidence that this situation already characterizes such basic industries as agriculture and energy. These trends in the productivity rate help to explain the lowered growth of real earnings over recent years. Whether the slowdown in productivity is permanent or temporary, and whether actions can be taken to prevent its continuation, are crucial issues for the future.

LABOR COSTS AND THE PRICE LEVEL

A comparison of earnings and productivity yields a measure of labor costs of production. If money earnings rise more rapidly than labor productivity, then the firm's labor costs per unit of output will be increased. If in the short run

---

[16] Council of Economic Advisers, *Economic Report of the President, 1977* (Washington, D.C.: U.S. Government Printing Office, 1977), pp. 45–48.

firms attempt to cover changes in costs by the price of the commodities they sell, then movements of costs are related to movements in the price level. However, the relationship between costs and prices may be viewed in two ways: a rise in money earnings at a rate more rapid than labor productivity may be held the cause of an increase in the price level, or increasing demand for goods may be considered the significant factor that lifts prices and in turn raises costs. The problem of evaluating these relationships first arose in the late 1950s, when the real value of money earnings to workers increased moderately from 1949 to 1959 while the labor cost per unit of output to employers showed a significant rise. These changes led to a controversy about the relationships of unions to labor costs and of labor costs to the level of prices that became especially heated during the more severe inflation of the 1970s. Did strong unions "cause" higher prices (cost-push inflation), or did higher demand lead to higher prices and hence to higher wages (demand-pull inflation)? Or was it possible that other special factors were more relevant?

Cost-Push Inflation

The concept of cost-push inflation is based on the assumption that unions can, through collective bargaining, initiate a wage increase that would otherwise not be forthcoming. This ability of unions to succeed in raising wages beyond the "natural" level presumably rests upon their power, through the threat of strikes, to command the higher wage level. Under such circumstances the employer's only alternative is to raise prices in order to recoup losses. If, because of the increased product price, the public chooses to buy less, unemployment among the workers in the firm will result. Unions can moderate this employment effect by organizing all firms within a given industry, thus removing the lower-priced competition.

If the union is able to increase wages and prices generally throughout a totally organized industry, it is argued that an employment effect, however modified, may nevertheless occur. If unions in other industries are not also demanding higher wages, thereby promoting a general rise in the wage level, a wage push in one or a few industries may lead to a dampening of employment opportunities in those industries. If the government is not willing to increase the supply of money in circulation in order to support a higher general level of prices, wages in nonunionized sectors of the economy will fall, resulting in a "distortion" of the wage structure and a misallocation of resources but no general rise in the price level.

When the government is willing to increase the flow of money in order to avoid the Scylla of unemployment or wage distortion, the economy may still be caught up in the Charybdis of inflation. Then, as unions attempt to raise their money wages, they will discover that the rising price level prohibits the translation of their monetary gains into real improvements in goods and services.[17] Inflation can be dangerous for several reasons. A continued rise in the price level of a country undermines its economic position with respect to other nations of the world. Depreciation of a nation's currency may lead to a flight of capital, a drain on monetary reserves, and an unwanted contraction of production and employment. As import prices rise due to the fall in value of the monetary unit, and if unemployment mounts, serious political repercussions may follow. Inflation also has a serious impact on various groups within a nation: while some, like debtors and profit receivers, may gain, others, including creditors and those on fixed incomes, suffer from the depreciation of the monetary unit. For these reasons most governments concerned with minimization of the effects of economic change upon the social and political system tend to urge the maintenance of a stable price level as a prime public goal. To those who subscribe to the union-power cost-push theory of the price level, achievement of that goal without reducing union power is an impossibility.

Demand-Pull Inflation

The alternate approach to price and wage levels within an economy is that an increase in aggregate demand will initially raise prices and profits. As businesses seek to produce more goods to meet rising demands, they will in turn bid for factors of production. In competitive markets, prices of products and factors will not rise if the elasticity of supply curves is high, since additional units of factors of production will be available at going wage levels. High elasticity of supply would be characteristic of an economy at less than full employment. As rising aggregate demand continues to reduce unemployment, however, the elasticity of supply will fall; that is, it will be necessary to raise factor prices to recruit more factors of production to produce more goods. With the economy near full employment, and with both prices and costs rising, it may not be obvious to the lay observer whether costs are pushing or following prices upward. While businesses may justify a price increase because of a rise in costs, and while workers may demand higher wages because prices are higher, the underlying situation is held to be the pull of rising aggregate demand.

Prices and wages may rise before full employment is reached even where firms or workers acting though unions have no market power because of bottlenecks or because the supply of various commodities and factors fails to increase uniformly as the economy moves toward full employment. Certain types of labor or capital goods may be in especially short supply, and their

---

[17] The use of escalator clauses in union contracts does not necessarily overcome the problem raised here, since the question is whether unions can capture excess gains, not whether they can maintain the "normal" rate of increase in wages. If all contractual incomes were to be "indexed"—that is, tied to a particular index of consumer prices—then the effects of price changes on income would show up as gains or losses in noncontractual shares, such as profits.

prices will necessarily rise before those of other factors. The bottleneck pattern during a particular business expansion need not be the same as that in others, because the composition of the additional aggregate demand by products and services may differ from one situation to another and because the supply characteristics of special factors of production may differ.

Whether a factor of production is in short supply because of a bottleneck or because of a generally inflationary situation at or near full employment, its price will rise, and the increase cannot be confined to changes in its average physical productivity.

The Phillips Curve

The relationship between the extent of unemployment in the labor market and changes in wages and prices was originally described by a curve named for its author, A. W. Phillips. Phillips showed with data from the British economy for a period of nearly a hundred years that annual wage increases tended to vary inversely with the rates of unemployment. The curve was convex to the origin: it was nonlinear in that wage increases were greater as the economy approached full employment. The present-day version of the curve, however, follows Paul A. Samuelson and Robert M. Solow, who examined American data in a similar way but added an important new variable. Finding also that wage increases were greater the lower the rate of unemployment, they stated that if the rate of change in labor productivity were taken into account, the wage change could be directly converted into a price level change. Curve A in Figure 15–1(A) illustrates the final result. As the unemployment rate, Ur, is reduced, the price level increases by a larger percentage. The intermediate steps by which the reduction in unemployment causes wages to rise relative to productivity are assumed but not shown.

The Phillips curve symbolized to many what came to be considered one of the major unresolved dilemmas of modern industrial economies: the impossibility of having full employment without inflation. The curve seemed to impose the harsh choice between living with unemployment in order to avoid inflation and accepting inflation as a cost of full employment. Although there was a range of possibilities between the two extremes—a little less inflation but a little more unemployment, for example—the outlook was not a rosy one. Still, many believed that a particular combination of inflation and unemployment could be decided upon and achieved through appropriate public monetary and fiscal policy. Determining the desired point on the curve was a matter of the value judgments not only of the policy makers but more fundamentally of the public, which expressed its views through the political process.

But more recent studies reveal that the relationships among money wages, unions, productivity, prices, and unemployment are more complex than those

A. Phillips Curve Shift

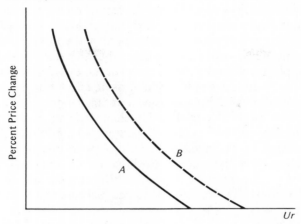

B. Inflationary Acceleration

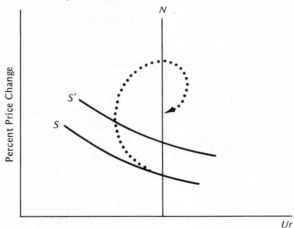

FIGURE 15-1   Phillips Curves

S ans S' are short-run Phillips curves.
N is the long-run, natural unemployment rate.
The dotted line shows the loop of year-to-year changes.

represented by the Phillips curve. In the first place, the curve was an average of wage/employment relationships over many years and could not be expected to give precise dimensions of changes for any specific period. Moreover, the curve reflected past policies, or lack of them, and could not therefore be used to forecast the effect of events and policies in new situations. For example, if aggregate demand is expanding (in a demand-pull manner), its composition may differ from one business cycle to another so that different sets of bottlenecks may be encountered, giving rise to different rates of price increases. If the particular motivation is wage-push because of union aggressiveness, it is possible that the sets of economic constraints that influence union power may also vary from one period to another. The curve "blurred" the distinction between demand-pull and cost-push inflation.[18]

Even recognizing the curve's limitations, the course of prices, wages, and rates of unemployment during the recession of the early 1970s was surprising and unexpected. With the combination of rising rates of unemployment and inflation—a situation that became known as stagflation—the older view of the Phillips curve as a stable relationship characterizing the American economy had to be abandoned. There developed two schools of thought. One denied the existence of the traditional Phillips curve except as a short-run, transient phenomenon; the other claimed that institutional and other factors had combined to shift the curve outward so that the economy had to face an even more painful dilemma in its choice between more inflation and unemployment.

In the view of those who held the first position, such as Milton Friedman, the Phillips curve describes what occurs as a nation attempts through an expansionary monetary and fiscal policy to move toward full employment in the short run but not in the long run.[19] The first effects of government attempts to reduce unemployment are that wages will begin to rise faster than productivity; the result is that prices move upward. But workers are disappointed when their increase in money wages is in part nullified by higher prices. They then demand even higher wages, with the same consequences of rising prices. As workers anticipate higher prices, the result is a wage-price spiral, an accelerating rate of wage changes and price inflation. Depending on the actions of the monetary authorities, the upward movement of both prices and wages can continue or can turn into a depression, with rising unemployment and falling prices and wages. In the latter case, the short-run curve becomes a loop, to be repeated when the process of artificial stimulation of the economy begins anew. See Figure 15–1(B). According to this analysis, the long-run curve becomes a vertical line indicating what is called the "natural" rate of unemployment—namely, the rate that would persist under equilibrium conditions in the long run, with the actual change in the price level dependent on monetary policy. Friedman recommends that monetary authorities increase the money supply each year only enough to ensure the maintenance of a stable price level, given the average annual rate of growth of goods and services, and not attempt to reduce unemployment from its natural rate. The result would be self-defeating.

Other analysts believe that the Phillips curve, while still a viable tool of analysis, has shifted outward, as shown by B in Figure 15–1(A). One explana-

[18] James Tobin, "Inflation and Unemployment," *American Economic Review,* 62 (March 1972), 2.

[19] Milton Friedman, "The Role of Monetary Policy," *American Economic Review,* 58 (March 1968), 1–11.

tion is that this has happened in part because of demographic changes in the composition of the unemployed. With a labor force that included proportionally more teenagers—whose unemployment rates are higher—one would expect that the average unemployment rate, given a specific level of economic activity, would also be higher. Hence the official unemployment rate was becoming a misleading indicator and the shift of the Phillips curve was more apparent than real.

A second, somewhat similar, explanation was the theory of structural transformation, meaning that the patterns of the demands for workers were becoming increasingly divergent from the patterns of skills of the work force. The outward shift of the curve represented the failure of markets to bring about rapid adjustments of supplies to demands. (These two points of view will be examined in detail in the following chapter.)

A third explanation of the outward movement of the Phillips curve invokes the theory of cost-push inflation. It emphasizes the market power of oligopolistic industries, in which unions are able to raise wages, a process that provides a rationale for firms to raise prices. While the general level of unemployment in the economy as a whole, as indicated on the Phillips curve diagram, can affect bargaining power, this line of argument stresses instead the market power of the firms (and unions) themselves. Critics of this explanation offer three counterarguments. One is that industry concentration and union power, while perhaps creating price and wage differentials with respect to competitive markets, have not been increasing in recent years, so that the shift in the Phillips curve remains unexplained. Another, the cyclical movement of union-nonunion wage differentials—examined in the previous chapter—would imply a diminution in the cost-push effect of unions during a business boom, for example, in the late 1960s, when the Phillips curve was believed to be shifting outward.[20] A final argument is that commodity price rises, such as those of American grain and oil from the Middle East, which played a significant role in the inflation of the early 1970s, had no relation to union wage action in the domestic economy.

Nonetheless, the question of the relationships of wages, productivity, and prices in an economy characterized by economic concentration and collective bargaining in its basic industries has not been satisfactorily answered, and the possibility of cost-push inflation cannot be entirely written off.

As noted in chapter 14, econometric studies have shown profits to be a significant economic variable in explaining wage changes. This relationship would seem to support the demand-pull explanation of wage increases. But to the extent that profits are greater in the concentrated than in the nonconcentrated industries, the implication could also be that it is oligopolistic market

---

[20] See, for example, Charles C. Holt, C. Duncan MacRae, Stuart O. Schweitzer, Ralph E. Smith, *The Unemployment-Inflation Dilemma: A Manpower Solution* (Washington, D.C.: The Urban Institute, 1971), esp. pp. 56–57; and James Tobin, "Inflation and Unemployment," pp. 13ff.

power that enables unions in those industries to bargain for, and obtain, wages higher than would be obtainable in other industries. A study of wages in manufacturing industries from 1950 to 1970 showed that profits had a greater impact on wage changes than did the unemployment rate.[21] An earlier econometric analysis of the effect of unions on the Phillips curve confirmed the general impression that strong unions were able to win higher wages for a given increase in profits, whether viewed in absolute or relative terms,[22] but the most strongly organized industries were also the most concentrated. This investigation concluded that the period of the guideposts—the early 1960s, when the United States first introduced a peacetime program, albeit modest, for price and wage restraint—had been successful in cutting wage increases below those that otherwise would have been expected to occur, and that the greatest effect was in those industries most strongly organized and, by implication, the most concentrated. But other studies stressed the role of oligopolistic pricing practices and deemphasized the power of unions to push up prices. In an empirical investigation of profit margins of firms in concentrated industries, Wachtel and Adelsheim showed that margins have increased during recessions since World War II because firms with market power typically seek a given target profit rate. When sales fall off with a business decline, the profit margin and the price markup are perversely raised. Unemployment, in short, can create pressures for price inflation rather that do not stem from union wage power at all.[23]

THE RECORD OF RECENT YEARS

The issue of cost-push inflation cannot easily be resolved. Since World War II, when the controversy became important, there have been six business

---

[21] William A. Howard and N. Arnold Tolles, "Wage Determination in Key Manufacturing Industries, 1950–70," *Industrial and Labor Relations Review*, 27 (July 1974), 543–559.

[22] Gail Pierson, "The Effect of Union Strength on the U.S. 'Phillips Curve,' " *American Economic Review*, 58 (June 1968), 462. The period covered by this analysis is 1953 to 1966.

[23] The authors present evidence that the perverse response has also been affecting industries of medium and low concentration. See Howard M. Wachtel and Peter D. Adelsheim, *The Inflationary Impact of Unemployment: Price Markups During Postwar Recessions, 1947–70*, Paper No. 1, Prepared for the Joint Economic Committee, Congress of the United States (Washington, D.C.: U.S. Government Printing Office, 1976), esp. ch. 4.

For other works that stress the primary role of monopolistic pricing practices, see L. Godfrey, "The Phillips Curve: Incomes Policy and Trade Union Effects," in H. G. Johnson and A. R. Nobay, eds., *The Current Inflation* (New York: St. Martin's, 1971), pp. 99–124. Among those who view unions' actions as a defense against rising prices (and tax increases), which diminish the workers' take-home pay, are Dudley Jackson, H. A. Turner, and Frank Wilkinson; see their *Do Trade Unions Cause Inflation?*, University of Cambridge, Department of Applied Economics, Occasional Paper 36 (Cambridge University Press, n.d.).

cycles: the first, from the end of the war to the boom in 1948 and the recession of 1949–1950; the second, through the high levels of output during the Korean hostilities to the recession of 1955–1956; the third, to the prosperity of 1957 and the sharp recession of 1958; the short fourth cycle, from 1958 to a peak early in 1960 and the recession of the fall of 1960 and of 1961; a long fifth cycle stimulated by the Vietnam War, which lasted until the recession of 1969–1971; and the sixth cycle, beginning in 1970, which ended in the recession of 1974–1975, the worst of the postwar period.

In the first cycle there can be no doubt that the boom reflected demand-pull factors. In the 1946–1948 period, the Consumer Price Index rose about 30 percent in two years, or more than 1 percent a month. This sharp price rise resulted from the removal of wartime price controls, the release of pent-up demands for consumer goods, a substantial rise in consumer credit, and sharply increased investments by businesses in new plants and equipment. Wages lagged despite unions' efforts, including strikes, to keep up with living costs. In the recession of 1949 the level of consumer prices dropped slightly, heralding the end of the immediate postwar boom. Earnings were maintained, however, despite the rising rate of unemployment. This was not the result of union resistance, because strikes were also fewer. Since both union and nonunion wage rates seemed to be inflexible downward, employers instead cut overtime, reduced hours of work, and laid off workers.

During the second cycle demand again expanded, but governmental spending for military items in the Korean situation was the initiating factor. From June 1950 to early 1951, when wage and price controls were imposed, the wholesale price index rose by about 16 percent and the Consumer Price Index by 8 percent. But the latter continued to rise until 1954, while the former began to fall and reached a low point in 1955. Average hourly earnings, on the other hand, had by 1952 begun to climb more rapidly than consumer prices. In view of these facts, it appears that the experience up to this time was quite consistent with the traditional demand-pull inflation hypothesis.

Beginning in 1955, however, several new cyclical features appeared and gave support to the cost-push hypothesis. Earnings during the period 1955–1958 increased by 13.4 percent, while consumer prices not only followed them during the upswing of the cycle but continued to advance during the recession of 1958, for a total gain of about 8 percent. This occurred during a boom marked by a relatively low increase in output and the existence of unused plant capacity.[24]

Not all the factors supported the cost-push analysis of the rise in prices, however. The component of the price index that revealed the greatest rise was the cost of services and shelter (rent), areas in which union pressures were

[24] See summary of the period in *Staff Report on Employment, Growth, and Price Levels*, Prepared for Consideration by the Joint Economic Committee, Congress of the United States, December 24, 1956, ch. 5.

minimal. On the other hand, the wholesale price rise was concentrated in metals and machinery, where unions were strong. One study found three-fourths of the 9 percent rise in this index due to metals—primarily iron and steel products, and machinery and metal products.[25] The importance of iron and steel in postwar inflation was borne out in another study. Steel prices rose 37 percent from 1951 to 1958, in comparison with 9 percent for all other commodities except farm and food products.[26] The direct and indirect impact of the increases in steel prices was held to account for 40 percent of the entire rise in wholesale prices from 1951 to 1958, and for 50 percent of the increase during 1953–1958.

The mechanism of inflation in steel prices was cost-push, with both the steel companies and the steelworkers' union using their market power: the strongly organized union was not able to cause the rise in cost and prices by itself.

The short fourth cycle, from 1958 to 1961, was characterized by only a limited recovery, as unemployment declined only to 5.5 percent; wholesale prices remained constant and consumer prices rose by slightly more than 1 percent per year. In the long 1959 steel strike the relationship of productivity and wage increases became a matter of major concern. The issue was finally resolved, after the strike had been halted by a Taft-Hartley Act injunction, with an increase of about 3.5 percent a year in wage costs, more or less consistent with productivity changes.

The boom of the 1960s began with an unemployment rate of 6.7 percent (in 1961) and a determination by the Kennedy administration to "get the economy moving again." Sensitive to the possibility of cost-push inflation, the Council of Economic Advisers, under the chairmanship of Walter Heller, recommended in 1962 that negotiated wage settlements, except in exceptional circumstances, should be guided by the average annual rise in productivity per man-hour of about 3.2 percent. In addition to this guideline for wage settlements, the council initiated a proposal for a major tax cut, carefully designed to increase aggregate demand and spur the economy to full employment. After this was adopted in 1964, under President Johnson, the unemployment rate began to fall, as predicted, but the unforeseen defense expenditures that soared with increasing involvement in the Vietnam War quickly converted the expansion into an inflationary boom. In the demand-pull inflation of 1961–1969, unemployment fell from 6.7 to 3.5 percent, while the rise in consumer prices was 22.8 percent, with 10 percent coming in the last two years. In the face of these inflationary pressures, the guideline policy of voluntary restraint on wages collapsed in 1966. Average hourly earnings rose 42.1 percent over the eight-year period, but after 1965 higher con-

[25] Ibid., p. 123.
[26] Otto Eckstein and G. Fromm, *Steel and the Postwar Inflation*, Study Paper No. 2. Prepared for the Joint Economic Committee, Congress of the United States, 1959.

sumer prices and taxes held the real net spendable earnings of workers in manufacturing to no gain.[27]

It was the recession of 1969–1971 that renewed fears of cost-push inflation and led to the introduction of the nation's first peacetime compulsory controls of wages and prices. In those two years, the unemployment rate jumped (on an annual basis) to 5.9 percent, the Consumer Price Index rose 10.7 percent, and average hourly earnings increased 13.2 percent. In this stagflation situation, President Nixon, on August 15, 1971, imposed a 90-day wage-price freeze and a variety of other measures designed to prevent further deterioration of the nation's balance of payments and stimulate domestic industry and investment.[28]

Union-negotiated wage increases were significant in this recession. While unemployment was rising, the average increase in wages in new contracts (for the first year) was nearly 9 percent in 1969 but about 12 percent in 1971. Although this suggests cost-push inflation, one study points out that these increases "had their roots in and were primarily the outgrowth of previous trends in prices and other wages."[29] In the late 1960s wage changes under long-term bargaining agreements with various terminal dates meant that while some workers could adjust their bargaining demands to new wage-price situations, others had to put up with rising prices and attempt to catch up later, when their contracts expired. The key was partly the expectation of future inflation but also, and more urgently, the recovery of lost real earnings and the reestablishment of former relative wage levels. One of the objectives of wage control was to prevent such leapfrogging.

The period of mandatory controls consisted of the initial freeze and Phase II, which ended in January 1973. Under Phase II the wage guidelines limited wage increases to 3 percent for productivity gains plus an additional 2.5 percent to offset an increase in consumer prices. Although the latter was a goal to be reached by the end of 1972, with measures restricting price increases—a goal which was not achieved—the rationale of the 5.5 percent wage guideline was that if the wage-price spiral were to be broken, limitations on wages should be imposed first. The controls turned out to be effective: rises in wages and prices were moderated, and the unemployment rate slowly fell to below 5 percent in early 1973.

---

[27] Take-home pay statistics of manufacturing workers are used in preference to those of the private economy because there has been less change in the relative importance of full- versus part-time workers than in other sectors such as trade.

[28] For a summary of the August 15, 1971, decisions and their background see Council of Economic Advisers, *Economic Report of the President, 1972* (Washington, D.C.: U.S. Government Printing Office, 1972), pp. 65ff.

[29] Marvin Kosters, Kenneth Fedor, and Albert Eckstein, "Collective Bargaining Settlements and the Wage Structure," Industrial Relations Research Association Series, *Proceedings of the Spring Meeting, 1973*. Reprinted from the *Labor Law Journal* (August 1973), p. 518.

With the end of Phase II and substitution of voluntary restraints under Phase III,[30] the economy was startled by a rapidly accelerating inflation. From January 1973 to January 1975, when business activity had already turned downward in its sixth post–World War II recession, the Consumer Price Index rose 22.2 percent, its food component 32.9 percent. As gross weekly earnings in manufacturing increased only 13.5 percent, the average worker suffered a decline of over 7 percent in real weekly earnings; a family with three dependents lost over 8 percent in net real spendable earnings. The main causes of this period of inflation were (1) the explosion of commodity prices, especially of grain prices, as a result of the poor harvests of 1974, and of oil prices, which quadrupled due to actions by the Organization of Petroleum Exporting Countries (OPEC); and (2) the international monetary crises, which had been fueled by the exportation of inflation during the Vietnam War period, when the dollar was overvalued, and which led to higher prices for imports after the dollar's depreciation in 1971–1973. Economists disagreed about which cause was most important, but they all agreed that wage-push was not the reason.

One conclusion drawn from the post–World War II record is that union-induced wage and price increases are less important than war expenditures and their legacy in boosting the price level. In such inflationary spirals workers suffer a lag in real, take-home pay; where inflation appears to be wage-induced, the price rises are not explosive.

INCOMES POLICIES

It had long been considered a basic theme of national wage and price level policy that three long-run possibilities were open to any economy: (1) if wages rise as rapidly as productivity, the price level can remain stationary; (2) if wages rise more rapidly, the price level will rise; and (3) if wages remain constant or increase less rapidly than productivity, then the general level of prices can decline, with the result that the general public will be able to share the gains resulting from technical progress through lower prices. The more acceptable objectives have been either a slightly rising or a constant level of prices. Advantages include equity considerations between debtor and borrower, and the stimulative effects of rising prices on business investment.

But with the demands for full employment that swept across the Western

---

[30] The Economic Stabilization Act of 1971, which gave legislative authority for wage and price controls, expired on April 30, 1974. Phase III maintained the wage guidelines of Phase II but on a self-administered basis. On June 13, 1973, a temporary price freeze was imposed, and in August 1973, Phase IV, a further modification of price regulations, was instituted.

nations after World War II—to be promoted by expansionary government fiscal and monetary policies—an inflationary potential became locked into the economy, as we have seen from the Phillips curve analysis. To avoid both inflation and unemployment, a number of Western European nations instituted what have become known as incomes policies. These measures seek to induce different price and wage decisions from those that otherwise would be made. Their primary assumption is that by controlling wage behavior so that wages increase only as much as productivity does (or by not much more), price rises can be checked; this benefits all classes, and the nation can gain the advantages of greater employment and output from existing resources. The issue of incomes policies raised the question of the involvement of the government as a third party in what were previously private decisions of firms, individual workers, and unions engaged in collective bargaining.

Attempts to Institute Controls

In certain respects the issue of governmental intervention was less agonizing in some European countries than in the United States. In Europe there was a greater acceptance of unionization by employers and the public. Also, with a history of labor parties, unions sought political leadership on the grounds that they spoke in the best interests of their country. These factors meant that the required incomes policies for the control of inflation could be readily integrated into broad social and political programs. In some countries voluntary agreements on wage and price restraint were worked out on a tripartite basis between national federations of employers, unions, and the government; in others, wage and price restraints were more legalistic and imposed unilaterally.[31] Nonetheless, because of the importance of collective bargaining, governments were inclined to accept greater union influence in broad areas of social and economic policy in exchange for the unions' surrender of their freedom in wage negotiations. The term "social compact" has been used to describe such an agreement that entailed expansion of governmental benefits for labor on the one hand and union pledges of moderate wage demands on the other.

In the United States, where unions have not sought to create a political party with its own social and economic objectives, the institutional base for incomes policies has been different. Fearful that their long and difficult

[31] For a systematic review of European experience, see Lloyd Ulman and Robert J. Flanagan, *Wage Restraint: A Study of Incomes Policies in Western Europe* (Berkeley: University of California Press, 1971). For a comparison of U.S. and European situations, see Derek Robinson, "The International Scene and Controls—A Comparative Overview," in *Proceedings of the Industrial Relations Research Association, 1973*, (Madison, Wis.: Industrial Relations Research Association, 1974), pp. 32–39.

struggles to win the right to free collective bargaining might be abruptly ended by governmental controls, unions have been reluctant, except in times of national emergency, to accept wage and price control programs. There have been five such programs: during World War II (1942–1945); in the immediate postwar conversion period (1945–1946); in the Korean War period (1951–1952); under the Kennedy-Johnson administration (1962–1966); and during the Nixon administration (1971–1974).[32] In the World War II and Korean War periods, labor was willing to accept third-party intervention. But during the reconversion period of 1945–1946, when the price level exploded, unions believed that they had no choice but to protect their members' economic interests with independent economic actions, including strikes (1946 was the biggest strike year in American history). The Labor-Management Conference called by President Truman in the fall of 1945 to achieve wage and price stability broke down. During the period of voluntary measures of price and wage restraint in the 1960s, it was again labor unrest, as prices began to rise, that led to the unions' unwillingness to adhere to the guidelines.[33] Under the Nixon controls, four of the five members of the tripartite Pay Board, led by President George Meany of the AFL-CIO, walked out in March 1972 in protest against the 5.5 percent standard for wage increases on the grounds that it was too low. Union leaders also complained that wage control formulas, arrived at without labor participation, applied only after delays, and administered without the guarantees of due process and appeals procedures, would undermine the institutions of democratic society.[34]

Some Difficulties

While it is undoubtedly true that labor bore the greater burden of the effects of the Nixon income policies, the conclusion is that unless all groups are willing to accept the restraints of wage-price interventions, the consensus essential for a workable program could be shattered. Advisory committees on labor-management relations were set up not only under President Truman

[32] Milton Derber, "The Wage Stabilization Program in Historical Perspective," in Industrial Relations Research Association, *Proceedings of the 1972 Spring Meeting,* reprinted from the *Labor Law Journal* (August 1972), pp. 453–462; Craufurd D. Goodwin, ed., *Exhortation and Controls: The Search for a Wage-Price Policy, 1945–1971* (Washington, D.C.: Brookings Institution, 1975).

[33] The case that broke the guideline involved the International Association of Machinists (IAM) and five airlines (Eastern, National, Northwest, Trans World, and United). Despite intervention by President Johnson, the wage settlement was 4.3 percent.

[34] The leading case was the contract of the West Coast longshoremen, which provided for a wage increase in excess of the guideline but reflective of the productivity changes agreed to in the negotiations. Although the Pay Board had permitted settlements to reach 7 percent in exceptional cases, approval of the contract's wage gain of more than twice that amount meant the end of fixed ceilings.

but also under Presidents Kennedy, Nixon, and Ford. In general, none could agree on basic principles for controls.[35] But it should be pointed out that these were appointed, ad hoc committees and not the type of representative organizations that would be necessary politically if a controls program were to be formulated.

Other difficulties with incomes policies arise out of the problems of adapting the control restraints to underlying shifts in market forces of supply and demand. While a free market does not necessarily bring about a reordering of labor supplies to new demands quickly and without social costs, a bureaucratic mechanism may be even more insensitive to the desirability of such shifts.[36] Most wage and price control systems attempt to allow for exceptions to an overall formula of wage control in order to remedy specific injustices, or to allow special adjustments—for example, the payment of higher wages to ease recruitment problems. But administrative rules and procedures can create obstacles that delay their implementation.

The history of incomes policies also raises doubts as to the adequacy of measures of productivity as a guide to wage changes. The productivity rates of 3.2 and 3 percent, laid down as the average, annual long-run rates of productivity changes under the Kennedy-Johnson guidelines and under Phase II of the Nixon controls, were often falsely assumed to be based on precise definitions and calculations unanimously agreed to by "experts." On the contrary, a specific rate will vary depending on the scope of the industries considered, the period of time used in its calculation, and the level of capacity operation of the economy. In scope, productivity rates can be calculated for the nonprivate sector, with or without agriculture, for manufacturing and/or selected other industries, or for the entire economy, including services and governments, where measures of output often cannot be quantified. Historical productivity rates depend on the number of years included in the base period and on whether that base is continuously recalculated; in addition, there is the question of whether a historical rate is appropriate for a current year

---

[35] One important exception was the development of a controls program in the construction industry. With John T. Dunlop as an intermediary, construction unions and contractors accepted wage stabilization formulas and a dual organization of bipartite craft dispute boards and a tripartite Construction Industry Stabilization Committee (CISC) established by President Nixon's Executive Order No. 11588 on March 29, 1971. Satisfactory settlements along with a gradual elimination of "leapfrogging" wages were achieved over its three-year life span. See Neil de Marchi, "The First Nixon Administration: Prelude to Controls," in Goodwin, *Exhortation and Controls*, esp. pp. 331–334.

[36] For a discussion of these and related issues arising from wage and price controls, see George P. Shultz and Kenneth W. Dam, "Reflections on Wage and Price Controls," *Industrial and Labor Relations Review*, 30 (January 1977), 139–151; Arnold R. Weber and Daniel J. B. Mitchell, "Further Reflections on Wage Controls: Comment," *Industrial and Labor Relations Review*, 31 (January 1978), 149–158; and George P. Shultz and Kenneth W. Dam, "Reply," ibid., pp. 159–160.

because short-run productivity changes do not necessarily coincide with long-run averages. As productivity tends to decline when an economy approaches full utilization of capital equipment, and rises during recoveries from recessions, a long-run average is not likely to be appropriate as a guide to wage increases for any specific year.[37]

Where the wage guideline is composed of both a productivity standard and a cost-of-living standard, as in the case of Phase II controls, the assumption is that the worker should be entitled to a real wage gain per year equal to greater productivity. But this makes the problem of wage control more complex. There is the necessity of deciding what index will be used to measure changes in costs of living, whether past or anticipated rises in prices should be grounds for allowing wage offsets, and whether the living cost allowance should be deliberately restrictive on the grounds that sacrifices must be imposed to restrain inflationary forces. None of these questions can be resolved by a mechanical formula: on the contrary, they raise political issues of the highest order.

Finally, there is the question of the applicability of a measure, once agreed to. A guideline represents an average of different rates of productivity change in different industries and firms. In a competitive economy, one would expect that in the long run those industries with higher rates of productivity advance would lower prices, and those with low productivity gains would be forced to raise their prices; through competition in the labor market, all workers—irrespective of the productivity of the industry in which they were employed—would eventually gain by the general advance in the nation's technological capabilities. To apply such principles to pricing decisions in particular industries requires detailed knowledge of an industry's cost structure and productivity changes. Under Phase II it was found that while attempts to measure productivity changes within specific firms were unsuccessful, a control system could be devised that relied on a designation of allowable costs and on specific limitations on profit margins. It focused on the large firms and unions for

---

[37] On the problems, both technical and political, of establishing productivity standards, see D. Quinn Mills, "The Problem of Setting General Pay Standards: An Historical Review," *Proceedings* of the Industrial Relations Research Association, 1973 (Madison, Wis.: Industrial Relations Research Association, 1974), pp. 9–16. On the cyclical behavior of productivity, see J. Randolph Norsworthy and Lawrence J. Fulco, "Productivity and Costs in Perspective," *Monthly Labor Review*, 98 (November 1975), 44–48.

It should be noted that although the guideline policy under President Kennedy was introduced in 1962, no single rate of productivity change was made explicit. The 3.2 percentage rate, based on a five-year annual average increase of output per man-hour, was included in a table in the 1964 Report of the Council of Economic Advisers but not mentioned in the text. With the periodic recalculation of the rate, the five-year average had risen to 3.6 in 1966, but a political decision was made to hold to the well-publicized 3.2 measure. See William J. Barber, "The Kennedy Years," and James L. Cochrane, "The Johnson Years," in Goodwin, *Exhortation and Controls*, pp. 159–63, 203, 243, and passim.

three reasons: these were the heart of the cost-push forces in the economy; because of their greater visibility, successful results would have an important psychological effect on smaller firms and unions; and the limited resources for administering controls would be most effectively employed.

Despite limitations, there is evidence that wage and price control measures, whether voluntary or compulsory, have had some restraining effects on wage and price behavior in the United States.[38] They have not, however, been able to cope with strong demand-pull inflationary pressures, and they have not curbed the exercise of market power of large firms in oligopolistic industries. The basic issue of inflationary pressures in the modern economy is so far unresolved.

SUMMARY

The long-run upward trend of real wages in the United States has been well documented, but there is evidence of a slowdown in the rate of increase since the 1950s—especially since 1969, when inflationary forces began to gather momentum.

The rise in labor productivity accounts for the long-run improvement in the economic position of American workers. In terms of macroeconomic analysis, the question is whether, if wages rise more rapidly than productivity, the increase in labor costs will lead to a rise in the general level of prices. The wage-push hypothesis is that this will occur. The demand-pull approach to inflation is that the culprit is too much aggregate demand. The modified Phillips curve attempts to describe what are considered stable relationships among price changes, unemployment, and labor costs (that is, wages and productivity), but the problems faced by policy makers show that those relationships are not stable.

In analyzing the causal factors of the worsening trade-off between inflation and unemployment, many writers point to the cost-push of unions, to oligopolistic pricing practices, or to both. This analysis has served as the theoretical foundation for the wage-price guidelines of the Kennedy-Johnson era, the price controls of the Nixon administration, and incomes policies generally. Although the effect of controls in restraining inflation is somewhat ambiguous, there can be little doubt that they had a detrimental impact on the position of the worker.

[38] Studies of these issues include George L. Perry, *Unemployment, Money Wage Rates and Inflation* (Cambridge, Mass.: M.I.T. Press, 1966); John Sheahan, *The Wage-Price Guideposts* (Washington, D.C.: Brookings Institution, 1967); Jerry E. Pohlman, *Economics of Wage and Price Controls* (Columbus, Ohio: Grid, Inc, 1972); John Kraft and Blaine Roberts, eds., *Wage and Price Controls: The U.S Experiment* (New York: Praeger, 1975); Arnold R. Weber, *In Pursuit of Price Stability: The Wage-Price Freeze of 1971* (Washington, D.C.: Brookings Institution, 1973); and Robert F. Lanzillotti, Mary T. Hamilton, and R. Blaine Roberts, *Phase II in Review, The Price Commission Experience* (Washington, D.C.: Brookings Institution, 1975).

DISCUSSION QUESTIONS

1. Changes in real wages in the long run are related to trends in labor productivity in the economy as a whole. Would you expect a similar long-run relationship to be found between real wages and productivity in specific industries? Why or why not?
2. To what factors can you attribute the slowdown in labor productivity that has apparently been occurring in the American economy since the 1960s? Do you believe that these factors represent permanent or temporary limitations in a long-run upward growth rate?
3. Workers have generally been losers in terms of real wages during periods of rapid inflation. What are the advantages and disadvantages of indexing workers' money wages?
4. Using the usual version of the Phillips curve, how would you represent (a) a period of stagflation, (b) a decline in the level of labor productivity, (c) an acceleration of inflationary expectations, (d) an increase in union bargaining power?
5. What reasons were advanced for the introduction of wage-price guidelines during the Kennedy-Johnson years? Was the system of controls set up by President Nixon in 1971 justified on the same grounds?
6. One of the problems in developing an incomes policy is how to determine the rate of labor productivity growth. Why is this important, and why is it hard to determine?

SELECTED READINGS

For studies of productivity and wages, see Edward F. Denison, *Accounting for United States Economic Growth, 1929–1969* (Washington, D.C.: Brookings Institution, 1974); H. M. Douty, "The Slowdown in Real Wages: A Postwar Perspective," *Monthly Labor Review*, 100 (August 1977), 7–12; and John W. Kendrick, *Productivity Trends in the United States* (Princeton, N.J.: Princeton University Press, 1961).

The following present different approaches to the relationships between wages and inflation: Charles C. Holt et al., *The Unemployment-Inflation Dilemma: A Manpower Solution* (Washington, D.C.: Urban Institute, 1971); Dudley Jackson, H. A. Turner, and Frank Wilkinson, *Do Trade Unions Cause Inflation?* University of Cambridge, Department of Applied Economics, Occasional Paper 36 (Cambridge, England: Cambridge University Press, n.d.); H. G. Johnson and A. R. Nobray, eds., *The Current Inflation* (New York: St. Martin's, 1971); and George L. Perry, *Unemployment, Money Wage Rates and Inflation* (Cambridge, Mass.: MIT Press, 1966). The monetarist position on inflation can be found in Milton Friedman, "The Role of Monetary Policy," *American Economic Review*, 58 (March 1968), 1–17; and in Edmund S. Phelps, *Inflation Policy and Unemployment Theory: The Cost-Benefit Approach to Monetary Planning* (New York: Norton, 1972).

For views on wage and price guidelines during the Kennedy and Johnson years, see George P. Shultz and Robert Z. Aliber, eds., *Guideposts, Informal Controls and the Market Place* (Chicago: University of Chicago Press, 1966); and John Sheahan, *The Wage-Price Guideposts* (Washington, D.C.: Brookings Institution, 1967). References to the wage-price controls of the Nixon administration are included in footnote 38.

APPENDIX

Wages and Labor Costs: Definitions and Problems of Measurement

The word "wages" has a variety of meanings. Most commonly it is understood to refer to the price of work presented as a monetary rate for a unit of time or a given amount of output—in other words, as a time rate or a piece rate. "Wages" is also used to designate the amount earned in a certain period of time—an hour, a week, or a year. Such earnings are of course not identical with the price of a unit of the worker's labor, or the wage rate, but relate also to the amount of work performed and the extent of premium pay.

Neither wage rates nor earnings are wholly satisfactory indications of either the benefit of wages received by the worker or the cost of labor to the employer. The worker considers certain monetary fringe benefits as well as the nonmonetary rights and privileges of the employment relationship. To employers, the labor cost of a unit of output is more important. Labor cost is affected by workers' productivity as well as by the wage rate.

Earnings

In the United States the best statistical information about wages involves earnings. Relatively few data are available on monetary wage rates as such. "Earnings" are defined as the gross monetary payment for current labor services for a particular period of time. Earnings data in the United States are obtained either from establishments or from households. The two types of information must be appraised differently. We consider first establishment data. Most important is the earnings series collected monthly by the United States Bureau of Labor Statistics (BLS) for most nonagricultural industries from a sample of firms. The data, which in the case of manufacturing provide a long historical series, refer to production workers only. The BLS also collects information on certain occupational wages from firms in various industries and locations.

The basic statistical information obtained from firms on the earnings of production workers consists of the number of workers employed during the same week (L), the number of man-hours worked (MH), and the total wages earned (W). From these reports, the ratio W/L gives average weekly earnings, W/MH the average hourly earnings, MH/L average weekly hours of work.

Several types of adjustments are often made with the available figures. Since the data include payments for overtime work, a series known as "straight-time average hourly earnings" is calculated by deflating the average hourly earnings by the extent of overtime work during any given week. As the result of such an adjustment, straight-time earnings are more indicative of changes in wage *rates* than are gross earnings.

Another adjustment is made to obtain *real* earnings, or a measure of the amount of goods and services that can be purchased with a given wage. To measure the change in real wages from one period to another, the money earnings are divided by the index of change in the prices of goods and services. For example, if money earnings double from $50 to $100 a week while the price level rises by 50 percent, earnings are $66.67 in constant dollars ($100/1.5), an increase of 33.3 percent.

The Consumer Price Index (CPI) published by the Bureau of Labor Statistics is undoubtedly the most satisfactory obtainable indication of current prices and is widely used to measure changes in the price level. But it must be interpreted carefully. The Bureau of Labor Statistics itself points out that the index cannot be used indiscriminately as a measure of the "cost of living." Rather it is a measure of the average change in prices of goods and services purchased by the families of wage earners and clerical workers in urban areas. The index uses an average "market basket" of goods and services derived from a study of expenditures of a sample of moderate-income urban families, and it is weighted by the relative importance of certain goods and services in those baskets. It cannot be considered applicable to any one family, since the composition of expenditures naturally varies with income level, family size, and tastes; the index is not meant to be representative, for example, of single persons, higher-income families, rural families, or elderly couples. Moreover, since expenditure studies are expensive and cannot be made frequently, they become out of date in terms of the relative weights given various products during the time between such studies. Also, new goods that become available after the expenditure study has been made and changes in quality of goods are difficult to take into consideration. A deterioration in quality will result in an underestimation of a price rise, and hence in an overestimation of a real wage increase. Improvements in quality, on the other hand, produce underevaluations of real wage increases.

Beginning in 1978, the Bureau of Labor Statistics publishes two consumer price indices. The old one is now known officially as the Consumer Price Index for Urban Wage Earners and Clerical Workers. The additional one, covering a broader range of families, is called the Consumer Price Index for All Urban Consumers. Whereas the first was representative of about 45 percent of the total noninstitutional population, the second has a coverage of approximately 80 percent. Rural families and military personnel are the principal groups whose expenditure patterns are not reflected. Both of the new indices use weights drawn from expenditure studies of 1972–1973; both use 1967 as the base year.

A third type of adjustment is often made in original earnings statistics to measure take-home pay, or net earnings after the deduction of federal income and Social Security taxes. The series, called "net spendable average weekly earnings," is calculated both for a worker with no dependents and for one with three dependents. "Real net spendable average weekly earnings" have been corrected for changes in the CPI. It should be noted that this measure of earnings does not purport to identify family earnings. The data from which the series is derived provide no information on the number of workers within the family unit, nor on whether the family worker holds two or more jobs.[1]

In calculating any one of these series of earnings, special attention should be given to the statistical problem of aggregation, since the BLS earnings series is an average of many firms and industries. If the number of workers in a high-wage industry increases and other factors remain equal, the national average earnings figure will rise; if it decreases, the average will fall. While this may seem highly reasonable, it leads to the possibility that a change in earnings may occur even if there is no change in wage rates. The BLS has introduced a new Hourly Earnings Index (HEI) that adjusts straight-time earnings for employment shifts among industry groups. The HEI comes closest of all indices to a measure of wage *rate* changes. It applies to production and nonsupervisory employees in the private nonfarm economy.[2]

Households are the second source of data on earnings. In this case earnings are classified by the residence of the worker rather than by the location of the firm. Information concerning income of households from all sources for a given period, such as the previous year, is regularly obtained from the U.S. Census and through the Current Population Survey sample. Since May 1967 a special question has been asked of wage and salary workers concerning "usual weekly earnings" from their principal job before deductions.

The chief advantage of data collected from households is that the personal characteristics of the wage earner and his or her family can also be obtained. Thus sex, race, family size, education, union membership, and similar factors can be directly related to earnings. This method also avoids double counting of individuals; in the establishment reports an individual who holds two jobs would be reported twice. The disadvantage of household reports is their lack of accuracy. Unlike reports from firms on payrolls, household responses are subject to bias and unintentional errors. Designations of occupations and industries are likely to be imprecise.

Labor Cost and Labor Productivity

Employers examine wages in terms of labor cost. Because they are primarily concerned with the cost of producing goods or services, they want to know not only the wage rate of the worker but also his or her output. Labor cost per unit of output is the ratio of the cost of labor to labor productivity. More specifically, the relationship is described in terms of the following symbols:

W, total money earnings

MH, total man-hours

---

[1] For the formulas used in calculations, see John F. Early, "Factors Affecting Trends in Real Spendable Earnings," *Monthly Labor Review*, 96 (May 1973), 16–19.

[2] A comparison of different measures of wages for the period 1964 to 1970 has been made by Thomas W. Gavett, "Measures of Change in Real Wages and Earnings," *Monthly Labor Review*, 95 (February 1972), 48–53. Also reviewed is a series called "real compensation per man-hour for the total private economy." This comprehensive series is unadjusted for overtime and employment shifts and includes payments to supervisory workers, the self-employed, farm employees, and private household workers. Estimates of fringe benefits are also taken into account.

O, output in units
W/MH, average hourly earnings
O/MH, output per man-hour (that is, average labor physical productivity)
MH/O, unit labor requirements (that is, average number of man-hours per unit of
    output)
W/O, labor cost per unit of output
The equation

$$\frac{W/MH}{O/MH} = \frac{W}{MH} \cdot \frac{MH}{O} = \frac{W}{O}$$

shows the relationship between average hourly earnings, W/MH; productivity, O/MH (or its inverse, unit labor requirements, MH/O); and labor costs, W/O. For example, a rise in earnings accompanied by the same relative increase in productivity (or decrease in unit labor requirements) will cause no change in labor cost per unit of output. If the rate of increase in productivity (or of decrease in unit labor requirements) is greater than the rise in earnings, labor costs will fall. If productivity does not rise as rapidly (or if unit labor requirements do not fall as rapidly) as earnings, labor costs will rise.

The definition of labor productivity used above, O/MH, is simply the relationship of physical output and labor inputs. An increase in labor productivity can result from improved efficiency of workers or from many other causes, such as an increase in capital per worker, improved technology, a better flow of material, and better management. The contrast in productivity between a pick-and-shovel worker and the operator of a power shovel, measured in cubic feet of earth moved per hour, should dispel the idea that greater worker effort necessarily lies at the heart of increased productivity. An index of labor productivity does not imply that labor produces all of the output, but simply relates an output resulting from many factors of production to only one of the inputs. A productivity measure relating output with any other units of input—for example, kilowatt hours of electricity or dollars of capital—could be made just as easily and logically.

Several problems in measuring labor productivity should be noted at this point. First, the unit of man-hours does not reflect changes in the quality of labor. For instance, if the operator of the power shovel in the above example is more skilled than the man with the hand shovel, perhaps his hour of labor should be regarded as more important than that of the unskilled digger. While the solution to this problem depends upon the objective of a particular productivity measure, it is apparent that if one hour of his labor is counted as more than one hour of unskilled labor, the long-run rise in productivity would be less than reported. The difference between the two levels of productivity could be attributed to investment in human capital—that is, to the costs related to the training and education of the worker in acquiring the quota skill—but most indices of labor productivity do not provide for this type of adjustment.

In most indices of productivity, labor inputs are measured only by man-hours of direct production workers, while the amount of indirect labor—clerical, administrative, or professional—is usually not included, largely because of a lack of a regular reporting procedure. Since the relative amount of indirect labor in manufacturing in the United States has been steadily increasing, productivity series based only on production workers tend to overstate the rise in productivity and hence understate labor costs.

A second problem relates to measures of output. While physical output can be counted, the constancy of quality of units produced and product mix must be considered; otherwise, the usual productivity and labor cost data will be misleading. For example, if no consideration is given to improvements in the quality of output, then productivity is understated and labor cost overstated. Product mix refers to the relative importance of one type of output to another in a multiproduct firm or industry, where the different products require different amounts of labor. This is a problem of aggregation, similar to that discussed above.

A final problem is measuring output related to those services that are essentially labor. Savings in the amount of labor per unit of service performed may not be possible except with a decline in the quality of the service. For example, a teacher may increase "productivity" by teaching 50, 100, or 1,000 students, rather than 20 students, but whether each student in the class will continue to receive the same quality of teaching services remains questionable. The problem of evaluating services in labor productivity studies has not been satisfactorily resolved. Perhaps increasing productivity in the services should be viewed simply as an undesirable goal because it decreases quality. From the point of view of the entire economy, the growth of services relative to the production of goods would imply a slowing up of the rate of productivity increase for the economy as a whole.

16

Unemployment

Its Costs, Characteristics, and Causes

One of the great social and political changes among industrial societies in the last four decades has been a shift in the public attitude toward unemployment. No longer is mass unemployment considered a private affair. Rather, the recognition that it creates urgent economic and political problems for much of the population has forced governments, despite lapses, to accept full-employment measures as a matter of high policy. Unemployment is in many respects the central economic problem of modern industrial nations.

Several reasons account for this. First of all, the sweep of industrialization has drawn workers away from farms and transformed them into wage and salary earners dependent on jobs in the market place. Secondly, although modern industry yields higher incomes, its fluctuations can bring greater economic hardship when unemployment strikes. Finally, it has gradually been realized that depressions are not natural phenomena, like droughts or floods, and that the basic economic causes of unemployment are subject to control.

The Depression of the 1930s first brought acceptance of these new attitudes. Although a good part of the present population of the United States never experienced the Great Depression, the general social attitude is shown by the fears of unemployment that mount with every business downturn, by the recognition that the costs of unemployment are serious for specific groups or localities whether the rate of unemployment for the nation is high or low, and by the dominance of unemployment issues in national elections held in times of recession.

With the downturn of the economy beginning in 1974, the nation entered its most serious recession since World War II. Although the official unemployment rate in 1975 of 8.5 percent was below the levels of the Great Depression—in 1933 about one-fourth of the labor force was unemployed—it was high enough to center attention again on some of the basic facts, theories, and policies for the mitigation of unemployment.

THE COSTS OF UNEMPLOYMENT

Unemployment imposes economic and psychological costs on the individual who is out of work and his or her family and social costs on the community and nation as a whole. However, unemployment of one particular type, although not without cost, can serve to make possible the adjustments necessary for a healthy, dynamic economy. This unemployment, known as *frictional*, is associated with the movement of workers to jobs in an economy that has relatively high levels of employment. Specifically, it includes the unemployment of workers who have left one job voluntarily and are looking for another, and also the involuntary separations from jobs through discharges and layoffs initiated by employers adjusting to changes in demand or to new production and work methods. In the latter case, a sufficient number of employment alternatives must be available elsewhere for those willing and able to work so that unemployment periods are short. Frictional unemployment is also associated with the movement of workers in and out of the labor force, especially with new entrants who shop in the market before finding jobs.

Unemployment associated with the failure of aggregate demand to provide a sufficient number of adequate employment opportunities for those who can and wish to work is the type that emerges in full force during serious recessions. Loss of a job with no alternative in sight after a lengthy search can mean hardship and perhaps disaster to the worker, for wages are usually the only source of income the family has. During the recession year of 1975 nearly 8 million workers were unemployed during the average week, but this did not include the number of those at part-time jobs who for economic reasons were not able to work more, nor those discouraged workers (excluded from the labor force totals) who wanted to work but believed that no jobs were available. Adding these to the reported unemployed, the adjusted total for 1975 becomes almost 12.7 million, or 13.5 percent of the adjusted civilian labor force (including the discouraged workers).[1] (See Table 16–1.) This adjusted unemployment rate was twice the rate of 1969.

The seriousness of joblessness to any individual or family rises sharply with its duration. Unemployment of short duration is characteristic of times of relatively full employment. In 1969, for example, when the reported unem-

---

[1] The Joint Economic Committee of the Congress of the United States uses a measure consisting of the unemployed who seek full-time jobs, half of the part-time job seekers, half of those working part-time for economic reasons, and the discouraged workers. Called the comprehensive unemployment rate and calculated on the basis of reported labor force, the measure reached nearly 12 percent in 1975. See the committee's *1976 Joint Economic Report* (Washington, D.C.: U.S. Government Printing Office, 1976), pp. 49, 50. "Hidden unemployment" in the sense used in chapter 3 above—that is, individuals not in the labor force even as discouraged workers who would be drawn into labor markets as the market improved—is not included in these measures.

Table 16-1
Unemployment Adjusted for Part-Time and Discouraged Workers, 1969–1975
(Numbers in thousands)

	Civilian Labor Force (Adj.)[a]	Total (Reported) Unemployed	Rate of (Reported) Unemployment (% of labor force)	Part-Time Unemployed[b]	Discouraged Workers[c]	Total Adjusted Unemployed	Percent of Labor Force (Adj.)[a]
1969	81,307	2,831	3.5	2,056	574	5,461	6.7
1970	83,353	4,088	4.9	",443	638	7,169	8.6
1971	84,887	4,993	5.9	2,675	774	8,442	9.9
1972	87,307	4,840	5.6	2,624	765	8,229	9.4
1973	89,393	4,304	4.9	2,519	679	7,502	8.4
1974	91,697	5,076	5.6	2,943	686	8,705	9.5
1975	93,695	7,830	8.5	3,748	1,082	12,660	13.5

[a] Civilian labor force plus discouraged workers.
[b] Persons on part time for economic reasons.
[c] Persons not in the labor force who want work but believe they cannot get a job.

Source: Employment and Training Report of the President, 1976.

Table 16-2
Duration of Reported Unemployment, 1969–1975 (Numbers in thousands)

	Civilian Labor Force	Unemployed Total	%[a]	Under 5 Weeks Total	%[a]	5–14 Weeks Total	%[a]	15 Weeks and Over Total	%[a]
1969	80,733	2,831	3.5	1,629	2.0	827	1.0	375	0.5
1970	82,715	4,088	4.9	2,137	2.6	1,289	1.5	662	0.8
1971	84,113	4,993	5.9	2,234	2.7	1,578	1.8	1,181	1.4
1972	86,542	4,840	5.6	2,223	2.6	1,459	1.7	1,158	1.3
1973	88,714	4,304	4.9	2,196	2.5	1,296	1.5	812	0.9
1974	91,011	5,076	5.6	2,567	2.8	1,572	1.8	937	1.0
1975	92,613	7,830	8.5	2,894	3.1	2,453	2.7	2,483	2.7

[a] Percent of civilian labor force.
Source: Employment and Training Report of the President, 1976.

ployment rate was 3.5 percent, nearly three out of five (57.5%) of the 2.8 million unemployed were out of work for less than five weeks; only 375,000 workers were unemployed 15 weeks or more. The number has risen during the 1970s with the recession of 1970–1971, with the less than satisfactory recovery in 1972–1973, and with the recession beginning in 1974. In 1975, 2.5 million persons were out of work for 15 weeks or more (see Table 16–2). This was nearly a third (31.7%) of the reported number of unemployed.

Unemployment compensation payments are important in easing the financial burdens of job loss, but coverage is incomplete and benefits are low compared to regular earnings. In 1975 some 4 million workers a week received benefits under regular state programs; under emergency acts passed in late 1974, another 2 million workers were able to receive additional benefits.[2] Altogether, more than 24.5 million persons received unemployment benefits at some time during the year. Not every unemployed person received benefits; moreover, about one out of every seven wage and salary workers was not covered by any program for unemployment compensation.

The amount of benefits per week under state laws is calculated on the basis of the wages earned by the worker in "covered" employment but is limited by certain minimum and maximum amounts. Although formulas vary widely by states, the general objective is to provide a 50 percent replacement of the wage. Because maximum limits as laid down by the states have not kept up with changes in wage levels generally, the actual replacement value of the benefit has been falling in recent years, especially for those who have higher earnings. In 1975 the average state benefit for workers fully unemployed was

[2] The Emergency Unemployment Compensation Act of 1974 extended benefit rights to a total of 65 weeks for those under state laws who had exhausted their benefits; the Emergency Jobs and Unemployment Assistance Act of 1974 provided benefits for certain groups of workers who were not covered by the state program. For further discussion of these acts, see chapter 18.

Table 16-3
Distribution of Family Units by Size of Liquid Asset Holdings,[a] 1965 and 1971

	1965	1971
All family units	100%	100%
Own no assets	20	16
Own assets	80	84
$1-$199	17	14
$200-$499	11	12
$500-$1,999	21	24
$2,000-$4,999	14	13
$5,000-$9,999	9	9
$10,000 and over	8	12
Median holdings	$575	$700
Median holdings in 1965 dollars[b]	$575	$545

[a] Includes checking and savings accounts, and nonmarketable U.S. savings bonds.
[b] Based on the Consumer Price Index.
Source: Statistical Abstract of the United States, 1974.

about $70 a week, or about 43 percent of the average weekly earnings of workers in private, non-agricultural jobs. This figure, however, overstates the replacement value. Workers typically do not file for benefits immediately upon becoming unemployed; when they do file there is a waiting period before benefits are paid; they are not compensated for the loss of fringe benefits; and they may remain unemployed after exhausting their benefits.[3]

Although unemployed workers may lessen their hardships by selling or borrowing on already accumulated assets such as savings accounts, bonds, insurance policies, automobiles, or real property, the average wage earner has little protection in terms of liquid assets from loss of income for more than a month or two. Data from 1971—the most recent available—are instructive. As shown in Table 16-3, 16 percent of all family units in 1971 owned no liquid assets; 42 percent held less than $500. The median holdings were $700, up in dollars from the median liquid assets of $575 in 1965 but actually 5 percent less in real terms because of the fall in the value of money by more than a fourth during that six-year period. Furthermore, by drawing on their assets or credit, workers incur capital drains that can only be replaced slowly over later years of work and savings—assuming that they become employed without subsequent layoffs.

[3] It is sometimes charged that unemployment benefit payments prolong the period of unemployment by reducing the incentive to find work. For example, see Martin Feldstein, "The Unemployment Caused by Unemployment Insurance," Industrial Relations Research Association, *Proceedings, 1975* (Madison, Wis.: Industrial Relations Research Association, 1976), pp. 225-233. Undoubtedly a weekly benefit may have a negative effect on a worker's efforts to search for a new job, but studies find the effect to be minimal. *Employment and Training Report of the President, 1976*, p. 52.

As any particular period of unemployment lengthens, workers will begin to make radical adjustments in their living habits. They may seek other types of work, usually those requiring lesser skills and training and yielding lower wages. If they decide to acquire the necessary skills for other, better-paying jobs, they will be forced to invest their time and energies when the burden of the costs of training are greatest. A progressive deterioration of normal levels of living can affect workers' efficiency and undermine their health and that of their families. It can produce anxiety and demoralization.

It is not only the individual worker and his or her immediate family that feel the effects of unemployment. If the unemployment level within a community increases, welfare costs rise, perhaps along with the incidence of illness, crime, and juvenile delinquency.[4] Increased financial outlays to allay distress force either a reduction in other types of government expenditure or an increase in taxes. Even if taxes are unchanged, the burden on the employed taxpayers will rise as those families with lowered incomes fail to pay their former share. Other social costs may indirectly affect the flow of public revenues and expenditures. For example, prolonged localized unemployment can cause deterioration of real property assets because repair and maintenance expenditures are postponed. Values of neighboring properties are then likely to be similarly affected, and investments for renovation or new construction may be shifted elsewhere.

During a recession fewer goods and services are produced on a national level. The Great Depression of the 1930s brought a total loss of goods and services about equal to the total gross national product of the entire year of 1941. But output not produced is, of course, gone forever, and there was no way of using the unemployment of the 1930s to produce military strength in the 1940s, even though the lost value of output was roughly the equivalent of the entire cost of the military production during World War II.

In the recession of the middle 1970s, it has been estimated that the losses in output, in terms of the gross national product, were some $400 billion in constant 1972 dollars for the period 1973–1975. In 1975, the GNP gap, as measured by the difference between actual and potential GNP as a percentage of potential, was 12.4 percent.[5] Although the measure of the potential

[4] For these social costs, see M. Harvey Brenner, *Estimating the Social Costs of National Economic Policy: Implications for Mental and Physical Health and Criminal Aggression,* a study prepared for the Joint Economic Committee of Congress (Washington, D.C.: mimeographed, 1976). Using data on unemployment, prices, and per capita income from a 34–year period (1940 to 1973), Brenner found that changes in the unemployment rate had the greatest impact of the three variables on seven indicators of stress: total mortality, homicide, suicide, cardiovascular-renal disease mortality, cirrhosis of the liver mortality, total state imprisonment, and state mental hospital admissions. The author emphasizes that the econometric analysis does not demonstrate causation but does establish a statistical linkage.

[5] Joint Ecomomic Committee, Congress of the United States, *The 1976 Joint Economic Report,* pp. 5, 31. Among the factors considered in estimating potential GNP are

and attainable gross national product at any given time is inexact and subject to differences in judgment, there is little doubt that the economic inefficiencies of unemployment are far more serious than any misallocation of national resources through union or governmental wage actions.

Unemployment has political effects on both the domestic and the international level. Radical movements of either the left or the right may seize upon economic crises in a struggle for power. The rise of the Nazis in Germany during the 1930s is a grim reminder of how a social system collapsing under mass unemployment and economic frustration can be transformed into a reign of terror. The current struggle by the United States to maintain political and economic leadership in a world where old patterns of power have been challenged by communist bloc nations and by the emergence of new, developing nations in Africa and Asia is clearly affected by the level of unemployment. Any sign of rising domestic unemployment can seriously undermine the prestige, power, and economic leadership of a nation in world affairs. The relationship between unemployment at home and economic leadership is especially simple and direct: when incomes fall, a nation's imports are reduced, and this immediately affects the level of income of the exporting country. If it in turn reduces its imports, a chain reaction of contractions can spread from one country to another, its effect depending upon the extent of participation in foreign trade.

At one time it may actually have been believed that mass unemployment was necessary or desirable in eliminating the unfit, in correcting an unbalanced economy, or in promoting industrial discipline. More recently, some have promoted rising unemployment as a cure for inflation. But such a policy is a clumsy blunderbuss, as dangerous to its user as to others. The costs of unemployment to individuals and society at large are much too great to be risked or tolerated. Excess unemployment can hardly be considered the most desirable device for correcting the ills of overbuilding in one industry or another, for promoting the spirit of workmanship, or for reducing inflationary pressures endemic in the world economy.

---

the size of the labor force, average hours worked, and productivity (output per man hour).

An early attempt to calculate the relationship between the unemployment rate and potential GNP was made by Arthur Okun in his "Potential GNP: Its Measurement and Significance," *Proceedings of the Business and Economics Statistics Section of the American Statistical Association*, 1962, pp. 98–104. His estimate was that an additional 1 percent of unemployment led to a 3.2 percent GNP gap. George L. Perry later recalculated the relationship to show that the increasing proportion of women and young people among the unemployed meant less lost production because of their lower productivities. To Perry, 1 percent unemployment now reduced GNP by 2.7 percent. See his "Labor Force Structure, Potential Output, and Productivity," *Brookings Papers on Economic Activity* (Washington, D.C.: Brookings Institution, 1971), no. 3, pp. 533–565.

CHARACTERISTICS OF THE UNEMPLOYED

The level of unemployment does not affect all classes of workers equally. At any national level the incidence of unemployment will differ significantly according to age groups, sex, race, types of industry, occupation, and geography. The characteristics of the unemployed will depend upon the point of time for analysis, because the "profile of the unemployed" varies with the stage of the business cycle, the season of the year, and the structure of the labor force as affected by long-run growth trends. Since no cycle, season, or year is an exact repetition of another, certain variations in the composition of unemployment must be expected, depending upon the peculiarities of whatever period is examined.

In the six postwar recessions, the peak unemployment rates by quarters have ranged from a low of 6.0 percent in both the 1954 and 1971 recessions to a high of 8.7 percent in 1975. However, there have been marked changes in the incidence of unemployment during these recessions. As shown in Table 16–4, the unemployment rates for teenagers of both sex has been stead-

Table 16–4
Unemployment Highs in Postwar Recessions

Age and Sex	1949 IV	1954 III	1958 II	1961 II	1971 III	1975 II
	Unemployment Rates (seasonally adjusted, quarterly averages)					
All workers	7.0	6.0	7.4	7.0	6.0	8.7
Both sexes, 16 to 19 years	15.0	13.7	16.3	16.3	17.0	20.2
Men, 20 to 24 years	11.1	11.0	13.7	11.9	10.3	14.7
Men, 25 years and over	5.9	4.9	6.2	5.5	3.5	5.7
Women, 20 to 24 years	8.6	7.8	9.9	11.0	9.1	12.8
Women, 25 years and over	5.3	4.8	6.2	6.1	5.0	7.4
	Percent Distribution					
Total unemployment	100.0	100.0	100.0	100.0	100.0	100.0
Both sexes, 16 to 19 years	15.1	14.1	13.9	16.1	25.5	22.0
Men, 20 to 24 years	12.1	8.9	10.3	10.0	12.8	13.4
Men, 25 years and over	50.5	49.6	48.7	44.2	29.2	30.3
Women, 20 to 24 years	5.4	5.0	5.0	6.0	9.3	9.6
Women, 25 years and over	16.9	22.3	22.1	23.7	23.3	24.6

NOTE: These are the actual highs of the seasonally adjusted unemployment rates and do not necessarily reflect the National Bureau of Economic Research troughs. Detail may not add to totals because of rounding.

Source: *Manpower Report of the President, 1975.*

ily increasing, reaching 20.2 percent in the 1975 peak quarter. Although the trends upward in unemployment rates of young men and women 20 to 24 years of age have been less steady, the rates of 14.7 and 12.8 percent in 1975 were higher than in any of the previous five recessions. For women 25 years of age and over, the 1975 rate was also the highest, but for men 25 years and over the rate was less than in two previous recessions, those of 1949 and 1958.

Age

In terms of the composition of the unemployed, the most significant trend has been the increasing number of those under 25 years of age. Teenagers 16 to 19 years of age comprised only some 14 percent of the unemployed in the recessions of the mid-1950s, but 22 percent in the 1975 recession. When this group is added to the unemployed of both sexes age 20 to 24, the total is 45 percent. In other words, nearly half the unemployed at the high point of 1975 were under the age of 25, in contrast to the 28 percent during the recessions of the mid-1950s.

Higher unemployment among youth appears to reflect two factors. First, the underlying demographic shift resulting from the baby boom after World War II led to a flood of youthful entrants into the labor market in the late 1960s and early 1970s. This alone would have meant that one could expect a rising proportion of youthful workers among the unemployed. But the increasing incidence of unemployment among this group, taken with the relatively low incidence among older workers (especially males 25 years and over), indicates a second factor: namely, the lack of employment opportunities in primary labor markets. The fact that youths are forced more and more into jobs in the secondary labor markets—where advancement possibilities are poor, training requirements are minimal, and unemployment is more likely—has led some observers to underscore the seriousness of the effects of a recession precisely at the time when a new generation of young workers was entering the labor market in larger numbers than ever. The inability to acquire skills and work experience, together with the lack of incentives for labor market participation and career advancement, can have serious implications for the nation's future.[6]

In analyzing the unemployment rates of older workers, one must distinguish between those 55 to 64 years of age and those 65 and over. The latter group have lower participation rates and, when unemployed, are likely to look for part-time rather than full-time jobs to supplement their savings, Social Security benefits, and other pension payments. The earnings limitation on those between the ages of 65 and 72 who wish to receive their full Social Security

---

[6] Peter B. Doeringer and Michael J. Piore, "Unemployment and the 'Dual Labor Market,'" *The Public Interest*, 38 (winter 1975), 74–75.

benefit payments undoubtedly reduces their labor force participation rate and inhibits the search for jobs. Even so, unemployment rates of this age group (both men and women) have been somewhat higher than those of the 55-to-64 age group since the early 1960s; previously the relationship of unemployment rates had been reversed. Although low in comparison with the overall average, the unemployment rates of those in the 55-64 age group tend to run higher than in the age groups of 25 to 44. Despite the fact that older workers are more likely to be protected by seniority during times of downturn, once they lose their jobs they have a more difficult time finding new ones and hence remain unemployed longer.

Race

Unemployment data by race show persistently higher rates for "Negro and other races" as compared with whites. From 1960 to 1976, the black employment rate has been twice or more the white rate except in four years (see Table 16–5). (It should be noted that in three of those years the black unemployment rate increased more than the white rate in absolute amounts.) Unemployment rate differentials occur in each of the major age-sex categories,

Table 16–5
Unemployment Rates by Race and Their Ratios, 1960–1976 (Annual averages)

| Year | Unemployment Rate | | Ratio: Negro and Other Races to White |
	Negro and Other Races	White	
1960	10.2	4.9	2.1
1961	12.4	6.0	2.1
1962	10.9	4.9	2.2
1963	10.8	5.0	2.2
1964	9.6	4.6	2.1
1965	8.1	4.1	2.0
1966	7.3	3.3	2.2
1967	7.4	3.4	2.2
1968	6.7	3.2	2.1
1969	6.4	3.1	2.1
1970	8.2	4.5	1.8
1971	9.9	5.4	1.8
1972	10.0	5.0	2.0
1973	8.9	4.3	2.1
1974	9.9	5.0	2.0
1975	13.9	7.8	1.8
1976	13.1	7.0	1.9

Source: U.S. Department of Labor, Bureau of Labor Statistics.

but the ratios of black to white are somewhat higher for men than for women, and most pronounced among teenagers. In 1973 the jobless rate for teenagers who were "Negro and other races" was 30.2 percent, or 2.4 times the white teenage rate of 12.4 percent. During the 1974–1975 recession, unemployment rates for young black males rose for certain age groups to nearly 40 percent.

Racial differentials in unemployment rates can be attributed to several factors. One is the concentration of black employment in industries and occupations in secondary labor markets, which are especially prone to employment fluctuations. Other factors are less education, probably a lower quality of education (although measures are not wholly satisfactory), discriminatory practices, and residential location. The last factor is significant for those blacks in big-city ghetto areas where commuting costs impose barriers to many suburban opportunities, and where alternative housing facilities near those opportunities are limited.[7] If one uses the census designation of poverty areas in metropolitan areas as indicative of ghettos, it is there that the highest unemployment rates in the nation are found: in 1975, the unemployment rate for all "Negro and other races" was 17.3 percent, and for teenagers alone 45.5 percent.[8]

Marital Status and Sex

Married men have a lower unemployment rate than single men, even of the same age. The lower rate probably reflects the pressure of greater family responsibilities on married men to obtain and to hold a job. One measure of the seriousness of a recession is the extent to which their unemployment rate rises. As shown in Figure 16–1, the rate for married men (wife present) reached its lowest point (1.5%) in 1969, doubled in the recession year of 1971, and then shot up rapidly in 1975 (standing at 5.1%).

In terms of hardship, unemployment undoubtedly has the greatest effect upon households headed by women. For female heads of family, unemployment rates are higher in good as well as bad times. Their unemployment rate in 1975 was nearly 10 percent. Among female-headed families, half of the women are divorced or separated, 37 percent are widowed, and 13 percent are unmarried. With dependent children to support, high child-care costs, and low earning potential, women who head families find it difficult to secure an

---

[7] It is erroneous to assume that all workers living within a metropolitan area have equal access to all jobs. Commuting costs, the extent of automobile ownership, the particular network of public transit facilities, and scheduling problems result in the creation of many submetropolitan labor markets. See Everett J. Burtt, Jr., "Workers Adapt to Plant Relocation in Suburbia," *Monthly Labor Review*, 91 (April 1968), 1–5.

[8] The poverty area classification is based on the 1970 designation of an area in which 20 percent or more of the residents were poor in accordance with the income standard adopted by a federal interagency committee in 1969. These standards vary by family size, composition, and residence (farm or nonfarm).

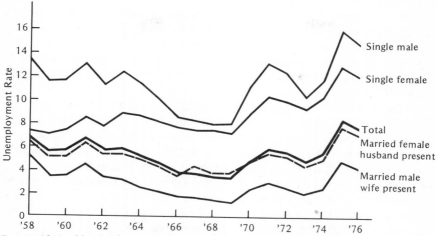

FIGURE 16-1 Unemployment by Sex and Marital Status

Source: *Employment and Training Report of the President, 1977.*

adequate income even in good times. In fact, in 1972, when one out of every 10 male-headed families had an income below the poverty line, more than five out of 10 female-headed families fell in that category. Many women are employed in part-time and secondary market type jobs that are particularly subject to high labor turnover. In 1973, of the 4.2 million women heads of families who worked or looked for work, 17.1 percent experienced some unemployment. Of these about one-fourth did not work during the entire year, while another fourth had a total unemployment of over six months.[9]

Industry and Occupation

The incidence of unemployment varies greatly among industrial and occupational groups. Classified according to the "last job held," workers in goods-producing industries reach higher unemployment levels during recessions than those in service industries, and blue-collar workers are affected more severely than those in white-collar occupations. Among industries, construction workers have borne the higher rate of unemployment. In 1975 nearly one in five construction workers (18.1%) was unemployed; the rate has regularly been about twice the national average. Between 9 and 12 percent of the nation's total unemployment over the years since 1948 has consisted of unemployed construction workers, even though they represent only about 5 percent of the civilian labor force. Although some part of this unemployment results from the intermittent, seasonal nature of the industry itself, construc-

[9] *Manpower Report of The President,* Submitted to the Congress April 1975 (Washington, D.C.: U.S. Government Printing Office, 1975), pp. 70–71.

tion activity is notably sensitive to cyclical changes in economic activity. Workers in manufacturing experience the second highest unemployment rate among the major industrial categories. A post–World War II low of 3.3 percent was reached in 1968–1969, but the rate rose to 10.9 percent in 1975. Unemployed manufacturing workers, the largest group of the nation's unemployed in good years or bad, have accounted for 23 to 30 percent of the total since 1960.

In the white-collar occupational categories, clerical workers, followed by those in sales, have higher unemployment rates than do professional, technical, and managerial workers, but the latter groups are not immune to business downturns. It was in the recession of 1970–1971 that they were first significantly affected by layoffs and hiring cutbacks. Among blue-collar workers, unemployment rates are highest for unskilled factory operatives and for service workers other than those in private households (see Figure 16–2). On the whole, craftsmen fare best. Of all unemployed workers with previous job experience, blue-collar and service workers compose about two-thirds. (Unemployed workers with no previous work experience are relatively more important in times of boom than in recessionary periods. They accounted for over 14 percent of all unemployed workers in 1969 but only 10 percent in 1975.)

Other Characteristics

Certain groups of workers have unique problems. Migratory farm workers and families face not only the hazards of low wages, substandard housing, and lack of educational facilities for their children, but also the costs of frequent unemployment that arise between the times when crops can be harvested.

FIGURE 16-2 Unemployment by Occupation

Source: Employment and Training Report of the President, 1977.

Unemployment of the handicapped presents a special problem of adjustment in the labor market. Although many handicapped persons can perform certain types of work quite satisfactorily, their range of job opportunities is limited. A measure of the inefficiency of the labor market mechanism is the high rate of unemployment of the handicapped, even when special efforts are taken by governmental agencies and other interested groups to inform the public of their abilities.

Finally, it should be repeated that the description of unemployment is obviously based on the means available for measuring it. The blurred boundary between the designations "out of work" and "out of the labor force" raises the question of whether the existing statistics adequately present the extent of the unemployment problem, especially for groups such as young people, older persons, and women. It should also be remembered that, since the boundary line between unemployment and employment is determined in such a way as to exclude part-time unemployment from the overall statistics, the extent of unemployment tends to be understated.[10]

CAUSES OF UNEMPLOYMENT

According to the usual classification, there are three basic types of unemployment: frictional (including seasonal), structural, and cyclical. Although these categories can be justifiably criticized on the grounds that they are not mutually exclusive, they do serve to identify important causes of unemployment. One of the problems of determining the "cause" of unemployment is that statistics are not, and probably could not be, collected for that purpose. It is doubtful whether the individual worker would have the necessary information to provide a satisfactory answer.[11] Employers who are laying off workers

---

[10] Also excluded are "unemployment on the job" and "disguised unemployment." The former term refers to workers on piece work who are forced to hold up production because of delays in the flow of materials, thereby losing income. The latter term refers to those who have lost their regular jobs but have taken less-skilled, lower-paying jobs as the best alternative available.

[11] Unemployed workers can, however, give information on the way in which they became unemployed. Since 1967, monthly data are collected from household interviews as to whether the unemployed worker lost the last job (a job loser), quit the last job (a job leaver), reentered the labor force (a reentrant who previously worked for at least two weeks in a full-time job but then dropped out of the labor force), or entered the labor force without previous full-time work experience of at least two weeks (a new entrant). Although useful for many purposes, these data cannot be unambiguously applied in the analysis of causes of unemployment. For example, although a worker who voluntarily quits (a job leaver) to search for a new job may appear to be "frictionally unemployed," the worker may have quit in anticipation of a plant shutdown, or to escape from the limited opportunities of a depressed area—that is, the basic cause could have been cyclical or structural. For an analysis of the trends by unemployment categories for 1967–1972, see Curtis L. Gilroy, "Job Losers, Leavers, and Entrants: Traits and Trends," *Monthly Labor Review*, 96 (August 1973), 5–15.

may be in no better position: even if they ascribe their actions to a decline in sales or to poor business conditions, they may not have perceived the basic cause. For example, a firm laying off workers during the usual seasonal slack period of the industry may be unaware that a cyclical downturn is in the making.

Frictional Unemployment

As we have already seen, frictional unemployment arises as workers shift from one job to another. Some of it is voluntary, in that a worker may resign from one job in order to look for another. But a worker who has come into the labor market from "out of the labor force" either as a new entrant or as a reentrant may also experience unemployment before finding the desired job. Workers who are discharged or laid off and endure a period of unemployment before finding new jobs are also said to be frictionally unemployed if the resultant unemployment period is short. The principal characteristic of frictional unemployment is its association with mobility in the labor market and the difficulty of making changes in jobs easily and with no lost time. Such unemployment can never be entirely eliminated in a free, dynamic economy— even one operating at "full employment."

Seasonal unemployment, often considered a part of frictional unemployment, is that which results from those fluctuations of business activity that occur regularly within a 12-month period. The causes of such seasonality are changes associated with weather conditions, buying habits, or recurring holidays. Some industries, such as agriculture, the processing of foods, and construction in the North, are directly affected by weather conditions. Among the industries affected by seasonal spending patterns are automobiles (where summer layoffs occur during model changeovers), Christmas toys, and garments that are dependent on seasonal fashions.

A decline in the seasonal demand for labor does not necessarily produce a proportionate rise in unemployment. The unpaid workers in agriculture may be family members, young people may work at summer jobs and return to school in the fall, or housewives may "retire" from the labor force when the seasonal jobs are ended (as in the Christmas retail trade or in canning industries). Furthermore, workers laid off seasonally in one industry may be able to shift to other industries that are seasonally expanding. But while the dovetailing of employment may be possible for certain workers, it can not be true for all because the aggregate seasonal variation of demand is substantial.

Another source of seasonal unemployment is fluctuation in the size of the labor force. The expansions and contractions of the labor force as youths enter it at the end of the school year and leave in the fall or as women temporarily enter it in the summer and again in the holiday season do not exactly coincide with the seasonal job changes. As a result, the actual seasonal unemployment pattern for the nation as a whole reflects the aggregate effects of the seasonal fluctuation of both demand and supply.

Structural Unemployment

Structural unemployment has traditionally been regarded as the result of major shifts in the structure of demand—shifts in consumer tastes that cause some industries to grow and others to decline, and geographical movements in industry location. Since in many cases scientific research and technology have given birth to new products or have altered the geographical pattern of production, technological changes are often included as causes of shifts in the structure of demand.

Structural unemployment is not easily remedied or corrected if the unemployed have acquired skills no longer useful in nearby industries. Time may be required to readjust labor supplies to demand, and it is such difficulty of mobility that gives structural unemployment its special significance. It is sometimes considered a form of frictional unemployment, though most writers apply the term "frictional" to unemployment of a short-term or temporary nature, while using "structural" to refer to unemployment of relatively long duration.

Structural unemployment also includes changes emanating from supply factors in the market. Changes in the composition of the labor force as the result of long-run demographic and cultural influences can result in excess supplies of certain types of labor. The relatively large number of young people entering the labor force in the 1970s as a result of high birth rates after World War II is a structural change that can lead to higher levels of unemployment if, as we have seen, adequate job opportunities are not available.

Technological change may lead to structural unemployment (what was at one time called technological unemployment), but the result is not certain. Technological unemployment results from the displacement of labor due to the introduction of new ways of combining capital and labor to produce old or new products. Such technological changes in regard to previously manufactured products are usually labor-saving in that less labor is required to produce a given amount, but they may be capital-saving in that they require less capital per unit of output. Labor-saving changes can result in immediate unemployment, but this effect need not continue (see chapter 4). If a firm reduces its product price in accordance with the decrease in production costs, increased consumer purchases may lead to an expansion of output and employment. If the demand for the product is elastic, the firm may eventually employ more workers than before. If the demand is inelastic, output cannot be increased proportionately to the price decline, and there will be a net decrease in employment.

If the introduction of new labor-saving equipment leads to unemployment in a given firm or industry, the problem of reemploying the technologically displaced workers again becomes one of mobility and of the adequacy of other employment opportunities in the economy. The mobility problem, although essentially the same as that for frictionally unemployed workers, will be difficult for the technologically unemployed if they have special skills no longer needed or are located in areas where similar jobs are scarce. In such cases, the unemployment would be considered structural.

On the other hand, technological change may have a favorable effect on the aggregate level of employment in the economy. The expansionary effect of newly created industries on total employment is direct and obvious. But whether the new technology leads to new industries or to labor-saving machinery in old ones, most types of innovations require capital outlays, which in turn have a stimulating impact on national income, output, and employment.[12] "The slowing down of technological change may lead to more unemployment than its acceleration, and may do so without yielding any of the advantages which flow from a rapid rate of technological improvement."[13]

Cyclical Unemployment

Unemployment arising from declines in the general level of business is the most dramatic and most serious of all types of unemployment. Cyclical fluctuations in business activity can be moderate: in only one of the six recessions since World War II, for example, was more than 8 percent of the labor force unemployed at the trough of the cycle. Yet it is clear that even in these declines the private and social costs of unemployment are high. Cyclical unemployment is essentially that attributable to inadequate aggregate demand, and in that sense cyclical unemployment can be said to exist even when peaks in the business cycle fall below reasonably full capacity levels. The half-hearted boom is not a rarity. The gap between actual peak employment and full capacity employment is called "growth-gap" unemployment.

It should be noted that the three types of unemployment are interrelated. If cyclical unemployment is remedied by the maintenance of adequate aggregate demand conditions for the economy as a whole through appropriate monetary and fiscal policies, structural unemployment would be more likely to disappear than if the economy experienced recession and growth-gap un-

---

[12] Capital-saving innovations, while not causing technological displacement of labor, may have an eventual adverse effect because they would not stimulate as high a rate of capital investment.

[13] *Higher Unemployment Rates, 1957–60: Structural Transformation of Inadequate Demand;* study paper prepared for the Subcommittee on Economic Statistics, Joint Economic Committee, 87th Congress, 1st Session (Washington, D.C.: U.S. Government Printing Office, 1961), p. 44.

Schumpeter's theory of innovation makes technological change central to business expansion. In this case unemployment declines as new processes and products are introduced and imitated by competitors, and rises when the spurt of innovation has spent itself.

employment. With sustained high levels of aggregate demand, only frictional unemployment would eventually remain, although the level of such unemployment might be somewhat higher in times of business boom because voluntary quits increase when job opportunities are widespread.

CONTROVERSIES OVER THE CAUSES OF UNEMPLOYMENT

The key role of maintaining aggregate demand in reducing unemployment was challenged in the late 1950s and early 1960s by a group called the structuralists. More recently it has been questioned by those who emphasize the frictional nature of unemployment.

The Structuralist Debate

In the structural/aggregate demand controversy, the structuralists argue that an imbalance between the skills of the unemployed and the demands of industry had developed because of new technology, shifts in the composition of demand, and shifts in the geographical location of economic activity. In the first instance, it was automation and the introduction of computers that raised the specter of mass technological unemployment. In the second, increasing dominance of the service industries tended·to make many skills obsolete. The third factor was the decline of such areas as Appalachia, afflicted by the depression in coal mining, and the older New England towns, whose industrial base had eroded with the movement southward of the textile industry. Charles C. Killingsworth, one of leading exponents of the new view of structural unemployment, emphasized the new skill requirements of the automation revolution to show what he called the "labor market twist."[14] As new jobs demanded more educated workers, the burden of the unemployment was falling more and more on the unskilled. The conclusions of the structuralists were that appropriate governmental policies should encourage human capital investment through training programs, and that increases in aggregate demand through tax cuts or other fiscal policy would be less effective. In short, the argument was that structural changes had shifted outward the Phillips curve relationship between unemployment and price increases.

The essential counterargument advanced against this position by proponents of fiscal policy was that a flourishing economy was the best cure for structural unemployment. It would facilitate the labor market adjustments

---

[14] Charles C. Killingsworth, "Automation, Jobs, and Manpower: The Case for Structural Unemployment," testimony from U.S. Senate Hearings, excerpted in Garth L. Mangum, ed., *The Manpower Revolution: Its Policy Consequences* (Garden City, N.Y.: Doubleday, 1965), esp. pp. 94–95.

needed to eliminate the imbalances of demand shortages and excess supplies. These economists claimed that no appreciable concentration of unemployment had been found among workers attached to specific industries and occupations, although there may have been some increase in *frictional* unemployment as greater female participation rasied turnover rates generally.[15]

As it turned out, the two approaches in the structuralist/aggregate demand controversy were not irreconcilable, since policies reflecting each approach were mutually reinforcing. The $14 billion tax cut, planned by the Council of Economic Advisers under the chairmanship of Walter E. Heller (an advocate of aggregate demand policies) and passed in 1964, provided a major stimulus to the economy, although its effects were soon overshadowed by rising Vietnam defense expenditures. At the same time new manpower training programs—spurred more by the civil rights movement than by the arguments of the structuralists—proliferated. (These will be reviewed in the next chapter.) Nonetheless, even as unemployment fell toward the 3.5 percent level of 1969, it was clear that while demand deficiencies as a cause of unemployment might have been eliminated, the continuing high unemployment rates of youths and blacks and other minorities revealed that structural factors had not in fact disappeared.[16]

The Frictionalist Debate

In the late 1960s and early 1970s a new challenge to those who stressed inadequate aggregate demand was advanced by economists concerned with what they believed were the inflationary dangers of policies of government expansion aimed at full employment. These writers stressed the frictional nature of unemployment.

The new approach to frictional unemployment led first to a reexamination of the nature and amount of labor turnover. One of the arguments advanced by the new school was that much unemployment tends to be of short dura-

---

[15] For statements of the aggregate demand hypothesis, see *Higher Unemployment Rates, 1957–60.* An early attempt to measure frictional unemployment is found in a study prepared for the Joint Economic Committee by the Bureau of Labor Statistics, U.S. Department of Labor, *The Extent and Nature of Frictional Unemployment*, Study Paper No. 6 (Washington, D.C.: U.S. Government Printing Office, 1959).

[16] Eleanor G. Gilpatrick concluded that "structural unemployment might account for as much as half the increase in unemployment rates above the frictional minimum in nonrecession years," and that there was no reason to assume that frictional unemployment should be more than 3 percent. See her *Structural Unemployment and Aggregate Demand: A Study of Employment and Unemployment in the United States, 1948–1964* (Baltimore: Johns Hopkins Press, 1966), pp. 202, 214. Killingsworth also held that structural unemployment was persisting during the boom, some of it as "hidden unemployment" as indicated by lower participation rates. See his statement before the Joint Economic Committee, U.S. Congress, August 6, 1971.

tion. (Most of these arguments were advanced before the sharp rise in cyclical unemployment in 1975.) The record indicated that in four of the seven years from 1969 to 1975, half or more of the unemployed were out of work less than five weeks. (For basic data see Table 16–2.) In 1975 the percentage dropped to 37. The average length of unemployment over the longer period of time from 1948 to 1969 was 5.5 weeks.[17] In addition, these writers pointed to work experience statistics indicating that unemployment tends to recur in a small proportion of the population. In 1973, for example, when the average monthly unemployment rate stood at 4.9 percent, 14.2 percent of those in the labor force during the year experienced some unemployment. Excluding those who did not work at all, 13 percent of the experienced workers had one or more spells of unemployment. Of these, nearly a third (32%) had two or more spells, and over half of those (52%) had three or more spells. In short, the conclusion was that the unemployment rate tends to reflect not an overall problem but a concentration of unemployment among workers subject to frequent periods of unemployment of relatively short duration.[18]

It was claimed, furthermore, that demographic changes in the American labor force have raised the frictional unemployment rate. The increasing importance of youths and women in the labor force, with their normally higher rates of labor turnover, caused the average unemployment rate to be higher than it would have been otherwise. The Council of Economic Advisers estimated, for example, that if the 1956 weights for age-sex specific labor force groups were used to calculate unemployment, the reported unemployment rate of 5.6 percent for 1974 would have been reduced to 4.8 percent. The implication was that although the absolute unemployment rate appeared to be relatively high, there was little in the way of remedial action that could be taken by governments to reduce it, especially action that would increase aggregate demand. Because, in terms of the Phillips curve analysis, higher frictional rates meant an outward movement of the curve, such action would tend to have undesirable inflationary consequences.[19]

A second aspect of the new approach to frictional unemployment was its emphasis on the concept of the job search as an extension of human capital

[17] Council of Economic Advisers, *Economic Report of the President*, transmitted to the Congress February 1975 (Washington, D.C.: U.S. Government Printing Office, 1975), p. 97.

[18] These relationships can be described in the equation U=DS, where U is the annual unemployment rate, D the average duration of a spell of unemployment as a fraction of 52 weeks, and S the average number of spells. If a particular age-sex group averages one and a half spells of unemployment of 5.2 weeks in duration (that is, 10% of a year), its unemployment rate is .15 = .1 × 1.5, or 15 percent.

[19] George C. Perry had earlier calculated that because of changes in the age-sex composition of the unemployed, a 4 percent unemployment rate meant a tighter labor market than in the 1950s with the result that it would lead to 1.5 percentage points more inflation. See his "Changing Labor Markets and Inflation," *Brookings Papers on Economic Activity* (Washington, D.C.: Brookings Institution, 1970), no. 3, pp. 411–441.

theory. Information concerning jobs and wages is imperfect, and it was held that the search for a job becomes an investment decision for workers. They set for themselves an acceptance wage based on their estimate of the probabilities of finding it, and calculate the costs they expect will be incurred. If the expected benefits outweigh the costs, they then make an "investment decision" to search. That decision may mean giving up one's job in order to search more efficiently. Hence, unemployment is rational and "productive" and can lead to more efficient resource allocation.[20] In the course of the search, however, workers may lower their aspirations—that is, they may be willing to take a lower wage—if their expectations are not fulfilled; they may even abandon the search and leave the labor force.

In pointing to the role of wage adjustments, these theorists placed the burden of responsibility for unemployment on the worker and on those institutions that fostered wage inflexibilities. In effect, they reverted to the pre-Keynesian position of denying the existence of unemployment due to inadequate aggregate demand. They sought to show that minimum wage laws, union-wage rigidities, and even unemployment compensation benefits—all of which, they claimed, prolonged job searching—were the institutional factors that aggravated "structural maladjustments" between demand and supply. The theory accepted the existence of cyclical unemployment but supported the concept of the emergence of the "natural" rate of unemployment in the long run. Although the precise numerical value of the natural rate could not be calculated and would probably change as circumstances changed, it was, as we have seen earlier, independent of the trade-off between inflation and unemployment as conceived by the Phillips curve theorists.

The analysis of the changing age-sex composition of unemployment and the concept of the job search, however, do not in themselves demand acceptance of any particular set of policy conclusions, as those who have criticized the "frictionalists" have been quick to point out. If the government adopts policies designed to maintain adequate aggregate demand, the costs of job search can be reduced, readjustments of labor supplies to demands can be made more readily and efficiently, and many workers who have dropped out of the labor market can be induced back into it. A model of wage flexibility as a viable alternative seems to many to be as unrealistic today as when Keynes first argued against it in the 1920s and 1930s. The nature of the structured markets of the primary sectors militates against it. The counterargument also points to the deceptive implications of aggregate turnover rates in the economy, which do not indicate that it is in the unstructured, secondary labor markets—with their poor opportunities for advancement and unstable job relationships—where the high turnover rates are found. If steps are taken to

[20] Edmund S. Phelps, "Introduction: The New Microeconomics in Employment-Inflation Theory," in Edmund S. Phelps, ed., *Micro-Economic Foundations of Employment and Inflation Theory* (New York: Norton, 1970), p. 17.

shift workers from secondary to primary types of markets, then the mainte-nance of high levels of employment becomes a necessary precondition for success. For primary market firms to expand their operations and to provide new opportunities for steady employment and advancement, "credible com-mitment to stable and continuous full employment" must be established at the national level.[21]

SUMMARY

Unemployment imposes costs on individuals, families, and society as a whole. Severe unemployment accentuates those costs, whether measurable (as in the case of estimated reduction of national output) or unmeasurable (in terms of social distress and political unrest).

Even during "normal" years the average rate of unemployment can be misleading as an indicator of hardship. High unemployment rates of youth, although expected because of more frequent job-changing, nonetheless im-pede the acquisition of skills and work experience and can have serious impli-cations for a nation's future. High rates for youths, blacks, and women may reflect entrapment in secondary labor markets where resources are underem-ployed. Even low unemployment rates for certain groups may be indicative of hardship—for example, households headed by women and older persons.

The three basic types of unemployment are frictional, structural, and cy-clical, although the lines between them are often unclear. Frictional unem-ployment arises from the movement of workers among jobs. Structural unemployment, which arises from imbalances between demands and sup-plies, is a form of frictional unemployment, but is of longer duration. Cyclical unemployment, resulting from declines in the general level of business, is the most dramatic and serious type.

The types of unemployment have had important policy implications. In the structuralist view, the increase of aggregate demand to eliminate unem-ployment is ineffective and inflationary when unemployment is structural, as they believed much of it to be, especially during the late 1950s and early 1960s. In the 1970s those who believed that frictional unemployment had increased because of the larger proportion of youth in the labor force also tended to be skeptical of aggregate demand policies as a solution for unemployment.

DISCUSSION QUESTIONS

1. Some commentators claim that unemployment among youths should be of less concern to society as a whole than the unemployment of experienced workers be-

---

[21] Doeringer and Piore, "Unemployment and the 'Dual Labor Market,' " p. 79.

cause, when employed, they contribute less to the nation's gross national product. Would you support this position? Why or why not?

2. How do you explain the facts that for youth in central cities, compared with the suburbs, (a) unemployment rates are higher, and (b) labor force participation rates are lower?

3. Distinguish between frictional and structural unemployment. Is each type affected in the same way by changes in the general level of economic activity? Explain.

4. Show how structural unemployment can arise out of changes on both the demand side and the supply side of labor markets.

5. How is the unemployment rate affected by the frequency of spells of unemployment? by the duration of unemployment?

6. In analyzing frictional unemployment, what are the principal issues between those who support the job search concept as a form of human capital investment and those who stress the dual labor market approach?

SELECTED READINGS

For basic discussions of unemployment, see Robert Aaron Gordon and Margaret S. Gordon, eds., *Prosperity and Unemployment* (New York: John Wiley & Sons, 1966); and Arthur M. Ross, ed., *Employment Policy and the Labor Market* (Berkeley and Los Angeles: University of California Press, 1965). The following present analyses of structural unemployment: Eleanor G. Gilpatrick, *Structural Unemployment and Aggregate Demand, A Study of Employment and Unemployment in the United States, 1948–1964* (Baltimore: Johns Hopkins Press, 1966); and Charles C. Killingsworth, "Automation, Jobs, and Manpower: The Case for Structural Unemployment," reprinted in *The Manpower Revolution: Its Policy Consequences* (Garden City, N.Y.: Doubleday, 1965).

Analysis of urban unemployment is found in David M. Gordon, *Theories of Poverty and Underemployment, Orthodox, Radical, and Dual Labor Market Perspectives* (Lexington, Mass.: D. C. Heath, 1972); and Stanley Friedlander, *Unemployment in the Urban Core* (New York: Praeger, 1972). Studies of urban ghetto problems are surveyed by Bennett Harrison, "Ghetto Economic Development: A Survey," *Journal of Economic Literature*, 12 (March 1974), 1–37.

For different approaches to recent debates over frictional unemployment, see Peter B. Doeringer and Michael J. Piore, "Unemployment and the 'Dual Labor Market,'" *The Public Interest*, No. 38 (Winter 1975), 67–79; and Edmund S. Phelps, ed., *Microeconomic Foundations of Employment and Inflation Theory* (New York: Norton, 1970).

17

Full-Employment Policies

During and after World War II the elimination of mass unemployment and the maintenance of full or high level employment became accepted as their responsibilities by the governments of many nations. Not only was full employment recognized as a paramount domestic objective, but nations with memories of the international ramifications of unemployment supported the pledge to pursue full-employment policies when they became members of the United Nations.

SOME ASPECTS OF POLICY MAKING

United States recognition of governmental responsibility for eliminating unemployment came with the passage of the Employment Act of 1946. The declaration of policy was set forth in Section 2:

> The Congress hereby declares that it is the continuing policy and responsibility of the Federal Government to use all practicable means consistent with its needs and obligations and other essential considerations of national policy, with the assistance and cooperation of industry, agriculture, labor, and State and local governments, to coordinate and utilize all its plans, functions, and resources for the purpose of creating and maintaining, in a manner calculated to foster and promote free competitive enterprise and the general welfare, conditions under which there will be afforded useful employment opportunities, including self-employment, for those able, willing, and seeking to work, and to promote maximum employment, production, and purchasing power.

Although the phrase "full employment" was not included, the act nonetheless marked a new era in national policy.

The government's initiation and implementation of specific programs that would in fact bring about high levels of employment were more complex. Though the act gave wide scope to whatever programs might seem feasible, it did set up a specific procedure to insure examination of unemployment and its remedies by both the president and Congress. The president is required to submit to Congress at the beginning of each regular session an economic report in which he reviews past and current economic trends, sets forth the level of employment consistent with Section 2, and recommends policies for legislative action that he feels will best promote that level. The act also authorized the formation in the executive office of the president of the Council of Economic Advisers, consisting of three people selected by the president with the consent of the Senate. The council's function is to assist and advise the president in the preparation of the economic report and on matters pertaining to the economy. In Congress the act established the Joint Economic Committee, composed of members from both the House and the Senate, to conduct investigations into proposed economic programs of the president and to make recommendations to Congress for any needed legislation.

The character, forcefulness, and effectiveness of government in pursuing the goals of the Employment Act have varied since its inception with changing business conditions and with the differing philosophies of presidents, Congress, and members of the council about the extent to which the government should become a prime factor in maximizing employment. Although the act provided a procedure for bringing economic problems relating to the national level of employment and production into the public arena for open debate and discussion, it did not legally obligate the government to provide jobs to any who wanted them, to take any action in time of depression, or to give priority to high levels of employment over other national objectives.

The range of possible lines of action under the Employment Act is wide, desirably so. The remedies for unemployment are not a matter of automatic prescription. Although the causes of unemployment may be analyzed, particular policies must suit the specific conditions of each situation. If a deficiency in aggregate demand is the major cause of large-scale unemployment, there are a variety of well-recognized methods by which the deficiencies may be overcome. Each method may have certain advantages and disadvantages in resolving the problems presented by a particular recession.

But national objectives other than full employment may be considered. A stable price level may be given a higher priority than low rates of unemployment, so that in terms of the Phillips curve trade-off the full employment and output that could have been gained under inflationary conditions are sacrificed in the interest of price stabilization. A conflict in national objectives can arise over the types of full-employment policies to be emphasized. For example, funds can be directed toward manpower programs that give work experience and training to the unskilled, or toward projects that utilize jobless skilled workers. Different objectives reflect different interest groups, and tugs of war among them are to be expected. Controversy persists among economists on these questions just as it does within the political process through which, in the last analysis, the decisions are finally made.

MAINTENANCE OF ADEQUATE AGGREGATE DEMAND

Acceptance of the obligation to achieve full employment by leading industrial nations after World War II marked a revolutionary change in domestic economic policy. Although government intervention to ease economic burdens had been substantial during the Great Depression, there had never before been the belief that governments not only should but could abolish the scourge of unemployment that afflicted developed nations. Earlier generations of economists had taken the position either that the business cycle was part of the nature of the capitalist economy that had to be endured as long as capitalism existed, or that whatever government intervention did occur in the economy was the more likely cause of the business cycle itself and the unemployment that went with it. Government spending, for example, was considered inflationary and, by distorting the normal tendencies toward full-employment equilibrium that were held pervasive in competitive market economies, eventually bound to lead to depressions as painful but inevitable correctives.

The theoretical underpinnings for the turnabout among economists came with the publication, over forty years ago, of *The General Theory of Employment, Interest, and Money* by John Maynard Keynes. Now elaborated and modified, but still the core of modern macroeconomics, the central proposition is that governments can so adjust their expenditure and taxation policies that the aggregate demand for goods and services will create a derived demand for labor sufficient to eliminate unemployment except for the frictional minimum.

Theory

The theory of the determination of the level of national income and output is now so well known that no more than its basic essentials need be stated here. Two aspects of the theory have been continuing sources of controversy, however, and therefore require emphasis. The first is the relevance of wage policy to the elimination of mass unemployment, and the second is the role of fiscal policy.

The several criticisms of general wage policy as an antidepression device laid down by Keynes were essential to the acceptance of his statement of national income determination. Orthodox economic theory had held the view that the price of labor served the same function in the labor market that prices did in other markets. If there were a surplus of potatoes, for example, the price of potatoes should fall, and—in the absence of artificial monopolistic restraints—the excess should disappear as the market was "cleared." In a similar fashion, it was argued, mass unemployment could as easily be eliminated if only wages would fall.

In an earlier chapter, Figure 4–6 presented a supply and demand schedule for a labor market at which the wage W_3 is too high. The quantity demanded, OF, is less than the quantity of labor able and willing to work at that wage, OG. The section of the labor supply curve to the right of OG represents those who are not willing to work at the existing wage and are *voluntarily* employed. If the figure is applied to a national labor market, orthodox economists held that those willing to work at the wage but who cannot find jobs, FG, are the involuntarily unemployed. They stated that the remedy for involuntary unemployment is a fall in the wage to W_2, where an equilibrium of supply and demand will be established. FB additional workers will be hired; *BG workers will become voluntarily unemployed, and the involuntarily unemployed* will have disappeared.

Keynes offered three direct criticisms of the theory that implied that a free labor market in which the wage was flexible enough to reflect supply and demand changes would guarantee the elimination of mass unemployment.[1] First, he pointed out that the vertical axis of the graph referred to real wages, not money wages, and asked how the real wage could be lowered. He contended that if in a specific market labor and management negotiate a cut in money wages, the price in that market will also fall, but that if a general wage cut is negotiated, the general price level will decline (assuming competition in product markets) and the real wage would not be reduced. Secondly, he pointed out that businessmen would not be inclined to expand investments or increase production when further price declines were anticipated, a situation that would be considered likely if wages and prices were already falling. Finally, Keynes argued, the belief that the labor supply schedule was a function of the real wage was erroneous, because workers react differently to a fall in money wages than they do to one in real wages. Whereas labor may be withdrawn when the money wage falls, a decline in real wages might have no such effect. If supply is not a sole function of the real wage, the theory "breaks down entirely and leaves the question of what the actual employment will be quite indeterminate."[2]

After indicating that wage flexibility cannot resolve the problem of involuntary unemployment, Keynes developed his concept of effective aggregate demand. This demand consists of the outlays consumers are willing to make

[1] John Maynard Keynes, *The General Theory of Employment, Interest, and Money* (New York: Harcourt Brace, 1936). These arguments are contained in chs. 2 and 19.
[2] Ibid., p. 8.

out of their current incomes and the investment outlays of businesses. Consumer expenditures for goods and services, Keynes held, are a function of income; as incomes rise, they will also rise, but will not do so proportionately. Investment outlays are related to profit expectations on the one hand (that is, the marginal efficiency of capital) and, on the other hand, to the costs of capital as expressed by the rates of interest on loans of various degrees of risk. The propensities to consume and to invest will determine a unique level of income and employment at which, as Keynes put it, an equality of the aggregate supply price of the output as a whole and its aggregate demand price will be achieved. He saw no reason why a particular equilibrium level of national income should be associated with full employment, which is only one of many possible equilibrium points.

Keynes believed that any government seeking to overcome a deficiency in aggregate demand could rely on fiscal policy—that is, on its powers to spend money and to tax. Government expenditures would offset savings and would create new income just as surely as new investment or new consumer outlays. A reduction in taxes could also stimulate the economy, because the additional outlays made by those who gained income from the tax cut would boost the aggregate level of output and employment.

Despite wide acceptance of the basic elements of this theoretical analysis, one school of critics, the monetarists, led by Milton Friedman, has advanced arguments remarkably similar to those that Keynes initially challenged. Their position is that workers are not deceived by a money illusion with respect to their wages. Whereas Keynes had assumed that workers who would resist a money wage cut would accept a real wage reduction if prices rose, the monetarists claim that workers would demand and receive higher money wages during inflationary periods to preserve their real wages. The result would nullify the employment expansion. Given the appropriate time lags for adjustment, the unemployment which was natural to the particular economic system would eventually reemerge undiminished by government actions designed to eliminate it. This "natural" rate of unemployment, as shown in Chapter 15, can be identified as a long-run, vertical "Phillips curve."

In addition, the monetarists decry the use of governmental fiscal policy as a device to stimulate the economy on two grounds. First, they argue, it is inflationary. Increases in governmental outlays and/or declines in taxes are likely to produce an expansion in monetary supplies through government borrowing. This need not be the case if governments were to draw funds directly from savers, but in that event the savings that would otherwise be available for private investment outlays would be diminished—"crowded out"— and the expansionary effects of government deficits would be offset by investment declines. With the elastic money supply mechanism of the banking system and the Federal Reserve Banks, however, the inflationary potential of governmental fiscal policy is high. Whatever increases the supply of funds over and above the minimum required for the normal growth of the economy's resources will cause the price level to rise. This relationship, which constitutes the basic article of faith for monetarists, leads them to advocate only one guide to governmental action—namely, a guarantee of a long-run, steady increase in the money supply at some fixed rate, such as the 4 percent a year which Friedman has estimated as normal.

The second argument against fiscal policy is essentially ideological. Although monetarists recognize that governmental spending may very well reduce unemployment in periods of recession, they claim that it has "continuously fostered an expansion in the range of governmental activities at the federal level" and hence contributed to greater intervention by the state in economic affairs.[3] Monetarists, as well as conservatives in general, believe that economic actions should be confined, in the greatest degree, to the private domain of the individual.

It is clear that although monetarists accept the basic proposition that governmental fiscal policy can reduce cyclical unemployment at least temporarily, they are fearful of inflationary consequences. The amount of unemployment that would occur "naturally" as the result of a steady increase in the supply of new money is not known, and probably could not be determined beforehand. But because the economy without controls also tends to fluctuate cyclically, one would expect the amount of unemployment to vary during the business cycle: presumably the natural rate of unemployment could be that which existed at any point.[4]

Public Policies

Government expenditure and tax policies to remedy unemployment cannot be applied in a vacuum; their impact upon other sections of the economy must be considered and evaluated. For example, increasing government expenditures would not cause an expansion of the economy if they caused private business to decrease investment outlays. And it is now understood that many combinations of policies—monetary as well as fiscal and foreign as well as domestic—should be considered in any full-employment program because problems arising from their interrelations are not easily resolved.

One problem concerns the timeliness of fiscal action. During a cyclical downturn it is important to act quickly with countermeasures, as it is more

[3] Milton Friedman, *Capitalism and Freedom* (Chicago: University of Chicago Press, 1962), p. 76. The presentation of the natural unemployment rate is found in his "Role of Monetary Policy," *American Economic Review*, 58 (March 1968), 1–11.

[4] Charles C. Holt, C. Duncan MacRae, Stuart O. Schweitzer, and Ralph E. Smith, in *The Unemployment-Inflation Dilemma: A Manpower Solution* (Washington, D.C.: Urban Institute, 1971), do not believe that an unemployment rate below the natural rate causes inflation to accelerate. Their econometric estimation of the natural rate leads them to conclude that it is "too high to be politically and economically tenable" (p. 32).

difficult to roll back a recession after it is fully under way than to nip it in the bud. Here we should distinguish between automatic stabilizers and discretionary fiscal policy.

A government program that serves as a built-in or automatic stabilizer either increases governmental outlays in recession and decreases them during booms, or decreases or increases taxes during recessions and booms respectively; in neither case is any specific administrative decision required, other than the original enabling legislation. One of the best examples is the unemployment compensation program, under which eligible workers who became unemployed receive weekly benefit payments. When the level of business activity falls and workers lose their jobs, the payment of benefits helps offset the decline in wage income. The level of consumer expenditures will still fall, but not as far as otherwise. The existing tax structure can be considered a built-in stabilizer to the extent that revenues increase and decrease more than proportionately with the rise and fall of national income: during a cyclical boom a general rise in incomes will be dampened if the relative share of tax payments is raised, and the loss will be partially offset if taxes decline more rapidly when income is falling.

A built-in stabilizer cannot prevent deflation or inflation, nor can it reverse the direction of the cyclical pattern. But by narrowing the range in the swings from peaks to troughs, it does reduce the extent of the unemployment resulting from a general business decline, and it does operate automatically.

In contrast to automatic stabilizers, discretionary fiscal policy offers a remedy for a deficiency in aggregate demand and can reverse an economic downturn. The impact of new money spent by governments for public transit systems, housing, new energy sources, grants-in-aid to cities, or defense contracts will add immediately to someone's income, and as the income is spent and respent by the receivers, the aggregate effect will be larger than the original outlay.[5] Similarly, a tax cut will add immediately to the disposable income of taxpayers and make possible new spending.[6]

But the timing of discretionary fiscal action is crucial and difficult. There must be adequate and current information concerning the state of business activity; the time lag between the collection and the publication of statistical information makes it difficult to determine what is happening in the economy at any exact moment. Even with the most up-to-date information, there re-

---

[5] As economics students know, this is the multiplier effect, the size of which is determined by the marginal propensity to consume. The formula is $k = 1/1 - c'$, where k is the multiplier and c' is the marginal propensity to consume. Although the new expenditures would increase the income stream immediately, the total multiplied effect would not be felt at once. For any given period of time, the effect is dependent on the velocity of money as well as c'.

[6] Other things being equal, the total multiplier effect of a dollar of tax cut is less than a new dollar of government expenditure. The latter directly adds to output (and income), in addition to the effect of its being spent and respent by income recipients.

main such problems as forecasting whether a small downturn actually indicates the beginning of a recession. Sophisticated econometric models in short-run forecasting have been less successful in foreseeing turning points in the business cycle, especially downturns, than in predicting growth rates during periods of business expansion. As in medicine, diagnoses may differ, and it may be only after the operation that the true nature of the illness can be ascertained. A time lag also arises between the decision to embark on remedial fiscal action and the effective execution of that action. If national legislation is required, time is necessary for congressional action on presidential proposals and for preparation of the procedure for approval of specifically projected expenditures; if the policy is to increase governmental expenditures, the money is generally not spent at once but is spread out over a period of time. From this point of view, the impact of a tax cut will be much more immediate than a construction project involving the same dollar value.

Another set of issues relate to the monetary policies required for supporting expansionary governmental outlays. It is one of the striking characteristics of the American monetary and banking system that the control of monetary supplies is in different hands from the determination of fiscal policy. The Federal Reserve system has the responsibility and power to influence the volume of money and interest rates, but according to the 1913 law establishing the system, it has remained independent of presidential and congressional controls. Although the president appoints the seven-man Board of Governors, with the advice and consent of the Senate, the term of office of each governor is fourteen years, with the term of only one governor expiring every two years. Moreover, the Federal Reserve does not come under the budgetary authority of Congress because the system more than pays its own way.

Under most circumstances cooperation between the "Fed" and United States Treasury operations is close and results in coordinated policies. But inconsistencies in fiscal and monetary actions can arise, and sometimes have. There have been instances when the government has attempted to promote an expansionary program but the Federal Reserve authorities have restricted monetary supplies and allowed interest rates to rise, thus dampening business expansion and endangering high employment levels.

Finally, specific programs must be selected. These can include those that increase consumer expenditures, increase private investment, or expand the public sector of the economy. Any one of these policies will affect the aggregate demand for goods and services and will help boost employment, but each will have unique effects on the economic interests of various groups within the economy.

Government policies affecting consumption outlays include increasing benefits under various social security programs, reducing personal income tax rates (especially in the lower income brackets), and introducing similar measures designed to enhance spending power. The principal advantage of such policies is that they tend to increase consumption expenditures at a time when consumers are presumably most in need of additional income. The principal limitation is that once the economy has reached a high level of employment, the rate of investment for long-term growth of the economy as a whole may be lower if a larger fraction of the full-employment output consists of goods and services for immediate consumption.

Government fiscal policies directed toward the stimulation of private investment outlays include reductions of taxes on corporation income, allowances for more rapid write-off of capital charges, and such direct subsidies as the purchase of goods for governmental stockpiles. Although each proposal must be carefully weighed according to a variety of criteria before its desirability is determined, the general policy of stimulation of private investment has one substantial advantage. New investment outlays not only lead to increased employment; if they are in the form of new plants and equipment, or lead indirectly to such investment, they also raise the productive capacity of the economy as a whole and increase the potential national output and income. Indiscriminate stimulation of private investment may not always lead to a continuing high growth rate, however. It has been a major source of business instability in the past, and an accelerated spurt of investment today might possibly lead to an accelerated decline in the near future. What is needed is the stabilization of the rate of investment at a relatively high level over a long period of time rather than the initiation of policies that might unduly accentuate short-run fluctuations.

Governmental outlays may be within the public sector itself. Such expenditures and countercyclical measures, often called public service employment, date from the New Deal, when programs like the Works Progress Administration and the Public Works Administration were designed to give jobs to the unemployed.[7] Funds for public service employment can be spent in capital-intensive types of projects for the construction of public facilities such as dams, hospitals, transit systems, and sewage disposal plants. They can be used for additional employment in conservation, parks and recreation, maintenance, and other labor-intensive occupations.

Four types of problems arise in connection with public service employment. The first is whether the projects should be designed to provide the services and facilities that meet high-priority, public needs, or whether they should be tailored to give jobs to those who have become unemployed in the private sector. In the latter case, then public service employment becomes primarily a countercyclical program, and projects will be undertaken only in connection with the expediences of the moment rather than being carried

---

[7] For a review of this history through the Emergency Employment Act of 1971, see William J. Spring, "Congress and Public Service Employment," in Harold L. Sheppard, Bennett Harrison, and William J. Spring, *Political Economy of Public Service Employment* (Lexington, Mass.: Heath, 1972).

through on their own merits. The second question is whether the workers most in need of assistance should be given preference in employment and in special training and other manpower services, even if fully qualified unemployed workers are available. Thirdly, the existence of collective bargaining rules and/or civil service regulations raises the question of whether new public service employees will be treated as temporary employees outside the established system or integrated in it. Some public-sector unions, for example, have been fearful that new workers could be a source of competition that would enable administrators to bypass union standards. Finally, the unique federal-state-local system of government imposes certain limitations on the program's effectiveness. Where federal funding requires later assumption by local governments of a portion of the costs, the grant-in-aid may be refused because of the limited fiscal capacity of the local government, or else lead to reductions in locally-funded programs and hence nullify the desired employment expansion.

Nonetheless, expenditures in the public sector, whether for specifically approved public works projects or more generally for state and local governments to hire at will within few guidelines, can constitute an important and speedy way to provide jobs for the unemployed.

FULL EMPLOYMENT, DEFICITS, AND THE PRICE LEVEL

Opposition to the maintenance of an adequate aggregate demand in peacetime often stems from reluctance to accept the possibility of governmental deficits and their inflation-generating potential. Federal expenditures during wartime are well-known examples of how unemployment can be reduced to a bare minimum but at a cost of mounting deficits and inflationary consequences. Yet the argument that similar evils are in store for peacetime deficit finance in times of recession has not been substantiated. On the contrary, it is often more accurate to conclude that it is recessions that create the deficits. With the tax structure so designed that revenues are sensitive to changes in levels of national income, federal deficits tend to diminish during business recoveries and to be transformed into budgetary surpluses during prosperity. It has been estimated that in the recession of the mid-1970s every percentage point of unemployment cost the federal government some $12 billion in lost tax revenues and additional costs estimated at about $5 billion in unemployment compensation outlays, food stamps, and other support programs. Thus $17 billion of federal deficit could be eliminated if the unemployment rate were reduced by 1 percent.[8]

The concept of the full-employment fiscal budget is used to indicate the

[8] Joint Economic Committee, Congress of the United States, *1976 Joint Economic Report*, p. 10.

relationships of the federal tax structure and levels of expenditures. If the budget were in deficit at a time of full employment, then the overall effect of federal fiscal policy is said to be stimulative; if in surplus, the budget is restrictive. Because the productive capacity and level of full employment income for the economy as a whole grows from year to year, a given tax structure will yield more revenues over time so that a full-employment deficit of one year may turn into a surplus of a later year. In the latter case, where there is "fiscal drag," either taxes should be reduced, expenditures increased, or some adjustments made in both, if fiscal policy is not to become unduly restrictive. Inflation can also influence the full-employment budget. During the recession beginning in late 1973, there was a perversity in the behavior of the full-employment budget as the result of the sharp rise in the price level which, despite the developing recession, brought an increased flow of tax revenues. A full-employment fiscal deficit of over $10 billion in 1972 turned into a surplus of more than $23 billion for 1974, largely the result of the 1973–1974 inflation.[9] The tax cut passed in the spring of 1975 attempted to redress the new restrictiveness of the federal budget.

The problem of whether full-employment objectives can be achieved in peacetime without inflation and without wage and price controls has been a dominant factor in the controversy over the setting of full-employment goals. If a primary concern is the problem of inflation, one would choose from the current Phillips curve analysis some tolerable combination of unemployment and expected price rises. To others, the appropriate method would be to estimate the amount of unemployment that could reasonably be expected even if the economy were at full employment. This would mean that estimates of the amounts of frictional, seasonal, and structural unemployment become the target for a minimum unemployment rate. A third approach that attempts to combine these considerations defines a full-employment goal as that situation when the number of vacancies equals the number of unemployed workers. In this case, the underlying assumptions are (1) that the point at which equality between vacancies and the number of unemployed occurs would in fact measure the extent of structural and frictional unemployment in the economy, and (2) that the equality would mean an "equilibrium" labor market in that wages would be expected to rise in accordance with productivity and hence the general price level would remain stable.[10]

In practice, there are difficulties with each method. The conventional Phillips curve is imprecise; it has shifted in the past and may shift again in the future. The curve, after all, represents past policy, or lack of it, and does not reflect events and policies in a new situation. The composition of aggregate demand may be different than in the past, so that with any new expansionary fiscal measures a different set of bottlenecks may lead to new patterns of price increases. Moreover, the power of firms and unions to divert new demands into higher prices and wages may have changed, as well as the government's willingness to try to restrain such power with threats of intervention or actual price and wage controls.

The measurement of minimal frictional and structural unemployment, although also imprecise, undoubtedly furnishes the best guide in determining full-employment levels. From such data one can determine the extent of unused but employable labor resources, including those outside the labor force that could be expected to be drawn into the labor market. With information concerning the productivity of the additional resources, the next step would be calculation of full-employment output and the full-employment fiscal budget. The difficulties with the third approach arise from the fact that data on vacancies have so far proven to be unreliable indicators of firms' labor requirements and can offer no sure guide for macro policy making.

Although fine-tuning an economy as complex as that of the United States in order to reach noninflationary full employment represents more a hope than an accomplished art, the costs of not trying to achieve such a goal are great. Moreover, the definition of the goal has significant implications. A 1 percent difference in the rate of unemployment amounts to nearly a million workers. Whether the goal should be 6 percent or 4 percent is not a measurement problem; it is a matter of value judgments. A government can opt for "high pressure" rather than "low pressure" policies for full employment.

This is precisely the type of social issue that was raised by the proposed legislation introduced in 1976 by Senator Hubert Humphrey and Representative Augustus Hawkins, entitled the Full Employment and Balanced Growth Act. The bill would require the federal government to formulate a program designed to reduce adult unemployment to 3 percent within a period of four years. Amending the Employment Act of 1946, the bill would establish a comprehensive planning process to achieve such a goal. The president would submit annually the targets, policies, and programs to reach full employment and to meet national needs. This plan would be reviewed by a consultative body established by Congress and composed of representatives of major groups within the nation. The Congress would review the proposed policies for appropriate action. The Federal Reserve Board would also be included in the planning process; it would submit annually its proposed policies concerning interest rates and the supply of money to help meet the national targets. Although the emphasis is on the provision of jobs in the private sector, the 1976 bill would guarantee jobs in the public sector as a last resort.

MANPOWER POLICIES

Since the 1960s it has become increasingly apparent that even with relatively low overall unemployment rates, some labor markets are disorganized—with segments of the labor force facing exceptionally high unemployment rates—and that discrimination, lack of training, and poor education can impose serious inefficiences in utilizing the nation's labor resources. While the maintenance of a high level of aggregate demand is the main line of attack on unemployment, measures designed to enhance the employment opportunities of specific groups of workers, known as manpower policies, have now become an integral part of the nation's full-employment strategy. Manpower policies can be interpreted narrowly to mean actions designed to minimize frictional and structural unemployment. A broader interpretation would include efforts to upgrade and develop all labor resources, whether unemployed or employed. In the latter case, manpower policy would cover policies of private firms directed toward raising the productivities of their own workers, union training programs, training of military personnel, and even the efforts of the educational system, public and private, at primary, secondary, college and university levels. The more restrictive point of view is taken here. In this section we examine, first, the initial efforts of government to organize free labor exchanges; second, the proliferation of manpower policies during the hectic 1960s; and, finally, the Comprehensive Employment and Training Act (CETA) of 1973, the present law which has attempted to reorganize and decentralize governmental manpower programs.

The United States Employment Service

The first involvement of government in labor markets in order to minimize the costs of frictional unemployment was the establishment of free public employment exchanges in some of the larger cities and states during the nineteenth century. The idea of bringing together unemployed workers and employers with unfilled jobs through a public exchange resulted from a recognition of both the private and social benefits of such a marketplace. That there was a private benefit was demonstrated by the willingness of buyers and sellers to pay for the services of private employment agencies, which recruited for employers and placed workers. Society gained from a more efficient worker/job matching through a reduction in the costs of unemployment and increased production of goods and services. Abuses by private agencies, which exploited workers with little knowledge of market conditions, motivated the public to accept the costs of free labor exchanges.

Although the federal government operated a number of employment offices during World War I, no permanent peacetime system was set up until 1933, when the Wagner-Peyser Act created a new United States Employment Service (USES, now called ES). The service was to encourage the establishment of state-administered employment offices, help pay administrative costs by federal grants, and coordinate their activities in a national employment-exchange system. All states soon joined in the ES, especially under the added impetus of the Social Security Act of 1935, which required state unemployment compensation programs to pay benefits only through the offices of the public employment system. The federal-state relationship established by the original act has continued except during World War II, when the ES was federalized and placed under the control of the War Manpower Commission.

According to the basic procedure of the ES, job applicants who register at the local employment service office are referred to those employers who list unfilled vacancies with the office if their experience and skill meet employers' job specifications. A worker who is not hired will continue to be referred to other employers with job openings; and to fill jobs that remain vacant, recruitment is conducted through other local offices and if necessary in other states.

The Employment Service has had only a limited role in bringing the unemployed into contact with employing firms. Its number of placements has declined during recent years. In fiscal year 1975, although over 15 million applicants were registered with the public employment service offices, nonagricultural placements totaled about 3 million. This level reflected not only the poor job market during the year but a long-run downward trend. In the middle of the 1950s, for example, when the labor force was much smaller, placements were from 14 to 15 million a year, of which about 5 million were nonagricultural.

The apparent reason for the relatively limited use of the ES is that many firms list their vacancies with the local offices only during times of labor shortage. Otherwise they prefer to recruit directly from high schools and colleges, through newspaper advertisements, or from friends and relatives of present employees. In certain industries, such as construction, firms rely on established methods of recruitment through unions, and governments typically use civil-service procedures. The failure of many private firms to use ES facilities in turn reflects the fact that workers in the white-collar, skilled, and technical occupations do not usually register at the public offices. Since it is these occupations that have grown the most rapidly in recent years, the inability of the ES to serve these groups effectively has been a real limitation to its overall expansion.

In addition, the ES in the 1960s changed from being primarily a job referral agency to becoming a center for the provision of manpower services. Officially retitled the United States Training and Employment Service, the agency was directed to serve the disadvantaged worker by job counseling, training, and referral to other supportive services that could improve the employability of those not yet ready for employment. To some employers and to other workers, these developments appeared to diminish the attractiveness of the public employment service system because of the possible implication that its applicants were less qualified.

The ES has sought, in some cases successfully, to improve its public image with the development of special offices for office and professional workers. In order to improve the efficiency of its operations it has begun the development of a computer-aided Job Service Matching System. This system is designed to bring the job applicant and available jobs together quickly. Already in operation are many "job banks"—local and state computerized informational systems that provide for immediate dissemination of current information on job-orders of employers. Now operating in 43 states as statewide systems and in major cities in other states, job banks operated in areas with almost 85 percent of the American population in the mid-1970s. Although still in the developmental stage, the matching system will provide information concerning the skills and other qualifications of job applicants so that referrals can be made quickly.

Manpower Programs of the 1960s

The decade of the 1960s marked the permanent entrance of the federal government into the area of manpower policy. Although federal programs were developed on a piecemeal, sometimes emergency basis, often in confusion and in competition with each other, manpower policy quickly became the dominant thrust of the federal government for giving training and work experience to the unemployed and the disadvantaged. The new direction of federal policy was a major break with older views of the role of the federal government in labor market affairs. The prevailing view had been that a fiscal policy to bring full employment on an overall basis, plus a system of free local employment service offices to act as referral agencies, were as far as the government should go in its attempts to seek the maximum employment levels specified in the Employment Act of 1946.

Three developments contributed to the new point of view. One was the controversy between the structuralists and advocates of aggregate demand, in which, as we have already noted, the existence of high rates of unemployment among various sectors of the labor force for the first time became a matter of national concern. With the persistence of such rates even as the government moved toward stimulation of the economy by tax cuts, manpower policy became not a competitive but a complementary way to attack the unemployment that remained as the economy expanded.

Secondly, the emergence of the civil rights movement in the late 1950s, culminating in the Civil Rights Act of 1964 and the Voting Rights Act of 1965, revealed that the exclusion of blacks and other minorities from full civil and political rights had been accompanied by exclusion from the expanding economic world of better-trained workers and white-collar occupations. The great black migration of the 1950s and 1960s from rural to urban areas meant that a new major population group with an obsolete agricultural background required a massive educational effort to prepare for participation in modern industrial society. The riots in the ghettos of big cities of the North in the mid-1960s gave impetus to the introduction of manpower programs on a crash basis.

A third factor, related to the second, was the rediscovery of poverty in America among whites as well as blacks, supported by new evidence from the Council of Economic Advisers, and the belief that the federal government could marshal its forces to eliminate it. Manpower programs were to have wider objectives than the elimination of structural unemployment: many of the poor were not only outside the labor force and could not reasonably be expected to obtain jobs (for example, the elderly) but some were already employed.

The result of these divergent influences was the development of many different manpower programs with varied objectives and with separate and sometimes overlapping administrations. The following is a brief review of some of the principal programs.[11]

The first act that demonstrated the federal government's willingness to intervene in labor markets for the benefit of specific groups of unemployed workers was the Area Redevelopment Act of 1961. This measure offered financial assistance to regions of "substantial and persistent unemployment and underemployment" in order to develop and expand new and existing facilities for the creation of new jobs. The act also introduced programs for training employed workers in depressed areas for new occupations, and provided for retraining subsistence benefits equal to the average unemployment benefit payment for a period of up to 16 weeks.

The concept of retraining allowances was incorporated into the Manpower Development and Training Act (MDTA) of 1962, which at first gave priority to the problems of the structurally unemployed worker. The act provided for institutional programs of training and retraining through utilization of educational institutions and local community agencies, and on-the-job training programs (OJT) in which subsidies were made available to employing firms to cover the costs of hiring and training less qualified workers for full-time jobs. The underlying assumption was that because certain skills had become obsolete as the result of automation and rapid technological change, and as shortages of workers with new skill requirements were in demand, government assistance for retraining would correct the underlying imbalances of the labor market.

As general business conditions improved and the overall unemployment rate, especially for experienced workers, began to decline, the objectives of

[11] One of the most comprehensive treatments of these programs is Sar A. Levitan and Garth L. Magnum, *Federal Training and Work Programs in the Sixties* (Ann Arbor, Mich.: Institute of Labor and Industrial Relations, 1969). A more recent review is Ewan Clague and Leo Kramer, *Manpower Policies and Programs: A Review, 1935–75* (Kalamazoo, Mich.: W.E. Upjohn Institute for Employment Research, 1976).

these programs shifted, as reflected in amendments to the MDTA in 1963, 1965, and 1966. Work experience requirements for those eligible for training programs were reduced, the minimum age for youth in training programs was lowered, and attention became increasingly directed toward school dropouts from disadvantaged families. As it was apparent that many of these trainees had poor educational backgrounds, authorized training periods were lengthened and the program extended to include basic education. In addition to the MDTA, the federal government embarked on programs to aid education. One was the Vocational Education Act of 1963; in 1965 the Elementary and Secondary Education Act authorized more federal funds, with emphasis on those in poverty areas.[12]

The "War on Poverty" became the new thrust of the federal government with the passage of the Economic Opportunities Act of 1964 and creation of the Office of Equal Opportunity (OEO). The new legislation comprised a variety of manpower programs to prepare the employable poor, especially youths, for jobs. The Job Corps provided a residential program for youths from disadvantaged poor families operated in many cases by private contractors. These centers were designed to provide basic education, vocational training, and in some cases work experience. The Neighborhood Youth Corps (NYC), established in 1965 for youths 16 to 21 years of age, was a work-training program for those in school, out of school, and on summer vacations; it quickly developed into the largest of all federally assisted programs in terms of enrollees, with a peak of over 500,000 in 1967. (In the Job Corps the peak was also reached that year, with 71,000 enrolled.) In addition, Operation Mainstream aimed at providing work experience for those over 55 years of age, while the Work Experience and Training Program sought to assist those on welfare, specifically, recipients of Aid to Families with Dependent Children (AFDC), whose numbers were expanding rapidly during the decade. In 1967 amendments to the Social Security Act set up a Work Incentive Program (WIN) requiring mothers on AFDC to register with their local employment office for work and training.

In 1968 on-the-job training programs under the MDTA were given a new emphasis with funds for a program called Job Opportunities in the Business Sector, or JOBS. To promote the support of the business community, President Johnson established the National Alliance of Businessmen (NAB) which encouraged some of the nation's leading firms to participate in contracts to

---

[12] The Higher Education Act was also passed in 1965. Although education has been traditionally within the domain of state and local government, federal assistance was by no means a unique development. Under the Morrill Act of 1862 the federal government established land-grant colleges; in 1917 the Smith-Hughes Act provided funding for vocational education; the GI Bill in 1944 enabled millions of ex-servicemen to pursue college education after World War II; and the National Defense Education Act of 1958 set up federal financing to develop scientific and technical manpower. It was the use of federal funds for the disadvantaged that represented the new departure of the 1960s.

employ and train the chronically unemployed. The federal government covered the special costs, over and above the firm's normal personnel operations, for added training, counseling, health services, day care for children, and similar types of supportive services. A somewhat different orientation of on-the-job training was initiated in 1969 with the New Careers program. This was directed toward preparing disadvantaged adults for paraprofessional jobs in public and nonprofit establishments in such fields as health, education, and welfare.

New Directions for Manpower Policy

Although the manpower concept of matching specific workers with specific jobs was the underlying justification for the creation of so many separate programs, it had become clear by the end of the 1960s that much of the manpower effort was duplicative, conflicting, and poorly administered. The programs had not been planned on the basis of any systematic identification of the needs of the disadvantaged but arose, as Levitan and Magnum point out, "to meet current crises, real or imagined, with little attention to their interrelations."[13] At the same time, federal manpower efforts, which necessarily had to be innovative and experimental because they sought to accomplish objectives never sought before, revealed that the problems of structural unemployment and underemployment, especially among those in the lowest income levels, were far more complex than previously realized. It was ironic that as the official, overall unemployment rate for the economy declined to below 4 percent, manpower administrators were finding their problems increasing. By 1968 total federal expenditures for manpower programs had risen to $2.2 billion (from only $250,000 in 1961),[14] but revelations of the scope of the problem of training and upgrading the skills of the disadvantaged labor force—estimated in 1967 at more than 13 million—made such expenditures merely a beginning.

The administrative difficulties created by the profusion of new programs, as well as attacks leveled against the growing costs of manpower programs, brought reorganizations that began in 1969 and eventually culminated in the Comprehensive Employment and Training Act of 1973. In 1968 three major governmental agencies—the Department of Labor, the Department of Health, Educations, and Welfare, and the Office of Economic Opportunity—had shared about equally in manpower funding. Now the responsibilities for the main programs in manpower began to be shifted to the Department of Labor and the role of the OEO was phased out. (The magni-

---

[13] Levitan and Magnum, *Federal Training and Work Programs*, p. 403.
[14] Ibid., p. 11.

tude of manpower programs under the Department of Labor is shown in Table 17-1.) In addition, the position of older agencies, such as the Employment Service, was enhanced in order to provide coordination of counseling, training, placement, and other manpower services in local areas. The initial groundwork for this had been laid with the establishment of the Concentrated Employment Program (CEP) and the Cooperative Area Manpower Planning System (CAMPS) in 1967, but tensions had persisted among the old-line agencies and the newer ones, which felt that the interests of their particular clientele, especially if disadvantaged, had been neglected. Finally, the anomalous position of the community action agencies, set up under the OEO outside of local governmental agencies, was ended with the channeling of federal funds to cities, counties, and states for manpower purposes.

The Comprehensive Employment and Training Act (CETA), passed on December 28, 1973, was a major, if limited, attempt to bring reform, reorganization, and consolidation to federal manpower policy. The primary objectives of the act were to decentralize manpower authority by transferring the responsibilities and administration of programs to the elected officials of states, counties, and cities (known as prime sponsors), with only a minimum of federal supervision, and to decategorize national programs so that a more flexible utilization of federal funds could be planned and directed to meet special problems by local prime sponsors. The new procedures rested upon a flow of federal funds through a form of revenue-sharing in which the federal government still retains the power to approve programs before funding and to monitor those that have been established.

Although CETA has brought about a reshuffling of manpower programs, the question of whether certain basic issues of manpower policy will be resolved still remains in doubt. The first issue relates to decentralization. While it can be argued that local governments know best what the local needs are and what measures are required to meet them, state and local governments have serious limitations for effective manpower action. They are no more likely to be efficient than the federal government—perhaps less so; they must heed local political pressure groups that may be reluctant to help minorities and disadvantaged workers in general; they are likely to have less experience in designing and planning efficient manpower programs; and they may develop policies in conflict with those of other areas and thus undermine any semblance of a sound national system.[15]

A second issue concerns decategorization, which, despite the stated CETA objective, was not in fact fully carried through. Although Title I of CETA established "comprehensive manpower services" and included funds for institutional and on-the-job training, the NYC, and other specific programs,

[15] Clague and Kramer, *Manpower Policies*, p. 72.

Table 17-1
Enrollment Opportunities and Federal Obligations for Work and Training Programs Administered by the Department of Labor, by Program, Fiscal Years 1963–1974 (Thousands)

Program	Total	FY 1974	FY 1973	FY 1972	FY 1971	FY 1970	FY 1969	FY 1968	FY 1967	FY 1963-66
ENROLLMENT OPPORTUNITIES										
Total	9,140.8	439.3	927.4	1,562.3	1,149.6	1,011.3	910.7	823.8	808.5	1,504.0
Manpower Development and Training Act	2,413.2	178.9	183.0	229.2	213.7	211.2	198.5	229.9	270.9	697.9
Institutional training[a]	1,532.8	108.4	116.3	138.7	144.5	147.2	120.7	131.1	126.4	499.5
JOP—OJT[b]	880.4	70.5	66.7	90.5	69.2	64.0	77.8	98.8	144.5	198.4
Neighborhood Youth Corps	5,396.8	177.3	661.3	863.0	698.9	600.0	539.7	537.7	512.8	806.1
In school	1,190.5	136.1	111.3	101.6	78.8	97.1	100.6	135.0	139.0	291.0
Out of school	562.3	41.2	38.7	41.6	40.1	45.4	51.9	63.6	79.5	160.3
Summer	3,644.0	(c)	511.3	719.8[d]	580.0[d]	457.5[d]	387.2[d]	339.1[d]	294.3	354.8
Operation Mainstream	163.9	35.8	32.3	22.3	23.3	17.8	13.5	10.9	8.0	
Public Service Careers	111.2	(c)	(c)	21.0	42.4	34.8	5.9	2.7	4.4	
Special Impact[e]	6.5						1.3	1.2	4.0	
Concentrated Employment Program[f]										
JOBS (federally financed)	361.1	26.4	33.1	60.6	88.2	60.1	52.8	31.5	8.4	
Work Incentive Program	384.8	(c)	(c)	149.5	60.7	65.7	99.0	9.9		
Job Corps	110.6	20.9	17.7	24.0	22.4	21.7				
Public Employment Program	192.7	(c)	(c)	192.7						
FEDERAL OBLIGATIONS	$14,366,600	$2,143,469	$2,753,485	$2,696,940	$1,485,466	$1,418,552	$1,029,730	$802,173	$795,950	$1,240,835

[a] Includes part-time and other training.

[b] Includes the JOBS-Optional Program (JOP), which began in fiscal 1971, and the MDTA on-the-job training (OJT) program, which ended in fiscal 1970 except for national contracts. Also includes Construction Outreach.

[c] Not available.

[d] Includes enrollment opportunities made available by MDTA supplemental funds; these were 307,900 in fiscal 1972, 145,000 in fiscal 1971, 64,500 in fiscal 1970, 36,200 in fiscal 1969, and 49,100 in fiscal 1968.

[e] Transferred to the Office of Economic Opportunity effective July 1, 1969.

[f] Data for fiscal 1974 and the total for the Comprehensive Manpower Program (CMP) are included with CEP: 43,000 first-time enrollments and $36,775,452 in allocations. Enrollment opportunities (slots) are not meaningful for CEP or CMP because the CEP and CMP approaches utilize a variety of program components—orientation, basic education, work experience, and other types of job training. An individual may be enrolled in one or in several components.

Source: *Manpower Report of the President, 1975.*

other parts of the act authorized a continuation of certain special federal responsibilities. Under Title III, these groups include AFDC families in the WIN program, older workers, American Indians, migrants, veterans, people in vocational rehabilitation programs, and workers in the JOBS program; Title IV maintains the Job Corps under federal supervision. Nonetheless, about two-thirds of CETA funding during its first year of operation was designated for Title I.

Finally, the goal of CETA training has never been satisfactorily answered. Both basic education and training for occupations with well-defined skills and requirements can readily be justified. But there are many other jobs in which the skill requirements are low and the number of openings uncertain. Instead of upgrading workers, funds might be better allocated to upgrading jobs. Manpower policy can not be efficient or successful unless not only the quality but the number of jobs makes the effort worthwhile.[16] Private contractors under the JOBS program, for example, were forced to break their training contracts when the recessions of 1971 and 1974–1975 forced reductions in their labor force.

Fears have also been expressed during cyclical downturns that manpower programs would become income-maintenance arrangements for new entrants and for jobless workers whose unemployment compensation benefits had run out. During recessions, government policy shifts, immediately even if not adequately, to public service employment arrangements. In 1971 Congress passed the Emergency Employment Act establishing a Public Employment Program (PEP), in which funds were designated for public service jobs in states and local communities. (The total number of individuals put to work under the program during the first fiscal year was 226,000.) Funds for public service employment at the local level were in CETA's Title II, and additional funding of such employment, set up by the Emergency Jobs and Unemployment Assistance Act of 1974, was added to CETA as Title VI.

These three issues—the appropriate arrangements for decentralizing and coordinating manpower programs, the degree to which funds should be allocated for specific groups of workers, and the extent to which quantity and quality of the demand for labor, both in and out of the public sector, should be influenced and controlled—remain unresolved and undoubtedly will continue to dominate manpower policy controversies in the years ahead.

---

[16] Garth L. Mangum writes: "The basic manpower obstacle is still the supply of jobs. Even during 1966–68 when labor markets in general were tight, there were never enough jobs in rural depressed areas or central city ghettos within the occupational ranges attainable by the disadvantaged which (1) paid as well as welfare, and (2) offered sufficient promise of advancement to be attractive to the young." See his "Manpower Research and Manpower Policy," in Benjamin Aaron and Paul Seth Meyer et al., A Review of Industrial Relations Research (Madison, Wis.: Industrial Relations Research Association, 1971), vol. II, pp. 109–110.

SUMMARY

Full employment as an objective of American economic policy is based on the Employment Act of 1946, passed at a time when the governments of many nations were expressing a determination to eliminate the scourge of unemployment and any further depressions like that of the 1930s. The act set up the Council of Economic Advisers to the President and the Joint Economic Committee of Congress to recommend legislation to achieve this objective.

The types of governmental actions designed to maintain full employment have been Keynesian in essence. Keynes had argued that wage flexibility was an ineffective remedy for depressions. Instead, government policies aimed at maintaining aggregate demand at full-employment levels were the only certain way of avoiding deflation and stagnation. Discretionary fiscal actions—manipulation of federal outlays and taxes—have since become the primary tools of full-employment policy. But the guidelines are still debatable: who should receive the benefits of tax relief during recessions? should government outlays take the form of public works projects or public service employment? what unemployment rate is acceptable as "full employment"?

While the maintenance of adequate aggregate demand was considered the main line of attack on unemployment, it was increasingly recognized during the 1960s that other policies were needed to reach segments of the labor force with intractably high unemployment rates. The explosion of manpower programs, fueled by the War on Poverty, represented an attempt to resolve what were seen as structural unemployment problems through training and the upgrading of skills. These programs were reorganized and consolidated by the Comprehensive Employment and Training Act (CETA) of 1973.

DISCUSSION QUESTIONS

1. It has been over thirty years since the 1946 Employment Act made "maximum employment" a goal of public policy. How important is such a declaration of policy? Would it be desirable if the goal were defined in terms of a specific minimum unemployment rate?
2. What approaches have been used to define "full employment"? What are the advantages and limitations of each approach?
3. In attempting to raise the level of employment through governmental fiscal policy, should governments also consider whether their actions affect the relative importance of the public sector in the economy as a whole? On what grounds would you support your position?
4. Should projects to provide public service jobs for the unemployed be labor-intensive? Why or why not?
5. In what ways would you expect manpower training and retraining programs to lead to a reduction in frictional and structural unemployment?

6. "Manpower training programs are essentially a mechanism for subsidizing the costs of specific human capital investment that would otherwise have to be made by employers." Discuss.
7. Do you believe that the success of government training programs depends, in the last analysis, upon the accuracy of forecasts concerning occupational job requirements in private industry? Explain your answer.
8. One of the fundamental issues of federally financed manpower training programs is the extent to which federal or state standards should be controlling. What are the advantages and disadvantages of local control of federal training funds?

SELECTED READINGS

For a discussion of public employment policy, see E. Wight Bakke. *A Positive Labor Market Policy* (Columbus, Ohio: Charles E. Merrill, 1963); R. A. Gordon, *The Goal of Full Employment* (New York: John Wiley & Sons, 1967); Richard A. Lester, *Manpower Planning in a Free Society* (Princeton, N.J.: Princeton University Press, 1966); Garth L. Mangum, "Manpower Policies and Worker Status Since the 1930s," in Joseph P. Goldberg et al., eds., *Federal Policies and Worker Status Since the Thirties* (Madison, Wis.: Industrial Relations Research Association, 1976), pps. 135–157; and Stanley H. Ruttenberg, assisted by Jocelyn Gutchess, *Manpower Challenge of the 1970's: Institutions and Social Change*, Policy Studies in Employment and Welfare No. 2 (Baltimore: Johns Hopkins Press, 1970).

For discussions of specific government training and manpower-related programs, see Frank H. Cassell, *The Public Employment Service: Organization in Change* (Ann Arbor, Mich.: Academic Publications, 1968); Alan Gartner, ed., *Public Service Employment: An Analysis of its History, Problems and Prospects* (New York: Praeger, 1973); Sar A. Levitan and Garth L. Mangum, *Federal Training and Work Programs in the Sixties* (Ann Arbor, Mich.: Institute of Labor and Industrial Relations, 1969); Ray Marshall, *Rural Workers in Rural Labor Markets* (Salt Lake City: Olympus, 1974); William Mirengoff and Lester Rindler, *The Comprehensive Employment and Training Act: Impact on People, Places, Programs—An Interim Report* (Washington, D.C.: National Academy of Sciences, 1976); Charles A. Myers, *The Role of the Private Sector in Manpower Development* (Baltimore: Johns Hopkins Press, 1971); and Harold L. Sheppard, Bennett Harrison, and William J. Spring, *Political Economy of Public Service Employment* (Lexington, Mass.: D. C. Heath, 1972).

18

Federal Programs
Against Economic
Hardship
and Insecurity

For workers in the modern industrialized and urbanized world of market economies, economic hardship results from inadequate wages, hazards of the workplace, and disruptions in the flow of income caused by unemployment, sickness, disability, and retirement. We have seen in the previous chapter how governments have attempted to reduce unemployment by policies to maintain high levels of aggregate demand and programs to provide training and other educational services so that workers could compete for better jobs in the market.

In this chapter we shall examine other federal programs that have as their target the reduction of poverty and the alleviation of economic insecurity. One is minimum wage legislation, which establishes a floor for wages so that those who work are not forced to accept poverty-level pay. Another, based on the Occupational Safety and Health Act of 1970, attempts to eliminate dangers in the work environment. A third is Social Security, which constitutes the primary defense against insecurities for most workers and their families in the United States today. Its social insurance provisions provide payments that help to offset income lost by unemployment, retirement, and disability. In addition, the act enables assistance benefits to be paid under certain conditions to individuals and families who have not established rights to social insurance through employment or are otherwise disqualified, and whose income and assets are considered to be insufficient to meet minimum standards. The final section of the chapter discusses the proposal known as the negative income tax, which has been advocated as a substitute for the present system of assistance.

MINIMUM WAGE LEGISLATION

The Fair Labor Standards Act, passed in 1938, was the first federal law to regulate minimum wages and maximum hours in the United States. Before that time some states had passed minimum wage laws under the general police powers reserved to them, but these had been struck down by the courts as unconstitutional. The grounds were that government-established wages infringed on the Fifth Amendment's constitutional guarantee of the individual's freedom "to contract about one's affairs."[1] It was not until 1937 that the Supreme Court reversed its position and upheld a Washington state law setting minimum wages for women. It was then argued successfully that the restraints on liberty of contract are not in violation of the Constitution if they are reasonable and "adopted in the interest of the community."[2]

Once the Supreme Court had cleared the way for such laws, not only were states encouraged to pass and strengthen similar measures, but the federal government also enacted the Fair Labor Standards Act (known as the Wage and Hour Law) in 1938. By 1970 some 38 states had minimum wage laws.

The state laws usually present one of two stated objectives. Most of the earlier group wished to set minimums designed to give workers a "living wage." But in the 1923 decision that struck down such laws, the Supreme Court's statement that the "value of the services rendered" by workers should have been considered led to the passage in several states of laws using the "value rendered" rather than the "living wage" as criterion for wage policy. Although the Supreme Court in 1936 invalidated a New York minimum wage law for women based on the value of service, both objectives are found in state laws today.

In the Fair Labor Standards Act both of the above objectives are combined with others. The act attempts to eliminate substandard wages as rapidly as "practicable," "without substantially curtailing employment" to maintain national purchasing power and eliminate unfair competition from low-wage employers.

Minimum wage laws are of two kinds—those that lay down a specific minimum that must be adhered to by employers and those that set up wage boards with the authority to determine the minimum in specified industries or for classes of workers. Many state laws are of the second type, and in the early days the federal act employed the wage board procedure as a supplement to legislated minimums.

---

[1] Supreme Court decision in *Adkins* v. *Children's Hospital,* 226 U.S. 525 (1923).
[2] *West Coast Hotel* v. *Parrish,* 300 U.S. 370 (1937).

The Fair Labor Standards Act

The Fair Labor Standards Act provided for the regulation of minimum wages, hours of work, and employment of child labor[3] in firms in interstate commerce of those industries not specifically excluded. The exclusions are agriculture, firms processing agricultural products, and government employees, as well as bona fide executive, administrative, and professional employees. For "covered employment," the original act set as the flat minimum $0.25 per hour for the first year and $0.30 the second year. The floor was to be raised to $0.40 per hour by the seventh year (October 24, 1945), but the act provided for the establishment of industry committees with power to raise the minimum to $0.40 before that date.

With the price rises and rapidly increasing money wages during and after World War II, the effectiveness of the minimum wage provisions was soon nullified, but the basic minimum, then at $0.40, was not raised until 1950, when it was increased to $0.75 per hour. There have been five major amendments to the law since then. The minimum was raised to $1.00 an hour in 1956; a two-step increase passed in 1961 led to a minimum of $1.25 in 1963; a similar two-step increase passed in 1966 raised the minimum to $1.60 beginning in 1968. In 1974 amendments to the law provided for a several-step increase to raise the minimum to $2.30: by January 1, 1976, for most non-farm workers; by January 1, 1977, for certain newly covered workers; and by January 1, 1978, for farm workers. With the 1977 amendments, levels were again raised to prevent further erosion of the minimum wage by the continuing rise in prises. The new requirement was $2.65 per hour beginning January 1, 1978, with a step-by-step annual increase to $3.35 per hour beginning in 1981. Under the provisions of the Equal Pay Act of 1963, discrimination in the payment of wages on the basis of sex is prohibited for employees covered by the Fair Labor Standards Act.

The amendments of 1961, 1966, and 1974 considerably increased coverage of nonsupervisory employees under the act. It has been estimated that in 1974 more than 48 million workers, or 83.7 percent of nonsupervisory employees in the private sector, came under the minimum wage provisions. The attempt by Congress in the 1974 amendments to extend coverage to employ-

---

[3] The child labor provisions prevent (a) employment of children under age 16 from working on goods to be shipped in interstate commerce, or from working in a firm within 30 days of shipment of such goods even though children did not work on the actual goods, and (b) employment of children aged 16 to 18 in hazardous occupations as defined by the Wage and Hour Division. Children under 16 may work on goods in interstate commerce if employed by a parent or guardian in industries other than mining, manufacturing, or hazardous occupations, or if a temporary work permit is issued by the Department of Labor. Two exemptions from the act are minors working in agriculture after school hours and those in motion pictures or theatrical productions.

ees of state and local governments, however, was declared unconstitutional by the Supreme Court in 1976.[4]

Forty years of experience with the federal minimum wage law have led to several conclusions concerning its effectiveness. First, there seems to be little doubt that many workers have benefited from it. This has been true in those manufacturing industries where wages have been exceptionally low, as well as in trade and service industries, to which coverage was extended by the 1961 and 1966 amendments. Secondly, it is clear that, once passed, a mimimum wage quickly becomes out of date in terms of its relationship both to a price level that appears to rise continuously and to the average level of wages. In amending the act periodically, Congress has been more than able to correct for the rise in prices, so that there has been considerable improvement in the real minimum wage. But in terms of the average rate of pay of production workers in manufacturing, the ratio—which had formerly remained in the range of 50 to 55 percent—fell after 1968 to less than 40 percent in 1973. With the new 1974 amendments, the ratio was about 46 percent. In comparison with the total compensation of wages and fringe benefits received by workers, the relative minimum wage is of course less.

Economic Implications of Legislated Wages

Examination of the economic effects of a government-directed wage rate raises a number of issues similar to those discussed earlier in connection with union-imposed wages. There are several differences, however. While unions bargain to set the complete wage scale for all workers within their jurisdiction, the wage rate we are now considering affects only the lowest wage category of workers. Secondly, in making decisions concerning wage demands, unions can consider a wide variety of objectives and use any of several types of policies. A union can, for example, attempt to limit labor supplies to remove downward pressures on wage rates, or it can moderate its wage demand if it wishes to maximize employment opportunities for its members. In the case of government-set minimum wages, however, no ancillary policies compensate for any direct effects of the legal minimum.

In theory, when a higher minimum wage is first imposed, the reaction of a particular firm would depend upon whether it had enjoyed any monopolistic advantages in the product or labor markets or had been forced to adjust to

---

[4] This decision in *League of Cities* v. *Usery* reversed an earlier decision of the court that had accepted a more limited extension of coverage, approved by Congress in 1961, to state and local government public school and hospital employees. See Rudolph A. Oswald, "Fair Labor Standards," in Joseph P. Goldberg et al., eds., *Federal Policies and Worker Status Since the Thirties* (Madison, Wis.: Industrial Relations Research Association, 1976), pp. 131ff.

For estimates of coverage see Peyton Elder, "The 1974 Amendments to the Federal Minimum Wage Law," *Monthly Labor Review*, 97 (July 1974), 35.

highly competitive conditions. In the first situation an enforced increase in wages may be readily absorbed by the firm, and productivity may be increased by better management through the "shock effect" of the higher costs. The extent to which this factor will offset the new mimimum depends upon the extent to which wages have been below the minimum, the relative number of workers affected, the proportion of labor costs to total costs, and the ability of the employer to compensate for cost increases. In the monopsonistic labor market the wage may be raised without an adverse employment effect as long as the new minimum is less than the firm's marginal revenue product.

In highly competitive industries, where firms have less "fat" to cover additional labor costs, they will attempt to raise the prices of their products as costs are increased. If the demand for products is relatively inelastic, the results of the wage increase can be passed on to consumers without as much loss of output and employment as would occur for firms that face a more elastic demand.

Another type of adjustment to the higher labor cost is the substitution of capital for labor. Introduction of new equipment or processes in a specific firm or industry may lead to reduced employment opportunities for labor.

In analyzing the extent to which the firms affected by minimum wage legislation have been in monopolistic or competitive situtations, some writers have emphasized the prevalence of highly competitive conditions in product and labor markets, while others have been more inclined to point out the noncompetitive elements, especially in labor markets.[5] On the one hand, it is argued that since the firms with low-wage labor are likely to be small plants with less capital per worker, where competition by entrepreneurs tends to prevail, the disemployment effects of a minimum wage would be major. On the other hand, it is difficult to argue that all firms, especially the small ones, are already utilizing the most efficient managerial methods and are unable to achieve additional productivity gains. They may be able, even if reluctantly, to absorb the added costs of a higher minimum.

If there is any significant employment effect resulting from the imposition of a minimum wage, the unemployment that results would have to be considered an offset to any gains that others receive. Some critics maintain that minimum wage legislation, if at all effective, is therefore inadequate as a measure to decrease poverty and in addition creates distortions in resource allocation. The issue has been raised in recent years with respect to the effect of minimum wages on youth employment. Because of youths' limited work skills and experience, some believe that they have been particularly hard hit

---

[5] For a "classic" statement of the first position, see George J. Stigler, "The Economics of Minimum Wage Legislation," *American Economic Review,* 36 (June 1946), 358–365. The contrary view is expressed by Richard A. Lester, "Marginalism, Minimum Wages, and Labor Markets," *American Economic Review,* 37 (March 1947), 142–146, with Stigler's comments, "Professor Lester and the Marginalists," Ibid., pp. 157ff.

by a minimum designed primarily for adult workers, which in effect contributes to the youth unemployment rate. In part, this argument has been incorporated since 1966 into present law, which allows full-time students employed on a part-time basis by retail and service establishments and in agriculture, under certificates issued by the Department of Labor, to be paid 85 percent of the applicable minimum. Congress did not, however, further broaden exceptions for youth—as proposed by the Nixon administration in 1971—partly on the grounds that as a solution to youth unemployment the proposed remedy of lower minimum wages was unproven, and partly because of fears that firms would tend to substitute youths for adults through wage competition.

A review of many studies of the effects of minimum wage changes indicates a considerable division of opinion. Yale Brozen studied unemployment rates for youth (seasonally adjusted) immediately before and immediately after minimum wage increases and found the rate had risen in six out of eight instances. Kosters and Welch estimated that youth's share in employment has decreased in comparison with what it might have been in the absence of minimum wage increases between 1954 and 1968, and they believed that teenage employment has become more sensitive to cyclical variations. But other studies do not show an adverse effect of minimum wages on youth employment. Kalachek's regressions indicated that the effects of state minimum wage laws on teenage employment were either statistically insignificant or were not consistent with those predicted by the usual economic analysis. A comprehensive study by the Bureau of Labor Statistics also did not support the view that minimum wage legislation led to teenage unemployment. Goldfarb's conclusion was that the employment effect of a higher minimum wage for teenagers is small.[6]

Also, the charge that minimum wage laws do not alleviate poverty but create it has not been substantiated. The evidence, on the contrary, is that the laws have raised wages and may even have increased labor's share of total personal income.[7] Moreover, the minimum is still low by official poverty

---

[6] Yale Brozen, "The Effect of Statutory Minimum Wage Increase on Teen-Age Employment," *Journal of Law and Economics*, 14 (April 1969), 109–122; Marvin Kosters and Finis Welch, "The Effects of Minimum Wages on the Distribution of Changes in Aggregate Employment," *American Economic Review*, 62 (June 1972), 323–332; E. Kalachek, *The Youth Labor Market* (Ann Arbor: University of Michigan Press, 1969); U.S. Department of Labor, *Youth Unemployment and Minimum Wages*, Bulletin 1657 (Washington, D.C.: U.S. Government Printing Office, 1970). The last publication contains an excellent review of other investigations in this field. Robert S. Goldfarb, "The Policy Content of Quantitative Minimum Wage Research," *Proceedings*, Industrial Relations Research Association, 1974, pp. 261–68.

[7] Gramlich's conclusion is that "they are not terribly harmful and in fact even have slightly beneficial effects both on low-wage workers and on the overall distribution of income." See Edward M. Gramlich, "Impact of Minimum Wages on Other Wages, Employment and Family Income," *Brookings Papers on Economic Activity*, Washing-

standards. (See the appendix to this chapter for poverty measures.) For a full-time, full-year worker receiving the minimum wage in 1974, total earnings barely met the low income level for a nonfarm family of two persons; for larger families the earnings would be below the official poverty level. This has been shown to be the case. In 1973, of the 4.8 million families officially classified as poor, nearly half the heads of families worked, and of these over 1 million worked full-time all year.

WORK SAFETY AND HEALTH

The first comprehensive federal law to assure "safe and healthful working conditions" for the nation's workers was the Williams-Steiger Occupational Safety and Health Act of 1970. The act was passed as the result of the realization in the late 1960s that the work hazards of modern industry had been growing, not diminishing, and that the voluntary efforts of employers and workers, together with state laws to promote safety and prevent occupational disease, were inadequate—often ineffective and in some cases nonexistent. Administered by the Occupational Safety and Health Administration (OSHA) of the Department of Labor, the new act provided for the setting of mandatory standards of safety and health, encouragement of voluntary efforts to reduce work hazards, and an enforcement program. Under certain circumstances, state governments may assume specified administrative and enforcement functions. But OSHA has overall responsibility, and it was the intervention of the federal government in controlling health and safety standards in the workplaces of the United States that made the act a major turning point.

Workmen's Compensation and Its Limitations

In the early days of industrial development employers had a relatively free hand in running their operations as they wished, whether or not they were safe. The assumption was that workers knew about the risks of a particular occupation and could accept or reject them. It was argued that in hazardous occupations the wage, under free market conditions, would be high enough to attract a sufficient flow of workers who would be willing to bear the risks. Under such circumstances, and in accord with common-law doctrines, a worker injured on the job could receive compensation from the employer

ton, D.C.: Brookings Institution,1976), no. 2, pp. 409–451. See also Jacob J. Kaufman and Terry G. Foran, "The Minimum Wage and Poverty," in Sar A. Levitan et al., eds., *Toward Freedom from Want* (Madison, Wis.: Industrial Relations Research Association, 1968), pp. 211ff.

only if it could be proved that the employer had been negligent. Workers rarely won such cases and in fact did not often bring suit. They lacked the funds to initate suits, and proofs of employer negligence were difficult to obtain. Under common law the firm had certain defenses. It could not be held liable if it could show either that an employee in accepting the job knew of the hazards, or that the worker, or even a fellow worker, had been negligent and in any way contributed to the accident.

Only after major disasters in which many workers lost their lives did these views begin to change. State inspection of mines in Pennsylvania was first authorized after an anthracite mine fire in 1870 killed 109 miners. Mandatory safety regulations concerning fire escapes came in after the 1911 Triangle Shirtwaist Company fire, in which over a hundred women in a crowded sweatshop died trying to escape the flames when the exit doors were locked. One new development was the introduction of workmen's compensation laws by state governments after the turn of this century. Although at first considered revolutionary, by 1920 such laws were enacted in 43 states, Alaska, Hawaii, and Puerto Rico. Workmen's compensation was a form of social insurance which required that workers be compensated for personal injuries occurring in connection with their employment, with the scale of benefits related to the nature of the injury. The employer was required to pay a premium to an approved insurance carrier. As the amount of the premium reflected the accident rate of the particular industry, the hope was that firms would have an incentive to lower costs by improving work conditions. The Supreme Court upheld the constitutionality of such laws in 1917, and by 1948 all states had adopted them in one form or other.

But workmen's compensation laws were not fully satisfactory answers to the problems of industrial hazards.[8] Coverage by industry and the amounts of compensation varied greatly among the states. In cases of total disability, whether temporary or permanent, laws provided for weekly payments at a percentage of the employee's weekly wages—ranging from 50 to 80 percent— but maximum limits on the benefits often meant that the compensation was less than half the state's average weekly wage. Moreover, the so-called incentive system built into the state laws could work to the disadvantage of the worker. Employers and insurance companies (most states rely on private insurance carriers) had an incentive to challenge worker claims so as to hold down costs, and workers were often forced to engage in litigation that might be expensive and time-consuming in order to collect their benefits. States also had an incentive to keep premium payments (and hence benefits) low to improve their competitive image in attracting business.

Finally, it was becoming apparent in the post–World War II era that nei-

---

[8] See *Report of the National Commission on State Workers' Compensation Laws* (Washington, D.C.: U.S. Government Printing Office, 1972).

ther workmen's compensation laws nor state safety standards were accomplishing what, in the last analysis, was their primary mission—namely, a reduction of occupational hazards. The long-run downward trend in the frequency of industrial injuries came to a halt in the 1950s, and the trend turned upward. Evidence began to accumulate that there were health hazards in the modern work environment that had either not been previously fully recognized or not fully understood. The new concern with occupational disease and health was dramatized by revelations of "black lung" (pneumoconiosis) among coal miners, "brown lung" (byssinosis) among textile workers, and of the toxic and carcinogenic effects of substances such as vinyl chloride and asbestos in other work environments.

OSHA Pro and Con

The passage of the Occupational Safety and Health Act (OSHA) of 1970 was recognition that a new emphasis was needed. In addition to compensation for on-the-job injuries, the objective was now prevention of "silent killers," those health hazards whose effects might be "slow, cumulative, irreversible, and complicated by nonoccupational factors."[9] Research on industrial disease was discovering that even brief exposures to certain toxic materials in a work environment could produce disease, sterility, and higher mortality rates. The Public Health Service estimates that 390,000 new cases of occupational disease occur annually, and that there are as many as 100,000 fatalities a year from disease hazards of the workplace.[10]

The objective of the 1970 act is to eliminate health hazards in the estimated 4 million workplaces that come under its jurisdiction. Under the law, the employer has a "general duty" to provide a place of employment "free from recognized hazards" and to comply with the act's standards of safety and health. In administering the act, OSHA inspectors have the right to enter a workplace and to inspect for compliance. Fines are mandatory where serious violations are found; if willful, violations subject an employer to possible imprisonment. Employees who believe that some plant condition threatens harm may request an inspection by OSHA, but they also have the responsibility of following employers' standards of safety and health and of reporting hazardous conditions to their supervisors.

In setting safety and health standards, OSHA is required by Congress to adopt existing consensus standards. These have been developed over the years through the voluntary cooperation of various business groups with the American National Standards Institute and the National Fire Protection As-

[9] Nickolas A. Ashford, "Worker Health and Safety: An Area of Conflicts," *Monthly Labor Review*, 98 (September 1975), 5.

[10] The number of on-the-job fatalities averages about 14,000 a year.

sociation.[11] OSHA also adopted certain federal safety standards that had already been established under such laws as the Walsh-Healey Public Contracts Act of 1936. Although the primary purpose of that act was to set minimum wages for employees of government contractors, the act also required the government to determine that the conditions of work were not unsanitary, hazardous, or dangerous.[12] Finally, OSHA cooperates with the National Institute for Occupational Safety and Health (NIOSH) of the Department of Health, Education, and Welfare in designating specific substances that are hazardous to workers' health. NIOSH, which has identified some 15,000 toxic substances, conducts research on the severity of the health hazard involved and makes recommendations for standards governing their use.

In its early operations, OSHA gave highest priorities for the use of its limited resources to several types of programs. One was the investigation of disasters and fatalities. Another was the designation of five target industries for special attention: marine cargo handling, roof and sheetmetal work, meat and meat products, miscellaneous transportation equipment (primarily mobile homes), and lumber and wood products. The workers employed in these industries in 1969 (over 1.25 million) had injury frequency rates that were twice as high as the average for manufacturing employment. OSHA also set up standards to govern the use of five toxic substances—asbestos, cotton dust, silica, lead, and carbon monoxide.

Controversy has marked nearly all aspects of OSHA programs, ranging from disagreements over the setting of health standards to inspection procedures.[13] A major complaint of employers was excessively detailed regulations which, they believed, ignored the realities of plant management; they held that even if nonconforming, certain safety measures taken by firms in accordance with their unique characteristic of operation were satisfactory. Unions, on the other hand, took the position that employers often forced standards to be modified to such a point that they became ineffective. Unions also be-

---

[11] For background on these voluntary safety programs, see Leo Teplow, "Comprehensive Safety and Health Measures in the Workplace," in Goldberg, *Federal Policies and Worker Status*, pp. 212ff.

[12] Other federal safety standards before 1970 dealt with specific industries: the Federal Coal Mine Safety Act of 1952, amended in 1966 and 1969; the 1958 amendments to the Longshoremen's and Harbor Workers' Compensation Act; the Federal Metallic and Non-Metallic Mine Safety Act of 1966; and the Construction Safety Act of 1969, which applied to federally financed construction. The mining acts are administered by the Secretary of the Interior. See Teplow, "Comprehensive Safety," pp. 216ff.

[13] See the views of Frank R. Barnako, Alexander J. Reis, and Michael Wood, expressing management, Department of Labor, and labor evaluations respectively, in "An Assessment of Three Years of OSHA," in *Proceedings of the Twenty-Seventh Annual Winter Meeting* (1974), Industrial Relations Research Association (Madison, Wis.: 1975), pp. 31–51.

lieved that the transfer of some administrative authority to state governments, urged by some employers, would weaken enforcement processes.

One question frequently raised concerns the cost burden imposed on employers who must make changes in the workplace in order to comply with safety and health standards. Where the remedy requires substantial outlays, the costs may appear excessive to some firms, even though they may eventually recover the additional expense through higher prices. The problem of occupational safety and health, however, like many other problems of the marketplace, involves what the economists call externalities—namely, the fact that all social costs of production are not necessarily included on a firm's profit-and-loss statement. The employer does not suffer the worker's injury or disease, and therefore lacks the full incentive to reduce it. As long as the outlays required for preventive measures are less than the social costs of disability among workers, higher fatality rates, and the diversion of medical resources, then the enforcement of safety and health standards is well worth it and society is the gainer.[14]

SOCIAL SECURITY

Governments have long recognized the responsibility of providing for the needy in society. In the United States prior to the Social Security Act of 1935, local governments bore the primary costs of relief for the poor, sick, and aged. Their assistance programs were generally organized to meet actual needs, as measured by the gap between some accepted minimum standard of income and the "means" available to the individual. The income and assets of the family unit therefore had to be investigated by a social worker or some welfare officer. Many limitations were placed on the granting of relief payments. For example, they were paid only to those who had resided in a community for a specified period of time, in order to prevent an overwhelming number of applicants from other areas. Communities would deny relief to those whose relatives were able to furnish support.

This system proved to be inadequate, especially during times of economic depression and mass unemployment, when communities faced sharply rising needs on the one hand and falling revenues on the other. During the Great Depression of the 1930s, localities could not meet mounting costs of relief and turned to the states for financial help, and the states soon turned to the federal government. The relief system also represented a failure to realize that need was in part a social responsibility, often beyond the individual's control, as in the case of cyclical unemployment. "Relief" carried the stigma of per-

[14] For an appraisal of these factors see Ashford, "Worker Health and Safety," pp. 9–10.

sonal failure, and many came to believe that it tended to undermine self-respect and to expose people to unnecessary humiliation.

Although relief of various kinds, usually called "assistance," is still part of the programs of local, state, and federal governments, the United States and most nations of the world have accepted social insurance as a basic method of reducing economic insecurities. "Social insurance" is defined as a system organized by the government for the payment of benefits for specific purposes out of a fund accumulated by regular payments. Such a system is almost always compulsory, in that all those who fall within the designated class must participate. Benefits are not necessarily related to contributions, if any, but may be established on the basis of previous earnings or some standard of need. The benefits are not established by contract, as in private insurance, but by law, and they can be changed by law. Funds for benefits are obtained through regular payments of employers, employees, or the government. A system is called "contributory" if some portion of the fund has been obtained from the potential beneficiaries. For example, the old age, survivors, disability, and health insurance (OASDHI) plan in the United States is contributory; but, except in three states, the unemployment insurance system is not. Unlike assistance programs, a social insurance system makes benefit payments a lawful right that is not dependent upon a means test.

Although, as we have seen, the introduction of the social insurance principle in the United States came with state workmen's compensation laws early in this century, it was not until the passage of the Social Security Act in 1935 that the federal government adopted the principle and accepted the responsibility of establishing programs for income security. Although the programs have since been expanded and elaborated, the act laid down the framework of the present system of social security. Briefly described, it provided for three major programs: unemployment compensation, old age insurance, and public assistance. The first two were social insurance systems in which the source of benefits came from funds built up through contributions. The public assistance program was a system of federal grants-in-aid to states for relief payments in accordance with state laws that met minimum federal standards. The Social Security Act provided for different administrative procedures in the different programs: the unemployment insurance system required passage of state laws and the setting up of state administrations under federal supervision; the old age insurance program was a national system operated by the federal government; and the administration of public assistance programs remained in the hands of the state and local government.

Unemployment Insurance

The unemployment insurance system of the United States consists of state laws that meet the minimum federal standards written into the Social Security Act as amended. As a result, there is no uniformity in the schedule of benefits, eligibility requirements, the actual payroll taxes levied on employers, or coverage of the act among states except as they adhere to minimum standards. The federal measure was an "enabling act" in that it gave an incentive to states to pass unemployment insurance laws, and after its passage in 1935 the states quickly enacted the desired legislation. The federal government then levied a 3 percent payroll tax to be paid by covered employers on the first $3,000 of an employee's wages per year but allowed the state to use 90 percent of it (2.7 percent of the total) for its own compensation fund if it passed the desired legislation. The remainder of the tax (0.3 percent) went to the federal government for administrative expenses. The standard tax is now 3.2 percent of wages up to $6,000 a year paid to an employee, and employers receive a 2.7 percent credit against that tax liability. Because the federal law sets only minimum standards, states are free to make certain adjustments in their own regulations. Three states, for example, also tax employees. Most jurisdictions also allow lower rates for certain employers. About a third of the states have a higher tax base than the minimum $6,000.

Coverage   Originally firms were subject to the unemployment compensation payroll tax if they employed eight or more employees during any twenty weeks of the calendar year. In 1938 some 20 million workers—about a third of the civilian labor force—were covered. Gradual increases in coverage as the result of legislation extended permanent coverage to an estimated 97 percent of all wage and salary workers by 1978. In 1954 coverage was broadened to include employers of four or more workers in 20 weeks in a calendar year, and in 1970 to one or more workers in commercial and industrial establishments. In addition, the 1970 amendments required that the laws apply to agricultural processing plants, nonprofit organizations employing four or more workers in 20 weeks, and to state hospitals and institutions of higher learning. In 1976 new amendments required that states extend coverage on a permanent basis to state and local government employees as well as to certain domestic and agricultural workers. (These workers had been given protection earlier under temporary legislation as authorized by the Emergency Jobs and Unemployment Assistance Act of 1974.)

Benefits and Eligibility[15]   Workers who find themselves out of work through no fault of their own are eligible for compensation benefits if they have been unemployed for longer than a specified waiting period, if they were employed in a covered industry during a base period, and if they are able and willing to work. The waiting period between the filing of a claim and receipt

[15] See "The Unemployment Insurance System: Past, Present, and Future," *Employment and Training Report of the President, 1976* (Washington, D.C.: Superintendent of Documents, 1976), p. 37. See also earlier discussion, pp. 391–392 above.

of the first benefit payment, which is usually one week, is designed to prevent those unemployed for a very short term from drawing benefits. The amount of benefits is related to the wages earned by the worker during the base period, which is generally a year prior to the time the worker becomes unemployed, often with the lag of a quarter. The willingness of the person to work is determined by the public employment office: the claimant must register and be available for referral to job openings, and a refusal to accept a reasonable job offer would be grounds for disqualification. But an applicant is not disqualified if he or she refuses to accept a job where a labor dispute is in progress or where wages and working conditions are substandard.

Workers who leave their jobs voluntarily, or who are discharged because of misconduct, are generally not eligible for unemployment compensation, and some laws also disqualify workers who become unemployed as a result of a labor dispute. Controversies over eligibility can be appealed through special procedures set up by state laws.

The amount paid in weekly benefits depends on the formula of the particular state law. Generally the amount varies with the wages earned in covered employment during the base period within statutory minimum and maximum limits. According to the original intent of the law, the average weekly benefit was to be the equivalent of half the worker's regular wage. But the rising wages of employed workers and the failure of state legislatures to raise the benefit allowances as rapidly have led to a decline in the ratio between benefits and the average wage. As noted earlier, this situation resulted in part from the failure of states to raise the statutory maximum benefit amount. There have been recent attempts to correct this, and in 1975, 11 states established a maximum at 65 percent of the statewide average weekly wage. But nine states still set their maximums below half the average wage. In 12 jurisdictions benefits may be increased by allowances to dependents.

Benefit duration when the program began was 16 weeks. The maximum number of weeks that benefits can be paid has gradually been lengthened. For most states it is 26 weeks: only Puerto Rico has less with 20 weeks, and several states allow additional weeks under certain circumstances. But these periods have been found inadequate to meet the problems of workers caught in periods when the job market did not rebound quickly. On several occasions the federal government has provided funds for temporary extensions of benefits beyond the state maximums, and in 1970, with the Federal State Extended Unemployment Compensation Act, a permanent program for 13 additional weeks of benefits was passed with 50–50 shared financing between federal and state governments. Because of the unusual severity of the 1974–1975 recession, two new procedures were authorized on a temporary basis. In 1974 a program for Federal Supplemental Benefits (FSB) for 13 more weeks was introduced with the Emergency Unemployment Compensation Act—bringing the total number of weeks to 52—for those states in which the unemployment rate of those insured by the state law was greater than 5 percent. In 1975 the Emergency Compensation and Special Unemployment Assistance Extension Act provided a further extension to 65 weeks when the state unemployment rate was 6 percent or more. These temporary programs were phased out during 1977 and 1978.

Financing Funds for unemployment insurance are obtained by the states from the tax on payrolls and deposited with the federal government in accounts segregated by states. Each state is entitled to tax the covered employer up to 2.7 percent of the first $6,000 of a worker's annual earnings, but experience rating, or merit rating, provisions—under which employers with a record of low unemployment compensable by benefits may enjoy a tax rate lower than the 2.7 percent—have been widely adopted. (The employers must of course continue to pay the federal tax.) Experience rating was strongly supported by employers from the earliest days of unemployment compensation laws because it served as an incentive for firms to minimize unemployment among their employees at the same time that it provided them with substantial savings.

Experience rating has been criticized on several grounds, however. In certain firms no efforts can stabilize employment because of the industry's seasonal and/or cyclical fluctuations. Employers in such industries are in effect penalized by having to pay higher taxes, while those in more economically stable industries gain. Moreover, once experience rating has been established, there is a strong tendency to resist any increase in rates because of the importance of the tax as a cost to a firm competing in interstate commerce. If a state raises its tax rates, some firms adversely affected may be tempted to relocate elsewhere.

Undoubtedly the pressure to keep taxes low has been a major factor restraining the rise in benefits and causing a decline in the ratio of benefits to average wages. Because the extent to which these practices occur varies from state to state, and because funds are segregated by states, it is possible for a state in times of a serious recession to find itself without adequate funds to pay unemployment benefits; though it cannot draw on the surpluses of other states, it can borrow from the Federal Unemployment Account, set up to handle emergency, short-term needs. In the 1974–1975 recession, 15 states had either received or applied for such emergency loans by the end of the calendar year 1975. Both the Federal Unemployment Account and the Extended Unemployment Compensation Account (which financed the federal share of the extended benefits programs) were exhausted and had to receive advances from general revenue sources. The unemployment insurance program, while able to handle its benefit obligations during modest downturns in business conditions, has to receive substantial infusions of funds when recessions are more severe. The fact that such allocations were made points to the significant role of the unemployment insurance system. It is sometimes argued that the system, by providing benefits to those who have been employed in amounts related to past earnings, is not an antipoverty program. Most workers who receive benefits had not been below the poverty line. Yet it is also clear that the system, along with the emergency financial procedures that may arise from the stresses and strains of a severe recession, is necessary in order to help prevent many workers from sinking below the low-income level.

The Old-Age, Survivors, Disability, and Health Insurance Program

The Social Security Act established a national social insurance system of old age payments with the objective of eventually including all retired workers. At the same time the public assistance provisions of the act provided for federal grants to states for old age assistance (OAA) to give adequate relief to the needy aged who had not been able to contribute and become eligible for the insurance payments. The assumption was that the OAA program would gradually decline in importance as workers acquired rights to retirement payments under the insurance system.

Coverage The trend toward increased coverage of workers under the insurance provisions of the act has been substantial. When the act was first passed, an estimated 60 percent of the labor force was covered; today it is 90 percent. Amendments extending coverage, passed since 1950, have brought groups under its provisions that have included the self-employed, members of the armed forces, farmers and farm workers, and domestic help. Coverage is optional for employees of state and local governments, but some 70 percent of such government workers are currently covered. The principal exceptions are federal employees and railroad workers; each group has its own pension system.

Although initially the act was designed to give protection to workers and their families against the loss of income resulting from retirement, amendments have extended the provisions in several ways. In 1939 survivors insurance was added, providing for monthly payments to the widow and dependent children of a deceased worker. In 1956 disability insurance was added so that a worker under the age of 65 and dependents could become eligible for benefits if the disability was prolonged and if the worker was otherwise covered by the act. In 1966 health insurance, or Medicare, was introduced for those 65 years of age and over. (Since then this entire system of benefits has been known as the Old-Age Survivors, Disability, and Health Insurance program, or OASDHI.) Health insurance offers two separate plans. One covers hospital costs in accordance with the deductible and copayment requirements of the law. The other, known as Part B, is a voluntary, supplementary plan for payment of doctors' bills. (Medicare contrasts with Medicaid, which is not an insurance but an assistance program. Based on federal grants-in-aid to states, it enables individuals, most of them under 65, to receive financial aid to meet the costs of specified medical services when the payment of such costs would entail financial hardship.) Other amendments modified the retirement age requirement of the original law (65 years), permitting early retirement with reduced pensions at age 62.

The effect of all these changes has been to make the act "one of the most far-reaching pieces of social legislation ever enacted by Congress."[16] In the mid-1970s, more than 30 million persons were drawing benefits under the program: over 20 million were retired workers and their dependents, 7 million were survivors of covered workers, and over 4 million were receiving disability payments. The total annual amount of benefits was about $75 billion. The medical insurance provisions apply to some 22 million aged persons as well as to the disabled, in accordance with a 1973 amendment. It can be said that the original goal of the act—to make it a matter of right for a retired person to receive a benefit that replaces, at least in part, the income lost by retirement—has largely been achieved. In 1950 16.4 percent of the aged population received Social Security benefits; the percentage in 1960 was 61.6; in 1974 it had risen to 88.3.[17]

Nevertheless, the assistance type of program for the aged has not disappeared. New legislation in 1972 combined OAA with two other assistance programs—aid to the blind and aid to the permanently and totally disabled—to form a federal system called Supplemental Security Income (SSI) that became effective in 1974. Replacing the former individual state programs, SSI was fully financed from general revenues, and set uniform benefits and eligibility requirements. States had the option of supplementing benefits, and were required to do so for recipients whose current benefits were above the new federal standard. The new income-maintenance program is in many ways a better program than the old, but it still relies on a means test. The benefit is reduced if the recipient has other income, earned or unearned, and will not be paid at all if the individual's assets exceed certain limits. In 1976 the benefit was about $168 a month for one person and $252 per month for a couple in cases where requirements were fully met. There were over 4 million beneficiaries of SSI, of whom nearly 2.5 million were aged persons. This constituted about 10 percent of the aged population of the United States.

Benefits While benefits under the SSI program are determined by "need" as defined in terms of income and assets, benefits under the social insurance provisions are related to the previous wages of the individual, or head

---

[16] Wilbur J. Cohen, "The Evolution and Growth of Social Security," in Goldberg et al., eds., *Federal Policies and Worker Status*, p. 63.

[17] Alicia H. Munnell, *The Future of Social Security* (Washington, D.C.: Brookings Institution, 1977), table p. 10.

of household, in accordance with the basic assumption that the benefit is partial replacement of wages lost through retirement. In calculating the benefit—known as the primary insurance amount (PIA)—the procedure calls first for finding the individual's average monthly earnings in covered employment. The period used in calculating the average includes the years after 1950 (or age 21, if later) to the year before the worker dies, is disabled, or reaches 62 years of age. Five years of lowest earnings can be omitted, and years of higher earnings after 62 can be substituted for earlier low earnings.[18]

In calculating average monthly earnings, only wages up to the amount of the base on which the tax was paid are considered; earnings in excess of that amount are excluded. (The wage base has increased from $3,600 in 1951 to $17,700 in 1978.) In addition, under the Social Security Act amendments of 1977, a person's previous earnings are indexed in order to reflect changes that occurred in the average level of wages during the person's worklife. Once the individual's average monthly indexed earnings are determined, the benefit is then calculated in accordance with a formula that is progressive, in the sense that it is weighted in favor of those with lower earnings.[19] The minimum monthly benefit in 1976 was $108; for a fully insured worker retiring at the age of 65 the maximum was $388. Benefits are adjusted annually to changes in the cost of living as measured by the Consumer Price Index. This procedure, introduced in 1972, obviates the necessity of legislative action by Congress to adjust the benefit structure to prevent erosion of the real value of benefits by inflation.[20]

Because the social insurance system attempts to achieve a variety of broad social goals, the benefit structure is highly complex. The primary insurance amount is paid in monthly installments to the insured worker at age 65 upon retirement. The amount is reduced proportionately for early retirement,

---

[18] The age of 62 was introduced for men in the 1972 amendments in order to eliminate a form of discrimination by sex. Under a 1956 amendment, women workers were required to use the 62-year cutoff, while men were allowed to include the additional years until 65 in calculating average monthly earnings (AME).

[19] The basic formula used in late 1976 consisted of eight steps, beginning with 137.77 percent of the first $110 of AME, and 50.11 percent of the next $290, and then ranging downward, with one exception, to 21.28 percent in the eighth step.

Under the earlier 1972 amendments, these percentages were adjusted annually by changes in the cost of living. Under the 1977 amendments, the new benefit formula (becoming effective in January 1979) reproduces roughly the same relative weighting as the old system but will be indexed by changes in the wage level. In this way, the worker's PIA would bear a relatively constant relationship to preretirement wages. For details see Social Security Administration, "Social Security Amendments of 1977," *Legislative Report Number 17* (mimeographed, December 16, 1977).

[20] An unintended double compensation for inflation was introduced in 1972, when the percentages used in calculating benefits from average monthly earnings were also indexed to the Consumer Price Index. This "coupled" system, would have created a much larger drain on financial resources. It was "decoupled" in 1977 with the new provisions for calculating average wages described in the previous footnote. For an analysis of "decoupling," see Munnell, *The Future of Social Security*, pp. 32ff.

which the worker may elect beginning at age 62. The act provides monthly benefits to dependents of the retired worker (the amount related to the primary benefit)—to the wife of a retired worker if she is 65 or over, to a dependent husband, to a child if dependent and under 18, or to a dependent grandchild. There is a maximum amount payable to the retired worker and dependents, which limits the total to less than twice the primary benefit. Benefits are paid to survivors of deceased workers and to disabled workers. A widow or dependent widower receives 100 percent of the worker's PIA, a surviving child 57 percent. For a worker who becomes totally and permanently disabled before 65 and can no longer be expected to work, benefits are paid equal to the PIA the person would receive at 65. Dependents receive benefits similar to those paid to dependents of retired workers.

The benefit structure of the Social Security system thus recognizes the family as the beneficiary unit. Because the calculation of the benefit amount is based on the individual's, not the family's, earning record, certain problems relating to equity have arisen, especially in connection with the increase of families having two wage earners.[21] A wife's earnings do not add to the retirement benefits of the family unless they yield a monthly payment greater than 50 percent of her husband's benefit. Despite the taxes she has paid, her earnings may not contribute to the family's retirement income. While some have argued that the dependency benefit should be reduced so that the second wage earner would have a clear right to a primary insurance amount, it is also true that the person who remains out of the labor market to assume household responsibilities is excluded from coverage. For such a person, the dependency payment is the only "retirement benefit."

The receipt of old age insurance payments requires that the insured person up the the age of 72 must be "retired" from gainful employment. (After 1981, the age is reduced to 70.) According to the definitions of the retirement test, an individual's Social Security benefit is reduced $1 for every $2 earned in excess of an annual exempt amount. Under the 1977 amendments, that amount—which was $4,000 in 1978 for beneficiaries age 65 and over—is increased in $500 steps for each year until it reaches $6,000 in 1982. Thereafter it will be raised automatically as wage levels rise.

The retirement test has been criticized because it appears to deny benefits for those who paid taxes on previous earnings. While this criticism would be justifiable in the case of commercial insurance, it is not compelling for a social insurance program that is explicitly designed to provide benefits for those retired. An exception is made for those 72 and over (70 and over beginning in 1980); but the numbers who work after that age are not large. The practical issue of the retirement test is its effect on the aggregate payments made under

---

[21] For a discussion of these problems see Joseph A. Pechman, Henry J. Aaron, and Michael K. Taussig, *Social Security, Perspectives for Reform* (Washington, D.C.: Brookings Institution, 1968), ch. V.

the Social Security program. Of the 21.8 million persons 65 years of age and over in 1976, some 1.5 million individuals, or 6 percent of the total number, were affected by the test. Of the 1.5 million, 1 million were receiving reduced benefits, while 500,000 had earnings high enough to reduce their benefits to zero. (For the latter group the cutoff point was reached when annual earnings equaled $8,280.) If the test were eliminated, nearly $7 billion more would have to be paid out annually to these relatively few workers, and to meet that cost either taxes would have to be increased or benefits to others reduced.

Financing Revenues to pay for Social Security benefits are obtained from payroll taxes on employees and employers in covered employment.[22] In 1978 the tax rate was 6.05 percent for each group on the first $17,700 of the worker's earnings during the calendar year, of which 1 percent is allocated for hospital benefits. This arrangement puts into motion a massive transfer payment from those currently paying taxes to those receiving benefits. There is no accumulated fund to meet future obligations as found in private insurance plans, nor could there be. The creation of a fund of the required magnitude—larger than the national debt—would be a fiscal impossibility; any attempt to build up a fund by increasing taxes beyond those necessary for payment of benefits would have serious deflationary effects upon the economy as a whole. There are Social Security trust funds, but they are relatively small. For a pay-as-you-go system of annual transfer payments, the financial underpinning is the government's power to tax, which in the last analysis rests upon the public's willingness to bear those taxes for the benefits that are forthcoming.

Although Social Security has wide public support, there has been concern that the public's expectations concerning the relationships of taxes and benefits may be unrealistic. In the 1970s studies indicated the likelihood of the development of an imbalance between revenue inflows and benefit outflows, the early exhaustion of trust funds (by 1982), and the necessity of an unexpectedly high payroll tax in the twenty-first century. One reason for the increasing disparity relates to fundamental demographic changes in the American economy. First, the post–World War II baby boom will lead to a "retiree boom" in the first part of the next century. Secondly, a trend toward low birth rates began in the latter part of the 1950s and now approximates a zero population growth rate; if this continues, the number of workers to support the greater outflow of retirement benefits will be relatively fewer. Although predicting future fertility rates is notoriously difficult, some estimates indicate that the ratio of beneficiaries to workers will be likely to rise from about three

[22] General revenues are used (1) for hospital benefits where individuals have less than specified amounts of coverage, (2) for retirement benefits for uninsured persons age 72 and over who do not otherwise qualify under the act and who are not eligible for assistance, and (3) for helping to finance the voluntary medical insurance plan.

for every ten workers in the 1970s to five for every ten by the middle of the next century. Other factors of importance in the imbalance of inflows and outflows of funds have been the recession of the middle 1970s, during which revenues from payroll taxes were adversely affected by employment cutbacks and slowdowns, and the overcompensation for inflation created by the 1972 amendments and not remedied until 1977.

In 1977 Congress acted to strengthen the Social Security system in several ways. By eliminating the double compensation for cost-of-living changes, the benefit formula is expected to reduce benefit levels, beginning in January 1979, by approximately 5 percent from what they would otherwise be.[23] In addition, tax revenues were increased both by raising the tax rate on payrolls and by extending the tax base upward. (The possibility of supplementing the payroll tax from the general revenues of the federal government was rejected.) The payroll tax rate on employees and on employers is scheduled to rise from 6.05 percent in 1978 to 7.05 percent in 1985; on self-employed the rate will increase from 8.10 to 9.90 percent. The tax base is scheduled to rise from $17,700 in 1978 to $29,700 in 1981 and to be adjusted automatically thereafter.

There is little dispute that raising the tax rate tends to make the system more regressive: the tax does not fall either on earnings above the tax base, or on income from property, which tends to be received primarily by those at higher income levels. Action taken to raise the tax base, however, offsets the first type of regressiveness, while reliance on the general revenues of the government would eliminate the second type as well. So far, there has been little support for reliance solely on general tax revenues. The payroll tax made it possible for the Social Security system to be established in the United States in the first place because, as a contributory social insurance program, it justified benefits as a right. That attitude is still strongly held. But the anticipated future financial requirements of the system may be too substantial to be borne without at least partial support from general tax revenues.

ASSISTANCE PROGRAMS AND THE NEGATIVE INCOME TAX

When the Social Security Act was passed, it was recognized that the insurance programs for unemployment and old age would serve the valuable function of partially replacing earnings lost through unemployment or retirement, but that they would be of little help to those who had not worked or could not work. The three assistance provisions that attempted to fill the gap aided old persons, the blind, and the totally and permanently disabled—now combined in Supplementary Security Income (SSI) and Aid to Families with De-

[23] Social Security Administration, *Legislative Report 17*, p. 2.

pendent Children (AFDC). While general assistance continues as a program funded by states and local governments, the federal government has developed and financed new means-tested programs. These attempt to meet a wide range of specifically identifiable problems of poverty and human needs. Among them are the Medicaid program under the Social Security Act, food stamps, subsidies for low-cost housing, rent supplements, and child care. Whether the assistance is "in kind" or in cash benefits, testing for eligibility in terms of income and assets is carried out in order to identify recipients as well as to limit the programs' cost. Nonetheless, assistance programs have greatly expanded. AFDC, for example, served some 3 million persons at a total cost of $3.7 billion in 1960; in 1974 aid was given to 11 million individuals (of whom nearly 8 million were children) at a total cost of about $21 billion. Other programs have also expanded substantially. It is currently estimated that means-tested, in-kind programs pay out more than $30 billion in benefits annually, while means-tested cash benefits cost more than $20 billion.[24]

Historically, the most rapid growth of "welfare"—a term applied especially to the federal-state AFDC program—occurred during the 1960s. While there is little doubt that many inconsistencies and injustices can be attributed to programs that grew so rapidly and required administration by so many layers of government, it does not necessarily follow that the system will continue to expand uncontrollably. In fact, evidence seems to indicate that the great welfare explosion of the mid-1960s was the result of a unique set of circumstances: (1) the technological transformation of southern agriculture and its displacement of many black families; (2) the high rate of migration to northern cities that were ill-prepared to provide needed jobs, housing, educational facilities, and other services; and (3) the civil rights movement, which gave voice to a displaced people. The fundamental problem was the failure of northern labor markets to absorb poorly trained workers. The result was the unemployment and subemployment of both male and female in-migrants, and a breakup of families, which then became eligible for AFDC payments. In this sense, AFDC became the system that attempted to meet basic needs, while the new manpower programs sought to bring to the ghettos and poverty areas of the big cities the counseling, training, and other services that would enable the new labor force to adjust to an urban marketplace.

One alternative to public assistance programs is the negative income tax, a proposal that has many variants. The essence of all the plans is that they would operate with federal income tax procedures so that a negative tax, or subsidy, would be paid by the government to those who claimed their income

---

[24] Robert J. Lampman, "An Overview: Issues and Choices," in *The Treatment of Assets and Income from Assets in Income-Conditioned Government Benefit Programs*, Institute for Research on Poverty (Washington, D.C.: Federal Council on the Aging, September 1, 1977), p. 4.

was below some designated "poverty level."[25] Such a means test, it is argued, would be simple, not demeaning, and would eliminate the unfairness and complexities that arise from the investigations required under present forms of assistance. Some proposals would eliminate not only assistance but all forms of categorical programs including Social Security benefits, veterans' benefits, rent subsidies, and subsidies for low-cost housing.[26] Any negative income tax scheme establishes a basic income guarantee and a specific offsetting tax rate. A family with no income would receive the basic subsidy of, say, $3,000, but if income were earned it would be offset by the special tax. If the tax rate were 50 percent, the family that earned $2,000 would repay $1,000 to the government so that its net subsidy would be the $3,000 minus $1,000, or $2,000. As the family earned more money, the tax offset would increase up to the break-even point at which it equaled the subsidy. In this example, the net benefit would become zero when the family earned $6,000. If the family earned more than $6,000 the family would receive no benefits and its earnings would be subject to the regular income tax schedule.

Advocates of the negative income tax emphasize work incentive aspect: workers receiving the subsidy do not have their benefits reduced dollar for dollar as they receive earnings from employment. But this means that, as long as the offsetting tax rate is less than 100 percent, subsidies would be paid to workers with incomes above the basic income. The lower the offsetting tax rate, the more families above the line would receive in subsidies. If in the above example the rate were 25 percent, the break-even point would not be reached until the worker earned $12,000. The dilemma of the negative income tax is that the only way to avoid the higher costs of subsidizing those above the basic amount is to raise the tax rate and thus diminish the work incentive.

There is no easy solution to the question of whether to subsidize higher-income workers in the interests of greater work incentives for lower-income

[25] A modest version of the negative income tax was incorporated in the Tax Reduction Act of 1975 in order to reduce the burden of the Social Security payroll tax on low-income workers who maintain a household and have dependent children. Known as Earned Income Tax Credit (EITC), this provision makes it possible for a worker to receive an income tax credit of 10 percent of family earnings up to $4,000 per year; the credit is reduced by 10 percent of earnings in excess of $4,000. The EITC has not been widely used: many workers are not eligible; low-paid workers may not file income tax returns; and some who do file fail to take advantage of the credit.

[26] Milton Friedman, an early proponent of a negative income tax, emphasized the broader scope. See his *Capitalism and Freedom* (Chicago: University of Chicago Press, 1962), ch. XII.

Negative income tax proposals should be distinguished from systems of allowances. The latter technically give subsidies irrespective of any means test. Many countries have allowances for all children irrespective of the family income level. One of the first to advocate a universal allowance for all citizens, financed by income taxes, was Lady Rhys-Williams, whose book, *Something To Look Forward To*, appeared in 1942. This plan would have substituted for social insurance and assistance programs in Great Britain a uniform income-maintenance system.

workers. To reduce costs, some proposals simply lower the basic minimum. But this merely allows poverty to continue. Under the Family Assistance Plan, proposed in 1969 by the Nixon administration but not passed, the recommendation was for payments of $500 per adult and $300 per child with a tax rate of 50 percent on earnings above the first $720. This meant that a family of four would receive a benefit of $1,600 per year that would not be fully offset until its earnings had reached $3,900—that is, $720 plus the 50 percent tax on the additional $3,200. In the welfare reform proposal of President Carter that was advanced in 1977, a family of four entitled to full support would receive $4,200 a year with earnings taxed at 50 percent. This meant that the benefits would be phased out when earnings reached $8,400. Although the Carter plan was more generous than the Nixon one in real income, both basic minimums were below the official poverty line; however, both plans sought continuation of state contributions to benefits, although at lower levels.

A final concern raised by the negative income tax relates to asset-testing. In the SSI program, eligibility depends upon certain asset limitations. An aged couple, for example, cannot have assets greater than $2,500 and qualify for benefits, although certain exclusions are permitted. These include a home, certain personal effects, the first $1,200 of value in an automobile, and a few other items. Other assistance programs have various specific rules limiting assets for determination of eligibility. Negative income tax proponents have only recently begun to evaluate the types of problems that could arise from the establishment of a federal asset-test. One question relates to the limit that is imposed. Another and more fundamental one is whether individuals should be placed in the position of having to divest themselves of assets in excess of allowable amounts in order to receive a minimum income-maintenance payment.

SUMMARY

Although work provides the source of income for most people, economic hardship can result from wages that are too low to meet minimum living standards, from job hazards, and from disruptions in the flow of income through unemployment and retirement.

In addition to the programs discussed in chapter 17, the federal government has passed legislation that attempts to reduce poverty and alleviate economic insecurity. Some of these actions mean that the government intervenes directly in the labor market and the workplace; others establish systems of government transfer payments either in the form of social insurance or assistance programs.

One direct attack on the poverty of those who work at low wages is the Fair Labor Standards Act, first passed in 1938. In 1978 it required that a minimum wage of $2.65 per hour be paid to workers in interstate commerce. Although some have argued that minimum wages promote unemployment, especially for low-skilled workers such as youth, the evidence is ambiguous; many Americans have gained from this program.

In 1970 the Occupational Safety and Health Act was passed to assure workers of "safe and healthful working conditions." Its administration requires inspection of firms and the establishment of standards in the use of hazardous and toxic materials.

The Social Security Act, passed originally in 1935, provides for systems of transfer payments: to the unemployed through unemployment insurance laws of states, in keeping with federal standards; to retired workers, dependents, and survivors through the Old Age, Survivors, Disability, and Health Insurance program; and assistance to families with dependent children and to the disabled.

The growth of such transfer programs has raised questions concerning the respective roles of social insurance and of income-maintenance (or means-tested) payments in helping individuals meet the economic insecurities of modern society. Both types of programs have their function. The negative income tax, which has been proposed in various forms, is an income-maintenance scheme that attempts to provide individuals with economic incentives often lacking in many welfare payment systems. It relies on tests of need as defined in terms of income and assets.

DISCUSSION QUESTIONS

1. High rates of unemployment for youth in the United States (as well as in many Western European countries) has led some observers to recommend a lower minimum wage rate for teenagers than for adults on the grounds of productivity. What are the arguments both pro and con? Do you believe that productivity should be the principal criterion for the setting of a minimum wage?

2. If there were no federal standards, how would a market economy adjust to problems of worker health and safety (a) under pure competition, (b) under conditions where immobilities were persistent, (c) under collective bargaining? Contrast each situation with one in which federal standards are imposed.

3. What is meant by experience rating in unemployment insurance programs? For what types of industries would such programs be most effective?

4. The Supplementary Security Income (SSI) system, introduced in 1972, increased the federal role, administratively and financially, for certain specific income-maintenance programs. What reasons were used to support this change? Do you believe these reasons would also be relevant to an increased federal role in the unemployment insurance system? Why or why not?

5. The costs of the Old Age and Survivors Insurance program are expected to mount in future years. Why? In what ways did the 1977 amendments attempt to offset that trend?

6. Under negative income tax proposals, what is the relationship between the amount

of tax incentives and the amount of subsidy to those above the poverty line? Illustrate with a hypothetical example.

7. In what ways, if any, should an individual's assets as well as income affect his or her eligibility for an income-maintenance program?

SELECTED READINGS

For a general review of many of the federal programs to prevent economic hardship and insecurity, see the articles by Wilbur J. Cohen on social security, Raymond Munts on unemployment insurance, Rudolph A. Oswald on fair labor standards, and Leo Teplow on worker health and safety in Joseph P. Goldberg et al., eds., *Federal Policies and Worker Status Since the Thirties* (Madison, Wis.: Industrial Relations Research Association, 1976).

Miminum wage legislation, which has long been a center of controversy among economists, has been analyzed recently by Marvin Kosters and Finis Welch in "The Effects of Minimum Wages on the Distribution of Changes in Aggregate Employment," *American Economic Review*, 62 (June 1972), 323–332; and by Edward M. Gramlich in his "Impact of Minimum Wages on Other Wages, Employment and Family Income," *Brookings Papers on Economic Activity #2*, 1976 (Washington, D.C.: Brookings Institution, 1976).

For an up-to-date review of the unemployment insurance system, see *Employment and Training Report of the President*, 1976 (Washington, D.C.: U.S. Government Printing Office, 1976), pp. 35–52. Two recent studies of occupational health and safety are Nicholas Askounes Ashford, *Crisis in the Workplace: Occupational Disease and Injury: A Report to the Ford Foundation* (Cambridge, Mass.: MIT Press, 1976), and Robert Stewart Smith, *The Occupational Safety and Health Act: Its Goals and Its Achievements* (Washington, D.C.: American Enterprise Institute for Public Policy Research, 1976).

For analyses of recent problems of the Social Security system, see Michael J. Boskin, ed., *The Crisis in Social Security: Problems and Prospects* (San Francisco: Institute for Contemporary Studies, 1977); and Alicia H. Munnell, *The Future of Social Security* (Washington D.C.: Brookings Institution, 1977).

APPENDIX

The Measurement of Poverty

The most commonly used measure of poverty in the United States today is the "low-income threshold," more popularly known as the "poverty line"—namely, the level of income below which a family can be said to be poor. Although estimates of a poverty line are by no means new, present concern with measurement of poverty began in the early 1960s. The Council of Economic Advisers published an analysis of poverty in the United States based on a poverty line of $3,000 for a family of four. About the same time, the Social Security Administration developed a different methodology that has subsequently been used in poverty statistics. This approach relates the poverty threshold to the cost of a minimum food budget. An economy food plan had been devised by the Department of Agriculture to define the minimum amount of foods that would be nutritionally adequate for a family for "emergency or temporary use when funds are low."

To derive the poverty line, the cost of the minimum food budget was multiplied by three on the grounds that for a family at that income level food costs are about a third of expenditures. If the food cost was $1,000 a year for a family of four, then the poverty line would be $3,000, of which $2,000 would have to provide shelter, clothes, transportation, medical, and all other costs. From this standard, poverty thresholds are determined for families of different sizes, for the number of children under 18, for families headed by women as well as men, for families whose head is 65 years of age and over, and for farm and nonfarm locations.

The poverty thresholds are revised yearly to reflect changes in costs. At first the changes reflected the prices of the specific foods that comprised the economy food budget; this procedure was changed in 1969, and adjustments are now made in accordance with the Consumer Price Index. Also in that year, following recommendations of a federal interagency committee, farm levels were raised from 70 to 85 percent of the corresponding nonfarm levels. Table 18–1 gives the low-income (poverty) thresholds for selected years.

Any measure of poverty is necessarily arbitrary. In the food budget approach, the key questions concern the elements to be included; they can be answered in various ways depending on prevailing value judgments. For example, the Department of Agriculture has prepared, in addition to the economy food plan on which the poverty line is based, a "low-cost food plan" on which a "near-poor" budget was defined by the Social Security Administration. This threshold was a third higher than the poverty line. If families spend less than the "low-cost food plan," diets are likely to have nutritional deficiencies: the poverty-line food plan, as noted above, is specifically designed for temporary situations. Both plans assume that families will purchase the most nutritious food, and that the preparation of meals will yield the highest nutritional values. But the poor (as well as others) are likely to lack such knowledge; they are often unable to spend the time in comparative shopping; and in poor neighborhoods retail prices are usually high.

A different approach specifies all items in a budget, in addition to foods, as requisite for a "poverty" or other income level and prices each separately. As with new products, standards of consumption change so that what may have been considered an absolute standard at one time becomes out of date and less relevant at another. An example of this approach is the budgets of the Bureau of Labor Statistics for urban families of four. Of the three published budgets—the lower, the intermediate, and the upper—the lower budget includes the low-cost food plan of the Department of Agriculture. These budgets identify specific items by quantity and quality, and the composition of the budget is adjusted in accordance with studies of actual consumer expenditures. In 1970 the average annual cost of all of the family consumption items in the lower budget for both metropolitan and non-metro-

Table 18-1

Average Low Income Levels for Nonfarm Families and Individuals,[a] by Size of Family and Sex of Head: 1959, 1970, and 1974 (in dollars)

Size of Family Unit	1959			1970			1974		
	Total Nonfarm	Male Head[b]	Female Head[b]	Total Nonfarm	Male Head[b]	Female Head[b]	Total Nonfarm	Male Head[b]	Female Head[b]
1 person (unrelated individual)	1,467	1,529	1,428	1,954	2,044	1,898	2,495	2,610	2,413
Under 65 years	1,503	1,569	1,451	2,010	2,092	1,935	2,562	2,658	2,458
65 years and over	1,397	1,409	1,391	1,861	1,879	1,855	2,364	2,387	2,357
2 persons	1,894	1,904	1,843	2,525	2,534	2,471	3,211	3,220	3,167
Head under 65 years	1,952	1,964	1,883	2,604	2,619	2,522	3,312	3,329	3,230
Head 65 years and over	1,761	1,762	1,752	2,348	2,349	2,336	2,982	2,984	2,966
3 persons	2,324	2,335	2,235	3,099	3,113	3,003	3,936	3,957	3,822
4 persons	2,973	2,974	2,957	3,968	3,970	3,948	5,038	5,040	5,014
5 persons	3,506	3,507	3,483	4,680	4,684	4,639	5,950	5,957	5,882
6 persons	3,944	3,944	3,941	5,260	5,263	5,220	6,699	6,706	6,642
7 or more persons	4,849	4,856	4,763	6,468	6,486	6,317	8,253	8,278	8,079

[a] Excludes inmates of institutions, members of armed forces living in barracks, and unrelated individuals under 14 years of age. Families and unrelated individuals are classified as being above or below the low income level, using the poverty index adopted by a Federal Interagency Committee in 1969.

[b] For unrelated individuals, sex of the individual.

Source: U.S. Bureau of the Census, *Current Population Reports,* series P-60, Nos. 81 and 98, and P-23, No. 28. Reprinted in *Statistical Abstract of the United States, 1975.*

politan areas was $5,553; other costs (such as occupational expenses), Social Security payments, and personal income taxes raised the total to $6,960. This figure was 75 percent higher than the official 1970 poverty line of $3,970 for a nonfarm family of four headed by a male.

Finally, it should be noted that measurement of low incomes can reflect geographical differences. Official poverty statistics do not differentiate among metropolitan areas and among regions of the country. BLS budgets, however, do measure differences among metropolitan areas. In 1970, for example, the lowest cost of the lower budget was $6,197 in Austin, Texas, and the highest in the continental United States was $7,686 for the San Francisco–Oakland area—a range of over 21 percent from the average of $7,061 for all metropolitan areas.

Even with the limitations of the current procedures for measuring low-income thresholds, it is apparent that poverty remains significant in the United States. An estimated 25.9 million persons, or 12.3 percent of the population, had incomes below the official line in 1975. Two-thirds of these individuals were white and one-third "Negro and other races." The incidence of poverty was greater among blacks (including other races) than whites, with 29.3 percent of the blacks and 9.7 percent of the whites falling below the poverty line. In recent years, nearly half the poor lived in families with female heads, over a third of all such families. About one of every six persons 65 and over had incomes below the poverty level.

The number of persons officially designated as poor has been decreasing. From a level of about 39 million at the beginning of the 1960s (some 22 percent of the population), the number declined with the growth of the American economy to a low of 23 million in 1973, and then rose moderately during the recessions of 1970–1971 and 1974–1975. As the economy had expanded, many workers were able to enter the labor market, women as well as men, and many of those who had been termed the "working poor" were able to rise above the poverty threshold. As a result, disability, responsibilities in the home, and retirement became more important characteristics of those who were poor. Nonetheless, low wages in labor markets remained a major factor. In 1973, of the 4.8 million families who were poor, nearly half the heads of families worked, and of these, over 1 million worked full-time all year. Of the total income received by the nearly 5 million poor families, including public assistance and Social Security benefits, 44.6 percent was derived from earnings.

Glossary

Commonly Used Terms in Labor Economics

additional worker hypothesis the view that persons not normally in the labor force will look for jobs during periods when employment declines and will leave the labor force when employment expands.

agency shop a form of union security under which employees in a bargaining unit must pay union dues even though they are not required to join the union.

arbitration a form of dispute settlement under which a third, impartial, party has the power to make a decision that is binding on both parties. It is *voluntary arbitration* when both parties are at liberty to agree to submit the dispute to an arbitrator. It is *compulsory arbitration* when both parties are compelled by law to submit the dispute to an arbitrator. See also **interest arbitration** and **rights arbitration**.

"Boulwareism" the refusal by a firm to modify its stated terms for a new labor agreement during negotiations with a union on the grounds that the firm, not the union, knows what is best for its employees (named after Lemuel R. Boulware, former official with General Electric Co.).

boycott the refusal by a union to deal with an employer in order to induce changes in the employment practices of that employer. It is a *primary boycott* when the union brings its pressure to bear directly upon the offending employer. It is a *secondary boycott* when the union induces or compels other employers to refuse to deal with the offending employer.

business agent a full-time elected official of a local union concerned with job assignments of workers to employers and with such other tasks as negotiating over grievances and similar problems; found in industries where the union jurisdiction covers a number of employers.

business unionism the philosophy of unions whose objectives are primarily to obtain higher wages and better working conditions solely for their own members. The term is used to distinguish such unions from those that have broader social reform and political objectives.

call-in pay guaranteed pay for a worker who is called to work during nonscheduled hours but finds no work available.

check-off an arrangement under which an employer regularly withholds union dues from wages of union workers and transmits such funds to the union.

closed shop a form of union security under which all employees in the bargaining unit must belong to the union before they are hired and must maintain their membership in the union as a condition of continued employment. Illegal under the Taft-Hartley Act.

collective bargaining negotiation of the terms and conditions of employment by a union representing the employees with the employer or a group of employers.

competitive hypothesis the view that wages and conditions of employment in an economy in the long-run conform to those which would occur if the economy were characterized by pure competition in both product and factor markets.

compulsory arbitration see **arbitration**.

conciliation intervention in a dispute by a third party who seeks through persuasion to induce both parties to reach an agreement. See **mediation**.

conspiracy doctrine the legal doctrine, once used in labor disputes, that concerted action by workers to better their conditions was unlawful even though such action, when taken by persons acting individually, was lawful.

contributory insurance or pension plan an insurance or pension plan for the benefit of the employee to which both the employer and employee contribute.

cost-of-living adjustment clause see **escalator clause**.

craft union labor organization of workers who work at jobs requiring a specific skill or related skills.

crowding hypothesis view that employment discrimination against workers by race, sex, or other characteristics, in certain, usually higher-paid, occupations leads to an oversupply of such workers in other occupations and to lower wages in the nondiscriminating occupations.

cyclical unemployment that unemployment which arises during a decline in the level of business conditions and which diminishes during periods of business expansion.

discouraged worker a person not actively looking for work because he or she does not believe that jobs are available.

discouraged worker hypothesis the view that workers will leave the labor force when they lose jobs during periods of employment decline and reenter when the general level of employment rises.

discrimination see **crowding hypothesis, employment discrimina-**

tion, statistical discrimination, wage discrimination.

disguised unemployment workers who have taken less skilled jobs at lower wages temporarily because of loss of regular positions. See also **hidden unemployment**.

dual labor market theory classification of labor markets as primary and secondary. *Primary markets* are characterized by administratively-determined rules and procedures and include internal markets (*q.v.*) of firms and also those employments governed by union rules. *Secondary markets* are those in which firms tend to be small, opportunities for advancement limited, wages low, and employment less stable.

dual unionism two or more unions that claim jurisdiction in organizing and representing in collective bargaining a particular group of workers identified by craft, industry, or area.

earnings remuneration of a worker or group of workers for services rendered, including wages, overtime pay, fringe benefits, bonuses, commissions, etc. These are usually expressed in terms of earnings per hour, week, month, or year. *Real earnings,* in contrast to money earnings, represent the goods and services that can be purchased with money earnings and are obtained by dividing money earnings by an appropriate index of consumer prices. See also **spendable earnings** and **straight-time hourly earnings**.

economic strike a work stoppage by workers in order to obtain an improvement in the terms and conditions of work from an employer. For comparison, see **unfair labor practices strike**.

employment discrimination the refusal to hire a worker because of race, sex, or other form of discrimination, even though the worker can meet the qualifications of the job in terms of productivity.

employment effect the change in employment resulting from a change in wages. If measured in percentage terms, it is the elasticity of the demand curve for labor.

equalizing wage differences the hypothesis that monetary wages by occupation, under competitive conditions, will differ in order to compensate for the noneconomic conditions of different employments.

escalator clause an arrangement in collective bargaining agreements that provides for an automatic wage adjustment in accordance with specified changes in an index designed to reflect changes in costs of living.

fact-finding a form of third-party intervention in a labor dispute to investigate the causes of the dispute and—usually—to make recommendations for settlement. In contrast to arbitration, acceptance of the decision is voluntary.

featherbedding union practices designed to create artificially more work, and hence more income, for union members.

final-offer arbitration a form of interest arbitration in which the award by the arbitrator is restricted to the last proposal for settlement of a dispute made by either party.

frictional unemployment unemployment that represents the temporary imbalances between the supply of and demand for labor even where there is an overall equality between job vacancies and the number seeking work.

full employment an objective for maximum utilization of labor resources, usually stated in terms of the minimum percentage of the labor force that can be acceptably unemployed.

general strike a concerted stoppage of work in a given area by workers in all industries and occupations to accomplish some objective important to all workers; it is usually political in nature.

grievance procedure the steps to be taken, as defined in a labor agreement, for settlement of disputes arising out of the interpretation and administration of the agreement.

growth-gap unemployment the unemployment that results if the expansion of aggregate demand, over time, is less than the growth of the labor force.

hidden unemployment the number of persons, not reported in official labor force statistics, who would seek work if employment opportunities were greater.

hot-cargo clause an agreement between a union and an employer in which the employer agrees not to do business with another employer with whom the union is involved in a labor dispute.

human capital investment use of resources in such forms as education and training to improve the earning capacity of a worker. If the investment is undertaken to provide a gain limited to employment in a particular firm, it is *specific*; if the investment yields a return irrespective of the particular firm, it is termed *general*.

incentive wage a system of remuneration within a firm designed to induce greater productivity. The term applies to piece rates and rates of pay per unit of output above some predetermined minimum, as well as to labor-management plans for sharing labor cost savings.

industrial union a labor organization whose jurisdiction includes all workers in a plant or industry irrespective of specific occupations.

interest arbitration a form of dispute settlement in which a third party makes a final and binding award on the terms of a new settlement. Compare with **rights arbitration**.

internal labor market allocation and pricing of labor within a firm in accordance with the firm's administrative rules and the collective bargaining agreement if one exists. The market is not immediately responsive to economic forces outside the firm.

international union a union with affiliates in more than one country. Most American international unions have affiliates only in Canada.

involuntary unemployment in Keynesian analysis, unemployed workers who seek jobs at the going money wage in an economy characterized by a deficiency in aggregate demand; frictional unemployment is excluded.

job evaluation use of various criteria—such as experience, skill, training—for ranking of specific jobs within a job hierarchy in order to establish equitable internal wage structures.

jurisdiction the designation by a union of the class of workers that it organizes and represents in collective bargaining. The designation may be by occupation, industry, or area.

jurisdictional strike a work stoppage to force an employer to assign work to members of the striking union rather than to members of competing unions. Prohibited by the Taft-Hartley Act.

labor force an estimate, prepared by the U.S. Bureau of Labor Statistics, of the sum of the employed and unemployed for a particular week during the month as determined from interviews of a sample of households conducted by the Bureau of the Census. It refers only to the noninstitutional population 16 years of age and over. Members of the armed forces are included in the *total labor force;* they are excluded from the *civilian labor force.*

labor force participation rate the percentage of a given population group who are classified as members of the labor force.

labor force turnover the ratio of those of a particular population group who are employed or unemployed at some time during a year to the average monthly labor force estimate for that group. The term also refers to entries into and exits from the labor force during specified periods of time.

labor turnover accessions and separations of employees of firms over a designated period of time. Rates of accessions and separations are calculated with respect to the average employment of the firm during the period. Accessions include new hires and rehires; separations include quits (voluntary separations), layoffs (involuntary separations), discharges (involuntary separations for cause), and miscellaneous (retirements, death, compulsory military service).

labor union in its broadest meaning, any organization of workers with the purpose of improving the economic position of its members. The term is sometimes used to designate a labor organization whose jurisdiction includes all workers, irrespective of occupation, industry, or area.

lockout refusal of a firm to allow employees to work at their jobs in order to force them to accept the firm's terms of employment.

maintenance-of-membership shop a form of union security in which a worker, once he agrees to join the union, must maintain his membership in it as a condition of continued employment.

means test an investigation of an individual's income and other financial resources to determine his or her eligibility for an income maintenance payment.

mediation third party intervention in a labor dispute to resolve differences through persuasion and compromise; the mediator may make proposals for settlement. See **conciliation.**

natural unemployment rate the unemployment that would occur if an economy conformed to the assumptions of the competitive hypothesis (*q.v.*).

negative income tax a system of guaranteed income under which an individual or a family with income less than the taxable level would file a tax return and receive a payment from the government.

non-contributory insurance or pension plan an insurance or pension plan for the benefit of the employee under which the entire cost is paid by the employer.

open shop a shop in which a worker is not required to join the union. Sometimes it means a shop that bars all union workers.

picketing the placing of workers and sympathizers with signs before the entrance to a business establishment to indicate that the firm is engaged in an unfair labor practice or that a strike is in progress, and to urge workers not to work and customers not to patronize the establishment.

portal-to-portal pay computation of hours worked and paid for to include travel time between entry on the firm's premises and the actual work site.

preferential shop a form of union security in which the employer gives preference in hiring to union members. Illegal under the Taft-Hartley Act.

primary boycott see **boycott.**

primary labor market see **dual labor market theory.**

real wages the goods and services that can be purchased with money wages. Over periods of time, changes in real wages are obtained by dividing indices of money wages by an appropriate index of consumer prices.

right-to-work law state legislation designed to prohibit union security clauses in collective bargaining agreements, such as the union shop.

rights arbitration a form of settlement of disputes by a third party over the interpretation of an existing labor agreement which defines the rights of the various parties. It is usually the last step in the grievance procedure. Compare with **interest arbitration**

secondary boycott see **boycott.**

secondary labor market see **dual labor market theory.**

secondary workers those persons whose attachment to the labor force is temporary or not as strong as that of the primary earner in the family.

segmented labor market a market for a particular class of workers whose mobility to enter other labor markets is unduly limited. Segmentation can arise from racial and sex discrimination in employment. Internal labor markets (*q.v.*) are a form of segmentation.

seniority use of length of service with an employer to determine eligibility of employees for promotion, specified benefits, or retention during layoffs.

shop steward a union official elected by union members within a department of an organized firm to investigate and handle employee grievances.

spendable earnings money earnings of workers minus amounts deducted for social security and income taxes. (In the statistical series of the U.S. Bureau of Labor Statistics, only federal income taxes are deducted.)

statistical discrimination refusal to hire a worker solely because he or she does not meet general hiring criteria, with no test of the applicant's actual productivity. It is also said to occur when the percentage of minorities and women working for an employer is smaller than the percentage found in the relevant labor market.

straight-time hourly earnings wages earned per hour but excluding premium payments for overtime and shift differentials.

strike a concerted work stoppage by workers to force an employer to accede to union demands or to protest employment practices or the terms and conditions of work imposed by the employer. See also **boycott, secondary; economic strike; general strike; jurisdictional strike; sympathetic strike; unfair labor practices strike;** and **wildcat strike.**

structural unemployment unemployment that results from long-run and persistent imbalances between the supply of and demand for labor by skills or areas.

structured labor market a market in which the allocation and pricing of labor is determined by administrative decisions in accordance with the rules and regulations of the firm and/or union. See also **dual labor market theory** and **internal labor market.**

sweetheart contract a collective bargaining agreement negotiated for the benefit of the employer and union leaders and not in the interests of the rank and file.

sympathetic strike a concerted work stoppage by workers to show support for a strike of some other union, even though they have no direct grievance against their own employer.

trade union often used in the general sense as an organization of workers with the objective of improving the terms and conditions of their employment; also used to designate those unions whose jurisdictions are limited to occupations requiring specific skills.

unemployment in labor force statistics, those persons in the noninstitutional population 16 years of age and over who did not work during a particular week of the month, and who were actively seeking work. For different types, see **frictional, growth-gap, hidden, involuntary, structural,** and **voluntary.**

unfair labor practices strike a work stoppage by workers to protest an unfair labor practice of the employer.

union for different types, see **craft, industrial, labor, trade.**

union security clauses in collective bargaining agreements designed to protect the existence of the union within the firm and to prevent discriminatory discharge of union members.

union shop a union security clause in collective bargaining agreements that requires all workers to be members of a union as a condition for continued employment. Newly-hired workers must join the union within a specified time period.

unstructured labor market allocation and pricing of labor resources primarily in response to market forces of supply and demand unimpeded by the rules and procedures administered by firms or unions.

voluntary arbitration see **arbitration.**

voluntary unemployment workers who are unemployed because they seek jobs at higher wages.

wage discrimination payment of a different wage because of discrimination by race, sex, or other personal characteristic even though the worker performs the same work as other workers.

wage rate direct payment to a worker based either on the period of time during which the work is performed (by the hour, day, week) or on output (number of units produced).

wage supplements indirect benefits (known also as fringe benefits) for workers in addition to wages. They include vacation and holiday pay, pensions, and various insurance and health benefits.

wildcat strike a work stoppage by workers unauthorized by the union leadership.

yellow-dog contract a contract that requires the worker to refrain from joining a union as a condition of continued employment. Illegal under federal law.

Index